THE COMMONWEALTH KING GEORGE VI POSTAGE STAMP CATALOGUE

19th Edition

Published by:

Murray Payne Ltd
P O Box 1135
Axbridge, Somerset
BS26 2EW, UK.

www.murraypayne.com

Tel: + 44 (0)1934 732511
Fax: + 44 (0)1934 733498
Email: info@murraypayne.com

VAT No. GB 570 3455 49

For John Martyn

1957- 2008

ISBN 978-1-901624-07-6

17th Edition (1997)
18th Edition (2000)
19th Edition (2008)

Printed by:
SP Press, Cheddar Business Park
Cheddar, Somerset
BS27 3EB, UK.

Preface

Welcome to the 19th Edition of The Commonwealth King George VI Catalogue. This is the third opportunity for us to produce the definitive catalogue of the Reign. Earlier Editions have allowed us to mould this reference work into a form that represents our house style whilst maintaining the very high standards that we set ourselves. We believed that after the 18th Edition it would merely be a case of 'fine tuning' for future Editions. However besides the discovery of new information and research, our drive for ever-increasing standards has resulted in a major re-examination of all that has gone before. This has extended the time between Editions to more than we had originally intended. Increasingly, demand has grown to such an extent that we could not delay any further. As any publisher will recognise it is possible to go fine-tuning ad infinitum. However I believe we have got to the point where what we have is a significant improvement on the previous edition in both terms of new research and up-to-date information, not to mention pricing.

There is significant new information, not least the addition of the Indian Feudatory States as a whole section. Again there are hundreds of additions in terms of new varieties, shades and watermarks. Particular attention has been paid to the description of the shades and printings, as these are significant especially where there is no reference to these in other catalogues. The expansion of the footnotes continues with the user-friendly theme adopted by us. Essentially we have maintained our approach that allows this catalogue to be at the very heart of a novice King George VI collection while at the same time delivering the extraordinary detail required by the more advanced specialist of the Reign, with one not mutually excluding the other! It was an editorial decision to remain essentially a 'black and white' production; colour would not have added significantly to the overall production, certainly not in the accuracy of information presented. Indeed we have come across incidences where collectors have tried to apply distinctions to shades within the same colour band by the images themselves (in other catalogues), which is impossible to do. If in the future we feel that colour would add significant benefits to the core of the catalogue, then we may embrace it, but at this juncture feel that the added expense to the collector would not be worth the return.

Since the publication of the previous Edition, we have witnessed extraordinary growth in the market with huge demand across all areas of this Reign. It is not unusual to witness five-figure sums for individual King George items these days. It seems that collectors are showing increasingly good taste as collectors migrate to this area of philately. The expansion of the Internet has allowed a much faster dissemination of information and this has been embraced by collectors around the world. Indeed our own web-site www.murraypayne.com has increased our ability to share information more readily with collectors through articles and listings. This facility neatly integrates with our bi-monthly newsletter *Sixth* Sense, a reference source in its own right.

Finally we would like to thank all of you who have contributed, commented and encouraged us in our endeavours. More particular 'thanks' are noted elsewhere, while as ever the extraordinary talents of Dickon Pollard as Editor should be recognised. Iain Murphy also requires recognition for his significant input for continuing what Tanzy Brown started in assembling the data and overseeing the typesetting. Seldom could an individual have such a baptism of fire, as this task began almost on his first day with the company. His calm exterior, good humour and organisational skills have often carried the day.

Stuart Babbington
Managing Director

Editorial Note and Acknowledgements

It seems to me that the principle function of editing a catalogue of this nature is to engender humility. It is a truism that the more one learns about an open-ended research area such as KGVI philately, the more one realises how much more there is yet to be learned. Some of the more gaping holes in our knowledge have been capably filled by those listed below, in every case cheerfully and without complaint. Some should have special recognition for their contribution – John Cruttenden, Tom Gosse (Indian States), Andrew Norris (Malaya); and Peter James, who acted as a kind of editorial long-stop, with great wisdom and patience. No blame for any errors in this edition attaches to them, or any of those others who have helped; our sincere apologies to anyone inadvertently omitted from this list –

Eric Abraham, Richard Baker, Michael Bale, Tony Belfield, Dave Boakes, Peter Brooks, Barry Burns, Jean Cheston, Andrew Claridge, Owen Cock, Peter Cockburn, Graham Cooper, Mike Cox, Michael Deverell, Michael Eastick, Steve Ellis, Charles Freeland, David Gillis, Harold Green, Dan Griffin, Richard Hale, Nick Halewood, Bob Hill, David Horry, Stephen Reah Johnson, Mike Ley, Richard Lockyer, Gary Lyon, Phil MacMurdie, Susan McEwen, Jeremy Martin, Graeme Murray, Graham Pound, George Rab (Pakistan Study Circle), Alan Rigby, Nigel Roberts, Brian Rogers, Doreen Royan, Mike Sanders, Robin Sherman, Simon Smith, Iain Stevenson, Richard Stock, Bob Tyrrell, Peter van der Molen, Rod Vousden, Frank Walton, Richard Warren (Burma (Myanmar) Study Circle), Gary Watson, Dick Williams, Neil Williams, Dave Wright, Paul Wright, Eric Yendall

Abbreviations

With the object of making lists not only complete but as concise as possible, where necessary the following abbreviations have been made:

Fluorescent Aniline - FA. Line-engraved - recess, Photogravure - Photo, Rotogravure - roto, Typographed - typo.
Paper: Ordinary - O, Chalk-surfaced - ch or C, Substitute - sub.
Perforation: Comb - C, Line - L.

Shades

It will facilitate the identification of catalogued shades if it is borne in mind that shade designations are fixed in relation to stamps in the same set. For instance, a stamp may be listed as yellow-green, but it may differ from a stamp in another set also classified thus, but it will be yellow-green compared with the other listed stamp in the set of which it is a shade variation. The first colour listed is the central colour (usually the vignette) and the second is the outer colour (usually the frame).

Paper

Early printings of KGVI stamps were often made on thick, 'chalk-surfaced' paper producing high-quality stamps with excellent image-definition. The surface is smooth and often exhibits small 'pits'. Due to shortages during the war years, 'ordinary' paper or 'substitute' papers came into use. With these, there are loose fibres on the surface and ink can 'bleed' into it, producing some blurring and indistinctness.

Traditionally, the 'silver test' has been used to differentiate between chalky and ordinary paper. If rubbed with silver, chalky paper exhibits a pencil-like mark; no mark is left on ordinary paper. However, this test is unreliable, can be destructive and should be discouraged.

Some wartime printings were made on a thin paper which gives a slight reaction to the silver test. Examples of this are Bahamas CW 15a, 16a, S13 and S16; Strait Settlements CW 17 and BMA Malaya CW 22d, 24b etc. This paper is not chalk-surfaced. It shows horizontal ribbing on the surface, visible when held at an angle to the light. Stamps printed on this paper are separately categorised as 'thin striated paper'.

Cancels

Prices given are for stamps with genuine postmarks. There are numerous forged cancellations in circulation - see the Madame Joseph book (vide bibliography). In addition, there are many dangerous forgeries on stamps of Indian Convention States. Care is necessary when buying stamps which are worth more used than mint.

Gum

The early printings of KGVI usually have a more yellowish thick gum than the post-war issues, which have a clear shiny gum. Of course, the climatic effect on gum in hot or humid countries must be allowed for - some of the high value issues made during the difficult war years have a streaky yellow gum, which was made up specially from glue when the more normal Arabic gum was not available.

Watermarks

All watermarks are illustrated as they appear from the front of the stamp. The following watermarks are common to most Crown Colonies and other territories and are illustrated here for convenience. Unless otherwise indicated, all KGVI colonial issues are on paper watermarked Multiple Script CA.

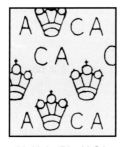
Multiple 'Block' CA

Multiple 'Script' CA

Certain stamps printed in 1950-52 showed variations in the Multiple Script CA watermark. These arose from damage to two of the Dandy Rolls used for impressing the watermark into the paper. On one a Crown 'bit' was lost from a Crown- only row (Type A), whereas on the other the Crown 'bit' was lost from a Crown CA row (Type B). In both cases the missing Imperial Crown 'bit' was subsequently replaced by a Crown of different shape, the St. Edward's Crown (reduced size illustrations).

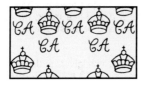

Type A

Postage stamps of Johore and Seychelles, Postage Due stamps of Barbados, Basutoland, British Guiana, Gold Coast, Grenada, Northern Rhodesia, St. Lucia, Swaziland and Trinidad & Tobago.

Type B

Postage stamps of Bahamas, British Guiana, St. Kitts-Nevis and Singapore.

The position in the sheet of the stamp affected varies between Types A and B and also according to the size of the stamps and sheet layout, but, in the case of the Type A variety on Postage Due stamps, this will invariably be found within the fifth and sixth vertical rows of the sheet (6 x 10).

Perforation

In detailing the perforations the first figure refers to the horizontal and the second figure to the vertical: thus, 'Perf 15 x 14' means that the perforations measure 15 at the top and bottom and 14 at both sides. Mixed perforations are given to the nearest decimal point, i.e. Perf 11.1 is Perf 11, Perf 11.2 is Perf 11¼. Where the perforations are different at the top/bottom and sides on vertical and horizontal format stamps the measurement given will be for the first value listed. If this is a horizontal format, for example it will be necessary to transpose the measurements for vertical format stamps.

Sheets

In describing the make-up of sheets the first figure gives the number of **vertical columns** and the second figure the number of **horizontal rows,** e.g. 12 x 20 means the sheet is made up of 20 horizontal rows each of 12 stamps. (12 stamps across and 20 down). Where sheets are printed in two panes, 'LP' indicates left pane and 'RP' right pane.

Sheet positions: The position in the sheet of a stamp with a listed variety is indicated, as for instance Row 1/2. The 1 signifies the first horizontal row and the 2 the second stamp in that row, and so on.

Symbols Used

The following symbols have been used in this catalogue:

†   Does not (or cannot) exist.
-     Pricing is impracticable.

Specimen Stamps

Collectors are warned that forgeries of Specimen stamps are widespread. Some are crude, but others are excellent. Hence, our advice is to buy such items as Victory or Coronation sets only from the most reputable sources. Indeed, all Specimen stamps need to be treated with great caution. All specimen stamps we offer are guaranteed to be genuine.

Exclusions

We do not list archival material. This includes Specimens not intended for UPU distribution, colour trials, proofs and essays. Because much of this material is unique, it is impractical to include it in a catalogue of this nature. Revenue stamps are no longer listed (it is hoped that a future publication will cover these). We do not list such transient errors as doctor blade flaws, offsets, dry or partial prints or 'confetti' flaws.

Pricing

Our prices are in pound (£) sterling, inclusive of VAT. Prices in the left column are for mounted (hinged) mint stamps. Unmounted (never-hinged) stamps command substantial premiums: please ask us to quote. Prices in the right column are for fine used, i.e. for examples with circular datestamp postmarks, not for slogan/wavy-line cancels. Set prices are discounted when practicable. Plate varieties, where not listed for each listed printing, are priced as for the cheapest variant. On 'better' printings prices will be higher.

UPU Presentation Folders

At the 1947 Congress of the UPU in Paris, the Secretary of State for the Colonies presented delegates with presentation folders for each colony. These folders had either red or blue covers, and contained the Victory stamps, plus the then-current definitives to the 10/- value (or equivalent). Similar items exists for Great Britain, Newfoundland, Canada and Palestine and possibly others. Prices range from £45 upwards depending on the colony.

German Propaganda Forgeries

In addition to the 'issues' for individual colonies, noted after each, much scarcer overprints for Rabaul, Bougainville, Grenada and St. Vincent also exist. There are also a series of political slogans.

Illustration of Varieties

The advent of scanning has made the job of illustrating varieties much easier, and it can largely be done in-house. However, there are certain types of variety which do not show up well on a scanned image. Re-entries, which are apparent as partial doublings of designs, are not possible to reproduce with a scanner unless they are extreme. Similarly, plate varieties on sets printed by photogravure (e.g. Seychelles 1938-49 set) barely show up, however big they are, because the stamp design is made up from small dots. We would undoubtedly list many more re-entries and photogravure plate varieties if this were not the case. As things are, where they can be adequately described by words alone, we have included some.

Expertisation

While we guarantee all stamps sold by ourselves as genuine, and/or as described, we recognise that customers may wish to have the backing of a second opinion. We especially recommend the professional body, B.P.A. Expertising Ltd., P.O. Box 137, Leatherhead, Surrey, KT22 0RG. A quicker opinion is obtainable from David Brandon, Wellington House, Guildford, Surrey GU3 1DE. Contact us for details of our own expertising service.

Terms of Business

We welcome Wants Lists and will be pleased to advise on prices and availability. All stamps sold by us are subject to customers' approval. We accept credit cards (Mastercard, Visa) for amounts of £30+ and can accept U.S. $ cheques; please contact us first if wishing to pay by U.S. $ cheque.

GREAT BRITAIN

All stamps are printed (photo) by Harrison and Sons Ltd. on 'Multiple Block GVIR' paper and perf. 14¾ x 14 (C), unless otherwise indicated. Sheets 12 x 20.

A considerable number of Great Britain King George VI issues exist as imperforate proofs, released by the British Postal Museum and sold in 1984-5. All are handstamped on the back 'Imprimatur'.

1937-47 Designs, King's Head with National Emblems in corners. Designers, E. Gill (frames) and E. Dulac (portrait), but 7d to 1/- designed entirely by the latter.

1	½d **deep green** (10/5/37)	.15	.15
2	1d **deep scarlet** (10/5/37)	.15	.15
3	1½d **deep red-brown** (30/7/37)	.15	.15
	a damaged crown	£75	-
	b pair imperf three sides	£3250	-
4	2d **deep orange** (31/1/38)	.60	.30
5	2½d **deep ultramarine** (10/5/37)	.20	.15
	a tete-beche pair	-	-
6	3d **violet** (31/1/38)	2.25	.60
	a imperf between stamp and top margin	-	-
7	4d **greenish grey** (21/11/38)	.30	.45
	a imperf pair	£5000	-
	b pair imperf three sides	£5000	-
8	5d **pale brown** (21/11/38)	1.50	.50
	a imperf pair	£5500	-
	b pair imperf three sides	£5000	-
9	6d **pale purple** (30/1/39)	.75	.35
	a reddish purple (/42)	£1	.35
10	7d **emerald-green** (27/2/39)	2.25	.40
	a pair imperf three sides	£5000	-
11	8d **deep rose** (27/2/39)	3.50	.50
12	9d **deep olive** (1/5/39)	3.25	.50
13	10d **deep grey-blue** (1/5/39)	3.25	.50
	a imperf pair	£5500	£2500
14	11d **deep plum** (29/12/47)	1.40	1.65

15	1/- **bistre-brown** (1/5/39)		4.25	.45
	a broken barb		£90	-
	b broken cross		£60	-
	c broken cross retouched		£90	-
1-15	**set** (15)		£21	6.50

The dates (supplied officially) refer to when they were issued to postmasters for use by the public.

Perforated or imperforate stamps with thick bars cancelling the stamps are Post Office Training School Stamps, or experimental material not issued for postal purposes.

3a R19/7 the left cross at the base of the crown is broken.

8a A sheet of stamps purchased at a Stockport P.O. had perforations missing on the first three rows.

13a A used block (3 x 2) with partial vertical perfs on top row is known with a Belfast postmark.

    15a   15b

15a R7/12, control S46, cyl. 16. The sepal (heraldic term barb) at the right side of the rose is broken short.

15b R18/2, control S46, cyl. 16. The base of the cross at the right side of the crown is missing. This was later retouched - CW 15c.

As before but watermark inverted (ex booklets)

1i	½d **deep green** (8/37)	£3	.40
2i	1d **deep scarlet** (3/37)	£12	£2
3i	1½d **deep red-brown** (8/37)	£5	.60
4i	2d **deep orange** (7/40)	£18	£3
5i	2½d **deep ultramarine** (7/40)	£15	£3
1i/5i	**set** (5)	£45	£8

As before but watermark sideways

1s	½d **deep green** (1/38)	.20	.30
2s	1d **deep scarlet** (2/38)	£7	£6
3s	1½d **deep red-brown** (2/38)	.35	.75
4s	2d **deep orange** (2/38)	£20	£16
5s	2½d **deep ultramarine** (10/37)	£20	£16
1s/5s	**set** (5)	£42	£35

COMPLETE BOOKLET PANES
(Unused)

		Wmk.	
		Upright	Invert
P1	½d pane of 6	£18	£35
P2	½d pane of 4	£25	-
P3	½d pane of 2	£32	£15
P4	1d pane of 6	£20	£175
P5	1d pane of 4	£55	-
P6	1d pane of 2	£35	£45
P7	1½d pane of 6	£15	£60
P8	1½d pane of 4 plus 2 labels	£50	£60
P9	1½d pane of 2	£12	£20
P10	2d pane of 6	£50	£275
P11	2½d pane of 6	£40	£225

P2, P5 have watermark sideways.

P8 sixteeen different advertisements on the labels exist.

1939-48 Designs and designers, 2/6 and 5/-
(King's head above Royal Arms, by E. Dulac);
10/- and £1 (King's head with frame of
National Emblems, by Hon. G.R. Bellew).
Printers (recess) Waterlow and Sons.
Watermark 'Crown on GVIR' (single). Perf.
14 (C). Sheets 8 x 5.

16	2/6 **brown** (4/9/39)	£15	£4
	a deep brown	£15	£4
	b re-entry	£95	£25
	c 'T' guide mark	£185	-
17	2/6 **green** (9/3/42)	£5	.90
	a re-entry	£60	£35
	b 'T' guide mark	£90	£35
18	5/- **red** (21/8/39)	£6	1.25
	a re-entry	£80	£35
	b "T" guide mark	£70	£30
19	10/- **dark blue** (3/10/39)	£90	£15
	a steel blue-black (/42)	£100	£20
20	10/- **ultramarine**	£12	£3
21	£1 **deep brown** (1/10/48)	£12	£12
16/21	**set** (6)	£125	£32

17a R1/7 and R5/2

There are a large number of re-entries, 'T' guide marks and other varieties on this set. Those listed are a sample of the most important. For full information, see Gerry Bater's book 'Waterlow Procedures King George VI "Arms to Festival" High Values - Design to Press'.

16b R4/3 this re-entry shows on the foreleg of the unicorn, under the unicorn and in the shield.

17a These re-entries show strong doubling of the harp and lower right quarter of shield (Row 5/2); and ragged left frame and extra vertical line between upper quarters of shield (Row 1/7).

18a R4/2 this re-entry shows as doubling of the lions in the shield.

16c, 17b, 18b "T" Guide Lines are found on a number of different positions (and in different forms; upright, inverted, partial or partly doubled) from different plates. (Image enhanced).

Number issued - 2/6 (16), 8,660,000; 2/6 (17), 56,000,000; 5/-, 27,380,000; 10/- (19 and 19a), 1,960,000; 10/- (20), 7,350,000; £1, 920,000.

1941-51 As Nos. 1 to 6 but backgrounds
lighter (a wartime economy measure).

22	½d **green** (1/9/41)	.10	.15
	a tete-beche horiz. pair	£13000	-
	b imperf pair (9/43)	£4750	-
	c dull green (/48)	.25	.15
23	1d **scarlet** (Type 1)	.15	.20
	(11/8/41)		

	a	scar on left cheek	£100	-
	b	thick paper (/42)	£12	2.50
	c	scarlet (Type 2) (/48)	.25	.15
	ca	imperf pair	£5500	-
	cb	pair imperf three sides	£5500	-
	cc	vertical pair imperf between	-	-
	cd	thick paper (/51)	£10	£2
24		1½d **red-brown** (29/9/42)	.20	.50
25		2d **dull orange** (6/10/41)	.20	.30
	a	tete-beche horiz. pair	£13000	-
	b	imperf pair (8/43)	£4750	-
26		2½d **ultramarine** (21/7/41)	.15	.15
	a	tete-beche horiz. pair	£13000	-
	b	imperf pair	£3600	-
	c	pair imperf three sides	£5500	-
	d	b for D variety (/48)	£38	-
	e	thick paper (/47)	£8	£1
27		3d **purple-violet** (2/11/41)	.45	.45
	a	major retouch	£35	£25
	b	imperf between stamp and top margin	-	-
22/27		**set** (6)	1.25	1.60

22a/25a/26a These tete-beche varieties came from faultily-assembled booklets (with an extra row of stamps doubled back).

22b Only one used block of four and a mint vertical pair are known, from a booklet bought in Huddersfield in 1943.

Type 1   Type 2

23 Type 1 - at the back of the King's head, an unshaded lock crosses the dark patch of hair. The upper lip is straight and a white mark is to be found alongside the front upper edge of the ear. All overprinted 1d scarlets are 1st State, except Eritrea No. 15, Morocco Agencies No. B2 and Tripolitania No. 15.

Type 2 - the lock and white mark have been eliminated by retouching, and the upper lip now curves inwards.

23a R3/4, control U47, Cyl. 149 a small oval-shaped flaw on the left cheek has the appearance of a scar.

23b/23d/26e In mint examples, the gum has an enamelled appearance and the watermark is barely visible.

25b A block of five from a booklet is known, with watermark normal.

26b A block of six (from a booklet), a block of four and pairs are known.

26d R18/3, Cyl. 239 '2½D' appears as '2½b' due to a plate flaw.

27a R9/10, cyl. 34 considerable retouching on the background, and the King's hair.

As before but watermark inverted (ex booklets).

22i		½d **green** (3/42)	1.50	.30
25i		2d **dull orange** (3/42)	£1	.60
	ia	imperf pair (/49)	£4750	-
26i		2½d **ultramarine** (3/42)	.40	.50
22i/26i		**set** (3)	2.50	1.20

As before but watermark sideways (ex coils).

23s		1d **scarlet** (1st state) (9/42)	£2	£3
	a	ditto (thick paper) (/51)	£18	£15
25s		2d **dull orange** (6/42)	£10	£10
26s		2½d **ultramarine** (8/42)	£5	£8
23s/26s		**set** (3)	£15	£19

COMPLETE BOOKLET PANES
(Unused)

			Wmk.	
			Upright	Invert
P12	½d	pane of 6	£10	£20
P13	½d	pane of 4	-	£20
P14	½d	pane of 2	£5	-
P15	1d	pane of 4	-	-
P16	1d	pane of 2	£5	-
P17	1½d	pane of 4	-	-
P18	1½d	pane of 2	£5	-
P19	2d	pane of 6	£10	£20
	a	imperf pane (/49)	£12500	-
P20	2½d	pane of 6	£8	£10
	a	imperf pane	£8500	-

P19a A block of six (from a booklet, with watermark inverted) was bought at a Cardiff P.O. in 1949. Three used examples (on cover) and a mint pair are also known.

1951 (May 3rd) As No. 22, etc., but colours changed (to conform with 'U.P.U.' regulations).

28		½d **dull orange**	.15	.20
	a	imperf pair	£3500	-
	b	tete-beche pair	£13000	-
29		1d **ultramarine** (2nd state)	.15	.20
	a	imperf pair	£3600	-
	b	pair imperf 3 sides	£4500	-
30		1½d **green**	.25	.35
31		2d **red-brown**	.30	.25
	a	tete-beche pair	£13000	-
	b	pair imperf 3 sides	£4500	-
	c	bright red-brown (/51)	.35	.35
32		2½d **scarlet**	.25	.25
	a	tete-beche pair	£2500	-
33		4d **light blue**	.80	£1
	a	double print	-	£5250
28/33		**set** (6)	1.80	£2

28a An imperforate booklet pane (perforated along the bottom) and an imperforate strip of three exist.

As before but watermark inverted (ex booklets).

28i	½d **dull orange**	.20	.25
29i	1d **ultramarine** (2nd state) (3/52)	£2	£1
30i	1½d **green** (3/52)	1.80	2.50
31i	2d **red-brown** (/51)	2.50	£3
	ia deep red-brown (/51)	3.50	4.50
32i	2½d **scarlet** (/51)	.50	.50
28i/32i	**set** (5)	6.50	6.50

As before but watermark sideways (ex coils).

29s	1d **ultramarine** (1st state) (3/51)	.35	.30
30s	1½d **green** (3/51)	1.50	£2
31s	2d **red-brown** (/51)	.75	1.25
	sa swan neck variety	£18	£22
	sb ditto (retouched)	£15	£20
	sc bright red-brown	1.75	1.75
32s	2½d **scarlet** (/51)	.50	.40
	sa long serif to S	£20	£25
29s/32s	**set** (4)	2.75	3.50

31sa/31sb This flaw on the large '2' exists in two types, the second showing also a vertical smudge. A subsequent retouch left a dark speck where the flaw had been.

32sa The serif of 'S' in 'POSTAGE' is to be found lengthened on every 25th stamp of certain coils with watermark sideways.

COMPLETE BOOKLET PANES
(Unused)

		Watermark Upright	Invert
P21	½d pane of 6	£4	£4
	a imperf pane	£11000	-
P22	½d pane of 4	£6	£6
P23	½d pane of 2	£5	-
P24	1d pane of 6	£10	£15
P25	1d pane of 4	£6	£10
P26	1d pane of 2	£5	-
P27	1d pane of 3 plus 3 labels		
	(Type 1 label)	£12	£12
	a Type 2 label	£35	£35
	ab partial tete beche pane	£4500	-
	b Type 3 label	£30	£30
P28	1½d pane of 6	£9	£15
P29	1½d pane of 4	£6	£8

P30	1½d pane of 2	£5	-
P31	2d pane of 6	£8	£35
P32	2½d pane of 6	£5	£6

P27 Type 1 'Minimum Inland Revenue Printed Paper Rate 1½d', set 17 mm high.

P27a Type 2 as P27, but set 15mm high.

P27b Type 3 'Shorthand in 1 week'.

1951 (May 3rd) Designs and designers, 2/6 'H.M.S. Victory' and 5/- 'The cliffs of Dover' by Miss M. Adshead; 10/- 'St. George and Dragon' and £1 'Royal Arms' by Percy Metcalfe. Printers (recess) Waterlow and Sons. Watermark 'Crown on GVIR' (single), Perf. 11 x 11¾ (C). Sheets 4 x 10.

34	2/6 **green**	2.50	.60
35	5/- **red**	£10	.90
36	10/- **ultramarine**	£8	£4
37	£1 **deep brown**	£18	£10
	a re-entry	£75	£30
34/37	**set** (4)	£35	£14

37a R5/1 and R5/4 "DIEU" is doubled.

Number issued - 2/6, 40,723,102; 5/-, 22,141,445; 10/-, 10,122,720; £1, 2,383,720.

SPECIAL ISSUES

1937 (May 13th) Coronation. Designer, E. Dulac. Sheets 6 x 20.

S1	1½d **dark maroon**	.10	.20
	a colon variety	£10	£10
	b crack in orb	£15	-

S1a   S1b

S1a R10/1, Cyl. 7 two dots appear between '12' and 'May'.

S1b a crack in the orb occurs on R4/1 Cyl. 20 no dot.

Number issued - 388,731,480

1940 (May 6th) Centenary of First Postage Stamps. Designer, H.L. Palmer. Perf. 14½ x 14 (C). Sheets 8 x 20.

S2	½d **deep green**	.15	.40
S3	1d **deep scarlet**	.40	.40
S4	1½d **deep red-brown**	.25	.80
S5	2d **deep orange**	.40	.40
S6	2½d **deep blue**	£1	.30
	a neck flaw	-	-
	b flaw retouched	£22	£15
S7	3d **violet**	1.25	£2
S2/7	**set** (6)	£2	3.90

S6a   S6b

S6a R20/2, cyl. 2 stop a small oval flaw on lower part of Queen's neck.

S6b the above flaw retouched by three short lines.

Number issued - ½d, 82,896,960; 1d, 232,903,680; 1½d, 40,412,880; 2d, 121,065,120; 2½d, 312,957,440; 3d, 22,128,000.

1946 (June 11th) Victory. Designs and Designers, 2½d (King's Head, with emblems of State and commerce, H.L. Palmer); 3d (dove and olive branch, by R. Stone). Sheets 6 x 20.

S8	2½d **ultramarine**	.10	.10
	a extra porthole at right	£30	-
	b extra porthole at left	£40	-
S9	3d **violet**	.10	.30
	a seven berries	£12	£12
	b glossy surface	.50	.45

S8a R5/6 Cyl 8 dot a white dot in line with, and to the right of, the two hawse-pipes at the bows of the ship.

S8b Similar to above, at the left of the two hawse pipes on R16/1, Cyl 11a.

S9a R12/5, Cyl. 4 an extra olive above the lower leaf at the right hand side of the branch.

S9b later releases (on slightly thicker paper) presented a shiny appearance.

Number issued - 2½d, 307,832,520; 3d, 43,185,720.

1948 (April 26th) Silver Wedding. Designs (from photographs by Dorothy Wilding), portraits of King and Queen. Designers, 2½d (G.T. Knipe), sheets 6 x 20; £1 (Joan Hassall), sheets 5 x 4.

S10	2½d **ultramarine**	.15	.15
	a extra jewel	£15	-
S11	£1 **deep blue**	£15	£22

S10a R15/1 has an extra jewel on the Queen's shoulder, cyl 5 no stop.

Number issued - 2½d, 147,500,000; £1, 419,628.

1948 (July 29th) London Olympic Games. Designs, King's head and various Olympic symbols. Designers, 2½d (P. Metcalfe); 3d (A. Games); 6d (S.D. Scott); 1/- (E. Dulac). Sheets 6 x 20.

S12	2½d **ultramarine**	.15	.10
S13	3d **violet**	.15	.30
	a crown flaw	£12	£12
	b flaw retouched	£25	£15
S14	6d **reddish purple**	.75	.25
	a "HLP"	£150	-
	b retouch	£100	-
S15	1/- **bistre-brown**	£1	.90
S12/15	**set** (4)	1.80	1.40

S13a   S13b

S13a/b R20/2 Cyl. 1 a white area at the left base of the crown, which was later retouched, leaving a small blotch.

S14a/b the initials H.L.P. (H.L. Palmer) exist on Cyl. 9 stop in the Jubilee lines below stamps Nos. 118, 119, 120. Touching-out of the letters occurred in three stages.

Number issued - 2½d, 155,350,000; 3d, 32,554,000; 6d, 24,397,000 (air letters with 6d. stamps, 4,060,000); 1/- 32,187,000.

1949 (Oct. 10th) U.P.U. Designs and designers, 2½d (globes by Mary Adshead); 3d (U.P.U. Statue at Berne, by P. Metcalfe); 6d (Goddess Concordia, by H. Fleury); 1/- (globe and horn, by Hon. G. Bellew). Sheets 6 x 20.

S16	2½d **ultramarine**	.15	.10
	a lake in Asia	£20	£15
	b lake in India	£20	£15
	c flaw retouched	£60	£30
	d America retouch	£35	-
S17	3d **pale violet**	.15	.30
S18	6d **reddish mauve**	.30	.45
S19	1/- **bistre-brown**	.60	.90
S16/19	**set** (4)	£1	1.50

S16a   S16b

S16a R14/1 Cyl. 3. a white blotch appears in Asia, resembling a lake.

S16b/c R8/2 cyl. 2 (no stop) a similiar 'lake' in a slightly lower position. This flaw was subsequently retouched.

S16d R18/2, cyl. 5 extensive retouching of Central and South America, etc.; Hawaii and Galapagos Islands are missing, etc.

S16d

Number issued - 2½d, 135,150,000; 3d, 16,400,000; 6d, 11,400,000.

1951 (May 3rd) Festival of Britain. Designs and Designers, 2½d "Cornucopia and Mercury" (E. Dulac); 4d "Festival Symbols" (A. Games). Sheets 6 x 20.

| S20 | 2½d **deep scarlet** | .10 | .10 |
| S21 | 4d **deep ultramarine** | .15 | .25 |

Number issued - 2½d, 260,142,000; 4d, 22,197,000.

POSTAGE DUE STAMPS

Stamps printed (Typo) in sheets 20 x 12, with watermark sideways (normally pointing to left of stamp). Perf 14 x 15.

1936 (Nov.)-37 Watermark Multiple Block E8R. Printed by Harrison and Sons.

ED1	½d **emerald** (6/37)	£6	6.50
ED2	1d **carmine** (5/37)	£1	£1
ED3	2d **agate** (5/37)	£6	£7
ED4	3d **violet** (3/37)	.75	1.25
ED5	4d **dull grey-green** (12/36)	£20	£20
ED6	5d **bistre-brown** (11/36)	£25	£18
ED7	5d **yellow-brown** (/37)	£12	£16
ED8	1/- **deep blue** (12/36)	£6	£6
ED9	2/6d **purple-yellow** (5/37)	£90	£7
ED1-9	**set** (8)	£150	£75

1937-51 Watermark Multiple Block GVIR.

PD1	½d **emerald-green** (5/38)	£6	3.25
PD2	1d **rose-red** (5/38)	£1	.30
	a watermark sideways inverted	£100	-
	b scarlet (/51)	1.50	.50
PD3	2d **agate** (6/38)	£1	.25
	a watermark sideways inverted	£10	-
PD4	3d **violet** (12/37)	£3	.30
	a watermark sideways inverted	£22	-
PD5	4d **grey-green** (9/37)	£30	£6
	a watermark sideways inverted	£100	-
	b dull grey-green (/51)	£30	£6
PD6	5d **light brown** (11/38)	£5	.50
	a watermark sideways inverted	£25	-
	b yellow-brown	£6	.50
PD7	1/- **blue** (10/37)	£22	.50
	a watermark sideways inverted	£50	-
PD8	2/6 **deep purple/pale yellow** (9/38)	£30	£1
	a purple/yellow (/50)	£35	1.50
PD1/8	**set** (8)	£90	£11

The dates (supplied officially) refer to when the postage due stamps were issued to postmasters for general release.

1951-2 As Nos. PD1, etc., but colours changed.

PD9	½d **dull orange** (10/51)	1.25	£2
	a orange (/53?)	£18	-
PD10	1d **cobalt** (6/51)	£1	.50
	a watermark sideways inverted	-	-
PD11	1½d **green** (4/2/52)	£1	1.30
	a watermark sideways inverted	£7	-
	b stop after "three"	£110	-
PD12	4d **light blue** (9/8/51)	£18	£14
PD13	1/- **bistre-brown** (29/11/51)	£10	2.50
	a watermark sideways inverted	-	-
PD9/13	**set** (5)	£28	£18

PD11b R1/7, 8, 9 a stop after the 'three' in the value tablet.

PD2, 3, 4, 5, 6, 7, 10, 11 all exist with watermark (sideways) inverted.

1952 (June 7th) No. 29 handstamped 'POSTAGE DUE' horizontally or diagonally in black at Bury St. Edmunds.

| PD13a | 1d **ultramarine** | - | - |

On the authority of the local Postmaster a half sheet was handstamped when supplies of No. PD10 ran out. Initially, two separate handstamps were used and the two words were spaced approximately 3mm apart; the two handstamps were then fixed together with 5mm between the two lines. 100 copies were used and 20 survived mint.

GERMAN PROPAGANDA LABELS

During 1944, the Germans prepared imitations of the GB 1935 Silver Jubilee ½d, 1937 Coronation 1½d and 1937 Definitives ½d to 3d. Their purpose was, apparently, to circulate these in neutral countries with the intention of discrediting Great Britain.

They were printed on poor quality paper with a wavy line watermark and were perforated 11½ (Line). The definitives were less altered than the two 'commemoratives'. The Cross on the Crown was replaced by the Star of David (which also appears in the thistle), a Hammer and Sickle was substituted for 'D' in the value circle, and also appears within the rose. The colours were generally well matched to Nos. 1-6.

The definitives also appeared with a variety of propaganda overprints ('Liquidation of Empire/Hong Kong' etc.) within thick regular frames, or within a star-shaped device, or in a straight line. These were also circulated stuck on a sheet headed with the G.P.O. symbol and a Hammer and Sickle, inscribed 'SPECIAL STAMP IN MEMORY OF THE FIRST DAY OF INVASION' (in English and Russian), the 'stamps' being cancelled with a c.d.s. 'LONDON/ AAAO/6 JUN 44/SPECIAL STAMP'.

Prices: (For Mint or Used)

1935 ½d **green**		£80
1937 1½d **maroon**		£80
1937 ½d-3d (set of 6)		£200

CHANNEL ISLANDS

Stamps issued and used during the German Occupation 1940-5.

GUERNSEY

The G.B. K.G. VI definitive 1d. was overprinted with a small swastika, and the Postal Centenary 2d. with two swastikas, when the Germans occupied Guernsey in 1940. They were not issued, and very few copies are known.

1940 (Dec. 27th) stamps of Great Britain bisected diagonally and used as 1d. stamps for Inter-Island Postage.

G1	2d (half) G.B. No. 4 used on piece (cover £18)	£12
G2	2d (half) G.B. No. S5, used on piece (cover £14)	£10

Covers with 2d stamps of 1912, 1924 and 1934 issues similarly bisected were used by philatelists.

The use of bisected stamps was authorised up to February 24th, 1941.

1941-4 Design, Guernsey Coat of Arms. Designer, E.W. Vaudin. Printers (typo) Guernsey Press Co. Roul. 14 and/or 7. No watermark Sheets 6 x 10.

G3	½d **emerald** (7/4/41)	£3	1.20
	a deep blue-green (11/41)	£18	£10
	b imperforate between horizontal pair	£550	-
	bb ditto, vertical pair	£600	-
	c bright green (2/42)	£12	6.50
	d dull green (9/42)	£2	1.25
	e olive-green (2/43)	£24	£15
	f deep yellow-green (7/43)	£2	1.80
	f f printed on gummed side	£175	-
	g pale yellow-green (11/44)	£2	1.80
	h imperf. pair	£300	-
G4	1d **carmine-red** (thin paper) (18/2/41)	£3	1.25
	a carmine-red (/41)	£2	1.25
	b imperf. pair	£110	£60
	bb imperforate between horizontal pair	£550	-
	c imperforate between vertical pair	£600	-

d golden red (7/43)	£2	1.50
e dull scarlet (12/43)	1.75	1.50
ea double printing	£125	-
G5 2½d **deep ultramarine** (12/4/44)	£6	7.50
aa ultramarine	£5	4.25
a imperf. pair	£550	-
b imperforate between horizontal pair	£750	-
G3/5 **set** (3)	£8	£6

G4 The design can be seen clearly through the back of the stamp, owing to the thin paper.

1942 Design as before, but stamps printed on coloured French Bank Note Paper. Watermark Loops. Roul. 14 and/or 17.

G6	½d **green/blue** (11/3/42)	£12	£14
	a green/grey-blue	£10	£14
G7	1d **deep red/blue** (7/4/42)	£7	£14
	a red/grey-blue	£7	£14

Most of the stamps are to be found rouletted 7 or 14 (the latter has the appearance of pin perf.) or a combination of both (same valuation). Both types occur in the same sheet.

JERSEY

On entering Jersey, the Germans ordered all current stamps found to be overprinted 'Jersey 1940', and with swastikas. Small quantities of KGVI definitive stamps from ½d to 10/- (less 1d and 11d) and the Postal Centenary issue (less 1d) were so treated, but none were officially issued owing to strong protests. Copies are rare, as very few escaped destruction.

A local printing of 1d stamps depicting the Arms of Jersey was made, but never issued. Imperforate examples exist with and without swastika overprint. Price from £750.

1941-3 Design, Jersey Coat of Arms. Designer Major Rybot. Printers (typo) Jersey Evening Post. Perf. 11 (L). No watermark. Sheets 6 x 10.

J1	½d **emerald-green** (29/1/42)	£4	3.75
	a emerald-green (thin paper) (8/42)	4.50	£4
	b imperforate between vertical pair	£600	-

	c ditto horizontal pair	£550	-
	d imperf. pair	£300	-
	e on newsprint (/43)	£5	£7
J2	1d **scarlet** (thin paper) (1/4/41)	£4	£3
	a scarlet (/41)	£4	£3
	b imperforate between vertical pair	£600	-
	c ditto horizontal pair	£550	-
	d chalky paper (/41)	£25	£28
	e on newsprint (1/43)	£7	8.50
	f imperf. pair	£325	-

J1a The design is visible through the back of the thin paper varieties.

J1e/2e This paper is coarse and greyish.

J2d The heavily chalk-coated paper has a strong glaze.

J1d/2f Faked imperforates exist on thin white wove paper in bright colours.

1943-4 Designs, Views of Jersey. Designer, E. Blampied. Engraver, H. Cortot. Printers (typo) French Govt. Printing Works, Paris. Perf. 13½ x 13¼ (C). No watermark. Sheets 120 - four panes, each 3 x 10.

J3	½d **green** (1/6/43)	£5	7.50
	a on newsprint (7/10/43)	6.50	8.50
J4	1d **scarlet** (1/6/43)	1.50	.30
	a on newsprint (28/2/44)	1.75	1.45
J5	1½d **brown** (8/6/43)	3.50	3.50
J6	2d **orange** (8/6/43)	3.50	1.25
J7	2½d **blue** (29/6/43)	1.50	.60
	a on newsprint (25/2/44)	.60	£1
	b thin paper	£225	-
J8	3d **purple-violet** (29/6/43)	1.50	1.75
J3/8	**set** (6)	£15	£13

J3a/4a/7a The dates given refer to printing dates. They were placed on sale, unnoticed, later on in the year.

7b the paper is so thin that the design shows through to the back of the stamp.

1948 (May 10th) Third Anniversary of Liberation. Designs and designers, 1d (gathering seaweed, by J.R. Stobie); 2½d (gathering seaweed, from painting by E. Blampied). Printers (photo) Harrison and Sons. Watermark as Great Britain. Perf. 14¾ x 14 (C). Sheets 6 x 20.

CIS1 1d **scarlet**	.10	.20
a rose-red	.30	.25
CIS2 2½d **deep ultramarine**	.15	.20
a wheel flaw	£8	£9
b crown flaw	£8	£9

Numbers issued - 1d., 5,934,000; 2½d., 5,398,000.

These two stamps were valid for postage throughout Great Britain.

CIS2a R20/5 A white blotch breaks rim of cartwheel.

CIS2b R1/1 A white line joins the central jewel of the crown to the base, at its left side.

ADEN

1937 (April 1st) Printers (recess) De La Rue. Perf. 13¼ x 12 (C). Sheets 8 x 10.

1	½a	light green	1.50	1.50
2	9p	deep grey-green	1.50	1.80
3	1a	sepia	1.50	.90
4	2a	scarlet	1.50	1.80
5	2½a	light blue	1.75	1.20
6	3a	carmine-rose	£4	£5
7	3½a	dull grey-blue	£3	2.75
8	8a	pale reddish purple	£10	£5
9	1r	brown	£19	£6
10	2r	orange-yellow	£35	£16
11	5r	purple	£65	£60
	a	bright aniline purple	£90	£75
12	10r	pale olive-green	£175	£275
1/12		set (12)	£375	£400
SP1/12		specimen perf (12)	£350	†

11a the shade is brighter and, especially with used examples, suffuses through to the back of the stamp. There is an aniline reaction under ultra-violet light.

1939 (Jan 19th)-48 Designs, ½a, 2a (Aidrus Mosque, Crater); ¾a, 5r (Adenese Camel Corps); 1a, 2r (Aden Harbour); 1½a, 1r (Adenese Dhow, "Al-Nars"); 2½a, 8a (Mukalla); 3a, 14a, 10r (Capture of Aden, 1839, H.M.S. "Volage"). Printers (recess) Waterlow and Sons. Perf. 12½ (L). Sheets ½a to 2½a and 8a, 5 x 16; 3a and 14a 8 x 10; Rupee values, 5 x 12.

13	½a	yellow-green	.40	.35
	a	green (7/42)	.50	.35
	b	blue-green (9/48)	1.60	£5
14	¾a	chocolate-brown	.80	.75
	a	red-brown (24/4/46)	.90	.75
15	1a	light blue	.30	.25
	a	bright blue (9/48)	.20	.25
16	1½a	scarlet-red	.60	.35
17	2a	sepia	.25	.15
	a	deep sepia (24/4/46)	.20	.15

18	2½a	deep ultramarine	.35	.20
19	3a	sepia and rose-carmine	£1	.25
	a	deep sepia and deep carmine (6/45)	.50	.15
20	8a	orange	£1	.25
	a	red-orange (10/50)	.75	.25
21	14a	sepia and pale blue (15/1/45)	1.25	.60
22	1r	emerald-green	1.50	1.40
	a	bright green (4/46)	£2	1.80
23	2r	indigo and magenta	£4	1.50
	a	blue-black and deep magenta (1/44)	3.50	1.25
24	5r	lake-brown and olive-green	£10	7.50
	a	lake-brown and deep olive (1/44)	£10	£8
25	10r	sepia and violet	£15	8.50
	a	bright sepia and bright violet (1/44)	£18	£10
13/25		set (13)	£32	£19
SP13/25		specimen perf (13)	£175	†

There are numerous re-entries on the 3a and 14a, as well as plate varieties and partial 'T' guidemarks.

1951 (Oct. 1st)-52. Nos. 15, etc., surcharged in black or red on introduction of British East African currency.

26	5c/1a	light blue	.10	.25
	a	bright light blue (3/52)	.25	.25
27	10c/2a	sepia	.25	.50
	a	brown-sepia	£4	.50
	b	deep sepia (18/3/52)	.15	.35
28	15c/2½a	deep ultramarine	.15	.75
	a	surcharge double	£750	-
29	20c/3a	sepia and rose-carmine	.15	.25
	a	dark sepia and carmine-rose (18/3/52)	1.75	1.25
30	30c/8a	orange (red opt.)	.15	.40
31	50c/8a	orange	.30	.20
	a	surcharge double, once albino	£1800	†
32	70c/14a	sepia and pale blue	1.25	£1
	a	dark sepia and bright pale blue (18/3/52)	£2	£1
33	1s/1r	emerald-green	.45	.20
34	2s/2r	greyish indigo and bright magenta	£6	2.75
	a	surcharge omitted (albino)	£500	-
	b	blue-black and magenta (3/52)	6.50	£5
35	5s/5r	lake-brown and olive-green	£11	7.50
	a	lake-brown and sage-green	£10	£8
36	10s/10r	sepia and violet	£14	£8
	a	bright sepia and bright violet	£15	£9
26/36		set (11)	£29	£19

28a One sheet of the 15c surcharge exists with double overprint. The variety varies over the sheet and the price quoted is for a well separated double - lesser doubles command lower prices.

31a A single mint example is known.

34/34b A printing of the surcharged stamps exists in which fluorescent aniline ink was used for the frames. Under ultra-violet they show up fluorescent salmon-pink and the centres appear greenish black, whereas the centres of all other printings are in varying shades of blue-black.

34a A sheet of sixty existed ex a new issue distribution.

SPECIAL ISSUES

1937 (May 12th) Coronation. Printers (recess) De La Rue. Perf 13¾ x 14 (C). Sheets 5 x 16.

S1	1a **sepia**	.30	.75
S2	2½a **light blue**	.40	.85
S3	3½a **blue-grey**	.50	1.75
S1/3	**set (3)**	1.10	£3
SP S1/S3	**specimen perf (3)**	£80	†

1946 (Oct. 15th) Victory. Printers (recess) De La Rue. Perf 13¾ x 14 (C). Sheets 6 x 10.

S4	1½a **carmine-red**	.10	.95
	a flaw above 'D'	£20	£25
S5	2½a **deep blue**	.15	.45
	a watermark inverted	£600	-
SP S4/5	**specimen perf (2)**	£55	†

S4a Flaw above the 'D' in 'Aden' on R7/1. Stamps from this position are known without the flaw; it has also been seen 'officially scratched out', an operation performed with a sharp instrument on the surface of the stamp itself.

1949 (Jan. 17th) Silver Wedding. Printers (low value) Waterlow and Sons (photo) and Perf. 14 x 14¾ (C). (Top Value) Bradbury Wilkinson (Design recess, name typo) and Perf. 11½ x 10¾ (C). Sheets 10 x 6 (low value), 6 x 10 (high value).

S6	1½a **scarlet**	.25	1.25
	a flaw on '4'	£15	£22
S7	10r **dull purple**	£14	£25

S6a R2/6 A flaw on the '4' of '1948'.

1949 (Oct. 10th) U.P.U. Designs (low value) Hermes, Globe and Transport. (Second value) Hemisphere, Plane and Steamer. (Third value) Hermes on Globe. (Top value) U.P.U. Monument, Berne. Printers (high and low values) Waterlow and Sons (recess) and Perf. 13½ x 13¾ (C). (Middle values) Bradbury, Wilkinson (Design recess, name typo) and Perf. 10¾ x 11½ (C). Sheets 5 x 12.

S8	2½a/20c **dull violet-blue**	.30	.90
S9	3a/30c **carmine**	£1	.90
S10	8a/50c **orange**	.85	1.20
S11	1r/1s **azure**	£1	£2
S8/11	**set (4)**	£3	4.50

The "U.P.U." stamps printed by Waterlow and Sons exist in two different perforations vertically, either 13.7 or 13.9, but the difference is too small to merit more than a general note. The surcharging of the Aden, Aden States and Somaliland sets was occasioned by an unexpected delay in the change of currency.

KATHIRI STATE OF SEIYUN

1942 (July 1st) - 50 Designs, ½a, ¾a, 1a
(Portrait of Sultan Jafar bin Mansar); 1½a
(Sultan's Palace, Seiyun); 2a (Palace, Tarim);
2½a (Mosque, Seiyun); 3a (Palace, Tarim); 8a
(Mosque, Seiyun); 1r (South Gate, Tarim); 2r
(Kathiri House); 5r (Mosque Door, Tarim).
Printers (recess) De La Rue. Sheets 6 x 10 or
10 x 6. ½a, ¾a, 1a perf 13¾ x 14 (C), 1½a -
5r perf 11¾ x 13.

2	½a **blue-green**	.10	.50
3	¾a **chestnut**	.15	1.50
4	1a **deep blue**	.30	.75
5	1½a **deep carmine**	£1	1.50
	a carmine (8/3/48)	.30	1.25
6	2a **sepia**	.50	1.25
	a sepia-brown (8/3/48)	.20	1.10
7	2½a **deep blue**	.50	1.10
8	3a **sepia and deep carmine**	.75	£2
	a sepia-brown and carmine (8/3/48)	£2	2.50
9	8a **vermilion-red**	.50	.40
10	1r **green**	£1.65	£2
11	2r **dark blue and deep purple**	£6	8.50
	a indigo and reddish purple (8/3/48)	£5	8.50
12	5r **chestnut and green** (1/10/42)	£12	£14
2/12	**set** (11)	£19	£30
SP2/12	**specimen perf (11)**	£150	†

5 this stamp fluoresces under ultraviolet light.

**1951 (Oct. 1st) Nos. 4, etc., surcharged in
black or red to bring in line with changed
currency.**

13	5c/1a **deep blue (red)**	.10	£1
14	10c/2a **sepia**	.15	.60
	a sepia-brown (1/10/51)	.75	£1
15	15c/2½a **deep blue**	.10	1.10
16	20c/3a **sepia and carmine**	.20	1.75
	a sepia-brown and deep carmine (1/10/51)	.75	2.50
17	50c/8a **vermilion-red**	.10	.60
18	1s/1r **green**	.40	£2
19	2s/2r **indigo and reddish purple**	£5	£20
	a dark blue & deep purple	£6	£22

20	5s/5r **chestnut and green**	£12	£30
13/20	**set** (8)	£16	£52

The 1r. (No. 10) exists with surcharge '5' in
black, the original value tablets being
overprinted with black circles. This was a
bogus production, made in Bombay.

SPECIAL ISSUES

**1946 (Oct. 15th) Victory. Nos 5 and 7
overprinted VICTORY ISSUE 8th JUNE 1946,
in black or red. Printers De La Rue.**

S1	1½a **deep carmine**	.10	.40
S2	2½a **deep blue (red)**	.10	.15
	a overprint inverted	£550	-
	b overprint double	£775	-
SP S1/2	**specimen perf** (2)	£40	†

S2a One sheet of 60 was purchased from the
Crown Agents. Distributed unnoticed, a number
of copies have not been traced.

S2b The 2½a surcharge double has the two
overprints almost coincident.

1949 (Jan. 17th) Silver Wedding. As Aden.

S3	1½a **scarlet**	.15	1.80
S4	5r **grey-green**	£8	£6

1949 (Oct. 10th) U.P.U. As Aden.

S5	2½a/20c **dull violet-blue**	.15	.40
S6	3a/30c **carmine**	.70	.90
S7	8a/50c **orange**	.20	£1
S8	1r/1s **azure**	.30	.60
S5/8	**set** (4)	1.20	2.60

QU'AITI STATE OF SHIHR AND MUKALLA

1942 (July 1st) - 50 Designs, ½a, ¾a, 1a (portrait of Sultan Salih bin Ghalib); 1½a (harbour, Mukalla); 2a (Gateway of Shihr); 2½a (Shibam, Qu'aiti Capital); 3a (Outpost Fortress, Mukalla); 8a ('Einat', City of Seiyids); 1r (Du'an); 2r (Mosque, Hureidha, at time of pilgrimage feast); 5r (Meshhed, Du'an Province). Printers (recess) De La Rue. Sheets 6 x 10 or 10 x6. ½a, ¾a, 1a perf 13¾ x 14, 1½a - 5r perf 11¾ x 13.

2	½a	blue-green	.50	.30
	a	deep olive-green (12/46)	£14	£25
3	¾a	chestnut	.90	.20
4	1a	blue	.50	.60
	a	dark blue (12/8/48)	.40	.60
5	1½a	carmine	1.25	.50
	a	deep carmine (6/3/50)	.85	.30
6	2a	sepia	.75	1.10
	a	yellowish brown (18/12/46)	£15	£20
	b	sepia-brown (12/8/48)	.90	1.25
7	2½a	deep blue	.25	.20
8	3a	sepia and carmine	.50	.45
	a	sepia and deep carmine (6/3/50)	.90	.60
9	8a	vermilion-red	.30	.25
10	1r	green	2.50	2.50
	a	'A' of watermark missing	†	£675
11	2r	deep blue and deep purple	£10	£8
	a	greenish blue and red-purple (6/3/50)	£7	£6
12	5r	light chestnut and green (1/10/42)	£10	7.50
2/12	set (11)		£22	£14
SP 2/12	specimen perf (11)		£150	†

5 shows fluorescent aniline reaction under ultra-violet.

1951 (Oct 1st) Nos 4, etc., surcharged in black or red to bring into line with changed currency.

13	5c/1a	deep blue (red)	.10	.15
	a	dark blue (red)	.25	.25
14	10c/2a	sepia	.10	.10
	a	yellowish brown	£18	£22
	b	sepia-brown	.30	.30
15	15c/2½a	deep blue	.10	.10
16	20c/3a	sepia and carmine	.15	.15
	a	sepia and deep carmine	.75	£1
	b	surcharge double one albino	£250	-
17	50c/8a	vermilion-red	.25	1.50
	a	scarlet-red (18/8/54)	.75	£2
18	1s/1r	green	£1	.35
19	2s/2r	greenish blue and red-purple	£4	£12
20	5s/5r	light chestnut and green	£8	£19
13/20	set (8)		£12	£30

SPECIAL ISSUES

1946 (Oct. 15th) Victory. Nos. 5 and 7 overprinted VICTORY ISSUE 8th JUNE 1946, in red or black. Printers De La Rue.

S1	1½a	carmine	.10	.60
S2	2½a	deep blue (red)	.10	.10
SP S1/2	specimen perf (2)		£55	†

1949 (Jan. 17th) Silver Wedding. As Aden.

S3	1½a	scarlet	.25	2.75
S4	5r	grey-green	8.50	£6

1949 (Oct. 10th) U.P.U. As Aden.

S5	2½a/20c	dull violet-blue	.15	.15
S6	3a/30c	carmine	.70	.50
S7	8a/50c	orange	.15	.50
S8	1r/1s	azure	.15	.30
	a	surcharge missing	£1600	-
S5/8	set (4)		£1	1.30

ADDIS ABABA
SEE BOIC
MIDDLE EASTERN FORCES

ANTIGUA

1938 (Nov. 15th) - 51 Designs, ½d, 2d (English Harbour), 1d, 1½d, 2½d, 10/- (Nelson's Dockyard); 3d, 2/6, £1 (Fort James); 6d, 1/-, 5/- (St. John's Harbour). Printers (recess) Waterlow and Sons. Perf. 12½ (L). Sheets 12 x 10 or 10 x 12; 1/- 10 x 6.

1	½d **yellow-green**	.20	.75
	a green (7/42)	.20	.75
2	1d **deep scarlet**	1.25	1.50
	a red (/42, /47)	1.50	1.80
3	1½d **chocolate-brown**	2.25	1.10
	a lake-brown (7/7/49)	£18	£12
	b red-brown (23/1/50)	1.75	1.25
4	2d **grey**	.40	.50
	a slate-grey (14/6/51)	£4	3.50
5	2½d **deep ultramarine**	.40	.50
	a ultramarine (12/43)	.60	.60
6	3d **orange**	.40	.50
	a pale red-orange (7/42)	.60	.60
7	6d **violet**	1.30	.60
8	1/- **black and chocolate**	£2	1.20
	a black and lake-brown (7/7/49)	£20	£8
	ab frame printed double, one albino	£4250	†
9	2/6 **purple-claret**	£19	£10
	a dull purple (7/42)	£12	£10
10	5/- **olive**	£6	5.50
	a grey-olive (26/6/44)	£10	6.50
11	10/- **deep magenta** (1/4/48)	£8	£19
12	£1 **greenish slate** (1/4/48)	£15	£28
1/12	**set** (12)	£45	£62
SP 1/12	**specimen perf** (12)	£150	†

3a/3b There is a somewhat purple tinge in the colour of 3a which is lacking in 3b, though the two are often confused. The best area on the stamp to observe this is the central hill.

8ab A few examples have been found showing a second, uninked impression of the frame.

SPECIAL ISSUES

1937 (May 12th) Coronation. As Aden, but printers, Bradbury, Wilkinson. Perf. 11 x 11¾ (C). Sheets 6 x 10.

S1	1d **carmine-red**	.35	1.50
S2	1½d **light brown**	.30	1.50

S3	2½d **blue**	£1	1.65
S1/3	**set** (3)	1.50	£4
SP S1/3	**specimen perf** (3)	£55	†

1946 (Nov. 1st) Victory. As Aden.

S4	1½d **chocolate-brown**	.10	.10
S5	3d **reddish orange**	.10	.30
SP S4/5	**specimen perf** (2)	£55	†

1949 (Jan 3rd) Silver Wedding. As Aden.

S6	2½d **ultramarine**	.25	1.75
S7	5/- **olive-green**	£6	6.75

1949 (Oct. 10th) U.P.U. As Aden

S8	2½d **dull violet-blue**	.20	.35
S9	3d **deep orange**	£1	1.50
S10	6d **purple**	.20	1.35
S11	1/- **beech-brown**	.20	.75
S8/11	**set** (4)	1.50	3.50

1951 (Feb. 16th) West Indies University College. Designs, 3c. (Arms of College); 12c. (Princess Alice, Chancellor). (Recess) Waterlow and Sons. Perf. 14 x 14¾ (C). Sheets 10 x 6.

S12	3c **black and brown**	.25	.90
S13	12c **black and violet**	.50	£1

Fourteen colonies participated in the issue, and they contributed to the University College funds the portion realised for the sales of the stamps over and above normal receipts.

ARABIAN GULF
SEE MUSCAT

ASCENSION

1938 (May 12th) - 40. Designs, ½d, 1/- (Georgetown, Clarence Bay); 1d, 6d, 10/- ("Three Sisters" Hills); 1½d, 2/6 (The Pier, Georgetown); 1d, 2d, 4d (Green Mountain); 3d, 5/- (Long Beach, opposite Georgetown). Printers (recess) De La Rue. Perf. 13½ (C). Centres black. Sheets 6 x 10.

1	½d **violet**	1.50	1.20
	a re-entry	£40	£40
	b long E	£100	£100
2	1d **green**		
	(Green Mountain)	£20	5.50
3	1d **orange-yellow** (8/7/40)	£5	£6
4	1½d **vermilion**	1.50	.85
	a davit flaw	£150	£120
5	2d **deep orange**	1.40	.60
6	3d **ultramarine**	£40	£16
7	3d **grey** (8/7/40)	£6	1.10
8	4d **ultramarine** (8/7/40)	£5	2.25
9	6d **grey-blue**	3.50	1.35
	a boulder flaw	£75	£60
10	1/- **sepia**	£5	1.10
	a re-entry	£90	£90
11	2/6 **carmine**	£16	£6
	a davit flaw	£750	£300
	b frame double		
	one albino	£3250	-
12	5/- **pale brown**	£38	5.50
13	10/- **bright red-purple**	£40	£25
	a boulder flaw	£175	£150
1/13	**set** (13)	£160	£65
SP1/13	**specimen perf** (13)	£600	†

As before but Perf. 13 x 12¾ (C). (Issued 17/5/44 unless otherwise indicated).

14	½d **violet**	.50	1.50
	a re-entry	£20	£25
	b long E	£45	£50
	c torpedo flaw	£40	£50
15	1d **orange-yellow** (5/42)	.20	.35
	a mountaineer flaw	£75	£95
16	1d **green**		
	("Three Sisters" 1/6/49)	.30	.90
	a re-entry	£24	£30
17	1½d **vermilion**	.40	.50
	a davit flaw	£85	£95
	b cut mast and railings	£85	£95
17c	1½d **rose-carmine** (25/2/53)	.30	£4
	d davit flaw	£70	£90
	e cut mast and railings	£70	£90
	f jibstay flaw	£50	£75

18	2d **deep orange**	.35	.25
	a mountaineer flaw	£140	£100
19	3d **dark grey**	.30	.50
	a grey-black (6/12/50)	£1	£1
	ab major retouch	£50	£60
20	4d **ultramarine**	£2	£2
	a mountaineer flaw	£225	£190
21	6d **grey-blue**	£4	3.75
	a boulder flaw	£65	£50
22	1/- **sepia**	£2	1.25
	a re-entry	£35	£40
23	2/6 **carmine**	£12	£19
	a davit flaw	£500	£650
	b cut mast and railings	£500	£650
24	5/- **light brown**	£18	£18
25	10/- **bright red-purple** (FA)	£25	£35
	a grey-black and		
	red-purple (14/2/45)	£25	£35
	b boulder flaw	£120	£120
14/25	**set** (13)	£60	£80

As before, but Perf. 14 (L) and colours changed (1½d and 2d).

26	1d **orange-yellow** (17/2/49)	.30	£10
	a mountaineer flaw	£75	£150
27	1½d **brownish vermilion**		
	(17/2/49)	£1	£8
	a davit flaw	£110	£150
	b cut mast and railings	£110	£150
28	1½d **rose-carmine** (1/6/49)	.30	.60
	a davit flaw	£80	£100
	b cut mast and railings	£80	£100
	c dull rose-carmine (1/6/49)	£4	£3
	ca davit flaw	£200	£200
	cb cut mast and railings	£200	£200
29	2d **deep orange** (17/2/49)	.80	£22
	a mountaineer flaw	£125	£200
30	2d **deep scarlet** (1/6/49)	.40	£1
	a mountaineer flaw	£100	£135
26/30	**set** (5)	2.50	£35

1b   14c

1a/14a Right frame lines strongly doubled. R2/2. Other lesser doublings on R2/3-6, R3/1.

1b, 14b Long centre bar to second 'E' in 'GEORGETOWN'. R2/3.

4a, etc There is a small davit-like object at top left of the pier. R5/1.   4a

9a, etc 'boulder' flaw. Occurs on part of the 1938 printing and all subsequent printings. R5/4

9a

10a, 22a Doubling of right vertical frame lines and value tablet. R6/4.

14c A diagonal line in the sea to the right of 'Georgetown', in the frameplate colour. 1944 printing only, R3/4.

15a, etc A flaw resembling a mountaineer on R4/4. Printings 1945 onwards.

16a Left vertical frame lines doubled. R4/6.

         17b   17f

17b, etc A broken diagonal line crosses the mast and railings. R3/1. Printings 1946 onwards.

17f On the main boom of the derrick a flaw appears centrally on the lower guy. R6/6, 1953-4 printings only.

19ab A major retouch above central mountain. R10/2, 1950 printing only. Other good retouches exist on R6/5 and 10/4.

25 The frame is fluorescent-aniline.

28c On greyish paper.

SPECIAL ISSUES

1937 (May 19th) Coronation. Perf. 13¾ x 14 (C). Printers (recess) De La Rue. Sheets 6 x 10.

S1	1d **green**	.25	.85
S2	2d **orange**	.50	.35
S3	3d **deep blue**	.50	.30
S1-3	**set** (3)	1.10	1.35
SP S1/3	**specimen perf** (3)	£225	†

1946 (Oct. 21st) Victory. As Aden

S4	2d **reddish orange**	.20	.60
S5	4d **deep blue**	.20	.35
SP S4/5	**specimen perf** (2)	£110	†

1948 (Oct. 20th) Silver Wedding. As Aden.

S6	3d **black**	.25	.20
S7	10/- **red-purple**	£24	£30

1949 (Oct. 10th) U.P.U. As Aden.

S8	3d **carmine-rose**		.50	1.20
S9	4d **indigo**		£2	.90
S10	6d **dull olive**		£1	2.25
S11	1/- **slate-black**		£1	.90
	a 'A' of watermark missing	£675	-	
S8/11	**set** (4)		£4	4.70

AUSTRALIA

1912-1947 THE KANGAROO TYPE ISSUES

The Kangaroo Type was designed by B. Young and engraved by S. Reading; the seventh and final issue was printed (typo) by W.C.G. McCracken.

1945 (Dec. 24th) The seventh and last Kangaroo Issue. The 2/- value from redrawn Die III.

G82	2/- **maroon** (24/12/45)	1.75	£3
G83	2/- **pale maroon** (1947)	1.75	£3
	a inverted watermark	†	-

The third die differs from Dies I and II (the earlier 2/- values) in that the new die has one coloured background line between the value circle and the 'SH' of Shillings, whilst stamps produced from Dies I and II show two coloured lines at the same position. Third multiple (C of A over Crown) watermark. Perf. 11¾ to 12. Sheets 120 - two panes, each 6 x 10.

1934 (Dec. 1st)-1948 Design, Hermes between the two hemispheres. Originally intended for the combined postage and air fee rate to Great Britain.

(I) (Recess) printed by John Ash on unwatermarked chalk-surfaced paper. Perf 11 (L). Sheets 80; two panes, each 4 x 10.

G236	1/6d **purple** (1/12/34)	£20	.60

(II) (Recess) printed by John Ash until April 1940, then by W.C.G. McCracken on chalk-surfaced paper, C of A multiple watermark. Perf 13¼ x 13¾ (C). Sheets 80; two panes, each 8 x 5.

G237	1/6d **brownish claret** (22/10/37)	5.50	.30
	a dull purple (1946)	5.50	.30

(III) As (II) previously but on thin uncoated paper.

G238	1/6d **dull purple** (12/2/48) £1.50	.85

Imperforate examples of G237 were not officially issued.

All stamps hereafter were printed (recess) at the Australian Note and Stamp Printing Works, Melbourne, on C of A Multiple watermark paper, unless otherwise mentioned.

1937-45 Designs, portraits of King and Queen (1d to 3d and 1/4d); Australian fauna (other values). Perf 13½ x 14 (C). Watermark sideways (5d and 9d), upright (other values). Designs, 5d, 9d, H. Sheets 160 - two panes, each 8 x 10 or 10 x 8.

1	½d **orange** (Kangaroo) (3/10/38)	1.25	.30
2	1d **emerald-green** (Queen) (10/5/37)	.40	.30
3	1½d **lake-brown** (King) (20/4/38)	4.50	2.75
4	2d **scarlet** (King) (10/5/37)	.40	.30
	a pale scarlet (/38)	.50	.40
5	3d **deep blue** (ch) Die 1, 1st printing (2/8/37)	£50	£50
	a dull blue (ch) Die 1, 2nd printing (2/8/37)	£25	£11
6	3d **dull blue** (ch) Die 1a (/38)	£50	4.50
7	3d **dull blue** (ch) Die 1b (3/38)	£22	3.25
	a blue, uncoated paper (21/12/38)	£22	2.25
8	4d **green** (Koala)	3.50	1.35
9	5d **dull purple** (Ram) (1/12/38)	.75	.35
10	6d **reddish brown** (Kookaburra) (2/8/37)	£8	.90
11	9d **sepia-brown** (Platypus) (1/9/38)	2.50	.90
12	1/- **dull green** (Lyre Bird) (2/8/37)	£24	1.50
13	1/4d **magenta** (King) (31/10/38)	£1	1.50
1/13	**set** (11)	£60	£11

5   5a

6   7

6 broken lines   7 firm lines

5 has letters TA (at right) clearly joined at base. The wattles and King's face have a whitish appearance, lacking much of the detail to be found in subsequent printings. The stamps are of a relatively deep blue shade, quite distinct from the paler chalky blue of later printings.

5a normally shows more detail on the wattles and King's face, and the joining of the letters TA is not so pronounced. The shade is pale chalky blue, but as the same plates were used for the printings of 5 and 5a only the shades are invariably different.

6 is as 5a but the letters TA have been clearly separated. The 'T' tapers at base.

7 a firm line has been added around the King's chin. The 'T' no longer tapers.

7a is as 7, but is printed on thinner paper; the shade is a deeper blue.

Imperforate examples of Nos. 8, 10, 11 and 12 were not officially issued.

1937-48 Designs, 5/-,10/-, £1 (King and Queen in State Robes). Perf 13¾ (C). (Watermark sideways, 5/- and 10/-; watermark upright, £1). Sheets 80; two panes, each 10 x 4 or 4 x 10.

15	5/- **red-claret** (ch) (1/4/38)	£7	1.20
	a uncoated tinted paper (12/47)	£3	£2
	b uncoated white paper (6/48)	1.50	1.50
16	10/- **dull purple** (ch) (1/4/38)	£18	£10
	a uncoated paper (11/48)	£22	£20
17	£1 **bluish slate** (ch) (1/11/38)	£25	£20
	a uncoated paper (/48)	£30	£40
15-17	**set** (3)	£40	£28

Specimen overprints - 10/- at £15, £1 at £275

Though Nos. 7a, 16a, 17a have been described as being on thin paper, they are actually similar in this respect to other Australian stamps not on chalk-coated paper. The difference arises from the latter being thicker than normal.

Care should be exercised in purchasing imperforate or tete-beche varieties issued between 1942-1950, some of which were unofficial leakages.

1938-51 As No 1 etc., but Perf 14¾ x 14 (C). (Nos. 19 to 24 have solid background, similar to No. 3).

18	½d **orange** (28/1/42)	.25	.10
	a brown-orange	£40	£25
	b coil pair, varied perf.	£7	£20
	ba coil block of 4	£400	-
	c tagged ear	£12	£10
19	1d **emerald-green** (11/7/38)	2.25	.35
	a thin paper (11/38)	£25	£15
20	1d **purple-brown** (10/12/41)	.70	.30
	a coil pair, varied perf	£6	£20
21	1½d **lake-brown** (11/41)	2.25	£6

22	1½d **emerald-green**		
	(10/12/41)	.50	1.10
23	2d **scarlet** (11/7/38)	1.75	.10
	a watermark inverted	£4	.50
	b medallion flaw	£150	£50
	c thin paper (/39)	£50	£20
	d coil pair, varied perf	£275	£350
	e coil pair, uniformly large		
	perf holes	£250	£300
24	2d **purple-mauve**		
	(10/12/41)	.20	£1
	a medallion flaw	£35	£40
	b coil pair, varied perf (/42)	£20	£40
	c watermark inverted		
	(from coils)	£100	£45
25	3d **blue** (Die 2) (11/40)	£20	2.25
26	3d **purple-brown**		
	(10/12/41)	.20	.10
	a thin paper	£30	£15
27	4d **green** (10/42)	.50	.10
	a inverted watermark	£1600	£1200
28	5d **dull purple** (12/45)	.25	1.20
29	6d **reddish brown** (6/42)	£1	.10
	a red-chocolate (/44)	1.25	.25
	b greyish brown (/51)	£1	.15
	c top hat flaw	£225	-
30	9d **sepia-brown** (/42)	.50	.15
	a thin paper	-	-
31	1/- **dull green** (3/41)	.65	.10
	a watermark inverted	£1600	£1200
	b roller flaw	£15	7.50
18/31	**set** (14)	£28	£11

For note on coil perf varieties see after 55.

Normal   'tagged ear'

18ca 'Tagged ear - an upwards line from the lower ear. R6/8 RP

23a from booklets

23b/24a A flaw obliterates the medallion which is normally below the end medal at left, on the King's left breast. R2/5 RP.

Die 1 eyebrow left to right   Die 2 eyebrow right to left

25 Notable differences between this die and the one in use previously (For Nos. 5-7a) is that more of the epaulette on the left shoulder shows and the King's left eyebrow is shaded from right to left (downwards - as you look at the stamp), instead of the reverse as previously.

29c this large flaw (variable in appearance) was constant for a brief period in early 1950. R3/3 sheet A.

30 The normal sideways watermark faces right when seen through the front of the stamp. On CW11, it faces left.

31b a flaw above the 'O' of 'ONE', R1-6/6 sheet A

1941 (Dec. 10th) Nos. 23, 25 and 9 surcharged in violet (2½d and 5½d) and yellow on black (3½d).

32	2½d/2d **scarlet**	.35	.40
	a medallion flaw	£175	£100
	b surcharge omitted in		
	pair with normal	£5500	-
33	3½d/3d **blue**	.50	1.35
34	5½d/5d **dull purple**	£2	3.30
32/34	**set** (3)	2.50	4.50

32a See 23b/24a.

32b Two examples of this error are known.

Numbers surcharged - 2½d, 32,366,400; 3½d, 2,946,080; 5½d, 3,820,500

1942-51 Designs, King and Queen's Portraits (1d-3½d), Emu (5½d), framed by design incorporating Australian Flora and Fauna. Perf 14¾ x 14 (C).

35	1d **plum** (Queen) (1/1/43)	.65	.10
	a coil pair, varied perf. (/44)	£11	£25
	b deep plum (/47)	.65	.10
36	1½d **green** (As No. 35)		
	(1/12/42)	.75	.10
	a deep green (/47)	.90	.10
37	2d **mauve-purple**		
	(King) (4/12/44)	.50	£1
	a coil pair, varied perf. (1/49)	£45	£90
	ab coil block of 4 (5/50)	£1200	-
	b bright mauve-purple (/47)	.50	£1
38	2½d **scarlet** (King) (7/1/42)	.20	.10
	a watermark inverted	2.50	£1
	b imperf. strip	£4000	-

39	3½d **blue** (King) (3/42)	.50	.35
	a deep violet-blue (8/51)	.60	.35
	b thin paper (/51)	£15	£15
40	5½d **slate** (Emu) (2/42)	.50	.10
	a bluish slate (/47)	.75	.10
35/40	**set** (6)	2.80	1.60

38a from booklets.

38b A quarter sheet (top right) bought at St. Kilda P.O. had the end vertical strip of five imperf, yielding 5 horizontal strips of 8 (with sheet margin at right). All other imperforate items were not officially issued.

For coil perf. varieties see note after 55.

1947-48 Design, Portrait of Princess Elizabeth. Perf. 14 x 14¾ (C). Watermark sideways. Sheets 160 - two panes, 10 x 8.

43	1d **dull purple** (20/11/47)	.10	.20
	a deep dull purple (/48)	.10	.20
	b dark purple		
	(no watermark) (8/48)	.10	.10
	bc coil pair, varied perf.	1.25	£3
	bd coil block of 4	2.50	£6

Imperf. varieties of No. 43 were not officially issued. See also note after 55.

1948-52 Designs, portraits of Royal Family (1½d, 2d, 3d and 7½d); 8½d Aborigine; 1/3d Bull; 1/6d Hermes and Globe; 2/- Aboriginal Art. Perf. 14¾ x 14 (C) (1½d to 8½d). Perf. 14½ x 14¾ (C) (other values).

44	1½d **deep green** (no watermark)		
	(Queen) (19/5/50)	.20	.25
46	2d **yellow-green** (as No. 44)		
	(no watermark) (28/3/51)	.10	.10
	a coil pair, varied perf	£3	£6
	b coil block of 4 (11/52)	£6	£10
	c green (1956)	.15	.15
47	2½d **scarlet** (King) (12/4/50)	.10	.10
48	2½d **purple-brown** (as No. 47)		
	(no watermark) (23/5/51)	.10	.20
49	3d **scarlet** (as No. 47)		
	(28/2/51)	.10	.15
	a coil pair, varied perf (5/51)	£8	£28

	b thin paper	£25	£15
	c weak entry	£25	£10
	d vertical strip of three ex		
	booklet printing with		
	margin top and bottom	£8	£12
50	3d **myrtle-green** (as No. 47)		
	(no wmk.) (14/11/51)	.10	.10
	a coil pair, varied perf. (12/51)	£12	£30
51	7½d **blue** (King) (31/10/51)	.10	.50
	a thin paper	£20	£15
	b vertical pair, imperf		
	three sides	£10000	-
52	8½d **brown**		
	(Aborigine) (14/8/50)	.10	.60
53	1/3d **purple-brown**		
	(Bull) (16/2/48)	.85	.65
	a deep purple-brown (/52)	.85	.65
	b thin paper (/52)	£30	-
54	1/6d **sepia-black**		
	(Hermes) (1/9/49)	.50	.10
	a black	.50	.10
55	2/- **deep chocolate**		
	(Crocodile) (16/2/48)	.75	.10
	a black-brown		
	(thin paper) (/51)	£25	£15
44/55	**set** (11)	2.75	2.50

The special perforation used for coils, had small holes at the side and large at the centre. Nos 37a, 43bc and 56c were also released in sheet form. No. 46a was issued only in sheet form.

CW 49c in pair with normal

49c The 'AUSTRALIA' panel is noticeably paler on R8/15 (ex sheets originally made up for booklets).

1948-56 As nos. 18, 36, 37, 27, 29, 30 and 31 but no watermark, perforated 14¾ x 14 or 14 x 14¾ (No. 61).

56	½d **orange** (15/9/49)	.10	.10
	a tagged ear	£15	£10
	b sky retouch	£22	£22
	c coil pair (1950)	.35	£2
	ca tagged ear	£40	-
	cb sky retouch	£135	-
	d coil block of 4	1.40	-
57	1½d **green** (17/8/49)	.50	£1
58	2d **bright purple** (20/12/48)	.40	£1
	a coil pair	1.50	£6
59	4d **green** (18/8/56)	£1	1.35
60	6d **purple-brown** (13/12/56)	2.75	.60
61	9d **chocolate** (12/12/56)	£10	2.25
62	1/- **grey-green** (13/12/56)	£2	.75
	a 'green mist' retouch	£1500	-
	b roller flaw	£18	£12
56-62	**set** (7)	£15	6.50

56a, ca see 18ca.

56cb is in pair with normal.

62a the sky to the left of the bird has been extensively recut. ULP R9/3.

62b see 31b.

56b, cb   62a

1949-51 Design, Commonwealth Coat of Arms. Perf. 14¼ x 13¾ (C). Sheets 8 x 10.

63	5/- **red-claret** (11/4/49)	1.50	.15
	a thin paper (/51)	£45	£6
64	10/- **purple-violet** (3/10/49)	£8	.50
65	£1 **deep blue** (28/11/49)	£16	£2
66	£2 **reseda-green** (16/1/50)	£45	8.50
	a roller flaw	£150	£30
63/66	**set** (4)	£65	£10
SP64/66	**specimen ovpt** (3)	£85	†

It is possible to find various thickness of paper on this issue, varying from thick to thin, with plenty of intermediates. We list the 5/- on thin paper, the listed variety being very obvious.

66a The flaw appears on Row 5/1 and Row 6/1 as a smudge under E. It can also be found retouched.

'roller' flaw

1951-52 Designs, King's Head. Perf. 14¾ x 14 (C) No. 69 watermark sideways. Perf. 14¾ x 14½ (C).

67	3½d **purple-brown** (28/11/51)	.10	.10
	a vertical pair, imperf between	£7500	-
68	4½d **scarlet** (20/2/52)	.10	.75
69	6½d **deep brown** (20/2/52)	.10	.60
	a re-entry	£10	£10
70	6½d **emerald-green** (9/4/52)	.10	.20
	a re-entry	£10	£10

71	1/0½d **slate-black** (19/3/52)	.30	.35
67/7	**set** (5)	.60	1.80

67a was from a booklet pane found in Wollongong Post Office. It is now split into pairs.

69a, 70a Re-entries occur - R1/7 left vertical frame re-cut; R2/8 right lower frame lines doubled; R10/4 all letters of Australia re-entered or doubled. Also left and right frame lines doubled.

SPECIAL ISSUES

All commemorative issues have multiple 'C of A' watermark upright, unless stated.

1937 (Oct. 1st) 150th Anniversary of Foundation of N.S.W. Design, Gov. Phillip and companions at Sydney Cove, from a painting by John Alcott. Perf. 13¼ x 13½ (C). Sheets 80 - two panes, each 8 x 5.

S1	2d **scarlet**	£1	.20
	a tail variety	£250	£60
S2	3d **blue**	£3	1.35
S3	9d **dull purple**	7.50	£6
S1/3	**set** (3)	10.50	£7

S1a A curved line extending from the right figure has the appearance of a tail. R7/1, left pane. This was retouched; various states exist.

Number issued - 2d, 71,668,000; 3d, 2,454,000; 9d, 512,000.

1940 (July 15th) War Effort. Designer, F. Manley from drawing by Virgil Reilly. Perf. 13¾ x 13¼ (C). Sheets 80 - two panes, each 8 x 5.

S4	1d **green**	.85	1.50
	a rifle flaw	£18	£14
S5	2d **scarlet**	.85	.90
S6	3d **blue**	£6	£6

S7   6d **brownish purple**   £10   £12
S4/7   **set** (3)   £16   £18

S4a A flaw on the butt of the soldier's rifle appears on R2/2.

Number issued - 1d, 61,240,000; 2d, 85,782,800; 3d, 3,078,240; 6d, 1,808,400.

1945 (Feb. 19th) Swearing-in of Governor-General, Duke of Gloucester. Designer, F. Manley. Perf. 14¾ x 14½ (C). Sheets 60 - two panes, each 5 x 6.

S8 2½d **carmine-lake**   .10   .10
S9 3½d **deep ultramarine**   .10   .65
S10 5½d **deep slate-blue**   .15   .65
S8/10   **set** (3)   .30 1.25

Number issued - 2½d, 88,290,000; 3½d, 4,048,320; 5½d, 5,886,900.

1946 (Feb. 18th) Peace. Perf. 14½ x 14¾ (C). Designs, 2½d star and wreath, 3½d flag and dove, 5½d angel. Designers, F. Manley and G. Lissenden. 5½d watermark sideways. Sheets 6 x 5 or 5 x 6.

S11 2½d **carmine-red**   .10   .10
S12 3½d **grey-blue**   .25   .90
S13 5½d **deep emerald-green**   .30   .55
S11/13   **set** (3)   .60 1.40

S11; examples exist without watermark, but they were never issued.

Number issued - 2½d, 93,985,500; 3½d, 5,448,600; 5½d, 7,840,500

1946 (Oct. 14th) Centenary of Discovery of pastoral lands in central Queensland. Design, portrait of Sir T. Mitchell. Designer, F. Manley. Perf. 14 ¾ x 14½ (C). Sheets 60 - two panes, each 5 x 6.

S14 2½d **carmine-red**   .10   .10
S15 3½d **blue**   .25   .75
S16 1/- **grey-green**   .25   .30
S14/16   **set** (3)   .50   £1

S14 imperforate examples were not officially issued.

Number issued - 2½d, 104,492,160; 3½d, 4,640,940; 1/-, 9,401,160.

1947 (Sept. 8th) 150th Anniversary of foundation of Newcastle, N.S.W. Designs, 2½d, (Lt. John Shortland); 3½d (Steel Foundry); 5½d (Coal cranes). Perf. 14¾ x 14 (C) (2½d) or Perf. 14½ x 14¾ (C) (other values). (S18-S19 on surfaced paper). 3½d watermark sideways. Sheets, 2½d, 160 - two panes, each 8 x 10; others, 60 - two panes, each 6 x 5.

S17 2½d **carmine-lake**   .10   .10
S18 3½d **blue** (shades)   .25   .75
S19 5½d **green**   .25   .40
S17/19   **set** (3)   .50 1.10

S17; the portrait was intended to be that of the discoverer of the Hunter River, but it is actually of his father.

S17; imperforate examples were not officially issued.

Number issued - 2½d, 105,840,000; 3½d, 4,531,500; 5½d, 7,516,380.

1948 (July 12th) William J. Farrer. (scientist who improved wheat breeds). Designer, F. Manley. Perf. 14¾ x 14 (C). Sheets 160 - two panes, each 8 x 10.

S20 2½d **scarlet**   .15   .10

Number issued - 74,168,000.

1948 (Sept. 13th) Sir F. von Mueller (botanist and explorer). Designer, F. Manley. Perf. 14¾ x 14 (C). Sheets 160 - two panes, each 8 x 10.

S21 2½d **lake-carmine**   .10   .10

Number issued - 73,754,880.

1948 (Nov. 15th) Pan-Pacific Scout Jamboree. Perf. 14 x 14¾ (C). Wmk. sideways. Sheets 160 - two panes, each 10 x 8.

S22 2½d **lake-carmine**   .10   .10

Number issued - 90,307,200.

1949 (June 17th) Anniversary of Birth of Henry Lawson (Poet and Author). Perf. 14¾ x 14 (C). No wmk. Sheets 160 - two panes, each 8 x 10.

S23 2½d **deep lake-maroon**   .15   .10

Number issued - 109,252,000.

1949 (Oct. 10th) U.P.U. Design, mounted postman. Designers, Sir D. Lindsay, F. Manley. No watermark, Perf 14½ x 14 (C). Sheets 6 x 14.

S24 3½d **bright ultramarine**   .20   .35

Number issued - 5,084,688.

1949 (Nov. 28th) Lord Forrest of Bunbury (explorer and politician). Designer, F. Manley. Perf. 14¾ x 14 (C). Sheets 160 - two panes, each 8 x 10.

S25 2½d **lake-carmine**   .15   .10

Number issued - 90,602,880.

1950 (Sept. 27th) Dual Centenary of Postage Stamps for N.S.W. and Victoria. Designs, adaptations of original stamps (se-tenant). Designers, G. Lissenden (S26), E.R.M. Jones (S27). No watermark. Perf. 14¾ x 14 (C). Sheets 160 - two panes, each 8 x 10.

S26 2½d **maroon (N.S.W.)**   .15   .10
S27 2½d **maroon (Victoria)**   .15   .10
     a se-tenant pair   .30   .40

Number issued - 47,040,000 each.

1951 (May 1st) Golden Jubilee of Commonwealth of Australia. Designs, 3ds (se-tenant), Sir Edmund Barton and Sir Henry Parkes; 5½d, opening First Parliament by Duke of York (later KGV); 1/6d, Parliament House, Canberra. Designer, F. Manley. No watermark. Perf. 14¾ x 14 (C). Sheets, 3d., 160 - two panes, each 8 x 10; others 6 x 14.

S28	3d **lake-carmine** (Barton)	.30	.10
S29	3d **lake-carmine** (Parkes)	.30	.10
	a se-tenant pair	1.10	1.50
S30	5½d **dark blue**	.15	1.35
S31	1/6d **red-brown**	.25	.30
S29a/31	**set** (4)	1.35	2.75

Number issued - 3d (each), 52,709,920; 5½d, 2,137,716; 1/6d, 6,351,576.

1951 (July 2nd) Gold Centenary and Victoria Government Centenary. Designs (se-tenant), E. H. Hargreaves (gold discoverer) and C. J. Latrobe, first Governor of Victoria. Designer F. Manley. No watermark Perf. 14¾ x 14 (C). Sheets 160 - two panes, each 8 x 10.

S32	3d **lake-maroon** (Hargraves)	.25	.10
S33	3d **lake-maroon** (Latrobe)	.25	.10
	a se-tenant pair	.75	1.75

Number issued - 32,023,360 (pairs).

POSTAGE DUE STAMPS

All the following were printed by J. Ash.

Type 1	Type 2	Type 3

Type 4	Type 5

1936-7 Additional values on paper watermarked Multiple Crown over A. Typo. Perf. 11 (L).

D101	3d carmine and yellow-green		
	- **Type 1** (4/47)	£40	£45
D103	6d carmine and yellow-green		
	- **Type 2** (8/36)	£200	£200

1938-9 (June) Value (typo) with ornamental frame (recess). Perf. 14¾ x 14 (C). Centres carmine.

PD1	½d **yellow-green** (1939) (1)	1.50	1.65
PD2	1d **yellow-green** (1)	4.50	.35
PD3	2d **yellow-green** (1)	£7	1.35
PD4	3d **yellow-green** (2)	£16	£11
PD5	4d **yellow-green** (1)	£6	.35
PD6	6d **yellow-green** (1)	£35	£28
PD7	1/- **yellow-green** (4)	£25	7.50
PD1/7	**set** (7)	£85	£45

This issue is in a different perforation from all previous issues. PD1-3, 5-6 have values as type 1 above, PD4 as type 2. PD7 has a small figure '1', as 4.

1946-57 As before, but with alterations in value tablet. ½d to 8d type 3, 1/- type 5. Centres carmine.

PD8	½d **yellow-green** (9/56)	.60	£2
PD8a	1d **yellow-green** (1/47)	.60	.50
	a watermark inverted		
PD9	2d **yellow-green** (9/46)	2.50	.75
PD10	3d **yellow-green** (9/46)	2.25	.75
PD11	4d **yellow-green** (11/52)	£4	1.50
	a deep green (/57)	£4	1.50
PD12	5d **yellow-green** (2/12/48)	£6	2.50
PD13	6d **yellow-green** (9/47)	£5	1.20
PD14	7d **yellow-green** (26/8/53)	1.50	£2
PD15	8d **yellow-green** (24/4/57)	£2	£10
PD16	1/- **yellow-green** (7/46)	£8	£1
	a deep green	£9	£6
PD8/16	**set** (10)	£30	£20

The coloured portion of the centre of the 'D' is half-moon shaped. The '1' of the '1/-' is larger than PD7; there are only three lines between the top of the figure and the frame.

BOOKLET PANES

P1	CW 23 pane of 6	£50	-
P2	CW 38 pane of 6	£40	-
P3	CW 67 pane of 6	£6	-

BOOKLETS

(B1-B4 are stapled)

B1	2/- **1938 black on green cover**		
	P1 2 panes of 6	£300	-
	a with waxed interleaves	£400	-

B2   2/- **1938 black on buff cover**
        P1 2 panes of 6   £400   -

Each exist watermark upright or inverted.

B3   2/6 **1942 black on buff
        cover**
        P2 2 panes of 6   £80   -
        a with waxed interleaves,
        postal rates on back cover £160   -

        Stamps upright in book.

B4   2/6 **1949 black on buff
        cover**
        P2 2 panes of 6   £55   -

Stamps sideways in book.

B5   3/6 **1952 orange and black
        on green cover**
        P3 2 panes of 6   £12   -
        a with waxed interleaves   £60   -

COMMONWEALTH OCCUPATION FORCES IN JAPAN

1946 (Oct. 11th)-48 Australian stamps overprinted B.C.O.F. JAPAN 1946, in black, at Hiroshima Printing Works, for use of Australian Occupation Force. Use ceased 12/2/49.

J1	½d **orange** (No 18)	£2	£5
	a narrow N	£85	£90
	b narrow B and A	£80	£85
	c 4 different fount	£80	£85
	d 6 different fount	£80	£85
	e stop after 'JAPAN'	£80	£90
J2	1d **deep plum** (No 35)	1.75	2.75
	a purple	2.50	3.50
	b deep blue overprint (/48)	£30	£65
J3	3d **purple-brown** (No 26)	1.25	£2
	a double overprint	£600	-
J4	6d **reddish brown** (No 29) (8/5/47)	£8	£9
	a narrow N	£140	£125
	b narrow B and A	£125	£125
	c 4 different fount	£125	£125
	d 6 different fount	£125	£125
	e stop after 'JAPAN'	£125	£140
J5	1/- **dull green** (No 31) (8/5/47)	£8	£10
	a narrow N	£150	£150
	b narrow B and A	£150	£150
	c 4 different fount	£150	£150
	d 6 different fount	£150	£150
	e stop after 'JAPAN'	£180	£200
	f 'roller' flaw	£65	£65
J6	2/- **maroon** (No G82) (8/5/47)	£18	£30
	a pale maroon (No G83)	£18	£30
	b narrow 4	£150	£150
	c narrow B	£150	£150
J7	5/- **red-claret** (No 15) (8/5/47)	£50	£80
	a thin paper (No 15b)(8/48)	£40	£80
J1/7	**set** (7)	£75	£125

1d and 3d values are overprinted in thick condensed type; other values as ½d illustrated.

Numerous small varieties exist amongst the overprints, but only those due to use of different founts have been listed; however, in the overprinting of the 5/- the A is in two founts but as these have been used indiscriminately they have been ignored.

J1a/J4a/J5a R1/8 (right pane).

J1b/J4b/J5b R4/5 (left pane).

J1c/J4c/J5c R2/27 (left pane).

J1c   J4b

J2a (a lighter shade) does not appear to exist without overprint.

'6' normal   '6' different fount

J1d/J4d/J5d the '6' of '1946' is in the wrong fount on R9/4 left pane.

J5f 'roller' flaw see Australia 31b

J6a a single mint example with clear double overprint is known.

J6b R2/7 (left pane).

J6c R5/2 (right pane).

Numbers issued - ½d, 189,670; 1d, 378,750; 3d, 891,643; 6d, 136,053; 1/-, 131,095; 2/-, 62,651; 5/-, 32,508 (approx. 6,000 thin paper No J7a).

Australian stamps supplied to the Army were charged at full face value, and it was consequently necessary for the Army to account for trial overprints submitted for approval. One sheet of 160 of each of the following rejected proofs was placed on sale with the normal stamps, this being an easier alternative to writing them off.

½d. thin overprint in red.
1d. thin overprint in black or red.
3d. thin overprint in black, red or gold.

They can be found used with A.P.O. cancellations. Prices, mint or used from £75 for the black overprints; £200 in red or gold. The gold overprint becomes brown with age.

BAHAMAS

1931 Seal of Colony. Printers (recess) Bradbury, Wilkinson. Watermark Multiple Script CA. Perf. 12. Thick paper with yellowish gum. Sheets 12 x 5.

G99	2/- **slate-purple and bright blue**	£10	£18
G103	3/- **slate-purple and green**	£12	£16
SP G99/103	**specimen (pair)**	£55	†

G99, 103 shades exist. However, there was no announced reprint of these values made until 1942. See 22 and 23.

1938-52 Printers (typo) De La Rue. Perf. 13¾ x 14 (C). Sheets 120 - two panes, each 6 x 10.

1	½d **green** (11/3/38)	.60	.75
	a blue-green (9/42)	.80	1.35
	b deep green (11/12/46)	3.50	£8
	c long 'E'	£80	£100
	d accent flaw	£275	-
2	½d **claret** (18/2/52)	.50	1.50
	a deep claret (9/52)	.60	2.50
	b long 'E'	£90	-
3	1d **rose-carmine** (11/3/38)	£4	1.50
	a white ear	-	-
4	1d **grey** (17/9/41)	1.50	£2
	a pearl-grey (27/6/50)	.30	.40
5	1½d **red-brown** (19/4/38)	.60	.75
	a deep red-brown (/42)	1.50	£1
	b very pale red-brown (19/4/48)	£3	1.50
6	2d **pale grey** (19/4/38)	£9	2.40
	a short T	£475	-
7	2d **dark scarlet** (17/9/41)	.50	.40
	a short T	£70	-
	b rose-red (12/46)	1.40	£2
	c dull carmine (19/4/48)	1.40	£2
	d value tablet doubly printed	†	£6750

8	2d **yellow-green** (1/5/51)	.80	.50
	a green and yellow-green (5/51)	£12	£4
9	2½d **blue** (11/3/38)	1.50	.90
10	2½d **dull violet** (1/7/43)	£1	1.25
	a violet (7/45)	.60	.75
	b value tablet doubly printed	£3000	-
11	3d **pale violet** (19/4/38)	£7	1.80
12	3d **blue** (4/43)	.30	.75
	a 'RENCE' flaw	-	-
	b bright blue (19/4/48)	1.90	2.80
13	3d **rose-carmine** (1/2/52)	.35	£2
14	10d **orange** (18/11/46)	1.20	.15
15	1/- **black and carmine** (ch) (15/9/38)	£9	£4
	a grey and scarlet (thin striated paper (4/42)	£250	£55
	b black and carmine (sub) (9/42)	£10	£4
	c grey and scarlet (sub) (6/3/44)	£7	.45
	d dull grey and deep crimson (ch) (19/4/48)	6.50	.90
16	5/- **pale lilac and blue** (ch) (19/4/38)	£45	£65
	a lilac and blue (thin striated paper) (7/41)	£1500	£400
	b purple-lilac and blue (sub) (9/42)	£12	£13
	c brown-mauve and deep blue (sub) (11/46)	£50	£40
	d deep purple and deep blue (ch) (19/4/48)	£15	£8
	e red-purple and bright blue (ch) (/51)	£12	£10
17	£1 **green and black** (ch) (15/9/38)	£100	£90
	a blue-green and black (sub) (13/4/43)	£30	£35
	b dull green and black (sub) (3/44)	£100	£75
1/17	**set** (17)	£70	£52
SP 1/17	**specimen perf** (14)	£350	†

Early printings are on thicker paper and are usually found with discoloured gum. This is particularly evident on the 1/-, 5/- and £1, where the gum is normally brown and inclined to streakiness.

1d a flaw after the first 'A' of 'BAHAMAS' resembles an accent, R1/5 RP.

1b muddy, unclear printing, a very poor DLR production.

1c, 2b R9/6 LP the bottom bar of the E of PENNY is longer and raised.

normal   CW 3a 'white ear'

3a a white patch on the ear. R2/6 LP. Traces remain on later printings.

6a/7a the stem of the T in TWO was cut short (the letters WO were also misshapen), R3/ 6 RP. Differing states may be found, including on the printings in green. A similar variety exists on R7/6 RP.

normal

CW 10b double

7d, 10b minor doubling in the value tablet is frequently met with, especially on the bottom row of the 2d value. The 'true' double prints are much more spectacular.

12a a large flaw on the 'P' of 'PENCE', quickly corrected. R9/3 RP.

15a, 16a were placed on sale shortly before the release of the "Landfall" set and most were utilised in its preparation. When held at an angle to the light, horizontal deeper-coloured striations are apparent on the surface of the stamps, especially on the nape of the neck.

16 the later printings are known faded or chemically changed in the pale grey colour of the 1/-.

Coils were prepared for the following values: ½d green, 1d red and 1d grey.

WATERMARK VARIETY (TYPE B)
(See introduction for details)

2c	½d Crown missing	£6500	-
2d	½d St Edward's Crown	£2750	£2500

1938 (July 1st) Designs, 4d (Sea Gardens, Nassau); 6d (Fort Charlotte, New Providence); 8d (flamingoes in flight). Printers (recess) Waterlow and Sons. Perf. 12½ (L). Sheets 5 x 12.

18	4d **light blue and orange-red**		.50	.60
19	6d **olive-green and light blue**		.35	.60
20	8d **ultramarine and red**		£4	1.50
18/20	**set** (3)		4.50	2.40
SP18/20	**specimen perf** (3)		£90	†

The 6d value was prepared in coil form.

1940 (Nov. 28th) No. 9 surcharged by the City Press, Nassau.

21	3d/2½d blue	.35	.25

1942-46 As Nos. G99/103 but on thin white paper with clear gum.

22	2/- **purple-slate and indigo-blue** (9/42)	£40	£24
	a 'A' of watermark missing	-	-
	b black and deep blue (13/4/43)	4.50	£5
	c black and steel-blue (1/10/46)	£8	£2
23	3/- **purple-slate and myrtle-green** (9/42)	£12	£16
	a black and deep yellow-green (13/4/43)	£4	£2
	b black and dull myrtle-green (1/10/46)	3.75	£5

22, 23 were released in the Colony late in 1942, but most of the printing was used for the "Landfall" issue. Specimens were not made for U.P.U. distribution.

22b, c, 23a, b the 'black' of these printings has suffused brownish tinge quite unlike 22 and 23.

For similar stamps on thick paper with yellowish gum see note after G99/103.

SPECIAL ISSUES

1937 (May 12th) Coronation. As Ascension.

S1	½d **green**	.10	.10
S2	1½d **light brown**	.15	.65
S3	2½d **blue**	.25	.65
S1/3	**set** (3)	.45	1.25
SP S1/3	**specimen perf** (3)	£65	†

1942 (Oct. 12th) - 43 450th Anniversary of Landfall on America. Nos. 1, etc., locally overprinted in black at the office of the Nassau Guardian.

S4	½d **green**	.15	.35
	a overprint double	£175	-
	b blue-green	.15	.35
	c long 'E'	£38	£45
	d accent flaw	-	-
S5	1d **pale grey**	.15	.35
S6	1½d **red-brown**	.20	.35
S7	2d **rose-carmine**	.20	.40
	a short T	£100	£100
S8	2½d **blue**	.20	.40
S9	3d **blue**	.15	.40
	a 'RENCE' flaw	£275	-
S10	4d **light blue and orange-red**	.20	.60
	a COIUMBUS	£550	£650
S11	6d **olive-green and light blue**	.20	£1
	a COIUMBUS	£550	£750
S12	8d **ultramarine and red**	.40	.40
	a COIUMBUS	£6500	£2500
S13	1/- **grey and scarlet** (thin striated paper)	3.75	2.50
	a black and carmine (sub) (/43)	3.75	5.50
	b grey-black and crimson	7.50	5.50
	c broken 'OF' and 'US'	£125	-
S14	2/- **black and deep blue**	£4	£6
	a purple-slate and indigo-blue (/42)	£6	£13
	b black and steel-blue	£12	£16
	c stop after COLUMBUS	£3250	-
S15	3/- **black and green**	£16	£22
	a purple-slate and myrtle-green (/42)	£4	£4
	b stop after COLUMBUS	£1500	-
S16	5/- **lilac and blue** (thin striated paper)	£20	£10
	a purple-lilac and blue (sub)	£12	8.50
	b broken 'OF' and 'US'	£275	-
S17	£1 **green and black** (ch)	£35	£55

	a green and black (sub)	£18	£15
	b broken 'OF' and 'US'	£450	-
S4/17	**set** (14)	£35	£35
SPS4/17	**specimen perf** (14)	£300	†

S4d see 1d.

S7a see note under 6a/7a.

S9; A double overprint is known on stamps perforated SPECIMEN.

S9a see 12a.

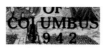

S10a/11a/12a - The L, lacking its foot, has been converted into an I. R5/2 (on one overprinting only). This was a progressive variety and can be found in varying states.

S13, S16, See note 15a, 16a.

S13c, 16b, 17b this progressive variety may be found in various states; only on the top three values. R2/6

1 4 9 2
LANDFALL
OF
COLUMBUS
1 9 4 2

S14c/15b. Row 2/12 on a very limited number of sheets. Less than 10 of the 2/- have been recorded, one of which is used.

S17 has brown gum whereas the gum of No. S17a is clear.

There are numerous varieties and three settings of the overprint, making this a fertile field for study.

1946 (Nov. 11th) Victory. As Aden.

S18	1½d **sepia-brown**	.10	.35
S19	3d **deep blue**	.10	.35
SP S18/19	**specimen perf** (2)	£60	†

1948 (Oct. 11th) Tercentenary of Eleutheran Settlement. Designs, ½d, 4d, 8d, 10d, £1 (buildings and scenes); 1d, 1½d, 2d, 2½d, 3d, 6d, 3/-, 10/- (island pursuits); 1/-, 2/- (sports); 5/- (transport). Printers (recess) Canadian Bank Note Co. No watermark. Perf. 12 (L). Sheets 120 - two panes, each 5 x 12.

S20	½d **orange**	.15	.90
S21	1d **sage**	.15	.20
S22	1½d **greenish bistre**	.15	.50
S23	2d **dull scarlet**	.15	.25
S24	2½d **dull indian red**	.30	.45
S25	3d **bright ultramarine**	£1	.50
S26	4d **grey-black**	.30	.40
S27	6d **emerald**	£1	.50
S28	8d **bright violet**	.60	.40
S29	10d **deep rose-carmine**	.60	.20
S30	1/- **sepia**	1.25	.30
S31	2/- **reddish purple**	£2	£5
S32	3/- **deep blue**	£5	£5
S33	5/- **deep lilac**	£8	£3
S34	10/- **deep grey**	£7	6.50
S35	£1 **vermilion-red**	7.50	9.50
S20/35	**set** (16)	£32	£30

1948 (Dec. 1st) Silver Wedding. As Aden.

S36	1½d **chestnut-brown**	.10	.15
S37	£1 **greenish slate**	£18	£20

1949 (Oct. 10th) U.P.U. As Aden.

S38	2½d **dull violet**	.20	.45
S39	3d **indigo**	£1	1.95
S40	6d **slate-blue**	.30	1.80
S41	1/- **rose-pink**	.30	.45
S38/41	**set** (4)	1.60	4.25

BOOKLET PANES
1938-52

P1	1d **CW 3** pane of 6	-	-
P2	1½d **CW 5** pane of 8	-	-

BOOKLETS

B1	2/- **1938 black on pink cover**		
	CW P1 x 2, P2 x 1	-	-

Some years ago, Murray Payne Ltd sold a 'dummy' booklet from the printer's archive. Since then, a single example of the issued booklet has been recorded.

GERMAN PROPAGANDA LABELS

The 1944 German imitations of the G.B. 1937 Definitive ½d. to 3d. (see after Great Britain for details) were also overprinted in black "LIQUIDATION/OF EMPIRE/BAHAMA IS" within a vertical rectangular frame.

BAHAWALPUR
SEE PAKISTAN

BAHRAIN

1938-41 Stamps of India (1937-46 issue) overprinted BAHRAIN. The overprint measures 13mm (low values), 19mm (rupee values).

1		3p **slate** (5/38)	7.50	2.75
2		½a **red-brown** (5/38)	£3	.10
3		9p **deep green** (5/38)	£5	5.50
4		1a **carmine** (5/38)	£5	.10
5		2a **vermilion** (/39)	2.75	2.25
6		3a **yellow-green** (/41)	£6	£5
7		3½a **blue** (7/38)	£3	£3
8		4a **deep brown** (/41)	£75	£42
9		8a **violet-slate** (/40)	£95	£22
10		12a **deep crimson** (/40)	£60	£30
11		1r **violet-grey and**		
		light brown (/40)	2.50	£1
12		2r **reddish purple and**		
		brown (/40)	£9	£5
	a	**deep purple and brown**	7.50	£5
13		5r **deep green and**		
		deep blue (/40)	£8	£7
14		10r **violet-purple and**		
		red-claret (/41)	£35	£30
15		15r **chocolate and**		
		deep green (/41)	£95	£125
	a	**watermark inverted**	£35	£45
16		25r **slate-violet and**		
		purple-violet (/41)	£60	£55
1/16		**set** (16)	£375	£230

1942-5 Stamps of India (1941-3 issue) overprinted BAHRAIN.

17		3p **slate** (/43)	1.50	1.50
18		½a **purple** (/45)	£2	1.80
	a	**defective 'H'**	£150	-
19		9p **green** (/43)	6.50	£12
20		1a **rose-carmine** (/44)	£3	.60
21		1a3p **bistre** (/43)	£4	£13
22		1½a **slate-purple** (/44)	£3	£5
23		2a **vermilion** (/42)	£3	£1
24		3a **bright violet** (/45)	£9	4.50

25	3½a	blue (/42)	2.40	£13
26	4a	brown (/42)	£2	1.20
27	6a	greenish blue (/42)	7.50	7.50
28	8a	violet-slate (/42)	3.50	2.50
29	12a	deep crimson (/42)	4.50	3.75
17/29		set (13)	£45	£60

18a R20/14. The 'H' in the overprint lacks the crossbar.

Crude, easily recognised, forged and bogus overprints exist on several values of the above. They were handstamped on used Indian stamps.

Although Indian stamps without overprint were not officially used in Bahrain at the time, such stamps (India KGVI 1941/43 and 1937 Rupee values) are known with forged Bahrain cancellations dated 26th January, 1942.

An American A.P.O. (#816) operated at Muharraq Airport from June 1944 to the end of 1945. Mail from American servicemen was carried free; but contractors' employees working on the erection of refinery installations in Bahrain were permitted the use of the A.P.O. as they were employed on a U.S. Government project, and postage on their mail was paid with U.S. stamps.

The Indian Victory stamps (S1-4) were issued (without overprint) in Bahrain in 1946, but are very scarce with Bahrain postmarks.

Casual carriage resulted in very occasional use in Bahrain in early 1948 of Indian stamps with Nasik "PAKISTAN" overprints. Such use was not intended and examples are extremely rare.

1948 (April 1st) -49 Stamps of Great Britain overprinted BAHRAIN and surcharged by Harrison and Sons. The change from Indian to British stamps coincided with the change of administration.

30	½a/½d	green	.25	.75
31	1a/1d	scarlet	.25	1.75
32	1½a/1½d	red-brown	.25	2.25
33	2a/2d	dull orange	.25	.15
34	2½a/2½d	ultramarine	.25	2.75
35	3a/3d	purple-violet	.25	.10
37	6a/6d	pale purple	.25	.10
38	1r/1/-	bistre-brown	.60	.10

39	2r/2/6	green	2.50	£3
	a	'T' Guide mark	£100	£100
40	5r/5/-	red	£3	£3
	a	re-entry	£100	£100
	b	'T' Guide mark	£60	£50
41	10r/10/-	ultramarine (4/7/49)	£40	£38
30/41		set (11)	£45	£45

39a, 40b see note after Great Britain Nos. 16-21

40a R4/2 see Great Britain 18a.

Number issued - ½a, 481,713; 1a, 465,689; 1½a, 213,418; 2a, 484,939; 2½a, 198,928; 3a, 1,138,523; 6a, 2,152,034; 1r, 423,706; 2r, 46,709; 5r, 43,379; 10r, 16,460.

From 1948 British Forces in Bahrain used stamps of the foregoing and following issues, which were cancelled with British F.P.O. date-stamps (#756 and, later, #518).

1950 (2nd October) - 55 As No. 30, etc., but colours changed (Nos. 48-50 as Nos. 34-6 of Great Britain), similarly overprinted and surcharged.

42	½a/½d	dull orange	1.25	1.80
43	1a/1d	ultramarine	1.80	.15
44	1½a/1½d	green	1.80	£7
45	2a/2d	red-brown	.90	.20
46	2½a/2½d	scarlet	1.80	£9
47	4a/4d	light blue (2/10/50)	2.75	.90
48	2r/2/6	green Type 1	£13	£7
	a	Type 2 ('53)	£55	£25
	b	Type 3 ('55)	£650	£60
	ba	inverted 'I'	£4500	£550
49	5r/5/-	red	£7	2.50
	a	third bar in overprint	£325	£275
50	10r/10/-	ultramarine	£15	£4
42/50		set (9)	£40	£30

48 "BAHRAIN" in sharp letters. "2" and "RUPEES" in line, overall measurement 16 mm.

Type 1

48a "BAHRAIN" in heavier, worn type with poorly-defined edges. "2" raised in relation to "RUPEES", overall measurement 15½ mm.

Type 2

48b As Type 2, but vertical distance between "BAHRAIN" and "2 RUPEES" is 15¾-16½ instead of 15mm, and the surcharge is set ¾ to 1½mm to the left of "BAHRAIN".

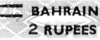

Type 3

48ba R2/1 The "I" in BAHRAIN is higher than the other letters.

49a R6/1 has a third (thinner) bar below the normal two bars, on part of the printing only.

Number issued - ½a, 407,547; 1a, 347,155; 1½a, 155,944; 2a, 374,277; 2½a, 171,900; 4a, 304,323; 2r, 58,184; 5r, 38,937; 10r, 28,994.

SPECIAL ISSUES

1948 (May 1st) Silver Wedding Issue of Great Britain surcharged and overprinted BAHRAIN.

S1	2½a/2½d **ultramarine**	.50	1.50
S2	15r/£1 **deep blue**	£18	£30

Number issued - 2½a, 186,095; 15r, 21,984.

1948 (July 29th) Olympic Games Issue of Great Britain, surcharged and overprinted BAHRAIN.

S3	2½a/2½d **ultramarine**	.50	2.50
	a surcharge double	£1300	£2250
S4	3a/3d **violet**	.50	2.25
S5	6a/6d **reddish purple**	.75	2.25
S6	1r/1/- **bistre-brown**	1.25	2.50
S3/6	**set** (4)	2.75	8.50

S3a The balance of a sheet of 120 was purchased by a serviceman in Muharraq Post Office after a number had been sold and used. Most of the 15 known used copies were cancelled "EXPERIMENTAL P.O. K - 121". Cyl. No. 2 stop, sheet No. 31430. A bogus double surcharge in three lines (as No. S1) exists.

Number issued - 2½a, 99,304; 3a, 112,515; 6a, 112,919; 1r, 87,858.

1949 (Oct. 10th) U.P.U. Issue of Great Britain, surcharged and overprinted BAHRAIN.

S7	2½a/2½d **ultramarine**	.30	1.35
	a Indian lake	£60	£90
S8	3a/3d **pale violet**	.35	2.50
S9	6a/6d **reddish mauve**	.30	1.90
S10	1r/1/- **bistre-brown**	.65	1.75
S7/10	**set** (4)	1.40	6.75

S7a see Great Britain S16b.

Number issued - 2½a, 93,689; 3a, 105,246; 6a, 105,064; 1r, 80,853.

BARBADOS

1938 (Jan 3rd.) - 48 Design, Seal of Colony. (Recess) De La Rue. Sheets 10 x 12, ½d-4d; 10 x 6, 6d-5/-.

(a) Perf. 13¼ x 13 (C).

1		½d **green**	2.25	.10
	a	deep green (/41)	2.50	.15
	c	recut frame	£80	£25
2		½d **yellow-bistre** (16/10/42)	.10	.20
	a	yellow-buff (5/8/48)	.10	.20
	b	'A' of watermark missing	£850	-
	c	recut frame	£13	-
3		1d **scarlet-red**	£100	2.50
	a	sky and 'TES' re-entry	£175	£28
4		1d **blue-green** (16/10/42)	£2	.75
	a	green (7/48)	2.50	.75
	b	sky and 'TES' re-entry	£20	£15
5		1½d **orange**	.15	.25
	a	red-orange (12/6/47)	.10	.25
	b	'A' of watermark missing	£850	-
6		2d **red-claret** (3/6/41)	.25	1.50
	a	extra frameline	£30	£45
7		2d **carmine-red** (20/9/43)	.10	.45
	a	extra frameline	£18	£25
	b	'A' of watermark missing	†	-
8		2½d **ultramarine**	.25	.35
	a	mark on ornament	£25	£25
	b	blue (17/2/44)	.75	£6
	bc	mark on ornament	£35	-
	bd	'A' of watermark missing	£750	-
9		3d **deep brown**	.10	£2
	a	brown (17/2/44)	.15	1.25
	b	line over horse's head	£55	£85
	c	'A' of watermark missing	£850	-
10		3d **blue** (1/4/47)	.10	£1
	a	line over horse's head	£55	£65
	b	ultramarine (18/12/47)	.25	1.25
11		4d **deep grey**	.10	.10
	a	black (18/12/47)	.50	.25
	b	grey-black (5/8/48)	.30	.20
	c	joined scroll	£60	£35
	d	flying mane	£65	£35
	e	shading omitted	£60	£35
	f	cracked plate	£95	£40
12		6d **violet**	.35	.25
	a	pale violet (9/44)	£6	.75
	b	deep bright violet (/48)	£3	.25
13		8d **deep magenta** (9/12/46)	.25	1.25
	a	magenta (18/12/47)	£1	1.25
14		1/- **olive-green**	£5	1.50
	a	olive (9/42)	£2	.10

	b brown-olive (19/11/45)	1.50	.35
	c deep olive-green		
	(11/12/46)	1.50	.75
	d olive-brown (5/8/48)	.50	£1
15	2/6 **reddish purple**	3.50	£1
	b bright red-purple (/42)	3.50	.90
16	5/- **greyish indigo** (3/6/41)	£5	5.50
	a blue-indigo (/49)	2.50	5.50
	b 'A' of watermark missing	£1300	-
SP1/16	**specimen perf** (16)	£250	†

(b) Perf. 13¾ x 14 (L).

17	1d **scarlet-red** (3/1/38)	£12	£4
	b sky and 'TES' re-entry	£50	-

As before but Perf. 14 (C or L). (Nos. 18, 19, 23 Line; Nos. 20a, 24 Comb; Nos. 20, 21, 22 Line and Comb.)

18	½d **sage-green** (4/42)	£30	£1
	a recut frame	£225	£45
19	1d **bright scarlet-red**		
	(10/42)	£6	.10
	a sky and 'TES' re-entry	£38	-
20	1d **blue-green** (16/10/42)	.20	.10
	a green (5/8/48)	.10	.10
	b printed double once albino	£500	-
	c sky and 'TES' re-entry	£14	-
	d 'A' of watermark missing	£850	-
21	1½d **orange** (12/41)	1.75	.45
22	2d **carmine-red** (11/9/44)	.25	£1
	a extra frameline	£25	-
23	3d **brown** (/41)	.10	.35
	a line over horse's head	£55	£65
24	4d **grey-black** (11/9/44)	.10	3.75
	a joined scroll	£60	£90
	b flying mane	£75	£100
	c shading omitted	£70	£90
	d cracked plate	£80	£90
1/24	**set** (16)	£15	£8

See the introduction for further details on gum and paper.

1c   3a   6a

1c, 2c, 18a the top inner frame on R10/6 has been roughly recut.

3a, 4b, 17b, 19a, 20c a re-entry to the top lines in the sky shows them doubled, as is the 'TES' of 'REGNANTES'. R11/2.

6a, 7a, 22a extra frameline on R11/9.

8a, 8bc shows a mark on the central ornament R1-3/3.

8a   9b

9b, 10a, 23a occurs on R4/10 on all printings until the last. Positional blocks without the variety are to be found from the final printing, 10b.

11c   11d

11e   11f

11c, 24a a curved line joins the top right scrolls, R7/8.

11d, 24b the horse has an upright tuft of mane, somewhat resembling a plume, R4/1.

11e, 24c the shading at the base is omitted on R8/10, probably from 1944 onwards.

11f, 24d shows a cracked plate through the value tablet on R6/10.

13, a the 8d displays an interesting range of reactions under ultra-violet.

20b brighter shade and woolly impression.

1947 (April 21st) Nos. 7 and 22 surcharged by the Barbados Advocate Co., Bridgetown.

(a) Perf. 13¼ x 13 (C).

25	1d/2d **carmine-red**	1.25	£3
	a broken Ns	£140	£150
	b short Y	£120	£150
	c broken E	£60	£85
	d extra frameline	£100	£120
	e double surcharge	£3500	†

(b) Perf. 14 (C).

26	1d/2d **carmine-red**	.80	1.80
	a broken N's	£80	-
	b short Y	£60	£80
	c broken E	£30	£35
	d extra frameline	£55	£60

The surcharge has many constant varieties, the most noteworthy being illustrated as follows:-

25a/26a

25b/26b

25c/26c

25a/26a damage to all 3 'N's' is present on later sheets only. R2/8.

25b/26b the short 'Y' is not constant on all sheets. R6/2.

25c/26c the short central bar of the 'E' of 'PENNY' is very similar on positions R7/4 and 11/4.

25d and 26d see 22a.

25e We have now seen a genuine example of the double surcharge, and learned of two others.

1950 (May 1st) Designs, 1c to 60c (views and scenes in Colony); $1.20 (map); $2.40 (Seal of colony). Designers, staff artists, Bradbury Wilkinson. (Recess) Bradbury, Wilkinson. Horizontal designs perf 11 x 11½, vertical designs perf 13½ (C). Sheets 10 x 10.

27	1c **slate-indigo**	.15	2.25
28	2c **emerald**	.10	1.50
29	3c **chocolate and greenish grey**	.60	£2
30	4c **rose-carmine**	.10	.25
31	6c **bright blue**	.15	1.35
32	8c **blue and purple-brown**	.75	1.80
33	12c **blue-green and olive-grey**	.50	.90
	a grey-green and olive-green (10/3/54)	£1	.75
34	24c **deep scarlet and grey-black**	.45	.30
35	48c **purple-violet**	£4	£4
36	60c **deep green and lake**	£4	6.50
37	$1.20 **deep carmine and olive-green**	£4	2.50
38	$2.40 **grey-black**	£12	£18
27/38	**set** (12)	£24	£36

SPECIAL ISSUES

1937 (May 14th) Coronation. As Ascension.

S1	1d **red**	.15	.10
S2	1½d **yellow-brown**	.25	.40
S3	2½d **blue**	.60	.45
S1/3	**set (3)**	.90	.90
SP S1/3	**specimen perf** (3)	£55	†

1939 (June 27th) Tercentenary of General Assembly. (Recess) De La Rue. Perf. 13½ x 14 (C). Sheets 6 x 10.

S4	½d **green**	1.35	.60
S5	1d **scarlet**	1.35	.75
S6	1½d **orange**	1.35	.35
S7	2½d **ultramarine**	1.50	4.25
S8	3d **light brown**	1.75	3.30
S4/8	**set** (5)	6.50	8.50
SPS4/8	**specimen perf** (5)	£130	†

1946 (Sept. 18th) Victory. As Aden.

S9	1½d **orange**	.10	.25
	a double flag	£15	£18
S10	3d **chocolate-brown**	.10	.25
	a 'kite' flaw	£10	£12
SP S9/10	**specimen perf** (2)	£50	†

S9a - This variety is in the form of a second flag (one below the other) at the stern of the launch, R5/2.

S10a - A flaw in the sky to the lower left of the portrait medallion. R10/4 (not on all sheets).

1948 (Nov. 24th) Silver Wedding. As Aden.

S11	1½d **orange**	.15	.30
S12	5/- **bluish slate**	£7	£6

1949 (Oct. 10th) U.P.U. As Aden.

S13	1½d **red-orange**	.25	1.20
S14	3d **indigo**	1.25	2.40
S15	4d **grey**	.25	1.95
S16	1/- **sage-green**	.25	.35
S13/16	**set** (4)	1.80	5.50

1951 (Feb. 16th) West Indies University College. As Antigua.

S17	3c brown and slate-green	.15	.25
S18	12c blue-green and		
	sepia-black	.35	1.35

1952 (April 15th) Centenary of first Barbados postage stamps. Design, replicas of original stamps. Printers (recess) Waterlow and Sons. Perf. 13¾ x 13¼ (C). Sheets 10 x 10.

S19	3c grey-green and		
	bluish slate	.15	.25
S20	4c blue and rose-carmine	.15	.60
S21	12c bluish slate and emerald	.15	.60
S22	24c red-brown and black	.20	.35
S19/22	set (4)	.60	1.60

Number issued - 3c, 574,860; 4c, 271,120; 12c, 339,854; 24c, 219,187.

POSTAGE DUE STAMPS

1934-48 (typo) De La Rue. Watermark Multiple Script CA. Perf. 13¾ x 14. Sheets 6 x 10.

PD1	½d deep green (10/2/35)	.60	£5
	a rough paper (/47)	2.40	£5
PD2	1d black (2/1/34)	.60	.75
	a bisect (½d.) on cover	†	£1500
	b rough paper (/47)	2.75	£1
PD3	3d carmine (13/3/47)	£10	£12
	a smooth paper (/48)	£10	£12
SP PD1/3	specimen set (3)	£65	†

PD2a - This bisect was officially authorised from March, 1934 until supplies of the ½d. stamp were available in February, 1935. In some cases the half stamp was surcharged ½d in red, or black, in manuscript.

PD3 The initial release was on rough paper.

1950 (Dec. 8th) As No. PD1, etc., but currency changed.

PD4	1c deep green	£2	£20
PD5	2c black	3.50	£10
PD6	6c rose-carmine	£8	£12

As Nos. PD4/6, but printed on chalk-coated paper.

PD7	1c dark green (29/11/51)	.20	£2
PD8	2c black (20/1/53)	.50	£4
PD9	6c carmine-red (20/1/53)	.50	£6

Watermark Varieties (Type A)
(See Introduction for details)

PD7a	1c Crown missing	£500	-
PD7b	1c St. Edward's Crown	£200	-
PD8b	2c St. Edward's Crown	£475	-
PD9a	6c Crown missing	£180	-
PD9b	6c St. Edward's Crown	£90	-

BOOKLET PANES

P1	½d CW 1 pane of 10	£500	-
P2	1½d CW 5 pane of 6	£500	-
P3	1d CW 17 pane of 10	£500	-

BOOKLETS

B1	2/- 1938 black on light blue	
	½d, 1d panes of 10,	
	1½d pane of 6	£2000	-

5,000 printed.

GERMAN PROPAGANDA LABELS

The 1944 German imitations of the G.B. 1937 Definitives ½d to 3d (see after Great Britain for details) were also overprinted in black "LIQUIDATION/OF EMPIRE/BARBADOS" within a vertical rectangular frame.

BASUTOLAND

1938 (April 1st) - 52 Printers (recess) Waterlow and Sons. Perf. 12½ (L). Sheets 6 x 10.

1	½d **yellow-green**	.20	.75
	a green (1/44)	.25	£1
	b pale green (14/5/52)	2.50	2.50
2	1d **scarlet**	.25	.45
	a tower variety	£90	£100
	b scarlet-rose (1/10/46)	.35	.45
	c tower variety	£90	£100
	d carmine-lake (/40?)	£200	£140
	e tower variety	-	£650
3	1½d **dull pale blue**	£1	.50
	a light blue (8/12/47)	.20	.30
4	2d **red-purple**	.25	.40
	a mauve-purple (8/12/45)	.15	.35
5	3d **dark blue**	.15	.75
	a bright deep blue (12/47)	.50	1.25
6	4d **grey**	£1	2.50
	a slate-grey (23/1/50)	1.25	2.25
7	6d **yellow-ochre**	.75	£1
	a orange-ochre (1/10/46)	.85	1.25
8	1/- **deep orange**	.75	.60
	a pale reddish-orange (14/5/52)	.85	£1
9	2/6 **sepia**	£6	£5
10	5/- **bright violet**	£16	£6
11	10/- **sage-green**	£17	£12
	a deep olive-green (1/10/46)	£18	£15
1/11	**set** (11)	£38	£26
SP 1/11	**specimen perf** (11)	£200	†

2a/c/e A flaw resembling a tower is to be found on the hilltop on R2/4.

SPECIAL ISSUES

1937 (May 12th) Coronation. As Ascension.

S1	1d **scarlet**	.20	.75
S2	2d **red-purple**	.30	.75
S3	3d **deep blue**	.40	.75
S1/3	**set** (3)	.80	£2
SP S1/3	**specimen perf** (3)	£40	†

1945 (Dec. 3rd) Victory. Nos. S33-5 of South Africa, overprinted Basutoland.

			Pair M	Pair U
S4	1d **deep brown and carmine**		.25	.50
	a barbed wire		£8	£10
S5	2d **slate blue and purple-violet**		.25	.35
S6	3d **deep blue and blue**		.25	.50
S4-6	**set** (3)		.70	1.20

S4a R9/6 See South Africa S33b

1947 (Feb. 17th) Royal Visit. Designs, portraits of Royal Family. Printers (recess) Waterlow and Sons. Perf. 12½ (L). Sheets 10 x 6 or 6 x 10.

S7	1d **scarlet**	.10	.10
S8	2d **green**	.10	.10
S9	3d **ultramarine**	.10	.10
S10	1/- **dull mauve**	.10	.10
S7/10	**set** (4)	.35	.35
SP S7/10	**specimen perf** (4)	£80	†

1948 (Dec. 1st) Silver Wedding. As Aden.

S11	1½d **ultramarine**	.10	.10
S12	10/- **olive-grey**	£19	£23

1949 (Oct. 10th) U.P.U. As Aden.

S13	1½d **dull ultramarine**	.15	.75
S14	3d **indigo**	£1	1.20
S15	6d **orange**	.60	2.40
S16	1/- **beech-brown**	.30	.75
S13/16	**set** (4)	1.90	4.75

POSTAGE DUE STAMPS

1937-46 Printers (typo) De La Rue. Perf. 13¾ x 14 (C). Sheets 6 x 10.

PD1	1d **carmine-red** (/37)	£1	£6
	a deep carmine-red (rough paper) (/46)	£15	£20

PD2 2d **purple-violet**   3.50   £12
     a rough paper (/46)   £15   £20
     b thick 'd'   £35   -
SP PD1/2 **specimen perf** (2)   £40   †

1951. As before, but printed on chalk-coated paper.

PD3 1d **deep carmine-red**
     (24/10/51)   .75   2.75
PD4 2d **purple-violet (6/11/52)** .20   £12
     a thick "d"   £8   £45

PD2b, PD4a The "d" and dot
below are thicker on R9/6 and
R10/6.

                    Normal   R9-10/6

WATERMARK VARIETIES (TYPE A)
(See Introduction for details).

PD3a 1d **Crown missing**   £160   -
PD3b 1d **St. Edward's Crown**   £65   -
PD4b 2d **Crown missing**   £190   -
PD4c 2d **St. Edward's Crown**   £75   -

BECHUANALAND

1938 (April 1st) - 52 (recess) Waterlow and Sons. Watermark multiple Script CA. Perf. 12½ (L). Sheets 6 x 10.

1	½d **green**	£1	£2
	a yellow-green (/41, /43)	£4	4.50
	b bluish green (11/9/44)	6.50	6.50
	c deep green (4/49)	1.75	6.50
2	1d **scarlet**	.40	.75
	a scarlet-rose (1/10/46)	.35	.30
3	1½d **dull pale blue**	£4	1.25
	a light blue (4/43)	.50	.60
4	2d **chocolate-brown**	.40	.50
	a red-brown (10/12/45)	.35	.30
5	3d **ultramarine**	£1	2.50
	a bright ultramarine (1/44)	.50	1.50
6	4d **orange**	.80	£2
7	6d **red-purple**	£2	£2
	ab 'A' of watermark missing	†	-
8	1/- **olive and black**	1.75	4.50
	a olive-green and grey-black (21/5/52)	£10	£20
9	2/6 **carmine and black**	£7	£9
	a scarlet and black (1/44)	£8	£11
10	5/- **deep ultramarine and black**	£15	£14
	a ultramarine and grey-black (shades) (10/46)	£40	£40
11	10/- **deep chocolate and black**	£10	£15
1/11	**set** (11)	£35	£45
SP 1/11	**specimen perf** (11)	£200	†

SPECIAL ISSUES

1937 (May 12th) Coronation. As Ascension.

S1	1d **scarlet**	.20	.25
S2	2d **yellow-brown**	.30	.60
S3	3d **deep blue**	.30	.75
S1/3	**set (3)**	.75	1.45
SP S1/3	**specimen perf** (3)	£68	†

1945 (Dec. 3rd) Victory. Nos. S33-5 of South Africa, overprinted Bechuanaland.

		Pair M	Pair U
S4	1d **deep brown and carmine**	.35	.75
	a **barbed wire**	£8	£12
S5	2d **slate-blue and purple-violet**	.25	.75
S6	3d **deep blue and blue**	.25	.90
	a **overprint omitted** (vert pair with normal)	£9000	-
S4-6	**set** (3)	.80	2.20

S4a R9/6 see South Africa CW S33b

S6a came from a sheet where the overprint was omitted from the first horizontal row. On the other stamps in the sheet, the overprints are at the top of the stamp, partly across the value: there is an extra row of overprints on the bottom selvedge.

1947 (Feb. 17th) Royal Visit. Designs, etc., as Basutoland, S7-10. Sheets 10 x 6 or 6 x 10.

S7	1d **scarlet**	.10	.10
S8	2d **green**	.10	.10
S9	3d **ultramarine**	.10	.10
S10	1/- **dull mauve**	.10	.10
S7/10	**set** (4)	.35	.35
SP S7/10	**specimen perf** (4)	£80	†

1948 (Dec. 1st) Silver Wedding. As Aden.

S11	1½d **ultramarine**	.15	.10
S12	10/- **black**	£18	£25

1949 (Oct. 10th) U.P.U. As Aden.

S13	1½d **dull ultramarine**	.20	.75
S14	3d **indigo**	.75	1.50
S15	6d **reddish mauve**	.40	1.80
S16	1/- **sage-green**	.40	.90
S13/16	**set** (4)	1.60	4.50

POSTAGE DUE STAMPS

1932 (Dec 12th) (typo) De La Rue. Perf 13¾ x 14 (C). Smooth cream paper. Sheets 6 x 10.

XPD1	½d **sage-green**	£3	£35
XPD2	1d **carmine**	3.50	£6

XPD3	2d **violet**	£5	£35
XPD1-3	**set** (3)	£10	£70
SPXPD1-3	**specimen perf** (3)	£60	†

1944 (July) As Nos XPD1-3 but on rough thick paper. Sheets 6 x 10.

PD1	½d **olive-green**	£3	£35
PD2	1d **deep carmine**	3.50	£5
PD3	2d **violet and purple-violet**	£5	£35
PD1-3	**set** (3)	£10	£70

1947 (July) As Nos. PD1-3, but smooth and thinner paper, and changed shades.

PD4	½d **dull olive-green**	£3	£35
PD5	1d **rose-carmine**	3.50	£8
PD6	2d **dull purple-violet**	£5	£38
	a **thick "d"**	£85	£150
	b **serif on 'd'**	£120	-
PD4-6	**set** (3)	£10	£75

PD6a, 9a The "d" and the dot after "2" are thicker on Row 9/6 and Row 10/6. See Basutoland PD4a.

PD6b, 9b The serif at the base of the 'd' on R1/6 is extended.

1958 (Nov.) chalk-surfaced paper.

PD8	1d **rose-carmine**	£1	£15
PD9	2d **dull purple-violet**	1.10	£14
	a **thick "d"**	£24	£100
	b **serif on 'd'**	£35	£125

BERMUDA

1936 (April 14th) various designs (recess)
Bradbury Wilkinson. Perf 12 (L). Watermark
multiple Script CA. Sheets 6 x 10.

G60	½d **green** (14/4/36)	.10	.10
	a bright yellow-green (3/43)	£5	£2
	b blue-green (9/51)	.10	.10
G66	6d **lake and violet**		
	(thick paper) (14/4/36)	.50	.10
	a claret and violet		
	(thin paper) (6/47)	£2	1.50
G68	1/6d **brown** (14/4/36)	.25	.10

**1938 (Jan. 20th)-53 Designs, 1d, 1½d ('J.W.
Clise' and 'Monarch of Bermuda' in Hamilton
harbour); 2d (yacht 'Lucie'); 2½d, 1/-
(Horseshoe Beach, Southampton Parish); 3d (St.
David's Lighthouse); 7½d ('Longtail' bird - with
Arms of Bermuda and flower) Printers (recess)
Bradbury, Wilkinson. Perf 12 (L). Sheets 6 x
10.**

1	1d **black and rose-red**	£20	£3
	a black and rose-scarlet (/40)	.60	.10
	b black and rose	.40	.10
2	1½d **deep blue and chocolate-brown** (/38)	£3	1.50
	a deep blue and brown (/43)	£4	£2
	b bright blue and purple-brown (9/45)	1.25	.90
	c 'A' of watermark missing	£1200	-
3	2d **sky-blue and blackish sepia**	£20	£5
	a sky-blue and sepia (/39)	£20	£5
4	2d **pale ultramarine and scarlet**	£2	1.50
	a pale ultramarine and carmine-red (7/42)	£45	£60
	b bright blue and scarlet (11/47)	.75	.60
5	2½d **light blue and dark blue**	£5	.75
6	2½d **sky-blue and sepia-grey** (18/12/41)	1.50	£2
	a pale blue and drab (5/3/43)	1.40	1.75
7	3d **black and scarlet**	£12	2.40
8	3d **black and deep blue** (7/41)	1.25	.25

	a black and greenish blue (7/42)	£15	£8
	b black and dark blue (7/43)	.90	.40
9	7½d **black, blue and pea-green** (18/12/41)	3.50	1.65
	a black, blue and green (5/3/43)	2.50	1.65
10	1/- **green**	£1	.30
	a yellow-green (thinner paper) (/42)	£5	2.50
	b blue-green (13/6/49)	£3	3.50

See also CW 28-34 for comb-perforated issues.

1 Examples with vermilion frames are mostly
changelings. However, there was a printing in
vermilion in 1940 which can be found unaffected
in mint condition. This printing is rare. The
original printing is best distinguished by the
(sometimes faint) gum cracking which is
invariably present.

4a This is a very elusive shade, rarely correctly
identified. A similar shade on whiter paper and
less pronounced, appeared in November 1947.

9 7½d typo reproductions by 'Helio Vaugirard'
exist in issued colours.

**Printer (typo) De La Rue. Perf 14 x 13¾ (C). £1
Watermark Multiple Crown CA. Sheets 12 x 5.**

11	2/- **purple and bright blue/ grey-blue** (ch) (11/37, 10/40, /40)	£40	£9
	a purple and deep blue/ mottled blue (sub) (10/41)	3.50	£1
	b purple and deep blue/ pale blue (sub) (3/43, 3/44, 6/45, 12/46)	£5	£1
	c brown-purple and bright blue/pale blue (sub) (7/47)	£16	£8
	d dull purple and blue/ pale blue (sub) (2/49) (centre FA)	£12	£6
12	2/6 **black and deep red/ grey-blue** (ch) (11/37,10/40)	£25	£7
	a black and carmine/ pale blue (sub) (12/41)	£8	£5

	b black and dull red/ pale blue (sub) (3/43,12/46, 6/48)	£8	£5
13	5/- **deep green and red/yellow** (ch) (11/37)	£55	£22
	aa pale green and red/yellow (ch)(1/39)	£150	£55
	ab bronze-green and carmine- red/yellow (sub) (11/41)	£600	£110
	a pale green and carmine/ pale yellow (sub) (3/43)	£45	£30
	b green and red/pale yellow (sub) (3/44, 12/46)	£20	£12
	c pea-green and carmine/ pale yellow (sub) (6/48)	£35	£18
14	10/- **green and deep lake/ bright green** (ch) (11/37)	£160	£250
	a blue-green and deep red/ green (ch) (1/39)	£100	£80
	b yellow-green and deep red /green (sub) (3/43,11/44)	£30	£38
	c green and red/green (emerald back)(sub)(12/46)	£35	£40
15	12/6 **deep grey and deep maize** (ch) (/37, 7/38)	£350	£400
	aa grey and maize (ch) (/37, 7/38, 8/38, 7/39, 10/40)	£40	£35
	a grey and maize (sub) (3/43, 12/46)	£40	£40
	b grey and yellow (sub) (6/46)	£400	£340
	c grey and maize (ch) (6/48)	£60	£75
16	£1 **pale purple and black/ crimson** (ch)(11/37)	£100	£60
	a pale purple anddull black/pale red (ch) (7/41)	£40	£45
	b purple and black/pale red (ch)(3/43)	£30	£40
	c deep purple and jet- black/pale red (ch) (6/45)	£35	£40
	d bluish purple and black/pale red (ch) (12/46)	£38	£42
SP1-16	**specimen perf** (16)	£1200	†

13ab, 15, 15b Expert Committee certificates are
advisable when purchasing these stamps.

15aa has thick brown gum; 15a has clear white
gum; 15c has clear colourless gum, and is also
known on thin paper, as is 15b

As No. 11, etc., but Perf 14¼ (L).

17	2/- **purple and bright blue/ grey-blue** (ch) (5/41)	£130	£60
18	2/6 **black and carmine/ grey-blue** (ch) (5/41)	£225	£75
19	5/- **dark green and carmine/yellow** (ch) (5/41)	£90	£25
20	10/- **yellow-green and carmine/green** (sub) (9/41)	£160	£90

As No. 11, etc., but Perf. 13¼ x 13 (C).

21	2/- **dull purple and deep blue/ light blue** (sub) (12/49)	£7	£10
	a greyish purple centre (sub) (8/50)	£5	£9
	b reddish purple centre (sub) (2/52)	£30	£35
22	2/6 **black and vermilion/ pale blue** (sub) (8/50, 11/51)	£8	7.50
	a black and carmine-red/ pale blue (sub) (4/52)	£7	£9
23	5/- **pea-green and carmine/ pale yellow** (sub) (12/49)	£12	£14
	a green and red/yellow (ch) (2/50)	£20	£40
	b pale green centre (ch) (4/52)	£40	£60
24	10/- **green and vermilion/ green** (sub) (6/51)	£18	£28
	a green and dull red/ green (sub) (1/53)	£20	£32
25	12/6 **grey and yellow** (ch) (8/50)	£40	£45
	a bluish grey and deep yellow (ch) (6/51, 9/52)	£60	£65
26	£1 **violet and black/crimson** (ch) (11/51, 4/52)	£20	£48
	a bright violet centre (ch) (10/52)	£125	£300
1-26	**set** (16)	£130	£120

21, a, b See under 'Identification 2/-' following
this listing.

£1 values with the violet vignette apparently
omitted are not errors but are the result of
exposure to sunlight or other ultraviolet source.

1940 (Dec. 20th) CW 1a (and shade)
surcharged HALF PENNY and original value
obliterated by 'X's at Hamilton Press.

27	½d/1d **black and rose-scarlet**	.20	1.20
	a black and scarlet	.50	1.50

Three printings of this provisional can be
identified. Spacings between the 'Xs' and 'Penny'
of 12½, 13½ and 14mm on the same sheet can
be found.

VARIETIES

For a fully-detailed account of all aspects of the Large Keyplates, see Eric Yendall's book 'The KG VI Large Key Types and Postage High Value Stamps 1937-53', RPSL, 2008

Type A
Scroll Flaw #60

Type B
Scroll Flaw #59

Type A Scroll Flaw: On stamp 60 (5/12). The flaw can be found in several states.

Type B Scroll Flaw: On stamp 59 (R5/11). Only on the line-perforated stamps.

Type C
Blank Scroll
#1

Type D
White Island #11

Type C Blank Scroll: On stamp 1 (R1/1). Only on March '43 2/- and £1.

Type D White Island: On stamp 11 (R1/11) on the £1 - a large frame flaw, on some sheets of the November 1951 printing only.

Type E
Crown Flaw

Type F
Gash in Chin #17

Type E Crown Flaw: On stamp 52 (R5/4), occuring, on the line-perforated 10/- and a few examples of the 2/- mottled only.

Type F Gash in Chin: On stamp 17 (R2/5) a large flaw in the King's chin.

Type G Missing Pearl: On stamp 49 (R5/1) the pearl to the left of centre at the bottom is missing. Occurs on the 5/- March 1944 printing only.

Type H Joined 'ER': On stamp 2 (R1/2). At its most pronounced on the first printing.

Type I Lower Right Scroll with Broken Tail: On stamp 22 (R2/10), line-perforated printings only.

All mint prices are for hinged or very fine used singles.

11a	2/-	Type A	£120	£65
		Type F	£140	£80
11b	2/-	Type A	£375	£250
		Type C	£1200	£600
		Type F	£400	£275
17	2/-	Type A	£1100	£450
		Type B	£1100	£450
		Type F	£1300	£550
		Type I	£2400	£800
12a	2/6d	Type A	£375	£225
		Type F	£450	£250
12b	2/6d	Type A	£375	£225
18	2/6d	Type A	£1200	£525
		Type B	£1200	£525
		Type F	£1400	£600
		Type I	£2400	£900
13a	5/-	Type A	£600	£350
		Type F	£600	£350
13ab	5/-	Type A	£4500	£1200
		Type F	£4500	£1200
13b	5/-	Type G	£550	£500
19	5/-	Type A	£600	£250
		Type B	£600	£250
		Type F	£850	£300
		Type I	£2000	£575
14b	10/-	Type A	£1500	£1300
		Type F	£1500	£1300
20	10/-	Type A	£1200	£575
		Type B	£1200	£575
		Type E	£1000	£600
		Type F	£1450	£650
		Type I	£3000	£950
15a	12/6d	Type A	£1400	£1500
		Type F	£1550	£1600
16	£1	Type H	£600	£375
16a	£1	Type A	£1200	£850
		Type C	£2250	-
		Type F	£1200	£850
		Type H	£375	£375
16b	£1	Type F	£1200	£1200
		Type E	£900	£700
		Type H	£275	£225
26	£1	Type D	£2400	-

GENERAL NOTES

The following is intended as a guide to identifying keytypes. It is worth remembering that there are many printings of this issue not listed separately here and some stamps may not exactly 'fit' the descriptions. For greater depth on printings of this issue, further study is required. Contact us if you need help!

Perforations:

It is important to use a good quality perforation gauge and to measure accurately. Keytypes were perforated by three different machines and fall into the following categories.

	2/-	2/6d	5/-	10/-	12/6d	£1
comb perf 14 x 13¾	CW 11-11d	12-12b	13-13c	14-14c	15-15c	16-16b
line perf 14.15	CW 17	18	19	20	-	-
comb perf 13¾ x 13	CW 21-21b	22-22a	23-23b	24-24a	25-25a	26-26a

Line Perforations:

Apart from the precise measurements of the line perfs, there are a couple of other pointers which may prove helpful. Firstly, comb-perforated stamps produce even **bottom** corners. Line-perforated stamps produce random corners, which may (rarely) confirm to the appearance of comb-perforated corners, but are mostly uneven.

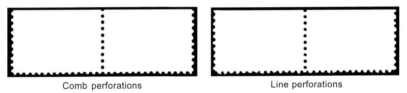

Comb perforations   Line perforations

The appearance of the line-perforated 2/-, 2/6d and 5/- values is such that there is some danger of confusion with the first printings. They are on chalk-surfaced paper and quite bright in shade. As with the 10/-, the gum is invariably streaky and brown. The 10/-, however, is on ordinary paper and often pale and weakly printed. Beware of used examples of this stamp with centre colour washed - these are usually overly yellow in appearance.

Ultraviolet Light:

We have tried to make identification simple for all and not use specialist equipment. However, in some cases UV is important for confirmation of a printing. It is almost essential for differentiating between CW 13a and b, 21, a and b, and vital for confirming the 12/6d grey and yellow ('lemon'). The paper under UV is whiter than the other ordinary paper printings, and the frame colour under UV is yellow-orange, not brownish orange.

Paper:

While the first group of chalk-surfaced papers show a diagnostic clarity of printing, mostly have brown, streaky gum, exhibit pitted paper and react to the 'silver test', later chalk-surfaced papers may not be so easy to distinguish as the surfacing can be inconsistent. Clarity of line is probably the most reliable characteristic, using a consistent point of reference, such as the lines over the King's head.

Postmark:

The following is a list of the earliest known dates. The dates in the main listing are the date of despatch to the colony, or the date of issue in London.

Perf 14 x 13¾ (C)

2/-	CW11 - 20/1/38 CW11c - 3/4/48	CW11a - 14/8/42 CW11d - 3/9/49	CW11b 17/11/44
2/6d	CW12 - 20/1/38	CW12a - 8/5/42	CW12b - 3/44
5/-	CW 13 - 20/1/38 CW13a - 25/5/43	CW13aa - 14/3/39 CW 13b - 23/5/45	CW13ab - 5/42 CW 13c - 4/4/49
10/-	CW14 - 20/1/38 CW14c - 30/6/47	CW14a - 6/39	CW14b - ?/44
12/6d	CW15 - 20/1/38 CW15b - 17/9/47	CW15aa - 9/39 CW15c - 2/49	CW 15a 2/3/44
£1	CW16 - 20/1/38 CW16c - ?/?	CW16a - 10/10/41 CW16d - ?/49	CW16b - 20/6/44

Perf 14¼ (L)

2/-	CW17 - 12/3/42
2/6d	CW18 - 6/41
5/-	CW19 - ?5/1/43
10/-	CW20 - /42

Perf 13¼ x 13 (C)

2/-	CW21 - 7/3/50	CW21a - 14/11/50	CW21b - 7/8/52
2/6d	CW22 - 27/10/50	CW22a - 22/7/52	
5/-	CW23 - 7/3/50	CW23a -1/6/51	CW23b - 26/8/52
10/-	CW24 - 10/10/51	CW24a - 1/5/53	
12/6d	CW25 - 11/50	CW25a - 31/10/52	
£1	CW26 - 30/1/52	CW 26a - ?/52	

Notes follow each flow chart with further information to guide you through the identification process. An 'R' after the printing dates denotes that the printing was a reprint.

Perf 14 x 13¾

CW 11a - This printing was carried out by Williams Lea. The paper was treated with a coat of deep blue ink and the stamps produced presented a blotched and/or lined appearance.

The 1943-47 printings (CW 11b, c) have much in common, but the brownish tinge to the vignette of the 1947 printing (CW 11c) is distinctive.

Perf 13

Aniline reaction of headplate under ultraviolet:

        CW 21 - no reaction
        CW 21a - relatively strong reaction (orange)
        CW 21b - slight reaction (pale pink)

Colour, although variable on the 1949 and 1950 printings, also helps. The final printing has a pinkish element in the head colour and is scarce. The 1949 printing has a very muddy headplate which has lost much detail.

Perforation: Comb 14 x 13¾

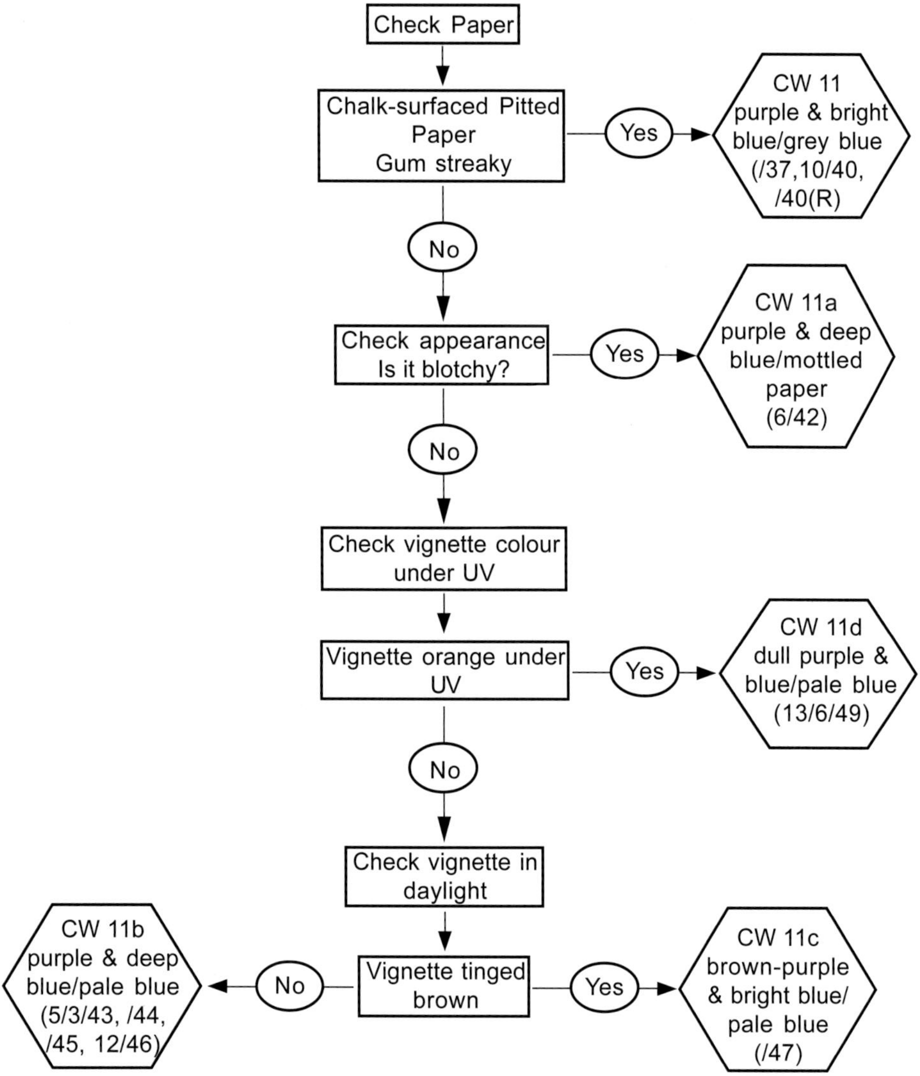

Check Paper

↓

Chalk-surfaced Pitted Paper Gum streaky — Yes → CW 11 purple & bright blue/grey blue (/37,10/40, /40(R)

No
↓

Check appearance Is it blotchy? — Yes → CW 11a purple & deep blue/mottled paper (6/42)

No
↓

Check vignette colour under UV

↓

Vignette orange under UV — Yes → CW 11d dull purple & blue/pale blue (13/6/49)

No
↓

Check vignette in daylight

↓

CW 11b purple & deep blue/pale blue (5/3/43, /44, /45, 12/46) ← No — Vignette tinged brown — Yes → CW 11c brown-purple & bright blue/ pale blue (/47)

Perf 14 x 13¾

CW 12a - The 1942 printing has a carmine frame, while all the later printings have the frame in various shades of brown-red, which are insipid in comparison.

Perf 13¼ x 13

Frame colour is an adequate distinguishing factor.

Perforation: Comb 14 x 13¾

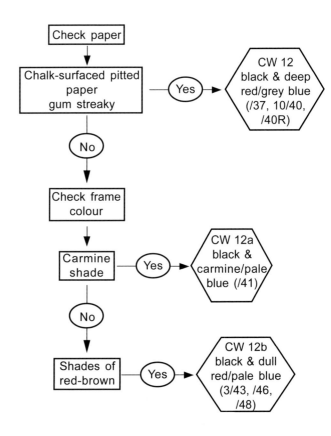

Perf 14 x 13¾

CW 13 the difference between the deep green vignette and the pale green of CW 13aa is quite distinctive. On the 13a the gum browning should be slight.

The remainder should have clear gum. Of these the Nov. 1941 printing (CW 13ab) is most distinctive. There was no London release. Most examples were used, and the majority have Ireland Island postmarks. The headplate colour is bronze or deep olive, entirely different from any other printing. If you are in doubt you probably don't have it!

CW 13b and c are more difficult and can be confusing to separate. The frame of CW 13b is very deep camine and the pale green vignette can be said to have an element of blue.

CW 13c this has a bright, yellowy 'pea-green' vignette, rather like the perf 13 vignettes.

As a rule, examples of CW 13c have paler frames with much less carmine or even no carmine. The vignette lacks the bluish element of CW 13b. It is between these printings that misidentification is most understandable, since considerable variation occurs.

Matters are much simpler if the frames of the 1943, 1944 and 1946 printings are viewed under ultraviolet. 1943 is bright red while the others are deep, almost blackish, lake.

Perf 13¼ x 13

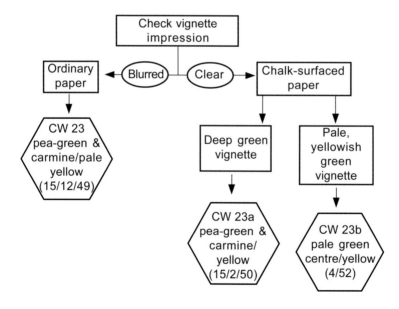

Perforation: Comb 14 x 13¾

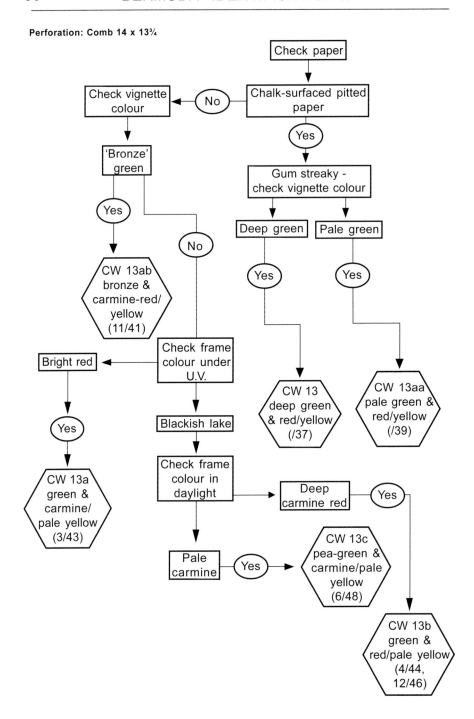

Perf 14 x 13 ¾

CW 14   The gum on this stamp tends to be relatively heavily streaked.

CW 14a   The gum is lightly streaked (sometimes almost clear); there is a distinctive bluish tinge to the vignette.

Perf 13¼ x 13

Frame colour is an adequate distinguishing factor.

Perforation: Comb 14 x 13¾

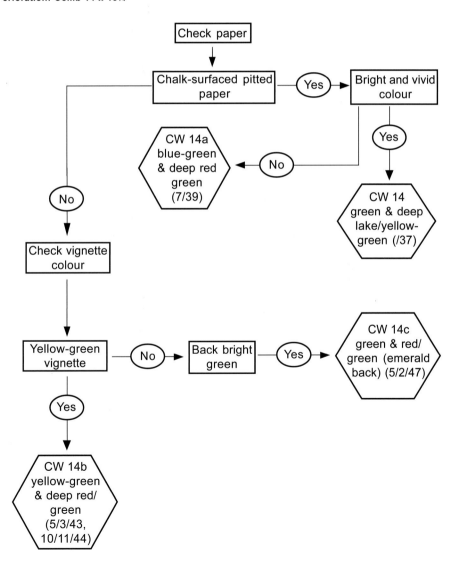

Perf 14 x 13¾

CW15 and 15aa; because of the gum, some colour alteration may have taken place. Few stamps qualify as 15, the qualification being, unfortunately, rather subjective. It is almost entirely on the amount of brown apparent in the frame that 15 is identified. We usually recommend an expertising certificate. However, the grey is a useful indicator, being quite deep on CW 15.

Perf 13¼ x 13

CW 25 - speckled headplate (dusty appearance)
CW 25a - clean headplate

Head plate colour also assists.

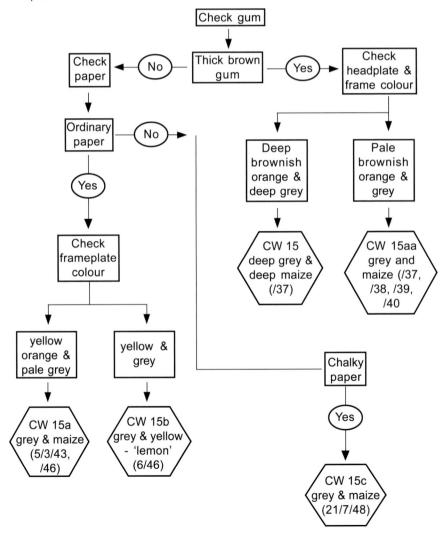

Perf 14 x 13¾

The crimson paper of 16 should be sufficient to identify it, but if further help is required, the vignette is noticeably pale and its line is appreciably finer.

Perf 13¼ x 13

The final printing has an extremely vivid headplate colour, to the extent that a true example verges on being uncomfortable to look at in daylight. Colours on the first two printings vary from pale to bright - because you have one of each doesn't mean you have the final printing! Almost every single example of 26a we have seen offered for sale has been incorrect. Great care is necessary when purchasing this stamp.

Perforation: Comb 14 x 13¾

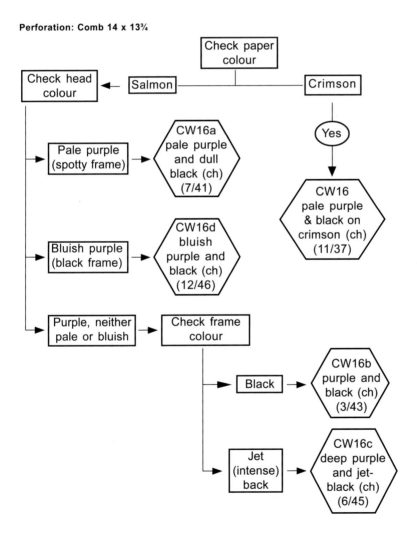

1950-1 As 1, etc., but Perf. 12 x 11¾ (C).

28	1d **black and scarlet-red**		
	(10/7/50)	1.75	2.50
	a black and dull red (9/52)	£2	2.50
29	1½d **deep blue and**		
	chocolate-brown		
	(10/10/50)	3.50	2.25
	a blue and purple-brown		
	(7/51)	2.50	£2
30	2d **pale ultramarine and**		
	carmine-red (10/7/50)	2.50	£3
	a bright blue and		
	deep carmine-red	7.50	£4
31	2½d **sky-blue and sepia-grey**		
	(23/9/52)	£2	1.50
32	3d **black and deep blue**		
	(2/7/51)	£2	£1
	a black and bright blue		
	(9/52)	7.50	£4
33	6d **lake and purple-violet**		
	(2/7/51)	£4	£2
	a carmine-lake and		
	purple-violet (1/52)	£6	£3
34	1/- **blue-green** (/51)	2.50	£2
	a deep blue-green		
	(10/12/52)	£4	4.50
28-34	**Set (7)**	£15	£13

The line-perforated stamps come from sheets perforated in the lower selvedge. The comb-perforated sheets have the lower selvedge imperforate.

SPECIAL ISSUES

1937 (May 14) Coronation. As Ascension.

S1	1d **scarlet**	.35	.75
S2	1½d **yellow-brown**	.30	1.10
S3	2½d **blue**	.35	1.10
S1/3	**set (3)**	.90	2.65
SP S1/3	**specimen** perf (3)	£130	†

1946 (Nov. 6th) Victory. As Aden.

S4	1½d **chocolate-brown**	.10	.10
S5	3d **deep blue**	.10	.20
SP S4/5	**specimen** perf (2)	£95	†

1948 (Dec. 1st) Silver Wedding. As Aden.

S6	1½d **chestnut-brown**	.15	.30
S7	£1 **rose-carmine**	£20	£30

1949 (April 11th) 100th Anniversary of Bermuda's First Stamp. Design; Postmaster Perot's Stamp, King's Portrait and Sisyrinchium Bermudiana. Printers (recess) Bradbury, Wilkinson. Perf 13¼ (C). Sheets 6 x 10.

S8	2½d **blue and grey-brown**	.20	.25
S9	3d **black and dull blue**	.20	.10
S10	6d **purple-violet and green**	.20	.10
S8/10	**Set (3)**	.55	.40

1949 (Oct. 10th) U.P.U. As Aden.

S11	2½d **slate**	.25	1.20
S12	3d **indigo**	.85	.75
S13	6d **purple**	.25	.45
S14	1/- **quartz-green**	.25	.90
S11/14	**Set (4)**	1.50	£3

BOOKLET PANES

1936-53 Low values

P1	1d **CW 1c** 1947 pane of 6	£18	-
P2	1½d **CW 2d** 1947 pane of 6	£18	-
P3	2d **CW 4c** 1947 pane of 6	£20	-
P4	2½d **CW 6c** 1947 pane of 6	£20	-
P5	3d **CW 8c** 1947 pane of 6	£20	-
P6	6d **CW G66ab** 1947 pane of 6	£22	-

BOOKLETS

A special printing of stamps for booklets was sent to the Colony between 10th November 1947 and 22nd January 1948.

B1	5/- **Pink cover** (14/4/48)		
	stapled at left or right, for		
	surface mail, contains		
	P1-5	£100	-
B2	10/6 **Blue cover** (9/3/48)		
	stapled left or right, for		
	Airmail. Contains P5 x 1,		
	P6 x 3	£125	-

It is assumed that 20,500 of each booklet were prepared.

BERMUDA

POSTAL FISCAL

1937 (Feb. 1st) (typo) De La Rue. Revenue stamp, authorised for postal use from Feb. 1st to April. As 11, etc, but with portrait of KGV and inscribed 'Revenue' on both sides. Chalk-surfaced paper.

PF1 12/6d **grey and orange**   £700   £1100

Examples with postmarks dated after April were cancelled by favour. Most used examples seen are without dates and are worth much less than the price quoted.

Plate varieties as listed in the 1980 'Five Reigns' catalogue may be found.

GERMAN PROPAGANDA LABELS

The 1944 German imitations of the G.B. 1937 Definitives ½d. to 3d. (see after Great Britain for details) were also overprinted in black 'LIQUIDATION/OF EMPIRE/BERMUDA Is', within a vertical rectangular frame.

BCOF (AUSTRALIA) SEE AUSTRALIA

BRITISH GUIANA

1934 (Oct. 1st) - 50 (recess) Waterlow and Sons. Watermark Multiple Script CA (sideways on horizontal designs). Sheets 6 x 10 or 10 x 6.

(a) Perf. 12½

G38	3c **scarlet**		.15	.10
	a watermark Crown missing (Type B)		£2250	-
G41	12c **red-orange**		.10	.15
G46	72c **deep red-purple**		.75	1.35

(c) Perf 13 x 14 (3c) or 14 x 13 (12c).

G50	3c **scarlet** (28/4/49)		.25	.15
G51	12c **red-orange** (1/5/50)		.30	.40

1938 (Feb. 1st)- 52 Designs, 1c, 3c, 6c, 24c, 60c (colonial activities); 2c, 12c, 36c, 48c, $1, $2 (views in Colony); 4c (map of South America); 96c (Sir Walter Raleigh & son); $3 (Victoria Regia lilies). Printers (recess) Waterlow & Sons. Watermark Multiple Script CA. Perf. 12½ (L). Sheets 10 x 6 or 6 x 10.

1	1c **yellow-green**		£6	.35
	a green (5/42)		.15	.10
2	2c **violet-black**		.25	.10
3	4c **red and grey-black**		.30	.20
	a pair imperf. horiz		£20000	£16000
4	6c **deep ultramarine**		.20	.10
	a ultramarine		.30	.10
5	24c **blue-green** (watermark upright) (3/4/38)		£10	£6
	a deep blue-green (watermark sideways (/41)		.75	.10
	b blue-green (watermark sideways)(/46?)		£3	.30
6	36c **violet** (7/3/38)		£1	.10
7	48c **orange**		.30	.30

8	60c **deep red-brown**	£6	5.50
	a brown (/43)	7.50	5.50
	b red-brown (8/4/46)	£6	£5
9	96c **deep plum**	2.50	1.75
10	$1 **bright violet**	£9	.20
11	$2 **reddish purple** (11/6/45)	£4	£13
12	$3 **reddish chestnut**		
	(2/7/45)	£15	£18
	a terracotta (13/12/46)	£17	£18
1/12	**set** (12)	£30	£26
SPI/12	**specimen perf** (12)	£150	†

No. 3a - Half a sheet imperf. horizontally was discovered in the colony in 1947. A few used pairs exist.

As before but Perf. 12½ x 13½ (L), 3ct (C) or (L).

13	3c **scarlet-red**		
	(30/12/43)	.30	.50
14	96c **deep plum**		
	(20/3/44)	£3	£5

As before but Perf. 12¾ x 13¾ (C).

15	1c **green** (/49)	.15	.50
16	2c **violet-black** (28/4/49)	.15	.10
17	3c **carmine-red** (/49)	.30	.50
18	4c **red and grey-black**		
	(12/1/52)	.25	.10
19	6c **deep ultramarine**		
	(24/10/49)	.30	.20
20	12c **vermilion** (1/7/50)	£4	£6
	a bright vermilion	.25	.60
21	36c **violet** (8/5/51)	1.25	.20
22	48c **orange** (8/5/51)	.85	.75
24	96c **dark plum** (8/2/51)	1.50	£4
25	$1 **bright violet** (/51)	£250	£375
26	$2 **reddish purple** (9/8/50)	£7	£13
27	$3 **reddish chestnut**		
	(29/10/52)	£16	£40
15/27	**set** (11) (less 25)	£24	£50

17 - See also No. G50.

20 - See also No. G51.

25 - $1 forgeries exist. Margins added and reperforated, stamp size incorrect.

Overprints "Marine Detatchment" on 1c, 2c, 3c, 6c, 12c, 36c, and $1 are bogus. A double overprint on the 36ct is recorded.

SPECIAL ISSUES

1937 (May 12th) Coronation. As Ascension.

S1	2c **light brown**	.10	.10
	a blocked pearl	£20	£20
S2	4c **grey-black**	.25	.25
S3	6c **blue**	.30	£1
S1-3	**set** (3)	.60	1.20
SP S1/3	**specimen perf** (3)	£60	†

S1a - a pearl on the Queen's necklace is coloured in. Position unknown.

1946 (Oct. 21st) Victory. As Aden.

S4	3c **carmine-red**	.10	.25
S5	6c **deep blue**	.25	.50
SP S4/5	**specimen perf** (2)	£55	†

Number issued; 3ct 2,727,240, 6ct 837,000.

1948 (Dec. 20th) Silver Wedding. As Aden.

S6	3c **scarlet**	.10	.25
S7	$3 **chestnut-brown**		
	(all recess)	8.50	£14

1949 (Oct. 10th) U.P.U. As Aden.

S8	4c **carmine-rose**	.15	.30
S9	6c **indigo**	£1	1.10
S10	12c **orange**	.15	.30
S11	24c **quartz-green**	.15	.40
S8/11	**set** (4)	1.30	1.90

1951 (Feb. 16th) West Indies University College. As Antigua.

| S12 | 3c **black and carmine-red** | .20 | .30 |
| S13 | 6c **black and blue** | .20 | .40 |

POSTAGE DUE STAMPS

1940 (March 1st) (typo) De La Rue. Perf. 13¾ x 14 (C). Smooth cream paper. Sheets 6 x 10.

PD1	1c **green**	£3	4.50
PD2	2c **black**	£12	1.50
PD3	12c **scarlet**	£12	7.50
	a deep scarlet (rough paper)		
	(?/45)	£15	4.50
PD1-3	**set** (3)	£24	£12
SPPD1/3	**specimen perf** (3)	£50	†

1952. Chalk-surfaced paper.

PD4	1c green	.75	£10
PD5	2c black	1.50	£3
PD6	4c blue	.15	7.50
PD7	12c scarlet	8.50	£18
PD4-7	set (4)	£10	£35

WATERMARK VARIETIES (TYPE A)
(See Introduction for details)

PD4a	1c Crown missing	£275	-
PD4b	1c St. Edward's Crown	£85	-
PD5a	2c Crown missing	£225	-
PD5b	2c St. Edward's Crown	£85	-
PD6a	4c Crown missing	£175	-
PD6b	4c St. Edward's Crown	£70	-

BOOKLET PANES

1934-52 booklet panes.

Perf 12½

P1	1c CW 1 pane of 4	£85	-
P2	1c CW 1b pane of 4	£18	-
P3	2c CW 2 pane of 4	£18	-
P4	3c CW G38 pane of 4	£18	-
P5	4c CW 3 pane of 4	£18	-

Perf 13 x 14

P6	3c CW G50 pane of 4	£18	-

Perf 12¾ x 13¾

P7	1c CW 15 pane of 4	£15	-
P8	2c CW 16 pane of 4	£15	-
P9	3c CW 17 pane of 4	£15	-

BOOKLETS

All booklets white-stitched except B1 (black), and B2 (black and white).

B1	36c **1938 black on orange-red** P3 x 2, P1, P5	£375	-
B2	24c **1944 black on orange-red** P1 x 2, P3 x 2	£350	-
B3	24c **1945-49 black on red** P1, P3, P4	£150	-
B4	24c **1945-49 black on red** P2, P3, P4	£45	-
B5	24c **1945-49 black on red** P2, P3, P9	£45	-
B6	24c **1945-49 black on red** P2, P3, P6	£45	-
B7	24c **1945-49 black on red** P2, P8, P4	£60	-
B8	24c **1945-49 black on red** P2, P8, P9	£60	-
B9	24c **1945-49 black on red** P7, P8, P6	£60	-

BRITISH HONDURAS

1938 (Jan 10th) - 47 Designs, 1c (Maya figurines); 2c, 3c, 4c, 5c, 10c, 50c, $2 (products of Colony); 15c, 25c, $1 (scenes in Colony); $5 (Arms of Colony). Printers (recess) Bradbury, Wilkinson. Perf. 11¼ x 11 ½ (C). Sheets 10 x 5 or 5 x 10.

1	1c **purple-magenta and green** (14/2/38)	.15	.90
	a violet-magenta and green (12/2/47)	.20	£1
2	2c **black and deep scarlet** (14/2/38)	.15	.60
3	3c **purple-violet and chocolate** (10/1/38)	.50	.50
	a dull purple-violet and brown (2/11/42)	.65	.50
4	4c **black and deep green** (10/1/38)	.75	.40
	a black and green (17/4/46)	.50	.40
5	5c **red-purple and slate-blue** (10/1/38)	1.25	.60
	a mauve-purple and slate-blue (21/2/45)	1.10	.60
6	10c **green and red-chocolate** (14/2/38)	1.25	.35
	a yellow-green and purple-brown (20/1/47)	£3	£1
7	15c **chocolate and grey-blue** (14/2/38)	£4	.40
	a deep chocolate and deep blue (20/1/47)	2.25	.40
8	25c **deep violet-blue and deep green** (14/2/38)	1.60	.75
	a deep blue and green (20/11/42)	2.25	£1
9	50c **black and deep purple** (14/2/38)	£9	£3
	a black and reddish purple (12/2/47)	7.50	2.25
10	$1 **deep scarlet and olive-green** (28/2/38)	£14	£6
11	$2 **indigo and maroon** (28/2/38)	£22	£12
12	$5 **deep carmine and deep brown** (28/2/38)	£22	£19
1/12	set (12)	£75	£40
SP 1/12	specimen perf (12)	£175	†

See introduction for further details on gum and paper.

1947. As No. 2 but Perf. 12 (L).

13	2c black and deep scarlet	1.25	.60

This stamp was sent out to the Colony on September 6th, 1946, and placed on sale early in 1947.

SPECIAL ISSUES

1937 (May 12th) Coronation. As Ascension.

S1	3c orange	.15	.20
S2	4c deep grey	.35	.20
S3	5c blue	.40	1.15
S1/3	set (3)	.80	1.40
SP S1/3	specimen perf (3)	£58	†

1946 (Sept. 9th) Victory. As Aden.

S4	3c chocolate-brown	.10	.15
S5	5c deep blue	.10	.15
SPS4/5	specimen perf (2)	£35	†

1948 (Oct. 1st) Silver Wedding. As Aden.

S6	4c green	.10	.35
S7	$5 chocolate	9.50	£29

1949 (Jan 10th) 150th Anniversary of Battle of St. George's Cay. Design, 1c to 4c, St. George's Cay; 5c to 15c, H.M.S. Merlin. Printers (recess) Waterlow & Sons. Perf. 12½ (L).

S8	1c ultramarine and yellow-green	.10	.75
S9	3c blue and light brown	.10	.90
S10	4c olive and pale violet	.10	.90
S11	5c chocolate-brown and grey-blue	.75	.45
S12	10c green and chocolate-brown	.75	.20
S13	15c emerald and slate-blue	.75	.20
S8/13	set (6)	2.30	£3

1949 (Oct. 10th) U.P.U. As Aden but all four values printed entirely by recess.

S14	4c green	.15	.20
S15	5c indigo	.75	.30
S16	10c dull brown	.20	1.80
S17	25c azure	.20	.30
S14/17	set (4)	1.20	2.35

1951 (Feb. 16th) West Indies University College. As Antigua.

S18	3c purple and brown	.25	.90
S19	10c green and brown	.25	.20

POSTAGE DUE STAMPS

1923-46 (typo) De La Rue. Watermark Multiple Script CA. Perf. 13¾ x 14. Sheets 6 x 10.

(a) Smooth paper (1923-44, 1948).

GD1	1c black	1.10	£8
GD2	2c black	1.10	£5
GD3	4c black	.65	4.50
	a missing serif	£20	-
	b inverted watermark	£200	-
GD1/3	set (3)	2.50	£15
SP GD1/3	specimen ovpt (3)	£50	†

(b) Rough paper (1944, 1946).

PD1	1c black	£5	£10
PD2	2c black	£10	£15
PD3	4c black	£8	£10
	a missing serif	-	-
PD1/3	set (3)	£20	£32

(c) Chalk-surfaced paper (25 September 1956).

PD4	1c black	.25	£16
PD5	2c black	.25	£15
PD6	4c black	.45	£14
	a missing serif	£20	-
PD4/6	set (3)	.90	£40

A 1964 printing of the 1ct was on white uncoated paper.

GD3a, PD3a, PD6a the top serif of the 'C' is omitted on R6/6.

BRITISH OCCUPATION OF ITALIAN COLONIES

ADDIS ABABA

After the occupation of Addis Ababa on April 5th 1941, British Forces administered the postal system. Unoverprinted British stamps were used until March 23rd, 1942, when Ethiopia stamps were available. Theoretically, all values to 1/- (½d to 3d both 'dark' and 'light' colours) could exist with Addis Ababa postmarks.

Prices for used are for stamps used within the territories for which they were issued. They were valid for use in the U.K. from 1950 and are worth much less with U.K. postmarks.

M.E.F.

The principal characteristics of the different overprints are as follows;

| square stops (1-5) | round stops (1a-5a) |

| Cairo stops (6-10) | Harrison stops (11-18) |

1-5 overprint 13½mm and letters somewhat uneven at edges. 1a-5a overprint 13½mm but ends of letters and stops rounded. These occured on the same setting of 10 rows of six stamps; rows 2, 3, and 7 being the 'square stops'. Most, but not all, sheets have the margin detached.

6-10 overprint 14mm letters and stops clear-cut and straight.

11-18 overprint 13½mm with letters and vertical oblong stops also clear-cut and straight, appearing slightly thicker then the other two printings. Stamp colour readily distinguishes all except CW5. This overprint is in glossy blue-black, as against the matt black of the previous overprint (most noticeable when light shines across the overprint). Also the stop between 'M' and 'E' is slightly nearer 'M' than 'E' in the case of CW 15, whereas it is exactly in the centre on CW 10.

1942 (Mar. 2nd) Stamps of Great Britain overprinted 'M.E.F.' at GHQ Middle East Land Forces, Nairobi, May 1941, for use in Eritrea.

1	1d **deep scarlet**	£30	£10
	a round stops	£25	7.50
	b se-tenant pair	£125	£65

2	2d **deep orange**	£50	£70
	a round stops	£40	£65
	b se-tenant pair	£225	£275
3	2½d **deep ultramarine**	£30	£5
	a round stops	£28	£4
	b se-tenant pair	£140	£45
4	3d **violet**	£80	£30
	a round stops	£75	£28
	aa overprint double	†	£3500
	b se-tenant pair	£275	£135
5	5d **pale brown**	£250	£75
	a round stops	£225	£65
	b se-tenant pair	£1000	£550

CW 1-5 quantities printed - 1d, 36,000; 2d, 12,000; 2½d, 36,000; 3d, 12,000; 5d, 5,280.

1942 (Mar. 2nd) As before but overprinted by the Army Printing Services at Cairo (MEF), June 1941, for use in Eritrea and Italian Somaliland.

6	1d **deep scarlet**	.75	1.65
	a sliced 'M'	£55	-
7	2d **deep orange**	.55	2.40
	a sliced 'M'	£40	-
8	2½d **deep ultramarine**	.45	.75
	a sliced 'M'	£45	-
9	3d **violet**	.40	.20
10	5d **pale brown**	.40	.20
	a sliced 'M'	£40	-
6-10	**set** (5)	2.30	4.75

6a-10a R6/10 the left leg of the 'M' of the overprint is cut away at the base.

1943 (Jan. 1st) - 47 Stamps of Great Britain overprinted 'M.E.F.' in blue-black or black (2/6, 5/- and 10/-) by Harrison and Sons, for use in Cyrenaica, Dodecanese Islands, Eritrea, and Tripolitania.

11	1d **scarlet**	.60	.10
12	2d **dull orange**	.60	.75
13	2½d **ultramarine**	.20	.10
14	3d **purple-violet**	.60	.10
15	5d **pale brown**	1.75	.10
16	6d **pale purple**	.20	.10
17	9d **deep olive**	.40	.10

18	1/- bistre-brown	.20	.10
	a broken barb	£90	-
	b broken cross	£90	-
19	2/6 green	3.25	.60
20	5/- red (27/1/47)	£8	£12
	a 'T' guide	£75	£75
21	10/- ultramarine (27/1/47)	£14	£6
11/21	set (11)	£26	£17
SP18/21	specimen ovpt (4)	£375	†

18a (R7/12); b (18/2); 20a (various positions); (see Great Britain 15a, b, 18b).

M.E.F. overprints on ½d and 1½d 1941 colours exist. These are presumed bogus, in the absence of any evidence to the contrary.

Number issued: 1d 2,338,263; 2d 2,387,731; 2½d 3,006,679; 3d 1,929,050; 5d 2,240,604; 6d 1,318,924; 9d 1,030,036; 1/- 2,060,434; 2/6 271,850; 5/- 101,830; 10/- 130,986.

POSTAGE DUE STAMPS

1942 (Mar. 2nd) Postage Due Stamps of Great Britain overprinted 'M.E.F.' in dark blue by Harrison and Sons for use as CW 11-21.

PD1	½d emerald-green	.15	£8
PD2	1d rose-red	.15	£1
	a watermark sideways		
	inverted	-	£35
PD3	2d agate	.60	.75
PD4	3d violet	.30	2.50
PD5	1/- blue	1.50	£8
PD1/5	set (5)	2.50	£18
SP PD5	1/- specimen ovpt	£120	†

PD2a crown pointing to left, as seen from reverse.

Numbers issued - ½d, 336,613; 1d, 243,941; 2d, 242,887; 3d, 294,394; 1/-, 260,344.

CYRENAICA

1950 (Jan 16th) Design, Mounted Mujahid. Printer (recess) Waterlow and Sons. No watermark Perf 12½ (L).

1	1m sepia	1.50	3.50
2	2m rose-red	1.50	3.50
3	3m orange-yellow	1.50	3.50
4	4m dull myrtle-green	1.50	3.50
5	5m brownish grey	1.50	2.25
6	8m orange	1.50	1.75
7	10m violet	1.50	1.50
8	12m scarlet	1.50	1.50
9	20m deep blue	1.50	1.50
10	50m ultramarine and deep brown	3.50	4.50
11	100m carmine and black	£7	6.50
12	200m violet and violet-blue	£9	£18
13	500m orange-yellow and green	£25	£45
1/13	set (13)	£52	£85

POSTAGE DUE STAMPS

1950 (Jan 16th) Design, POSTAGE DUE in ornamental frame. Printers (recess) Waterlow and Sons. No watermark. Perf 12½ (L).

PD1	2m sepia	£28	£65
PD2	4m green	£28	£65
PD3	8m carmine-red	£28	£75
PD4	10m dull scarlet	£28	£75
PD5	20m yellow-orange	£28	£80
PD6	40m blue	£28	£110
PD7	100m slate-black	£28	£120
PD1/7	set (7)	£175	£550

ERITREA

1948 (May 27th) - 49 Stamps of Great Britain surcharged and overprinted B.M.A. ERITREA etc., for civilian use and to replace M.E.F.-overprinted stamps.

1	5c/½d green	.85	.40
2	10c/1d scarlet	.70	1.50
3	20c/2d dull orange	.70	1.35
4	25c/2½d ultramarine	.60	.35
5	30c/3d purple-violet	.70	2.75
6	40c/5d pale brown	.70	2.50
7	50c/6d pale purple	.30	.60

8	65c/8d **deep rose** (1/2/49)	£3	1.25
9	75c/9d **deep olive**	.85	.45
10	1s/1s **bistre-brown**	.70	.30
11	2s50/2/6 **green**	£4	£6
	a misplaced stop	£85	£110
	b T guide mark	£125	£125
12	5s/5s **red**	£4	£10
	a re-entry	£125	£150
	b T guide mark	£85	£100
13	10s/10s **ultramarine**	£11	£13
1/13	**set** (13)	£25	£36

11a R4/7; the stop after SH is smaller and next to the '50' of the surcharge.

11b,12b see note after Great Britain 16-21.

12a R4/2 (see Great Britain 18a).

Number issued - 5c, 171,441; 10c, 232,179; 20c, 327,677; 25c, 434,917; 30c, 218,741; 40c, 319,432; 50c, 338,946; 65c, 316,958; 75c, 173,926; 1s, 213,267; 2s50c, 71,608; 5s, 70,864; 10s, 89,912.

1950 (Feb. 6th) As before, but overprint altered to B.A. ERITREA

14	5c/½d **green**	.70	£5
15	10c/1d **scarlet** (2nd state)	.20	£2
16	20c/2d **dull orange**	.20	.50
17	25c/2½d **ultramarine**	.20	.35
18	30c/3d **purple-violet**	.20	1.35
19	40c/5d **pale brown**	.45	£1
20	50c/6d **pale purple**	.20	.15
21	65c/8d **deep rose**	1.50	.90
22	75c/9d **deep olive**	.30	.15
23	1s/1s **bistre-brown**	.20	.10
24	2s50/2/6 **green**	3.50	£3
	a re-entry	£85	£100
25	5s/5s **red**	3.50	7.50
	a 'T' Guide mark	£75	£80
26	10s/10s **ultramarine**	£30	£35
14/26	**set** (13)	£37	£52

24a R1/7 (see Great Britain 17a).

25a see Great Britain 18b.

Number issued - 5c, 116,664; 10c, 169,469; 20c, 313,389; 25c, 248,558; 30c, 365,280; 40c, 232,561; 50c, 532,559; 65c, 808,273; 75c, 328,275; 1s, 394,870; 2s50, 98,367; 5/-, 78, 823; 10/-, 111, 647

1951 (May 28th) As No. 14, etc., but colours changed (Nos. 31-3 as Nos. 34-6 of G.B.)

27	5c/½d **dull orange**	.40	.45
28	10c/1d **ultramarine**	.40	.45
29	20c/2d **red-brown**	.40	.20
30	25c/2½d **scarlet**	.40	.20
31	2s50/2/6 **green**	5.50	£14
32	5s/5s **red**	£10	£14
33	10s/10s **ultramarine**	£11	£16
27/33	**set** (7)	£25	£40

Number issued - 5c, 131,716; 10c, 174,181; 20c, 261,294; 25c, 261,712.

POSTAGE DUE STAMPS

1948 (May 27th) Postage Due Stamps of Great Britain overprinted B.M.A. ERITREA

PD1	5c/½d **emerald-green**	4.50	£13
	a no stop after A	-	-
PD2	10c/1d **rose-red**	4.50	£15
	a no stop after B	£100	-
PD3	20c/2d **agate**	£6	£10
	a no stop after A	£35	-
	b no stop after B (R1/9)	£110	-
PD4	30c/3d **violet**	£5	£10
PD5	1s/1s **blue**	£9	£20
PD1/5	**set** (5)	£26	£62

PD2a, PD3b R1/9.

PD3a Various positions.

Number issued - 5c, 22,991; 10c, 26,164; 20c, 40,436; 30c, 52,000; 1s, 22,264.

1950 (Feb. 6th) As before, but overprint altered to B.A. ERITREA

PD6	5c/½d **emerald-green**	£6	£30
PD7	10c/1d **rose-red**	£6	£12
	a 'ENTS' for 'CENTS'	£2000	-
	b 'C' omitted & quad for 'E'	£3750	-
PD8	20c/2d **agate**	£6	£12
PD9	30c/3d **violet**	£8	£17
	a sideways-inverted watermark	-	£35
PD10	1s/1s **blue**	£8	£18
	a no stop after A	£300	-
PD6/10	**set** (5)	£32	£80

PD10a Various positions.

PD7a, 7b The C in CENTS of surcharge was omitted in the first releases (Row 7/17) but almost immediately the omission was rectified. A variety with the 'C' omitted and a "vertical oblong for E" (a printer's quad) also exists.

PD9a crown to left, as seen from reverse.

Number issued - 5c, 19,917; 10c, 32,761; 20c, 40,349; 30c, 39,267; 1s, 26,234.

SOMALIA

1943 (Jan 1st)-46 Stamps of Great Britain, overprinted E.A.F. (blue), for use in Somalia.

1	1d scarlet	.45	.35
2	2d dull orange	.75	.90
3	2½d ultramarine	.60	£2
4	3d purple-violet	.60	.10
5	5d pale brown	£1	.25
6	6d pale purple	.75	.75
7	9d deep olive	£1	1.40
8	1/- bistre-brown	1.50	.10
9	2/6 green (14/1/46)	8.50	£5
	a re-entry	£95	£125
	b 'T' Guide mark	£75	£80
1/9	set (9)	£13	£10
SP8/9	specimen ovpt (2)	£200	†

9a R1/7, R5/2 (see Great Britain 17a).

9b see Great Britain 17b.

Number issued - 1d, 160,991; 2d, 204,321; 2½d, 150,505; 3d, 310,111; 5d, 178,410; 6d, 132,386; 9d, 157,081; 1/-, 323,781; 2/6, 84,127.

1948 (May 27th) Stamps of Great Britain surcharged and overprinted B.M.A. SOMALIA to replace the E.A.F. issue.

10	5c/½d green	.60	1.25
11	15c/1½d red-brown	.80	£9
12	20c/2d dull orange	1.50	2.75
13	25c/2½d ultramarine	1.10	2.75
14	30c/3d purple-violet	1.10	5.50
15	40c/5d light brown	.60	.15
16	50c/6d pale purple	.25	1.25
17	75c/9d deep olive	£1	£12
18	1s/1/- bistre-brown	.60	.15
	a broken barb	£120	£120
19	2s50/2/6 green	£2	£15
	a misplaced stop	£60	£160
	b 'T' guidemark	£175	£175
20	5s/5/- red	5.50	£25
	a 'T' guide mark	£65	£100
10/20	set (11)	£13	£68

18a R7/12 (see Great Britain 15a).

19a R4/7 (see Eritrea 11a).

19b, 20a see note after Great Britain 16-21.

Numbers issued - 5c, 123,200; 15c, 29,094; 20c, 80,033; 25c, 277,790; 30c, 42,107; 40c, 88,235; 50c, 102,984; 75c, 31,500; 1/-, 140,873; 2s50c, 29,057; 5s, 20,082.

1950 (Jan 2nd) As before but overprint altered to B.A. SOMALIA

21	5c/½d green	.10	1.80
22	15c/1½d red-brown	.35	£10
23	20c/2d dull orange	.35	4.50
24	25c/2½d ultramarine	.25	5.25
25	30c/3d purple-violet	.60	£3
26	40c/5d pale brown	.25	.60
27	50c/6d pale purple	.25	.60
28	75c/9d deep olive	£1	4.50
29	1s/1/- bistre-brown	.30	£1
30	2s50/2/6 green	£2	£15
	a re-entry	£95	£125

31	5s/5/- **red**	5.50	£23
	a 'T' guide mark	£75	£125
21/31	**set** (11)	£10	£62

30a R1/7 see Great Britain 17a.

31a see Great Britain 18b.

Number issued - 5c, 45,811; 15c, 28,094; 20c, 34,522; 25c, 109,461; 30c, 29,236; 40c, 36,748; 50c, 56,418; 75c, 26,145; 1s, 58,170; 2s50c, 20,884; 5s, 19,310.

TRIPOLITANIA

1948 (July 1st) Stamps of Great Britain, surcharged and overprinted B.M.A. TRIPOLITANIA to replace the M.E.F. issue.

1	1l/½d **green**	.50	£1
2	2l/1d **scarlet**	.25	.15
3	3l/1½d **red-brown**	.25	.30
	a misplaced 3	£22	£30
4	4l/2d **dull orange**	.25	.40
	a misplaced 4	£22	£35
5	5l/2½d **ultramarine**	.25	.15
6	6l/3d **purple-violet**	.25	.25
7	10l/5d **pale-brown**	.25	.15
8	12l/6d **pale purple**	.25	.15
9	18l/9d **deep olive**	.50	.40
10	24l/1s **bistre-brown**	.50	.90
	a broken barb	£90	£100
11	60l/2/6 **green**	£2	7.50
	a 'T' guide mark	£100	-
12	120l/5/- **red**	£8	£15
	a 'T' guide mark	£75	£120
13	240l/10/- **ultramarine**	£12	£65
1/13	**set** (13)	£22	£80

3a, 4a figure of value set further right than normal, almost over the stop after 'A'. R8/8, 18/8.

10a see Great Britain 15a.

11a, 12a see note after Great Britain 16-21.

Number issued - 1l, 91,405; 2l, 396,555; 3l, 115,888; 4l, 221,453; 5l, 303,580; 6l, 194,095; 10l, 380,896; 12l, 151,505; 18l, 90,208; 24l, 77,993; 60l, 31,048; 120l, 19,127; 240l, 14,793.

1950 (Feb. 6th) As No 1, etc., but overprint altered to B.A. TRIPOLITANIA.

14	1l/½d **green**	1.50	£8
15	2l/1d **scarlet** (2nd state)	1.40	.25
16	3l/1½d **red-brown**	.85	£8
	a misplaced 3	£48	£125
17	4l/2d **dull orange**	£1	£3
	a misplaced 4	£55	£75
18	5l/2½d **ultramarine**	.50	.40
19	6l/3d **purple-violet**	.85	£2
20	10l/5d **pale-brown**	.60	2.50
21	12l/6d **pale purple**	1.25	.30
22	18l/9d **deep olive**	1.50	1.75
23	24l/1/- **bistre-brown**	1.50	2.25
24	60l/2/6 **green**	£5	7.50
	a re-entry	£125	-
25	120l/5/- **red**	£11	£14
	a 'T' guidemark	£75	-
26	240l/10/- **ultramarine**	£19	£45
14/26	**set** (13)	£40	£85

16a and 17a see 3a and 4a.

24a see Great Britain 17a.

25a see Great Britain 18b.

Number issued - 1l, 79,973; 2l, 319,109; 3l, 108,391; 4l, 354,698; 5l, 450,690; 6l, 302,847; 10l, 622,901; 12l, 233,534; 18l, 118,337; 24l, 91,583; 60l, 34,400; 120l, 18,020; 240l, 14,220.

1951 (May 3rd) As No. 14, etc., but colours changed (Nos. 32-4 as Nos. 34-5 of GB).

27	1l/½d **dull orange**	.10	£4
28	2l/1d **ultramarine**	.10	.60
29	3l/1½d **green**	.15	£5
30	4l/2d **red-brown**	.10	.75
31	5l/2½d **scarlet**	.15	4.50
32	60l/2/6 **green**	£4	£14
33	120l/5/- **red**	4.75	£16
34	240l/10/- **ultramarine**	£20	£38
27/34	**set** (8)	£26	£75

Number issued - 1l, 74,590; 2l, 200,530; 3l, 72,077; 4l, 126,803; 5l, 222,817; 60l, 19,148; 120l, 17,037; 240l, 12,858.

POSTAGE DUE STAMPS

1948 (July 1st) Postage Due Stamps of Great Britain, overprinted B.M.A. TRIPOLITANIA

PD1	1l/½d **emerald-green**	2.75	£35
	a no stop after A	£45	-
PD2	2l/1d **rose-red**	1.25	£25
	a no stop after A	£30	-
	b no stop after M	£85	-
PD3	4l/2d **agate**	5.50	£25
	a no stop after A	£90	-
	b no stop after M	£120	-
PD4	6l/3d **violet**	3.75	£15
PD5	24l/1/- **blue**	£15	£60
PD1/5	**set** (5)	£25	£145

PD1a-3a the stop after A in B.M.A. is missing. Various positions.

PD2b, PD3b the stop after M in B.M.A. is missing. R1/17.

Number issued -1l, 20,863; 2l, 22,742; 4l, 19,649; 6l, 17,702; 24l, 10,640.

1950 (Feb. 6th) As before but overprint altered to B.A. TRIPOLITANIA

PD6	1l/½d **emerald-green**	£6	£55
	a no stop after B	£100	-
PD7	2l/1d **rose-red**	2.75	£16
	a no stop after B	£55	-
PD8	4l/2d **agate**	3.25	£24
	a no stop after B	£60	-
PD9	6l/3d **violet**	£9	£45
	a no stop after B	£140	-
	b watermark sideways-inverted	17.50	-
PD10	24l/1/- **blue**	£24	£85
	a no stop after B	£300	-
	b no stop after A	£300	-
PD6/10	**set** (5)	£40	£200

PD6a-10a The stop after B in B.A. is missing. R11/10.

PD9b watermark crown pointing to left, as seen from reverse.

PD10b The stop after A in B.A. is missing. R11/2.

Number issued - 1l, 16,404; 2l, 20,312; 4l, 19,008; 6l, 24,137; 24l, 10,682.

BRITISH SOLOMON ISLANDS SEE SOLOMON ISLANDS

BRITISH POSTAL AGENCIES IN EASTERN ARABIA (MUSCAT)

An Indian Postal Agency was opened at Muscat on May 1st, 1864, and contemporary Indian stamps were used without overprint (except S1-15 and O1-O10) until December 29th, 1947 when Indian stamps to 2r overprinted 'PAKISTAN' (See Pakistan 1-15) were introduced. The use of Indian and Pakistani stamps throughout this period may only be recognised by the cancellation '309', '29', 'K-4', 'MASKAT' and finally 'MUSCAT'.

At Guadur, a dependency of Muscat until September 8th, 1958, an Indian Postal Agency was opened on April 12th, 1868. The use of Indian and, from November 1947, Pakistani stamps (see Pakistan 1-17, 21-37, S1-7, etc.) may be recognised by the cancellations '24', 'K41', 'GWADUR' and 'GUADUR'. Surcharged GB stamps were not used at Guadur.

Preceding the Nasik 'PAKISTAN' overprints, a very small number of Indian stamps from 3p-2r were handstamped 'PAKISTAN' and put on sale in Muscat Post Office on December 20th, 1947. These covers are exceedingly rare and less than six covers have survived. Although the handstamped overprints were not sold in Guadur Post Office, they were valid for use there and the ½a and 2a values are known on cover.

An Indian Postal Agency was opened at Dubai on August 19th, 1909; Indian stamps were used without overprint until October 1947 when Indian stamps to 2r overprinted 'PAKISTAN' (see Pakistan 1-15) were introduced. Their use during this period may be recognised by the named DUBAI cancellation; EXPERIMENTAL P.O. K-46 and K-77 cancellations may be found on mail emanating from Dubai and Sharjah during the period 1941-43, but these cancellations were applied in Karachi on Paquebot letters.

The issue of GB stamps surcharged in Annas and Rupees coincided with the change of administration. They were valid for general use in all British Postal Agencies in the area. They were used in Bahrain and Kuwait as well as Muscat, Dubai and (from August 1950) Doha (Qatar). CW7 and 8 were sold in Kuwait Post Offices in 1951 and 1953 due to shortages of these values overprinted KUWAIT.

FOR USE IN MUSCAT AND GUADUR

1947 (Dec. 20th) Stamps of India (Nos. 20, 21, 3, 23, 25 and 26) handstamped 'PAKISTAN' diagonally, reading up or down, by the Postmaster at Muscat. The overprint is in black seriffed capitals and normally measures 20mm x 3mm, but heavy applications of the rubber stamp occasionally give an overprint measuring up to 22mm.

M1	3p **slate**	-	-
M2	½a **purple**	-	-
M3	9p **deep green**	-	-
M4	1a **rose-carmine**	-	-
M5	1½a **slate-purple**	-	-
M6	2a **vermilion**	-	-

Although all values up to 2r are believed to have been oveprinted, we only list those which are known to have survived.

Although a large variety of 'PAKISTAN' handstamped overprints were made on the stamps of India in 1948, this overprinted issue was peculiar to Muscat. It was on sale for only nine days until Pakistan stamps (Nos. 1-15) were introduced on December 29th, 1947; the unsold stock was then destroyed, but the stamps were valid for use until March 31st, 1948 in Muscat, and thereafter in Guadur.

FOR GENERAL USE

1948 (April 1st) Stamps of Great Britain surcharged (½a-1r) by Harrison and Sons, London; 2r on 2/6d by Waterlows.

1	½a/½d **green**	1.30	4.50
2	1a/1d **scarlet**	1.50	.20
3	1½a/1½d **red-brown** Type I	5.50	2.25
4	1½a/1½d **red-brown** Type II	5.50	2.25
	a se-tenant pair	£150	-
5	2a/2d **dull orange**	£1	1.95
6	2½a/ 2½d **ultramarine**	1.75	£5
7	3a/3d **purple-violet**	1.75	.10
8	6a/6d **pale purple**	£2	.10
	a surcharged omitted in pair with normal	-	†
9	1r/1/- **bistre-brown**	£2	.35
10	2r/2/6 **green**	£5	£25
	a 'T' guidemark	-	-
1/10	**set** (9)	£19	£37

3/4/13/13a
Type I; the large figure '1' measures 3¼ mm (top half of sheet). Type 2 (lower half of sheet) measures 3½mm. In Type 1, the '1' is level with the '2' in '½';

8a A single example of this variety is known, R20/2 bearing only a faint impression of 'AS' of 'ANNAS' (Cylinder 36; Sheet No. 27204).

10a a single mint example has been reported.

Number issued ½a, 138,285; 1a, 117,548; 1½a, 97,146; 2a, 77,116; 2½a, 78,759; 3a, 356,061; 6a, 385,885; 1r, 56,179; 2r, 20,518.

From 1950 British Forces in Sharjah and elsewhere in Eastern Arabia used stamps of the foregoing and following issues; these were cancelled with British F.P.O. datestamps (Nos. 171 and 756 and, later, No. 518 and others).

1951 (May 3rd)-55. As No. 1, etc., but colours changed (No. 17 as No.34 of Great Britain), similarly surcharged.

11	½a/½d **dull orange**	.35	5.50
12	1a/1d **ultramarine**	.15	4.50
13	1½a/1½d **green** Type I	5.50	£20
13a	1½a/ 1½d **green** Type II	5.50	£20
	b se-tenant pair	£150	-
14	2a/2d **red-brown**	.15	£5
15	2½a/ 2½d **scarlet**	.15	£10
16	4a/4d **light blue** (2/10/50)	.25	£2
17	2r/2/6 **green** Type 1	£15	4.25
	a Type 2 (/55)	£125	£40
	aa raised 's'	-	£200
11/17	**set** (7)	£19	£45

Type 1

17 (Type 1) '2' and 'RUPEES' level, and in line with the lower of the two bars cancelling '2/6'; overall measurement 15¾ mm.

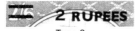

Type 2

17a (Type 2) '2' raised in relation to 'RUPEES', and the whole surcharge is below the lower bar; overall measurement 15½ mm.

17aa the 'S' of 'Rupees' is raised on R9/3 and 10/3. 2,000 printed.

Number issued ½a, 181,280; 1a, 143,706; 1½a, 77,953; 2a, 110,786; 2½a; 67,748; 4a, 103,516; 2r, 34,859.

SPECIAL ISSUES

FOR USE IN MUSCAT ONLY

1944 (Nov. 20th) Bicentenary of Al-Busaid Dynasty. Stamps of India (No. 20 etc.,) overprinted 'AL-BUSAID 1363' (in Arabic).

S1	3p **slate**	.15	4.50
	a watermark inverted	3.50	-
S2	½a **purple**	.15	4.50
S3	9p **green**	.15	4.50
S4	1a **rose-carmine**	.15	4.50
S5	1½a **slate-purple**	.15	4.50
	a double overprint	£1500	-
S6	2a **vermilion**	.20	4.50
	a watermark inverted	-	-
S7	3a **bright violet**	.50	4.50
	a watermark inverted	-	-
S8	3½a **blue**	.50	4.50
S9	4a **brown**	.60	4.50
S10	6a **greenish blue**	.60	4.50
S11	8a **violet-slate**	.75	4.50
S12	12a **deep crimson**	.75	4.50
S13	14a **purple**	£2	7.50
S14	1r **violet-grey and light brown**	.85	£7
S15	2r **violet-purple and brown**	2.25	£10
S1/15	**set** (15)	£4	£70

Some values from this set exist with 'ghost' second overprints resulting from a 'flap' in the press. Since these are not proper double overprints, they are not listed. However, S5a is genuinely doubled.

Forged overprints and cancels are known, forged cancels being particularly widespread.

FOR GENERAL USE

1948 (May 1st) Silver Wedding Issue of Great Britain surcharged.

S16	2½a/ 2½d **ultramarine**	1.25	2.25
S17	15r/£1 **deep blue**	£12	£22

Number issued 2½a, 137,789; 15r, 20,656.

1948 (July 29th) Olympic Games Issue of Great Britain surcharged.

S18	2½a/2½d **ultramarine**	.20	1.50
S19	3a/3d **violet**	.25	1.50
	a crown flaw	£45	-
S20	6a/6d **reddish purple**	.25	1.65

S21	1r/1/- **bistre-brown**	.60	2.25
	a surcharged double	£850	-
S18-21	**set** (4)	1.20	£6

S19a See Great Britain S13a (R20/2).

S21a A sheet of 120 stamps sold in London was found with a double surcharge. No used examples are known (Cylinder 3; Sheet No. 21164).

Number issued 2½a, 73,998; 3a, 72,225; 6a, 68,904; 1r, 66,867.

1949 (Oct. 10th) UPU Issue of Great Britain surcharged.

S22	2½a/2½d **ultramarine**	.30	1.80
	a Lake in India	£55	-
S23	3a/3d **pale violet**	.30	2.25
S24	6a/6d **reddish mauve**	.30	1.65
S25	1r/1/- **bistre-brown**	£1	3.75
S22-25	**set** (4)	1.70	8.50

S22a See Great Britain S16b (R8/2).

Number issued 2½a, 70,462; 3a, 64,843; 6a, 62,797, 1r, 60,093.

OFFICIAL STAMPS

Prior to 1948 Indian Service stamps were occasionally used in Muscat, Guadur and Dubai.

FOR USE IN MUSCAT ONLY

1944 (Nov 24th) Bicentenary of Al-Busaid Dynasty. Stamps of India (No. 9, etc.) overprinted 'AL BUSAID 1363' (in Arabic).

O1	3p **slate**	.30	£9
O2	½a **deep purple**	.40	£9
O3	9p **green**	.35	£9
O4	1a **rose-carmine**	.35	£9
O5	1½a **slate-purple**	.50	£9
O6	2a **vermilion**	.75	£9
O7	2½a **purple-violet**	£3	£9
O8	4a **brown**	1.25	£9
O9	8a **violet-slate**	2.25	£10
O10	1r **violet-grey and**		
	light brown	1.75	£14
O1/O10	**set** (10)	£10	£85

Forged cancellations are common.

BRITISH VIRGIN ISLANDS

1938-47 (Issued 1 August 1938 unless indicated otherwise). Design, head of King, with badge of Colony in bottom right corner. Printers (photo) Harrison and Sons. Watermark Multiple Script CA. Perf. 14 (C). Sheets 8 x 15.

1	½d **green** (ch)	£1	1.80
	a green (sub) (2/10/43)	.35	.60
2	1d **scarlet** (ch)	£1	.75
	a scarlet (sub) (2/10/43)	.75	.35
3	1½d **red-chocolate** (ch)	£2	3.50
	a red-chocolate (sub)		
	(2/10/43)	.75	.60
	b inverted watermark	-	£1000
4	2d **pale grey (ch)**	£2	1.35
	a pale grey (sub) (2/10/43)	.85	.55
5	2½d **ultramarine** (ch)	1.50	.75
	a ultramarine (sub)		
	(2/10/43)	.90	1.50
6	3d **orange** (ch)	2.25	.40
	a orange (sub) (2/10/43)	.40	.50
7	6d **purple-violet** (ch)	2.75	.60
	a purple-violet (sub)		
	(2/10/43)	1.75	.50
8	1/- **brown-olive** (ch)	5.50	£2
	a brown-olive (sub)		
	(2/8/42)	.75	.40
9	2/6 **sepia** (ch)	£20	4.75
	a sepia (sub) (2/8/42)	8.50	£2
10	5/- **dull claret** (ch)	£20	5.50
	a dull lake (sub) (2/8/42)	£7	2.50
11	10/- **blue** (ch) (1/12/47)	3.50	£5
12	£1 **black** (ch) (1/12/47)	£5	£12
1/12	**set** (12)	£27	£23
SP 1/12	**specimen perf** (12)	£220	†

1952 (April 15th) Designs, 1c (Sombrero Lighthouse); 2c, 4c, 8c, 12c, $4.80 (maps of various islands); 3c, 5c (sheep and cattle scenes); 24c (Presidency Badge); 60c, $1.20, $2.40 (seascapes). Printers (recess) De La Rue. Perf. 12½ x 13 or 13 x 12½ (C). Sheets 10 x 5 or 5 x 10.

13	1c **black**		.15	.55
	a re-entry		£15	£28
14	2c **deep green**		.15	.20
15	3c **black and sepia-brown**		.15	.55
16	4c **carmine-red**		.15	.55
17	5c **claret and black**		.40	.30
18	8c **blue**		.15	.50
19	12c **violet**		.20	.60
20	24c **sepia**		.20	.20
21	60c **sage-green and blue**		1.25	£7
22	$1.20 **black and blue**		1.75	7.50
23	$2.40 **deep green and**			
	red-brown		£5	£8
24	$4.80 **deep blue and**			
	rose-carmine		5.50	8.50
13/24	**set** (12)		£13	£30

13a doubling of the lines and lettering below lighthouse on Row 5/5.

SPECIAL ISSUES

1937 (May 12th) Coronation. As Antigua.

S1	1d **chestnut-red**		.20	1.95
S2	1½d **light brown**		.30	1.80
S3	2½d **deep ultramarine**		.25	.90
S1/3	**set** (3)		.65	£4
SP S1/3	**specimen perf** (3)		£60	†

1946 (Nov. 1st) Victory. As Aden.

S4	1½d **chestnut-brown**		.10	.10
S5	3d **yellow-orange**		.10	.20
SP S4/5	**specimen perf** (2)		£55	†

1949 (Jan. 3rd) Silver Wedding. As Aden.

S6	2½d **ultramarine**		.10	.10
S7	£1 **grey-black**		6.50	£10

1949 (Oct.10th) U.P.U. As Aden.

S8	2½d **dull violet-blue**		.15	.60
S9	3d **orange-yellow**		.75	1.50
S10	6d **reddish mauve**		.25	.25
S11	1/- **sage-green**		.20	.30
S8/11	**set** (4)		1.20	2.40

1951 West Indies University College (See Antigua).

S12	3c **black and red-brown**			
	(10/4/51)		.20	1.35
S13	12c **black and violet** (16/2/51)	.30	£1

The issue of the 3c value was delayed due to late arrival in the colony.

1951 (April 2nd) Restoration of Legislative Council, 1950. Design, map of islands. Printers (recess) Waterlow and Sons. Perf. 14¾ x 14 (C). Sheets 6 x 10.

S14	6c **orange**	.25	.90
S15	12c **purple-violet**	.25	.30
S16	24c **brown-olive**	.25	.30
S17	$1.20 **claret**	.65	.60
S14/17	**set** (4)	1.25	1.90

BRUNEI

The stamps current in 1937 were as follows: 1c black, 2c green, 4ct orange, 5c chocolate, 6c scarlet, 8c grey-black, 12 blue, 25c slate-purple, 30c purple and orange-yellow, 50c black on emerald, $1 red and black on blue, $5 carmine on green, $25 black on red. They were despatched in 1935, except the 5c in 1936, and the $5 and $25 which were rarely used and were despatched in 1924.

1937 single plate printings. Watermark multiple Crown CA. Sheets 10 x 5. Line perf 14 x 14½.

G26	10c **purple/yellow**	£12	£16

Brunei was occupied by the Japanese from December 16th, 1941 to June 10th, 1945 and current stamps were overprinted with Japanese characters. During the occupation Brunei, North Borneo and Sarawak were administered as a single territory (North Borneo) and the overprinted stamps of all three states were used throughout the whole area. Following the re-occupation in 1945 the State was under British Military Administration and the BMA issues of North Borneo and Sarawak were in use until January 2nd 1947.

1941 (Dec.) Prepared for use but, because of the invasion, not officially issued without Japanese overprint. 6c perf. 14 x 11½ (L), remainder perf. 14. Sheets 10 x 5.

G33	2c **orange-brown**	£30	-
G34	3c **blue-green**	£200	-
G35	6c **slate-green**	£50	-
G36	8c **red**	£30	-
G37	15c **ultramarine**	£75	-
G33/37	**set** (5)	£350	-

Used examples are known. Most mint examples are discoloured on reverse; prices are for fine examples.

The 3c is in blue-green as opposed to earlier printings in green. The design measures 30mm vertically, instead of 29½mm.

1947 (Jan. 2nd)-51. Designs, 3c, 6c water village; other values, river view. Printers De La Rue. Sheets 10 x 5 or 5 x 10. (a) Perf. 14 (1947-50).

1	1c brown	.20	1.20
	a A of watermark missing	£800	-
	b weak entry	£10	£18
2	2c slate-grey	.30	£3
3	3c grey-green	.50	3.50
4	5c orange	.40	.75
	a '5c' inserted	£45	£55
5	6c black	.50	2.50
6	8c scarlet	.20	.60
7	10c purple-violet	.90	.20
	a sky retouch	£14	-
8	15c ultramarine	.85	.40
9	25c red-purple	1.30	.60
10	30c black and orange	1.20	.60
11	50c black	1.75	.50
12	$1 black and scarlet	£5	.45
	a black and carmine-red (15/2/50)	£30	£20
14	$5 green and vermilion (2/2/48)	£10	£12
15	$10 grey-black and plum (2/2/48)	£40	£18
1/15	set (14)	£55	£40
SP1/15	specimen (14)	£200	†

1b R4/4 shows the design at left very weak in comparison to other stamps in the sheet.

normal   CW 4a   normal   CW 1b

4a, 18a R1/8 has the top left value engraved by hand. This is characterised by distinct vertical lines in the figure '5'. The 'C' is also a different shape.

normal   CW 7a

7a, 19a R2/10 top of sky roughly retouched.

12a the carmine shade is so distinct that it almost qualfies as an error of colour. It is very deep in comparison with earlier issues.

(b) Perf. 14½ x 13½ (1950-51).

16	2c slate-grey (25/9/50)	.80	£3
17	2c black (27/6/51)	.80	£4
	a sky retouch	£45	-
18	5c orange (25/9/50)	£2	£9
	a '5c' inserted	£80	£150
19	10c purple-violet (25/9/50)	£1	3.50
	a sky retouch	£20	-
20	25c red-purple (25/1/51)	1.25	5.50
21	30c black and orange (25/1/51)	.90	£7
16/21	set 5 (16, 18-21)	5.50	£26

17a R1/1. A major retouch appears in the sky at top left corner.

18a R1/8 see No. 4a.

19a R2/10 see No. 7a.

Many other retouches exist.

(c) Perf. 13¼ x 13 (C) (1950-51).

22	8c scarlet (25/1/51)	.25	5.75
23	50c black (25/9/50)	.85	£10

1952 (1 March)-1958 Designs (1c - 50c) showing Sultan Omar Ali Saifuddin, $1-$5 showing water village. All with black vignette, frame plate colours as noted. Printers De La Rue. Watermark Multiple Script CA. Ordinary paper Perf 13 (C). Sheets 5 x 10.

24	1c black	.10	.30
25	2c orange	.10	.30
26	3c lake-brown	.10	.20
27	4c green	.10	.15
28	6c grey	.20	.10
29	8c crimson	.20	.35
	a crimson-lake (15/2/56)	4.50	.15
30	10c sepia	.10	.10
31	12c violet	2.50	.10
32	15c pale blue	1.50	.10
33	25c purple	1.20	.10
	a reddish purple (8/10/53)	£2	.55
34	50c ultramarine	£1	.10
	a blue (22/6/55)	3.50	.10
35	$1 green	.75	.85
	a bronze-green (23/7/58)	£3	1.80
36	$2 scarlet	£2	1.50
37	$5 maroon	£9	£5
	a brown-purple(15/2/56)	£12	£5
24/37	set (14)	£17	-

SPECIAL ISSUES

1949 (Sept. 22nd) Silver Jubilee of Sultan Ahmad Tajuddin. Recess De La Rue. Watermark Multiple Script CA. Perf 13 x 12¾ (C). Sheets 5 x 10.

S1	8c **black and rose-carmine**	.50	.75
S2	25c **purple-lake**		
	and red-orange	.50	£1
S3	50c **black and blue**	.50	£1
S1/3	**set** (3)	1.35	2.50

1949 (Oct. 10th) U.P.U. As Aden.

S4	8c **carmine-rose**	.50	.90
S5	15c **indigo**	1.75	.90
S6	25c **reddish mauve**	.50	.90
S7	50c **slate-black**	.50	.75
S4/7	**set** (4)	2.90	£3

BURMA

Contemporary Indian stamps without overprint were used in Burma from 1854 until March 31st, 1937.

1937 (April 1st) Stamps of India (1926-36 issues) inscribed 'INDIA POSTAGE'. Watermark Multiple Star, overprinted 'BURMA' at the Nasik Security Press. The overprint measures 15 mm. on the low values and 17½ mm. on the rupee values.

G1	3p **slate**	.50	.10
	a inverted watermark	3.50	.80
G2	½a **green**	.50	.10
	a inverted watermark	3.50	.80
G3	9p **deep green**	.50	.10
	a inverted watermark	3.50	.80
G4	1a **chocolate**	1.25	.10
	a inverted watermark	3.50	.80
G5	2a **vermilion** (small die)	.35	.10
G6	2½a **orange**	.30	.10
	a inverted watermark	3.50	.80
G7	3a **carmine**	1.10	.20
	a inverted watermark	£5	1.75
G8	3½a **deep blue**	1.75	.10
	a inverted watermark	£2	.20
G9	3½a **grey-blue**	£8	£5
	a inverted watermark	£5	2.75
G10	4a **sage-green**	.50	.10
	a inverted watermark	-	£45
G11	6a **bistre**	.50	.20
	a inverted watermark	-	£45
G12	8a **reddish purple**	£1	.10
G13	12a **claret**	3.75	£1
	a inverted watermark	£12	£2
G14	1r **chocolate and green**	£15	2.25
G15	2r **carmine and orange**	£15	£11
	a inverted watermark	£28	£12
G16	5r **ultramarine and purple**	£18	£14
	a inverted watermark	-	£125
G17	10r **green and scarlet**	£50	£48
	a inverted watermark	†	-
G18	15r **blue and olive**		
	(inverted watermark)	£200	£90
G19	25r **orange and blue**	£400	£225
	a inverted watermark	£425	-
G1/19	**set** (18)	£1000	£350

Forged overprints on Indian KG V high values are known for both postage and service issues.

The overprint is at the top on all values except G7.

All the following stamps were printed by offset-lithography at the Security Printing Press, Nasik, India, on "Elephant's Head" (multiple) watermarked paper, unless otherwise indicated.

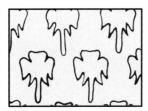

1938 (Nov. 15th)-40 Designs, 1p-2a, 4a King's head (small format) and perf. 13¾ x 14 (C); 2½a-8a (less 4a) scenes in Burma and perf. 13 (C); 1r-10r King's head (large format) and perf. 13¾ (C). Sheets 1 - 7 and 11, 16 x 20; other anna values 8 x 16; rupee values 10 x 12.

1	1p **vermilion** (1/8/40)	1.25	.90
2	3p **violet**	.10	1.20
3	6p **bright blue**	.10	.10
4	9p **yellow-green**	.50	.90
5	1a **chocolate-brown** (litho)	.10	.10
	a (typo)	1.25	1.50
6	1½a **turquoise-green**	.10	1.50
7	2a **deep carmine-rose**	.50	.30
8	2a6p **claret**	£7	1.50
	a birds above trees	£45	£30
9	3a **purple-violet**	£7	1.80
10	3a6p **ultramarine and blue**	1.25	£4
	a tick bird	£30	£40
	b extra trees	£55	£50
	c vignette double	£40	-
11	4a **greenish blue**	.85	.10
12	8a **myrtle-green**	£2	.35
13	1r **deep purple and deep blue**	£2	.35
14	2r **chocolate-brown and purple**	£7	£2
15	5r **violet and red**	£25	£22
16	10r **brown and myrtle**	£28	£40
1/16	**set** (16)	£75	£70

5a See Note after India 32 for details of printing differences.

CW 8a   CW 10a

8a R15/3 a flaw gives the appearance of birds in flight above the trees at left.

10a R9/5 A "tick bird" appears on the flank of the nearest buffalo.

10b R11/8 a flaw shows as a large clump of trees in front of the background hills, above the farmer's head.

10c the lines of the vignette are strongly doubled. Less clear examples exist.

Burma was occupied by the Japanese from early 1942 until the recapture of Rangoon in May 1945.

Prior to the issue of stamps by the Japanese Army Administration in June 1942, stocks of the pre-war stamps (G1-G8 and G08, 2-14 and 01-09) were overprinted in the Irrawaddy Delta area with representations of a Peacock.

1945 (June 8th) As No. 1 etc. but overprinted 'MILY ADMN'.

17	1p **vermilion**	.10	.10
	a double overprint	£20	£20
	b overprint omitted in pair with normal	£1200	-
18	3p **violet**	.10	.75
19	6p **bright blue**	.10	.20
20	9p **yellow-green**	.15	.75
	a basic stamp doubly printed	£70	-
21	1a **chocolate-brown** (typo)	.10	.10
22	1½a **turquoise-green**	.10	.10
23	2a **deep carmine-rose**	.10	.10
24	2a6p **claret**	£1	1.35
	a birds above trees	£18	£25
25	3a **purple-claret**	.75	.15
	a double overprint	£30	£30
26	3a6p **ultramarine and blue**	.10	.45
	a double overprint	£25	£30
	b vignette double	£35	£35
	c worn vignette	£18	£35
	d tick bird	£20	£30
	e extra trees	£20	£30
27	4a **greenish blue**	.10	.40
28	8a **myrtle-green**	.10	.75
29	1r **deep purple and deep blue**	.20	.30
30	2r **chocolate-brown and purple**	.20	.75
31	5r **violet and red**	.20	.75
32	10r **brown and myrtle**	.25	.75
17/32	**set** (16)	3.25	£7

Number issued - 1p, 3,744,00; 3p, 2,391,00; 6p, 2,804,000; 9p, 813,000; 1a, 11,702,720; 1½a, 3,957,440; 2a, 1,348,000; 2½a 2,005,120; 3a, 69,120; 3½a, 379,648; 4a, 463,616; 8a, 730,624; 1r, 265,920; 2r, 215,000; 5r, 183,000; 10r, 78,600.

24a, etc. For descriptions of the positional varieties see 1938 set.

26a 'MILY ADMN' printed doubly, well separated. There are many double overprints showing slight separation, worth little or no premium.

26b see 10c.

26c The centre plate became so worn that the inscription "Burma Rice" is virtually omitted.

This set came on the market in quantity after issue and was available at under face value.

1946 (Jan. 1st) As No. 2, etc., but colours changed. (Issued when the Civil authorities took over from the Military Administration).

33	3p **chocolate-brown**	.10	1.80
34	6p **purple-violet**	.10	.20
35	9p **grey-green**	.10	2.75
36	1a **deep blue** (typo)	.10	.15
37	1½a **vermilion**	.10	.10
38	2a **dull claret**	.10	.30
39	2a6p **greenish blue**	1.35	3.50
	a birds above trees	£20	£30
40	3a **dull violet**	£3	£4
41	3a6p **black and ultramarine**	.75	2.25
	a vignette double	£45	-
	b tick bird	£45	£50
	c extra trees	£45	£50
42	4a **mauve-purple**	.25	.35
43	8a **maroon**	.90	£3
44	1r **slate-violet and claret**	.60	1.20
45	2r **brown and dull vermilion**	£3	£3
46	5r **green and chocolate-brown**	3.50	£14
47	10r **red-claret and grey-purple**	7.50	£18
33/47	**set** (15)	£19	£50

39a, etc. For descriptions of the positional varieties see 1938 set.

1947 (Oct. 1st) As No. 33, etc., but overprinted 'INTERIM GOVERNMENT' (in Burmese) in Rangoon.

48	3p **chocolate-brown**	.60	.40
	a first character error	£40	-
	b overprint inverted	£15	-
	c overprint double	£15	-
	d end character error	£40	-
49	6p **purple-violet**	.10	.20
	a first character error	£28	-
	b overprint inverted	£15	-
	c overprint double	£15	-
50	9p **grey-green**	.10	.25
	a overprint inverted	£15	£20
	b overprint double	£10	-
51	1a **deep blue**	.10	.20
	a overprint inverted	£10	-
	b overprint double, both inverted	£14	-
	c vertical pair, one with overprint omitted	£750	-
52	1½a **vermilion**	.85	.10
	a overprint inverted	£10	-
	b overprint double, both inverted	£10	-
	c double print of entire stamp	£80	-
53	2a **dull claret**	.15	.10
	a first character error	£40	-
	b overprint inverted	£12	-
	c horizontal pair, one with overprint omitted	£750	-
54	2a6p **greenish blue**	.85	.60
	a overprint inverted	£15	-
	b birds above trees	£25	£25
55	3a **dull violet**	1.20	£1
	a overprint inverted	£10	-
	b overprint double	£10	-
	c overprint double, both inverted	£15	-
56	3a6p **black and ultramarine**	.60	1.35
	a overprint inverted	£12	-
	b overprint double	£10	-
	c tick bird	£40	£45
	d extra trees	£40	£45
57	4a **mauve-purple**	.80	.20
	a overprint inverted	£12	-
	b overprint double, both inverted	£12	-
58	8a **maroon**	.80	1.75
	a overprint inverted	£12	-
	b overprint double, both inverted	£12	-

59	1r **slate-violet and claret**	2.75	1.35
	a overprint inverted	£14	-
	b overprint double, both inverted	£14	-
	c frame printed double	-	-
60	2r **brown and dull vermilion**	2.75	3.75
61	5r **green and chocolate-brown**	2.75	3.50
62	10r **red-claret and grey-purple**	1.85	3.50
48/62	**set** (15)	£15	£16

The majority of the overprint errors on the market are forgeries, mostly of poor quality. Use of a good magnifying glass to examine the overprint is strongly advised.

It is not certain that all the inverted, double and double (one inverted) overprint errors exists genuinely overprinted. Comment is welcome.

48a   Inverted Overprint

48a/49a/53a The first character of the overprint was transposed to the end of the same line in error (R6/15). Some examples of these, and 48d, exist with the error corrected by handstamp.

48d The two end characters of the first line of the overprint were transposed to the front of same line (R14/14).

54b, etc. For descriptions of the positional varieties see 1938 set.

SPECIAL ISSUES

1940 (May 6th) Centenary of first postage stamps. No. 8 overprinted and surcharged at Security Printing Press, Nasik. Sheets 16 x 8.

S11a/2a6p **claret**	£2	1.25
a broken bar	£30	£35
b birds above trees	£30	£35

S1a the top bar obliterating 'TWO' is broken on R17/6.

S1b See 8a.

1946 (May 2nd) Victory. Designer, A.G.I. McGeoch. Perf. 13 (C). Watermark sideways. Sheets 16 x 8.

S2	9p **turquoise-green**	.10	.15
S3	1½a **purple-violet**	.10	.10
S4	2a **carmine-rose**	.10	.10
S5	3a6p **ultramarine**	.25	.15
	a bearded King	£140	
S2/5	**set** (4)	.50	.45

S5a a flaw on the King's chin resembles a beard. Position unknown.

Burma became an independent republic on 4th January, 1948, and these Victory designs were adapted (with changed portrait) to commemorate the change in status: they are outside the scope of this catalogue.

OFFICIAL STAMPS

Contemporary Indian "Service" stamps were used in Burma until March 31st, 1937.

1937 (April 1st-June) Stamps of India (1926-36 Issues) inscribed 'INDIA POSTAGE', Watermark Multiple Star, overprinted 'BURMA SERVICE' at the Nasik Security Press.

The overprint is spaced 11½mm between lines. Measurements of BURMA as on ordinary issue: SERVICE 13½mm (anna values); 19½mm (rupee values). The bulk of the overprinting was done in one operation, but quantities of certain values were overprinted in two operations.

GO1	3p slate	£2	.10
	a watermark inverted	-	£22
GO2	½a green	£9	.10
	a watermark inverted	†	-
GO3	9p deep green	£3	.60
GO4	1a chocolate	£4	.10
GO5	2a vermilion (small die)	£9	.30
	a watermark inverted	-	£22
GO6	2½a orange	£4	1.50
GO7	4a sage-green	£4	.10
GO8	6a bistre	£4	7.50
GO9	8a reddish purple	£4	1.50
GO10	12a claret	£4	£6
GO11	1r chocolate and green	£15	4.25
GO12	2r carmine and orange	£30	£35
	a watermark inverted	£20	£40
GO13	5r ultramarine and purple	£95	£35
GO14	10r green and scarlet	£260	£120
GO1/O14	set (14)	£425	£190

1939 (April 1st) No 2, etc, overprinted 'SERVICE'.

O1	3p violet	.10	.15
O2	6p bright blue	.10	.15
O3	9p yellow-green	£2	£3
O4	1a chocolate-brown (litho)	.10	.10
	a ditto (typo)	£2	1.50
O5	1½a turquoise-green	1.75	1.35
O6	2a deep carmine-rose	.60	.15
O7	2a6p claret	£14	£11
	a birds above trees	£85	-
O8	4a greenish blue	2.25	.75
O9	8a myrtle-green	7.50	2.50
O10	1r deep purple and deep blue	£8	3.50
	a frame doubled	-	-
O11	2r chocolate-brown and purple	£15	£10
O12	5r violet and red	£12	£19
O13	10r brown and myrtle	£70	£23
O1/13	set (13)	£120	£68

1942 PROVISIONAL ISSUE - CHIN HILLS DISTRICT

When the Japanese occupied the remainder of Burma in March 1942, a substantial area of the Chin Hills remained in British hands until it was finally overrun between November 1943 and March 1944. Covers and pieces from this period may be found, with Burma or Indian stamps with or without 'OHMS' handstamped, typewritten or in manuscript. This is a complex area, which has been fully covered by the Burma (Myanmar) Philatelic Study Circle in their Journal 'The Burma Fantail', Vol. 5 no.3, July 2008; this contains a full census of known covers, carried out by Richard Warren.

1946 (Jan. 1st) Civil Administration, No. 33, etc., overprinted "SERVICE".

O14	3p chocolate-brown	1.50	2.75
O15	6p purple-violet	1.10	1.40
O16	9p grey-green	.30	2.75
O17	1a deep blue (typo)	.10	1.20
O18	1½a vermilion	.10	.15
O19	2a dull claret	.10	1.20
O20	2a6p greenish blue	£1	5.50
	a birds above trees	£35	-
O21	4a mauve-purple	.10	.45
O22	8a maroon	1.85	£3
O23	1r slate-violet and claret	.40	4.50
O24	2r brown and dull vermilion	£4	£30
O25	5r green and chocolate-brown	7.50	£35
O26	10r red-claret and grey-purple	8.50	£42
O14/26	set (13)	£24	£115

O20a see 8a

1947 (Oct. 1st) Interim Government. No. O14, etc., overprinted 'INTERIM GOVERNMENT' as Nos. 48/62.

O27	3p chocolate-brown	.50	.25
O28	6p purple-violet	1.85	.10
O29	9p grey-green	2.50	.55
O30	1a deep blue (typo)	2.50	.50
O31	1½a vermilion	4.25	.20
O32	2a dull claret	2.50	.10
O33	2a6p greenish blue	£15	£8
	a bird above trees	£75	-
O34	4a mauve-purple	£9	.25
O35	8a maroon	£9	2.50
O36	1r slate-violet and claret	7.50	1.50
O37	2r brown and dull vermilion	7.50	£12
O38	5r green and chocolate-brown	7.50	£12
O39	10r red-claret and grey-purple	7.50	£18
O27/39	set (13)	£70	£50

O27 exists with additional overprint on top selvedge.

O33a see 8a.

GERMAN PROPAGANDA LABELS

The 1944 German imitations of the Great Britain 1937 definitives ½d to 3d (see after Great Britain for details) were also overprinted in black 'LIQUIDATION/OF EMPIRE/RANGOON' within a vertical rectangular frame.

CANADA

IMPERFORATE STAMPS

It was formerly the practice to distribute by favour four imperforate sheets of certain stamps, a fifth sheet being placed in the Post Office archives. These exist for 1-11, 15-28, A1, A2-3, S1, S2-4, SD10, AS 1-6.

Note:- All Canadian stamps are Perf 12 unless specified. Used Canadian stamps are plentiful. Nice examples used with circular datestamps are much scarcer. Our prices are for average-to-good CDS-used; very fine examples will be more expensive. Various values exist printed on paper with ribbed effect on the underside. The wire mesh on which the pulp is laid in the first instance is the cause of this, and the variety has no connection with laid paper.

1937-41 Definitives. Designs, 1c-8c (portrait of King from photo by Bertram Park); 10c (Memorial Chamber, Parliament Buildings, Ottawa); 13c (entrance, Halifax Harbour); 20c (Fort Garry Gate, Winnipeg); 50c (entrance, Vancouver Harbour); $1 (Chateau de Ramezay, Montreal). CW1-6 panes of 100 (10 x 10); CW 7 panes of 50 (10 x 5); CW 8-11 panes of 50 (5 x 10).

1	1c **green** (1/4/37)	.60	.10
2	2c **brown** (1/4/37)	.75	.10
3	3c **carmine-red** (1/4/37)	.75	.10
	a crease on collar	£35	£20
4	4c **yellow** (10/5/37)	2.50	£1
5	5c **blue** (10/5/37)	2.50	.10
6	8c **orange** (10/5/37)	2.50	1.80
7	10c **pale rose-carmine**		
	(15/6/38)	£2	.20
	a rose-carmine (3/8/38)	£2	.10
8	13c **blue** (15/11/38)	£10	1.20
9	20c **light brown** (15/6/38)	£10	1.20
10	50c **green** (15/6/38)	£20	£8
11	$1 **purple-violet** (15/6/38)	£25	£8
	a vertical pair,		
	imperf. between	£2750	-
	b aniline printing (/41?)	£30	£8
1/11	**set** (11)	£70	£19

7 under UV shows a cold purple reaction, 7a has a bright rosy-red glow.

11b These fluorescent-aniline stamps can be readily distinguished from the ordinary shade, as the ink is visible through the back of the stamp, apart from the fluorescent reaction under the ultraviolet lamp.

Number issued - 1c, 1,393,677,600; 2c, 1,163,103,550; 3c, 2,633,940,000; 4c, 24,074,000; 5c, 133,102,302; 8c, 14,035,353; 10c (CW 7) 10,186,690; 10c (CW 7a) 54,019,523; 13c, 13,028,291; 20c, 30,499,240; 50c, 4,924,100; $1, 2,210,219.

As before, but Imperf. x Perf. 8 (Coils).

12	1c **green** (15/6/37)	1.60	2.25
13	2c **brown** (18/6/37)	1.60	2.75
14	3c **carmine-red** (15/4/37)	£10	.75
12/14	**set** (3)	£12	£5

Number issued - 1c, 23,021,500; 2c, 34,565,000; 3c, 57,827,000.

1942 (July 1st) - 43 War Effort. Designs, 1c - 5c (less 4c slate) (King's portrait); 4c slate (Grain Elevator); 8c (farm scene); 10c (Parliament buildings); 13c (tank); 20c (Corvette); 50c (munitions); $1 (H.M.C.S. 'Iroquois'). CW 15-22 panes of 100 (10 x 10); CW 23-28 panes of 50 (5 x 10).

15	1c **green**	.65	.10
16	2c **brown**	.85	.10
17	3c **carmine-red**	.60	.35
18	3c **purple** (30/6/43)	.40	.10
19	4c **slate**	2.50	.90
20	4c **carmine-red** (9/4/43)	.30	.10
21	5c **blue**	1.30	.10
22	8c **red-brown**	2.50	.45
23	10c **brown**	4.50	.10
24	13c **grey-green**	3.50	£5
25	14c **grey-green** (16/4/43)	£9	.60
26	20c **deep chocolate-brown**	£8	.25
27	50c **bright blue**	£12	3.30
28	$1 **blue**	£20	£5
15/28	**set** (14)	£60	£15

Number issued - 1c, 2,533,900,000; 2c, 470,710,000; 3c (No. 17), 605,750,000; 3c (No. 18), 2,118,190,000; 4c (No. 19), 7,900,000; 8c, 22,978,621; 10c, 157,680,577; 13c, 4,000,000; 14c, 14,878,673; 20c, 62,028,166; 50c, 16,486,515; $1, 6,195,600.

As before but Imperf. x Perf. 8 (Coils).

29	1c **green** (9/2/43)	.45	.90
30	2c **brown** (6/10/42)	.90	1.25
31	3c **carmine-red** (6/10/43)	.80	4.75
32	3c **purple** (18/8/43)	4.50	3.75
33	4c **carmine-red** (18/8/43)	£3	.90
29/33	**set** (5)	£9	£10

Number issued - 1c, 26,000,000; 2c, 8,465,000; 3c (No. 31), 9,975,000.

As before but Imperf. x Perf. 12 (Booklets).

34	1c **green** (23/12/46)	1.50	.75
35	3c **purple** (23/12/46)	1.50	.90
36	4c **carmine-red** (23/12/46)	1.50	1.10
34/36	**set** (3)	£4	2.50

These stamps are from booklets, printed in strips of three, with outer edges imperf.

As before, but Imperf. x Perf. 9½ (Coils).

37	1c **green** (13/7/48)	1.50	2.75
38	2c **brown** (1/10/48)	3.50	£12
39	3c **purple** (2/7/48)	2.25	3.75
40	4c **carmine-red** (22/7/48)	3.25	2.25
37/40	**set** (4)	9.50	£18

The dates given beside Nos. 37-40 refer to when the stamps were delivered to Post Office Dept.; all were issued to the public shortly afterwards.

Number issued - 1c, 8,675,000; 2c, 3,195,000; 3c, 45,990,000; 4c, 47,590,000.

1946 (Sept. 16th) Designs, 8c (Ontario farm scene); 10c (Great Bear Lake); 14c (St. Maurice River power station); 20c (combine harvester); 50c (lumbering in Br. Columbia); $1 (Train Ferry 'Abegweit'). Panes of 50 (5 x 10).

41	8c **dull red-brown**	.50	1.50
42	10c **sage-green**	.80	.10
43	14c **deep sepia**	1.80	1.35
44	20c **slate-grey**	1.30	.10
45	50c **deep green**	7.50	2.50
46	$1 **reddish purple**	£12	2.50
41/46	**set** (6)	£22	£7

43 exists on thin ribbed paper.

Number issued - 8c, 15,100,000; 10c, 118,250,000; 50c, 13,970,000; $1, 15,375,000.

1949 (Nov. 15th) - 51 Designs, 1c-5c (King's portrait from photographs by Dorothy Wilding; POSTES POSTAGE incorporated in design); 10c (fur drying and wigwam); 50c (Oil Well); $1 (fish and fisherman). CW 47-53 panes of 100 (10 x 10); CW 54-56 panes of 50 (5 x 10).

47	1c **green**	.10	.10
48	2c **deep sepia**	.75	.30
49	2c **sage-green** (25/7/51)	.65	.10
50	3c **purple**	.15	.10
51	4c **carmine-red**	.10	.10
52	4c **orange-vermilion** (25/7/51)	.25	.10
53	5c **blue**	.85	.25
54	10c **dark purple-brown** (1/10/50)	1.75	.10
55	50c **deep green** (1/3/50)	2.75	.60
56	$1 **ultramarine** (1/2/51)	£18	£3
47/56	**set** (10)	£23	4.25

Number issued - 1c, 802,855,400; 2c (No. 48), 201,920,000; 2c (No. 49), 652,946,800; 3c, 1,357,100; 4c (No. 51), 709,940,000; 4c (No. 52), 790,680,000; 5c, 95,308,100; $1, 4,460,000.

As No. 47, etc., but Imperf. x Perf. 9½ (Coils).

57	1c **green** (18/5/50)	1.25	.90
58	2c **deep sepia** (18/5/50)	3.50	3.75
59	2c **sage-green** (9/5/51)	.80	2.25
60	3c **purple** (18/5/50)	1.10	1.80
61	4c **carmine-red** (18/5/50)	£6	5.50
62	4c **orange-vermilion** (27/10/51)	1.25	1.65
57/62	**set** (6)	12.50	£14

Number issued - 1c, 8,675,000; 2c (No. 58), 3,195,000; 2c (No. 59), 7,331,500; 3c, 26,625,000; 4c (No. 61), 10,980,000; 4c (No. 62), 9,645,000.

As No. 47, etc., but Imperf. x Perf. 12 (Booklets).

63	1c **green** (18/5/50)	.25	£1
64	3c **purple** (18/5/50)	.60	.60
65	4c **carmine-red** (18/5/50)	6.50	5.50
66	4c **orange-vermilion** (9/10/51)	3.50	4.50
63/66	**set** (4)	9.75	10.50

These were issued only in booklet panes of 3 with outer edges imperforate.

1950 (Jan. 19th) Designs as No. 47, etc., but POSTES POSTAGE omitted. Panes of 100 (10 x 10).

67	1c **green**	.25	.40
68	2c **deep sepia**	.25	£2
69	3c **purple**	.25	.40
70	4c **carmine-red**	.25	.15
71	5c **blue**	.25	.90
67/71	**set** (5)	1.10	3.50

Stamps without inscription POSTES and POSTAGE were printed and ready for issue, when a decision was made to incorporate the two words in the design. Later, the original stamps were released for sale at the Philatelic Bureau, Ottawa, to avoid speculation in stamps which were said to have leaked out.

Number issued - 1c, 84,000,000; 2c, 10,200,000; 3c, 101,300,000; 4c, 101,100,000; 5c, 5,000,000.

As No. 67, etc., but Imperf. x Perf. 9½ (Coils).

72	1c **green** (20/1/50)	.15	.60
73	3c **purple** (20/1/50)	.40	.90

Number issued - 1c, 2,660,000; 3c, 3,085,000.

AIR STAMPS

1938 (June 15th) Design, Seaplane over Riverboat S.S. 'Distributor III' on Mackenzie River. Panes of 50 (5 x 10).

A1	6c **blue**	5.50	.90

Number issued - 29,008,650.

1942-3 Design, Harvard Plane, etc. Panes of 50 (5 x 10).

A2	6c **blue** (1/7/42)	£11	5.75
A3	7c **blue** (16/4/43)	£2	.10
	a dull grey-blue (/45)	£3	.30

Number issued - 6c, 14,990,000; 7c, 97,793,352.

1946 (Sept. 16th) Design, Geese in Flight. Panes of 50 (5 x 10).

A4	7c **blue**	2.25	.10
	a ditto (thin paper) (/49)	£55	£12

A4a is usually very poorly centred.

Number issued - 72,350,000.

SPECIAL ISSUES

1937 (May 10th) Coronation. Panes (5 x 10).

S1	3c **carmine-red**	.80	.90

Number issued - 51,400,000.

1939 (May 15th) Royal Visit. Designs, 1c (Princesses Elizabeth and Margaret); 2c (National War Memorial, Ottawa); 3c (King and Queen). Panes of 50 (S2, S4 5 x 10; S3 10 x 5).

S2	1c black and green	.90	.15
S3	2c black and brown	.90	.75
S4	3c black and carmine	.70	.15
S2/4	set (3)	2.25	.90

Number issued - 1c, 50,043,000; 2c, 50,224,000; 3c, 100,000,000.

1947 (March 3rd) 100th Anniversary of Birth of Alexander Bell. Panes of 50 (10 x 5).

| S5 | 4c light blue | .10 | .20 |
| | a blue | .75 | .40 |

Number issued - 25,050,000.

1947 (July 1st) Canadian Citizenship. (Actually issued on the 80th Anniversary of Founding of Dominion). Panes of 50 (10 x 5).

| S6 | 4c blue | .10 | .15 |

Number issued - 25,100,000.

1948 (Feb. 16th) Marriage of Princess Elizabeth. Design from photograph by Dorothy Wilding. Panes of 100 (10 x 10).

| S7 | 4c blue | .10 | .10 |

Number issued - 50,010,000.

1948 (Oct. 1st) Centenary of Responsible Government. Panes of 50 (5 x 10).

| S8 | 4c slate | .10 | .10 |

Number issued - 50,300,000.

1949 (April 1st) Newfoundland's entry as Tenth Canadian province. Design, Cabot's ship 'Matthew' (from model by Ernest Maunder). Panes of 50 (5 x 10).

| S9 | 4c green | .15 | .10 |

Number issued - 50,850,000.

1949 (June 26th) 200th Anniversary of Founding of Halifax, Nova Scotia. Design after painting by C.W. Jefferies. Panes of 50 (5 x 10).

S10   4c **purple-violet**   .10   .10

Number issued - 25,450,000.

1951 (June 25th) Prime Ministers. Designs, 3c (Sir R.L. Borden), 4c (Rt. Hon. W. L. Mackenzie King). Panes of 100 (10 x 10).

S13   3c **turquoise-green**   .10   .45
S14   4c **carmine-rose**   .10   .10

Number issued - 3c, 50,800,000; 4c, 49,953,000.

1951 (Sept. 24th) Centenary of first postal service of provinces. Designs, 4c (Train of Bytown and Prescott Railway, 1851, and diesel electric locomotive drawing regular passenger train); 5c (side-paddle wheel steamship 'City of Toronto' and Canadian National Steamship 'Prince George'); 7c (stagecoach of 1851 and 'North Star' airliner); 15c (reproduction of 'Three Penny Beaver'). S20-22 Panes of 50 (5 x 10); S23 panes of 100 (10 x 10).

S20   4c **black**   .20   .10
S21   5c **purple**   .30   1.25
S22   7c **blue**   .20   .75
S23   15c **red**   .55   .10
S20/23   **set** (4)   1.10   £2

Number issued - 4c, 49,750,000; 5c, 5,050,000; 7c, 19,900,000.

1951 (Oct. 26th) Royal Visit. Panes of 50 (5 x 10).

S24   4c **violet**   .10   .10

Number issued - 50,300,000.

SPECIAL EXPRESS DELIVERY STAMPS

1938-9. Design, Canadian Coat of Arms on lined background. Panes of 50 (5 x 10). Perf 12.

SD7   10c **green** (1/4/39)   £9   2.50
SD8   20c **carmine-red**
      (15/6/38)   £20   £17

Number issued - 10c, 2,305,450; 20c, 200,000.

1939 (March 1st) No. SD8 surcharged. Panes of 50 (5 x 10).

SD9 10c/20c **carmine-red**   £4   8.50

Number issued - 300,000.

1942 (July 1st) Design, Coat of Arms flanked by Flags. Panes of 50 (5 x 10).

SD10 10c **green**   3.50   .20

Number issued - 3,276,404.

1946 (Sept. 16th) Design, Coat of Arms flanked by olive and laurel branches (emblems of Peace and Victory). Panes of 50 (5 x 10).

SD11 10c **green** 2.25 .20

SPECIAL AIR EXPRESS DELIVERY STAMPS

1942-3. Design, Trans-Canada Plane in Flight (flying to left). Panes of 50 (5 x 10).

AS1 16c **deep ultramarine** (1/7/42) 2.50 .30
AS2 17c **deep ultramarine**
(16/4/43) £2 .35

Number issued - 16c, 814,841; 17c, 868,689.

1946 Designs, Trans-Atlantic Plane over Quebec (flying to right). Panes of 50.

(a) Circumflex accent over E in EXPRES.

AS3 17c **dull ultramarine** (16/9/46) £2 £4

(b) Grave accent over E in EXPRES.

AS4 17c **dull ultramarine** (12/46) £3 3.50

AS3 AS4

Number issued - AS3, 300,000.

OFFICIAL STAMPS

The perforated initials (O.H.M.S.) are to be found inverted, sideways, etc., with valuations the same.

Collectors are warned that many of the perforated OHMS stamps on the market were produced at a later date, using the original perforating dies. These are not distinguishable from originals and buyers should take this into account.

Numbers in brackets after the description refer to the number of the stamp prior to perforation or overprinting.

Five Hole Punch   Four Hole Punch

We have decided to list the 4 and 5 hole punch 'OHMS' separately. The numbers have been altered as follows:

19th edition	18th edition
O1-O11	O1a-O11a
O12	-
O13-O16	-
O17-27	O1-O11
O28-O29	-
O30-O43	O12-O25
O44-O49	O26-O31
O50-O51	O32-O33
O52-O60	O34-O42
O61-O66	O43-O48
O67-O80	O49-O62
OS1-OS5	-
OS6-8	OS2-4
OA1-OA3	-
OA4-9	OA1-6
OSD1-OSD5	-
OSD6	OSE1
OSD7	-
OSD8-11	OSE2-6

1937-38 Nos. 1-11 perforated 'O.H.M.S.', five punch holes high.

O1	1c **green**	-	£2
O2	2c **brown**	-	£2
O3	3c **carmine-red**	-	£2

O4	4c **yellow**	-	6.50
O5	5c **blue**	-	4.50
O6	8c **orange**	-	£9
O7	10c **pale rose-carmine**	-	£14
	a rose-carmine	-	£15
O8	13c **blue**	-	£20
O9	20c **light brown**	-	£20
O10	50c **green**	-	£40
O11	$1 **purple-violet**	-	£65
O1/11	**set** (11)	-	£185

1937 No. 14 imperf x perf 8 (Coil), perforated 'O.H.M.S.', five punch holes high.

O12	3c **carmine-red**	-	£ 48

1939 stamps of King George V 1935 set, perforated 'O.H.M.S.', four punch holes high.

O13	10c **red**	£45	£28
O14	13c **purple**	£50	£28
O15	20c **green**	£55	£36
O16	50c **violet**	£40	£28
O13/16	**set** (4)	£170	£110

1939 (July) Nos. 1-11 perforated 'O.H.M.S.', four punch holes high.

O17	1c **green**	£1	.20
O18	2c **brown**	1.50	.20
O19	3c **carmine-red**	1.65	.20
O20	4c **yellow**	3.25	1.50
O21	5c **blue**	2.25	.30
O22	8c **orange**	8.50	2.70
O23	10c **pale rose-carmine**	£35	£2
	a rose-carmine	7.50	.25
O24	13c **blue**	£12	£1
O25	20c **light brown**	£24	1.50
O26	50c **green**	£35	£5
O27	$1 **purple-violet**	£75	£19
O17/27	**set** (11)	£150	£29

1939 No. 13-14 imperf x perf 8 (Coil), perforated 'O.H.M.S.', four punch holes high.

O28	2c **brown** (18/6/37)	£50	£30
O29	3c **carmine-red** (15/4/37)	£50	£30

1942-3. Nos. 15-28 (War activities), perforated 'O.H.M.S.', four punch holes high.

O30	1c **green**	.35	.10
O31	2c **brown**	.35	.10
O32	3c **carmine-red**	1.20	.45
O33	3c **purple**	.75	.10
O34	4c **slate**	£3	.90
O35	4c **carmine-red**	.35	.10
O36	5c **blue**	.75	.20
O37	8c **red-brown**	4.25	1.40
O38	10c **brown**	2.50	.15
O39	13c **grey-green**	4.75	£5
O40	14c **grey-green**	£5	.80
O41	20c **deep chocolate-brown**	8.50	.60
O42	50c **bright violet**	£20	3.75
O43	$1 **blue**	£48	£16

O30/43	**set** (14)	£90	£27

1946. Nos. 41-46 (Peacetime activities), perforated 'O.H.M.S.', four punch holes high

O44	8c **dull red-brown**	£12	2.50
O45	10c **sage-green**	1.50	.10
O46	14c **deep sepia**	3.50	.90
O47	20c **slate-grey**	£4	.30
O48	50c **deep green** (45)	£15	£5
O49	$1 **reddish purple**	£35	£10
O44/49	**set** (6)	£65	£17

1949 (Nov.) Nos. 48 and 50, perforated 'O.H.M.S.', four punch holes high.

O50	2c **deep sepia**	£1	1.50
O51	3c **purple**	£1	1.50

1949 (Sept-Oct) overprinted 'O.H.M.S.' on various stamps.

O52	1c **green** (No. 15) (22/9/49)	1.75	£2
	a stop after S omitted	£110	£50
O53	2c **brown** (No. 16)	£6	7.50
	a stop after S omitted	£100	£70
O54	3c **purple** (No. 18)	.90	1.50
O55	4c **carmine-red** (No. 20)	1.40	1.50
O56	10c **sage-green** (No. 42)	£2	.10
	a stop after S omitted	£75	£30
O57	14c **deep sepia** (No. 43)	£3	2.25
	a stop after S omitted	£85	£45
O58	20c **slate-grey** (No. 44)	£6	.40
	a stop after S omitted	£110	£40
O59	50c **deep green** (No. 45)	£90	£80
	a stop after S omitted	£1000	£500
O60	$1 **reddish-purple** (No. 46)	£25	£30
	a stop after S omitted	£3250	-
O52/60	**set** (9)	£120	£110

Missing stop errors on 1c, 2c, 5c (R6/2); 10c, 14c, 20c, 50c, $1 (R10/2), both lower left panes.

Number issued - 1c, 1,500,000; 2c, 500,000; 3c, 1,500,000; 4c, 3,000,000; 10c, 1,000,000; 14c, 600,000; 20c, 400,000; 50c, 30,000; $1, 65,000.

1949 (April)-50 Nos. 47-51 and 55 overprinted 'O.H.M.S.'

O61	1c **green** (No. 47)	1.50	.90
O62	2c **deep sepia** (No. 48)	1.60	.90
O63	3c **purple** (No. 50)	1.25	.90
O64	4c **carmine-red** (No. 51)	1.25	.10
	a stop after S omitted	-	-
O65	5c **blue** (No. 53) (15/11/49)	2.75	1.25
	a stop after S omitted	£55	£35
O66	50c **deep green** (No. 55)		
	(1/3/50)	£15	£18
O61/66	**set** (6)	£23	£20

O64a and O65a Missing stop; R8/8 upper left pane, R6/2 lower left pane.

CANADA

Number issued - 1c, 2,000,000; 2c, 1,000,000; 3c, 2,000,000; 4c, 5,500,000; 5c, 800,000; 50c, 95,000.

1950 (Oct. 24th) - 51 Stamps overprinted 'G'.

O67	1c **green** (No. 47)	.70	.10
O68	2c **deep sepia** (No. 48)	1.40	2.25
O69	2c **sage-green** (No. 49)		
	(25/7/51)	.85	.10
O70	3c **purple** (No. 50)(30/9/50)	1.10	.10
O71	4c **carmine-red** (No. 51)		
	(30/9/50)	1.30	.60
O72	4c **orange-vermilion**		
	(No. 52)(1/5/52)	1.30	.35
O73	5c **blue** (No. 53)	1.50	£1
O74	10c **sage-green** (No. 42)	1.30	.10
O75	10c **dark purple-brown** (54)	£2	.10
	a overprint omitted in		
	pair with normal	£425	£320
O76	14c **deep sepia** (No. 43)	8.50	£5
O77	20c **slate-grey** (No. 44)	£16	.20
O78	50c **deep green** (No. 55)	£7	9.75
O79	$1 **reddish purple** (No.46)	£40	£45
O80	$1 **ultramarine** (No. 56)		
	(1/2/51)	£32	£45
O67/80	**set** (14)	£100	£100

O75a should, ideally, be collected in positional blocks. A Certificate from a reputable expertising body is essential.

Number issued - 2c (O68), 1,500,000; 4c (O71), 10,000,000; 10c (O74), 975,000; 14c (O74), 600,000; 20c, 700,000; $1 (O79), 60,000; $1 (O80), 40,000.

OFFICIAL SPECIAL ISSUES

1937 (May) Coronation No. S1, perforated 'O.H.M.S.', five punch holes high.

OS1	3c **carmine-red**	-	£35

1939 Nos. S2-S3 (Royal Visit),perforated 'O.H.M.S.', five punch holes high.

OS2	1c **black and green**	-	£35
OS3	2c **black and brown**	-	£38
OS4	3c **black and carmine**	-	£35
OS2/4	**set** (3)	-	£100

1939 (July) Coronation No. S1, perforated 'O.H.M.S.', four punch holes high.

OS5	3c **carmine-red**	£55	£35

1939 (May) Nos. S2-S3 Royal Visit, perforated 'O.H.M.S.', four punch holes high.

OS6	1c **black and green**	£65	£28
OS7	2c **black and brown**	£65	£28
OS8	3c **black and carmine**	£65	£28
OS6/8	**set** (3)	£180	£75

OFFICIAL AIR

1938 No. A1 (Air), perforated 'O.H.M.S.', five punch holes high.

OA1	6c **blue**	-	£24

1939 Air (1928), perforated 'O.H.M.S.', four punch holes high.

OA2	5c **brown**	£18	£12

1939 Air (1935), perforated 'O.H.M.S.', four punch holes high.

OA3	6c **brown**	£40	£35

1939 No. A1 (Air), perforated 'O.H.M.S.', four punch holes high.

OA4	6c **blue** (/39)	2.50	.75

1942-43 Nos. A2-A3 (Air) perforated 'O.H.M.S.', four punch holes high.

OA5	6c **blue** (1/7/42)	2.50	2.25
OA6	7c **blue** (16/4/43)	£2	.20

1946 Nos. A4 (Air) perforated 'O.H.M.S.', four punch holes high.

OA7	7c **blue** (16/9/46)	£2	£1

1949 (Sept.) No. A4 (Air) overprinted 'O.H.M.S.'

OA8	7c **blue**	£11	£4
	a stop omitted after S	£100	£50

OA8a R10/2 lower left pane.

Number issued - 400,000.

1950 (Sept. 30th) No. A4 (Air) overprinted 'G'.

OA9	7c **blue**	£11	£9

Number issued - 400,000.

OFFICIAL - SPECIAL EXPRESS DELIVERY

1938-39. Nos. SD7 and SD8 perforated 'O.H.M.S.', five punch holes high.

OSD1	10c **green** (/39)	-	£35
OSD2	20c **carmine-red** (/38)	-	£55

1940 No. SD9 perforated 'O.H.M.S.'. five punch holes high.

OSD3	10c/20c **carmine-red** (/39)	-	£55

1939 Special Delivery (1932) perforated 'O.H.M.S.', four punch holes high.

OSD4	20c **reddish-brown**	£130	£65

1939 Special Delivery (1935) perforated 'O.H.M.S.', four punch holes high.

OSD5	20c **carmine-red**	£70	£32

1939. No. SD7 perforated 'O.H.M.S.', four punch holes high.

OSD6	10c **green** (/39)	4.50	£4

1939 No. SD9 perforated 'O.H.M.S.'. four punch holes high.

OSD7	10c/20c **carmine-red** (/39)	£90	£50

1942 No. SD10 perforated 'O.H.M.S.', four punch holes high.

OSD8	10ct green	4.50	£5

1946 No. SD11 perforated 'O.H.M.S.'. four punch holes high.

OSD9	10c **green**	£4	£3

1950 No. SD11 overprinted 'O.H.M.S.'

OSD10	10c **green**	£8	£16

1950 No. SD11 overprinted 'G'

OSD11	10c **green**	£12	£18

OFFICIAL - AIR SPECIAL EXPRESS DELIVERY

1946 Nos. AS1, 2 perforated 'O.H.M.S.', four punch holes high.

OAS1	16c **deep ultramarine**	£10	£10
OAS2	17c **deep ultramarine**	£8	£6

1946 Nos. AS3, 4 perforated 'O.H.M.S.', four punch holes high.

OAS3	17c **deep ultramarine** (AS3)	£30	£18
OAS4	17c **deep ultramarine** (AS4)	£50	£50

POSTAGE DUE STAMPS

1935-48. Panes of 100 (10 x 10).

PD1	1c **purple-violet** (14/10/35)	.40	.10
PD2	2c **purple-violet** (9/9/35)	1.75	.10
PD2a	3c **purple-violet** (4/65)	£3	£3
PD3	4c **purple-violet** (2/7/35)	.75	.10

PD4	5c **purple-violet** (11/8/48)	£3	2.25
PD5	6c **purple-violet** (16/1/59)	£1	1.80
PD6	10c **purple-violet** (16/9/35)	.35	.10
PD1/6	**set** (7)	£9	6.75

BOOKLET PANES
(Mint)

1937 K.G.VI issue.

P1	1c **CW 1** (pane of 4 + 2 labels)	£12	-
P2	1c **CW 1** (pane of 6)	2.50	-
P3	2c **CW 2** (pane of 4 + 2 labels)	£24	-
P4	2c **CW 2** (pane of 6)	4.50	-
P5	3c **CW 3** (pane of 4 + 2 labels)	£2	-

1942 War Effort issue.

P6	1c **CW 15** (pane of 4 + 2 labels)	£12	-
P7	1c **CW 15** (pane of 6)	1.25	-
P8	1c **CW 34** (pane of 3)	£4	-
P9	2c **CW 16** (pane of 4 + 2 labels)	£13	-
P10	2c **CW 16** (pane of 6)	£9	-
P11	3c **CW 17** (pane of 4 + 2 labels)	£2	-
P12	3c **CW 18** (pane of 4 + 2 labels)	2.50	-
P13	3c **CW 18** (pane of 6)	£6	-
P14	3c **CW 35** (pane of 3)	£4	-
P15	4c **CW 19** (pane of 6)	1.50	-
P16	4c **CW 36** (pane of 3)	£4	-

1946 Peace Issue.

P17	7c **CW A4** (pane of 4)	£4	-

1949 'POSTES-POSTAGE' issue.

P18	1c **CW 63** (pane of 3)	.75	-
P19	3c **CW 64** (pane of 3)	1.75	-
P20	3c **CW 50** (pane of 4 + 2 labels)	£1	-
P21	4c **CW 65** (pane of 3)	£20	-
P22	4c **CW 51** (pane of 6)	2.50	-
	a stitched	-	-
P23	4c **CW 52** (pane of 6)	£3	-
	a stitched	-	-
P24	4c **CW 66** (pane of 3)	£10	-

Fine used (C.T.O.) panes are, in theory, worth similar prices to mint. In reality, they are more difficult to obtain, especially cancelled in the correct period.

COMPLETE BOOKLETS

1937-41 definitives

Initial colours given indicate colour of the covers.
All are stapled, unless otherwise stated.

B1	25c **1937 green on white**			
	P2 x 4			
	English text	£25	-	
	a French text	£35	-	
B2	25c **1937 brown on white**			
	P4 x 2			
	English text	£30	-	
	a French text	£45	-	
B3	25c **1937 red on white**			
	P5 x 2			
	English text	£15	-	
	a French text	£35	-	
B4	25c **1937 blue on white**			
	P1, 3, 5			
	English text	£50	-	
	a French text	£70	-	

1942 War Effort

B5	25c **1942 25c green on white.**			
	P6 x 4			
	English text	£5	-	
	a French text	£8	-	
	b Bilingual text	£15	-	
B6	25c **1942 25c brown on white.**			
	P9 x 2 **English text**	£25	-	
	a French text	£45	-	
B7	25c **1942 red on white**			
	P11 x 2 **English text**	£4	-	
	a French text	£5	-	
B8	25c **1942 purple on white**			
	P6, 9, 11 **English text**	£32	-	
	a French text	£50	-	
B9	25c **1943 25c purple on white**			
	CW P11 of 4 + 2 labels x 2			
	English text	£5	-	
	a French text	£15	-	
	b Bilingual text	£10	-	
B10	25c **1943 25c orange on white**			
	P12 **English text**	£2	-	
	a French text	£6	-	
	b Bilingual text	£8	-	
B11	25c **1943 25c black on white**			
	P8, 14, 16 **English text**	£12	-	
	a French text	£18	-	
	b Bilingual text	£17	-	
B12	$1 **1947 'Gift' brown on orange**			
	P13, 15, 2 x 17			
	English text	£12	-	
	a French text	£20	-	

1949 Postes-Postage issue

B13	25c **1950 violet on white**			
	P20 x 2 **English text**	2.50	-	
	a Bilingual text	2.50	-	
B14	25c **1950 orange on white**			

	P22 **English text**	£20	-	
	a Bilingual text	£20	-	
B14b	25c **1951 orange on white**			
	(stitched) P22a **English text**	£35	-	
B15	25c **1950 black on white**			
	P18, 19, 21 **English text**	£20	-	
	a Bilingual text	£25	-	
B16	25c **1951 orange on white**			
	P23 **English text**	£3	-	
	a Bilingual text	£6	-	
B16b	25c **1951 orange on white**			
	(stitched)			
	P23a **English text**	£9	-	
B17	25c **1951 black on white**			
	P18, 19, 24 **English text**	£18	-	
	a Bilingual text	£20	-	

There are many variations of text (length of inscriptions, etc.) and postal rates which we do not list. For fuller details, we recommend the 'Canadian Booklet Catalogue', by Bill McCann, published by Unitrade Press in Toronto in 1988.

CAYMAN ISLANDS

1938 (May 5th) -47. Designs, ¼d, 1½d and 2/- (beach view); 1d and 3d (map of Islands); ½d and 1/- (Dolphin fish); 2½d and 5/- (schooner); 2d, 6d, 10/- (Hawksbill turtles). Sheets of horizontal designs, 5 x 12; others 10 x 6 or 6 x 10.

(a) Perf. 12½ (L). Printers (recess) Waterlow.

1	¼d orange	.30	.35
	a bright red-orange (17/12/45)	.35	.75
2	1d rose-red	.15	.45
	a scarlet-red (17/12/45)	.25	.60
3	1½d black	.15	.10
4	2½d light blue	.20	.15
5	2½d reddish orange (25.8.47)	1.50	.30
6	3d orange	.60	.50
	a reddish orange (17/12/45)	.20	.10
7	3d light blue (25/8/47)	1.50	.20
8	2/- yellow-green	£20	£9
	a green (16/7/43)	£12	5.50
	b deep green (26/8/48)	£20	£10
9	5/- lake	£15	£9
	a crimson-lake (16/7/43)	£30	£13

(b) Perf. 11¾ x 13 (C). Printers (recess) De La Rue.

10	½d green	.40	.35
11	2d violet	£1	.25
12	6d deep olive-green	3.50	2.50
	a brown-olive (8/7/47)	1.50	£1
13	1/- chestnut-brown	2.50	.90
	a red-brown (17/12/45)	£3	1.25
14	10/- chocolate	£12	5.50
	a sepia (12/3/45)	£12	6.50
SP1/14	specimen set (14)	£225	†

As No. 1 but Perf. 13½ x 12½ (L).

15	¼d orange (16/7/43)	.10	.50

As Nos. 10-14 but Perf. 14 (L).

16	½d green (16/7/43)	.60	.85
	a yellow-green	.80	.85
	b 'A' in watermark missing	£800	-
17	2d violet (16/7/43)	.30	.20
18	6d deep olive-green (16/7/43)	1.50	.75

19	1/- red-brown (16/7/43)	£2	1.25
	a 'A' in watermark missing	£900	-
20	10/- chocolate-brown (16/7/43)	£13	5.50
	a sepia-brown (17/12/45)	£13	6.50
	b watermark inverted		
1-20	set (14)	£45	£21

1950 (Oct. 2nd) Designs, ¼d (Cat Boat); ½d, 1½d, 6d, 9d (island views and scenes); 1d (turtle); 2d (Cayman seamen); 2½d (map of islands); 3d (Parrot fish); 1/- (turtles in "Crawl"); 2/- ("Ziroma"); 5/- (boat-building); 10/- (Government Offices, Grand Cayman). Printers (recess), Bradbury, Wilkinson. Perf. 11½ x 11¼ (C). Sheets 5 x 12.

21	¼d ultramarine and rose	.10	.35
22	½d purple and green	.10	.75
23	1d olive and deep grey-blue	.30	.45
24	1½d green and greyish brown	.15	.45
25	2d purple and lake-carmine	.50	.90
26	2½d turquoise and grey	.25	.35
27	3d emerald and light blue	.70	.90
28	6d red-brown and deep blue	£1	.75
29	9d carmine-red and grey-green	£5	1.20
30	1/- brown and orange red	1.50	1.75
31	2/- grey-violet and dull lake	3.75	£5
32	5/- olive and grey-violet	£9	4.25
33	10/- black and rose	£10	£8
21/33	set (13)	£32	£23

SPECIAL ISSUES

1937 (May 13th) Coronation. As Antigua.

S1	½d green	.15	1.15
S2	1d carmine	.25	.15
S3	2½d deep blue	.50	.25
S1/3	set (3)	.80	1.40
SP S1/3	specimen perf (3)	£95	†

1946 (Aug. 26th) Victory. As Aden.

S4	1½d black	.15	.10
	a re-entry	£35	£40
S5	3d yellow-orange	.15	.10
	a stop after date	£15	£15
SP S4/5	specimen perf (2)	£75	†

S4a   S5a

S4a R8/3 (Plate A1) Thickening of top framelines above and below 'IS' of Islands.

S5a R2/1 (plate B1) Full stop appears after the date.

1948 (Nov. 29th) Silver Wedding. As Aden.

S6	½d **green**	.10	.60
S7	10/- **slate-violet**	£9	£14

1949 (Oct. 10th) U.P.U. As Aden.

S8	2½d **orange-yellow**	.15	.60
S9	3d **indigo**	.75	1.35
S10	6d **dull olive**	.30	1.35
S11	1/- **beech-brown**	.30	.30
S8/11	**set** (4)	1.40	3.30

CEYLON

All stamps printed (recess) by De La Rue, unless otherwise stated.

1938-49, 2r (Guard Stone, Anuradhapura), other values (views and scenes in Ceylon). Watermark upright, except where indicated 'S' (sideways). Sheets 6 x 10 or 10 x 6.

(a) Perf. 13 x 11¾ (C).

1	2c	**black and deep carmine** (25/4/38)	£6	£1
		a comma flaw	-	-
2	3c	**black and bottle green** (21/3/38)	£4	.90
3	50c	**grey-black and purple-violet** (25/4/38)	£65	£32

(b) Perf. 11¼ x 11½ (C). Printers (recess) Bradbury, Wilkinson.

4	2c	**black and brownish carmine-lake** (17/2/44)	.35	.50
		a black and deep carmine-red (23/7/45)	.35	.50
		b watermark inverted	-	£550
5	3c	**grey and myrtle-green** (1942, 1943)	.30	.10
		a grey and deep dull green (1945)	.40	.10
		b inverted watermark	†	-
		c 'A' of watermark missing	£750	£750
6	6c	**black and grey-blue** (1/2/38)	.15	.10
		b black and steel-blue (22/9/47)	.20	.15
7	10c	**black and blue** (S) (1/2/38)	1.25	.10
		a black and dull blue (1/6/44)	1.25	.30
		b black and dark blue (7/7/48)	1.75	.60
8	15c	**deep blue-green and red-brown (S)** (1/1/38)	.80	.10
		a deep blue-green and lake-brown (S) (4/9/42)	£1	.20
		b deep blue-green and reddish brown (23/7/45)	1.25	.35
9	20c	**black and blue** (15/1/38)	1.40	.10

10 25c **deep prussian blue and purple-brown**
        (S) (15/1/38)   1.75 .20
    a indigo and chocolate
        (S) (19/2/43)   £2   .35
    b prussian blue and red-brown (thin paper)
        (4/45)   1.50 .20
    c dark blue and reddish brown (10/10/51) 2.75 .10
    d inverted watermark   -   -
11 30c **crimson and grey-green**
        (S) (1/2/38)   4.75 1.80
    a deep red and deep green
        (16/4/45)   4.75 2.75
12 50c **black and deep reddish lilac** (14/5/42) £2   1.80
    a deep grey-black and deep blackish purple
        (2/43)   £6   £5
    b black and deep dull purple (1/44) £4 £5
    c 'A' of watermark missing £650 -
13 1r **deep bluish violet and purple-brown**
        (S) (1/2/38)   £8   .75
    a deep violet and chocolate (thin paper)
        (S) (2/43)   £8   .75
    b deep bluish violet and purple-brown (/44) £6 1.35
14 2r **grey-black and carmine**
        (1/2/38)   £5   1.80
    a deep grey and rose-carmine (2/43) £6 £2
    b 'A' of watermark missing - -
15 2r **grey-black and violet**
        (15/3/47)   1.25 1.35

Bradbury, Wilkinson took over printing of the 2c, 3c, 50c values from De La Rue, when the works of the latter firm were bombed.

(c) Perf. 13½ (C). (As Nos. 1-3 plus 5c "Palm" design).

16 2c **black and deep carmine**
        (25/4/38)   .75   .10
17 3c **grey-black and bottle green** (21/3/38) 1.25 .10
    a grey-black and deep grey-green 2.50 .40
18 5c **sage-green and red-orange** (1/1/43) .15 .10
    a apostrophe flaw   £45   £26
19 50c **black and deep lilac**
        (25/4/38)   £7   .20

18a a flaw between the N and U of 'coconut' on R6/6 gives the impression of an apostrophe. This occurs on the 1943 printing only. Plate 1A-1.

COCONUT PALM

(d) Perf. 13½ x 13 (C). As Nos. 1-3.

20 2c **black and carmine-lake**
        (/38)   £45   £1
    a comma flaw   -   -
21 3c **grey-black and bottle-green** (/38) £100 7.50
22 50c **grey-black and deep lilac** (/38) £140 1.65

As Nos. 2 and 3 but Perf. 14 (L).

23 3c **black and bottle green**
        (7/41)   £50   .60
24 50c **grey-black and deep red-lilac** (4/42) £45 £17

As Nos. 1-3 and 18 but Perf. 12 (C).

25 2c **black and bright carmine**
        (22/4/49)   £1   2.25
26 3c **black and bottle green**
        (14/1/46)   .30   .50
27 5c **deep dull yellow-green and orange-red** (/47) .85 .20
    a pale dull yellow-green and orange-red (8/3/48) .85 .20
28 50c **black and deep lilac**
        (14/1/46)   1.75 .15

There were a very large number of printings of most values in this set. This results in a quantity of shades, plate number combinations, papers and shades; they may be collected in far greater detail than the above listing.
There are a number of re-entries on various values. Information as to positions, plate numbers etc is solicited.

1938-52 Perf. 13¾ x 14 (C) (typo). Sheets 120 - two panes, each 6 x 10.

29 5r **grey-green and sepia-brown** (ch)
        (10/10/38)   £18   £5
    a grey-green and dull brown (sub)
        (19/2/43)   £9   3.30
    b dull green and purple-brown
        (ch) (3/48)   £16   £5
30 10r **grey-green and orange** (ch) (1/2/52) £45 £28
1/29   **set** (cheapest 14) £35   £10
SP 1/29 **specimen** set perf (14) £340 †

30 - First issued for revenue purposes, it was subsequently authorised for postal use from 1 December 52 - 14 March 54. Dates outside this period must be assumed to be fiscally used. Most examples of this stamp offered for sale have large fiscal cancels.

1940-1. Nos. 6 and 9 surcharged 3 cents.

31	3c/6c **black and grey-blue** (16/5/41)		.30	.10
32	3c/20c **black and slate-blue** (5/11/40)		1.75	1.20

Crude forgeries of 31 and 32 exist with the overprint double and/or inverted.

Number issued - 3c/6c 1,800,000; 3c/20c, 900,000.

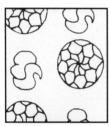

1950 (Feb. 4th) Designs, 4c (dancer); 15c (Vesak orchid); other values (views and scenes in Ceylon). Printers (recess) Bradbury, Wilkinson. Watermark Lotus Flowers and "Sri". Sheets 10 x 5.

(a) Perf. 12 x 12¾ (C).

34	4c **purple-brown and deep scarlet**		.10	.10
35	5c **green**		.10	.10
38	15c **deep emerald and purple-violet**		£1	.30
39	30c **yellow and carmine-red**		.15	.40

(b) Perf. 11¼ x 11½ (C).

40	75c **ultramarine and vermilion**		2.75	.15
41	1r **indigo and brown**		.80	.20
34/41	**set** (6)		4.50	1.10

1951-4. Designs, 2c (Ruhuna National Park); 3c (ancient Guard Stone, Anuradhapura); 6c and 10r (harvesting rice); 10c (Coconut Palms); 10c (King Coconuts); 25c (Sigiriya fresco); 35c (Star orchid); 40c (rubber plantation); 50c (outrigger canoe); 85c (tea plantation); 2r (River Gal Dam); 5r (Bas-relief, Anuradhapura). Printers (photo) Courvoisier, Switzerland. Perf. 11¾ (C). No watermark. Granite paper. Sheets 10 x 10.

42	2c **brown and blue-green** (15/5/54)		.10	.75
43	3c **black and violet** (15/5/54)		.10	.60
44	6c **sepia-black and green** (15/5/54)		.10	.20
45	10c **grey and deep green** (1/8/51)		.45	.40
45a	10c **orange and brown** (1/12/54)		.10	.10
46	25c **orange and ultramarine** (15/3/56)		.10	.15
47	35c **brown-red and dark green** (Type 1) (1/2/52)		.70	£1
	a ditto (Type 2) (/54)		2.50	.35
48	40c **dark brown** (15/5/54)		£2	.60
49	50c **bluish slate** (15/3/54)		.15	.10
50	85c **black and grey-green** (15/5/54)		.35	.20
51	2r **sepia-brown and light blue** (15/5/54)		3.50	.75
52	5r **brown and orange** (15/3/54)		2.25	.85
53	10r **brown** (15/3/54)		£20	9.50
42/53	**set** (12)		£27	£13

Type 1   Type 2

47 Type 1 - In the second line of the Tamil inscription at the top of the stamp, there is no dot above the third character.

47a Type 2 - Dot added in corrected inscription.

SPECIAL ISSUES

1937 (May 12th) Coronation. As Antigua.

S1	6c carmine-red	.30	.60
S2	9c green	1.25	2.75
S3	20c deep blue	1.75	2.40
S1-3	set (3)	£3	£5
SP S1/3	specimen perf (3)	£70	†

1946 (Dec. 10th) Victory. As Aden.

S4	6c deep blue	.15	.20
S5	15c dark brown	.15	£1
	a reddish brown	.25	1.25
SP S4/5	specimen perf (2)	£60	†

S5, S5a The 15ct from Plate B1 is dark brown, while the A1 shade is reddish brown

1947 (Nov. 25th) New Constitution. Designs, views in Ceylon. Designers, R. Tenison and M.S.V. Rodrigo. Printers (recess) Bradbury, Wilkinson. Perf. 11¾ x 11 (C). Sheets S6, S8, 5 x 12; S7, S9, 10 x 6.

S6	6c black and blue	.10	.10
S7	10c black, orange and carmine	.10	.25
S8	15c myrtle-green and purple	.15	.50
S9	25c ochre and emerald-green	.15	£1
S6-9	set (4)	.45	1.65
SPS6/9	specimen perf (4)	£68	†

1949 First Anniversary of Independence. Designs, 4c and 15c (Dominion Flag); 5c and 25c (Dr S. Senanayake, Prime Minister). Printers (recess, but flag typo) Bradbury, Wilkinson. Perf. 12¾ x 12½ (C) 15c, other values perf. 12 x 12¾ (C). Wmk. Script C.A. (4c and 5c) and Lotus Flowers and "Sri" (15c and 25c). Sheets 10 x 10.

S10	4c yellow, carmine and light brown (4/2/49)	.10	.15

S11	5c sepia and myrtle (4/2/49)	.10	.10
S12	15c yellow, carmine and salmon (5/4/49)	.50	.25
S13	25c sepia and blue (5/4/49)	.10	.60
S10/13	set (4)	.70	£1

Number issued (locally) - 4c, 9,171,071; 5c, 16,755,839; 15c, 1,393,777; 25c, 1,176,693.

1949 (Oct. 10th) U.P.U. Designs (globe and methods of mail transport). Printers (recess) De La Rue. Watermark Lotus Flowers and "Sri". Perf. 12 (C) 5c, 15c; perf. 13¼ x 13 (C) 25c. Sheets 5 x 10 or 10 x 5.

S14	5c chocolate and myrtle-green	.35	.10
S15	15c black and carmine-lake	.60	1.65
S16	25c grey-black and ultramarine	.60	.65
S14/16	set (3)	1.50	2.25

Number issued locally - 5c, 14,436,792; 15c, 1,097,631; 25c, 1,601,542.

1952 (Feb.) Columbo Plan Exhibition, design Ceylon Mace and symbols. Printers Harrison (photo). Watermark Lotus flowers and "Sri". Perf 14½ x 14.

S17	5c green	.10	.20
S18	15c blue	.10	.35

BOOKLET PANES

1937-50

P1	6c **S1** pane of 10	-	-
P2	9c **S2** pane of 10	-	-
P3	6c **CW 6** pane of 10	-	-
P4	20c **CW 9** pane of 5	-	-
P5	20c **CW 9** pane of 10	-	-
P6	3ct/6ct **CW 31** pane of 10	-	-
P7	5c **CW 35** pane of 4	-	-

P8   5c **CW 35** pane of 10   -   -
P9 75c **CW 40** pane of 4   -   -

BOOKLETS

B1 1r 80 **1937 Coronation**
         (P1 x 3)   £875   -
B2 2r 70 **1937 Coronation**
         (P2 x 3)   £950   -
B3 1r 80 **1938 black on blue**
         (P3 x 3)   £1000   -
B4   3r **1938 black on grey**
         (P4, P5)   £1100   -
B5 1r 80 **1941 black on pink**
         (P6 x 6)   -   -
B6 1r 80 **1941 black on blue**
         (P6x 6)   -   -
B7   1r **1951 black on buff**
         (P7x 5)   £8   -
B8   1r **1951 black on buff**
         (P8 x 2)   £30   -
B9   6r **1952 black on green**
         (P9 x 2)   £12   -

The following booklets contain airmail labels: B1, B2, B3, B4, B7, B9.

CHAMBA
SEE
INDIA

CHANNEL ISLANDS
SEE
GREAT BRITAIN

CONVENTION STATES
SEE
INDIA

COOK ISLANDS

1933-38. Designs, 1/- (portrait of King, from photo by B. Park);other values (island scenes). Designer, J. Berry. Printers (recess) Govt. Printing Office, Wellington (from plates engraved by Bradbury, Wilkinson). Watermark 'N.Z. Star' (single). Perf. 14 (L). Sheets 8 x 10 or 10 x 8.

X1	½d	**black and green** (25/5/33)	.50	2.75
		a watermark inverted	-	£60
X2	1d	**black and scarlet** (4/35)	.60	1.25
		a watermark inverted and reversed	-	-
X3	2d	**black and brown** (1/4/36)	.75	.30
		a watermark inverted	-	-
X4	2½d	**black and blue** (10/32)	.75	1.35
X5	4d	**black and bright blue** (1/4/36)	.75	.30
X6	6d	**black and orange** (1/4/36)	.80	1.50
1		1/- **black and violet** (/38)	£4	7.50
2		2/- **black and reddish chocolate** (/38)	£8	£8
		a watermark inverted	-	-
3		3/- **blue and emerald-green** (/38)	£22	£23
X1/3		**set** (9)	£35	£40

Number printed - X1, 600,000; X2, 560,000; X3, 560,000; X4, 72,960; X5, 56,000; X6, 72,000; 1 and 2, 60,000 each; 3, 40,000.

1936-44 stamps of New Zealand overprinted 'COOK ISLANDS'. 2/- and 3/- 1927 'Admiral' type, others Arms of Dominion (type New Zealand F48). Thick, opaque Cowan paper. Watermark 'NZ Star' single. Perf 14.

X7	2/-	**blue**	£6	£32
X8	3/-	**mauve**	£6	£45
X9	2/6d	**brown**	£12	£50
X10	5/-	**green**	£14	£65
X11	10/-	**carmine-lake**	£32	£130
X12	£1	**pink**	£45	£160
X7/11		**set** (6)	£100	£430

1940-? as X9-12 but on thin, hard Wiggins Teape paper.

X13 2/6d **brown** (12/40)	£85	£80
X14 5/- **green** (10/40)	£325	£275
X15 10/- **carmine-lake** (11/44)	£95	£145
X16 £3 **green** (?)	£275	£460
X 13/16 **set** (4)	£700	£875

1940 (Sept. 2nd) Printers (recess) Bradbury, Wilkinson. Watermark 'N.Z. Star' (multiple) Perf. 13½ x 14 (C). Sheets 8 x 10.

4 3d/1½d **black and red-purple**	.35	.35

A change in postal rates prior to issue created a demand for a 3d stamp, hence the surcharging. This stamp was not issued without surcharge, although examples without overprint exist ex the printers' archives. These have no gum.

Number issued - 333,680.

1943-50. As X13-16, but with watermark 'NZ Star' multiple.

5	2/6 **brown** (3/46)	£35	£55
	a watermark inverted (4/51)	£12	£15
6	5/- **green** (red) (11/43)	4.50	£15
	a watermark inverted	£13	£18
7	10/- **rose-carmine** (10/48)	£40	£80
	a watermark inverted	£32	£60
8	£1 **dull pink** (11/47)	£30	£60
	aa watermark inverted	£60	£65
8a	£3 **green** (red) (28/5/53)	£480	£650
	b watermark inverted	£30	£110
8c	£5 **blue** (red) (25/10/50)	£160	£250
	d watermark inverted	£125	£225
5/8c	**set** (6)	£210	£450

1944-6 Designs, ½d (Capt. Cook landing); 1d (Capt. Cook); 2d (Maori canoe); 2½d (working cargo); 4d (Port Avarua); 6d (R.M.S. 'Monowai'). Designer, L. Mitchell. Printers (recess) Govt. Printing Office, Wellington (from plates engraved by Perkins, Bacon). 1/- to 3/- (as Nos. 1-3). Watermark 'N.Z. Star' (multiple), sideways on ½d, 1d, 1/- and 2/-. Perf. 14 (L). Sheets 8 x 10 or 10 x 8.

9	½d **black and myrtle-green** (11/44)	.85	2.50
	a watermark sideways inverted	3.50	£6
10	1d **black and deep carmine** (3/45)	£1	.60
	a watermark sideways inverted	£4	£2
	b watermark sideways reversed	-	-
11	2d **black and light brown** (2/46)	1.10	£6
12	2½d **black and grey-blue** (5/45)	.50	1.25
13	4d **black and deep blue** (4/44)	2.75	£11
	a watermark inverted and reversed	£30	£30
14	6d **black and orange** (6/44)	1.75	1.25
15	1/- **black and violet** (9/44)	1.50	1.50
16	2/- **black and chestnut** (8/45)	£16	£29
17	3/- **blue and emerald-green** (6/45)	£18	£19
	a centre printed double	£75	-
	b watermark inverted	£75	-
9/17	**set** (9)	£27	£45

17a the vignette appears blurred. Under magnification, doubling can be seen. This may be because a batch of sheets had the vignette printed a little weakly, and was put through the press a second time.

Number issued - ½d, 299,640; 1d, 160,240; 2d, 150,400; 2½d, 113,200; 4d, 95,280; 6d, 79,200; 1/-, 68,400; 2/-, 38,320; 3/-, 43,280.

1949 (Aug. 1st) Designs, 1d (Capt. Cook and map, Hervey Is.); 2d (Rev. J. Williams and map, Rarotonga); 3d (map, Aitutaki and palms); 1/- (map and statue of Capt. Cook); 3/- (M.V. "Matua"); other values (views and scenes). Designer, J. Berry. Printers (recess) Waterlow and Sons. Watermark 'N.Z. Star' (multiple). Perf. 13¼ x 13½ (C). Sheets 12 x 10 or 10 x 12.

21	½d **purple-violet and red-brown**	.10	.75
22	1d **orange-brown and green**	1.75	1.35
23	2d **chocolate and deep crimson**	£1	1.35
24	3d **emerald-green and ultramarine**	1.35	1.20
	a watermark inverted	£75	-
	b watermark sideways (22/5/61)	2.25	1.50
25	5d **emerald and violet**	£3	.90
26	6d **black and carmine**	2.75	1.65
27	8d **sage and orange**	.30	2.25
	a watermark inverted	£80	£40
28	1/- **pale blue and chocolate-brown**	£2	2.25
29	2/- **yellow-brown and carmine-rose**	1.50	£8
	a watermark sideways inverted	-	-
30	3/- **pale blue and blue-green**	6.50	£14
21/30	**set** (10)	£18	£32

24b this stamp is on white opaque paper.

SPECIAL ISSUES

1937 (June 1st) Coronation. New Zealand Nos. S1-3, overprinted "COOK IS'DS".

S1	1d **carmine**	.20	.50
	a small 'S'	£9	£10
S2	2½d **deep blue**	.40	.85
	a small 'S'	£14	£16
S3	6d **reddish orange**	.40	.35
	a small 'S'	£14	£16
S1/S3	**set** (3)	.90	1.50

S1a-3a R1/2 (first printing) the second S of "IS'DS" is smaller. It also occurs on R8/4 first printing and R6/10 on the 2nd printing only. On the third printing all were corrected.

COOK IS'DS.

Number issued - 1d, 737,572; 2½d, 569,108; 6d, 541,657.

1946 (June 1st) Peace. New Zealand Nos. S19, S21, S25, S26 overprinted 'COOK ISLANDS' in blue or black.

S4	1d **emerald-green**	.15	.10
S5	2d **purple (blue)**	.15	.30
S6	6d **chocolate and vermilion**	.50	.75
S7	8d **black and lake (blue)**	.30	.75
S4/7	**set** (4)	£1	1.75

Number issued - 1d, 720,000; 2d, 720,000; 6d, 480,000; 8d, 480,000.

CYPRUS

1938 (May 12th) - 55. Designs, 4½p (map of Cyprus); 45p (forest scene); 90p and £1 (portrait, King George VI); other values (ruins and existing buildings of historical importance). Printers (recess) Waterlow and Sons, Perf. 12½ (L). Sheets 6 x 10.

1	¼p **ultramarine and buff-brown**	.40	.25
	a **ultramarine and red-brown** (16/7/45)	.50	.30
2	½p **deep green**	.75	.15
	a **green** (16/10/44)	.80	.20
3	½p **bright violet** (2/7/51)	£1	.25
4	¾p **black and pale violet**	£8	.60
5	1p **orange**	.75	.15
6	1½p **carmine**	2.50	.90
7	1½p **bright violet** (15/3/43)	.75	.30
8	1½p **green** (2/7/51)	1.75	.45
9	2p **black and red** (2/2/42)	£1	.15
10	2½p **deep ultramarine**	£12	1.50
11	3p **deep ultramarine** (2/2/42)	1.25	.25
	a **deep violet-blue** (19/8/47)	1.25	.25
12	4p **deep ultramarine** (2/7/51)	£2	.35
13	4½p **grey**	.85	.15
	a **slate-grey** (16/10/44)	£1	.15
14	6p **black and pale blue**	1.50	.60
	a **black and pale bright blue** (4/42)	1.25	.75
15	9p **black and deep purple**	1.50	.25
	a **black and bright red-purple** (15/6/55)	1.25	.30
16	18p **black and olive-green**	£6	.60
	a **black and deep olive** (16/10/44)	£5	.60
	b **black and sage** (19/8/47)	£7	£1
17	45p **green and black**	£15	2.25
18	90p **mauve and black**	£14	£4
19	£1 **scarlet and blue-black**	£28	£15
	a **re-entry**	£225	£125
1/19	**set** (19)	£90	£25
SP 1/19	**specimen perf** (16)	£425	†

19a left value tablet doubled vertically on both sides, R3/6.

1944. As Nos. 5 and 9 but perforations changed.

Perf. 13½ x 12½ (L).

20	1p **orange**	£275	£16

20 Forgeries exist, made by cutting down and reperforating examples of CW5.

Perf. 12½ x 13½ (L).

21	2p **black and red**	1.25	5.75

SPECIAL ISSUES

1937 (May 12th) Coronation. As Antigua.

S1	¾p **grey**	.75	.45
S2	1½p **carmine-red**	£1	.90
S3	2½p **blue**	1.35	1.50
S1/3	**set** (3)	2.75	2.50
SP S1/3	**specimen perf** (3)	£120	†

1946 (Oct. 21st) Victory. As Aden.

S4	1½p **slate-violet**	.15	.10
	a **spot in value tablet**	£20	£20
S5	3p **grey-blue**	.15	.20
SP S4/5	**specimen perf** (2)	£110	†

S4a a spot occurs between the '1' and '½' in the right value tablet on R7/1 (Plate B1).

1948 (Dec. 20th) Silver Wedding. As Aden.

S6	1½p **bright violet**	.35	.25
	a **extra decoration**	£25	£28
S7	£1 **bluish slate**	£25	£42

S6a A flaw on the King's uniform appears as an extra medal on R3/5.

1949 (Oct. 10th) U.P.U. As Aden, but all recess.

S8	1½p **dull violet**	.30	.75
S9	2p **carmine**	.75	.90
S10	3p **dull indigo**	.50	.60
S11	9p **purple**	.50	1.65
S8/11	**set** (4)	1.80	3.50

CYRENAICA
SEE
B.O.I.C.

DOMINICA

There are a number of instances of doubling of parts of the design on many values. These are highly collectable. Examples are 2½d R5/5, 3d R4/2 and 6d R2/10.

1938 (Aug. 15th) - 49 Designs, ½d, 6d, 7d, 2/6d (Fresh Water Lake); 1d, 3d, 2/-, 5/- (Layou River); 1½d, 2½d, 3½d (picking limes); 2d, 1/-, 10/- (Boiling Lake). Printers (recess) Waterlow and Sons. Perf. 12½ (L). Sheets 10 x 6.

1	½d red-brown and yellow-green	.15	.10
	a chocolate and green (3/2/44)	.10	.10
2	1d grey and scarlet	.15	.15
	a grey and carmine-red (15/11/49)	.20	.15
3	1½d green and purple-violet	.20	.40
4	2d dull carmine and grey	.25	1.20
	a bright carmine-rose and grey (3/2/44)	.40	1.50
5	2½d purple and blue	£2	1.10
	a purple and ultramarine (11/42)	.10	1.25
	b imperf between stamp and bottom margin	†	-
6	3d olive and light brown	.15	.30
	a olive and red-brown (2/48)	.25	.35
7	3½d ultramarine and purple (15/10/47)	1.10	1.20
8	6d emerald and violet	£1	.90
	a deep emerald and violet (5/11/49)	£3	1.25
9	7d green and light brown (15/10/47)	£1	.90
10	1/- violet and olive-green	£2	.90
	a violet and sage-green (15/11/49)	2.50	.90
11	2/- deep slate and purple-violet (15/10/47)	3.50	5.50
12	2/6d black and vermilion	£6	£3
13	5/- light blue and sepia-brown	4.50	£5
14	10/- black and orange-brown (15/10/47)	£8	£10

1 - A bisected ½d on a newspaper wrapper, paying island newspaper rate of ¼d, is known and two others have been reported. In late 1951 E.P. Arrowsmith, the Administrator in the colony, confirmed and emphasised that no offical permission was ever given for the use of a bisected ½d stamp.

5b - Used examples from the bottom row of the sheet with lower margin imperforate have been found.

1940-4. Printers (photo) Harrison and Sons. Perf. 14¾ x 14 (C). Sheets 12 x 10.

15	¼d chocolate (ch) (14/4/40)	.50	.15
	a chocolate (sub) (/42)	.20	.25
	b dull chocolate-brown (sub) (/44)	.10	.25
1-15	set (15)	£25	£27
SP1-15	specimen perf (15)	£175	†

1951 (July 1st) Printers (photo) Harrison and Sons. Perf. 14¾ x 14 (C). Sheets as before.

16	½c brown (ch)	.10	.10
	a reddish brown (10/52)	£1	1.50

1951 (July 1st) Designs, 6c (Botanical Gardens); 12c, $1.20 (Fresh Water Lake); 14c (Layou River); 24c (Boiling Lake); other values (scenes depicting local occupations and industries). Printers (recess) Bradbury, Wilkinson. Perf. 13 x 13½ (C) $2.40 perf 13½ x 13. Sheets 5 x 10.

17	1c black and vermilion	.10	.20
18	2c chocolate and grey-green	.10	.20
19	3c emerald and purple	.15	1.65
20	4c brown-orange and sepia	.35	.45
	a red-orange and deep sepia (21/4/54)	£1	2.50

21	5c black and carmine	.40	.20
22	6c olive and chestnut	.50	.20
23	8c blue-green and deep blue	£1	.50
24	12c black and emerald	.35	.75
25	14c ultramarine and purple	.60	1.65
26	24c purple and rose-carmine	.35	.20
27	48c emerald and vermilion	1.75	£6
28	60c scarlet and black	1.75	4.50
30	$1.20 emerald-green and black	2.25	£4
31	$2.40 deep orange and black	£12	£30
16/31	set (15)	£19	£45

WATERMARK ERRORS

17b	1c A of watermark missing £300	-
18a	2c C of watermark missing £350	-
b	A of watermark missing £350	-
19a	3c C of watermark missing £300	-
20b	4c C of watermark missing £350	-
c	A of watermark missing £350	-
21a	5c C of watermark missing £475	-
b	A of watermark missing £475	-
22a	6c C of watermark missing £350	-
b	A of watermark missing £600	-
23b	8c A of watermark missing	-	-
24a	12c C of watermark missing £750	-
25a	14c C of watermark missing £750	-
b	A of watermark missing	-	£475
26a	24c C of watermark missing £750	£600
27a	48c C of watermark missing £750	-
b	A of watermark missing £750	-
30a	$1.20 C of watermark missing £850	-
b	A of watermark missing £850	-

Apart from the watermark errors (missing letters on the dandy roll) listed above, other broken or partially-missing letters are known. The "A" varieties, listed above, all have a small portion of the right curve of the letter remaining. A variety with 'J' for 'C' in 'CA' is recorded on the 1c, 2c, 3c, 5c, 14c, 48c, and 60c.

SPECIAL ISSUES

1937 (May 12th) Coronation. As Antigua.

S1	1d carmine-red	.20	.10
S2	1½d light brown	.20	.10
S3	2½d deep blue	.30	£1
S1/3	set (3)	.70	1.10
SPS1/3	specimen perf (3)	£60	†

1946 (Oct. 14th) Victory. As Aden.

S4	1d carmine-red	.10	.10
	a scratched value tablet	£10	£10
S5	3½d grey-blue	.10	.10
SP S4/5	specimen perf (2)	£35	†

S4a R3/5 a prominent scratch across the right value tablet.

Number issued; 1d 675,000, 3½d 617,100.

1948 (Dec. 1st) Silver Wedding. As Aden.

| S6 | 1d scarlet | .10 | .10 |
| S7 | 10/- chestnut-brown | £9 | £14 |

1949 (Oct. 10th) U.P.U. As Aden.

S8	5c dull ultramarine	.10	.10
S9	6c brown	.65	1.65
S10	12c purple	.20	£1
	a A of watermark missing	-	£350
S11	24c sage-green	.15	.20
S8/11	set (4)	£1	2.70

1951 (Feb. 16th) West Indies University College. As Antigua.

| S12 | 3c green and mauve | .25 | .75 |
| S13 | 12c deep green and carmine | .40 | .25 |

1951 (Oct. 15th) New Constitution. No. 19, etc, overprinted "New Constitution 1951" in black or red.

S14	3c emerald and purple	.10	.40
S15	5c black and carmine	.10	.75
S16	8c blue green and deep blue (red overprint)	.10	.10
S17	14c ultramarine and purple (red overprint)	.50	.15
S14/17	set (4)	.70	1.25

Number issued (London only) - 3c, 66,140; 5c, 64,960.

WATERMARK ERRORS

| S14b | 3c C of watermark missing £350 | £400 |
| S17a | 14c A of watermark missing £550 | - |

The variety with 'J' for 'C' in 'CA' is recorded on the 5c and 8c. For information on these and the missing letters, see the notes after CW 30a.

BRITISH FORCES IN EGYPT

Between 1932 and 1936 mail to Great Britain from British Forces stationed in Egypt could be carried at concessionary rates, indicated by purchasing and affixing special seals made available at the N.A.A.F.I. The seals were replaced from 1936 to 1941 by Army Post stamps issued by the Egyptian postal authorities. These are printed by photogravure by the Survey Department, Cairo, on paper watermarked Multiple Crown above Arabic letter.

EAF
SEE
BOIC - SOMALIA

ERITREA
SEE
BOIC

1936 Portrait of King Fuad. Perf 13½ x 14.

1	3m **green (9/11/36)**	.50	£1
2	10m **carmine (1/3/36)**	£3	.10
	a watermark inverted	-	-

1939 (Dec. 12th) Portrait of King Farouk. Perf 13 x 13½.

3	3m **green**	2.50	£5
4	10m **carmine**	3.50	.10
	a watermark inverted	-	-

Though the reduced rates were operative until 1951, the stamps were not used after 1941.

FALKLAND ISLANDS

1938 (Jan. 3rd) - 49 Designs, 6d and 9d (ships); £1 (Arms of Colony); other values (scenes and fauna of Islands). Designers, 6d and 9d The Discovery Committee; 1/3d K. Lellman; remainder, G. Roberts. Printers (recess) Bradbury, Wilkinson. Perf. 12 (L). Centres black except where mentioned. Sheets 6 x 10.

1	½d **yellow-green** (/37)	.40	.75
	a green (/42)	.15	.45
	b blue-green(thin paper)(/47)	1.25	2.25
2	1d **carmine-rose** (/37)	£10	.50
	a scarlet (/37)	1.50	.55
3	1d **bright violet** (/41)	£1	1.20
	a purple-violet (/42)	£4	1.20
4	2d **deep violet** (/37)	.50	.30
	a pale violet (/38)	.50	.30
	b imperf between stamp and top margin	-	†
5	2d **carmine** (14/7/41)	.75	£2
	a carmine-red (thin paper)(/42)	£1	1.50
	b deep red (49)	1.50	£2
6	2½d **blue** (sheep) (/37)	.25	.20
7	2½d **blue** (goose) (15/6/49)	2.50	4.50
8	3d **greyish black and blue** (14/7/41)	2.50	£2
	a slate-black and deep blue (/42)	£5	1.80
9	4d **bright purple** (/37)	1.25	.75
	a grey-black and dull purple (/38)	1.25	.75
10	6d **slate-black and sepia-brown** (/37)	£4	£3
	a sepia-brown (/38)	£3	3.50
	b dark brown (/38)	1.75	£1
11	6d **black**(thin paper)(15/6/49)	2.75	£3
12	9d **slate-black and dull grey-blue** (/37)	£10	£2
	a sepia and grey-blue (/38)	£9	£2
	b pale grey-blue (thin paper) (/47)	£15	£15
13	1/- **pale blue** (/37)	£25	£12
	a dull greenish blue (/38)	£18	£2
	b dull blue (/44)	£10	£100
	c deep blue (thin paper) (27/5/47)	£30	£75
14	1/3d **carmine-rose** (10/12/46)	£1	£1
15	2/6d **slate-black** (/37)	£22	9.75
16	5/- **blue and light brown** (/37)	£58	£45
	a indigo and pale yellow-brown (/38)	£450	£60

	b dull deep blue and deep yellow-brown (/44)	£50	£250
	c bright blue and buff-brown (thin paper) (/49)	£100	£230
17	10/- **brownish orange** (/37)	£60	£30
	a light orange (/38)	£140	£25
	b orange (/44)	£40	£250
	c deep reddish orange (thin paper) (/49)	£200	£250
18	£1 **dull violet** (/37)	£100	£35
	a reddish violet (/38)	£80	£35
	b grey-black and bluish violet (/64)	£50	£200
	c bright violet (thin paper)(/49)	£185	£240
1/18	**set** (18)	£225	£120
SP 1/18	**specimen perf** (16)	£1300	†

Dates given are those of printing. In general, early printings have cracked cream gum and are printed on thick creamy paper. Later printings have thinner paper and gum, the final printings being on white thin paper with transparent gum.

4, 4a there is variation of shade. The gum cracking on 4 is more pronounced.

4b three examples are known.

1944 printings. In addition to the 1/-, 5/-, 10/- and £1 listed above, the ½d, 1d, 2d, 3d, 4d, 6d, 9d, and 2/6d were reprinted. All are on 'greyish' paper with a high rag content, which under a magnifying glass shows as coloured fibres on the surface of the stamps. No despatch to the colony was made, so used examples are scarce.

Forged postmarks are known, and in other cases cancellations have been applied which are genuine but improperly used; in some cases the date may precede the release of the stamps.

1952 (Jan 2nd) Designs, 1d (R.M.S. 'Fitzroy'); 2½d (map of Islands); 3d (Arms of Colony); 4d ('Auster' Aircraft); 6d (M.S.S. 'John Biscoe'); £1 (hulk of 'Great Britain'); other values (scenes and fauna of Islands). Printers (recess) Waterlow and Sons. Perf. 13½ x 13¼ (C), except Nos. 23, 27, 29 and 30, perf 13¼ x 13½ Designer, V.H. Spencer. Sheets 6 x 10 or 10 x 6.

19	½d **green**	.45	.40
	a yellow-green	1.50	£2
20	1d **scarlet**	£1	.25
21	2d **violet**	1.80	1.50
22	2½d **black and light ultramarine**	.75	.30

23	3d ultramarine	.90	.60
24	4d magenta-claret	4.50	£1
25	6d light brown	£5	.60
26	9d orange-yellow	3.75	1.25
27	1/- black	£10	.50
28	1/3d vermilion	6.50	3.50
29	2/6d olive-green	£8	6.75
30	5/- purple	£7	5.50
31	10/- slate-grey	11.50	7.50
32	£1 black	£14	£12
19/32	set (14)	£68	£38

BOOKLET

A 2/4d (containing 1d x 8 and 2½d x 8) booklet produced around 1940 is thought to exist. Little is known of this and more information is solicited.

SPECIAL ISSUES

1937 (May 12th) Coronation. As Antigua.

S1	½d green	.15	.10
S2	1d carmine-red	.50	.30
S3	2½d deep blue	.75	.85
S1/3	set (3)	1.25	1.10
SP S1/3	specimen perf (3)	£125	†

Number issued - S1, 318,420; S2, 330,000; S3, 268,140.

1946 (Oct. 7th) Victory. As Aden.

S4	1d violet-grey	.15	.40
S5	3d grey-blue	.20	.30
	a flaw and re-entry		
	to crown	£35	£40
SP S4/5	specimen perf (2)	£250	†

S5a R8/5 (Plate 1) a flaw affects the left side of the crown and the surrounding area has been re-entered in an attempt to conceal the damage. Positional blocks from Plate 1 without the damage are also valuable.

Number issued - S4, 883,080; S5, 804,300.

1948 (Nov. 1st) Silver Wedding. As Aden.

| S6 | 2½d ultramarine | £1 | .60 |
| S7 | £1 dull purple | £45 | £36 |

Number issued - S6, 171,326; S7, 22,956.

1949 (Oct. 10th) U.P.U. As Aden.

S8	1d dull violet	.85	.60
S9	3d indigo	2.50	1.65
S10	1/3d green	1.60	1.35
S11	2/- azure	1.50	4.80
S8/11	set (4)	£6	7.50

Number issued - S8, 618,000; S9, 467,400; S10, 507,000; S11 497,880.

FALKLAND ISLANDS DEPENDENCIES

If purchasing any of the following issues in 'SPECIMEN' form, please bear in mind that (in our experience) a minimum of two out of every three 'SPECIMEN' sets on the market are faked. Expertisation is essential.

GRAHAM LAND

1944 (Feb 13th) - 45 As Falklands CW 1 etc., but overprinted 'GRAHAM LAND/ DEPENDENCY OF' in red. Printers Bradbury Wilkinson. Perf 12. Centres black, except 1a, 6a, 8.

1	½d green	.15	£1
	a blue-slate and green (/44)	£800	£600
2	1d violet	.15	.60
3	2d carmine-rose	.25	.60
4	3d blue	.25	.60
5	4d purple	£1	£1
6	6d sepia-brown	7.50	1.50
	a bluish slate and		
	sepia-brown (24/9/45)	7.50	-
7	9d dull grey-blue	.60	.75
8	1/- slate-blue	.60	.75
1/8	set (8)	9.50	£6
SP1/8	specimen perf (8)	£400	†

1a a rare and distinctive shade. Intermediate examples exist and an expert society certificate is essential.

SOUTH GEORGIA

1944 (Feb 24th) - 45 As before, but overprinted 'SOUTH GEORGIA/DEPENDENCY OF', in red. Centres black except 14a,16.

9	½d green	.15	.60
	a watermark sideways	£3250	†
10	1d violet	.15	.60
11	2d carmine-rose	.25	.60
12	3d blue	.25	.60
13	4d purple	£1	£1
14	6d sepia-brown	7.50	1.50
	a bluish slate and		
	sepia-brown (24/9/45)	7.50	-
15	9d dull grey-blue	.60	.75
16	1/- slate-blue	.60	.75
9/16	set (8)	9.50	£6
SP9/16	specimen perf (8)	£400	†

SOUTH ORKNEYS

1944 (Feb 21st) - 45 As before, but overprinted 'SOUTH ORKNEYS/DEPENDENCY OF', in red. Centres black except 22a, 24.

17	½d **green**	.15	.60
18	1d **violet**	.15	.60
	a watermark inverted	£4000	†
19	2d **carmine-rose**	.25	.60
20	3d **blue**	.25	.60
21	4d **purple**	£1	£1
22	6d **sepia-brown**	7.50	1.50
	a bluish slate and		
	sepia-brown (24/9/45)	7.50	-
23	9d **dull grey-blue**	.60	.75
24	1/- **slate-blue**	.60	.75
17/24	**set** (8)	9.50	£6
SP17/24	**specimen perf** (8)	£400	†

SOUTH SHETLANDS

1944 (Feb 5th) - 45 As before, but overprinted 'SOUTH SHETLANDS/DEPENDENCY OF' in red. Centres black except 30a, 32.

25	½d **green**	.15	£1
26	1d **violet**	.15	.60
27	2d **carmine-rose**	.25	.60
28	3d **blue**	.25	.60
29	4d **purple**	£1	£1
30	6d **sepia-brown**	7.50	1.50
	a bluish slate and		
	sepia-brown (24/9/45)	7.50	-
31	9d **dull grey-blue**	.60	.75
32	1/- **slate-blue**	.60	.75
25/32	**set** (8)	9.50	£6
SP25/32	**specimen perf** (8)	£400	†

6a, 14a, 22a, 30a These printings were not sent to the islands. Used examples do exist, sent out by dealers and collectors, but are scarce. Beware of forged cancellations.

ISSUED FOR THE ENTIRE TERRITORY (REPLACING INDIVIDUAL SETS)

'Thick Map'

'Thin Map'

1946 (Feb 1st) Design, 'Thick Map' of islands (litho), in coloured frame (recess). Printers, De La Rue. Perf. 11¾ (C). Watermark sideways. Centres black. Sheets 10 x 6.

33	½d **green**	.50	2.25
34	1d **violet**	.50	£1
35	2d **carmine**	.50	1.50
36	3d **ultramarine**	.50	£3
37	4d **reddish claret**	£1	£3
	a deep lake	£5	£15
38	6d **orange**	1.50	£3
	a yellow-ochre	£25	£65
39	9d **deep brown**	.80	2.25
40	1/- **deep purple**	.80	2.50
33/40	**set** (8)	5.50	£17
SP33/40	**specimen perf** (8)	£650	†

This set can be distinguished from that which follows by differences in the vignettes. The lines are thick and coarse; the line of the 50° meridian protrudes slightly beyond the frame line at the upper left corner, and the meridian passes through the 'S' in 'COATS'.

No. 38a - Also exists in an almost black colour, due to poor mixing of ink, which oxidised.

Type A

Type Ab

Type A: Broken Arc. R1/4, 1/9, 3/4, 3/9, 5/4, 5/9. A break occurs in the 80th parallel, 6 times on every sheet.

Type Ab: Enlarged South Georgia. Occurs only in conjunction with Type A. R 5/9 (Plate 2).

Type B

Type C

Type B: Extra Island. An extra island (a large round dot) appears in the left top corner. Occurs only in conjuction with Type A. R3/9 (Plate 1).

Type C: Missing 'I'. The 'I' in 'SHETLAND Is.' is missing. R1/2 (Plate 1).

Type D

Type E

Type D: South Poke. The 'I' of 'Pole' in damaged. R6/8 (Plate 2).

Type E: Spot on Oval. There is a large spot by the portrait oval. R4/6 (Plate 1).

33	½d Type A	1.25	£4
	Type Ab	£15	£20
	Type B	£100	£125
	Type C	£95	£115
	Type D	£85	£125
	Type E	£100	£125
34	1d Type A	1.50	2.75
	Type B	£68	£78
	Type C	£60	£75
	Type E	£68	£78
35	2d Type A	1.50	3.30
	Type B	£110	£120
	Type C	£100	£120
	Type E	£110	£120
36	3d Type A	1.50	£5
	Type B	£90	£125
	Type C	£85	£110
	Type E	£90	£120
37	4d Type A	2.75	£6
	Type Ab	£20	£30
	Type D	£100	£120
37a	4d Type A	£10	£22
	Type Ab	£35	-
38	6d Type A	3.50	£6
	Type Ab	£25	£35
	Type B	£110	£120
	Type C	£100	£120
	Type D	£95	£125
	Type E	£110	£120
38a	6d Type A	£3	£6
	Type Ab	£25	£35
	Type B	£275	-
	Type C	£275	-
	Type D	£275	-
	Type E	£275	-
39	9d Type A	2.25	£5
	Type Ab	£20	£30
	Type D	£95	£125
40	1/- Type A	2.50	5.50
	Type Ab	£20	£30
	Type D	£85	£125

1948 (Feb. 16th) - 49 As before, 'Thin Map' (vignette) redrawn. Centres black.

41	½d **green**	£1	8.50
	a dot on 'T'	2.75	£22
42	1d **violet**	.60	£11
	a dot on 'T'	1.85	£25
43	2d **carmine**	1.25	£15
	a map double	£1200	-
	b dot on 'T'	3.25	£35
44	2½d **dark blue** (6/3/49)	£3	2.50
	a dark grey-blue (6/3/49)	£5	£3
45	3d **ultramarine**	1.25	2.40
	a bright ultramarine	2.50	£4
	b map double	-	-
	c dot on 'T'	3.25	6.75
46	4d **reddish claret**	£7	£17
	a map double	-	-
	b dot on 'T'	17.50	£38
47	6d **orange**	£10	£4
	a dot on 'T'	£30	£12

48	9d **deep brown**	£10	£4
	a dot on 'T'	£30	£12
49	1/- **deep purple**	£10	£4
	a dot on 'T'	£30	£12
41/49	set (9)	£40	£60

In the re-drawn map the lines are finer than before; the meridian O° does not cut through the 'S' in 'COATS'.

41a. etc. A dot on the right arm of 'T' in 'SOUTH' (except on 2½d). R5/2, 5/4, 5/6, 5/8, 5/10.

41 exists with frame printed double, once albino and inverted. One example has been reported showing map double.

43a a complete sheet was found in a London dealer's supply. The variety was caused by a blanket offset print.

SPECIAL ISSUES

1946 (Oct. 4th) Victory. As Aden.

S1	1d **violet-grey**	.25	.30
S2	3d **grey-blue**	.35	.30
SP S1/2	**specimen perf** (2)	£185	†

Number issued; S1, 860,520; S2, 831,000.

1948 (Dec. 6th) Silver Wedding. As Aden; 1/- printed wholly by recess.

S3	2½d **ultramarine**	.85	1.50
S4	1/- **slate-violet**	£1	1.50

Number issued; S3, 299,063; S4, 210,779.

1949 (Oct. 10th) U.P.U. As Aden.

S5	1d **dull violet**	.50	1.50
S6	2d **carmine**	2.50	2.25
S7	3d **dull indigo**	1.75	.75
S8	6d **orange**	£2	1.80
S5/8	set (4)	£6	5.50

Number issued; S5, 513,600; S6, 405,000; S7, 385,200; S8, 391,380.

FIJI

1938-50 Designs, ½d (sailing canoe); 1d (village); 1½d (canoe); 2d, 2½d, 6d (map); 2d (Gov. Offices); 3d (canoe and Arms of Fiji); 1/- (spearing fish); 2/- (Suva Harbour); 2/6 (river scene); 5/- (chief's hut); 10/- (Paw-paw tree); £1 (Police bugler). Designers, ½d, 1/-, 2/6 (V.E. Ousey); 3d, 5/- (I. Stinson); 1d, 1½d, 5d (C.D. Lovejoy); 2d (Map), 2½d, 6d, 2/- (A.V. Guy). Printers (recess) De La Rue, ½d, 1½d, 2d, 2½d, 6d, 8d, 1/5, 1/6. Other values, Waterlow and Sons. Perf. 13½ (C) ½d, 1½d, 2d, 2½d, 6d (Die 2). Perf. 13 x 11¾ (C) 6d (Die 1). Perf. 13¾ x 14 (C) 8d, 1/6. Perf. 14 (L) 1/5. Perf. 12½ (L) 1d, 3d, 5d, 1/-, 2/-, 2/6, 5/-, 10/-, £1. Sheets 10 x 6, 6 x 10 or 5 x 12.

1	½d **green** (5/4/38)	.10	.45
2	1d **light brown and blue** (5/4/38)	.35	.15
	a red-brown and blue (7/6/50)	.25	.15
3	1½d **carmine** (Die 1) (5/4/38)	7.50	.20
4	1½d **carmine** (Die 2) (27/9/40)	.60	1.80
	a deep carmine (Die 2) (10/1/44)	1.75	.75
5	2d **red-brown and green** (Map) (Die 1) (5/4/38)	£18	.25
	a extra line	£350	£45
	b 'Garrick line'	£350	£45
6	2d **red-brown and green** (Die 2) (27/9/40)	£8	£10
	a Vatulele curl	£35	£38
7	2d **yellow-green and magenta** (Gov. Building) (19/5/42)	.20	.35
	a scratched buildings	£14	£20
8	2½d **red-brown and green (Die 2)** (6/1/42)	.45	.50
	a red-brown and blue-green (10/1/44)	1.50	£2
	b Vatulele curl	£12	£12
	c extra island	£28	£28
9	3d **blue** (5/4/38)	.50	.20
	a bright blue	.75	.20
	b re-entry	£45	£45
	c spur on oval	£200	£110
10	5d **blue and red** (5/4/38)	£20	6.50
11	5d **pea-green and red** (1/10/40)	.10	.20
12	6d **black** (Die 1) (5/4/38)	£26	7.50

13	6d **black** (Die 2) (1/10/40)	1.50	1.35
	a slate-black (Die 2) (10/1/44)	£12	£18
14	8d **carmine-red** (5/11/48)	.40	1.50
15	1/- **yellow and black** (5/4/38)	.45	.40
16	1/5 **black and carmine** (13/6/40)	.10	.10
17	1/6 **bright ultramarine** (1/8/50)	1.50	1.75
18	2/- **orange and purple-violet** (5/4/38)	1.25	.25
19	2/6 **emerald and brown** (5/4/38)	1.60	£1
20	5/- **deep green and purple** (5/4/38)	1.50	£1
21	10/- **brown-orange and emerald** (13/3/50)	£20	£25
22	£1 **ultramarine and cherry-red** (13/3/50)	£26	£30
SP 1/20	**specimen perf** (18)	£350	†

As Nos. 1,4 and 8 but Perf. 14 (L).

23	½d **green** (/41)	£8	£2
24	1½d **carmine** (Die 2) (/42)	£10	£12
25	2½d **red-brown and green** (6/1/42)	.75	.60
	a Vatulele curl	£12	£12
	b extra island	£35	£30

As Nos. 1,4,7,8 and 13 but Perf. 12 (C).

26	½d **green** (26/8/48)	.45	1.80
	a extra frond	£50	-
27	1½d **carmine** (21/7/49)	.70	.75
	a re-entry	£35	£40
28	2d **yellow-green and magenta** (27/5/46)	.45	.40
	a scratched buildings	£15	£18
29	2½d **red-brown and green** (19/1/48)	.45	.30
	a Vatulele curl	£12	-
	b extra island	£28	£18
30	6d **black** (Die 2) (5/6/47)	.75	£1

As Nos. 14 and 17 but Perf. 13 x 13¼ (C).

31	8d **carmine-red** (7/6/50)	.35	1.75
32	1/6 **ultramarine** (16/2/55)	.65	£10
1-32	**set** (22)	£120	£80

On most of the early printings in this set, streaky brown gum is normal. White gum (where possible to find) will command a premium over prices quoted for CW 3, 5, 10, and especially 12.

1½d Die 1; without person in boat. Die 2; person added.

2d and 6d Die 1; without 180° under ISLANDS. Die 2; 180° added.

5 with blue-green frame is a changeling.

5a   6a

5a extra line left of 'Fiji' R10/2.

5b a strong scratch through the value (named after its discoverer). R5/1.

6a, etc brown arc ('Vatulele curl') in the sea near the left point of 'VITILEVU'. R9/6.

7a   8c

7a, 28a the buildings in the foreground have a diagonal scratch. R10/2, Plate 1-1.

8c, etc an 'extra island' just to the left of 'TAVEUNI'. R10/5.

9b Top frameline is doubled at right. R2/2, Plate 1.

9c   26a

9c There is a spur from the bottom of the Arms oval on R4/2. Plate 2 printings from 1939.

26a Extra frond on R5/8.

27a Top frameline is doubled at right. R4/2.

Apart from the plate varieties listed and described, there are many, many others, chiefly affecting the DLR ½d - 2½d values.

1941 (Feb 10th) No. 6 surcharged 2½d.

| 33 | 2½d/2d **red-brown and green** | £1 | .40 |
| | a Vatulele curl | £12 | £12 |

There are two types of surcharge, one of which has a small spur at the left of the head of "2" and which appears on the 1st, 3rd and 5th vertical rows. The other type appears on the 2nd, 4th and 6th vertical rows.

SPECIAL ISSUES

1937 (May 12th) Coronation. As Antigua.

S1	1d **deep purple**	.30	.75
S2	2d **deep grey**	.30	1.35
S3	3d **deep prussian blue**	.30	1.35
S1/3	**set** (3)	.80	£3
SP S1/3	**specimen perf** (3)	£65	†

1946 (Aug 17th) Victory. As Aden.

S4	2½d **green**	.10	.90
	a double print,		
	one albino	£275	-
S5	3d **grey-blue**	.10	.10
SP S4/5	**specimen perf** (2)	£65	†

S4a - One sheet was discovered which had been through the press twice, once uninked. Hence a second, albino impression is visible from the back of the stamp. From the numbers available it is possible that there was more than one sheet.

1948 (Dec 17th) Silver Wedding. As Aden.

| S6 | 2½d **green** | .20 | £1 |
| S7 | 5/- **slate-violet** | £7 | £5 |

1949 (Oct 10th) U.P.U. As Aden.

S8	2d **magenta**	.15	.45
S9	3d **indigo**	£1	2.25
S10	8d **carmine-red**	.15	2.40
S11	1/6 **azure**	.20	£1
S8/11	**set** (4)	1.35	5.50

HEALTH (CHARITY) ISSUE

1951 (Sept 17th) Designs, 1d + 1d (Fijian boys bathing); 2d + 1d (Fijian rugby footballer). Printers (recess) Bradbury, Wilkinson. Perf. 13¼ x 13½ (C). Sheets 10 x 6 or 6 x 10.

| H1 | 1d+1d **sepia-brown** | .10 | .75 |
| H2 | 2d+1d **green** | .20 | .75 |

Number issued - 1d+1d, 465,646; 2d+1d, 465,743.

POSTAGE DUE STAMPS

1940 (July 1st) Design, value in white circle. Printers (recess) Waterlow and Sons. Watermark Multiple Script CA Perf 12 ½ (L). Sheets 12 x 10.

PD1	1d **emerald**	£4	£45
PD2	2d **emerald**	£6	£45
PD3	3d **emerald**	7.50	£48
PD4	4d **emerald**	£8	£50
PD5	5d **emerald**	£9	£50
PD6	6d **emerald**	£10	£60
PD7	1/- **deep crimson**	£12	£80
PD8	1/6 **deep crimson**	£12	£125
PD 1/8	**set** (8)	£60	£450
SPPD1/8	**specimen perf** (8)	£140	†

Used examples should be purchased with great care. Most currently on the market show no portion of the central date-slug in the cancel. These were cancelled to order, probably in the 1980s. We do not sell these; the prices quoted above are for examples which show a portion of the central date-slug.

BOOKLET PANES

P1	½d **CW 1** pane of 8	-	-
P2	½d **CW 1** pane of 10	-	-
P3	1d **CW 2** pane of 8	-	-
P4	1d **CW 2** pane of 10	-	-
P5	2d **CW 5** pane of 6	-	-
P6	2d **CW 5** pane of 9	-	-

These are normally found with brown, streaky gum and are often affected by foxing.

BOOKLETS

1938 Booklets produced locally in Suva, stapled. No advertising interleaving.

B1	3/-	**1938 black on pale greenish blue, stapled;** ½d, 1d each pane of 8; 2d two panes of 6	£850	-
B2	5/9d	**1938 black on deep green, stapled;** ½d, 1d each pane of 10, 2d 2 panes of 9	£2250	-

1940 Booklets produced in England by De La Rue, stapled. With advertising interleaving.

B3	3/-	**1940 black on buff;** as B1 with 3 panes of adverts; 1 pane of rates	-	-
B4	5/9d	**1940 black on pink;** as B2 with 3 panes of adverts; 1 pane of rates	-	-

GAMBIA

1938 (April 1st) - 50 Design, Elephant and Palm (Badge of Colony). Printers (recess) Bradbury, Wilkinson. Perf. 12 (L). Sheets 10 x 6.

1	½d black and emerald-green	.10	.40
2	1d mauve-purple and chocolate	.15	.30
3	1½d brown-lake and carmine	£75	7.50
	a brown-lake and rose-scarlet (/40)	1.50	1.80
	b brown-lake and vermilion	.25	1.20
4	1½d dull blue and black (2/1/45)	.15	.95
5	2d dull blue and black	£4	£2
6	2d brown-lake and rose-scarlet (1/10/43)	.30	1.35
7	3d light and deep blue	.15	.10
8	5d sage and purple-brown (13/3/41)	.25	.30
9	6d olive-green and claret	.75	.20
	a deep olive and deep claret (30/1/50)	£1	.40
10	1/- slate and purple-violet	1.50	.15
11	1/3 chocolate and dull blue (28/11/46)	1.60	1.50
12	2/- carmine and blue	£3	£2
	a deep carmine and dark blue (9/4/45)	£4	£2
13	2/6 sepia and greyish olive	£6	1.50
14	4/- vermilion and deep purple	£12	1.50
15	5/- dark blue and vermilion	£13	2.50
16	10/- deep orange and black	£13	£5
1/16	set (16)	£50	£18
SP 1/16	specimen perf (16)	£275	†

3 is a much-misidentified stamp; numerous examples exist with erroneous expert society certificates. The 'real thing' has an unmistakable carmine frame, alongside which 'possibles' rapidly revert to scarlet.

SPECIAL ISSUES

1937 (May 12th) Coronation. As Antigua.

S1	1d light brown	.15	.75
S2	1½d carmine-red	.15	.75

S3	3d blue	.30	1.20
S1/3	set (3)	.50	2.40
SP S1/3	specimen perf (3)	£55	†

1946 (Aug 6th) Victory. As Aden.

S4	1½d black	.10	.15
S5	3d deep blue	.10	.25
SP S4/5	specimen perf (2)	£50	†

Number Issued; 1½d 689,700, 3d 673,920.

1948 (Dec 24th) Silver Wedding. As Aden.

S6	1½d black	.15	.10
S7	£1 dull purple	£9	£10

1949 (Oct 10th) U.P.U. As Aden.

S8	1½d slate	.15	.90
S9	3d indigo	.60	1.20
S10	6d reddish mauve	.40	1.65
S11	1/- dull violet	.25	.35
S8/11	set (4)	1.25	3.75

GIBRALTAR

1938-51 (½d-3d issued 25/2/38; other values 16/3/38, unless indicated otherwise). Designs, ½d and £1 (King's head); other values (views of colony), based on photographs from Beanland Malin postcards. Printers (recess) De La Rue. Wmk. Multiple Script CA. Watermark upright, except where indicated 'S' (sideways). ½d and £1 sheets of 120 in two panes, each 6 x 10: 1d - 10/- sheets of 60 (6 x 10).

(a) Perf. 13½ x 14 (C).

1	½d **deep green**	.10	.25
	a olive-green (28/4/49)	.10	.25
2	£1 **orange**	£18	£30

(b) Perf. 14 (C) (6d line). Sheets 6 x 10.

3	1d **dull chestnut**	£10	1.50
4	1½d **red**	£10	.45
5	2d **grey**	£11	.25
	a ape on rock	£240	-
6	3d **blue**	£48	£3
7	6d **carmine and violet-grey** (25/4/41)	£38	.75
8	1/- **black and green**	£14	£14
9	2/- **black and chestnut**	£24	£14
10	5/- **black and carmine-red**	£35	£120
11	10/- **black and deep blue**	£28	£80

(c) Perf. 13½ (C).

12	1d **dull chestnut**	£10	1.40
	a chestnut-brown (S) (/41)	£2	4.50
13	1½d **red**	£95	£20
14	2d **grey**	1.30	.20
	a grey (S) (/40)	£400	£25
15	3d **blue**	£8	.60
16	6d **carmine and violet-grey**	£16	£2

17	1/- **black and green** (4/40)	£25	3.75
18	2/- **black and chestnut-brown** (11/40)	£25	£22
19	5/- **black and carmine-red** (2/40)	£16	£9

5a a mark on the rock resembles an ape R1/5.

14a Forgeries exist, some printed photo-litho but mostly reperforated ordinary stamps. 14a normally has clipped perfs at top or bottom of stamp.

As before but Perf. 13 x 12¾ (C).

20	1d **chestnut** (S) (4/42)	.20	.35
	a chocolate (S) (27/3/44)	.75	2.25
	b reddish chestnut (S) (25/2/46)	.75	£1
	c red-brown (28/4/49)	1.25	£1
21	1½d **purple-slate** (1/1/43)	.20	.90
	a violet-slate (27/3/44)	.15	.90
22	2d **grey** (S) (2/42)	.40	.90
	a 'A' of watermark missing	£900	-
23	2d **carmine-red** (S) (15/7/44)	.20	.35
	a rose-carmine (S) (15/7/47)	.40	.35
24	3d **dull grey-blue** (4/42)	.20	.20
	a blue (23/4/45)	.25	.20
	b dull greenish blue (8/2/51)	1.75	.90
25	5d **orange** (1/10/47)	.50	.75
26	6d **carmine and violet-grey** (/42)	£2	£1
	aa re-entries from	£10	£8
	a scarlet and violet-grey (23/4/45)	2.50	2.25
	b re-entries from	£12	£12
27	1/- **black and green** (4/42)	1.25	2.50
	a grey-black and green (/44)	1.25	2.50
	b re-entry	£20	£20
	c broken 'R'	£285	-
28	2/- **black and chestnut-brown** (4/42)	£3	£5
	a black and red-brown	2.50	£4
	aa pale red-brown (2/46)	2.50	£4
	b re-entry	£40	£30
	c broken 'R'	£300	-
	d seagull flaw	£220	-
29	5/- **black and deep scarlet** (27/3/44)	£10	£11
	a black and pale carmine (22/11/49)	£12	£13
	b black and deep carmine (/51)	£15	£15
	c re-entry	£60	£50
	d broken 'R'	£450	-
30	10/- **slate-black and deep blue** (25/4/43)	£15	£16
	a black and dark blue (27/3/44)	£15	£16
	b re-entry	£70	£55
	c broken 'R'	£650	-

1/30	**set** (14)	£65	£60
SP 1/30	**specimen perf** (14)	£600	†

1, 1a, 3, 5, 12, 14a, 22 and 23 are known from coils.

Prices for used are for CDS-used examples. Stamps with parcel cancels are worth considerably less.

26aa, etc. There are a number of re-entries affecting stamps in this set. The 6d value and S14 have two particularly fine examples on R1/3-4. The centre plate of this stamp also has numerous re-entries. The 1/- to 10/- values show doubling to the castle at the top right and the frames.

27c, etc	28d

27c, etc, R9/4 (Frame Plate 2). The second 'R' in 'GIBRALTAR' is damaged, to a varying extent.

28d A flaw occurs on the statue on R9/3 on the perf 13 x 12¾ printings.

SPECIAL ISSUES

1937 (May 12th) Coronation. As Antigua.

S1	½d **green**	.15	.30
S2	2d **grey**	.75	1.95
S3	3d **blue**	1.35	1.95
S1/3	**set** (3)	£2	3.75
SP S1/3	**specimen perf** (3)	£120	†

Number printed: ½d 1,071,000; 2d 1,146,540; 3d 670,020.

1946 (Oct 12th) Victory. As Aden.

S4	½d **pale green**	.10	.75
S5	3d **ultramarine**	.25	.75
SP S4/5	**specimen perf** (2)	£75	†

Number sold: ½d 917,478; 3d 732,465.

1948 (Dec 1st) Silver Wedding. As Aden

S6	½d **green**	.60	1.50
S7	£1 **orange-brown**	£26	£45

Number sold: ½d 782,692; £1 26,110.

1949 (Oct 10th) U.P.U. As Aden.

S8	2d **carmine-rose**	.50	.75
S9	3d **indigo**	£1	.90
S10	6d **purple**	.60	1.20
S11	1/- **quartz-green**	.50	£2
S8/11	**set** (4)	2.75	4.50

Number sold: 2d 429,270; 3d 266,520; 6d 205,640; 1/- 91,250.

1950 (Aug 1st) Legislative Council. Nos. 23, etc., overprinted (letterpress) "NEW CONSTITUTION 1950" by De La Rue, in black or red.

S12	2d **carmine-red**	.15	.90
S13	3d **dull greenish blue**	.30	.60
S14	6d **carmine and violet-grey**	.35	1.20
	a overprint double	£750	£875
	b re-entries from	£10	£10
S15	1/- **black and green** (red)	.35	1.20
	a broken 'R'	£60	-
	b re-entry	£10	£10
S12/15	**set** (4)	£1	3.50

Number sold: 2d 1,188,594; 3d 1,082,084; 6d 417,084; 1/- 125,954.

S14b, S15b, see 26aa.

S15a see 27c.

GILBERT AND ELLICE ISLANDS

1939 (Jan 1st) - 55 Designs, ½d (Frigate Bird); 1d (Pandanus Pine); 1½d (canoe crossing reef); 2d (house and canoe); 2½d (native house); 3d (palms and sea); 5d (Ellice Is. canoe); 6d (Coconut palms); 1/- (cantilever jetty, Ocean Is.); 2/- (H.M.C.S. "Nimanoa"); 2/6 (Gilbert Is. canoe); 5/- (Coat of Arms). Watermark multiple script CA sideways. ½d, 2d, 2/6d printed by Bradbury, Wilkinson, perf. 11½ x 11¼ (C), sheets 5 x 12. 1d, 5d, 6d, 2/-, 5/- printed by Waterlow and Sons, perf. 12½ (L), sheets 10 x 6. 1½d, 2½d, 3d, 1/- printed by De La Rue, perf. 13½ (C), sheets 6 x 10.

1	½d	**bluish slate and deep green**	.30	.60
	a	bluish slate and green (5/43)	1.50	£2
	ba	'A' of watermark missing	-	-
2	1d	**blue-green and dull rose-lilac**	.15	.90
	a	blue-green and pale reddish lilac (5/51)	1.50	£3
3	1½d	**black and carmine-red**	.15	.75
	a	slate-black and carmine (12/5/43)	.75	£1
4	2d	**chestnut and deep grey**	.35	.60
	a	deep red-brown and grey (30/10/44)	.50	1.50
	b	light red-brown and pearly grey (5/51)	.75	1.50
5	2½d	**black and green-olive**	.25	.40
	a	slate-black and deep yellow-green (12/5/43)	2.75	2.25
	b	grey-black and olive (14/11/46)	£1	1.75
6	3d	**black and ultramarine**	.25	.60
	a	slate-black and bright ultramarine (12/5/43)	£4	£5
	b	black and blue (10/44)	.75	£1
7	5d	**deep blue and sepia**	2.25	.90
	a	ultramarine and brown-sepia, perf 12¾ (12/5/43)	3.50	£10
	b	dull ultramarine and sepia (10/10/44)	2.25	3.50
8	6d	**yellowish olive and violet**	.30	.35
	a	olive and cold violet, perf 12¾ (12/5/43)	2.50	£3
9	1/-	**black and turquoise-blue**	£8	1.35
	a	slate-black and dull turquoise-blue (12/5/43)	£4	£2
	b	greyish black and greenish turquoise (4/46)	£5	£3

10	2/-	**dark blue and dull vermilion**	£6	£6
	a	dark violet-blue and vermilion, perf 12¾ (12/5/43)	£10	£12
	b	violet-blue and reddish vermilion (10/10/44)	£5	£15
11	2/6	**blue and deep emerald-green**	£5	£7
12	5/-	**red-carmine and dark blue**	£12	8.50
	a	red and ultramarine, perf 12¾ (12/5/43)	£15	£18
	b	carmine-red and deep blue (30/10/44)	6.50	£10
SP1/12		specimen perf (12)	£290	†

As Nos. 6 and 9 but Perf. 12 (C).

13	3d	**black and deep blue** (25/7/55)	.30	1.35
14	1/-	**greyish black and turquoise-blue** (8/5/51)	1.50	£10
	a	black and light turquoise-blue (6/3/52)	£12	£15
1-14		**set** (12)	£20	£25

2a, 13 these stamps are on brittle white paper. Other values exist printed on the same paper.

1943 perf 12¾ printings (5d, 6d, 2/-, 5/-). Be wary of relying solely on perforation measurements, since other printings vary between 12.4 to 12.6. It is wise either to be precise with measurement, or to pay attention to the shade as well.

SPECIAL ISSUES

1937 (May 12th) Coronation. As Ascension.

S1	1d	**violet**	.15	.40
	a	light violet	.30	.40
S2	1½d	**carmine**	.15	.40
S3	3d	**blue**	.20	.40
S1/3		**set** (3)	.45	1.10
SP S1/3		specimen perf (3)	£85	†

1946 (Dec. 16th) Victory. As Aden.

S4	1d	**reddish purple**	.10	.30
S5	3d	**deep blue**	.10	.30
SP S4/5		specimen perf (2)	£40	†

1949 (Aug. 29th) Silver Wedding. As Aden.

S6	1d	**bright violet**	.25	.45
S7	£1	**rose-carmine**	£7	£14

1949 (Oct. 10th) U.P.U. As Aden.

S8	1d	**dull purple**	.20	.75
S9	2d	**dark slate**	£1	1.80
S10	3d	**dull indigo**	.25	1.80
S11	1/-	**azure**	.25	1.20
S8/11		**set** (4)	1.50	£5

POSTAGE DUE STAMPS

1940 (Aug.) Printers (typo) Bradbury, Wilkinson. Perf. 12 (L). Watermark CA. Sheets 12 x 10.

PD1	1d **pale emerald**	£5	£15
PD2	2d **red**	£5	£15
PD3	3d **brown**	7.50	£16
	a small "b"	£350	£600
PD4	4d **blue**	£8	£22
PD5	5d **myrtle-green**	£11	£22
PD6	6d **magenta**	£11	£22
PD7	1/- **violet**	£12	£30
PD8	1/6 **pale blue-green**	£24	£55
PD1/8	**set** (8)	£75	£175
SP PD1/8	**specimen set** (8)	£140	†

PD3a R10/5 the top loop of 'B' in 'Gilbert' is obscured by a plate flaw, resembling a 'b'.

GOLD COAST

All definitive stamps were printed (recess) by Bradbury, Wilkinson.

1938 (April 1st) Design, Christiansborg Castle, Accra. Watermark Multiple Script CA. Perf. 12 (L). Sheets 6 x 10 or 10 x 6.

1	½d **pale green**	2.50	1.35
2	1d **red-brown**	3.50	.20
3	1½d **scarlet**	3.50	2.25
4	2d **slate**	3.50	.90
5	3d **blue**	2.75	.60
6	4d **deep magenta**	£3	1.80
7	6d **red-purple**	£5	.30
8	9d **orange**	£4	£1
9	1/- **black and olive**	6.50	1.35
10	2/- **deep blue and violet**	£18	£12
11	5/- **deep olive-green and carmine**	£35	£15
1/11	**set** (11)	£80	£33

As No. 1, etc., but Perf. 12 x 11¾ (C).

12	½d **green** (/40)	.15	.30
	a emerald-green (22/7/47)	.20	.30
13	1d **red-brown** (/39)	.15	.10
14	1½d **scarlet** (/40)	.20	.30
	a carmine-red (21/1/46)	.20	.30
15	2d **slate** (/40)	.20	.10
	a deep grey (10/2/44)	.30	.10
16	3d **blue** (/40)	.20	.20
17	4d **deep magenta** (/42)	.50	£1
	a bright magenta (7/47)	£1	.75
18	6d **purple** (/39)	.40	.15
19	9d **orange** (/44)	.65	.40
	a reddish orange (16/5/45)	.65	£1
20	1/- **black and deep olive** (/40)	.75	.40
	a black and olive-green (21/1/46)	£1	.40
21	1/3 **chestnut and turquoise-blue** (12/4/41)	£1	.30
	a chocolate and deep turquoise-blue (10/2/44)	1.25	.30
22	2/- **blue and red-violet** (/40)	2.50	£10
	a greenish blue and purple-violet (10/2/44)	3.50	£11
23	5/- **olive-green and carmine** (/40)	£6	£12
	a deep olive and deep carmine (10/2/44)	£6	£15

24	10/-	**black and violet** (7/40)	£4	£16
		a slate-black and		
		deeper violet (2/44)	£10	£25
12/24		**set** (13)	£15	£36
SP 1-11,21,24		**specimen** perf (13)	£185	†

Officially, no stamps were perforated 12 (line) after 1938, but the first recorded supplies of the comb-perforated stamps (12 x 11¾) were not sent out to the Colony until 1939. There was more than one printing of the line-perforated stamps, but no official record can be found of this. Comb-perforated stamps were placed on sale as and when required. No record was kept of release dates, but stamps postmarked with the year as given above have been noted. 1939 1d (coils), ½d, 1d and 6d; 1940 ½d (coils), 1½d, 2d, 3d, 1/-, 2/-, 5/- and 10/-; 1941, 1/3; 1942, 4d; 1943, 9d. The comb perf ½d and 1d also exist in coil form.

1948 (July 1st) Designs, ½d (mounted constabulary); 1d (Christiansborg Castle); 1½d (Council emblem); 2d (drums); 2½d (map); 3d (Manganese mine); 4d (Lake Bosumtwi); 6d, 1/- (cocoa industry); 2/- (Trooping the Colour); 5/- (surfboats); 10/- (forest scene). Watermark Multiple Script CA. Perf 11¾ x 12 except Nos 25, 28, 32, 36 Perf. 12 x 11¾ (C). Sheets 6 x 10 or 5 x 12.

25	½d	**emerald**	.10	.20
26	1d	**deep blue**	.10	.10
27	1½d	**scarlet**	.60	.50
28	2d	**chocolate-brown**	.30	.10
		a deep brown (24/6/52)	£4	1.50
29	2½d	**carmine-red and**		
		bistre-brown	£1	2.50
30	3d	**greyish blue**	1.75	.30
31	4d	**lake-magenta**	1.75	1.95
32	6d	**black and orange**	.20	.20
33	1/-	**black and red-orange**	.75	.20
		a inverted watermark	†	-
34	2/-	**sage and rose-carmine**	1.75	1.80
35	5/-	**purple and grey-black**	£12	£5
36	10/-	**black and sage-green**	5.50	£5
25/36		**set** (12)	£23	£16
SP 25/36		**specimen** perf (12)	£230	†

33a a single used example has been reported to us.

The ½d and 1d values were issued in coil form.

SPECIAL ISSUES

1937 (May 12th) Coronation. As Antigua.

S1	1d	**light brown**	.85	1.50
S2	2d	**slate**	.85	2.70
S3	3d	**blue**	£1	1.65
S1/3		**set** (3)	2.50	5.25
SP S1/3		**specimen** perf (3)	£60	†

1946 (Oct. 14th) Victory. As Aden.

(a) Perf. 13¾ x 14 (C).

S4	2d	**violet**	6.50	1.65
S5	4d	**dull lake**	£1	2.25

(b) Perf. 13¾ x 13½ (C).

S6	2d	**violet-grey**	.10	.10
		a inverted watermark	-	†
S7	4d	**dull lake**	.70	£2
SP S4,7		**specimen** perf (2)	£60	†

S6a a single mint example has been found.

Nos. S4 and S5 were mostly sold in the Colony and Nos. S6 and S7 in London.

1948 (Dec. 20th) Silver Wedding. As Aden.

S8	1½d	**scarlet**	.15	.40
S9	10/-	**grey-olive**	£11	£18

1949 (Oct. 10th) U.P.U. As Aden.

S10	2d	**beech-brown**	.15	.15
		a 'A' of watermark omitted	-	-
S11	2½d	**orange**	.75	2.50
S12	3d	**dull indigo**	.20	£1
S13	1/-	**quartz-green**	.20	.20
		a 'A' of watermark omitted	†	-
S10/13		**set** (4)	1.20	3.50

POSTAGE DUE STAMPS

1923 Printers (typo) De La Rue. Perf. 13¾ x 14 (C). Uncoated thick creamy paper. Clear impression.

PDX1	½d	**black**	£7	£75
PDX2	1d	**black**	.35	.75
PDX3	2d	**black**	£6	2.25
PDX4	3d	**black**	£10	1.35
PDX1-4		**set** (4)	£20	£75

These stamps have more-or-less toned gum.

1945 as before, but rough paper. Deep colour and woolly impression.

PD1	1d **black**	£5	£12
PD2	2d **black**	£5	£10
PD3	3d **black**	£5	£8
PD1-3	**set** (3)	£14	£18

These stamps have clear gum.

1951-54 as before, but chalk-surfaced white paper.

PD4	2d **black** (13/12/51)	1.50	£15
	c thick 'd'	£10	-
	d serif on 'd'	£30	-
PD5	3d **black** (13/12/51)	1.50	£14
	c damaged serif	£25	-
PD6	6d **black** (1/10/52)	.85	£6
PD7	1/- **black** (1/10/52)	.85	£40
	a upright diagonal	£8	£65
PD4/7	**set** (4)	4.25	£68

PD4c The 'd' of '2d' is thicker on R9/6 and 10/6.

PD4d The serif at the base of the 'd' extends to the right. R1/6.

PD5c The bottom serif of the '3' is damaged on R9/1.

PD7a The diagonal line in value is more upright than is normal on No. 5 of all rows (10 x 6). The height, position and angle of the '/' in the value varies.   Each vertical column differs. Those in column 5 show the '/' more nearly upright than the others. See also Trinidad & Tobago.

WATERMARK VARIETIES (TYPE A)
(See Introduction for details)

PD4a	2d **Crown missing**	£650	-
PD4b	**St. Edward's Crown**	£325	-
PD5a	3d **Crown missing**	£600	-
PD5b	**St. Edward's Crown**	£300	-
PD6a	6d **Crown missing**	£975	-
PD6b	**St. Edward's Crown**	£575	-
PD7b	1/- **St. Edward's Crown**	£650	-

GRAHAM LAND
SEE
FALKLAND ISLAND
DEPENDENCIES

GREAT BRITAIN
SEE FRONT OF BOOK

GRENADA

1937-50 Design, King's head. Printers (photo) Harrison and Sons. Perf. 14¾ x 14 (C). Sheets 12 x 10.

1	¼d **chocolate-brown** (ch) (12/7/37)	.85	.10
	a chocolate-brown (sub) (11/42)	.20	.90
	b chocolate (sub) (2/1/45)	.20	.90
	c chocolate (ch) (16/8/50)	.85	£5

1938 (Mar. 16th)-50 Designs, ½d (Grand Anse Beach); 1½d (Grand Etang Lake); 2½d (St. George's); other values (King's head and Badge of the Colony). Printers (recess) Waterlow and Sons. Centres black except Nos. 2, 6, 12, 15a, 16. Perf. 12½ (L). Sheets 6 x 10 or 10 x 6.

2	½d **yellow-green**	£3	.90
	a blue-green (10/9/43)	.25	.75
3	1d **sepia**	.40	.15
	a deep sepia (10/9/43)	.40	.15
4	1½d **deep scarlet**	.25	.60
	a scarlet-red (10/9/43)	.25	.60
5	2d **orange**	.15	.30
	a bright orange	.30	.30
6	2½d **deep blue**	.15	.20
	a bright blue (20/3/50)	.30	.20
7	3d **olive-green**	£5	.85
	a olive (/40)	1.50	£1
	b deep olive (16/8/50)	.20	1.20
8	6d **purple-lake**	£1	.25
	a purple (2/1/45)	.80	.25
9	1/- **light brown**	1.20	.25
10	2/- **ultramarine**	£11	£1
	a bright ultramarine (/43)	£12	1.25
11	5/- **violet**	1.75	£2

As Nos. 2, etc. but Perf. 13¼ x 12¾ (C) horizontal designs; 12¾ x 13¼ (C) vertical designs.

12	½d **yellow-green**	2.50	.75
	a blue-green (/41)	£3	£8

13	1d **sepia**	.20	.30
	a deep sepia (/40)	.40	.40
14	1½d **carmine-red**	£1	.20
15	2d **orange**	£1	.50
	a grey and orange	£1	1.50
16	2½d **blue** (/50)	£5500	£130
17	3d **olive-green** (/41)	3.50	.60
	a brown-olive (11/42)	.15	.60
	b deep olive (15/7/47)	.15	1.20
	c colon flaw	£55	-
18	6d **deep purple** (11/42)	1.25	.50
	a purple (15/7/47)	£1	.30
19	1/- **light brown** (11/42)	1.50	£1
20	2/- **ultramarine** (/41)	£11	£1
	a bright ultramarine (15/7/47)	£12	1.50
21	5/- **violet** (15/7/47)	1.50	3.50

Values in both perforations (where no dates are given) were issued at the same time in 1938, along with No. 22.

16 Beware of 'mint' forgeries of this stamp. An expert committe certificate is advisable for mint examples.

No. 7 with frames in bright green or orange are fakes with chemically-altered colours, and may be found with the words 'colour fake' handstamped on reverse.

17c R5/6 a flaw resembling a colon under the '3d' on the August 1950 printing only. Stamps can be found showing wear in this position, so care is necessary when purchasing the variety.

A flaw on R1/1 of the 'badge of the colony' values may be found, consisting of a line across the sail. We do not list this variety because there are a number of confusing states.

Nos. 2, 3, 12, and 12a were issued in coils as well as sheets.

Design, Seal of Colony. Printers (recess) De La Rue. Sheets 6 x 10.

Perf. 11¾ x 13 (C), narrow frame.

22	10/- **steel-blue and carmine** (16/3/38)	£20	£6

Allocation of the Grenada 10/- to CW numbers

22 and 24 have unique perforations.

23 also has a unique, but less distinctive, perforation. It is, however, the only stamp whose steel-blue vignette is identical to that of 22.

25 has a blurred vignette: 25a has a sharper vignette. The crow's nest is the best place to look for the distinction. 25a is on pinkish-surfaced paper. 25c has whiter gum than 25 or 25a and has a sharp vignette.

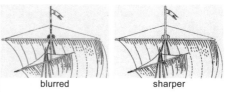

26 and 26a each have deep frames. The 'claret' contains an element of lake which is lacking in the carmine, and it is a common printing in used condition.

blurred   sharper

26b is on white paper.

Stamps with narrow frames, usually 23½-23¾ mm wide, were printed on dampened paper. Stamps with wide frames, about 24½ mm wide, were printed on dry paper.

Perforation 14 x 14

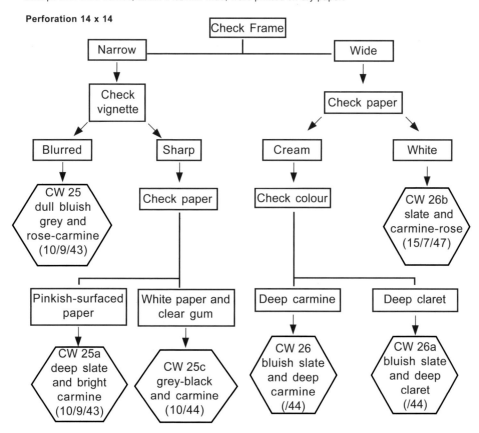

Perf. 13¾ x 14 (L), narrow frame.

23	10/- **steel-blue and carmine** (/40)	£80	£30

Perf. 11¾ (L), narrow frame.

24	10/- **bluish slate and dull carmine** (10/9/43)	£285	£1200

780 copies printed. Most used examples bear forged cancellations; an expert committee certificate is essential when purchasing.

Perf. 14 (L), narrow frame.

25	10/- **dull bluish grey and rose-carmine** (10/9/43)	£90	£75
	a deep slate and bright carmine (10/09/43)	£12	£6
	ab double print of frame, one albino	£3500	-
	c grey-black and carmine (10/44)	£12	£6

25a is on pinkish-surfaced paper.

Perf. 14 (L), wide frame (24¼ mm)

26	10/- **bluish slate and deep carmine** (/44)	£65	£50
	a bluish slate and deep claret (/44)	£45	£6
	b slate and carmine-rose (15/7/47)1-26	£10	£20
1-26	**set** (12, cheapest)	£30	£11
SP1-11,22	**specimen perf** (12)	£180	-

1951 (Jan. 8th) Designs, ½c - 12c (portrait of King); other values (Badge of Colony). Sheets 10 x 10.

(a) Perf. 11½ (C). Printers (recess) Bradbury, Wilkinson. Centres black.

27	½c **red-brown**	.10	£1
28	1c **emerald**	.10	.15
29	2c **sepia**	.10	.30
30	3c **carmine**	.10	.10
31	4c **orange**	.20	.25
32	5c **violet**	.10	.10
33	6c **olive-green**	.15	.35
34	7c **blue**	.80	.10
35	12c **purple**	£1	.20

(b) Perf. 11½ x 12 ½ (C). Printers (recess) De La Rue. Sheets 10 x 5.

36	25c **sepia**	£1	.50
37	50c **deep blue**	£3	.25
38	$1.50 **orange**	3.50	£4

(c) Perf. 11¾ x 13 (C). Printers (recess) De La Rue (large format).

39	$2.50 **slate-blue and carmine-rose**	3.50	3.50
	a value tablet re-entry	£40	£45
27/39	**set** (13)	£12	£10

39a occurs on nos. 1, 4 and 6 of the bottom row of ten. Each is different: the top and bottom framelines of the value tablets show varying duplication, as do the values themselves. We have not yet been able to illustrate these re-entries satisfactorily.

SPECIAL ISSUES

1937 (May 12th) Coronation. As Antigua.

S1	1d **violet**	.20	£1
S2	1½d **carmine-red**	.20	.30
S3	2½d **blue**	.40	.75
S1/3	**set** (3)	.70	1.85
SP S1/3	**specimen perf** (3)	£55	†

1946 (Sept. 25th) Victory. As Aden.

S4	1½d **carmine-red**	.10	.30
S5	3½d **grey-blue**	.10	.60
SP S4/5	**specimen perf** (2)	£55	†

1948 (Oct. 27th) Silver Wedding. As Aden.

S6	1½d **carmine-red**	.10	.10
S7	10/- **greenish slate**	£8	£10

Number issued (Colony only) - 1½d., 98,110; 10/-, 4,160.

1949 (Oct. 10th) U.P.U. As Aden.

S8	5c **dull violet-blue**	.10	.10
S9	6c **deep olive**	.75	1.50
S10	12c **reddish mauve**	.10	.20
	a 'A' of watermark omitted		
S11	24c **beech-brown**	.10	.25
S8/11	**set** (4)	£1	1.80

Number issued (Colony only) - 5c, 61,824; 6c, 29,593; 12c, 35,076; 24c, 27,580.

1951 (Feb. 16th) West Indies University College. (See Antigua).

S12	3c **black and deep red**	.25	.75
S13	6c **black and olive**	.25	.30

Number issued (Colony only) - 3c, 85,685; 6c, 63,967.

1951 (Sept. 21st) New Constitution. No. 29, etc., overprinted in black or red by Bradbury, Wilkinson.

S14	3c **black and carmine**	.15	.35
S15	4c **black and orange**	.15	.35
S16	5c **black and violet** (red)	.15	.50
S17	12c **black and purple**	.15	.60
S14/17	**set** (4)	.50	1.60

Number issued - 3c, 106,140; 4c, 104,576; 5c, 114,659; 12c, 113,221.

POSTAGE DUE STAMPS

1921(Dec.)-22 Printers (typo) De La Rue. Watermark Multiple Script CA. Perf. 14. Uncoated thick creamy paper. Clear impression. Sheets 6 x 10.

PDX1	1d **black**	.75	.60
PDX2	1½d **black** (15.12.22)	£4	£15
PDX3	2d **black**	£1	£1
PDX4	3d **black**	£1	2.75
PDX1-4	**set** (4)	£6	£17

These stamps have more-or-less toned gum.

1945 as before, but rough paper. Deep colour and woolly impression.

PD1	1d **black**	£3	£2
PD2	3d **black**	£5	£3

These stamps have clear gum.

1952 (March 1st). As before, but values in cents and printed on white chalk-surfaced paper.

PD3	2c **black**	.15	£5
PD4	4c **black**	.15	£9
PD5	6c **black**	.25	7.50
PD6	8c **black**	.35	7.50
PD 3/6	**set** (4)	.80	£26

WATERMARK VARIETIES (TYPE A)
(See Introduction for details)

PD3a	2c **Crown missing**	£110	-
PD3b	**St. Edward's Crown**	£35	-
PD4a	4c **Crown missing**	£100	-
PD4b	**St. Edward's Crown**	£35	-
PD5a	6c **Crown missing**	£150	-
PD5b	**St. Edward's Crown**	£60	-
PD6a	8c **Crown missing**	£250	-
PD6b	**St. Edward's Crown**	£120	-

GUERNSEY
SEE
CHANNEL ISLANDS

GWALIOR
SEE
INDIA

HONG KONG

1938-52 (typo) De La Rue. Perf. 13¾ x 14 (C). Sheets 120, two panes each of 6 x 10. (See footnote).

1	1c **brown** (24/5/38)	£1	£2
	a deep brown (9/4/46)	.75	£2
	b light brown (4/2/52)	£1	£4
2	2c **grey** (5/4/38)	.80	.20
	a pale slate (9/4/46)	.80	.20
3	4c **orange** (5/4/38)	£2	1.80
	a pale orange (2/46)	£2	1.80
4	5c **green** (24/5/38)	.60	.10
	a yellow-green (4/2/52)	£4	.30
5	8c **red-brown** (1/11/41)	.80	1.50
	aa stop after 'CENTS'	£125	£80
	a imperf pair (12/46)	£22000	†
	b deep brown (9/4/46)	£1	1.50
6	10c **violet** (13/4/38)	£20	.45
	a reddish lilac (8/4/46)	3.50	.60
	b pale lilac (9/4/47)	£8	.15
7	15c **scarlet-red** (13/4/38)	.80	.20
	a broken character	£45	£20
	b carmine-red (9/4/46)	.80	.20
8	20c **black** (1/2/46)	.65	.20
9	25c **blue** (5/4/38)	£15	1.65
	a brighter blue (/39)	£12	1.85
10	30c **yellow-olive** (13/4/38)	£45	£2
11	50c **purple** (13/4/38)	£25	.45
	a purple (9/4/46)	£7	1.20
	b bright red-purple (ch) (9/4/47)	4.50	.15
12	80c **carmine-rose** (ch) (2/2/48)	3.50	.60
	a bright rose (ch) (2/52)	2.50	£1
13	$1 **dull lilac and blue** (ch) (27/4/38)	£3	£2
	a red-lilac and blue (sub) (/41)	£6	£8
	b short R	£80	£110
14	$2 **red-orange and green** (ch) (25/5/38)	£35	£13
15	$5 **dull lilac and red** (ch) (2/6/38)	£20	£35
16	$10 **green and violet** (ch) (2/6/38)	£220	£75

Many of the first printings (especially the $5 and $10) usually have brown, streaky gum. Examples with white gum may occasionally be found, and are worth a considerable premium.

During the war years some printing was undertaken on behalf of De La Rue by Harrison, Williams, Lea and Bradbury Wilkinson. The 4ct (possibly the 8ct as well) was produced in single-pane sheets of 120.

1 A printing by Williams, Lea was made in late 1941.

1b/4a First released in Colony, and later in London on 27/2/52.

5aa A small dot appears after 'CENTS' on R4/2 LP. This occurs on part of requisition B.

5a One sheet was found imperforate in a branch post office, but most were used up as singles, on letters to China. A mint vertical strip of 5, however, was bought and preserved. It was split by H. da Luz into a strip of 3 and a pair. Forgeries exist.

6 The initial printings are distinctive, being at once deeper, brighter and more clearly printed than subsequent stamps.

7a damage to bottom left characters. R6/6 LP, first three printings only.

壹　壹
角　角
伍　伍
分　分
7　7a

13a The surfacing of this stamp smears easily. A Williams, Lea production.

13b R3/1 LP and R7/3 RP; the diagonal stroke of the 'R' of 'DOLLAR' is shorter than usual.

16 Most used examples are more-or-less washed in appearance. Price for a fine example.

1941-45. Design as No 1, etc., but printed on rough paper by Bradbury, Wilkinson (from De La Rue plates), except 4c, which was printed on smooth paper by Harrison and Sons. Perf. 14¾ x 14 (C). The printing plate was set in such a way that the design appears embossed on the back of the stamp.

17	2c **slate-grey** (12/41)	.75	£3
18	4c **orange** (28/9/45)	£2	£2
19	5c **green** (12/41)	1.25	£3
20	10c **pale violet** (12/41)	£4	.10
22	30c **sage** (12/41)	£8	£5
23	50c **red-purple** (12/41)	£12	.70

23 A variety of this stamp exists referred to as "printed both sides, inverted on the reverse". In our opinion, this is the result of a double offset.

As far as is known, No. 18 was not released in London at the end of 1941 with the other values. Supplies which were sent to the Colony were diverted to Australia and South Africa, and were not placed on sale in Hong Kong until the re-opening of the Post Office under British Administration in 1945.

Hong Kong was occupied by the Japanese from December 25th, 1941 to August 14th, 1945, and throughout this period unoverprinted Japanese stamps were in use. Three such stamps were surcharged specifically for use in the Colony.

Immediately following the Japanese surrender, mail was franked 'HONG KONG/1945/POSTAGE PAID' within an octagonal frame until the pre-war stamps were re-issued on September 28th, 1945.

1946-52. As No. 1, etc., but colours changed.

24	20c **scarlet** (1/4/48)	£3	.25
	a pale carmine-red (24/4/51)	£8	3.50
25	25c **pale sage** (24/9/46)	£2	1.35
26	30c **blue** (27/12/46)	£3	.15
	a bright blue (21/2/50)	3.50	.15
27	$1 **orange and green** (sub) (8/4/46)	6.50	.20
	a orange and green (ch) (21/6/48)	£20	1.50
	b red-orange and deep green (ch) (30/8/50)	£20	2.25
	c yellow-orange and green (ch) (6/11/52)	£30	£10
	d short R	£100	£38
28	$2 **violet and red** (sub) (8/4/46)	£15	3.50
	a purple-violet and red (ch) (9/4/47)	£18	.60
	b violet and red (ch)	£18	.60
29	$5 **yellow-green and violet** (sub) (8/4/46)	£110	£14
	a bluish green and violet (sub) (8/4/46)	£35	£7
	b deep yellow-green and violet (ch) (9/4/47)	£50	2.50
	c green and violet (ch) (2/2/48)	£65	£3
30	$10 **deep violet and blue** (sub) (8/4/46)	£100	£22
	a pale violet and blue (sub) (8/4/46)	£60	£22
	b red-violet and blue (ch) (9/4/47)	£80	£13
	c red-purple and blue (ch) (21/2/50)	£100	£13
1/30	**set** (23)	£440	£140
SP 1/30	**specimen perf** (23)	£1600	†

24 Plate proofs in scarlet on blue-green paper exist, from Plate 2, probably printed in 1952.

27d See note after 13b.

29b, c, 30b, c There were 8 printings of the $5 on chalky paper, and five of the $10. All are distinguishable and collectable.

SPECIAL ISSUES

1937 (May 12th) Coronation. As Antigua.

S1	4c **green**	£2	3.30
S2	15c **carmine-red**	£5	£2
S3	25c **blue**	£6	2.40
S1/3	**set** (3)	11.50	£7
SP S1/3	**specimen perf** (3)	£200	†

1941 (Feb. 26th) Centenary of British Occupation. 2c (street scene); 4c ('Empress of Japan' and junk); 5c (University); 15c (harbour); 25c (Hong Kong bank); $1 (China Clipper and seaplane). Designer, W. E. Jones. (Recess) Bradbury, Wilkinson. Perf. 13½ x 13 or 13 x 13½ (C). Sheets 10 x 6 or 6 x 10.

S4	2c **orange and chocolate**	2.50	1.20
S5	4c **purple-mauve and carmine**	£3	2.40
S6	5c **black and green**	1.25	.30
S7	15c **black and scarlet**	2.75	1.20
S8	25c **chocolate and deep blue**	£6	£4
S9	$1 **ultramarine and brown-orange**	£20	5.75
S4/9	**set** (6)	£32	£13
SP S4/9	**specimen perf** (6)	£350	†

Numbers printed - S4, 1,500,000; S5, 1,000,000; S6 4,500,000; S7, 1,600,000; S8, 720,000; S9, 480,000.

1946 (Aug. 29th) Victory. Designer, E. I. Wynne-Jones. (Recess) De La Rue. Perf. 13 x 12¾ (C). Sheets 6 x 10.

S10 30c **scarlet-red and**
        deep blue   1.25   £1
    a scarlet-vermilion
        and blue   £250   £150
    b extra stroke   £45   £35
S11 $1 **scarlet-red and sepia** £2   .45
    a extra stroke   £60   £35
SPS10/11 **specimen pair**   £150   †

S10b, 11a R1/2 extra stroke at top left
of Chinese character in left-hand
shield. Both values from this position
can be found without the variety.

1948 (Dec. 22nd) Silver Wedding. As Aden.

S12 10c **purple**   1.50   .60
    a toe to 'N' of 'KONG'   £40   £35
S13 $10 **rose-carmine**   £175   £65

S12a R2/9 the left stroke of the
'N' of 'KONG' has an extension.
This variety is present on the
imperforate proof sheet in the British Library.

1949 (Oct. 10th) U.P.U. As Aden.

S14 10c **dull violet**   £2   .60
S15 20c **carmine**   £7   2.70
S16 30c **dull indigo**   £7   2.70
S17 80c **magenta**   £17   £5
S14/17   **set** (4)   £30   £10

POSTAGE DUE STAMPS

**1938 (Feb.) - 50 (typo) De La Rue. Watermark
Multiple Script CA, sideways. Perf. 14. Sheets
10 x 10.**

PD1 1c **light brown** (2/38)   1.25   2.25
PD2 2c **grey** (2/38)   £6   £6
     a slate (rough) (2/46)   £9   £7
PD3 4c **orange** (2/38)   £8   £4
     a deep orange (rough)(4/46) £10   £5
PD4 6c **scarlet** (2/38)   £4   3.50
     a rose-red (30/8/50)   £5   £5
PD5 8c **deep chestnut**
        (rough) (26/2/46)   2.50   £22
     a chestnut (/50)   2.50   £20
PD6 10c **violet** (2/38)   £15   .30
     a bright violet (/50)   £15   .30
PD7 20c **black** (rough)
        (26/2/46)   £8   £2
     a black (/50)   5.50   £2
PD8 50c **deep blue** (19/8/47)   £24   £10
PD1/8   **set** (8)   £60   £45
SP PD2/8 **specimen perf** (7)   £300   †

The above are on ordinary paper. The 'rough
paper' issues are unmistakable, being printed on
paper that is extremely rough to the touch and
with a woolly impression. Stamps similar in
design, but on chalky paper, appeared from
March 1956 onwards.

PD1 Earlier stamps with sideways watermark,
from 1931, were in deeper shades.

POSTAL FISCAL

**1938 (Jan. 11th) (typo) De La Rue. Revenue
stamp, authorised for postal use for a period
of eleven days. Watermark Multiple Script
CA. Perf. 14. Sheets 120 - two panes, each 6
x 10.**

F15 5c **dull green**   £40   £8

The authorisation for postal use of this stamp
was necessitated by a shortage of the KG V 5ct.
Forged cancellations are known.

Numbers sold (Jan. 11th-21st, 1938) - 170,709,
of which many were used for fiscal purposes.

GERMAN PROPAGANDA LABELS

The 1944 German imitations of the G.B. 1937
Definitives ½d to 3d (see after Great Britain for
details) were also overprinted in black
"LIQUIDATION/OF EMPIRE/HONG KONG" within
a vertical rectangular frame.

INDIA

1932-41 Further printings of KG V 1¼a definitive of 1932. Printers (offset-litho) Security Printing Press, Nasik. Watermark Multiple Star. Perf. 14.

G55 1a 3p	**mauve** (/32)	.50	.10
a	Die II	£1	.55
b	double print (Die II)	£20	£20

G55 exists in three sizes, with minor variations due to paper shrinkage:
(i)   18.7mm wide: 1932 Sheet printing (no 'Jubilee' line) Die I.
(ii) 18.25mm wide: 1932 Booklet printing (with 'Jubilee' line) Die I.
(iii) 18.4mm wide: 1941 Sheet printing (no 'Jubilee' line) Die II.

The dies are distinguishable as follows:

DIE I (1932) Thin letters. Large coloured areas enclosed within letters O,A,R,P.

DIE II (1941) Thick letters. Smaller coloured areas enclosed within letters O,A,R,P.

Nos. 1/52 are printed (typo) by Security Printing Press, Nasik, on paper watermarked Multiple Star, except for lithographed values noted.

1937 (23rd August - Dec 15th). Designs, 3p - 1a and 1r - 25r (portrait of King-Emperor); 2a - 14a (methods of mail transport). Perforations; 3p - 14a, perf 13¾ x 14 (C); other values, perf. 13¾ (C). Sheets: 1-4, 16 x 20; 5-13, 8 x 20; 14-19, 120 - six panes, each 5 x 4.

1	3p	**slate**	.50	.10
2	½a	**red-brown**	£3	.10
		a watermark inverted		
3	9p	**deep green** (23/8/37)	£4	.35
		a watermark inverted		
4	1a	**carmine** (23/8/37)	.75	.10
		a tete-beche vert. pair	1.75	1.25
		ba watermark inverted	£1	£1
5	2a	**vermilion**	3.50	.20
		a watermark inverted	-	-
6	2½a	**violet**	.75	.15
		a watermark inverted		£18
7	3a	**yellow-green**	£4	.20
		a watermark inverted		£18
8	3½a	**blue**	£3	.30
		a watermark inverted		
9	4a	**deep brown**	£6	.15
		a watermark inverted		£18
10	6a	**greenish blue**	£7	.50
11	8a	**violet-slate**	3.50	.30
		a watermark inverted		
12	12a	**deep crimson**	£9	.65
		a watermark inverted		
14	1r	**violet-grey and light brown**	.75	.10
		a watermark inverted		
15	2r	**reddish purple and brown**	3.50	.20
		a deep purple and brown	3.50	.20
		b watermark inverted	£24	-
16	5r	**deep green and deep blue**	£14	.30
		a watermark inverted	£40	-
17	10r	**violet-purple and red-claret**	£10	.50
		a watermark inverted	-	£45
18	15r	**chocolate and deep green**	£45	£42
		a watermark inverted	£100	£80
19	25r	**slate-violet and purple-violet**	£70	£15
		a watermark inverted		
1/19		**set** (18)	£170	£55

4a this variety is from sheets of stamps which were prepared for making up into booklets. It can be found with or without interpanneau margin between the tête-beche stamps.

A postal forgery of the 1r (No 14) was made in Nepal and used only from the Indian Embassy in Khatmandu. It was lithographed and perf. 11½ on unwatermarked paper, and is 1mm taller than the genuine stamps.

Original printings of the 1½a and 3a were printed offset-litho without Jubilee Lines. Later printings were typo, with Jubilee Lines. The general appearance of litho printings is clean with distinct fine lines, whereas typo has a fuzzy appearance with thicker lines which tend to run together. Five points provide positive identification on both values:-

Lytho   Typo

1940-3 3a -12a Designs 3p-12a King-Emperor against a white background, 14a mail plane and portrait. Designer, T I Archer. Perf. 13¾ x 14 (C). Sheets 20-32 16 x 20, 32a 8 x 20.

20	3p **slate** (1/12/41)		.15	.10
	a watermark inverted		£5	-
21	½a **purple** (1/10/41)		.45	.10
	a watermark inverted		-	£10
22	9p **green** (16/8/41)		.45	.10
	a watermark inverted		-	£12
23	1a **rose-carmine** (1/4/43)		.60	.10
	a watermark inverted		-	£14
24	1a3p **bistre** (1/2/41)		.40	.10
	a watermark inverted		-	-
25	1½a **slate-purple** (litho) (20/5/42)		£2	.25
	a watermark inverted		-	-
	b slate-purple (typo) (/43)		.60	.15
	ba watermark inverted		£10	
26	2a **vermilion** (15/5/41)		.60	.10
	a watermark inverted		£22	£12
27	3a **bright violet** (litho) (5/1/41)		4.50	.25
	a bright violet (typo) (/43)		£2	.10
	b watermark inverted		-	£8
28	3½a **blue** (15/5/41)		.55	.45
	a watermark inverted		-	-
29	4a **brown** (15/5/41)		.55	.10
	a watermark inverted			
30	6a **greenish blue** (15/5/41)		1.75	.10
	a watermark inverted		-	£26
31	8a **violet-slate** (15/5/41)		.70	.20
	a watermark inverted		-	£30
32	12a **deep crimson** (15/5/41)		£3	.60
32a	14a **purple** (15/10/40)		£10	1.20
20/32a	**set** (14)		£19	£3

1. Litho: The outline of the King's nose is thin and clean.
   Typo: The line is thicker and ragged and in some cases the tip of the nose becomes pointed.
2. Litho: The background colour of the value tablets and "INDIAN POSTAGE" panel is evenly inked with very few blemishes or spots.
   Typo: The background colour has numerous small white specks in it. (These can vary considerably).
3. Litho: The base line is thin and has sharp edges.
   Typo: The base line is thick and has ragged edges.
4. Litho: The inside frame lines of the rows of pearls thick and clean.
   Typo: The lines are thick and ragged.
5. Litho: The curves on frame lines remain an even width.
   Typo: They bulge and get thicker at the top of curve.

1946 (Aug 8th) No. 24 surcharged.

33	3p/1a3p **bistre**	.10	.10

1949 (Aug 15th)-51. Designs, architectural and archaeological subjects. Designers, T.I. Archer and I.M. Das. Low values typo, rupee stamps offset-litho. 3p-2a, 1r-10r perf. 13¾ x 14; 2½a-12a perf. 13¾; 15r perf. 13. Watermark Multiple Star, sideways on 6p, 1r and 10r. Sheets; 3p - 12a, 16 x 20; 1r - 10r, 8 x 20 or 20 x 8; 15r, 8 x 16.

34	3p **deep slate-violet**	.10	.10
	a slate-violet (/51)	.20	.10
	b watermark inverted	-	-
35	6p **purple-brown**	.15	.10
	a red-brown (/51)	.30	.10
	b watermark inverted (sideways)	£1	.75
36	9p **pale green**	.20	.10
	a watermark inverted	-	£45
37	1a **turquoise** (Die I)	.30	.10
	a greyish turquoise (Die I)	£2	.10
	b watermark inverted	-	-
38	1a **turquoise** (Die 2) (15/7/50)	£2	.10
	a watermark inverted	-	£14
39	2a **carmine-red**	.40	.10
	a watermark inverted	£16	£1
40	2½a **maroon-lake** (30/4/51)	1.50	£2
41	3a **deep vermilion**	.85	.10
	a watermark inverted	-	£55
42	3½a **bright blue** (30/4/51)	.75	£3
43	4a **maroon-lake**	£2	.30
	a watermark inverted	£18	£2
44	4a **bright blue** (30/4/51)	£3	.10
	a watermark inverted	-	-
45	6a **violet**	£1	.10
	a watermark inverted	£2	1.25
46	8a **turquoise-green**	.85	.10
	a watermark inverted	-	£45
47	12a **dull blue**	£1	.20
	a watermark inverted	£14	£2
48	1r **purple-violet and green**	£8	.10
	a watermark inverted (sideways)	£15	.75
	b double print (frame)	-	-
49	2r **claret and purple-violet**	£7	.15
	a watermark inverted	£45	£2
50	5r **grey-green and maroon**	£14	£1
	a watermark inverted	£60	2.50
51	10r **maroon and dark blue**	£32	6.50
	a double print (centre)	-	-
	b maroon and light blue (/52?)	£50	3.50
	ba watermark sideways-inverted	£110	£45
52	15r **chocolate and maroon-lake**	£8	£15
	a watermark inverted	-	-
34/52	**set** (19)	£75	£23

Sideways watermarks - The normal has the top point of the star to the left on the 6p and right on the 1r and 10r, as seen from the back of the stamp.

37 the design wrongly depicted Bodhisattva with left arm outstretched. This was rectified in Die 2 (38) and the right arm is outstretched instead.

Lithographed postal forgeries of Nos. 46 and 48 exist, perf. 11 x 12½ on unwatermarked paper.

SPECIAL ISSUES

Printed offset-litho by Security Printing Press, Nasik, unless otherwise stated. Watermark Multiple Star.

1946 Victory. Designers, Dorothy Cronan and Edward Johangs. Perf. 13 (C). Sheets 8 x 16.

S1	9p **green** (8/2/46)	.35	.90
S2	1½a **purple-violet** (2/1/46)	.15	.20
	a watermark inverted	-	£20
S3	3½a **blue** (2/1/46)	.45	.75
S4	12a **dull crimson** (8/2/46)	.70	.75
S1/4	**set** (4)	1.50	2.35

1947 Dominion Status. Designs, 1½a (Asokan capital); 3a (National Flag); 12a (aeroplane). Perf. 14 x 13¾ (C). Sheets: S5, 12 x 12; S6, 8 x 12; S7, 8 x 20.

S5	1½a **grey-green** (15/12/47)	.10	.10
S6	3½a **orange, green and blue** (21/11/47)	.50	1.35
	a watermark inverted	£10	£10
	b teardrop flaw	£18	£19
S7	12a **ultramarine** (15/12/47)	£1	1.65
S5/7	**set** (3)	.75	2.80

S6b R5/6 a marked flaw appears above the 7.

1948 (May 20th) Inauguration of India-U.K. Air Service. Design, Lockheed Constellation. Perf. 13¾ x 14 (C). Sheets 8 x 20.

S8   12a black and ultramarine   .75   1.80

1948 (Aug. 15th) First Anniversary of Indian Independence. Design, Mahatma Gandhi. Printers (photo) on granite, chalk-surfaced paper by Courvoisier, Switzerland. Perf 11¾ (C). No watermark. Sheets 10 x 5.

S9	1½a chocolate-brown	2.50	.45
S10	3½a dull violet	£3	1.65
S11	12a greyish green	£4	1.50
S12	10r brown and lake	£60	£45
S9/12	set (4)	£65	£45

Number issued - 1½a, 24,680,924; 3½a, 2,226,324; 12a, 3,096,824; 10r, 229,974.

1949 (Oct. 10th) U.P.U. Design, Asokan Capital and Globe. Perf. 13¼ x 13 (C). Sheets 8 x 16.

S13	9p myrtle-green	£1	£2
S14	2a deep rose	£1	1.80
S15	3½a blue	£1	1.80
S16	12a maroon-lake	1.50	1.80
S13/16	set (4)	£4	6.50

1950 (Jan. 20th) Inauguration of Republic. Designs, allegorical scenes. Designers, D J Keymer and Co. Perf. 13¼ x 13 (C). Sheets 8 x 16.

S17	2a rose-carmine	£1	.30
	a watermark inverted	£18	£3
S18	3½a ultramarine	1.25	2.40
S19	4a violet	1.25	.75
S20	12a dull lake	1.75	1.50
	a watermark inverted	£24	5.75
S17/20	set (4)	4.75	4.50

Number issued 2a, 19,667,712; 3½a, 1,171,200; 4a, 6,674,048; 12a, 2,483,968.

1951 (Jan. 13th) Centenary of Geological Survey of India. Design, Stegodon ganesa. Perf. 13¼ x 13 (C). Sheets 8 x 16.

S21   2a black and claret   £1   .75

1951 (Mar. 4th) First Asian Games. Perf 14 x 13¾ (C). Sheets 20 x 8.

S22	2a claret and red-orange	.50	.60
S23	12a chocolate and blue	2.25	1.35

1952 (Oct. 1st) Indian Saints and Poets.
Designs, 9p Kabir; 1a Tulsidas; 2a Meera; 4a
Surdas; 4½a Ghalib; 12a Tagore. (Photo).
Perf. 14 x 13¾ (C). Sheets 160; 2 panes, each
8 x 10.

S24	9p emerald-green	.15	.35
S25	1a carmine-red	.15	.15
S26	2a orange-red	.75	.20
S27	4a blue	1.25	.35
S28	4½a magenta	.25	.75
S29	12a deep brown	£2	.60
S24/29	set (6)	£5	2.20

OFFICIAL STAMPS

1941 CW G55a overprinted SERVICE.

GO39b	1a3p mauve (Die II)	-	-

1937-47 Issue of 1937 overprinted SERVICE.

O1	½a red-brown (12/3/38)	8.50	.60
O2	9p deep green (5/10/37)	8.50	.60
O3	1a carmine (1/11/37)	1.75	.10
O4	1r violet-grey and light brown (25/4/38)	.25	.30
O5	2r reddish purple and brown (25/4/38)	.85	1.50
	a deep purple and brown (/47)	.85	1.50
	b watermark inverted	-	£25
O6	5r deep green and deep blue (10/10/38)	£3	4.25
	a watermark inverted	-	£40
O7	10r violet-purple and red-claret (29/9/39)	£7	£6
	a watermark inverted	£65	£40
O1/O7	set (7)	£27	£12

1939 KGV Official Stamp (GO39: Die 1),
surcharged, with bars obliterating original
value.

O8	1a/1¼a red-purple (20/4/39)	£6	.15
	a watermark inverted	-	£4

1939 (June 1st) - 42 perf. 13¾ x 14 (C). Sheets
16 x 20.

O9	3p slate	.30	.10
O10	½a red-brown	£4	.10
O11	½a deep purple (1/10/42)	.15	.10
O12	9p green	.15	.10
O13	1a rose-carmine	.15	.10
O14	1a3p bistre (2/6/41)	1.75	.40
	a watermark inverted	-	-
O15	1½a slate-purple (1/9/42)	.30	.10
	a watermark inverted	-	-
O16	2a vermilion	.30	.10
	a watermark inverted	-	-
O17	2½a purple-violet	.35	.75
O18	4a deep brown	.30	.10
O19	8a violet-slate	.45	.20
O9/O19	set (11)	7.50	1.50

1948 (Aug.5th) CW S9-12 overprinted
'SERVICE', for use by the Governor-General's
Secretariat.

O19a	1½a chocolate-brown	£25	£25
O19b	3½a dull violet	£775	£500
O19c	12a greyish green	£2500	£1600
O19d	10r brown and lake	£20000	-

Nos O19a-d Forged overprints of all values exist
and an expert committee certificate should be
obtained for the higher values.

O19a exists with genuine overprint, but with
backdated cancellation struck after the issue
was withdrawn.

Number overprinted 1½a, 15,950; 3½a, 1,350;
12a, 250; 10r, 20.

Three sheets of each overprinted value were officially reprinted for the 1954 Centenary Exhibition.

1950 (Jan. 2nd) - 51. Typo, 3p-8a (small format), perf. 13½ x 14 (C). Sheets 16 x 20. Litho, 1r-10r (large format), perf. 13¾ (C). Watermark Multiple Star. Sheets 1r - 5r 11 x 14; 10r 10 x 12.

O20	3p **blackish violet** (1/7/50)	.10	.10
O21	6p **deep chocolate** (1/7/50)	.15	.10
O22	9p **deep emerald-green** (1/7/50)	.60	.10
O23	1a **deep turquoise** (1/7/50)	.60	.10
O24	2a **crimson** (1/7/50)	.80	.10
	a watermark inverted	-	-
O25	3a **vermilion** (1/7/50)	£2	1.50
O26	4a **deep lake** (1/7/50)	£3	.15
O26a	4a **deep blue** (1/10/51)	.25	.10
O27	6a **purple-violet** (1/7/50)	£2	1.20
O28	8a **cinnamon-brown** (1/7/50)	£1	.10
	a watermark inverted	£12	-
O29	1r **purple-violet**	1.50	.10
	a watermark inverted	-	-
O30	2r **lake-red**	.50	.60
O31	5r **grey-green**	£1	1.20
O32	10r **maroon-brown**	1.75	£15
O20/32	**set (14)**	£13	£18

The rupee values later appeared with watermark Asokan Capital. The 10r with this watermark is quite common in used condition and is often wrongly offered as CW O32.

BOOKLET PANES

P1	1a3p **CW G55** pane of 4	-	-
P2	1a **CW 4** pane of 4	-	-

see notes after G55.

STAMP BOOKLET

Booklets were made up by the Security Printing Press, Nasik.

B20	1r **1937 brick-red cover,** stitched (black thread) P2 x 4	£250	-

INDIAN NATIONAL ARMY

In anticipation of the 'liberation' of India by the Japanese, Subhas Chandra Bhose (leader of the Independence Movement) arranged for the printing at the Government Printing Bureau in Berlin of stamps inscribed 'Azad Hind' (Free India). Some 80,000 sets (to 12a) and only 4,500 of the R1 + R2 of these unissued stamps came on to the market after the war. Very few of the R1 + R2 survived.

1943 Designer, Von Axster Heudtlass. Printed (photo) in sheets of 100 (10 x 10). No watermark. Imperf. or Perf. 10½ (anna values). R1 + R2 imperf only. Prices for mint examples.

A1	½a **green**	2.50	-
A2	1a **carmine**	2.50	-
A3	2½a **orange**	2.50	-
A4	1a+1a **brown**	2.50	-
A5	2a+2a **carmine**	2.50	-
A6	2½a+2½a **blue**	2.50	-
A7	3a+3a **red**	2.50	-
A8	8a+12a **deep violet**	2.50	-
A9	12a+R1 **magenta**	2.50	-
A10	R1+R2 **black**	£140	-
A11	R1+R2 **black and orange**	£140	-
A12	R1+R2 **slate black, orange and green**	£140	-
A1-9	**set (9)**	£18	-

A1-3 (500,000 each) are believed to have been intended for use in the Andaman and Nicobar Islands. A4-9 (1,000,000 each) and A10-12 (13,500 total) were intended for use in India.

Although these stamps were never valid for postal use, A1-9 are nevertheless known used on covers postmarked 'NETAJI BHAVAN/CALCUTTA 23.1.46'.

Indian Army soldiers, held prisoners of war in Singapore, were coerced into joining the Indian National Army for service with the Japanese in their attempted invasion of India from Burma. Stamps inscribed "CHALO DELHI" ("On to Delhi") were said to have been issued for use by the I.N.A. in the occupied areas of India during the march on Imphal where the Japanese invasion was halted.

1944. Printed typo in Rangoon. No gum. Perf. 11½ or Imperf.

A13	1p (¼a) **plum**	£50	-
A14	1a **green**	£85	-

Forgeries in slightly larger size were made in Calcutta. The 1a value also exists in red, believed to be a proof.

CONVENTION STATES OF INDIA

* Denotes dates when stamps were despatched from Central Stamp Store to Post Office. No records of actual dates of issue were kept.

In recent years there have been many forgeries of Convention States stamps. Forged overprints have been seen, occasionally certified as genuine by expert committees, but these are generally easy to distinguish since either the overprints are crude, being very rough and sometimes not even straight; or the overprint is more convincing, but the edges thereof are rough under a magnifying glass.

As far as cancellations on used stamps are concerned, the discrepancy between the values of used and mint means that forgers have been unable to resist faking postmarks on genuinely-overprinted stamps. Do not purchase the 'better' used Convention States stamps at bargain prices, whether through auction or from a dealer. Bargains in this particular field are rarely what they seem. Whenever practicable, obtain an Expert Committee Certificate or, if buying through auction, obtain an extension from the auctioneer for this purpose.

The King George V values which are included in this listing, issued from 1936 onwards, are inscribed 'POSTAGE', rather than 'POSTAGE & REVENUE'.

CHAMBA

1936-7 Stamps of India (1927-37 issue), watermark multiple star, overprinted 'CHAMBA STATE'.

G1	4a **sage-green** (1936)	3.50	£14
G2	6a **bistre** (watermark inverted)(/37)	£18	£150

1938 Stamps of India (1937 issue), overprinted 'CHAMBA STATE'.

1	3p **slate** (1/9/38)*	6.50	£18
2	½a **red-brown** (1/9/38)*	£1	£12
3	9p **green** (1/9/38)*	£6	£32
4	1a **carmine** (1/9/38)*	1.20	£3
5	2a **vermilion** (27/8/38)*	£5	£14
6	2½a **violet** (17/8/38)*	5.25	£25
7	3a **yellow-green** (27/8/38)*	5.50	£22

8	3½a blue (27/8/38)*	5.50	£24
9	4a deep brown (27/8/38)*	£13	£24
10	6a greenish violet (27/8/38)*	£16	£55
11	8a violet-slate (27/8/28)*	14.50	£50
12	12a deep crimson (27/8/38)*	£11	£50
13	1r violet-grey and light brown (1/9/38)*	£20	£58
14	2r violet-purple and brown (1/9/38)*	£35	£275
15	5r deep green and deep blue (1/9/38)*	£55	£390
16	10r violet-purple and red-claret (1/9/38)*	£90	£650
17	15r chocolate and deep green (1/9/38)*	£100	£875
18	25r slate-violet and purple-violet (1/9/38)*	£140	£975
1/18	set (18)	£480	£3250

1942 (May 7th) As 2 etc., overprinted 'CHAMBA'.

19	½a red-brown	£30	£38
20	1a carmine	£45	£48
22	1r violet-grey and light brown	£12	£55
23	2r reddish purple and brown	£15	£225
24	5r deep green and deep blue	£28	£250
25	10r violet-purple and red-claret	£42	£425
26	15r chocolate and deep green	£90	£725
	a watermark inverted	£275	£950
27	25r slate-violet and purple-violet	£85	£725
19/27	set (8)	£300	£2250

1942-7 Stamps of India (1941-3 issue), overprinted 'CHAMBA'.

28	3p slate (7/5/42)*	.75	4.50
29	½a purple (25/6/43)*	.45	5.50
30	9p green (7/5/42)*	.65	£16
31	1a rose-carmine (25/6/43)*	£1	4.50
32	1½a slate-purple (23/6/43)*	1.20	£12
33	2a vermilion (23/6/43)*	£5	£14
34	3a bright violet (typo) 97/5/42) *	£14	£40
	a bright violet (litho) (23/6/43)*	12.50	£40
35	3½a blue (7/5/42)*	6.50	£38
36	4a brown (7/5/42)*	£9	£12
37	6a greenish blue (7/5/42)*	£10	£35
38	8a violet-slate (7/5/42)*	£11	£40
39	12a deep crimson (7/5/42)*	£14	£55

39a	14a purple (15/10/47)*	8.50	2.50
28/39	set (13)	£72	£280

OFFICIAL STAMPS

1936-1939 watermark Multiple Star. Overprinted 'Chamba State Service'.

GO1	2a vermilion (/39)	£5	£15
GO2	4a sage-green (/36)	£5	£6
GO3	2r carmine and orange (/39)	£18	£220
GO4	5r blue and purple (/39)	£30	£250
GO5	10r green and scarlet (/39)	£45	£250

GO2 measures 18.4 x 21.8 mm, earlier issues measuring 19 x 22.6 mm.

1938-40 Postage stamps of India (1937 issue), overprinted 'CHAMBA STATE SERVICE'.

O1	9p deep green (1/9/38)*	£15	£60
O2	1a carmine (1/9/38)*	£18	£5
O3	1r violet-grey and light brown (12/12/38)*	£175	£650
O4	2r reddish purple and brown (12/12/40)*	£25	£350
O5	5r deep green and deep blue (9/11/39)*	£35	£400
O6	10r violet-purple and red-claret (9/11/39)*	£50	£675
O1/O6	set (6)	£285	£1900

1940-3 Official stamps of India (1939 issue), overprinted 'CHAMBA'.

O7	3p slate (12/12/50)*	.40	£1
O8	½a red-brown (12/12/40)*	£18	£3
O9	½a deep purple (25/6/43)*	.40	£3
O10	9p green (12/12/40)*	£4	£10
	a watermark inverted	£15	£15
O11	1a rose-carmine (23/1/41)*	.60	2.25
O12	1a 3p bistre (15/7/41)*	£60	£17
	a watermark inverted	-	-
O13	1½a slate-purple (25/6/43)*	4.50	6.50
O14	2a vermilion (12/12/40)*	4.50	6.50
O15	2½a purple-violet (23/1/41)*	2.70	£20

O16   4a deep brown
         (12/12/40)*   4.50   £15
O17   8a violet-slate
         (12/12/40)*   £10   £60
      a watermark inverted £10   £60
O7/O17 set (11)   £100   £130

1942 (May 7th) As O3-O6, but overprinted 'CHAMBA SERVICE'.

O18   1r violet-grey and
         light brown   £12   £200
O19   2r reddish purple and
         brown   £22   £250
O20   5r deep green and
         deep blue   £40   £375
O21 10r violet-purple and
         red-claret   £45   £650
O18/O21 set (4)   £110 £1350

GWALIOR

1938-48 Stamps of India (1937) issue, overprinted GWALIOR in English and Hindi.

1   3p slate (26/8/38)*   5.75   .10
2   ½p red-brown (20/6/38)*   5.40   .10
3   9p deep green
         (30/6/39)*   £30   £3
4   1a carmine (28/7/38)*   £5   .15
5   3a yellow-green
         (30/6/39)*   £17   3.50
6   4a deep brown
         (18/6/38)*   £27   2.50
7   6a greenish blue
         (30/6/39)*   2.50   £8
8   1r violet-grey and
         light brown (10/9/42)* 7.50   1.25
9   2r reddish purple and
         brown (17/8/48)*   £30   6.50
10   5r deep green and
         deep blue (17/8/48)*   £19   £30
11   10r violet-purple and
         red-claret (17/8/48)* £19   £35
12   15r chocolate and
         deep green (17/8/48)* £55   £130
13   25r slate-violet and
         purple-violet (17/8/48)* £50 £110
1/13   set (13)   £250   £300

Nasik   Alizah

1942-5 Stamps of India (1941-3 issue), overprinted (Nasik) 'GWALIOR' in English and Hindi.

14   3p slate (26/9/42)*   .30   .10
      a watermark inverted   -   £15
15   ½a purple (20/5/43)*   .60   .10
16   9p green (20/5/42)*   .30   .10
17   1a rose-carmine (20/5/43)* .60 .10
      a double overprint   -   £140
18   1½a slate-purple
         (litho) (10/9/42)*   5.50   1.25
      a slate-purple
         (typo) (20/5/43)*   4.50   .30
19   2a vermilion (26/9/42)* .90   .20
20   3a bright violet
         (litho) (26/9/42)*   9.50   1.20
      a bright violet
         (typo) (20/5/43)   12.50   2.50
      ab overprint double   -   £160
21   4a brown (26/9/42)*   £2   .20
22   6a greenish blue (1/8/45)* 8.50 £22
23   8a violet-slate (3/6/44)* 2.25 £2
24   12a deep crimson (20/5/43)* 3.50 £19
14/24 set (11)   £30   £40

1949 As before but overprinted locally at the Alizah Printing Press.

25   3p slate   1.20   .40
26   ½a purple   1.20   .40
27   1a rose-carmine   £1   .40
28   2a vermilion   £18   1.50
29   3a bright violet   £50   £22
30   4a brown   4.50   2.25
31   6a greenish blue   £40   £50
32   8a violet-slate   £80   £45
33   12a deep crimson   £325 £125
25/33 set (9)   £475   £225

Due to pressure of other work, Nasik was unable to overprint further supplies of stamps, and the work was undertaken at the Gwalior Government Printing Works (Alizah Press). The type used differs from that used in Nasik and the overprint measures 17mm instead of 13mm as previously.

OFFICIAL STAMPS

The official stamps of Gwalior are overprinted in Hindi only.

1937 Postage stamps of India overprinted (in Hindi) 'GWALIOR SERVICE'.

GO1	4a sage-green	.40	.50

1938-47 Postage stamps of India (1937 issue) overprinted (in Hindi) 'GWALIOR SERVICE'.

O1	½a red-brown (5/7/38)*	£4	.25
O2	1a carmine (5/7/38)*	£1	.15
O3	1r violet-grey and light brown (7/8/42)*	£6	£18
O4	2r violet-purple and brown (7/8/42)*	12.50	£85
O5	5r deep green and deep blue (20/5/43)*	£20	£475
O6	10r violet-purple and red-claret (12/7/47)*	£50	£1000
O1/O6	set (6)	£85	£1450

1940-2 Official stamps of India (1939 issue) overprinted (in Hindi) 'GWALIOR'.

O7	3p slate (8/7/40)*	.30	.10
O8	½a red-brown (8/7/40)*	2.50	.20
O9	½a deep purple (15/10/42)*	.30	.10
O10	9p green (15/10/42)*	.45	.45
O11	1a rose-carmine (8/7/40)*	1.50	.10
O12	1a3p bistre (11/2/42)*	£30	1.30
	a watermark inverted	-	£16
O13	1½a slate-purple (10/9/42)*	.75	.30
O14	2a vermilion (8/7/42)*	.75	.30
O15	4a deep brown (7/8/42)*	.75	£2
O16	8a violet-slate (7/8/42)*	£3	6.50
O7/O16	set (10)	£36	£10

1942 KGV stamp of India G55, overprinted in 1933 (in Hindi) 'GWALIOR SERVICE' now surcharged '1A. - 1A.'

O17	1a/1¼a red-purple (Die 1)	£15	£2
	a watermark inverted	£22	5.50

JIND

1937 Stamps of India. Watermark multiple star. Overprinted 'JIND STATE'.

G1	3a6p ultramarine (1937)		2.75	£18
	a watermark inverted		.40	£14
G2	6a bistre (1937)		.50	£16
	a watermark inverted		£5	-

1937 (May 10th) Stamps of India (1937 issue) overprinted 'JIND STATE'.

1	3p slate	£6	£2
2	½a red-brown	.45	£4
3	9p green (5/11/37)*	.45	3.50
4	1a carmine (5/11/37)*	.45	.40
5	2a vermilion	1.10	£17
6	2½a violet	.75	£20
7	3a yellow-green	£4	£18
8	3½a blue	£2	£20
9	4a deep brown	5.75	£17
10	6a greenish blue	3.75	£25
11	8a violet-slate	£3	£20
12	12a deep crimson	1.65	£25
13	1r violet-grey and light brown	7.50	£35
14	2r reddish purple and brown	£9	£110
15	5r deep green and deep blue	£18	£75
16	10r violet-purple and red-claret	£30	£70
17	15r chocolate and deep green	£65	£700
18	25r slate-violet and purple-violet	£375	£875
1/18	set (18)	£475	£1850

1941 (Aug. 7th)* As before, but overprinted 'JIND'.

19	3p slate	8.50	£19
20	½a red-brown	.60	£2
21	9p deep green	£7	£18
22	1a carmine	.60	£5
23	1r violet-grey and light brown	5.50	£23
24	2r violet-purple and brown	£11	£30
25	5r deep green and deep blue	£24	£85
26	10r violet-purple and red-claret	£35	£75
27	15r chocolate and deep green	£80	£140

28	25r **slate-violet and**		
	purple-violet	£40	£300
19/28	**set** (10)	£190	£625

1941-3 Stamps of India (1941-3 issue) overprinted 'JIND'.

29	3p **slate** (11/4/42)*	.30	£1
30	½a **purple** (17/6/43)*	.30	1.50
31	9p **green** (11/4/42)*	.45	£3
32	1a **rose-carmine**		
	(11/4/42)*	.60	£1
33	1a3p **bistre** (7/8/41)*	.60	£4
34	1½a **slate-purple**		
	(litho) (29/8/42)*	£5	3.75
	a slate-purple (typo)	£7	7.50
35	2a **vermilion** (7/8/41)*	1.10	£4
36	3a **bright violet**		
	(litho) (11/4/42)*	£15	£4
	a bright violet (typo)	£20	£9
37	3½a **blue** (7/8/41)*	5.50	£9
38	4a **brown** (7/8/41)*	3.50	£4
40	6a **greenish blue** (7/8/41)*	£4	£13
42	8a **violet-slate** (7/8/41)*	2.50	£12
43	12a **deep crimson** (7/8/41)*	8.50	£14
29/43	**set** (13)	£24	£68

OFFICIAL STAMPS

1937 Postage stamps of India overprinted 'JIND STATE SERVICE'. Watermark multiple Star.

GO1	2a6p **orange**	.80	£16
GO2	6a **bistre**	2.25	-
	a watermark inverted	3.50	£13

1937-40 Postage stamps of India (1937 issue) overprinted 'JIND STATE SERVICE'.

O1	½a **red-brown** (13/12/38)*	£40	.20
O2	9p **deep green** (5/11/37)*	1.25	£13
O3	1a **carmine** (5/11/37) *	£1	.25
O4	1r **violet-grey and**		
	light brown (7/5/40)*	£20	£45
O5	2r **reddish purple and**		
	brown (7/5/40)*	£30	£200
O6	5r **deep green and**		
	deep blue (7/5/40)*	£50	£325
O7	10r **violet-purple and**		
	red-claret (7/5/40)*	£275	£850
O1/O7	**set** (7)	£375	£1300

1939 (Dec. 12th)-43 Official stamps of India (1939 issue), overprinted 'JIND'.

O8	3p **slate**	.35	1.50
O9	½a **red-brown**	1.25	.75
O10	½a **deep purple** (17/6/43)*	.35	.20
O11	9p **green**	£2	£10
O12	1a **rose-carmine**	2.25	.15
O13	1½a **slate-purple** (12/9/42)*	5.50	1.50
O14	2a **vermilion**	£5	.25
	a watermark inverted	£8	£3
O15	2½a **purple-violet**	£3	7.50
O16	4a **deep brown**	£5	£4
O17	8a **violet-slate**	5.50	£6
O8/O17	**set** (10)	£27	£28

1942 (Sept. 18th) As O4-7, but overprinted 'JIND SERVICE'.

O18	1r **violet-grey and**		
	light brown	£10	£45
O19	2r **reddish purple and**		
	brown	£25	£135
O20	5r **deep green and**		
	deep blue	£42	£350
O21	10r **violet-purple and**		
	red-claret	£85	£475
O18/O21	**set** (4)	£145	£900

NABHA

1937 Postage stamps of India overprinted 'NABHA STATE'. Inscribed 'POSTAGE'.

G1	3a **carmine**	2.75	£14
G2	4a **slate-green**	£4	3.75

1938 (June 20th*, unless otherwise indicated), stamps of India (1937 issue), overprinted 'NABHA STATE'.

1	3p **slate**	5.50	£1
2	½a **red-brown**	£4	1.25
3	9p **deep green**	£12	£4
4	1a **carmine**	1.80	.70
5	2a **vermilion**	.75	5.50
6	2½a **violet**	.75	£10
7	3a **yellow-green**	.85	4.50
8	3½a **blue**	.95	£20
9	4a **deep brown**	4.50	£5
10	6a **greenish blue**	£2	£22
11	8a **violet-slate**	1.35	£20
12	12a **deep crimson**	1.50	£20
13	1r **violet-grey and**		
	light brown	7.25	£29

14	2r **reddish purple and brown**	£14	£110
15	5r **deep green and deep blue**	£25	£175
16	10r **violet-purple and red-claret** (16/6/38)*	£36	£330
17	15r **chocolate and deep green** (16/6/38)*	£120	£700
18	25r **slate-violet and purple-violet** (16/6/38)*	£95	£700
	a watermark inverted	£200	£850
1/18	**set** (18)	£300	£1950

1942 (May 30th) As before, but overprinted 'NABHA'.

19	3p **slate**	£25	£4
20	½a **red-brown**	£50	£5
21	9p **deep green**	£7	£12
22	1a **carmine**	7.50	3.25
19/22	**set** (4)	£80	£22

1941-5 stamps of India (1941-3 issue), overprinted 'NABHA'.

23	3p **slate** (2/5/42)*	.75	.60
24	½a **purple** (9/1/43)	1.80	£1
25	9p **green** (2/5/42)*	1.50	£1
26	1a **rose-carmine** (4/7/45)*	.60	3.50
27	1a3p **bistre** (30/5/41)*	.60	£3
28	1½a **slate-purple** (litho) (22/9/42)	1.50	2.25
	a slate-purple (typo) (4/7/42)*	£5	£4
29	2a **vermilion** (18/6/43)*	.65	3.50
30	3a **bright violet** (16/6/43)*	£4	£4
31	3½a **blue** (31/1/44)*	6.50	£50
32	4a **brown** (30/5/41)*	£1	.75
33	6a **greenish blue** (16/6/43)*	8.50	£45
34	8a **violet-slate** (16/6/43)*	£8	£35
35	12a **deep crimson** (16/6/43)*	6.50	£55
23/35	**set** (13)	£38	£185

OFFICIAL STAMPS

1937 Postage stamps of India, overprinted 'NABHA STATE SERVICE'. Inscribed 'POSTAGE'

GO1	4a **sage-green** (1942?)	£16	£2
GO2	8a **reddish purple** (1937)	.80	2.25

1938 (June 20th) Postage stamps of India (1937 issue), overprinted 'NABHA STATE SERVICE'.

O1	9p **deep green**	£3	£3
O2	1a **carmine**	£11	.85

1940-3 Official stamps of India (1939 issue), overprinted 'NABHA'.

O3	3p **slate** (2/5/42)*	.75	1.40
O4	½a **red-brown** (22/8/42)*	.65	.20
O5	½a **deep purple** (16/6/43)*	£4	1.20
O6	9p **green** (10/4/40)*	0.75	.20
O7	1a **carmine** (2/5/42)*	.35	.20
O8	1½a **slate-purple** (22/9/42)*	.40	.30
O9	2a **vermilion** (22/9/42)*	1.35	1.20
	a watermark inverted	£4	£2
O10	4a **deep brown** (22/9/42)*	2.25	2.50
O11	8a **violet-slate** (22/9/42)*	3.50	£18
O3/O11	**set** (9)	12.50	£23

1942 (May 2nd) Postage Stamps of India (1937 issue), overprinted 'NABHA SERVICE'.

O12	1r **violet-grey and light brown**	£5	£35
O13	2r **violet-purple and brown**	£18	£165
O14	5r **deep green and deep blue**	£150	£500
O12/4	**set** (3)	£155	£630

PATIALA

1936 stamps of India overprinted 'PATIALA STATE'. Inscribed 'POSTAGE'

G1	½a **blue-green** (1937)	.60	.20
G2	1a **chocolate** (1936)	.85	.15
G3	2a **vermilion** (1936)	.30	£1

1937-8 (June 1st) Stamps of India (1937 issue), overprinted 'PATIALA STATE'.

1	3p **slate**	£12	.30
2	½a **red-brown**	4.75	.40
3	9p **deep green** (16/10/37)*	£3	.70
4	1a **carmine** (16/10/37)*	1.65	.20
5	2a **vermilion**	£1	6.75
6	2½a **violet**	3.25	£20
7	3a **yellow-green**	3.50	6.50
8	3½a **blue**	£4	£24

9	4a deep brown	£14	£15
10	6a greenish blue	£15	£50
11	8a violet-slate	£16	£36
12	12a deep crimson	£15	£58
13	1r violet-grey and light brown	£16	£36
14	2r reddish purple and brown	£18	£90
15	5r deep green and deep blue	£23	£200
16	10r violet-purple and red-claret	£30	£350
17	15r chocolate and deep green	£80	£575
18	25r slate-violet and purple-violet	£90	£575
1/18	set (18)	£320	£1850

1941 (May 29th)*-46 As before, but overprinted 'PATIALA'.

19	3p slate	6.50	£2
20	½a red-brown	£4	1.60
21	9p deep green	£250	£6
	a watermark inverted	-	-
22	1a carmine	£15	1.75
23	1r violet-grey and light brown (22/6/46)*	£9	£65
19/23	set (5)	£260	£70

1942-5 Stamps of India (1941-3 issue), overprinted 'PATIALA'.

24	3p slate (2/5/42)*	2.40	.15
25	½a purple (29/4/43)*	2.40	.15
	a overprint omitted in pair with normal	£6000	-
26	9p green (2/5/42)*	.90	.15
	a overprinted omitted in pair with normal	£3250	-
27	1a rose-carmine (12/4/45)*	.60	.10
28	1a3p bistre (29/5/41)*	£1	£3
29	1½a slate-purple (litho) (10/9/42)*	£10	£5
	a slate-purple (typo)	£7	£3
30	2a vermilion (12/4/44)*	5.50	.35
31	3a bright violet (12/4/44)*	£5	£2
32	3½a blue (12/4/44)*	£12	£32
33	4a brown (12/4/44)*	5.50	3.50
34	6a greenish blue (12/4/44)*	£2	£24
35	8a violet-slate (12/4/44)*	1.80	£12
36	12a deep crimson (17/5/45)*	£14	£70
24/36	set (13)	£55	£135

OFFICIAL STAMPS

1936-39 stamps of India overprinted 'PATIALA STATE SERVICE'. Inscribed 'POSTAGE'

GO1	½a green (1936)	.10	.10
GO2	1a chocolate (1936)	.25	.25
GO3	2a vermilion (1939)	£13	£4
GO4	4a sage-green (1936)	£2	1.25

GO3 measures 18.4 x 21.8 mm, rather than 19 x 22.6 mm.

1937-39 Postage stamps of India (1937 issue), overprinted 'PATIALA STATE SERVICE'.

O1	½a red-brown (1/6/38)*	.45	.20
O2	9p deep green (1/6/38)*	£8	£60
O3	1a carmine (5/11/37)*	.45	.30
O4	1r violet-grey and light brown	.75	£6
O5	2r reddish purple and brown (16/2/39)*	£4	£4
O6	5r deep green and deep blue (16/2/39)*	£12	£60
O1/O6	set (6)	£23	£120

Number issued; O2, 4,800 (15 sheets).

1939-40 KGV stamp of India (G55).

(a) Previously overprinted 'PATIALA STATE/ SERVICE', now surcharged '1A-1A'.

O7	1a/1½a red-purple (Die 1) (/38)	£7	2.50
	a watermark inverted	6.50	2.25

(b) Previously overprinted 'PATIALA STATE', now further overprinted 'SERVICE' and surcharged '1A-1A' (in one operation).

O8	1a/1½a red-purple	£6	2.25
	a watermark inverted	£6	£3

In O7 the 'S' and final 'E' of 'SERVICE' (which measures 9½ mm) always lie under the 'T' of 'PATIALA' and the 'A' of 'STATE' respectively; and the position of the surcharge varies in relation to the previous overprint.

In O8 'SERVICE' measures 8¾ mm, and always appears in constant position relative to the surcharge, but varying in relation to the position of the previous overprint.

1939-44 Official stamps of india (1939 issue) overprinted 'PATIALA'.

O9	3p **slate** (10/6/40)*	£1	.10
O10	½a **red-brown** (12/12/39)*	£3	.10
	a watermark inverted	-	£15
O11	½a **deep purple** (29/4/42)*	.60	.10
O12	9p **green** (30/10/39)*	.60	.35
	a watermark inverted	-	-
O13	1a **carmine** (30/10/39)*	£2	.10
O14	1a3p **bistre** (18/6/41)*	.75	.20
O15	1½a **slate-purple** (7/7/44)*	£4	.90
O16	2a **vermilion** (10/6/40)*	£6	.25
	a watermark inverted	£12	-
O17	2½a **purple-violet** (5/10/40)*	2.25	.70
O18	4a **deep brown** (29/4/43)*	£1	1.75
O19	8a **violet-slate** (7/7/44)*	£3	£6
O9/O19	**set** (11)	£22	£9

1943-44 As O4-6, but overprinted 'PATIALA SERVICE'.

O20	1r **violet grey and light brown** (29/4/43)*	£3	£9
O21	2r **violet-purple and brown** (7/7/44)*	£8	£60
O22	5r **deep green and deep blue** (7/7/44)*	£12	£78
O20/O22	**set** (3)	£20	£130

Introduction

Please read the introduction. It's quite short, and is there to help you use the catalogue.

BARWANI

There were eight settings of the issue; four 'narrow', width 21½ - 23mm and height 25-27½mm; one medium, width 26½mm and height 31mm; three wide, width 23-23½mm and height 29-30mm. Measurements include the borders around the design.

All the stamps listed were issued in booklets, in panes of four. The setting measurements given refer to the vertical distance between the stamp impressions. Pairs of CW 5 and CW 10 are shown above.

1933-1941 Design, Rana Ranjit Singh. Various portraits. ¼a - 2a 'BARWANI POSTAGE' at left , 4a 'BARWANI STATE' at base.

C - Narrow setting (3-4½mm). Thick, cream surfaced wove paper.

11	¼a black	3.75	£65
12	½a blue-green	7.50	£28
	a yellowish green (1941)	7.50	£25
13	1a brown (shade)	£18	£25
14	4a sage-green	£35	£90

1932-1947 (Oct.) Design Rana Devi Singh. Medium to thick wove paper. 'BARWANI STATE' at top.

A - Close setting (2½-4½mm). Perf 11, 12 or compound (1932-1941).

1	¼a slate	£2	£20
2	½a blue-green	£3	£20
3	1a brown	£3	£20
	a imperf between horizontal pair	£1250	-
4	2a purple (shades)	£3	£38
5	4a olive-green	4.50	£38

B - Wide setting (6-7mm). Perf 11 (1945-47).

6	¼a slate	3.75	£28
7	½a blue-green	£4	£20
8	1a brown	£10	£20
	a chocolate (perf 8½) 1947	£10	£45
9	2a rose-carmine (1945)	£325	£550
10	4a olive-green	£20	£42

D - Wide setting (7-10mm). Medium to thick wove paper (1939-1947).

15	¼a black	£4	£35
16	½a yellowish green (1945)	£4	£36
17	1a brown (shades)	£12	£25
	a Perf 8½, 5mm (1947)	£10	£45
18	2a bright purple (1939)	£85	£350
19	2a rose-carmine (1945)	£20	£125
20	4a sage-green	£28	£60
	a pale sage-green	£12	£40

There were two 'narrow' settings, 25mm wide x 29mm high and five 'wide' settings, width 26½ - 31mm and height 31½ - 36mm. (17a was in a 'medium' setting, width 26½mm x 31mm.)

E - 1938 perf 11.

20   1a **brown**   £35   £70

Stamps printed in red with designs similar to 1a and 4a were intended for fiscal use.

BOOKLETS

The 'Times of India' press made 9 printings of these booklets from 1932-47, usually containing eight panes of 4. All were stapled at left.

1941 Buff card cover, inscribed 'Barwani State Postage Stamps' booklet value in brackets and number and value of stamps. 4 panes with margins at left only. Stapled.

Booklet size 59mm x 55mm.

B1   8a ¼a (No.1) x 32   £900   -
B2   1r ½a (No. 2) x 32   £1100   -
B3   2r 1a (No. 3) x 32
      (green cover)   £1100   -
B4   4r 2a (No. 4) x 32   £450   -
B5   8r 4a (No. 5) x 32   £675   -

B1, B4 The second issue of each was in uninscribed covers.

Booklet size 63mm x 60mm.

B6   1r ½a (No. 12a) x 32   £1000   -

Booklet size 73mm x 72mm with blue cover.

B7   8r 4a (No. 19) x 32   £1300   -

1947 Grey tissue cover inscribed '32 Stamps Value ...' Panes of 4 with margins all around. Stapled at left.

Booklet size 70mm x 95mm.

B8   1r ½a (No. 6) x 32   £550   -
B9   2r 1a (No. 8) x 32   £1100   -
B10   8r 4a (No. 10) x 32   £1000   -

Booklet size 76mm x 95mm.

B11   8a ¼a (No. 15) x 32   £850   -
B12   4r 2a (No. 18) x 32   £900   -
B13   8r 4a (No. 19a) x 32   £450   -

1947 Buff paper cover with violet handstamp inscribed '32 Stamps Value Rs2/-'. Panes of 4 with margins all round. Stitched (with twine) at left.

Booklet size 71mm x 69mm.

B14   2r 1a (No. 8a) x 32   £500   -

Booklet size 71mm x 73mm.

B15   2r 1a (No. 16a) x 32   £400   -

1947 Grey tissue cover inscribed '32 Stamp value As 8'. Panes of 4 with margins all round. Stapled at left.

Booklet size 70mm x 75mm.

B16   8a ¼a (No. 6) x 32   £250   -

Booklet size 85mm x 75mm.

B17   8a ¼a (No. 15) x 32   £300   -

Barwani became part of Madhya Bharat by 1st July 1948.

BHOPAL

The basic Postage stamps of Bhopal were made obsolete in 1908. All 1935-49 issues were overprinted or inscribed 'SERVICE'.

OFFICIAL

1935-1936 Arms of Bhopal stamps, surcharged in figures or words of various colours and with 'SERVICE' overprints.

Value in figures;

O1	¼a/½a **yellow-green** (R)	£24	£10
	a surcharge inverted	£150	£65
O2	¼a/2a **ultramarine** (R)	£22	£15
	a surcharge inverted	£150	£60
O3	¼a/4a **chocolate**(R)	£800	£250
O4	¼a/4a **chocolate** (Black)	£60	£20

Value in words;

O5	3p/½a **yellow-green** (R)	£3	2.75
	a 'THEEE PIES'	£58	£40
	b 'THRFE PIES'	£58	£40
	c surcharge inverted	£60	£30
O6	3p/2a **ultramarine** (R)	3.25	£3
	a surcharge inverted	£60	£30
	b 'THEEE PIES'	£60	£38
	ba as above, surcharge inverted	£550	£450
	c 'THRFE' PIES	£60	£38
	ca as above, surcharge inverted	£550	£450
O7	3p/4a **chocolate** (R)	£120	£50
	a 'THEEE PIES'	£600	£400
	b 'THRFE PIES'	£600	£400
O8	3p/4a **chocolate** (Black)	1.75	2.40
	a 'THRER PIES'	£300	£170
	b 'FHREE PIES'	£350	£250
	c 'THREE PISE'	£550	£400
	d 'THREE PIFS'	£300	£170
O9	1a/½a **yellow-green** (V)	£4	1.10
	a surcharge inverted	£55	£35
	b inverted N	£65	£48
	ba as above, surcharge inverted	£550	£400
O10	1a/2a **ultramarine** (R)	1.60	1.50
	a surcharge inverted	£65	£30
	b inverted N	£60	£42
	ba as above, surcharge inverted	£550	£400
O11	1a/2a **ultramarine** (V)	£40	£42
	a surcharge inverted	£70	£70

	b inverted N	£500	£500
	ba as above, surcharge inverted	£950	£1000
O12	1a/2a **ultramarine** (Black)	.50	£2
	a 'ONE ANNO'	£1750	-
O13	1a/4a **chocolate** (Blue)	£5	3.75
	a inverted N	£95	£65
	b perf 14	£10	£5
	ba inverted N	£200	£75

Vertical se-tenant pairs, upper stamp surcharged in figures, lower stamp surcharged in words;

O14	¼a/½a (**O1, O5**) (R)	£38	£18
	a surcharge inverted	£375	£160
O15	¼a2a, 3p/2a (**O2, O6**) (R)	£35	£24
	a surcharge inverted	£375	£150
O16	¼a/4a, 3p/4a (**O3, O7**) (R)	£1300	£450
O17	¼a/4a, 3p/4a (**O4, O8**) (Black)	£90	£40

O1-17 were printed together in sheets, giving rise to the various combinations listed above.

O5a, 6b, 7a, 'THEE PIES' R7/10
O5b, 6c, 7b 'THRFE PIES' R10/6
O8a 'THRFR PIES' R8/2
O8b 'FHREE PIES' R3/10
O8c 'THREE PISE' R10/10
O8d 'THREE PIFS' R7/9
O9b-13ba inverted first 'N' R4/5
O12a 'ONE ANNO' position not known

1935-39 Designer T. I. Archer. Printed (Litho) by the Indian Government Printing Works, Nasik. Inscribed 'Bhopal Govt. Postage', overprinted 'SERVICE', 13½mm, perf 13½.

O18	1a3p **blue and claret**	£3	1.20

As above, printed (typo) by the Bhopal Government Printing Works. Overprinted 'SERVICE', 11mm, perf 12.

O19	1a6p **blue and claret** (1937)	£2	.75
	a imperf between pair	£160	£180
	b overprint omitted	£150	£110
	c ovpt. double, one inverted	£400	£400
	d imperf pair	†	£150
	e blue printed double	†	£140

O20 1a6p **claret** (1939) £5 1.25
  a imperf between pair £160 £175
  b overprint omitted - £375
  c ovpt. double, one inverted - £375
  d overprint double - £375

All future issues were printed by the Bhopal Government Printing Works in typography.

1936-1938 Overprinted 'SERVICE', Perf 12.

O21 ¼a **orange** (Br) .70 .45
  a imperf between (vert pair)£140 -
  b imperf between (horiz pair) † £300
  c overprint inverted £350 £250
  d black overprint 6.50 .60
  da overprint inverted † £340
  db overprint double † £250
O22 ½a **yellow** (Br) 3.50 1.10
O23 1a **scarlet** 1.10 .10
  a imperf between (vert pair) † £240
  b imperf between (horiz pair) £120 £110
  c imperf internally
    (block of 4) £350 £350
  d imperf vertically (horiz pair) † £125

1936-1949 Designs; ½a the Moti Mahal; 2a the Moti Masjid; 4a Taj Mahal and Be-Nazir Palaces; 8a Ahmadabad Palace; 1r Rait Ghat. Perf 12. Overprinted 'SERVICE', various settings.

A - 'SERVICE' 13½mm

O24 ½a **purple-brown and yellow-green** .50 .55
  a imperf between (vert pair) † £160
  b imperf between (horz pair) † £190
  c overprint double £220 £130
  d frame doubled £95 £11
  e purple-brown and green (1938) .50 .30

B - 'SERVICE' 11mm

O25 2a **brown and blue** (1937) 1.50 .65

  a imperf between (vert pair) † £270
  b imperf between (horiz pair) † £190
  c overprint inverted £225 £300
  d overprint omitted £300 -
  e pair, with and without ovpt £525 -
  ea as above, ovpt inverted £775 -
O26 2a **green and violet** (1938) £9 .20
  a imperf between (vert pair) † £220
  b imperf between
    (vert strip of 3) £120 £160
  c frame doubled † £240
  d centre doubled † £260
O27 4a **blue and brown** (1937) £3 .40
  a imperf between (horiz pair) † £550
  b overprint omitted † £240
  c overprint double † £120
  d centre doubled † £320
  e blue and reddish brown (1938) 2.75 .40
  ea frame doubled † £240
O28 8a **bright purple and blue** (1938) 4.50 1.75
  a imperf between (vert pair) † £340
  b overprint omitted † £130
  c overprint double † £125
  d imperf vert (horiz pair)
    and ovpt omitted † £240
  e imperf (pair), ovpt omitted † £240
O29 1r **blue and reddish purple** (Br)(1938) £16 6.50
  a imperf horiz (vertical pair) † £1200
  b overprint in black 12.50 3.50
  ba light blue and bright purple £32 £23
  bb on laid paper £650 £650

C - 'SERVICE' 11½mm, with serifs.

O30 1r **blue and bright purple** (Blk)(1949) £36 £75
  a 'SREVICE' error £100 £190
  b 'SERVICE' omitted £750 -

O30a 'SREVICE' for 'SERVICE', R6/6.

D - 'SERVICE' 13½mm, with serifs.

O31 8a **bright purple and blue** (1949) £65 £90
  a 'SERAICE' error £375 £425
  b '1' for 'I' £375 £425

O31a 'SERAICE' for 'SERVICE', R6/5.

O31b The figure '1' appears in 'SERVICE' instead of 'I' on R7/1.

1940 Animals, designs ½a tiger; 1a spotted deer. Perf 12.

O32	¼a **bright blue**	£4	1.25
O33	1a **bright purple**	£20	2.40

1941 As CW O18, but coloured centre inscribed 'SERVICE'. Perf 12.

O34	1a3p **emerald-green**	1.50	1.75
	a imperf between (pair)	£375	£400

1944-47 Similar to O25-O29, but smaller. Designs; ½a the Moti Mahal, 2a The Moti Masjid; 4a Be-Nazir Palaces. Perf 12.

O35	½a **green**	.65	.70
	a imperf (pair)	†	£70
	b imperf pair (vert pair)	†	£145
	c doubly printed	†	£125
O36	2a **violet**	8.50	£3
	a imperf (pair)	†	£75
	b bright purple (1945)	2.75	£3
	c mauve (1947)	8.50	£11
	d chocolate (imperf)	£200	£200
O37	4a **chocolate**	5.50	1.80
	a imperf (pair)	†	£100
	b imperf vert (horiz pair)	†	£200
	c doubly printed	-	-

O36d This is an error of colour.

1944-49 Arms of Bhopal.

O38	3p **bright blue**	.70	.60
	a imperf between (vert pair)	£110	£120

	b imperf between (horiz pair)	†	£225
	c stamp doubly printed	£45	-
O39	9p **chestnut** (shades)(1945)	7.50	2.75
	a imperf (pair)	†	£150
	b orange-brown	1.50	3.50
O40	1a **purple** (1945)	3.75	1.25
	a imperf horiz (vert pair)	†	£340
	b violet (1946)	£7	2.50
O41	1½a **claret** (1945)	1.10	.95
	a imperf between (vert pair)	†	£325
	b imperf between (horiz pair)	†	£300
O42	3a **yellow**	£10	£12
	a imperf (pair)	†	£145
	b imperf horiz (vert pair)	†	£190
	c imperf vert (horiz pair)	-	-
	d orange-brown (1949)	£65	£90
O43	6a **carmine**	£14	£45
	a imperf pair	†	£220
	b imperf horiz (vert pair)	†	£250
	c imperf vert (horiz pair)	†	£250

1949 (July) as above, perf 12, surcharged.

O44	2a/1½a **claret**	£2	6.50
	a stop omitted	£10	£25
	b imperf (pair)	£200	£240
	ba stop omitted		
	(imperf pair)	£500	£600
	c '2' omitted in pair		
	with normal	£850	-

O44a This variety occurs on positions 60 and 69 in the sheet of 81. (9 x 9).

1949, as above, imperf. Surcharged.

O45	2a/1½a **claret**	£850	£900
	a perf 12	£950	£1000

There are 3 different settings of the '2' on O45.

There are numerious forgeries of the surcharge. A BPA Certificate is strongly recommended.

On June 1st 1949 the administration was transferred to India.

BIJAWAR

1935-1936 (1st July). Design; portraits of Maharaja Sarwant Singh. Printed by Lakshmi Art Printing Works, Bombay. Perf 11.

1	3p **brown**		4.50	£5
	a imperf pair		6.50	-
	b imperf between (vert pair)		£65	-
	c imperf horiz (vert pair)		£35	-
2	6p **carmine**		£4	£5
	a imperf pair		£65	-
	b imperf between (vert pair)		£60	-
	c imperf between (horiz pair)		£65	-
	d imperf horiz (vert pair)		£65	-
3	9p **violet**		£5	4.50
	a imperf pair		£110	-
	b imperf between (vert pair)		£68	-
	c imperf between (horiz pair)		£60	-
	d imperf horiz (vert pair)		£65	-
4	1a **blue**		£6	£5
	a imperf pair		£65	-
	b imperf between (vert pair)		£68	-
	c imperf between (horiz pair)		£120	-
	d imperf horiz (vert pair)		£70	-
	e imperf vert (horiz pair)		£135	-
5	2a **deep green**		5.50	4.50
	a imperf pair		£70	-
	b imperf horiz (vert pair)		8.50	-
	c imperf between (vert pair)		£26	-
	d imperf between (horiz pair)		£35	-
1/5	**set** (5)		£24	£20

1936 Similar to above, but Roul 7.

6	3p **brown**	£4	4.50
	a printed on gum	£425	-
7	6p **carmine**	£5	£18
8	9p **violet**	£4	£95
9	1a **blue**	£6	£110
10	2a **deep green**	£8	£120
6/10	**set** (5)	£24	-

1937 (May) Design; portraits of Maharaja Sarwant Singh. Printed by Lakshmi Art Printing Works, Bombay, (Typo). Perf 9.

11	4a **orange**	£9	£75
	a imperf pair	£110	-
	b imperf between (vert pair)	£160	-
12	6a **lemon**	9.50	£75
	a imperf pair	£120	-
	b imperf between (vert pair)	£160	-
13	8a **emerald-green**	£11	£110
	a imperf pair	£180	-
14	12a **greenish blue**	£11	£110
	a imperf pair	£200	-
15	1r **bright violet**	£32	£160
	a '1Rs' error	£40	-
	b imperf (pair)	£230	-
	ba '1Rs' error	£650	-
11/15	**set** (5)	£65	-

15a/ba On R1/2 '1Rs' appears instead of '1R'.

The stamps of Bijawar were withdrawn in 1941.

BUNDI

1935-41 Design, Raja protecting sacred cows. Printed typo on ungummed paper. Rouletted.

These designs were printed from separate cliches as a block of four. These are identified by the bottom and top of the tablets.

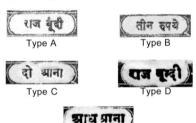

Type A   Type B

Type C   Type D

Type E

Type A - Top: This has a large loop usually joined to the main character, but can sometimes be detached.

Type B - Bottom:

Type C - Bottom: As B, but has a redrawn character to the second word. This has the line at top extending over the entire character.

Type D - Top:

Type E - Bottom: Similar to C but with characters larger and bolder.

Medium wove paper:

1	¼a **cobalt** (1937)(A, B)	£20	£16
2	¼a **cobalt** (1937) (A, C)	£20	£15
3	½a **black** (1938) (D, E)	£60	£60
4	1a **rosine** (1938) (D, E)	£15	£35
5	4a **emerald** (1938) (D, E)	£16	£25
6	3r **grey-blue and chocolate** (1941)(A, B)	£100	-
	a chocolate inverted	-	-
7	4r **yellow-green and vermilion** (1941) (D, E)	£160	-
8	5r **vermilion and yellow-green** (1941) (D, E)	£200	-

1939-1941 As above, printed on gummed medium wove paper, perf 11.

9	¼a **ultramarine** (D, E)	£20	£35
	a **greenish blue** (1941)	1.25	£45
10	½a **black** (D, E)	£25	£28
11	½a **black** (1940)(D,C)	£140	£85
12	1a **scarlet-vermilion** (1940)(D, E)	£110	£50
	a **rose** (1940)	£10	£45
13	2a **bright apple-green** (1940) (D, C)	£40	£45
14	2a **yellow-green** (1941)(D, E)	£12	£70

Collectors are warned that these issues were extensively used for fiscal purposes. Many 'used' examples have had fiscal cancels removed and faked postal cancels added.

1941-44 Design, Arms of Bundi, (typo). Perf 11. The first printing of this set was printed on gummed paper, further supplies were on ungummed paper.

15	3p **bright blue**	£2	£4
16	6p **deep blue**	3.50	7.50
17	1a **orange-red**	£5	£8
18	2a **chestnut**	6.50	£14
	a **deep brown** (1944)	£12	£15
19	4a **bright green**	£12	£45
20	8a **dull green**	£15	£160
21	1r **deep blue**	£35	£250
15/21	**set** (7)	£70	£450

18a was only printed on ungummed paper.

'Used' examples of the higher values usually have faked cancellations.

1947 Design, ¼a, ½a, 1a (Maharao Raja Bahadur Singh in uniform); 2a, 4a (Maharao in Indian dress); 8a, 1r views of Bundi. Printed (typo) by Times of India Press, Bombay. Perf 11.

22	¼a **blue-green**	1.75	£35
23	½a **violet**	1.60	£28
24	1a **yellow-green**	1.60	£28
25	2a **vermilion**	1.50	£60
26	4a **orange**	1.75	£80
27	8a **ultramarine**	2.25	-
28	1r **chocolate**	£12	-
22/28	**set** (7)	£20	-

Most 'used' examples bear faked cancellations.

OFFICIAL STAMPS

1941 Nos. 15-21 overprinted 'SERVICE'.

O1	3p **bright blue** (R)	4.50	£13
O2	6p **deep blue** (R)	£12	£13
O3	1a **orange-red**	£11	£9
O4	2a **brown**	£12	£10
O5	4a **bright green**	£40	£100
O6	8a **dull green**	£140	£500
O7	1r **deep blue** (R)	£200	£600
O1/7	**set** (7)	£375	£1100

Bundi had become part of the Rajasthan Union by 15 April 1948.

CHARKHARI

1930-45 Designs, Arms of Charkhari (left- hand sword over right). Wove paper, no gum, imperforate.

1	1p **deep blue**	.45	£11
	a vert pair one printed on reverse	£10	-
	b tête-bêche (vert pair)	£325	-
	c perf 11 x imperf (horiz-pair)	£60	£60
	d bluish slate	£18	-
	e laid paper (1944)	-	-
2	1p **green** (shades)(1943)	£45	£190
3	1p **violet** (1943)	£15	£140
	a tête-bêche (vert pair)	£40	-
4	½a **deep olive**	1.50	£11
5	½a **red-brown** (1940)	4.25	£20
	a tête-bêche (vert pair)	£390	-
6	½a **black** (1943)	£45	£160
7	½a **red** (shades) (1943)	£15	£35
	a tête-bêche (vert pair)	£35	-
	b laid paper (1944)	-	£300
8	½a **grey-brown**	£55	£68
9	1a **green**	1.50	£13
	a emerald (1938)	£40	£70
10	1a **chocolate** (1940)	£10	£22
	a tête-bêche (vert pair)	£60	-
	b lake-brown	-	£55
11	1a **red** (1940)	£110	£55
	a carmine	-	£55
	b laid paper (1944)	-	£325
12	2a **light blue**	.90	£14
	a tête-bêche (vert pair)	7.50	-
13	2a **greenish grey** (1941?)	£45	£65
	a tête-bêche (vert pair)	£90	-
	b laid paper (1944)	-	£340
	c greyish green	£70	£160
14	2a **yellow-green** (1945)	-	£800
15	4a **carmine**	£2	£16
	a tête-bêche (vert pair)	£11	-

Stamps with the right sword over the left are from an earlier (1909-1919) printings.

1a one stamp is normal (upright), the other is printed inverted on the reverse.

2, 6 on pelure (very thin, transparent) paper.

1940 As before but surcharged.

16	½a/8a **brown-red**	£26	£110
	a missing space	£26	£110
	b surcharge inverted	£230	£350
	c inverted '1'	£225	-

17	1a/1r **chestnut** (1As)	£100	£350
	a surcharge inverted	£250	-

18	1a/1r **chestnut** (1 ANNA)	£900	£850

16a The space between the '½a' and 'As' is missing.

16c The '1' of '½' is inverted.

18 overprinted '1 ANNA' rather than '1a'.

Many values from the 1930-45 series are found with faked postmarks. There are many forgeries of the surcharges, especially the '1 ANNA' on 1r (no.18). Expertisation is strongly advised.

COCHIN

Stamps of Cochin were valid on mail posted to Travancore, as well as within Cochin.

Recess and litho printing

Recess printing gives a crisp, clear result with raised lines of the design. Perkins, Bacon.

Litho printing generally gives a blurred result, with a flat surface. Associated Printers, Madras.

'Umbrella'
Watermark
(actual size 15.6 mm)

Portrait 1

All stamps to No. 28 are watermarked 'Umbrella'. Shades, many of which are consistent and dramatic, exist throughout. Stamps with colours not included in the listings are either unissued values, or trials.

All stamps X1-9 and 1-25 are Portrait 1.

1933-38 Maharaja Rama Varma III (Portrait 1). Recess printed. Perf 13 x 13½.

X1	2p brown	.55	.30
X2	4p green	.40	.10
X3	6p red-brown	.50	.10
X4	1a brown-orange	.55	.15
X5	1a8p carmine	2.25	£4
1	2a grey	£4	£1
X6	2¼a yellow-green	1.10	.20
2	3a vermilion	3.50	£1
X7	3a4p violet	1.10	£1
X8	6a8p sepia	1.10	£10
X9	10a blue	£2	£12

1938 As Portrait 1, Litho. Perf 11.

3	2p brown	.75	.35
	a watermark inverted	£125	£60
4	4p green	.75	.20
	a watermark inverted	-	-
5	6p red-brown	1.75	.10
	a watermark inverted	†	-
6	1a brown-orange	£55	£80
	a watermark inverted	-	-
7	2¼a sage-green	4.75	.15

1938 As 3-7 , Perf 13 x 13½.

8	2p brown	£5	.50
9	4p green	6.50	£15
10	6p red-brown	†	£2500
11	1a brown-orange	£75	£100
12	2¼a sage-green	£12	4.75

The 1a values in the above sets were mostly used for fiscal purposes. Beware of cleaned and regummed 'mint' examples, or cleaned and falsely-postmarked 'used' examples.

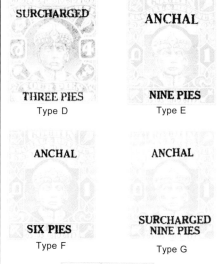

ANCHAL
Type A

ANCHAL
Type B

THREE PIES
Type C

SURCHARGED

ANCHAL

THREE PIES
Type D

NINE PIES
Type E

ANCHAL

ANCHAL

SIX PIES
Type F

SURCHARGED
NINE PIES
Type G

SIX PIES

Type H

1a stamps from 1916 onwards had been inscribed 'Anchal and Revenue' ('Anchal' meaning 'Postage'). In 1939 a decision to differentiate between 1a stamps for postal and revenue uses was made; 1a stamps intended for postal use were overprinted 'Anchal'.

1939 Overprinted large 'ANCHAL', type A. No 13 is perforated 13 x 13½, while No 14 is perforated 11.

13	1a **brown-orange** (recess)	£4	1.25
	a watermark inverted	†	£115
14	1a **brown-orange** (litho)(**X4**)	£285	1.25
	a watermark inverted	†	-
	b perf 13 x 13½ (**11**)	-	£300

1939 Overprinted small 'ANCHAL' type B. Litho. Perf 11.

15	1a **brown-orange** (**6**)	.60	1.25
	a perf 13 x 13½ (**11**)	£10	.40

1942-44 Various overprints and surcharges. Printed Recess. Perf 13 x 13½.

Overprinted solely with new values. Type C.

16	3p/1a8p **carmine**	£200	£75
17	6p/1a8p **carmine**	2.75	£16

Overprinted 'SURCHARGED' and new values. Type D. Perf 11.

18	3p/1a8p **carmine**	4.50	7.50
19	1a3p/1a8p **carmine**	.80	.40

1942-44 Various overprints and surcharges. Litho. Perf 11.

Overprinted 'SURCHARGED' and new value, Type D

20	3p/4p **green**	£5	3.50
	a perf 13 x 13½	12.50	3.50

Overprinted large 'ANCHAL' and new values, Type E.

21	6p/1a **brown-orange** (**6**)	£400	£225
	a 'SIX PIES' double	†	£1000
22	9p/1a **brown-orange** (**6**)	£110	£120

Overprinted small 'ANCHAL' and new value, Type F.

23	6p/1a **brown-orange** (**6**)	£220	£170
	a perf 13 x 13½ (**11**)	£125	£55
24	9p/1a **brown-orange**		
	perf 13 x 13½ (**11**)	£325	£35

Overprinted 'ANCHAL/SURCHARGED/NINE PIES'. Type G. Perf 13 x 13½.

25	9p/1a **brown-orange** (**11**)	.19	5.50

Portrait 2

All stamps 26-48 are Portrait 2.

1943 Portrait of Maharaja Kerala Varma II (Portrait 2), Litho. Inscribed 'ANCHAL & REVENUE'. Perf 13 x 13½.

26	2p **grey-brown**		2.75	3.50
	a perf 11		†	£1600
27	4p **green**		£750	£300
28	1a **brown-orange**		£85	£100

Approx size 169mm x 82mm

Due to the size of the watermark parts appear on some, but not all stamps.

1943 Portrait 2 but watermark altered to 'Government of Cochin'. Litho. Frame of 1a inscribed 'ANCHAL & REVENUE'.

Perf 13 x 13½.

29	2p **grey-brown**	£25	£3
30	4p **green**	£6	£18
31	6p **red-brown**	£3	.10
32	1a **brown-orange**	£185	£150
33	2¼a **yellow-green**	£22	£2

1943 As 29-33, but Perf 11. 6p - 2¼a no gum.

34	2p **grey-brown**	†	£2650
35	4p **green**	3.25	4.75
36	6p **red-brown**	6.50	1.35
37	9p **ultramarine**	£36	£1
	a imperf between		
	(horiz pair)	£1750	-
38	1a **brown-orange**	£180	£150
39	2¼a **yellow-green**	£22	£7

1943 Portrait 2 with various surcharges or overprints. Litho Perf 13 X 13½. Watermark Umbrella.

40	3p/4p **green** (D)(**27**)	£75	£17
41	9p/1a **brown-orange** (F)(**28**)	£5	£3
42	9p/1a **brown-orange** (G)(**28**)	5.75	2.50
43	1a3p/1a **brown-orange** (D)(**28**)	-	£3750

All stamps from 44-84 are watermarked 'Goverment of Cochin' (except 73-4)

1943 Portrait 2 with various surcharges. Litho. Perf 13 x 13½ unless stated. 44a, 47a no gum.

44	2p/6p **red-brown** (C)(**31**)	.60	3.25
	a perf 11(**36**)	.75	2.30
45	3p/4p **green** (C) perf 11(**35**)	5.50	.10
46	3p/4p **green** (D)(**30**)	4.50	.10
47	3p/6p **red-brown** (C)(**31**)	.75	.20
	a perf 11(**36**)	.75	.60
48	4p/6p **red-brown** (C)(**31**)	£4	£10

Portrait 3

1944 Maharaja Ravi Varma (Portrait 3). Litho. No gum. Perf 11. Type 1.

49	9p **ultramarine**	£14	3.50

1946-48 Portrait 3, Type 2. Perf 13 (Line) or 13 x 13½ (comb). No gum.

50	9p **ultramarine** (1946)	£14	£15
	a perf 13 x 13½	£42	£3
51	1a3p **magenta** (1948)	£6	6.50
	a perf 13 x 13½	£250	£50
52	1a9p **ultramarine** (1948)	£7	£14

Type 1   Type 2

There is shading on the Maharaja's lower cheek in Type 1. This is absent in Type 2.

Portrait 4

1946-48 Maharaja Ravi Varma (Portrait 4), 1a inscribed 'ANCHAL & REVENUE'. Litho. No gum. Perf 13.

53	2p **chocolate**	2.25	.15
	a imperf horiz (vert pair)	£2200	£2200
54	3p **carmine**	.40	.25
55	4p **green**	£2200	£65
56	6p **red-brown** (1947)	£20	£5
57	9p **ultramarine**	1.25	.10
	a imperf between (horiz pair)	†	£2000
58	1a **orange** (1948)	£7	£25
	a imperf between stamp and top margin	-	-
59	2a **black**	£100	6.50
60	3a **vermilion**	£70	1.10

Most examples of No 58 were used fiscally. The 1a3p magenta, issued overprinted as O58, is known without 'O.C.G.S.' overprint. It was probably not issued.

1946-1948 As before (Portrait 4), but perf 11 and with gum.

61	2p **chocolate**	£6	.45
	a perf 11 x 13 (no gum)	£325	£110
62	6p **red-brown**	£140	£4
63	1a **orange**	£450	-
64	2a **black**	£125	5.50

Portrait 5

2p Die 1   2p Die 1

2p Die 2   2p Die 2

1948-1950 Maharaja Kerala Varma III (Portrait 5). Litho. Watermark upright or inverted. Perf 11 with gum.

65	2p **grey-brown, Die 1**	1.50	.15
	a imperf between (horiz pair)	-	£2000
	b Die 2	£125	£2
66	3p **carmine**	1.20	.15
	a imperf between (vert pair)	-	£1500
67	4p **green**	£14	£3
	a imperf between (horiz pair)	£225	£275
68	6p **chestnut**	£15	.20
	a imperf between (horiz pair)	£650	-
	b imperf between stamp and margin	†	-
69	9p **ultramarine**	£2	.35
70	2a **black**	£50	£2
	a imperf between stamp and margin	-	†
71	3a **orange-red**	£55	.80
	a imperf between (horiz pair)	£2200	-
72	3a4p **violet** (1950), Die 1	£55	£350
	a tail to turban	£200	£750
	b Die 2	£175	-

72a a tail on the turban occurs on R1/7.

3a4p Die 1

3a4p Die 2

72, 72b Die 1 Two white lines below value; frame around head broken by value tablets. Die 2 One white line below value, frame around head unbroken.

1949 Pictorials. 2a Chinese Nets; 2¼a Dutch Palace. Litho. No Watermark. Perf 11.

73	2a **black**	£4	£7
	a imperf between (horiz pair)	£420	-
74	2¼a **green**	2.50	£8
	a imperf between (horiz pair)	£420	-

1949 Portrait 3, as 1944-48 surcharged with type H. Litho. Perf 13, no gum.

75	6p/1a3p **magenta** (51)	4.50	3.25
	a extended tail	£32	£25
76	1a/1a9p **ultramarine** (R) (52)	1.90	£1

normal   extended tail

75a The first character in the second group has a 'tail' which extends below the level of the other characters in the group. See also note after 81a.

1949, Portrait 4, as 1946-48 surcharged with type H. Litho. Perf. 13, no gum.

77	3p/9p **ultramarine** (69)	£9	£16
78	6p/1a3p **magenta**	£12	£11
	a surcharge double	†	£450
	b extended tail	£75	£70
79	1a/1a9p **ultramarine** (R)	2.75	1.60
	a surcharge in black	-	£2250
	b smaller black surcharge	-	£3250

78b See 75a

79b The native characters are 7½mm instead of 10mm long.

1948-1950 Portrait 5, surcharged type H. Litho. Perf 11.

80	3p/9p **ultramarine** (69)	£2	1.50
	a larger surcharge	£2	.40
	b imperf between (vertical pair)	-	£1500
	c surcharge double	£450	-
	d surcharge both sides	£320	-
81	3p/9p **ultramarine** (R)(69)	£4	2.25
	a extended tail	£24	£20
82	6p/9p **ultramarine** (R)(69)	1.25	.30

80a The native characters are 20mm instead of 16½mm long.

81a occurs 4 times in the setting twice as described under 75a, and twice with the extended tail affecting the second character.

The 9p ultramarine (Portrait 4) surcharged 6p (type H) in red was prepared for use but not issued.

1949 Portrait 4 surcharged type C. Litho. Perf 13, no gum.

83	6p/1a **orange (58)**	£50	£120
84	9p/1a **orange (58)**	£75	£120

OFFICIAL

Type I
Grander 'O'
'N' without serifs

Type J
Curved sides to
'O' and 'C'

Type K
Large type

Type L
Circular 'O' 'N'
with small serifs

Type M
Flat, oval 'O'

Type N
Pronounced serifs

Type O
Straight sides of
'O' and 'C'

Type P
Small 'ON'

1933-38 Portrait 1, recess, overprinted Type O. Watermark 'Umbrella'. Perf 13 x 13½.

XO1	4p **green**	3.25	.10
XO2	6p **red-brown** (1934)	£3	.10
XO3	1a **brown-orange**	£12	.10
XO4	1a8p **carmine**	1.25	.25
XO5	2a **grey**	£14	.10
XO6	2¼a **yellow-green**	4.50	.10
XO7	3a **vermilion**	£38	.10
XO8	3a4p **violet**	1.25	.15
XO9	6a8p **sepia**	1.25	.20
XO10	10a **blue**	1.25	.70

1937-38 As Portrait 1, recess, overprinted Type L. Watermark 'Umbrella'. Perf 13 x 13½.

O1	1a **brown-orange** (1937)	£35	.50
O2	2a **grey-black (2)**	£18	1.50
O3	3a **vermilion (3)**	£9	1.90

1938-44 As above, Portrait 1, litho. Various overprints. Watermark 'Umbrella'. Perf 11.

O4	4p **green** (J)(4)	£22	£2
	a inverted 'S'	£26	£2
O5	6p **red-brown** (J)(5)	£20	.30
	a inverted 'S'	£23	.40
O6	1a **brown-orange** (K)(6)	£250	£2
O7	2a **grey-black** (J)(1)	£15	.70
	a inverted 'S'	£16	.70

1938-44 As above, Portrait 1, litho except O12 recess. Various overprints. O8-10 Perf 13 x 13½, O11 and O12 Perf 11.

O8	4p **green** (J)(9)	£18	£2
O9	6p **red-brown** (M)(10)	£8	3.25
O10	6p **red-brown** (N)(10)	£750	£350
O11	1a **brown-orange** (L)(11)	.80	.10
O12	3a **vermilion** (L)(2)	2.50	1.25

1942-1943 Unissued stamps, Portrait 1, litho. Overprinted type M. Watermark 'Government of Cochin'. Perf 11.

O13	4p **green**	£60	£12
O14	6p **red-brown**	£130	9.50
O15	1a **brown-orange**	£10	£4
O16	2a **grey-black** (1943)	£60	.70
	a overprint omitted	-	£1200
O17	2¼a **sage-green**	£1350	£5
O18	3a **vermilion**	£15	£6

1942-43 As above, Portrait 1, but perf 13 x 13½.

O19	4p **green**	1.90	.60
O20	6p **red-brown**	£16	.75
	a overprint on both sides	†	£130
O21	1a **brown-orange**	1.30	£4
	a overprint on both sides	†	£125

Portrait O6

1943 stamp of 1921, Portrait O6, surcharged. Printed Recess. Watermark Umbrella. Perf 13½ to 14.

O22	9p/1½a **purple** (C)	£550	£20

1943 Portrait 1, with various surcharges and overprints. Recess. Watermark Umbrella. Perf 13 x 13½.

O23	3p/1a8p **carmine** (D, O)(18)	4.75	2.25
O24	9p/1a8p **carmine** (C, O)	£110	£24
O25	1a9p/1a8p **carmine** (C, O)	£2	£2
O26	1a9p/1a8p **carmine** (D, O)	1.25	.30

1943 Portrait 1. Litho. Watermark Umbrella. Perf 11.

O27	3p/1a **brown-orange** (L, C)(11)	1.75	£3
O28	9p/1a **brown-orange** (L, C)(11)	£225	£45
O29	1a3p/1a **brown-orange** (L, D)(11)	£240	£80

1943 Portrait 1, Litho. Watermark Umbrella. Perf 13 x 13½.

O30	3p/4p **green** (J, C)	£24	£8
	a surcharge double	£365	£150
O31	3p/4p **green** (J, D)	£140	£50

O32-82 all have watermark 'Government of Cochin'.

1943 Portrait 1, Litho. Perf 13 x 13½.

O32	3p/4a **green** (M, C)	£80	£45
O33	3p/4a **green** (M, D)	£1350	-
O34	3p/1a **brown-orange** (M, C)	£130	£65
	a perf 11	£95	£60

1944 Portrait 2 overprinted Type M or L. Litho. Perf 13 x 13½ (C).

O35	4p **green**(O20)	£34	5.50
	a perf 13 (L)	£400	£55
O36	6p **red-brown**(O21)	£2	.10
	a overprint double	-	£60
	b perf 13 (L)	£6	£2
O37	1a **brown-orange**(O22)	£2600	£50
O38	2a **black**	5.50	.80

O39	2¼a **yellow-green**	3.50	.85
	a overprint on both sides	†	£110
O40	3a **vermilion**(33)	£8	1.30

1944 Portrait 2, overprinted Type M, Perf 11.

O41	4p **green**	£120	£4
O42	6p **red-brown**	.80	.10
	a overprint double	-	£65
O43	3a **vermilion**	£8	.30

1944 Portrait 2, stamps with Type M plus surcharge as listed. Perf 13 x 13½.

O44	3p/4p **green** (C)	£3	.10
	a perf 11	£6	.50
	b type M on both sides	†	£120
O45	3p/4p **green** (D)	£4	.30
	a perf 11	£340	£150
O46	3p/1a **brown-orange** (C)	£22	£6
O47	9p/6p **red-brown** (C)	£9	£3
	a printed on both sides	-	£400
O48	9p/6p **red-brown** (D)	3.75	.30
O49	1a3p/1a **brown-orange** (C)	£11	£2
O50	1a3p/1a **brown-orange** (D)	£3	.10

1946-47 stamps of 1944-48, Portrait O3 (Type 2) overprinted with Type M. Litho. Perf 13.

O51	9p **ultramarine**	2.25	.10
	a stamp printed both sides	†	£450
	b perf 13 x 13½	£4	.10
O52	1a3p **magenta** (1947)	1.30	.20
	a double overprint	£15	£10
	b overprint on both sides	-	-
	ba ovpt both sides, double inverted on reverse	£45	-
O53	1a9p **ultramarine** (1947)	.30	.75
	a overprint double	-	-
	b overprint omitted in pair with normal	†	£1100

1948 Portrait 4 and unissued values overprinted with Type P. Litho. Perf 13.

O54	3p **carmine**	£1	.10
	a stamp printed both sides	-	£500
O55	4p **grey-green**	£24	£5
O56	6p **red-brown**	£11	1.25
O57	9p **ultramarine**	.60	.10
O58	1a3p **magenta**	3.25	1.10
O59	1a9p **ultramarine**	3.75	.30
O60	2a **black**	£12	2.50
O61	2¼a **yellow-green**	£18	3.75

1949 Portrait 5 and unissued values, overprinted with Type J. Litho. Perf 11.

O62	3p **carmine**	£1	.15
O63	4p **green**	1.25	.30
	a imperf bet (horiz or vert pair)	-	£1300
	b ovpt on reverse	£60	£60
O64	6p **chestnut**	2.25	.25
	a imperf between (vert pair)	-	£1600
O65	9p **ultramarine**	2.40	.10

O66	2a **black**	£2	.15
O67	2¼a **yellow-green**	2.75	£5
O68	3a **red-orange**	.90	.80
O69	3a4p **violet** Die 1	£36	£35
	a tail to turban	£225	£250
	b Die 2	£80	£80

O69a See No 72a, O69b see No. 72b

As O63-70 but overprinted 'On CCS'.

O70	3p **carmine**	£12	2.50
O71	4p **green**	£12	£4
O72	6p **chestnut**	£20	£3
O73	9p **ultramarine**	£21	£3
O74	2a **black**	£21	3.50
O75	2¼a **yellow-green**	£23	£42
O76	3a **red-orange**	£15	£9
O77	3a4p **violet** Die 1	£225	£250

1949 Various issues, surcharged with Type H. Litho.

Portrait 3, Perf 13.

O78	1a/1a9p **ultramarine** (R)	.50	.55

Portrait 4, Perf 13.

O79	1a/1a9p **ultramarine** (R)	£19	£14

Portrait 5, Perf 11.

O80	6p/3p **carmine**	£1	.55
	a imperf between		
	(vert pair)	†	£1000
	b surcharge double	†	£300
	c 'C' for 'G'	£12	£8
	d extended tail	£12	£8
O81	9p/4p **green** (18 mm long)	.60	2.25
	a imperf between		
	(horiz pair)	£550	£650
	b native characters		
	larger 22 mm long	.90	.85
	ba as above, imperf		
	between (horiz pair)	£500	£550
	bb extended tail	£15	£13
	c 'C' for 'G'	£15	£22
	ca as above, native		
	characters 22 mm	£16	£13

O81bb see 75a

The 'ON CCS' variety occurs on R1/4.

1949 Portrait 5, surcharged Type H, overprinted 'Service'. Litho. Perf 11.

O83	3p/9p **ultramarine**	.50	.60
	a imperf between		
	(horiz pair)	†	£1600
	b imperf between stamp		
	and margin	†	-

On July 1st, 1949 Cochin became part of Travancore-Cochin. Cochin stamps remained valid and were used together with those of Travancore, the latter being surcharged in the new currency,

DUNGARPUR

1933-47 Designs Arms of Dungarpur, printed by Shri Lakshman Bijaya Printing Press, Dungarpur (litho). Perf 11.

1	¼a bistre-yellow	-	£200
2	¼a rose (1935)	-	£700
3	¼a red-brown (1937)	-	£400
4	1a pale turquoise-blue	-	£175
5	1a rose (1938)	-	-
6	1a3p deep reddish-violet (1935)	-	£275
7	2a deep dull green (1947)	-	£375
8	4a rose-red (1934)	-	£700

No 2 and 5 are known in se-tenant strips of 3, the centre stamp being No. 5.

1939-46 Designs, Maharawal Lakshman Singh with various frames. Printers L. V. Indap & Co, Bombay (typo). Various perfs.

9	¼a orange	£900	£85
10	½a vermilion, Die 1 (1940)	£300	£70
	a Die 2 (1944)	£300	£80
	ab Pair showing Die 1 and 2	£750	£200
	b Die 3 (1945)	£400	£65
	c imperf between (vert pair)	†	-
11	1a deep blue	£325	£60
12	1a3p bright mauve (1944)	£900	£250
13	1½a deep violet (1946)	£1000	£250
14	2a bright green (1943)	£1400	£475
15	4a brown (1940)	£1000	£200

No 9, perf 12, 11, 10½ or 10
No 10, perf 12, 11 or 10½
No 10a, perf 10½
No 10b, perf 10
No 11, perf 12, 11, 10½ or 10
No 12, perf 10½ or 10
No 13, perf 10
No 14, perf 12 or pin perf 11½
No 15, perf 10½ or 10

Stamps with various perforations were printed in sheets of 12 (4 x 3). These were imperforate along the top, bottom and sometimes on the right side. Hence the various combinations, with some examples being imperforate on one or two sides. Perf 10 examples were printed in sheets of 4, some of these were fully perforated.

Dungarpur became part of Rajasthan by 15 April 1948.

HYDERABAD

Watermark Urdu script ('Sirkar Asafia')

1931-1947 Designs 4p, 8p Arms of Hyderabad; 1a the Char Minar; 2a High Court; 4a Osman Sagar Reservoir; 8a entrance to Ajanta Caves; 12a Bidar College; 1r Victory Tower, Daulatabad, 12a Bidar College. Plates De La Rue, printers (Recess) Stamps Department, Hyderabad. Watermark Urdu script, perf 13½.

1	4p black (shades)	.25	.10
	a laid paper	£2	£5
	b imperf pair	£40	£85
2	8p green (shades)	.35	.10
	a imperf between (vert pair)	-	£550
	b imperf pair	£48	£90
	c laid paper	2.50	3.75
3	1a brown (shades)	.35	.10
	a imperf between (horiz pair)	-	£575
	b perf 11	†	£650
4	2a violet (shades)	2.25	.10
	a imperf pair	£110	£225
5	4a ultramarine	1.30	.50
	a imperf pair	£120	£240
6	8a orange	£5	£3
	a yellow-orange (1944)	£60	£25
7	12a scarlet	5.50	£9
8	1r yellow	£4	£4
1/8	set (8)	£17	£15

1a/2c These printings have a large sheet watermark 'The Nizam's Government Hyderabad Deccan' and arms within a circle. This watermark does not appear on every stamp.

1937 (13 Feb.) Printer Indian Security Printing Press, Nasik (litho). Inscribed 'H.E.H. The Nizam's Silver Jubilee'. Designs, 4p Unani General Hospital; 8p Osmania General Hospital; 1a Osmania University; 2a Osmania Jubilee Hall. Perf 14.

9	4p slate and violet	.40	1.70
10	8p slate and brown	.65	1.70
11	1a slate and orange-yellow	£1	£1
12	2a slate and green	1.10	3.50
9/12	set (4)	£3	£7

1945 (6 Dec) Victory. Design, family reunion by T I Archer, on wove paper. Watermark Urdu script. Perf 13½.

13	1a blue	.10	.10
	a imperf between (vert pair) £550	-
	b laid paper	.60	.60

13b Has the same watermark as Nos 1a and 2c.

1947 Reformed Legislature. Design, Town Hall by T I Archer. Litho, Government Press. Perf 13½.

14	1a black	1.20	1.50
	a pair, imperf between	-	£775

1947-49 Various designs by T I Archer. 1a4p power house, Hyderabad; 3a Kaktyai Arch, Warangal Fort; 6a Golkunda Fort. Typo. Watermark Urdu script. Perf 13½.

15	1a4p green	.85	1.60
16	3a greenish blue	1.40	3.25
	a bluish green	2.50	£4
17	6a sepia	3.25	£14
	a red-brown (1949)	£15	£25
	b imperf (pair)	£120	-
15/17	set (3)	£5	£17

1947 Arms of Hyderabad, inscribed 'Postage and Receipt'. Watermark Urdu script. Perf 13½.

18	½a claret	2.25	.50
	a imperf between (horiz pair)	-	£275
	b imperf between (vert pair)	-	£525

Slightly reduced

An imperforate set of 4 (4p, 8p, 1a and 2a) was prepared for the independence commemorations in 1948 but were not issued.

1948 As above, but inscribed 'Postage' at foot. Perf 13½.

19	6p claret	7.50	£6

In September 1948 the state postal system was taken over by the Dominion authorities.

1949 Arms of Hyderabad, as No. 1. Watermark Urdu script, perf 13½.

20	2p bistre-brown	£2	2.20
	a imperf between (horiz pair)	†	£675
	b imperf pair	£120	£400

OFFICIAL STAMPS

1934-44 As Nos. 1-8, overprinted 'SARKARI' (Official) in Urdu.

O1	4p **black**	2.25	.10
	a imperf pair	£60	-
	b imperf between (vert pair)	£550	£500
	c imperf between (horiz pair)	-	£500
O2	8p **green**	.95	.10
	a overprint inverted	†	£125
	b imperf between (horiz pair)	-	£500
	c overprint double	†	£95
	d imperf pair	£140	£175
O3	1a **brown**	1.50	.10
	a imperf between (vert pair)	£500	£450
	b imperf between (horiz pair)	-	£400
	c imperf pair	£110	£130
	d overprint double	-	£130
O4	2a **violet**	£6	.10
	a imperf pair (horiz pair)	†	£1000
O5	4a **ultramarine**	£3	.20
	a overprint double	†	£400
	b imperf between (horiz pair)	†	£1250
O6	8a **orange**	£10	.45
	a yellow-orange	-	£35
O7	12a **scarlet** (1935)	£10	1.25
O8	1r **yellow** (1935)	£15	£2
O1/O8	set (8)	£45	£4

1947-50 As nos. 18, 19 and 20, overprinted.

O9	½a **claret**	4.50	£5
	a pair, one missing ovpt	-	-
O10	2p **bistre-brown**	4.50	£7
O11	6p **claret**	5.50	£15

IDAR

1932-43 Designs, Maharaja Himmat Singh. Printers M N Kothari & Sons, Bombay (typo). Perf 11.

1   2

The panels down the side are white on No. 1, on No. 2 they have dots of colour in the panels.

1	½a **light green**	-	£35
	a pale yellow-green (1939)	£20	£22
	b emerald (1941)	£16	£22
	ba imperf between (pair)	£1600	-
	c yellow-green (1943)	£13	£22
	ca imperf between (horiz pair)	£1400	-

1a is on thicker paper.

2	½a **pale yellow-green (1939)**	£32	£26
	a emerald (1941)	£20	£24
	b yellow-green (1943)	£10	£22

2 is on thicker paper.

1944 (21 Oct) Designs, Maharaja Himmat Singh. Printers P G Mehta & Co, Hitmatnagar (typo). Perf 12.

3	½a **blue-green**	2.40	£70
	a imperf between (vert pair)	£225	-
	b yellow-green	£3	£70
	ba imperf between (vert pair)	£9	-
4	1a **violet**	2.40	£60
	a imperf pair	£160	-
	b imperf vert (horiz pair)	£175	-
5	2a **blue**	2.60	£95
	a imperf between (vert pair)	£65	-
	b imperf between (horiz pair)	£160	-

6	4a **vermilion**	£3	£100
	a doubly printed	£1000	-
3/6	**set** (4)	9.50	£300

1-6 the postage stamps of Idar were printed as booklet panes of 4, imperforate on the outer edges. Single stamps therefore have one or two sides imperforate.

6 is known in violet, believed to be a colour trial.

POSTAL FISCAL STAMPS

1940?-45 Designs, Maharaja Himmat Singh. Perf 12 on two or three sides.

F1	1a **violet**	-	£140
	a perf 11	£125	£140
F2	1a **violet** (1943)	£95	£140
F3	1¼a/1a **violet**	£140	£350
F4	1¼a **yellow-green** (1945)	£16	-
	a imperf between (vert pair)	£35	-
	b imperf between tête-beche		
	horizontal pair	-	-
	c blue-green (1945)	£65	£125

F3 was surcharged with a handstamp in Gujerati.

Idar became part of Bombay Province on 10 June 1948.

BOOKLETS

1943-4 card covers inscribed 'IDAR STATE' with number and value of 'POSTAGE TICKETS', and price of the booklet. 8 panes of 4 with margin at left only.

Booklet size 63-65mm x 52-62mm (cover colour given).

B1	1r **½a (no. 3)** x 32 (light green) -	-
B2	1r **½a (no. 3b)** x 32 (light blue) -	-
B3	2r **1a (no. 4)** x 32 (white)	-	-
B4	2r **1a (no. 4)** x 32 (light green) -	-
B5	2r **1a (no. 4)** x 32 (purple)	-	-
B6	4r **2a (no. 5)** x 32 (blue)	-	-
B7	8r **4a (no. 6)** x 32 (white)	-	-

Booklet size 70 x 69mm.

| B8 | 2r **1a (no. F2)** x 32 (purple) | - | - |

Booklet size 180 x 65mm, thin paper cover with panes of 12.

| B9 | 7r8a **1¼a (no. F4c)** x 96 (beige) - | - |

INDORE

From 1908 the stamps of Indore were restricted to official mail only.

1927-37 Design, Maharaja Yeshwant Rao Holkar II. Printers Perkins, Bacon & Co. Perf 14 (L) - see footnote.

X1	¼a **orange**	.50	.20
X2	½a **claret**	1.75	.10
X3	1a **green**	2.25	.10
X4	1½a **green**	3.25	.65
X5	2a **sepia**	6.50	£2
1	2a **bluish green** (1936)	£11	£2
	a imperf (pair)	£20	£150
X6	3a **deep violet**	1.60	£8
X7	3a **Prussian blue** (1935)	£15	-
	a imperf (pair)	£24	£400
X8	3½a **violet** (1934)	5.25	7.50
	a imperf (pair)	£50	£400
X9	4a **ultramarine**	5.25	£4
2	4a **yellow-brown** (1937)	£28	1.50
	a imperf (pair)	£23	£300
X10	8a **slate-grey**	5.50	3.75
3	8a **red-orange** (1937)	£22	£18
X11	12a **carmine** (1934)	£4	£8
X12	1r **black and light blue**	6.50	12.50
X13	2r **black and carmine**	£45	£50
X14	5r **black and brown-orange**	£75	£85

Several different perforating heads were used; both comb and line.

The listed imperforate pairs were ordered in 1933, and are known postally used.

Other imperforate pairs are Plate proofs (the 1r is known postally used).

1940 (1 Aug) As above, but different values and surcharged. Overprinted by Times of India Press, Bombay. Various perfs.

4	¼a/5r	black and brown-orange	£12	1.50
		a surcharge double (Black & Green)		£400
5	½a/2r	black and carmine	£20	2.75
6	1a/1¼a	green	£20	0.60
		a surcharge inverted	£70	-
		c surcharge doubled	£375	-
4/6		set (3)	£48	4.50

6 Exists perforated 13.2, 13.8 or 14.2 (L)

1940-46 Design, Maharahja Yeshwant Rao Holkar II. Printers Times of India Press, Bombay. Perf 11.

7	¼a	red-orange	1.50	.10
8	½a	claret (1941)	£3	.10
9	1a	green (1941)	£9	.10
10	1¼a	yellow-green (1941)	£12	1.80
		a imperf pair	£200	-
11	2a	turquoise-blue (1941)	£8	0.80
12	4a	yellow-brown (1946)	£12	£11
13	2r	black and carmine (1943)	£10	£150
14	5r	black and yellow-orange (1943)	9.50	£200
7/14		set (8)	£58	£330

The 2r and 5r and often found with faked postmarks. Care is advisable when purchasing.

Indore was incorporated into Madhya Bharat by 1 July 1948.

JAIPUR

As is often the case with stamps printed by Nasik, double prints of the frame are frequently encountered. These are worth a premium, but not the large premium sometimes asked.

In any case when used is worth more than mint, beware of faked cancellations.

1932-46 Designs, Maharaja Sawai Man Singh II. Inscribed 'POSTAGE AND REVENUE'. Designer, T I Archer. Printers, Indian Security Printing Press, Nasik (litho). Perf 14

1	1a	black and blue	2.50	1.30
2	2a	black and buff	3.50	£2
3	4a	black and grey-green	3.50	£10
4	8a	black and chocolate	4.75	£12
5	1r	black and yellow-bistre	£22	£120
6	2r	black and yellow-green	£60	£450
1/6		set (6)	£85	£525

1932-46 As above, but inscribed 'POSTAGE'.

7	¼a	black and brown-lake	.30	.40
8	¾a	black and brown-red (1943?)	£6	£4
9	1a	black and blue (1943?)	£8	£4
10	2a	black and buff (1943?)	£8	4.50
11	2½a	black and carmine	3.75	£3
12	3a	black and green	3.25	.50
13	4a	black and grey-green (1943?)	£40	£150
14	6a	black and deep blue	4.75	£26
		a black and pale blue (1946)	£7	£70
15	8a	black and chocolate (1946)	£22	£120

16	1r black and yellow-bistre		
	(1946)	£15	£175
7/16	set (10)	£100	£430

1936 No.6 and 1931 5r, surcharged 'One Rupee'.

17	1r/2r black and		
	yellow-green (R)	6.75	£100
18	1r/5r black and purple	6.75	£80

1938 (Dec.) 1931 ½a, surcharged 'Quarter Anna' in Devanagari.

19	¼a/½a black and violet (R)	£11	£15

1947-48 Silver Jubilee of Maharaja's Accession. Designs, ¼a palace gate; ¾a map of Jaipur; 1a observatory; 2a Wind Palace; 3a coat of arms; 4a Amber Fort gate; 8a Chariot of the Sun; 1r Maharaja's portrait. Printers, De La Rue (recess). Perf 13½ x 14.

20	¼a red-brown and green		
	(5/48)	.75	£4
21	½a green and violet	.25	3.75
22	¾a black and lake (5/48)	.75	4.50
23	1a red-brown and		
	ultramarine	.50	£4
24	2a violet and scarlet	.50	£4
25	3a green and black (5/48)	.90	£5

26	4a ultramarine and brown	.50	£4
27	8a vermilion and brown	.50	4.50
28	1r purple and green (5/48)	1.50	£40
20/28	set (9)	5.50	£65

1947 (Dec.) Design as No. 7, etc. No wmk.

29	3p/½a black and violet (R)	12.50	£22
	a 'PIE' for 'PIES''	£38	£95
	b bars at left vertical	£55	£100
	c surcharge inverted	£38	£35
	ca as above, one bar at left	-	-
	cb as above with error 'PIE'	£200	£200
	d surcharge double,		
	one inverted	£55	£40
	da as above, one bar at left	-	-
	db as above with error 'PIE'	£350	£340

There were 3 settings of 6 x 5 (quarter sheets).

29a 'PIE' for 'PIES' occurs on R5/5 on 2 of the 3 settings.

29b The left bars are vertical on R6/1 on one setting.

OFFICIAL STAMPS

1931-7 values (inscribed 'POSTAGE') overprinted 'SERVICE' in red. Designs, ½a portrait; 1a elephant and banner; 2a sowar in armour; 4a elephant carriage.

XO1	½a black and violet	.25	.10
XO2	1a black and blue	£225	2.25
XO3	2a black and buff (1936)	3.50	4.50
O1	4a black and olive-green		
	(1937)	£40	£32

1932-7 Portraits (inscribed 'POSTAGE AND REVENUE') overprinted 'SERVICE' in red.

XO4	1a **black and blue**	3.50	.10
XO5	2a **black and buff**	£4	.10
O2	4a **black and grey-green**		
	(1937)	£325	£8
XO6	8a **black and chocolate**	£9	.85
XO7	1r **black and yellow-bistre**	£24	£22

1936-46 Portrait (inscribed 'POSTAGE') overprinted 'SERVICE' in red

O3	¼a **black and brown-lake**		
	(1936)	.30	.10
O4	¾a **black and brown-red**		
	(1944)	1.20	.40
O5	1a **black and blue**		
	(1941?)	3.75	.25
O6	2a **black and buff**	£3	2.75
O7	2½a **black and carmine**		
	(1946)	£8	£100
O8	4a **black and grey-green**		
	(1942)	4.75	£6
O9	8a **black and chocolate**		
	(1943)	£3	6.75
O10	1r **black and yellow-bistre**	£30	-
O3/O10	**set** (8)	£50	-

1936 No. O4, overprinted 'SERVICE' locally in black.

O11	¼a **black and red-brown**	£70	£60

1947 No. O6, surcharged '9 PIES'.

O12	9p/1a **black and blue (R)**	£3	£3

1947 (Dec.) As No. 29, overprinted 'SERVICE' in red.

O13	3p/½a **black and violet**	4.50	£11
	a surcharge double,		
	one inverted	£40	£40
	ab as above, error 'PIE'	£225	£240
	c surcharge inverted	-	£1250

1949 As XO1, surcharged in Devanagri; in red 'THREE-QUARTER ANNA'.

O14	¾a/½a **black and violet**	£15	£16
	a surcharge double	£1250	£1200

There are 3 settings of this surcharge.

Jaipur became part of Rajasthan by 7 April 1949.

JASDAN

1942-47 Design, Sun. Printers L V Inap & Co, Bombay (typo). Various perfs. 1-4 imperforate on one or two sides, from booklet panes of four; 5-6 from booklet panes of 6, perforated all round.

1	1a **deep myrtle-green** (p10½ x imperf)	£1100	£800
2	1a **light green** (p12 x imperf)	£575	£600
3	1a **light green** (1943) (p10½ x imperf)	£130	£160
4	1a **pale yellow-green** (p8½ x imperf)	£15	£140
5	1a **dull yellow-green** (1946) (p10)	£22	£150
6	1a **bluish green** (1947) (p9)	£19	£130

A 1a rose, with the arms of Jasdan in the centre, is a fiscal stamp.

Jasdan was merged with the United State of Kathiawar by April 1948.

KISHANGARH

1943-47 Design, Maharaja Yagyanarayan Singh. Thick, soft, unsurfaced paper. Mostly poor impressions, pin-perf.

2	¼a **pale dull blue** (1945)	3.50	£12
	a imperf pair	£28	-
3	¼a **greenish blue** (1947)	2.75	£8
	a imperf pair	£24	-
4	½a **deep green** (1944)	1.30	2.25
	a imperf pair	£20	£20
	b pair imperf between (vert or horiz)	£40	-
5	½a **yellow-green** (1946)	5.75	£8
	a imperf pair	£32	£32
	b pair imperf between (vert or horiz)	£40	-
6	1a **carmine** (1944)	6.50	3.50
	a double print	£260	-
	b imperf pair	£32	£32
	c pair imperf between (vert or horiz)	£40	-
	d red-orange (1947)	£70	£35
	e imperf pair	£125	£90
7	2a **bright magenta**	£10	£11
	a imperf pair	£60	£65
8	2a **maroon** (1947)	£80	£15
	a imperf pair	£40	£45
	b pair imperf between (horiz or vert)	£110	-
9	4a **brown**	£20	£15
	a imperf pair	-	-
10	8a **violet** (1945)	£40	£150
11	1r **green** (1945)	£50	£160
	a imperf pair	£185	£325
12	2r **yellow**	-	-
	a imperf pair	£500	-
13	5r **claret** (1945)	£600	£700
	a imperf pair	£325	-

Earlier issues were on thick, surfaced paper.

Kishangarh became part of Rajasthan by 15 April 1948.

MORVI

1935-48 Design, Maharaja Lakhdirji. Printers, Morvi Press (typo). Rough perf 11.

1	3p **scarlet** (shades)	1.50	£4
	a imperf between		
	(horiz pair)	£1250	-
2	6p **grey-green**	1.50	£3
	a emerald-green (1944-8)	6.75	£25
	b yellow-green	£7	-
3	1a **brown**	£9	£13
	a pale yellow-brown (1944-8)	£12	£20
	b chocolate (1944-8)	£16	£25
4	2a **dull violet** (shades)	1.75	£15
1/4	**set** (4)	£12	£32

Morvi merged with the United State of Kathiawar by 15 April 1948.

ORCHHA

1939-1942? Design, Maharaja Vir Singh II. Printers, Indian Security Printing Press, Nasik (litho). Nos 1-10 perf 13½ x 14, Nos 11-16 perf 14 x 13½.

1	½a **chocolate**	£3	£75
2	½a **yellow-green**	£3	£60
3	¾a **bright blue**	4.25	£90
4	1a **scarlet**	£3	£15
5	1¼a **blue**	3.50	£90
6	1½a **mauve**	3.75	£110
7	2a **vermilion**	£3	£65
8	2½a **turquoise-green**	4.50	£200
9	3a **slate-violet**	£5	£200
10	4a **slate**	5.75	£110
11	8a **magenta**	£9	£22
12	1r **grey-green**	£16	£200
13	2r **bright violet**	£38	£500
14	5r **yellow-orange**	£120	£700
15	10r **turquoise-green** (1942)	£400	£1600
16	15r **slate-lilac**	-	-
17	25r **claret**	-	-

The vast majority of 'used' stamps from this set have faked cancellations.

Orchha became part of Vindhya Pradesh by 1 May 1948.

RAJASTHAN

Rajasthan was made up of a number of smaller states, including Bundi, Jaipur and Kishangarh, whose own posts also ran until closed on April 1st 1950.

example with handstamp    machine overprint

BUNDI

1949   Handstamped in black

1	¼a **blue-green**	£4	-
2	½a **violet**	£4	-
3	1a **yellow-green**	£3.75	-
4	2a **vermilion**	£11	-
5	4a **orange**	£38	-
6	8a **ultramarine**	6.75	-

Overprinted in violet

7	¼a **blue-green**	4.50	-
8	½a **violet**	4.50	-
9	1a **yellow-green**	£12	-
10	2a **vermilion**	£24	-
11	4a **orange**	£24	-
12	8a **ultramarine**	6.75	-
13	1r **chocolate**	£220	-

Overprinted in blue

14	¼a **blue-green**	£28	-
15	½a **violet**	£40	-
16	1a **yellow-green**	£38	-
17	4a **orange**	£110	-
18	8a **ultramarine**	£65	-
19	1r **chocolate**	£80	-

Most of the above are known with the handstamps inverted, double or sideways.Pairs are known with and without handstamp.

As above, but machine-printed in black. An impression of the overprint shows on the back of the stamps.

24	2a **vermilion**	£7	£60
	a overprint inverted	£250	-

25	4a **orange**	£3	£60
	a overprint double	£250	-
26	8a **ultramarine**	£14	-
	a overprint inverted	£575	-
	b overprint double	£350	-
27	1r **chocolate**	£6	-

JAIPUR

1950 Stamps of Jaipur overprinted in various colours.

28	¼a **black and brown-lake** (B)	£5	£20
29	½a **black and violet** (R)	£4	£20
30	¾a **black and brown-red** (B-Blk)	£6	£22
	a overprint in pale blue	£10	£40
31	1a **black and blue** (R)	4.75	£40
32	2a **black and buff** (R)	£5	£55
33	2½a **black and carmine** (B)	£6	£25
34	3a **black and green** (R)	£7	£60
35	4a **black and grey-green** (R)	£6	£65
36	6a **black and pale blue** (R)	£6	£100
37	8a **black and chocolate** (R)	£10	£140
38	1r **black and yellow-bistre** (R)	£14	£220
28/38	**set** (11)	£65	£700

Most 'used' examples on the market bear forged cancellations.

KISHANGARH

1948-1949 Various stamps of Kishangarh, as detailed.

On the 1899-1901 issue, handstamped in red as no.1. 39 imperf, 40-6 pin-perf 12½ or 14.

39	¼a **rose-pink** (B)	£225	-
40	¼a **rose-pink**	-	£225
41	½a **deep blue**	£500	-

42	1a **brown-lilac**	£10	£40
	a imperf pair	£32	£85
	b violet handstamp	-	£400
	c black handstamp	-	£450
43	4a **chocolate**	£70	£95
	a violet handstamp	-	£525
44	1r **dull green**	£250	£285
45	2r **brown-red**	£325	-
46	5r **mauve**	£300	£300

On the 1904-1910 issue, handstamped in red as No. 1.

47	½a **chestnut**	-	£175
48	1a **blue**	-	£225
49	4a **brown**	£10	-
	a blue handstamp	£200	-
50	8a **grey**	£95	£130
51	8a **violet**	£8	-
52	1r **green**	£9	-
53	2r **olive-yellow**	£14	-
54	5r **purple-brown**	£20	-
	a blue handstamp	£400	-

On the 1912-1916 issue, handstamped in red as no.1

55	½a **green**	£400	£200
56	1a **red**	-	£250
57	2a **deep violet**	£500	-
58	2a **purple**	2.25	£7
	a pair with and without h/s	£375	-
59	4a **bright blue**	-	£480
60	8a **brown**	3.75	-
	a pair with and without h/s	£375	-
61	1r **mauve**	6.50	-
62	2r **deep green**	6.50	-
63	5r **brown**	£400	-

On the 1928-36 issue, handstamped in red as no.1.

64	½a **yellow-green**	£160	-

65	2a **magenta**	-	£550
66	4a **chestnut**	£260	-
67	8a **violet**	£4	£50
	a pair, with and without h/s	£350	-
68	1r **light green**	£15	-
69	2r **lemon-yellow**	£12	-
70	5r **claret**	£12	-

On the 1943-7 issue, handstamped in red, as no.1

71	¼a **pale dull blue**	£95	£100
72	¼a **greenish blue**	£38	£42
	a imperf pair	£200	-
73	½a **deep green**	£24	£28
	a violet handstamp	-	£270
74	½a **yellow-green**	£30	£35
	a imperf pair	£200	-
	b blue handstamp	-	£250
75	1a **carmine-red**	£60	£65
	a violet handstamp	-	£250
76	1a **orange-red** (imperf)	£150	-
	a blue handstamp	£160	-
77	2a **bright magenta**	£185	£200
78	2a **maroon** (imperf)	£200	-
79	4a **brown**	£2	6.75
80	8a **violet**	£12	£50
81	1r **green**	4.50	-
82	2r **yellow**	£80	-
83	5r **claret**	£42	-

A 1 anna in deep violet was issued for revenue purposes; it is known postally used.

A good deal of care is necessary when purchasing the more expensive stamps of Rajasthan. Forged cancellations and handstamps abound.

SORUTH

1929 (1 Oct.) Designs, 3p and 3a Junagadh City; ½a and 4a Gir Lion; 1a and 1r Nawab Mahabat Khan III; 2a, 8a Kathi horse. Inscribed 'POSTAGE'. Designers, Amir Sheikh Mahamadbhai. Printed litho, Indian Security Printing Press, Nasik, Perf 14.

X1	3p **black and blackish green**	.60	.10
X2	½a **black and deep blue**	£4	.10
X3	1a **black and carmine**	£3	.70
X4	2a **black and dull orange**	£8	1.40
	a **grey and dull yellow**	£20	1.20
X5	3a **black and carmine**	£4	9.50
X6	4a **black and purple**	£8	£19
X7	8a **black and yellow-green**	£12	£16
X8	1r **black and pale blue**	£10	£22
X1-8	**set** (8)	£45	£60

1936 Design, Nawab Mahabat Khan III. Inscribed 'POSTAGE AND REVENUE'. Printers Indian Security Printing Press, Nasik (litho). Perf 14.

1	1a **black and carmine**	6.50	.65

OFFICIAL STAMPS

1938 No. 1 overprinted 'SARKARI' in vermilion.

O1	1a **black and carmine**	12.50	1.50
	a brown-red overprint	£10	£1

The state was occupied by Indian troops on 9 November 1947 following the flight of the Nawab to Pakistan.

UNITED STATE OF SAURASHTRA

Junagadh, where the following issues are believed to have been used, joined the United State of Saurashtra on 20th January 1949, after a referendum.

The following issues were surcharged at the Junagadh State Press. Overprint varieties on nos. 2-5 are numerous. Only the most significant are listed.

1949 (June) x2 surcharged in red.

2	1a/½a **black and deep blue**	6.50	3.75
	a surcharge double	†	£450
	b 'AFNA' error	£2400	-
	c large first 'A' in 'ANNA' (R2/5)	£60	£45
	d small 'V' (R2/3)	£60	£45
	e small 'N' in 'REVENUE' (R2/4)	£60	£45
	f small 'E' in 'POSTAGE' (R3/2)	£60	£45
	g thick 'A' in 'POSTAGE' (R4/4)	£60	£45
	h inverted 'N' in 'REVENUE', small second 'A' in 'ANNA' (R4/5)	£60	£45
	i small 'O' (R6/1)	£60	£45

j small 'V' and 'U' (R6/3) £60 £45
k small 'N' in 'ONE' (R7/2) £60 £45

2b The overprint reads 'AFNA' instead of 'ANNA'. It also has an inverted 'N' in 'REVENUE'.

1949 (2 Feb.) X4a surcharged in green.

3 1a/2a **grey and dull yellow** £12 £20
   a 'EVENUE' omitted - £600

1949 Court Fee Stamp of Bhavnagar State overprinted 'SAURASHTRA' and 'U.S.S. REVENUE & POSTAGE' in black. Perf 11.

4 1a **purple** 6.50 6.50
   a overprint double £275 £325
   b 'POSTAGE' omitted (R2/1) £275 £180
   c small 'S' in 'POSTAGE'
     (R2/1) £50 £40
   d small 'N' in 'REVENUE'
     (R2/7) £50 £40
   e small 'U' in 'REVENUE'
     (R3/2) £50 £40
   f small 'V' in 'REVENUE'
     (R3/8, 5/5) £50 £40
   g small 'O' in 'POSTAGE'
     (R4/7) £50 £40

1950 (March) X1. Surcharged 'POSTAGE & REVENUE ONE ANNA'.

5 1a/3p **black and blackish green** £28 £40
   a 'P' of 'POSTAGE' omitted
     (R8/1) £375 £450
   b 'O' of 'ONE' omitted
     (R6/1) £600 -
   c small second 'A' in 'ANNA'
     (R1/2) £90 £120
   d small 'S' and 'V' (R2/3, 3/1) £90 £120

OFFICIAL STAMPS

SARKARI Type 1

SARKARI Type 2

SARKARI Type 3

1948 (July-Dec.) X4a, X5-7 overprinted 'SARKARI' (type 1) and 'ONE ANNA' (2¼mm high), by Junagadh State Press.

O2 1a/2a **grey and
      dull yellow (B)** £15000 £19
O3 1a/3a **black and carmine** £3500 £50
      a surcharge double † £3250
O4 1a/4a **black and purple** £325 £50
      a 'ANNE' error £2500 £350
      b 'ANNN' error £2500 £350
O5 1a/8a **black and yellow-green** £275 £38
      a 'ANNE' error £2500 £275
      b 'ANNN' error £2500 £275

O4a/O5a R5/4 'ANNE' for 'ANNA'.

O4b/O5b R7/5 'ANNN' for 'ANNA'.

1948-9 handstamped 'SARKARI' and 'ONE ANNA' (4mm high).

O6 1a/1r **black and pale blue**
      (Type 1) £2000 £38
O7 1a/1r **black and pale blue**
      (Type 2) £800 £40
O8 1a/1r **black and pale blue**
      (Type 3) - £65

1949 (Jan) As 1929 issue overprinted 'SARKARI', (type 3) in red.

O9   3p **black and
       blackish green** £200 £13
O10 ½a **black and deep blue** £500 £11
O11 1a/2a **grey and dull yellow** £70 £19

O11 is No. 3 overprinted.

Various errors occur on these overprints.

Mauscript overprints are known reading 'Service', in English or Gujerati script, usually in red. These provisionals were used at Gadhda and Una between June and December 1949. Stamps known are X1, X2,1, 2, 3 and 4.

The United State of Saurashtra postal service was incorporated into that of India 31 March 1950. The use of Soruth stamps was permitted until the end of April.

TRAVANCORE

Watermark
Conch Shell

Image 1

1937-39 Design, conch shell. Watermark, Conch shell. Various perfs. On machine made paper.

1	¾ch **mauve** (8/37) P 12½		7.50	.45
2	¾ch **reddish violet** perf 12			
	(/39)		2.75	.45
	a perf 12½		3.50	.35
	b comp P12 and 12½		5.50	1.50
	c perf 11		-	£80
	d comp P12 and 11		-	£80

Compound perfs occur when two different perforating heads are used to perforate the same sheet. The top, bottom or either side measures differently from the others.

Image 2

1937 (29 March) Image 2, Temple Entry Proclamation. Designs, 6ca, Maharaja Bala Rama Varma XI and Subramania Shrine; 12a, Sri Padmanabha; 1½ca, Mahadeva; 3ch Kanyakumari. Plates by Indian Security Printing Press, Nasik. Typo Stamp Manufactory, Trivandrum. Watermark Conch Shell. Perf 12.

3	6ca **carmine**		1.70	.85
	a imperf between			
	(horiz. strip of 3)		£450	-
	b imperf between stamp			
	and margin		-	-
4	12ca **bright blue**		2.50	.30
5	1½ch **yellow-green**		£1	1.40
	a imperf between (vert pair)		£300	-
6	3ch **violet**		3.25	1.50
	a imperf between stamp			
	and margin		-	-

1937 Image 2, perf 12½.

7	6ca **carmine**	1.70	1.25
8	12ca **bright blue**	£3	.50
	a imperf between (vert. pair)	£400	-
	b imperf between stamp and margin	-	-
9	1½ch **yellow-green**	£22	£5
	a imperf between stamp and margin	-	-
10	3ch **violet**	3.75	2.75

1937 Image 2, compound perf.

11	6ca **carmine**	£32	£38
12	12ca **bright blue**	£55	-
13	1½ch **yellow-green**	-	-

Image 3 (slightly reduced) Image 4

1939 (9 Nov) Image 3 and 4, Maharaja's 27th birthday. Designs 1ch, Lake Ashtamudi; 1½ch, 2ch, 3ch Maharaja Bala Rama Varma XI; 4ch, Sri Padmanabha Shrine; 7ch, Cape Comorin; 14ch Pachipari Reservoir. Plates by Indian Security Printing Press, Nasik. Typo Stamp Manufactory, Trivandrum. Watermark Conch Shell. Perf 12½.

14	1ch **yellow-green**	£4	.10
	a imperf between (horiz pair)	£6	-
15	1½ch **scarlet**	2.75	3.50
	a double print	£300	-
	b imperf between (horiz pair)	£22	-
	c imperf between (vert pair)	£18	-
	d imperf pair	£25	-
16	2ch **orange**	£5	1.50
17	3ch **brown**	4.75	.10
	a double print	-	£130
	b imperf between (horiz pair)	£35	£55
18	4ch **red-brown**	5.50	.30
19	7ch **pale blue**	£7	£16
20	14ch **turquoise-green**	£5	£55

As Images 3 and 4, perf 11.

21	1ch **yellow-green**	£10	.10
	a imperf between (vert pair)	£32	£42
	b imperf between (vert strip of 3)	£18	£32
22	1½ch **scarlet**	3.50	£22
	a imperf horiz (vert pair)	£7	-
23	2ch **orange**	£14	.70
24	3ch **brown**	4.75	.10
	a double print	£35	£50

25	4ch **red-brown**	£32	.35
26	7ch **pale blue**	£75	£30
	a **blue**	£70	£28
27	14ch **turquoise-green**	£10	£100

As Image 3 and 4, perf 12.

28	1ch **yellow-green**	£22	1.75
	a imperf between (horiz pair)	£18	-
	b imperf between (vert pair)	£40	-
29	1½ch **scarlet**	£32	£5
30	2ch **orange**	£100	£5
31	3ch **brown**	£35	£3
	a imperf between (vert pair)	£125	£140
32	4ch **red-brown**	£30	£8

As Images 3 and 4, compound perf.

33	1ch **yellow-green**	£25	£3
	a imperf between (vert pair)	£130	-
34	1½ch **scarlet**	£45	£7
35	2ch **orange**	£100	£7
36	3ch **brown**	£35	.80
37	4ch **red-brown**	£160	£130
38	7ch **pale blue**	£100	£40

As Image 4, perf 13½.

39	1½ch **scarlet**	£15	£60

Image 5

1941 (20 Oct) Image 5, Maharaja's 29th birthday. Designs 6ca Maharaja and Aruvikara Falls, ¾ch Maharaja and Marthanda Varma bridge. Plates by Indian Security Printing Press, Nasik. Watermak conch shell. Perf 12½.

40	6ca **blackish violet**	5.75	.10
41	¾ch **brown**	6.50	.15

As Image 5, perf 11.

42	6ca **blackish violet**	£5	.10
	a imperf between (vert. pair)	£15	-
	b imperf horiz (vert. pair)	£40	£58
43	¾ch **brown**	£8	.15
	a imperf between (horiz. pair)	£150	-
	b imperf between (vert. pair)	£25	£40
	c imperf between (vertical strip of 3)	£25	-
	d block of 4 (imperf internally)	£200	-

As Image 5, perf 12.

44	6ca **blackish violet**	£20	1.75
	a imperf between (horiz pair)	£20	-
	b imperf between (vert pair)	£45	-
	c imperf between (vert strip of 3)	£18	-
45	¾ch **brown**	£45	£8

As Image 5, compound perf.

46	6ca **blackish violet**	6.50	£1
47	¾ch **brown**	£12	£1

Image 6

1943 (17 Sept), surcharged as Image 6. Perf 12½.

48	2ca/1½ch **scarlet** (No 15)	1.20	£1
	a imperf between (vert pair)	£38	-
	b imperf between stamp and margin	-	-
	c '2' omitted	£275	£275
	d 'CA' omitted	£400	-
	e 'ASH' omitted	£400	-
49	4ca/¾ch **brown** (No 43)	£3	1.25
50	8ca/6ca **scarlet** (No 42)	3.75	.10

50 is as No 42 but with colour changed.

As Image 6, perf 11.

51	2c/1½ch **scarlet**	.30	.20
	a 'CA' omitted	£400	-
52	4ca/¾ch **brown**	£4	.20
53	8ca/6ca **scarlet**	£3	.10
	a imperf between (horiz pair) £34		-

As Image 6, perf 12

54	4ca/¾ch **brown**	-	£140
55	8ca/6ca **scarlet**	-	£78

As Image 6, compound perf

56	2ca/1½ch **scarlet**	.60	£1
	a imperf between (vert. pair)	£130	-
	b '2' omitted	£300	-
57	4ca/¾ch **brown**	4.50	.85
58	8ca/6ca **scarlet**	£14	£7

Image 7

1946 (24 Oct) Maharaja's 34th birthday (Image 7). Plates by Indian Security Printing Press, Nasik. Typo Stamp Manufactory, Trivandrum. Watermark Conch shell. Perf 12½.

59	8ca **scarlet**	£22	2.50
	a perf 11	£1	1.50
	b perf 12	£35	1.75
	c imperf between (horiz pair)	£32	£50
	d imperf between (horiz strip of 3)	£48	-
	e compound perf	-	-

1946 No. O45 validated for ordinary postage. Overprinted 'Special' in orange. Watermark Conch shell. Perf 12½.

60	6ca **blackish violet**	£5	2.25
	a perf 11	£35	£5
	b compound perf	£5	£5

OFFICIAL STAMPS

Type A	Type B

1939-1941 Image 1. Overprinted Type A. Perf 12½.

O1	6ca **brown-red** (1941)	.60	.20
	a perf 11	£1	.60
	b perf 12	.55	.20
	c compound perf	.50	.90
O2	¾ca **reddish violet**	£130	£68
	a perf 12	£24	£1
	b compound perf	£125	£60

Type A measures 13 mm across and the tail of the R is curved. Type B measures 13½ mm and the tail to the R is straight.

1939 (Nov. 9th) Image 3, overprinted Type A. Perf 12½.

O3	1ch **yellow-green**	5.50	.30
O4	1½ch **scarlet**	£6	£1
	a 'SESVICE'	£85	£22
O5	2ch **orange**	£6	£6
	a 'SESVICE'	£80	£110
O6	3ch **brown**	£5	.20
	a 'SESVICE'	£70	£16
O7	4ch **red-brown**	12.50	4.50
O8	7ch **pale blue**	£13	£3
O9	14ch **turquoise-green**	£16	5.50

As Image 3, Perf 12.

O10	1½ch **scarlet**	£50	£10
	a 'SESVICE'	-	£150
	b imperf between (horiz pair)	†	£225
O11	3ch **brown**	£26	.40
	a 'SESVICE'	£250	£45

As Image 3, compound perf.

O12	1½ch **scarlet**	£15	2.50
O13	2ch **orange**	£120	£120
O14	3ch **brown**	£10	£4

1940(?)-45 Image 1, overprinted Type B. Perf 12½.

O15	¾ch **reddish violet** (No. 2a)	£16	.15
	a imperf between (horiz pair)	£135	£150
	b Perf 11	£55	£1
	c Perf 12	£20	.20
	d compound perf	£40	.65
O16	1½ch **rose** (1945)	£12	6.50
	a Perf 12	£4	.80
	b compound perf	£20	£12

O16 was overprinted from an early (1932) printing.

1939 Image 3, overprinted Type B. Perf 12½.

O17	1ch **yellow-green**	£1	.10
	a Imperf between (vert pair)	£40	£45
	b overprint inverted	†	£36
	c overprint double	£20	-
O18	1½ch **scarlet**	£4	.10
	a double overprint in pair with normal	-	-
	b imperf between (horiz pair)	£55	-
O19	2ch **orange**	2.25	.25
O20	3ch **brown**	1.75	.10
	a imperf between (vert pair)	†	£525
O21	4ch **red-brown**	3.25	.75
O22	7ch **pale blue**	7.50	.25
O23	14ch **turquoise-green**	£13	.55

As Image 3, Type B. Perf 11.

O24	1ch **yellow-green**	.55	.10
	a imperf between (vert pair)	£36	-
	b overprint double	£120	£120
	c imperf between stamp and margin	-	-
O25	1½ch **scarlet**	£2	.15
	a imperf between (vert pair)	£120	£120
	b imperf between (vert strip of 3)	£80	-
	c imperf between (horiz pair)	†	£125
O26	2ch **orange**	£9	1.75
	a imperf between (vert pair)	†	£550
O27	3ch **brown**	£3	.10
O28	4ch **red-brown**	3.75	.40
O29	7ch **pale blue**	£5	£4
	a blue	£12	5.50
O30	14ch **turquoise-green**	£13	1.20

As Image 3, Type B. Perf 12.

O31	1ch **yellow-green**	2.75	.40
	a imperf between (vert pair)	£80	£80
	b stamp doubly printed	£120	-
	c overprint inverted	†	£120
	d overprint double	£20	£25
	e overprint double in pair with normal	-	-
O32	1½ch **scarlet**	5.50	.50
	a imperf between (vert strip of 3)	£160	-
O33	2ch **orange**	£100	£100
	a imperf between (vert pair)	£500	£500
O34	3ch **brown**	5.50	£2
	a imperf between (vert pair)	£500	£500
O35	4ch **red-brown**	£18	5.50

O36	7ch **pale blue**	£22	£9
	a blue	£8	5.50
O37	14ch **turquoise-green**	£9	£2

As Image 3, Type B (Nos. O17-O23), compound perf.

O38	1ch **yellow-green**	£6	1.25
	a imperf between (vert pair)	†	£160
O39	1½ch **scarlet**	3.50	.25
	a imperf pair	£22	-
O40	2ch **orange**	£100	£100
O41	3ch **brown**	£19	.65
O42	4ch **red-brown**	£52	£22
O43	7ch **pale blue**	£20	4.50
	a blue	£26	£16
O44	14ch **turquoise-green**	£65	£8

1942 Image 5, overprinted Type B.

O45	6ca **blackish violet**	.45	.50
	a perf 11	.55	.10
	b perf 12	£65	£8
	c compound perf	1.25	.90
O46	¾ca **brown**	£5	.10
	a imperf between (vert pair)	†	£375
	b perf 11	6.50	.10
	c perf 12	£65	2.50
	d compound perf	£9	.65

1943 Image 4 surcharged and overprinted 'SERVICE'. Perf 12½

O47	8ca/6ca **scarlet**	2.75	.25
	a perf 11	£1	.10
	ab surcharge inverted	†	£1000
	c compound perf	6.50	1.25

1945 Image 6 surcharged with Type B, perf 12½.

O48	2ca/1½ch **scarlet**	.50	.75
	a perf 11	.35	.15
	aa pair, with and		
	without surcharge	£275	-
	b compound perf	.50	1.25

	ba '2' omitted	£375	£375
	c perf 12	-	-
O49	4ca/¾ch **brown**	£3	.30
	a perf 11	2.25	.20
	b compound perf	£2	1.25

1947 Image 7, overprint type B. Perf 12½.

O50	8ca **carmine**	2.75	£1
	a stamp doubly printed	£25	-
	b perf 11	1.90	.65
	ba imperf between (horiz. pair)	£35	-
	bb imperf between (vert. pair)	†	£190
	bc overprint double	†	£230
	c perf 12	2.75	1.10
	ca stamp doubly printed	£35	-

From 1 July 1949 Travancore became part of the new State of Travancore-Cochin.

TRAVANCORE-COCHIN

The United States of Travancore and Cochin came into being on 1st July 1949. The name was changed to State of Travancore-Cochin on 26th January 1950.

Stamps of Travancore-Cochin were valid externally from 6th June 1950.

1949 (1 July) Stamps of Travancore (Nos. 41, 59, 14, 16, etc) surcharged 'PIES' or 'ANNAS'. Perf 12½.

1	2p/6ca **blackish violet** (R)	2.25	1.25
	a surcharge inverted	£35	-
	b character error	£120	£80
	c 'O' inverted	£32	12.50
2	4p/8ca **carmine**	1.10	.20
	a surcharge inverted	£40	-
	b 'S' inverted	£70	£35
3	½a/1ch **yellow-green**	2.50	.20
	a 'NANA' error	£120	£65
	b inverted 'H'	-	£80
	c imperf between (vert pair)	†	£120
4	1a/2ch **orange**	2.50	.20
5	2a/4ch **red-brown**	2.50	.40
	a surcharge inverted	†	£225
	b 'O' inverted	£36	£14
6	3a/7ch **pale blue**	7.50	£4
7	6a/14ch **turquoise-green**	£13	£25
	a accent omitted	£250	-

റണ്ട് ൭൭പ്ൻ
normal

റണ്ട് റ൭പ്ൻ
CW 1b, etc character error

1b, 8c, 15d, 33a an error occurs on R14/2 RP where the wrong character starts the second group.

1c, 5b, 8d, 12a, 15g, 19a, the 'O' is inverted. See Officials.

2b, 9e, 16d, the 'S' is inverted.

3a, 10c, 17d R3/3 LP has been overprinted 'NANA' instead of 'ANNA' 3b, 10d, the 'H' is inverted.

7a, 14a, 21a, 30a, the accent on the native surcharge is omitted on R13/4 RP.

As above, Perf 11.

8	2p/6ca **blackish violet** (R)	1.25	.20
	a imperf between (vert. pair)	£160	£160
	b pair with and without surcharge	£90	-
	c character error	£130	£75
	d 'O' inverted	£32	£15
9	4p/8ca **carmine**	1.80	.20
	a imperf between (vert pair)	£150	£150
	b surcharge inverted	£90	-
	c pair, with and without surcharge	£120	-
	d 'FOUP' error	£150	£85
	e 'S' inverted	£68	£38
10	½a/1ch **yellow-green**	2.50	.20
	a imperf between (vert pair)	£23	-
	b surcharge inverted	†	£175
	c 'NANA' error	£160	£90
	d inverted 'H'	-	£70
11	1a/2ch **orange**	.50	.20
	a surcharge double	£38	-
12	2a/4ch **red-brown**	2.40	.40
	a 'O' inverted		£15
13	3a/7ch **pale blue**	£4	2.75
	a blue	£55	3.75
	b '3' omitted	†	£550
14	6a/14ch **turquoise-green**	£13	£20
	a accent omitted	£240	£260

9d, 16c, 'FOUP' for 'FOUR'.

13b, '3' omitted from overprint.

As above, Perf 12.

15	2p/6ca **blackish violet** (R)	.35	.15
	a imperf between (horiz pair)	£55	-
	b imperf between (vert pair)	£5	£13
	c surcharge inverted	£90	-
	d character error	£120	£70
	e imperf between (vert strip of 3)	£26	-
	f block of 4 imperf between (horiz and vert)	£52	-
	g 'O' inverted	£30	£15
	h imperf between (horiz. strip of 3)	£58	-
16	4p/8ca **carmine**	1.25	.20
	a imperf between (vert pair)	£16	-
	b pair with and without surcharge	£110	-
	c 'FOUP' error	£110	-

d 'S' inverted		£85	£40
e surcharge inverted		£120	-
17 ½a/1ch **yellow-green**		.65	.25
a imperf between			
(horiz pair)		£50	£55
b imperf between			
(vert pair)		4.50	£11
c surcharge inverted		£4	-
d 'NANA' error		£200	£95
e block of 4 imperf			
between (horiz and vert) £42			-
18 1a/2ch **orange**		3.25	.35
a imperf between			
(horiz pair)		£6	-
b imperf between			
(vert pair)		£4	£10
c block of 4 imperf			
between (horiz and vert) £38			-
19 2a/4ch **red-brown**		2.40	.40
a 'O' inverted		£40	£15
20 3a/7ch **pale blue**		9.75	2.25
21 6a/14ch **turquoise-green**		£15	£26
a accent omitted		£250	£260

As above, Perf 14.

22 2p/6ca **blackish violet** (R)		†	£500
23 ½a/1ch **yellow-green**		†	£400

As above, compound perf.

24 2p/6ca **blackish violet** (R)		-	£34
25 4p/8ca **carmine**		-	£36
26 ½a/1ch **yellow-green**		-	£32
27 1a/2ch **orange**		£35	£20
28 2a/4ch **red-brown**		£40	£24
29 3a/7ch **pale blue**		-	£60
a blue		-	£85
30 6a/14ch **turquoise-green**		£35	£42
a accent omitted		£400	-

As above, Perf 13½.

31 4p/8ca **carmine**		†	£600
32 1a/2ch **orange**		£165	1.50

As above, imperforate pairs.

33 2p/6ca **blackish violet**		6.75	-
a character error		£225	-
34 4p/8ca **carmine**		£60	-
35 ½a/1ch **yellow-green**		£7	£16
36 1a/2ch **orange**		6.75	-
37 6a/14ch **turquoise-green**		-	-

1949 No 58 of Cochin overprinted 'U.S.T.C.'.

38 1a **orange**		4.50	£65
a no stop after 'S'		£60	-
b raised stop after 'T'		£60	-

38a there is no stop after the 'S' on R1/6.

38b the stop after the 'T' on R4/1 is raised.

1950 (1st April) No 58 of Cochin overprinted 'T.-C.'.

39 1a **orange**		5.50	£60
a No stop after 'T'		£45	£250
b overprint inverted		£225	-
ba No stop after 'T'		£1500	-

39a, ba R1/5, 1/8.

1950 (1st April) As above, surcharged.

40 6p/1a **orange**		3.25	£50
a no stop after 'T'		£16	-
b surcharge error		£12	-
ba no stop after 'S'		£160	-
bb raised stop after 'T'		£160	-

41 9p/1a **orange**   3.25   £42
   a no stop after 'T'   £16   -
   b surcharge error   £130   -
   ba no stop after 'S'   £600   -
   bb raised stop after 'T'   £600   -

40a, 41a no stop after 'T' occurs on R1/5.

overprint error

40b, 41b surcharge overprinted on CW 38 instead
of CW 39.

40ba, 41ba see 38a.

40bb, 41bb see 38b.

**1950 (24 Oct.) 2p Conch shell, 4p Palm
trees. Printers, Indian Security Printing
press, Nasik (Litho). Watermark multiple
star (as India). Perf 14.**

42 2p **rose-carmine**   £2   £3
43 4p **ultramarine**   2.75   £14

The ordinary issues of Travancore-Cohin became
obsolete on 1 July 1951.

OFFICIALS

These stamps were valid for use throughout India
from 30 September 1950.

Type 1 'Service' sans-serif

'Inverted O'   'FOUB' error

**1949 (1 July)-1950 Stamps of Travancore,
surcharged as Nos 1-7, etc, then overprinted
'SERVICE' (Type 1). No gum. Perf 12½.**

O1	2p/6ca	**blackish violet** (R)	1.50	.55
		a imperf between		
		(vert pair)	£160	£160
		b character error	£30	£20
		c 'O' inverted	£20	£11
		d pair, with and		
		without surcharge	£150	-
O2	4p/8ca	**carmine**	£3	.90
		a 'FOUB' error	£160	£100
O3	½a/1ch	**yellow-green**	.75	.20
		a pair, with and		
		without surcharge	£80	-
		b surcharge inverted	£20	-
		c 'NANA' error	£225	£65
O4	1a/2ch	**orange**	£14	5.50
		a surcharge inverted	£65	-
		b pair, with and		
		without surcharge	£550	-
O5	2a/4ch	**red-brown**	1.75	.75
O6	3a/7ch	**pale blue**	5.25	£2
		a imperf between		
		(vert pair)	£15	-
		b blue	£40	6.50
O7	6a/14ch	**turquoise-green**	£13	£8
		a imperf between		
		(vert pair)	£22	-

O1c, O8c, O12b, O15d, O18a, O34a, O40a, O46b
inverted 'O' see 1c, etc.

O2a, O8c, O16a, O31a, O37c, O43d 'FOUB' for
'FOUR' occurs on R2/3 LP.

O3c, O10c, O17a 'NANA' error for 'ANNA' occurs on R3/3 LP.

O1b, O8b, O15c 'Character error' see note below CW 7.

As above, overprinted Type 1. Perf 11.

O8	2p/6ca **blackish violet** (R)		.80	.15
	a imperf between			
	(vert pair)		£160	£160
	b character error		£33	£25
	c 'O' inverted		£20	£10
O9	4p/8ca **carmine**		£3	.25
	a 'FOUB' error		£75	£25
O10	½a/1ch **yellow-green**		.90	.20
	a pair, with and			
	without surcharge		£140	-
	b surcharge inverted		£55	-
	c 'NANA' error		£225	£75
O11	1a/2ch **orange**		£12	£6
	a pair, with and			
	without surcharge		£600	-
O12	2a/4ch **red-brown**		£5	.75
	a surcharge inverted		£800	-
	b 'O' inverted		-	£36
O13	3a/7ch **pale blue**		£3	.75
	a blue		£40	6.50
O14	6a/14ch **turquoise-green**		£12	8.50

As above, overprinted Type 1. Perf 12.

O15	2p/6ca **blackish violet** (R)		.45	.35
	a imperf between			
	(horiz pair)		6.50	£16
	b imperf between			
	(vert pair)		£5	-
	c character error		£30	£22
	d 'O' inverted		£20	-
	e block of 4 imperf			
	between (horiz and vert) £22			-
O16	4p/8ca **carmine**		£3	.40
	a 'FOUB' error		£100	£45
	b 'FOUR PIES' omitted			
	in pair with normal		£650	-
O17	½a/1ch **yellow-green**		£9	1.60
	a 'NANA' error		£360	£130
	b pair, with and			
	without surcharge		£95	-
	c surcharge inverted			
	on back		£260	-
O18	2a/4ch **red-brown**		£5	4.50
	a 'O' inverted		-	£65
	b pair, with and			
	without surcharge		£260	-
O19	3a/7ch **pale blue**		3.50	£4
	a imperf between			
	(horiz pair)		£15	-
	b imperf between			
	(vert pair)		6.75	-
	c block of 4 imperf			
	between (horiz and vert)		£34	-
	d blue		£40	3.75
O20	6a/14ch **turquoise-green**		£42	£9
	a imperf between			

(horiz pair)	£21	-
b imperf between		
(vert pair)	£28	-
c block of 4 imperf		
between (horiz and vert)	£55	-

As above, overprinted Type 1, compound perf.

O21	2p/6ca **blackish violet** (R)	£55	-
O22	4p/8ca **carmine**	£15	£15
O23	½a/1ch **yellow-green**	-	£18
O24	2a/4ch **red-brown**	-	£28

As above, imperforate pairs.

O25	2p/6ca **blackish violet**	6.50	£18
	a character error	£225	-
O26	2a/4ch **red-brown**	£10	-
O27	3a/7ch **pale blue**	£9	-
O28	6a/14ch **turquoise-green**	£12	-

1949-51 As No O1, etc but watermark 'Government of Cochin'. Various perfs. Overprinted Type 1.

O29	2p/6ca **blackish violet**			
	(R) P12½		.30	1.25
	a overprint double		£15	-
	b perf 11		.35	1.25
	c perf 12		.90	1.25
O30	2a/4ch **red-brown** P12½		2.25	1.25
	a perf 11		.65	.55
	ab imperf between			
	(vert pair)		£240	£250
	b perf 12		-	£65
	c compound perf		£50	£24

Type 2 'SERVICE' with serifs

'AANA' for 'ANNA'

Inverted 'C'

SERVICE

normal

SERVICE

Inverted 'S'

1949-51 As No. O1, etc but overprinted Type 2. Perf 12½. Watermark as Travancore.

O31	4p/8ca **carmine**	.75	.15
	a 'FOUB' error	£85	£32
	b 'E' error	£100	£42
	c inverted 'S'	-	£55
	d imperf between		
	(vert pair)	-	£135
O32	½a/1ch **yellow-green**	.75	.15
	a 'AANA' error	£160	£55
O33	1a/2ch **orange**	.30	.20
	a imperf between		
	(vert pair)	-	£135
	b imperf between		
	(horiz pair)	-	£135
O34	2a/4ch **red-brown**	3.25	.60
	a inverted 'O'	£75	£32
O35	3a/7ch **pale blue**	6.50	.85
	a inverted 'S'	£60	£25
	b inverted first 'E'	£130	£100
	c inverted 'C'	£75	£60
	d inverted second 'E'	£125	£100
O36	6a/14ch **turquoise-green**	1.10	3.75
	a accent omitted	£12	£10
	b inverted 'S'	£65	£34

O31b, O37d, O43e, O56e, 'E' error - the second 'E' in 'SERVICE' is in the wrong font.

O31c, O35a, O36b, O37e, O41a, O42b, O47a, O48b, 'S' in 'Pies' is inverted.

O32a, O38d, O44c, O51a, 'AANA' for 'ANNA' error occurs on R13/1 RP.

O35c and O35d the first or second 'E' is inverted.

O35c inverted 'C' on R4/1 or R5/1 LP.

O36a, O42a, O48a see 7a, etc.

O43f, 'FOUK' for 'FOUR'.

As above, Type 2. Perf 11.

O37	4p/8ca **carmine**	.35	.15
	a imperf between		
	(horiz pair)	£4	-
	b imperf between		
	(vert pair)	£32	-
	c 'FOUB' error	£75	£28
	d 'E' error	£100	£52
	e inverted 'S'	-	£65
	f block of 4 imperf		
	between (horiz and vert)	£30	-
O38	½a/1ch **yellow-green**	.35	.15
	a imperf between		
	(horiz pair)	£65	£65
	b imperf between		
	(vert pair)	£8	-
	c block of 4 imperf		
	between (horiz and vert)	£52	-
	d 'AANA' error	£60	£30

O39	1a/2ch **orange**	£3	.35
	a imperf between		
	(horiz pair)	6.50	£16
	b imperf between		
	(vert pair)	£85	£85
O40	2a/4ch **red-brown**	1.10	.85
	a inverted 'O'	£60	£32
O41	3a/7ch **pale blue**	1.10	.80
	a inverted 'S'	£40	£24
O42	6a/14ch **turquoise-green**	£11	£3
	a accent omitted	£45	£15
	b inverted 'S'	£110	£40

As above, Type 2. Perf 12.

O43	4p/8ca **carmine**	.20	.15
	a imperf between		
	(horiz pair)	£5	-
	b imperf between		
	(vert pair)	1.75	-
	c block of 4 imperf		
	between (horiz and vert)	£12	£22
	d 'FOUB' error	£95	£32
	e 'E' error	£110	£40
	f 'FOUK' error	-	-
	g imperf between		
	(horiz. strip of 3)	£40	-
	h imperf between		
	(vert. strip of 3)	£40	-
O44	½a/1ch **yellow-green**	.95	.15
	a imperf between		
	(horiz pair)	£3	-
	b imperf between		
	(vert pair)	£3	9.50
	c 'AANA' error	£85	£42
	d block of 4 imperf		
	between (horiz and vert)	£20	-
O45	1a/2ch **orange**	.35	.20
	a imperf between		
	(horiz pair)	£6	-
	b imperf between		
	(vert pair)	£3	£12
	c block of 4 imperf		
	between (horiz and vert)	£16	-
O46	2a/4ch **red-brown**	£7	.85
	a imperf between		
	(vert pair)	£100	£110
	b 'O' inverted	£110	£32
	c pair, with and		
	without surcharge	†	£800
O47	3a/7ch **pale blue**	£3	1.25
	a inverted 'S'	£110	£60
O48	6a/14ch **turquoise-green**	£32	3.75
	a accent omitted	£110	£23
	b inverted 'S'	£225	£50

As above, Type 2. Perf 13½.

O49	4p/8ca **carmine**	3.50	£1

As above, Type 2. Compound perf.

O50	4p/8ca **carmine**	6.50	6.50
O51	½a/1ch **yellow-green**	£20	£15
	a 'AANA' error	-	£200

O52 1a/2ch **orange** £28 £20
O53 2a/4ch **red-brown** £22 £12
O54 3a/7ch **pale blue** - £50
O55 6a/14ch **turquoise-green** £75 £85

As above, Type 2. Imperforate pairs.

O56 4p/8ca **carmine** 4.50 -
    a 'E' error £160 -
O57 ½a/1ch **yellow-green** £6 £15
O58 1a/2ch **orange** £12 -
O59 3a/7ch **pale blue** £40 -

1949 (July 1st)-51. Watermark 'Government of Cochin'. Various perfs.

O60 ½a/1ch **yellow-green** perf 12½ 2.25 .50
    a perf 11 .30 .30
    b perf 12 £16 £10
    c compound perf £10 2.50
O61 1a/2ch **orange** perf 12½ 1.75 .70
    a perf 11 .40 .30
    b perf 12 £10 £3
    d perf 13½ 1.50 £1
    e compound perf £4 2.25

The Official stamps became obsolete in September 1951.

IRELAND

DEFINITIVE ISSUES

Typographed by the Government Printers, Dublin Castle. Printed on Gaelic 'SE' watermark paper.

1922 (Dec. 6th)-35. Designs and designers: ½d, 5d, 6d, 8d, 1/- Sword of Light, J J O'Reilly; 1d, 1½d, 2d Map of Ireland, J. Ingram; 2½d, 4d, 9d Arms of Ireland, Miss M. Girling; 3d, 10d, 11d Celtic Cross, Miss L. Williams. Perf 15 x 14 and (Nos 31/3) 14 x 15. ½d - 1/-, sheets 240 (2 panes, 12 x 10 each). Watermark Gaelic SE.

G82 ½d **bright green** (20/4/23) 1.10 .55
    c watermark inverted £20 £25
G83 1d **carmine** (23/2/23) .50 .10
    a watermark inverted £30 £6
G84 1½d **claret** 1.10 1.50
    a watermark inverted £900 -
G85 2d **grey-green** .75 .10
    ac watermark inverted
     & reversed £28 £10
    ad watermark inverted £18 £5
G86 2½d **red-brown** £2 2.50
    a watermark inverted £40 £18
G87 3d **blue** (16/3/23) 1.10 .60
    a watermark inverted £48 £20
G88 4d **slate-blue** 1.20 £2
    a watermark inverted £95 £35
G89 5d **bright violet** £5 £6
    a watermark inverted - -
G90 6d **claret** 2.50 £2
    a watermark inverted £110 £50
G91 9d **bright violet** £8 £5
    a watermark inverted - -
G92 10d **brown** 5.50 £12
    a watermark inverted - -
G93 1/- **light blue** £10 3.75
    a watermark inverted - -
G82/93 **set** (12) £35 £33

1937 (Sept. 8th) Design, St. Patrick invoking Blessing on Paschal Fire, framed by an outline of the 11th Century Shrine of St. Patrick's Bell. Designer, R J King. Watermark Gaelic SE. Perf 14 x 15. Chalk-surfaced paper. Sheets 8 x 5.

14	2/6d **green**	£70	£45
	a watermark inverted	£400	£200
15	5/- **maroon**	£90	£75
	a watermark inverted	£350	£175
16	10/- **deep blue**	£70	£35
	a watermark inverted	£500	-
14/16	**set** (3)	£210	£140

1940-52 Various designs as 1922-35 and 1937 definitives but watermark Gaelic E. Designs and designers as previous set. Perf 15 x 14 and (Nos 31/3) 14 x 15. ½d - 1/-, sheets 240 (2 panes, 12 x 10 each), 2/6d - 10/- as above.

17	½d **emerald-green**		
	(24/11/40)	£1	.25
	a watermark inverted	£40	£15
18	1d **carmine** (26/10/40)	.15	.10
	a watermark inverted	£1	.20
19	1½d **ruby** (12/40)	£7	.20
	a watermark inverted	£30	£6
20	2d **pearl-green** (2/40)	.15	.10
	a watermark inverted	£2	£1
21	2½d **light brown** (3/41)	4.50	.10
	a watermark inverted	£12	£4
	b deep brown (/52)	£5	.10
22	3d **blue** (12/40)	.35	.10
	a watermark inverted	£3	£1
	b ultramarine (/52)	£1	.10
	c watermark inverted	£6	£1
23	4d **steel-blue** (12/40)	.30	.10
	a watermark inverted	£9	£5
24	5d **violet** (7/40)	.35	.10
	a watermark inverted	£22	£10

25	6d **purple** (cream paper)		
	(6/42)	1.10	.30
	a watermark inverted	£16	£5
26	8d **bright red** (12/9/49)	.40	.50
	a watermark inverted	£36	£15
27	9d **violet** (7/40)	.75	.50
	a watermark inverted	£7	£2
28	10d **brown** (7/40)	.30	.50
	a watermark inverted	£7	£3
29	11d **cerise** (12/9/49)	.75	1.50
30	1/- **azure** (6/40)	£32	£11
	a watermark inverted	£550	£150
31	2/6d **emerald-green**	£20	£2
	a pale emerald	£20	£2
	c watermark inverted	£60	£20
32	5/- **ruby** (15/12/42)	£20	£2
	a deep ruby	£20	£2
	b watermark inverted	£125	£30
	c line flaw	£125	£30
33	10/- **deep blue**	£30	£4
	b pale blue	£30	£4
	c watermark inverted	£110	£45
17/33	**set** (17)	£110	£21

32c A line connects the ornament to the lowest horizontal line above the left '5/-' R3/7.

It is not possible to be more specific about dates of issue, as stamps with Gaelic E watermark were put into circulation without any official record being kept. Some of the shades formerly listed have been removed, belonging to 1967-8 issues. These are on very white paper, which distinguishes them from those listed above. Our price for the set is for stamps listed above, not the later printings.

As No 18, but perf 13¾ x imperf (Coils) (thin paper).

34	1d **carmine** (/41)	£30	£40

As No 18, but perf 14¾ x imperf (Coils) (thin paper).

35	1d **carmine** (20/3/46)	£20	£12
	a watermark inverted	£20	£12

AIR STAMPS

1948-67 Designs, 1d, 1/3d, 1/5d (Angel Victor over Rock of Cashel, Munster); 3d (Angel Victor over Lough Derg, Ulster); 6d (Angel Victor over Croagh Patrick, Connaught); 1/- (Angel Victor over Glendalough, Leinster). Designer, R J King. Printers (recess) Waterlow and Sons. Perf 14½ x 14 (C). Watermark Gaelic E. Sheets 120 - two panes, each 6 x 10.

A1	1d **sepia** (4/4/49)	1.25	2.50
A2	3d **blue** (7/4/48)	1.50	1.65
	a major re-entry	£70	£70
A3	6d **wine** (7/4/48)	.50	£1
	a re-entry	£45	£50
	b watermark inverted	-	-
A4	8d **brown-lake** (13/13/54)	£3	5.50
A5	1/- **dark green** (4/4/49)	.50	1.20
A6	1/3 **red-orange** (13/12/54)	£4	.75
	a extra feather	£550	£400
	b watermark inverted	£400	£250
A7	1/5 **dark blue** (1/4/65)	1.75	1.20
	b retouch	£35	£15
A1/7	**set** (7)	11.50	£12

A2a R6/3 (sheets with bottom margin perforated) The 'H' of 'Hibernia', the bottom left frame line, and the '3' are partially doubled.

A3a R3/3 The lower background is extensively re-entered.

A6a R4/6 A forward-projecting feather on the left wing.

A7b R10/5, Plate 2B. Lines below wing at left are re-cut and strengthened.

SPECIAL ISSUES

Nos. S11/35 were typographed by the Government Printers, Dublin Castle, and (except where noted) Perf 15 x 14. Nos S11-16 are on paper watermarked Gaelic SE, S17-40 are on paper watermarked Gaelic E.

1937 (Dec 29th) Constitution Day. Design, Allegory of Eire and New Constitution. Designer R J King. Sheets 120 - two panes, each 6 x 10.

S11	2d **ruby**	£1	.15
	a watermark inverted	-	£140
S12	3d **blue**	2.25	2.25

A 3d in brown and 5d in green in the same design were issued in 1958.

Number issued 2d, 36,175,095; 3d, 1,129,299.

1938 (July 1st) Temperance Crusade Centenary. Design, Head of Father Mathew. Designer S. Keating. Sheets as before.

S13	2d **agate**	1.25	.30
	a damaged 8 in 18	£300	£70
	b inverted comma	-	£500
	c watermark inverted	£200	-
S14	3d **deep blue**	£6	£4

S13a R20/6 first 8 in 1838 damaged at base.

normal   damaged 8

S13b R2/2 (some sheets only) 'Inverted Comma' below 19 of 1938.

Number issued 2d, 46,973,640; 3d 1,387,320.

1939 (Mar. 1st) 150th Anniversary US Constitution and Installation of First President. Designer G Atkinson. Sheets as before.

| S15 | 2d **scarlet** | £1 | .60 |
| S16 | 3d **deep blue** | 1.75 | 2.85 |

Number issued 2d, 27,950,880; 3d, 1,100,493.

1941 (April 12th) 25th Anniversary of 1916 Easter Rising (provisional issue). Design, as No 20 (colour changed) and No. 22, but overprinted in green (2d) and violet (3d).

S17	2d **orange-yellow**	£1	.50
	a snub-nosed e	£100	£60
S18	3d **blue**	12.50	6.75

S17 there were at least two printings, the final printing being in a paler orange and with a paler green overprint.

S17a R5/3 the 'e' at the end of the second line of the overprint is damaged. From final printing.

Number issued - 2d, 28,162,320; 3d, 1,187,280.

1941 (Oct. 27th) 25th Anniversary of Easter Rising. Design, Volunteer and GPO, Dublin. Designer V. Brown. Sheets 120 - two panes, each 6 x 10.

S19	2½d **blue-black**	1.50	.75
	a broken pillar (a)	£4	£2
	b cracked statue (b)	£4	£2
	c damaged capital (c)	£15	£5
	d broken windows (d)	£22	£10

S19a	S19b	S19d

The break in the right pillar (a), and also the crack in the statue (b) on the top centre of the building, occur in each of the 12 stereos of ten subjects which make up the printing plate. The damaged capital (c) of the right pillar is on R2/4 (lower pane). The nine damaged windows (d) to the left of the building are on R10/1 (upper pane).

Number issued 32,394,840.

1943 (July 31st) 50th Anniversary of Founding of Gaelic League. Design, Portrait of Dr. D. Hyde. Designer S. O'Sullivan. Sheets 240 - two panes, each 12 x 10.

S20	½d **green**	.60	.20
S21	2½d **ruby**	£1	.10

Number issued ½d, 26,202,965; 2½d, 32,394,840.

1943 (Nov. 13th) Centenary of Announcement of Discovery of Quaternions. Design, portrait of Sir W. R. Hamilton. Designer S. O'Sullivan. Sheets 240 - two panes, each 12 x 10.

S22	½d **deep green**	.20	.40
	a watermark inverted	-	-
S23	2½d **chocolate-brown**	1.10	.10

Number issued ½d, 28,079,520; 2½d, 37,267,200.

1944 (June 30th)-52 Tercentenary of Death of Michael O'Clery. Design, portrait of Brother O'Clery. Designer R J King. Watermark sideways. Perf 14 x 15. Sheets 240 - two panes, each 10 x 12.

S24	½d **emerald-green**	.10	.10
	a watermark inverted	.30	.15
S25	1/- **brown**	.60	.10
	a dark brown (/52)	£1	.30
	b watermark inverted	1.50	.45

S24a, 25a the inverted watermark shows the top of the 'e' facing right, as seen from the reverse.

Adopted as definitive stamps to replace Nos 17 and 30.

1944 (Aug. 29th) Centenary of Irish Christian Brothers. Design, portrait of Edmund Ignatius Rice. Designer S. O'Sullivan. Sheets 240 - two panes, each 12 x 10.

S26 2½d **slate** .85 .25
    a watermark inverted - £175

Number issued 37,671,840.

1945 (Sept 15th) Centenary of Death of Thomas Davis, founder of Young Ireland Movement. Design, Sower of Seeds of Freedom. Designer R J King. Sheets as before.

S27 2½d **blue** .75 .45
    a watermark inverted - £150
S28 6d **red-purple** £3 3.50

Number issued 2½d, 70,528,080; 6d, 5,564,136.

1946 (Sept. 16th) Centenary of births of Michael Davitt and Charles Stewart Parnell. Design, country and homestead. Designer R. J. King. Sheets 120 - two panes, each 6 x 10.

S29 2½d **scarlet** 1.25 .15
S30 3d **blue** 1.75 2.50

Number issued 2½d, 36,938,550; 3d, 2,095,590.

1948 (Nov. 19th) 150th Anniversary of Insurrection of 1798. Design Theobald Wolfe Tone, framed with laurel leaves and flanked by pikeman and ships, depicting French expedition. Designer K. Uhlemann. Sheets as before.

S31 2½d **ruby** .50 .10
    a watermark inverted - -
S32 3d **violet** 1.65 2.50

Number issued 2½d, 38,066,160; 3d, 2,158,560.

REPUBLIC OF IRELAND

1949 (Nov. 21st) International Recognition. Design, Leinster House and Arms of the Four Provinces. Designer Mrs M. Brandt. Sheets as before.

S33 2½d **chocolate-brown** .85 .10
    a watermark inverted † -
S34 3d **deep blue** £3 2.50
    a dot over chimney £100 £40

S34a R1/1 dot above and to right of left-hand chimney.

Number issued 2½d, 53,913,020; 3d, 3,449,900.

1949 (Dec. 5th) Centenary of death of James Clarence Mangan, poet. Design, portrait. Designer R. J. King. Sheets 240 - two panes, each 12 x 10.

S35 1d **green** .75 .15
    a watermark inverted † -

Number issued 29,992,680.

1950 (Sept 11th) Holy Year (Annus Sanctus).
Design, statue of St. Peter. Printers (recess) Waterlow and Sons. Perf 12½ (C). Sheets 120 - two panes, each 10 x 6.

S36	2½d **bright violet**	.50	.25
S37	3d **light blue**	£4	£7
S38	9d **sepia-brown**	£4	7.50
S36-8	**set** (3)	7.50	£13

Sold in sheets of sixty. Gutter pairs do not exist.

Number issued 2½d, 12,887,140; 3d, 890,620; 9d, 1,588,240.

1952 (Nov. 10th) Centenary of death of Thomas Moore.
Design, from portrait by Sir M. Archer Shee. Engraver W. Vacek. Printers (recess) De La Rue (Clonskeagh, Dublin). Perf 13¾ x 13 (C). Sheets as before.

S39	2½d **claret**	.50	.10
	a re-entry	£55	£25
	b plate crack	£80	£70
S40	3½d **deep olive**	.85	2.50

S39a R3/6 (Plate 1B) 'Thomas Moore' doubled.

S39b R4/9-10, Plate 2A.

Number issued 2½d, 21,574,336; 3½d, 1,308,256.

POSTAGE DUE STAMPS

1925 (typo) Government Printing Works.
Watermark Gaelic SE. Perf 14 x 15. Issued in sheets of 60 from printers' sheets of 180.

PD1	½d **emerald-green**	£6	£10
PD2	1d **carmine**	7.50	£2
	a watermark sideways	£650	£300
	b watermark inverted	£275	£60
	c watermark inverted and reversed	£120	£120
PD3	2d **deep green**	£19	3.25
	a watermark sideways	£40	£12
	b watermark inverted	£70	£24
PD4	6d **plum**	3.25	4.50
PD1-4	**set** (4)	£32	£18

1940-52 As above, watermark Gaelic E.

PD5	½d **emerald-green** (/42)	17.50	£15
	a light emerald (/45)	17.50	£15
	b watermark inverted	£175	£300
PD6	1d **scarlet** (/41)	.75	.40
	a watermark inverted	£40	£5
	b deep golden-scarlet (/52)	£1	.50
PD7	1½d **vermilion** (10/11/52)	1.35	4.50
	a watermark inverted	£12	£15
PD8	2d **deep olive-green** (/40)	1.50	.40
	a watermark inverted	£250	£50
PD9	3d **blue** (10/11/52)	1.50	£2
	a watermark inverted	£4	£3
PD10	5d **violet-black** (3/3/43)	2.50	£2
	a watermark inverted	£4	£5
PD5/10	**set** (6)	£22	£22

6d-1/- values were issued from 1960 onwards.

BOOKLET PANES (MINT)

Prices are for panes with average perforations.

1922-35 watermark SE.

P1	½d **CW G82** pane of 6	£375	-
P2	1d **CW G83** pane of 6	£325	-
	a CW G83a pane of 6	£350	-
P3	1d **CW G83** pane of 3 + 3 labels	£450	-
	a CW G83a pane of 3 + 3 labels	£450	-
P4	2d **CW G85** pane of 6	£350	-

1940-52 watermark E. Perf 14 x 15

P5	½d **CW 17** pane of 6	£250	-
P6	1d **CW 18** pane of 6	£8	-
	a CW 18a pane of 6	£10	-

P7	1d **CW 18** pane of 3 + 3 labels	£2000	-
	a CW 18a pane of 3 + 3 labels	£2000	-
P8	1½d **CW 19** pane of 6	£60	-
P9	2d **CW 20** pane of 6	£15	-
P10	2½d **CW 21** pane of 6	£50	-
P11	3d **CW 22** pane of 6	£18	-
P12	4d **CW 23** pane of 6	£25	-
P13	½d **CW S24** pane of 6	£20	-
	a CW S24a pane of 6	£20	-

P8 is from a 4/- booklet, issued in 1954

BOOKLETS

Ireland's first booklet (1931-40) is listed for completeness. A useful feature of Irish booklets is the year and serial number printed on the front of the booklet, in that order until 1937, subsequently serial number followed by year. Watermarks upright or inverted are found in equal numbers. Our listing is based on the composition of each booklet.

B1   2/- **1931-40 Black on Red**
P1, P2 or P2a, P3 or 3a,
P4 £200 -
Serial No. 1-21

B2   2/- **1940 Black on Red**
P1, P2 or P2a, P7 or 7a£7000
Serial No. 22

B3   2/- **1940 Black on Red**
P5, P6 or P6a, P7 or 7a,
P9 £7000 -
Serial No. 23

B4   2/- **1941-44 Black on Red**
P5 x 2, P6 or P6a, P9 £975
Serial No. 24-26

B5   2/- **1945 Black on Red**
P5 x 2, P6 or P6a, P9 £975
Serial No. 27

B6   2/- **1946 Black on Buff**
P5 x 2, P6 or P6a, P9 £600
Serial No. 28

B7   2/- **1946-47 Black on Buff**
P13 x 2, P6 or P6a, P9 £290
Serial No. 29-30

B8   2/6d **1948-50 Black on Red**
P6 or P6a, P9, P13, P13a £175
Serial No. 31-33

B9   2/6d **1951-53 Black on Buff**
P6 or P6a, P9, P13, P13a £60
Serial No. 34-36

Numbers issued: B1 approx 100,000 of each; B2-7 250,000; B8 #31 350,000, #s 32-3 500,000 each; B9 #s 34, 36 500,00 each; #35 632,000.

B5 has no advertisement on the cover.

Prices are for the commonest serial number in a given group.

JAMAICA

1938 (Oct. 10th)-52 Designs, ½d, 1d, 1½d (King's head); 2d (Coco palms, Columbus Cove); 2½d (Wag Water River, St. Andrew); 3d (bananas); 4d (citrus grove); 6d (Priestman's River, Portland); 9d (Kingston Harbour); 1/- (sugar industry); 2/- (Bamboo Walk); 5/- (Isle of Wood and Water); 10/- (KGVI); £1 (cigar making). Printers (recess) De La Rue: ½d-1½d, perf 13½ x 14 (C); 5/-, 10/- perf 14 x 13¾ (C). Other values (recess) Waterlow and Sons, perf 12½ (L). Sheets: ½d, 1d, 1½d 120 in two panes, each 6 x 10. Other values: horizontal format, 5 x 12; vertical 10 x 6 or 6 x 10; 5/- and 10/-, 6 x 5 or 5 x 6; £1 6 x 5.

1	½d **deep green** (10/10/38)	.80	.10
	a green (5/42)	.85	.10
	b watermark sideways	-	£3750
2	½d **orange** (25/10/51)	.65	.20
	a deep orange (30/6/52)	£1	.25
3	1d **scarlet** (10/10/38)	.50	.10
	a carmine-red (30/1/50)	.60	.10
4	1d **green** (25/10/51)	£1	.10
5	1½d **light brown** (10/10/38)	.60	.10
	a chocolate-brown (/41)	.75	.10
	b light red-brown (/44)	£225	£60
	c pale brown (1/50)	4.50	.35
6	2d **grey and green**	.50	.50
	a grey and deep emerald-green (26/2/47)	.75	.60
	b man fishing	£18	£15
	c extra frond	£18	£15
7	2½d **grey-green and ultramarine**	£2	1.35
8	3d **pale ultramarine and green**	.60	1.25
	a pale ultramarine and deep green (26/2/47)	.50	£1
	b 'A' of watermark missing	£750	-
9	3d **pale green and ultramarine** (15/8/49)	£1	.75
10	3d **green and red** (1/7/52)	1.50	.20
11	4d **light brown and green**	.25	.10
	a light brown and blue-green (4/9/44)	.35	.10
12	6d **grey and red-purple**	2.75	1.25
	a grey and red-claret (15/4/46)	3.25	.20
	b exhaust pipe	£140	-

13	9d **lake**	.25	.30
	a claret (5/42)	.35	.30
	b 'A' of watermark missing	-	-
14	1/- **yellow-green and deep purple-brown**	£4	.15
	a blue-green and purple-brown (5/42)	3.75	.20
	b broken chimney	£375	£65
15	2/- **dull blue and chocolate-brown**	12.50	.60
	a pale blue and brown (2/47)	12.50	.60
16	5/- **grey-blue and yellow-ochre**	£7	2.50
	a deep blue and deep orange (5/42)	£7	2.25
17	10/- **myrtle-green**	£5	5.75
18	£1 **deep brown and violet** (15/8/49)	£19	£18
SP1/17	**specimen perf** (13)	£225	†

As No. 6 and 12, but Perf. 12¾ x 13¾ (C).

19	2d **grey and green** (/39)	1.25	.30
	a 'C' of watermark missing	£750	-
20	6d **grey and red-purple** (10/10/50)	£1	.10

As Nos. 16 and 17, but Perf 13¼ x13 (C).

21	5/- **blue-black and ochre** (blued paper) (24/10/49)	£4	2.50
	a deep blue and brownish orange (10/10/50)	3.50	£2
22	10/- **myrtle-green** (10/10/50)	£6	£4
	a light myrtle-green (8/1/52)	£8	£8

As No. 6, but Perf 12¾ x 13(C).

23	2d **grey and green** (/51)	.55	.10

As No. 16, but Perf 14.15 (L).

23a	5/- **grey-blue and red-orange** (/41)	£3000	£125
1-18	**set** (18)	£55	£26

5b this particular printing was on sale in the Colony (only) for a short period about the middle of 1944. It should be purchased only from a reputable source, since there are other printings which superficially resemble it.

6b R6/10 left figure appears to be holding a fishing rod. From (unnumbered) Centre Plate 1.

6c R6/1 a large extra palm frond.

12b R10/1 a flaw at the back of the car resembles an exhaust pipe.

14b R11/1 two short lines cut through the smoke from the smaller chimney, on either side of the large chimney, on all printings up to 1947.

15, a the 2/- has been seen with yellow-olive frame. Despite the fact that one has been seen on cover, we presume these to be changelings.

21a has a slight blue tinge on the surface, but not as pronounced as 21.

23a all this printing was released in Colony only. Used price for examples with slightly heavy CDS, as usually found.

SPECIAL ISSUES

1937 (May 12th) Coronation. As Ascension.

S1	1d **red**	.15	.10
S2	1½d **deep grey**	.30	.20
S3	2½d **blue**	.50	.40
S1/3	**set** (3)	.85	.65
SPS1/3	**specimen perf** (3)	£60	†

1945 (Aug. 20th) New Constitution. Designs, 1½d (Courthouse, Falmouth); 2d (Charles II and KGVI); 3d and 10/- (Institute of Jamaica); 4½d (House of Assembly); 2/- (Symbols of Arts and Learning); 5/- (Jamaican Flag). Designers 1½d, 3d, 4½d, 10/- Board of Governors of the Institute of Jamaica; 2d Hugh Paget (British Council); 2/- Miss Rhoda Jackson; 5/- G. C. Gunter. Printers (recess) Waterlow and Sons. Perf 12½ (L). Sheets 10 x 6 or 6 x 10.

S4	1½d **sepia-brown**	.10	.20
S5	2d **green**	£5	.55
S6	3d **ultramarine**	.10	.30
S7	4½d **slate-black**	.15	.20
S8	2/- **chocolate-brown**	.15	.30
S9	5/- **dark blue**	.75	.60
S10	10/- **green**	.75	2.50
SPS4/10	**specimen perf** (7)	£110	†

As Nos. S4 and S5 but Perf. 12¾ x 13¼ (C).

S11	1½d **sepia-brown** (/46)	£2	.35
S12	2d **green** (/45)	.15	.30

As Nos S6 and S7 but Perf. 13¼ x 13 (C).

S13	3d **ultramarine**	1.20	1.65
S14	4½d **slate-blue** (/46)	1.50	£2
S4/14	**set** (7)	1.90	3.75

1946 (Oct. 14th) Victory. As Aden.

(a) Perf. 13¾ x 14 (C).

S15	1½d **purple-brown**	£1	.10
S16	3d **grey-blue**	1.50	1.50
SPS15/16	**specimen perf** (2)	£55	†

(b) Perf. 13¾ x 13¼ (C).

S17	1½d **purple-brown**	.15	£2
S18	3d **grey-blue**	.15	3.25

1948 (Dec. 1st) Silver Wedding. As Aden.

S19	1½d **chestnut-brown**	.15	.10
	a 'flash' in neckline	3.50	£3
S20	£1 **rose-carmine**	£13	£40

S19a R1/1-6 white mark in neckline of dress above 'd'of '1½d'.

1949 (Oct. 10th) UPU. As Aden.

S21	1½d **beech-brown**	.15	.10
S22	2d **deep green**	.60	2.50
S23	3d **dull indigo**	.25	.90
S24	6d **purple**	.25	1.50
S21/24	**set** (4)	1.10	4.50

1951 (Feb. 16th) West Indies University College. As Antigua.

S25	2d **black and chocolate**	.15	.30
S26	6d **grey-black and purple-lake**	.20	.20

1952 (Mar. 5th) First Caribbean Scout Jamboree. Designs, 2d (Scout Badge and Map of Caribbean); 6d (Scout Badge and Map of Jamaica), adapted from designs by C. de Souza. Printers (litho) Bradbury, Wilkinson. Perf 13½ x 13 (C). Sheets S27, 6 x 10; S28, 5 x 12.

S27	2d **blue, black and green**	.15	.10

S28	6d **green, black and crimson**	.35	.35

Number issued 2d, 2,864,153; 6d, 899,723.

Booklet Panes

P1	½d CW1 pane of 6	£15	-
P2	½d CW 2 pane of 6	£12	-
P3	1d CW 3 pane of 6	£15	-
P4	1d CW 4 pane of 6	£12	-
P5	1½d CW S11 pane of 4	£45	-

BOOKLETS

B1	2/- **1938 black on deep emerald** P1 x 2, P3 x 3	£340	-
B2	2/- **1938 black on light emerald** P1 x 2, P3 x 3	£320	-
B3	2/- **1938 black on light green** P1 x 2, P3 x 3	£300	-
B4	2/- **1938 black on light blue** P1 x 2, P3 x 3	£200	-
B5	2/- **1938 black on light yellow** P1 x 2, P3 x 3	£75	-
B6	2/- **1946 New Constitution, black on light blue** P5 x 4	£150	-
B7	2/- **1951 black and pale yellow** P2 x 2, P4 x 3	£18	-

B1-7 many are affected by foxing and care is needed when purchasing.

GERMAN PROPAGANDA LABELS

The 1944 German imitations of the GB 1937 definitives ½d to 3d (see after Great Britain for details) were also overprinted in black 'LIQUIDATION/OF EMPIRE/JAMAICA' without vertical rectangular frame.

JERSEY
SEE
CHANNEL ISLANDS

JIND
SEE
CONVENTION STATES
OF INDIA

JOHORE
SEE
MALAYA

JORDAN
SEE
TRANSJORDAN

KATHIRI
SEE
ADEN STATE (SEIYUN)

KEDAH
SEE
MALAYA

KELANTAN
SEE
MALAYA

KENYA, UGANDA AND TANGANYIKA

1938 (April 11th) - 54. Designs: 1c, 20c, 40c, 10/- (crowned cranes); 5c, 25c, 50c (dhow on Lake Victoria); 10c, 1/-, 3/- (Lake Naivasha); 15c, 2/- (Mount Kilimanjaro); 30c, 5/- (Jinja Railway Bridge); £1 (lion and palms). Printers (recess) De La Rue, except £1 (typo). Sheets 10 x10.

(a) Perf. 13¼ (C).

1	1c	black and reddish brown	£1	.50
2	15c	black and red	£8	.35
3	20c	black and orange	£14	.20
4	30c	black and deep blue	£19	.25
5	2/-	maroon and bright mauve	£40	1.35
		a maroon and dull purple (39/40)	£110	1.35
6	5/-	black and carmine	£55	£10
7	10/-	pink and bright blue	£45	£13
		a lake and blue (39/40)	£80	-

3 is known imperforate, but is of doubtful status.

(b) Perf. 13 x 11¾ (C).

8	5c	black and green (11/4/38)	1.75	.30
9	5c	chocolate and orange (1/6/49)	.30	2.25
10	10c	chocolate and orange	.90	.10
		a watermark inverted	-	-
11	10c	black and green (1/6/49)	.15	.90
		a mountain retouch	£40	£50
		c double print of frame (one albino)	-	-
12	50c	deep purple and black	£6	.60
		a short stay	£150	£160
		b dull claret and black (7/47)	£40	£5
		c brown-purple and black (4/48)	£40	4.50
		d reddish purple and black (4/49)	£16	£3

13	1/-	black and brown	£9	.20
		a black and dark brown (8/42)	£5	.20
		ab mountain flaw (?/49)	-	-
		ac mountain retouch (/49)	£600	£200
		ad watermark inverted	†	£2000
14	3/-	blue and black	£15	£3
		a dark blue and black (29/7/47)	£20	5.75
		b mountain flaw (?/49)	£1800	-
15	£1	black and crimson (ch)	£120	£90
SP 1/15		specimen perf (13)	£500	†

R6/7   R5/10

11a, 13ac R6/7 and (later) R5/10 show substantial retouches to the top of the mountain. These differ. The flaw that necessitated the retouch on R5/10 has never been found. It is possible to find blocks of the 10ct with R6/7 retouched and 5/10 normal. The 3/- (14b) is not known in the retouched state.

11c a sheet of 100 is reported to exist. Plate 9/7B.

13ab, 14b R6/7 (Plate 7B) marks on the mountain peak appeared at some time in 1949. The 1/- value is not known mint, and very few 3/- seem to exist.

12a on the KG V 50ct, the rope at the top of the mast failed to join it. The same centre plate was used for the first printing of the KGVI 50c, after the short stay had been lengthened on 99 subjects on the plate. The exception was on R2/ 5 where the correction was overlooked: a number of sheets were printed and placed on sale in May 1938. The Die was then corrected and a new plate was laid down; stamps printed from this plate were placed on sale in September 1938 and the remainder of the first printing was withdrawn. The gum on mint examples is normally brown and streaky.

Type 1   Type 2

In Type 1 the stay rope was not attached to the upper point of the sail. The correction (Type 2) was made only on the last printing (late 1937) of the KGV 5c; it was not corrected on the 50c.

As No. 10, etc, but Perf 14. (L).

16	10c **chocolate and orange** (/41)	£45	£4
17	20c **black and orange** (/41)	£22	1.10
18	30c **black and deep blue** (/41)	£55	£7
19	2/- **maroon and purple-mauve** (/41)	£30	7.50
20	5/- **black and carmine** (/41)	£22	1.50
21	10/- **deep purple and deep ultramarine** (/41)	£25	£12
	a red-purple and bright ultramarine (4/49)	£19	£35
22	£1 **black and crimson** (ch) (/41)	£12	£10
	a black and crimson (sub) (24/2/44)	£13	£12

As No. 1, etc., but Perf. 13¼ x 13¾ (C).

23	1c **black and red-brown** (/42)	.15	.30
	a flawed tablet	£45	-
	b retouched tablet	£25	£45
	c tadpole flaw	£45	-
	d break in bird's breast	£45	-
	e 'A' of watermark missing	£200	-
	f black and dark brown (/48)	£1	1.25
	fa retouched tablet	£40	£60
	g black and red-chocolate (26/9/51)	1.50	2.25
24	15c **black and red** (2/43)	2.50	2.25
	a 'A' of watermark missing	-	-
25	15c **black and green** (1/4/52)	£1	3.25
26	20c **black and orange** (/42)	£3	.10
	a black and deep orange (26/9/51)	7.50	£1
	b watermark inverted	†	-
27	30c **black and deep blue** (9/42)	1.25	.10
	a slate-black and deep blue (24/2/44)	5.50	.40
	b black and violet-blue (29/7/47)	2.50	.60
28	30c **purple and sepia-brown** (1/4/52)	.75	.25
29	40c **black and deep blue** (1/4/52)	.80	£2
30	2/- **maroon and purple-mauve** (24/2/44)	£12	.20
31	5/- **black and carmine** (24/2/44)	£16	.90
32	10/- **purple and blue** (24/2/44)	£18	2.75
	a purple and steel-blue (/54)	£45	£8

23a   23b

23a R9/6 FP2 a flaw in the left value tablet left it almost unshaded.

23b, fa the above flaw was crudely retouched (probably in the press) and exists on printings 1942-6.

23c   23d

23c a flaw at the left of the portrait vignette resembles a tadpole. R10/8, Plate 2-4B.

23d R2/5, Centre Plate 4A. A break in the left crane's breast. This break varies considerably in size.

26a imperforate examples have been recorded. It seems likely that these are 'escapees' from De La Rue's premises. Definite information to the contrary is solicited.

32a this printing has a lovely dark frame shade, used in conjunction with the new head plate (which shows as bright and sharp). It is often optimistically identified.

As No. 9, etc, but Perf. 13 x 12½ (C).

33	5c **chocolate and orange** (14/6/50)	.75	1.80
34	10c **black and green** (14/6/50)	£1	.10
35	10c **brown and grey** (1/4/50)	.50	.35
36	25c **black and red** (1/4/52)	.75	1.25
37	50c **red-purple and black** (10/49)	£3	.35
	a watermark inverted	-	£2900
	b dot removed (7/6/50)	£8	.35
	c pair with/without dot	£240	£100
38	1/- **black and brown** (10/49)	£5	.35
	a black and deep brown (14/6/50)	£10	1.35
39	3/- **dark blue and black** (14/6/50)	£16	2.75

37a/b The dot which was to be found previously on the scroll at the bottom left corner has been removed by retouching on Frame Plate 3 except on R5/2, 6/1, 7/2, 7/4 and 9/1. Traces are still visible on some other positions, however, where the retouching was not completely effective. Illustration shows scroll with dot.

38a The new centre plate used for this printing shows much more detail, particularly in the foreground and sky.

As No. 15, but Perf. 12½ (L).

39a £1 black and crimson
(21/1/54) 6.50 £25
1/39a set (20) all colours £85 £25

1941 (July 1st)-42 stamps of South Africa, surcharged and overprinted.

			Pair Mint	Pair Used
40	5c/1d	grey and carmine-red	.60	£1
	a	grey and red-carmine	£5	£5
41	10c/3d	ultramarine	£2	5.50
42	20c/6d	green and deep orange	1.75	2.25
	a	green and brownish orange (/42)	2.25	2.25
43	70c/1/-	sepia and chalky blue (20/4/42)	£8	£3
	a	crescent moon	£40	-
40/43		set (4 pairs)	£11	£11
SP40/43		specimen handstamped (4 pairs)	£200	†

South African stamps were utilised because of the difficulty in obtaining supplies from London, due to the war.

40 this stamp measures 18½ x 22½mm.

40a measures 18¼ x 22¼mm.

43a A flaw on R20/4 resembles a crescent moon above the gnu.

These stamps exist overprinted SPECIMEN in sans-serif capitals, 26 x 3mm reading diagonally downwards. This overprint was locally handstamped, and should not be confused with a much larger hand-stamp with seriffed letters later applied to stamps used at the Postal Training School outside Nairobi.

SPECIAL ISSUES

1937 (May 12th) Coronation. As Ascension.

S1	5c	green	.10	.10
S2	20c	orange	.20	.20
S3	30c	blue	.30	£1
S1/3		set (3)	.55	1.20
SPS1/3		specimen perf (3)	£65	†

1946 (Nov. 11th) Victory. As Aden.

S4	20c	reddish orange	.15	.10
S5	30c	deep blue	.15	.45
SPS4/5		specimen perf (2)	£60	†

Placed on sale prematurely on October 15th at Lindi (Tanganyika).

1948 (Dec. 1st) Silver Wedding. As Aden.

S6	20c	orange	.10	.15
S7	£1	rose-carmine	£21	£42

1949 (Oct. 10th) UPU. As Aden.

S8	20c	red-orange	.10	.10
S9	30c	indigo	.85	1.35
S10	50c	grey	.25	.35
S11	1/-	beech-brown	.25	.25
S8/11		set (4)	1.30	1.80

1952 (Feb. 1st) Royal Visit. Design as CW 11 and 13, with inscription ROYAL VISIT 1952 added to frame plate. Perf 13 x 12½ (C). Sheets 10 x 10.

S12	10c	black and green	.15	.90
S13	1/-	black and brown	.55	1.25

Number issued 10c 1,020,044; 1/- 320,409.

BOOKLET PANES

P1	CW 2 pane of 4	£70	-
P2	CW 3 pane of 4	£120	-
P3	CW 33 pane of 4 (stapled)	-	-
P4	CW 33 pane of 4 (stitched)	£20	-
P5	CW 34 pane of 4 (stapled)	-	-
P6	CW 35 pane of 4	£15	-

BOOKLETS

B1	3s40c **1938 black/pink** P1 x 3, P2 x 2	£125	-
B2	1/- **1952 blue/yellow** P3 x 1, P5 x 2; stapled	£425	-
B3	1/- **1952 blue/yellow** P4 x 1, P6 x 2; stitched	£25	-

POSTAGE DUE STAMPS

1935 (May 1st) Printers (typo) De La Rue. Smooth paper in dull colours. Watermark Multiple Script CA. Perf 14. Sheets 10 x10.

GD7	5c **violet**	1.20	£1
GD8	10c **carmine**	.15	.30
GD9	20c **green**	.20	.30
GD10	30c **brown**	.60	.30
GD11	40c **ultramarine**	.75	1.80
GD12	1/- **grey**	£8	£14
GD7/12	**set** (6)	£10	£17
SPGD7/12	**specimen** (6) (opt. or perf)	£70	†

1942-43 Printers (typo) De La Rue. Rough paper. Perf 13¾ x 14 (C). Sheets 12 x 20.

PD1	5c **purple-violet** (/43)	£4	£3
PD2	10c **carmine-red** (/43)	£4	£3
PD3	20c **myrtle-green** (/43)	£4	£3
PD4	40c **deep ultramarine** (/43)	£6	£8
PD1/4	**set** (4)	£16	12.50

1950 re-issued on smooth paper with somewhat brighter colours.

PD5	5c **purple-violet**	1.50	1.25
PD6	10c **carmine-red**	£1	1.25
PD7	20c **myrtle-green**	£1	1.25
PD8	30c **brown**	£1	1.25
PD8	40c **deep ultramarine**	£3	£4
PD10	1/- **grey**	£10	£25
PD5/10	**set** (4)	£16	£32

KUWAIT

1939-45 Stamps of India (1937-46 issue), overprinted 'KUWAIT'. The overprint measures 12mm (low values), 19mm (rupee values).

1	½a **red-brown**	3.50	1.25
2	1a **carmine**	3.50	1.20
3	2a **vermilion**	3.50	1.65
4	3a **yellow-green**	3.50	1.20
5	4a **deep brown**	£19	£11
6	6a **greenish blue**	12.50	6.75
7	8a **violet-slate**	£14	£19
8	12a **deep crimson**	£10	£45
10	1r **violet-grey and light brown**	£10	2.50
	a extended T	£375	-
	b first repair	-	-
	c overprint treble, one inverted	-	-
11	2r **reddish purple and brown**	2.50	£10
	a extended T	£375	-
	b 1st repair	£450	-
	c deep purple and brown	2.50	£10
12	5r **deep green and deep blue**	8.50	£13
	a extended T	£500	-
	b 2nd repair	-	-
13	10r **violet-purple and red-claret**	£35	£52
	a extended T	£700	-
	b 2nd repair	-	-
	c overprint double	£350	-
14	15r **chocolate and deep green**	£120	£190
	a extended T	£1000	-
	b 2nd repair	-	-
	c watermark inverted	£50	£110
1/14	**set** (13)	£160	£250

10a/14a The stem of T in Kuwait extends downwards ¾mm on the lower left pane, R3/2. This was subsequently repaired in two stages, leaving minor traces.

extended T

1st Repair

2nd Repair

10c Only one copy has been recorded.

11b Only the first shade of the 2r has been recorded with 1st repair.

13c Only one sheet of 120 is known, on which the double overprint is less prominent on the right hand side. R3/2 of the lower left pane shows the 2nd repair (as 13b).

Forged overprints on the rupee values may be readily recognised, being only 16½mm in length.

Between May 1941 and 1945 Indian stamps without overprint were in use and may be recognised by the cancellations; 'SUPDT. OF POST OFFICES/PERSIAN GULF' from 25 May 41 to 6 June 41, 'EXPERIMENTAL P. O. K-79' from 10 June 41 to 30 August 41, and named KUWAIT cancellations from October, 1941.

Between May 1941 and January 1942 the very small amount of mail to the UK was despatched in the Diplomatic Bag to London, where it was franked with Great Britain stamps and posted.

Collectors are warned of forged 'KUWAIT PERSIAN GULF' cancellations dated 19th November, 1942, or with date omitted, on Indian stamps without overprint (1941/1943 issue and 1937 Rupee values).

The Indian Victory stamps (S1-4) were issued in Kuwait in 1946, but are very scarce with Kuwait postmarks.

1945 Stamps of India (1941-3 Issue), overprinted 'KUWAIT'.

15	3p **slate**	1.60	3.75
16	½a **purple**	.85	2.50
17	9p **green**	1.85	7.25
18	1a **rose-carmine**	1.10	1.35
19	1½a **slate-purple**	£2	£5
20	2a **vermilion**	£2	3.25
21	3a **bright violet**	2.75	5.75
22	3½a **blue**	£2	£6
23	4a **brown**	3.25	2.25
24	6a **greenish blue**	£7	7.75
25	8a **violet-slate**	3.50	4.50
26	12a **deep crimson**	4.25	3.25
26a	14a **purple**	7.50	£11
15/26a	**set** (13)	£35	£57

A similar overprint on the 1¼a of this issue of India is bogus.

Control of the postal service passed from Indian to Pakistan in August 1947, then to Great Britain from 1st April 1948.

1948 (April 1st)-49 Stamps of Great Britain overprinted 'KUWAIT', and surcharged (½a-1r) by Harrison, (2r-10r) by Waterlow.

27	½a/½d **green**	1.10	1.35
28	1a/1d **scarlet**	1.10	£1
29	1½a/1½d **red-brown**	1.25	£1
30	2a/2d **dull orange**	1.10	£1
31	2½a/2½d **ultramarine**	1.25	.60
32	3a/3d **purple-violet**	1.10	.50
	a overprint albino in pair with normal	£3000	-
34	6a/6d **pale purple**	1.10	.45
35	1r/1/- **bistre-brown**	2.25	1.20
36	2r/2/6d **green**	2.50	3.25
	a 'T' guide mark	£125	£140
37	5r/5/- **red**	3.50	3.25
	a 'T' guide mark	£50	£50
38	10r/10/- **ultramarine** (4/7/49)	£22	£5
27/38	**set** (11)	£35	£16

32a Five sheets of the 3a value were sold in Kuwait in early 1949 on which a small number of stamps in the lower left corner were wholly, or partly, without overprint and/or surcharge on account of inadequate inking of the plate. A mint sheet with 6 stamps affected survives, as do a handful of other mint and used examples.

36a, 37a see note after Great Britain Nos. 16-21

Number issued ½a, 443,355; 1a, 460,535; 1½a,424,579; 2a, 479,423; 2½a, 394,239; 3a, 1,243,707; 6a, 1,853,344; 1r, 445,074; 2r, 48,807; 5r, 43,154; 10r, 19,351.

Crude, easily-recognised forged and bogus overprints exist on many values in all the foregoing issues. They were handstamped on used Indian (or Great Britain) stamps.

1951 (May 3rd)-55 As No 27, etc., but colours changed (Nos 45-7 as Nos 34-6 of Great Britain), similarly overprinted and surcharged.

39	½a/½d **dull orange**	1.25	.90
40	1a/1d **ultramarine**	1.25	£1
41	1½a/1½d **green**	1.25	1.35
42	2a/2d **red-brown**	1.25	.90
43	2½a/2½d **scarlet**	1.25	1.65
44	4a/4d **light blue** (2/10/50)	1.25	.90
45	2r/2/6d **green** (Type 1)	9.50	£3
	a extra bar in overprint	£500	£325
	b Type 2 (/53)	£150	£30
	c Type 3 (/55)	-	£200
46	5r/5/- **red**	£13	3.75
	a extra bar in overprint	£300	£250
47	10r/10/- **ultramarine**	£19	£6
	a Type 2 (/53)	£170	£35
	b Type 3	-	£250
39/47	**set** (9)	£44	£14

CW 45 Type 1

45 Type 1 'KUWAIT' in sharp letters. '2' and 'RUPEES' in line, overall measurements 16mm.

CW 45b Type 2

45b Type 2 'KUWAIT' in slightly heavier, worn type. '2' raised in relation to 'RUPEES', overall measurements 15½mm.

CW 45c Type 3

45c Type 3 As Type 2, but space between bars and 'K' of 'KUWAIT' is only 2½mm instead of 3mm. The surcharge is set slightly further to the left of KUWAIT.

45a A third thinner bar appears between the normal two bars. R7/2, on part of the printing only. A single example has been recorded on which a third thinner bar appears below the normal two bars (sheet position not known).

46a A third thinner bar appears above the normal two bars. R2/2, on part of the printing only.

CW 47 Type 1

47 Type 1 Letters clean-edged and with D-shaped loops to 'R' and 'P'. '1' and '0' spaced 1mm.

CW 47a Type 2

47a Type 2 Letters worn and with small circular loops to 'R' and 'P'. '1' and '0' spaced ¾mm (the '0' being further away from 'R').

KUWAIT

10 RUPEES

CW 47b Type 3

47b Type 2 Appearance as Type 2, but the two lines of overprint are 10mm apart instead of 9mm. Only a few used examples have been recorded.

Number issued ½a, 446,569; 1a,486,629; 1½a, 253,725; 2a, 467,487; 2½a, 245,675; 4a, 433,391; 2r, 59,975; 5r, 48,117; 10r, 36,050.

SPECIAL ISSUES

1948 (May 1st) Silver Wedding Issue of Great Britain, overprinted 'KUWAIT' and surcharged.

S1	2½a/2½d **ultramarine**	1.10	1.50
S2	15r/£1 **deep blue**	17.50	£23
	a short bars	£100	£110

normal   short bars

S2a The bars cancelling the sterling value on R3/4 are 3mm long, compared with 3½mm on the rest of the sheet. There are other positions where the bars are slightly shorter than normal, but R3/4 stands out.

Number issued 2½a, 179,060; 15r, 21,703.

1948 (July 29th) Olympic Games Issue of Great Britain, overprinted 'KUWAIT' and surcharged.

S3	2½a/2d **ultramarine**	.60	1.80
S4	3a/3d **violet**	.60	1.80
S5	6a/6d **reddish purple**	.75	1.80
	a HLP retouch	£200	-
S6	1r/1/- **bistre-brown**	.75	1.80
S3/6	**set** (4)	2.50	6.50

S5a See Great Britain S14b.

Number issued 2½a 89,264; 3a, 91,203; 6a, 83,677; 1r, 83,395.

1949 (Oct. 10th) UPU Issue of Great Britain, overprinted 'KUWAIT' and surcharged.

S7	2½a/2½d **ultramarine**	.60	£2
	a Lake in India	£45	£60
S8	3a/3d **pale violet**	.60	2.25
S9	6a/6d **reddish mauve**	.60	2.25
S10	1r/1/- **bistre-brown**	.60	£1
S7/10	**set** (4)	2.20	6.75

S7a See Great Britain S16b.

Number issued 2½a, 90,781; 3a, 89,968; 6a, 92,987; 1r, 77,904.

SEMI-POSTAL ISSUE

Labels having the appearance of postage stamps, but without denomination, were supplied by the State Secretariat to the Post Office in celebration of the anniversary of accession of Shaikh Ahmad al Jabir (1921-50).

The Post Office affixed them to both incoming and outgoing letters and, although they had no postal validity, they are occasionally found with postal cancellations.

reduced size

(a) Booklet of 10 panes (5 x 2 with narrow margin all round), stapled. Line Perf.

SP1	1947 **reddish violet** (P 11)	£10 -
SP2	1948 **bluish violet** (P 11½)	£15 -

(b) Sheets, with Serial number (vertically upwards) in left margin opposite bottom row.

SP3	1949 **emerald** (P 11½)	£20 -

LEEWARD ISLANDS

1938 (Nov. 25th)-51 Printers (typo) De La Rue.
Perf 13¾ x 14 (C). Small format, sheets of
120 - two panes, each 6 x 10.

1	¼d **brown**	.20	£1
	a light brown (29/9/47)	.20	1.50
	b deep brown (ch) (13/6/49)	.15	£1
2	½d **green**	.30	.40
	a blue-green (3/42)	.25	.40
	b 'I.' for 'L'	£58	£60
3	1d **scarlet** (Die A)	3.50	1.50
	a scarlet (Die B) (/40)	£1	£1
	b carmine (8/42)	.60	£5
	c rose-scarlet (10/5/44)	.60	£1
	d 'DI' flaw	£120	£100
	e pale pinkish scarlet (13/9/48)	£2	2.50
	f 'DI' flaw (13/9/48)	£120	£100
4	1½d **dull red-brown**	.40	.30
	a deep red-brown (3/12/43)	.50	.50
5	2d **grey**	1.25	.90
	a slate (8/42)	2.50	1.50
	b pale grey (11/42)	£3	£4
	c short 'I'	£25	
	d silver grey (9/47)	5.50	£6
6	2½d **blue**	6.50	1.50
	a light bright blue (11/42)	.40	.75
	b pale blue (10/5/44)	£1	£1
7	3d **deep orange** (ch)	£9	1.75
	a orange (sub) (3/42)	.30	.50
	b pale orange (thin paper) (10/5/44)	.20	.50
8	6d **dull and red-purple** (ch)	£7	£4
	a pale and bright purple (sub) (3/42)	3.50	1.65
	b broken 'E'	£225	£275
	c deep and red-purple (ch) (29/9/47)	£4	2.25
	d broken 'E'	£250	£300
	e purple and bright purple (ch) (24/10/51)	4.50	£3
9	1/- **black/emerald-green** (ch)	5.50	1.25
	a 'DI' flaw	£275	£350
	b black/green (sub) (3/42)	1.80	.60
	c grey and black/green (sub) (8/42)	£7	2.50
	d black and grey/green (sub) (11/42)	£50	6.75

10	2/- **purple and deep blue/dull blue** (ch)	£7	£2
	a red-purple and deep blue/blue (sub) (3/42)	£5	1.20
	b deep purple and deep blue/pale blue (sub) (29/9/47)	5.50	1.50
11	5/- **green and red/yellow** (ch)	£20	£12
	a broken E	£600	£400
	aa damaged tablet	£550	£400
	b green and scarlet/pale yellow (sub) (3/12/43)	£14	£10
	ba broken E	£500	£400
	bb retouched tablet	£450	£400
	c light green and deep red/pale yellow (ch) (/51)	£30	£75

Large format. 10/- watermark Multiple Script
CA, £1 watermark Multiple Crown CA. Perf
14 x 13¾ (C). Sheets 12 x 5.

12	10/- **bluish green and red/green** (ch)	£80	£80
	a pale green and pale red /green (sub) (3/42)	£300	£240
	b green and red/green (sub) (3/12/43)	£60	£50
	c deep green and red /green (sub) (10/5/44)	£50	£75
13	£1 **deep purple and black/crimson-red** (ch)	£150	£225
	a purple and black/deep brick-red(ch) (11/38)	£150	£240
	b deep purple and black /carmine-red (ch) (3/42)	£60	£50
	c purple and black/deep carmine-red (ch) (10/42)	£40	£30
	d purple and black/salmon-red (ch) (9/12/43, 7/6/44)	£14	£15
SP 1/13	**specimen perf** (13)	£375	†

VARIETIES (¼d -5/-) + NOTES

2, 3 the ½d and 1d values exist in coil form, constructed from ordinary sheets. Printings in 1940, 1943 and 1944.

  2b   3d   5c

8b, 8d   11a, 11ba   11aa, 11bb

2b 'I.' for 'L' on R1/2 RP.

   Die A   Die B

3 the top of the 1 in Die A is more pointed than in Die B.

3a Die B was not released in London until 1942, but used examples exist postmarked as early as 1940.

3d/3f R7/3 LP the base of the letters 'D' and 'I' are cut away.

3e exists printed in fluorescent aniline ink.

5, 5a, 5b All printings from 1938 to 1943 exist with extensive damage to value and country tablets on many positions. In some cases, the damage was concealed by hand-retouching at the printers.

5c R4/2 RP the short 'I' can be found hand-retouched.

7 the paper used until 1942 for the 3d stamps was similar to that used for the 6d value; later, thin paper, as used for lower values, was employed.

7a exists on varying thicknesses of paper.

8a printings from 1942-4 are all on paper which is inclined to appear rubbed or blurred.

8b, 8d R4/1 RP the top bar of the second 'E' of 'LEEWARD' is missing. This flaw was corrected in the June 1949 release.

9a R9/6 RP. Similar to R7/3 LP on the 1d.

9c, 9d are often confused. The first colour refers to the portrait and the second to the duty and name tablets.

11a, 11 ba R4/3 LP the second 'E' of LEEWARD is broken at top.

11aa, 11bb R3/5 LP major damage to top right of value tablet, retouched before second printing.

11b the 1943 and 1944 printings are very similar and have horizontal striations on the surface, which are lacking in 11 and 11c.

11c most used examples are more-or-less washed. Price for a fine example.

NOTES (10/-, £1)

12, 13 do not rely on the silver test to identify the high values. Sheets have been found to react in some areas and not in others. Of the 10/-s, 12c has an emerald back; 12a (printed by Williams Lea) is very pale; 12 and 12b can be difficult to distinguish. The best indicator of 12 is the bluish colour of the headplate. The £1s listed can be separated by paper colour, except for 13b and 13c, best separated by the lines of shading above the head. In the February 1942 printing these are blurred, in the October 1942 printing they are clear.

VARIETIES (10/-, £1)

See Bermuda for images of these varieties.

Type A Scroll Flaw: On stamp No. 60 (R5/12); 10/- March 1942, £1 February/October 1942 printings.

Type B Scroll flaw: On stamp #59 (R5/11). March 1942 10/- only.

Type F Gash in Chin: On stamp 17 (R2/5) a large flaw on the King's chin. March 1942 10/- only.

Type G Missing Pearl: On stamp 49 (R5/1) the first pearl to left of centre at the bottom is missing. May 1944 10/-, June 1944 £1 only.

Type H Damaged cliche: On stamp 44 (R4/8) severe damage to the plate of the 10/- affects the right value tablet and 'TEN SHILLINGS' on CW 12, 12a, 12b. Occurs in various states including cases where the damage has been partially retouched by hand at the printers.

		from	
12-b	10/- Type H	£600	£600
12a	10/- Type A	£2500	£2500
12a	Type B	£2750	£2750
12a	Type F	£2500	£2500

12c	Type G	£1000	–
12c	Type H	£600	£600
13b	£1 Type A	£1000	£500
13b	Type F	£1000	£500
13c	Type A	£950	£550
13c	Type F	£950	£500
13d	Type G	£800	–

1949 (July 1st) - 51. As 1-11, but colours changed and stamps printed on chalk-coated paper.

14	½d **grey**	.75	.90
	a slate	£1	£1
15	1d **green**	.25	.10
	a DI flaw	£100	£120
16	1½d **orange and black**	.40	.25
17	2d **scarlet**	.60	.75
18	2½d **black and red-purple**	.25	.10
19	3d **deep blue**	.30	.10

14, 14a both shades occur on the initial printing.

15a see note under 3d above. The full 'DI' flaw occurs only on the first batch of the first printing in green. The second batch of the first printing had the 'DI' flaw corrected, but the accompanying dent in the top of the value tablet remained. The dent was corrected for the 1949 and subsequent printings.

As No. 13, but Perf. 13¼ x 13 (C).

21	£1 **violet and black/crimson**		
	(13/12/51)	£12	£30
	a watermark sideways	£3250	–
	aa frame doubly printed,		
	once albino	£2500	–
	b watermark inverted	£3250	–
1/21	set (19)	£85	£75

21aa One sheet showed the lower rows with an albino second print of the frame, clearly visible when stamp is held at 45 degrees to a light source.

£1 values with violet vignette omitted are not errors; this is the result of exposure to sunlight or other bright light.

Numbers printed: 10/- CW 12 (10/38) 9,900; CW 12a (3/42) 5,880; CW 12b (12/43) 15,180; CW 12c (5/44) 37,140.

£1 CW 13 (11/38) 5,580; CW 13a (11/38) 2,340; CW 13b (3/42) 6,000; CW 13c (10/42) 13,860; CW 13d (12/43) 12,120; CW 13d (6/44) 22,860; CW 21 (12/51) 31,020.

Earliest known postmark dates for 10/- and £1:

CW 12	25.11.38
CW 12a	26.6.44
CW 12b	22.2.45
CW 12c	17.7.48
CW 13	25.11.38
CW 13a	9.1.39
CW 13b	1.10.42 (fiscal use)
CW 13c	.47
CW 13d	5.2.45
CW 21	4.1.52

SPECIAL ISSUES

1937 (May 12th) Coronation. As Ascension.

S1	1d **scarlet**	.40	.45
S2	1½d **light brown**	.40	.85
S3	2½d **blue**	.45	.85
S1/3	**set** (3)	1.10	1.90
SPS1/3	**specimen** perf (2)	£65	†

1946 (Nov. 1st) Victory. As Aden.

S4	1½d **light brown**	.10	.45
S5	3d **reddish orange**	.10	.45
SPS4/5	**specimen** perf (2)	£60	†

1949 (Jan 2nd) Silver Wedding. As Aden.

| S6 | 2½d **ultramarine** | .10 | .10 |
| S7 | 5/- **grey-green** | 2.25 | 2.75 |

1949 (Oct. 10th) UPU. As Aden.

S8	2½d **slate**	.10	1.35
S9	3d **indigo**	£1	1.35
S10	6d **reddish mauve**	.10	1.35
S11	1/- **quartz-green**	.10	1.35
S8/11	**set** (4)	1.20	4.75

1951 (Feb. 16th) West Indies University. As Antigua.

| S12 | 3c **orange and black** | .15 | £1 |
| S13 | 12c **carmine and deep lake** | .35 | £1 |

MALACCA
SEE
MALAYAN STATES

MALAYAN STATES

STRAITS SETTLEMENTS

1937-41 Printers (typo) De La Rue. Perf 13¾ x 14 (C). Chalk-surfaced paper unless otherwise indicated. Sheets 10 x 10.

(a) Die 1.

1	1c **black** (1/1/38)	3.50	.10
2	2c **yellow-green** (6/12/37)	£7	.15
3	4c **orange** (1/1/38)	8.50	.15
4	5c **chocolate** (19/11/37)	8.50	.20
5	6c **scarlet-rose** (10/1/38)	£5	.30
	a scarlet (/41)	£5	.30
6	8c **grey** (26/1/38)	£16	.10
7	10c **deep purple** (8/11/37)	3.50	.10
8	12c **ultramarine** (10/1/38)	3.50	.30
9	25c **purple and carmine** (10/1/38)	£18	.65
10	30c **purple and orange** (1/12/37)	£9	1.20
11	40c **scarlet and purple** (20/12/37)	6.50	1.35
12	50c **black on emerald** (26/1/38)	4.50	.10
	a brownish grey and black on green (/39)	£14	£1
	b black on green (/41)	£6	.10
13	$1 **black and carmine on blue** (26/1/38)	£8	.20
	a black and scarlet on blue (/40)	£6	.15
14	$2 **green and carmine** (26/1/38)	£14	5.50
15	$5 **green and carmine/ green** (26/1/38)	£12	2.75
	a green and scarlet (/41)	£12	3.50

(b) Die 2. CW 21 is perf 14¾ x 14 (C).

16	2c **green** (28/12/38)	£25	.25
	a yellow-green (/41)	£28	.35
17	2c **orange** (thin striated paper) (6/10/41)	.80	£9
18	3c **green** (sub) (5/9/41)	3.50	2.50
	a yellowish green (sub) (/41)	£5	2.50
19	4c **orange** (29/10/38)	£32	.10
20	5c **chocolate** (18/2/39)	£12	.10
21	15c **ultramarine** (sub) (6/10/41)	£3	£6
	a deep ultramarine (sub)	£5	£6
1/21	**set** (18)	£120	£27
SP1/21	**specimen** perf (18)	£400	†

Die 1   Die 2

Die 1 These stamps were printed in two operations. They can be distinguished from Die 2 by the lower tip of the frond at the right side of the stamp, which terminates with two points.

Die 2 These stamps were printed in one operation. The palm fronds are cut clear of the oval frame, and the lower frond terminates in a single point.

17 A Japanese Occupation 2ct orange overprint is known on substitute paper which may, therefore, exist in unoverprinted state. See introduction.

After the issue of the 8ct rose overprinted 'B.M.A.', unoverprinted examples leaked out. Some exist with Singapore cancellations. They were used by a British stamp dealer on self-addressed letters in combination with legitimate issues, to avoid detection. Price (mint) £5. The 6ct in grey was also prepared, but no leaked examples are known.

SPECIAL ISSUES

1937 (May 12th) Coronation. As Ascension, perf 13¾ x 14 (C). Sheets 5 x 10.

S1	4c **orange**	.25	.10
S2	8c **deep grey**	.50	.10
S3	12c **blue**	1.25	.60
S1/3	set (3)	1.80	.65
SP S1/3	**specimen** perf (3)	£40	†

BOOKLET PANES

P1	5c **CW 4** pane of 10	-	-
P2	8c **CW 6** pane of 10	-	-
P3	5c **CW 20** pane of 10	-	-

BOOKLETS

B1	$1 **black on buff** (1938) P1 or P3 x 2	£3250	-
B2	$1.30 **black on grey-green** (1938) P1 or P3, P2	£3500	-

There were four issues of these booklets. In the first issue for each, the 5ct was from Die 1: in the subsequent issues, from Die 2. These booklets are extremely rare.

1937-41 POSTAL FISCAL

(Large Keytypes)

PF1 $25 **grey-purple and
blue on blue**   £400   £275

The $25 was postally used prior to the fall of Malaya to the Japanese, primarily for mailing large batches of sensitive documents back to the U.K. Postally-used examples are scarce.

BMA MALAYA

1945-8. As Strait Settlements, but overprinted (in London, Melbourne or Kuala Lumpur) 'B M A' (British Military Administration) in black or red, for use throughout Malaya. Chalk-surfaced paper, unless otherwise indicated. Setting generally 100, made up of four 5 x 5 units.

(a) Die 1 (see Straits Settlements for Die differences).

22	1c **black** (sub) (red) (19/10/45)	.10	.10
	a jet black (9/11/45)	£2	£1
	b magenta overprint	£2500	£375
	c black (10/45)	£3	.45
	ca opt double, once albino	-	-
	d black (thin striated paper) (8/46)	£18	£12
	e jet black (3/49)	£4	1.50
23	2c **orange** (sub) (9/46)	£12	2.50
24	10c **deep purple** (sub) (19/10/45)	.25	.10
	a deep brown-purple (9/11/45)	2.25	.50
	b dull purple (thin striated paper) (8/46)	£14	£10
	c purple (FA) and dull purple (11/47)	£8	£1
	d purple (fugitive) (sub) (1/48)	.50	.25
	e magenta-purple (FA) (22/3/48)	2.25	.20
	f reddish purple (FA) (13/5/48)	£1	.20
25	12c **ultramarine** (9/11/45)	.75	£6
26	25c **purple and carmine-red** (sub) (3/12/45)	.70	.20
	a pale purple (fugitive) and carmine-red (sub) (4/46)	1.25	.40
	ab 'A' of watermark omitted	-	-
	b purple and deep carmine (thin striated paper) (8/46)	£12	£5
	ba double overprint	£4250	-
	c purple and scarlet (sub) (6/47)	£1	.20
	d purple and deep scarlet (22/3/48)	£11	1.50
27	50c **black on green** (sub) (red) (11/45)	.35	.10
	a black on green (12/45)	£18	1.50
	b black on green (FA ovpt.) (sub) (5/46)	3.50	.50

	c jet black on green			
	(dark red opt.) (sub)(12/47)	£5	.75	
	d shiny metallic overprint	-	£12	
28	$1 **black and carmine**			
	(sub) (26/10/45)	£1	.10	
	a black and deep scarlet			
	(sub) (27/3/46)	1.50	.10	
29	$2 **green and carmine-red**			
	(sub) (3/12/45)	1.25	.45	
	a green and scarlet			
	(sub) (4/46)	£4	.60	
30	$5 **green and scarlet on green** (9/11/45)	£45	£75	
31	$5 **purple and brown-orange** (sub)			
	(4/46)	1.85	£2	
	a red-purple and yellow-orange (sub)			
	(6/7/47)	£8	£5	

22a is on toned paper with brown gum; 22e on very white paper, with white gum.

22b the magenta overprint is in a distinctly different colour, rather than merely a shade of red. Only one mint example is known to us. Extreme care is necessary when purchasing this stamp.

22d, etc thin striated paper - see introduction.

24a is on toned paper with brown gum.

24c, 24e, f, 27b 'FA' indicates that these stamps show a fluorescent aniline reaction under an ultraviolet lamp.

26ab one defective used example is known.

27d this stamp is not known to us in mint condition. No information as to printing date is available.

30 this stamp is known with forged overprint. It was not issued in Specimen form.

31a the appearance of this stamp is smeary.

b) Die 2. 38 is Perf 14¾ x 14 (C).

32	2c **orange** (sub) 19/10/45)	.10	.10
	a orange (white forehead) (sub) (/46)	2.25	.75
	b orange (thin striated paper) (7/46)	£10	£5
	c orange-yellow (sub) (21/7/47)	.40	.20
	d orange (8/7/47)	£3	£1
	e orange-yellow (12/10/48)	£4	.90
	f watermark inverted	-	£1200
33	3c **green** (sub) (19/10/45)	.85	.30
	a blue-green (sub) (27/1/47)	2.50	2.50
	b green (7/47)	£9	.30
	c blue-green (/48)	7.50	1.50

34	5c **chocolate** (26/10/45)	.30	.60
35	6c **slate-grey** (sub) (19/10/45)	.15	.15
	a slate (thin striated paper) (6/46)	£10	£8
	b slate-grey (white forehead) (sub) (/46)	.75	.50
	c slate (/47)	£15	£3
	d slate-grey (22/3/48)	£12	£4
36	8c **rose** (sub) (10/10/45)	.15	.10
	a red-scarlet (sub) (2/46)	.75	.10
	b deep red (thin striated paper) (6/46)	£10	£12
37	10c **reddish purple** (28/7/48)	£8	2.50
38	15c **ultramarine** (black) (sub) (9/11/45)	£1	5.50
	a overprint on selvedge	£42	£60
39	15c **ultramarine** (red) (sub) (12/45)	.35	.10
	a dull ultramarine (sub) (15/10/46)	.40	.10
	b blue (27/1/47)	£30	.60
	c steel-blue (sub) (8/7/47)	£65	7.50
	d ultramarine (22/3/48)	£20	.60
	e opt double, once albino	-	-
22/39	**set** (15)	£48	£78
SP22/38	**specimen perf** (14)	£425	†

normal   'white'

32a, 35b on certain stamps within the sheets of these printings, the forehead appears white. The lines which normally shade the forehead are shorter than normal. Strips may be found showing a progression from 'normal' to 'white forehead'.

32b, etc thin striated paper - see introduction.

38a normally found on the left selvedge of the sheet; less often found on the bottom selvedge.

39c steel-blue is deeper than the normal blue and is a very distinct colour.

39e we have seen a single mint example with the albino overprint placed diagonally.

Whilst stamps overprinted 'B.M.A.' were not placed on sale until 19/10/45, the BMA was in control prior to this date. Mail was carried free of charge from 17/9/45; thus stamps were not necessary. The 'BMA' stamps were withdrawn on July 10th 1951.

Postal forgeries exist of the 50c BMA, made from the 1c with paper dyed green and the value altered to 50c.

When the British Authorities returned in 1945, a quantity of the Straits Settlements 8ct grey was found in Kuala Lumpur and overprinted 'B.M.A.'. A supply of the 8ct rose arrived, and the 8ct grey was not issued because of the clash of colours with the 6ct grey. Price £240 mint. Used examples are known, mostly cancelled 'par complaisance', although some did go through the post - probably sent by collectors.

The BMA issues were withdrawn and replaced over a period of years, beginning with Singapore on 1 September 1948 and ending with Kelantan on 11 July 1951.

SPECIAL ISSUES

Victory stamps for Malayan Union exist, but extant examples of the 8ct carmine were obtained during a destruction operation and were never officially issued. Many are singed and discoloured by flames, and/or without gum; fine examples are difficult to obtain. Price *from* £175, according to condition. No examples of the 15ct value have appeared on the market, so presumably all were successfully destroyed.

POSTAGE DUE STAMPS

1936-8 Printers (typo) Waterlow and Sons. Watermark Multiple Script CA. Perf 14¾ x 14 (c). Sheets 10 x 10.

PD1	1ct **violet-maroon** (1938)	4.50	.40
GPD1	4ct **green** (9/36)	£11	.60
GPD2	8ct **scarlet** (6/36)	6.50	1.65
GPD3	10ct **yellow-orange** (6/36)	9.50	.20
GPD4	12ct **pale ultramarine** (9/36)	9.50	8.50
PD2	50ct **black** (1/38)	£14	2.75
PD1-2	**set** (6)	£50	12.50
SPPD1-2	**specimen** perf (6)	£175	†

1945-51 As above but new values, colours and papers.

PD3	1ct **purple**	1.50	1.20
	a purple-violet (/49)	£3	1.75
PD4	3ct **yellow-green**	£3	£3
	a emerald-green (/49)	£4	£4
PD5	5ct **scarlet** (/45)	£3	£2
	a bright scarlet (/49)	£4	£3
PD6	8ct **ochre** (/45)	6.50	£9
PD7	9ct **orange-yellow**	£18	£25
PD8	15ct **slate-violet**	£60	£17
PD9	20ct **deep blue** (/48)	£5	£4
	a deep violet-blue (6/3/51)	£4	£3
PD3-9	**set** (7)	£85	£55
SPPD6,9	**specimen perf** (2)	£120	†

The 1936-8 values are on smooth paper. Of the 1945-51 values, PD3, 4, 5 7 and 8 were on rough paper giving a coarse impression.

1951-4 As above, perf 14.

PD10	1ct **violet** (21/8/52)	.35	£1
PD11	2ct **deep slate-blue** (16/11/53)	.60	1.35
PD12	3ct **deep green** (21/8/52)	£12	£7
PD13	4ct **sepia** (16/11/53)	.35	£4
PD14	5ct **vermilion** (8/8/51)	£24	£7
PD15	8ct **yellow-orange** (8/8/51)	1.10	£3
PD16	12ct **bright purple** (1/2/54)	.60	3.60
PD17	20ct **blue** (8/8/51)	£3	£4
PD10-17	**set** (8)	£38	£28

JOHORE

All stamps were printed (typo) by De La Rue on chalk-surfaced paper unless otherwise stated.

1922-40 Design, portrait of Sultan Sir Ibrahim. Perf. 13¾ x 14 (C). Chalk-surfaced paper. Sheets 12 x 10, also 10 x 10, and 120; 2 panes, each 6 x 10.

X1	1c **dull purple and black**	.15	.15
X2	2c **green** (/28)	.25	.25
X3	3c **purple and sepia**	.70	£1
X4	4c **purple and carmine** (/24)	1.25	.15
X5	5c **dull purple and sage-green**	.15	.20
	a watermark inverted	-	-
X6	6c **dull purple and claret**	.25	.30
X7	10c **dull purple and yellow** (/22)	.25	.15
	a thin striated paper	£75	£150
X8	12c **dull purple and blue**	.50	.75
X9	12c **ultramarine** (/40)	£20	£2
X10	21c **dull purple and orange** (/28)	£1	£2
X11	25c **dull purple and myrtle**	1.85	.60
X12	30c **dull purple and orange** (/36)	4.50	£5
X13	40c **dull purple and brown** (/36)	4.50	5.50
X14	50c **dull purple and red**	1.85	£1
	a thin striated paper	£100	£200
X15	$1 **green and mauve**	1.85	.75
	a thin striated paper	£50	£60
X16	$2 **green and carmine** (/23)	£20	£15
	a thin striated paper	£5	2.50
X17	$3 **green and blue** (/25)	£32	£55
X18	$4 **green and brown** (/26)	£50	£120
	a watermark inverted	£550	-
X19	$5 **green and orange**	£30	£30
	a thin striated paper	£60	-
X20	$10 **green and black** (/24)	£150	£250
	a thin striated paper	£425	-
X21	$50 **green and ultramarine**	£650	-
X1/20	**set** (20)	£275	£250
SPX1/21	**specimen overprinted and perf** (21)	£650	†

X7a, etc In 1941 Williams Lea produced a printing which probably accounts for the 10ct-$10 on thin striated paper listed above. The 1ct, 2ct and 6ct were included in the same requisition, but have not yet been reported on the thin paper. See introduction. Most $ values were used for fiscal and telegraphic purposes.

X1-5 in booklet panes of 10 and X5 in panes of 6 exist from booklets printed 1928-30.

1940 (Feb.) Design, Sultan Sir Ibrahim. Perf. 13½ (C). Recess-printed on uncoated paper by De La Rue. Sheets 10 x 5.

1	8c **black and light blue**	£10	.60
	a black and pale ultramarine	£10	.60
SP1	**specimen perf**	£65	†

1949 (May 2nd) - 52 Design, Sultan Sir Ibrahim. Perf 17½ x 18 (C). Sheets 10 x 10.

3	1c **black**	.25	.10
4	2c **orange**	.10	.10
	a yellow-orange (22/1/52)	.75	1.35
	b pale yellow (9/12/58)	£3	£5
5	3c **green**	.25	.60
	a light green (2/9/49)	.25	.60
	b yellow-green (22/1/52)	£10	£3
6	4c **brown**	.50	.10
	a light brown (13/3/57)	.75	.35
7	6c **grey**	.30	.15
	a light grey (22/1/52)	.30	.30
	b greenish grey (16/12/52)	.50	.50
8	8c **scarlet**	1.75	.75
9	10c **reddish purple**	.35	.10
	a deep red-purple (24/5/56)	£1	.10
	b light red-purple (9/12/58)	.75	.10
	c imperf pair	£2250	-
10	15c **bright ultramarine**	1.75	.10
	a blue (22/1/52)	£2	.10
11	20c **black and green**	.50	.60
12	25c **red-purple and orange**	1.50	.10
	a deep red-purple and orange (22/2/51)	3.75	.25
13	40c **scarlet and red-purple**	2.75	£8
14	50c **black and violet-blue**	1.75	.10
	a black and blue (21/2/52)	£2	.10
	b black and pale blue (10/12/57)	£6	.75
15	$1 **ultramarine and deep red-purple**	3.75	1.75
	a blue and red-purple (17/12/52)	£5	1.20

	b pale blue and purple			
	(10/12/57)	£10	£4	
16	$2 **green and carmine-red**	£9	5.50	
17	$5 **green and deep brown**	£20	8.50	

WATERMARK VARIETY (TYPE A)
(See Introduction for details)

7c	6c **St Edward's Crown**	£1600	-

1952 (Sept.1st) - 56 As before, but new values or colours.

18	5c **magenta**	.35	.20
	a bright magenta (18/8/53)	.50	.20
	b pale magenta (10/12/57)	£2	£4
19	8c **green**	2.75	1.35
20	12c **scarlet**	£3	3.50
21	20c **deep blue**	.50	.10
	a bright blue (23/3/55)	.70	.10
22	30c **scarlet and red-purple**		
	(4/9/55)	£1	1.65
	a scarlet and dull lake-purple		
	(24/5/56)	£2	1.65
23	35c **scarlet and red-purple**	3.25	.75
3/23	**set** (21)	£50	£30

SPECIAL ISSUES

1948 (Dec. 1st) Silver Wedding. As Aden.

S1	10c **purple**	.10	.45
S2	$5 **grey-green**	12.50	£25

1949 (Oct. 10th) U.P.U. As Aden

S3	10c **dull purple**	.15	.25
S4	15c **indigo**	£1	.75
S5	25c **orange**	.30	£2
S6	50c **slate-black**	.60	2.25
S3/6	**set** (4)	1.90	4.75

Number issued 10c, 684,457; 15c, 156,319; 25c, 117,176; 50c, 90,450.

POSTAGE DUE STAMPS

1938 (Jan. 1st). Printers (typo) Waterlow and Sons. Perf. 12½ (L). Uncoated paper. Sheets 10 x 10.

PD1	1c **crimson**	£8	£32
PD2	4c **green**	£20	£30
PD3	8c **ochre**	£24	£120
PD4	10c **deep brown**	£24	£38
PD5	12c **deep purple**	£28	£90

PD1/5	**set** (5)	£95	£280
SPPD1/5	**specimen perf** (5)	£125	†

Beware of faked cancellations.

KEDAH

1937 (June 30th). Design, Sultan Abdul Hamid Halim Shah. Printers (recess) Waterlow and Sons. Perf 12½ (L). Sheets 6 x 10.

1	10c ultramarine and sepia	2.25	£1
2	12c black and violet	£24	2.75
	a 'A' of watermark missing	-	-
3	25c ultramarine and red-purple	4.75	2.75
4	30c green and red	4.25	£6
5	40c black and red-purple	£2	£10
6	50c deep brown and blue	4.50	2.75
7	$1 black and green	£2	£6
8	$2 green and deep brown	£65	£45
9	$5 black and red	£16	£150
1/9	set (9)	£80	£200
SP1/9	specimen perf (9)	£150	†

The vast majority of 'used' $5 values from this set bear faked postmarks.

1938-40. Printers (recess) De La Rue. Sheets 120, 10 x 12.

Perf. 13¾ (L).

10	1c black (/38)	£65	1.80

Perf. 14 (L).

10a	1c black (/40)	£65	1.80
11	2c green (/40)	£135	£4
11b	6c carmine (/40)	£8	£32

1922 Issue　　　　1938 Issue

10, 10a there were three printings from the new plate (Plate 2) which can be distinguished from that issued in 1922 by the shape of the '1's. 10 exists in two sizes, 18¾ x 22½mm and 19¼ x 22¾mm, having been printed on damp and dry paper respectively, the former being worth a premium. 10a was printed on dry paper only.

1922 Issue　　　　1938 Issue

11 in this die the '2's have round drops instead of oval, and the 'c's are larger than the 1921 issue. It measures 19½ x 22¾mm.

11b measures 19¼ x 22½mm and is line-perforated.

1950 (June 1st)-56. Designs, sheaf of rice (1c-20c), Sultan Tengku Badlishah (other values). Printers (typo) De La Rue. Perf 17½ x 18 (C). Sheets 10 x 10.

12	1c black	.25	.20
13	2c orange	.25	.10
14	3c green	£1	.60
15	4c brown	.35	.10
	a deep brown (24/3/54)	.75	.75
16	6c grey	.35	.10
	a greenish grey (27/11//52)	£1	.30
	b pale grey (19/12/56)	£3	£1
17	8c scarlet	.85	2.25
18	10c red-purple	.35	.10
	a deep red-purple (8/2/56)	£1	.10
19	15c bright ultramarine	1.25	.20
20	20c black and green	1.10	1.50
21	25c deep purple and orange	.75	.20
	a red-purple and orange (27/6/51)	£1	.20
22	40c scarlet and red-purple	1.85	£4
23	50c black and violet-blue	1.50	.20
	a black and deep blue (27/11/52)	2.50	.20
	b black and pale blue (23/4/54)	£5	£7
24	$1 ultramarine and red-purple	1.60	3.30
	a blue and deep red-purple (18/2/53)	4.50	£4
25	$2 green and carmine-red	£10	£16
26	$5 green and deep brown	£21	£33

1952 (Sept. 1st) - 56. As before, but new values or colours.

27	5c **magenta**	1.35	1.50
	a bright magenta (24/9/53)	1.35	.60
	b dark magenta (25/5/55)	£5	£4
28	8c **green**	£1	1.25
	a deep green (24/9/53)	£8	£12
29	12c **scarlet**	1.10	1.75
30	20c **blue**	.75	.10
	a deep blue (8/2/56)	£4	.60
31	30c **scarlet and red-purple**		
	(4/9/55)	1.85	.75
32	35c **scarlet and red-purple**	1.50	£1
12/32	**set** (21)	£45	£60

SPECIAL ISSUES

1948 (Dec. 1st) Silver Wedding. As Aden.

S1	10c **purple**	.10	.25
S2	$5 **rose-carmine**	£14	£25

1949 (Oct. 10th) U.P.U. As Aden.

S3	10c **dull purple**	.10	.75
S4	15c **indigo**	£1	.90
S5	25c **orange**	.30	1.35
S6	50c **slate-black**	.50	2.25
	a 'A' of watermark missing £550		-
S3/6	**set** (4)	1.70	4.75

Number issued 10c, 283,010; 15c, 89,652; 25c 84,456; 50c, 74,500.

KELANTAN

1937-40. Design, Sultan Ismail. Printers (recess) Bradbury, Wilkinson. Perf. 12 (L). Sheets 10 x 10.

1	1c **olive and ochre** (7/37)	.85	.35
2	2c **emerald-green** (7/37)	£3	.15
3	4c **scarlet-red** (7/37)	£3	.60
4	5c **deep chestnut** (7/37)	2.35	.10
5	6c **crimson-lake** (10/37)	£5	£6
6	8c **olive** (7/37)	2.25	.10
7	10c **deep purple** (10/37)	£10	1.75
8	12c **blue** (7/37)	£3	3.75
9	25c **vermilion and purple** (7/27)	£3	2.20
10	30c **purple and scarlet** (10/37)	£22	12.50
11	40c **red-orange and green** (7/37)	£4	£18
12	50c **olive and red-orange** (10/37)	£28	£5
13	$1 **purple and green** (10/37)	£20	£8
14	$2 **maroon and crimson** (3/40)	£110	£150
15	$5 **vermilion and crimson-lake** (2/40)	£250	£550
1/15	**set** (15)	£400	£700
SP1/15	**specimen perf** (15)	£500	†

14-15 most used examples were utilised for accounting purposes within the Post Office, and many faked cancels also exist. An expert committee certificate (of recent vintage) is advisable when purchasing used examples.

1951 (July 11th) - 55. Design, portrait of Sultan Tengku Ibrahim. Printers (typo) De La Rue, on chalk-surfaced paper. Perf 17½ x 18 (C). Sheets as before.

16	1c **black**	.25	.20

17	2c **orange**	.60	.25
	a orange-yellow (11/5/55)	£3	2.50
	b minute stop	£16	£20
18	3c **green**	£2	.75
19	4c **brown**	.60	.10
20	6c **light grey**	.35	.15
	a greenish grey (16/7/53)	.35	.15
21	8c **scarlet**	1.75	£2
22	10c **red-purple**	.30	.10
	a claret (8/12/53)	.25	.10
23	15c **bright ultramarine**	2.50	.30
24	20c **black and green**	1.50	5.50
25	25c **red-purple and orange**	.75	.35
	a deep red-purple and		
	orange (8/12/53)	1.75	.85
26	40c **scarlet and red-purple**	£6	£12
27	50c **black and blue**	2.50	.25
28	$1 **ultramarine and deep**		
	red-purple	£4	5.50
	a ultramarine and red-purple		
	(12/2/53)	£8	7.50
29	$2 **green and carmine-red**	£14	£24
30	$5 **green and deep brown**	£25	£35
	a green and sepia (8/12/53)	£60	£75

17b R1/2 the stop under 'c' in the right hand panel is almost completely missing. Occurs on both shades.

1952 (Sept. 1st) - 56. As before, but new values or colours.

31	5c **magenta**	.75	£1
	a bright magenta (8/12/53)	1.35	.60
32	8c **green**	1.25	£1
33	12c **scarlet**	1.75	1.35
34	20c **blue**	.75	.15
35	30c **scarlet and red-purple**		
	(4/9/55)	.65	2.25
	a scarlet and lake-purple		
	(27/3/56)	£4	£4
36	35c **scarlet and red-purple**	.75	.90
16/36	**set** (21)	£60	£85

SPECIAL ISSUES

1948 (Dec. 1st) Silver Wedding. As Aden.

| S1 | 10c **purple** | .35 | 1.65 |
| S2 | $5 **rose-carmine** | £14 | £32 |

Number issued 10c, 225,572; $5, 18,633.

1949 (Oct. 10th) U.P.U. As Aden.

S3	10c **dull purple**	.15	.20
S4	15c **indigo**	1.10	£1
S5	25c **orange**	.20	2.75
S6	50c **slate-black**	.35	1.80
S3/6	**set** (4)	1.60	5.25

Number issued 10c, 193,979; 15c, 69,160; 15c, 69,618; 25c, 72,435.

MALACCA

1949 (Mar. 1st)-52. Printers (typo) De La Rue, on chalk-surfaced paper. Perf 17½ x 18 (C). Sheets 10 x 10.

1	1c **black**	.15	.40
2	2c **orange**	.40	.30
3	3c **green**	.15	.85
4	4c **brown**	.15	.10
5	6c **greenish grey**	.35	.50
6	8c **scarlet**	.35	3.75
7	10c **red-purple**	.15	.10
8	15c **bright ultramarine**	1.35	.35
9	20c **black and green**	.35	4.25
10	25c **deep red-purple and**		
	orange	.35	.40
	a bright red-purple and		
	orange (13/11/52)	1.50	.75
11	40c **scarlet and red-purple**	.75	£8
12	50c **black and violet-blue**	.75	.75
	a black and blue		
	(13/11/52)	2.50	£2
13	$1 **blue and deep**		
	red-purple	5.50	£15
	a light blue and red-purple		
	(22/11/51)	£7	£14
14	$2 **green and carmine-red**	£10	£14
15	$5 **green and deep brown**	£25	£24

1952 (Sept. 1st) As before, but new values or colours.

16	5c **magenta**	.30	.90
	a purple	£1	£1
17	8c **green**	£2	£3
18	12c **scarlet**	£2	4.50
19	20c **blue**	£3	1.50
20	35c **scarlet and purple**	1.85	1.80
1/20	**set** (20)	£50	£75

SPECIAL ISSUES

1948 (Dec. 1st) Silver Wedding. As Aden.

| S1 | 10c **purple** | .15 | £1 |
| S2 | $5 **chocolate** | 14.50 | £24 |

Number issued 10c, 375,006; $5, 18,889.

1949 (Oct. 10th) U.P.U. As Aden.

S3	10c **dull purple**	.15	.30
S4	15c **indigo**	£1	1.65
S5	25c **orange**	.20	£4
S6	50c **slate-black**	.30	2.75
S3/6	**set** (4)	1.50	£8

Number issued 10c, 328,057; 15c, 79,242; 25c, 81,297; 50c, 69,213.

NEGRI SEMBILAN

All stamps were printed (typo) by De La Rue on chalk-surfaced paper except where otherwise mentioned.

1935-41. Design, Arms of Territory. Perf 13¾ x 14 (C). Sheets 10 x 10.

X1	1c **black**	.50	.10
X2	2c **green**	.50	.15
1	2c **orange** (thin striated paper)		
	(11/12/41)	£2	£50
2	3c **green** (sub)	£9	£5
	a thin striated paper (21/8/41)	£4	£6
X3	4c **orange**	.85	.10
X4	5c **brown**	.85	.10
3	6c **scarlet** (1/1/37)	£8	1.65
	a stop omitted	£350	-
4	6c **grey** (19/12/41) (sub)	1.35	£250
	a stop omitted	£140	-
X5	8c **grey**	£1	.10
X6	10c **purple**	.60	.10
X7	12c **blue**	1.50	.30
5	15c **ultramarine**		
	(1/10/41) (sub)	£5	£38
X8	25c **purple and scarlet**	.75	.40
	a thin striated paper (?/41)	-	-
X9	30c **dull purple and orange**	1.75	1.20
X10	40c **scarlet and purple**	1.50	1.20
X11	50c **black/emerald**	£3	1.20
X12	$1 **black and red/blue**	2.25	2.50
X13	$2 **green and scarlet**	£19	£11
X14	$5 **green and red/emerald**	£12	£150
X1/14	**set** (19)	£60	£475
SPX1/14	**specimen perf** (15)	£325	†

Used Stamps. The prices for the 1941 new colours or values are for clearly identifiable 1941 cancellations. The 6c grey in particular is usually found with either forged or post Japanese Occupation cancels when it was also valid for use. Prices for this stamp in this later period are about a third of those shown.

The $5 was primarily used for fiscal purposes and some copies used thus have subsequently been provided with obliterations, either forged or genuine by par complaisance, to disguise this. Such stamps often show traces of green crayon marks. Furthermore this stamp was relatively common in mint blocks and has in more recent times been provided with imitation fake cancels which have been applied to both singles and blocks of four of this value. These initially came on to the market through sales on EBay.

Gum. Some values from the Colonial releases, including the dollar values, had gum that browned in the climate to varying degrees. This is normal and is especially to be expected on stamps with genuine Japanese Occupation handstamps and overprints, but stamps released in London to the philatelic trade with paler or white gum are worth a premium.

Printings were made of the 1c,, 2c or., 3c, 25c and 30c on striated paper. The 25c has been reported on a local cover just before the Japanese occupation otherwise the 1c and 30c and not known without Japanese Occupation handstamps or overprints. The 2c and 3c were all (?) printed on striated paper and issued both before and during the Occupation.

3a, 4a R10/4 the stop under 'C' in the right value tablet is missing.

An 8ct rose was prepared for issue in 1941, but the Japanese occupation prevented this. It was, however, overprinted by the Japanese and, later, unoverprinted copies leaked out.

1949 (April 1st)-52 Design, Arms of Territory. Perf 17½ x 18 (C). Sheets as before.

6	1c **black**	.50	.10
7	2c **orange**	.25	.10
	a yellow-orange (8/1/52)	.30	.£3
8	3c **green**	.25	.20
9	4c **deep brown**	.15	.10
	a brown (16/6/54)	.75	.10
10	6c **greenish grey**	.85	.10
	a deep greenish grey (13/13/50)	£1	.10
	b grey (13/12/50)	£1	.10
	c silver-grey (13/12/56)	2.50	£2
11	8c **scarlet**	.25	.45
12	10c **deep red-purple**	.30	.10
	a claret (8/1/52)	.15	.10
	b red-purple (22/2/56)	1.50	.10
13	15c **deep blue**	1.60	.10
14	20c **black and green**	.50	.75
15	25c **deep red-purple and orange**	.50	.10
	a red-purple and orange (30/12/52)	£1	.10
16	40c **scarlet and red-purple**	1.60	£3
17	50c **black and violet-blue**	£2	.15
	a black and blue (8/1/52)	1.85	.15

18	$1 **blue and deep red-purple**	£3	1.35
	a blue and red-purple (30/12/52)	2.25	2.50
19	$2 **green and carmine-red**	6.50	£14
20	$5 **green and deep brown**	£25	£40

1952 (Sept. 1st) - 56. As before, but new values or colours.

21	5c **magenta**	.50	.35
	a bright magenta (25/8/53)	.30	.30
22	8c **green**	1.75	£1
23	12c **scarlet**	1.75	1.65
24	20c **blue**	.60	.10
	a deep blue (22/2/56)	£3	.20
25	30c **scarlet and deep red-purple** (4/9/55)	.60	1.50
	a scarlet and red-purple (22/2/56)	£4	£2
26	35c **scarlet and red-purple**	.85	.60
6/26	**set** (21)	£43	£60

SPECIAL ISSUES

1948 (Dec. 1st) Silver Wedding. As Aden.

S1	10c **purple**	.20	.30
S2	$5 **grey-green**	£10	£18

Number issued 10c, 496,250; $5, 19,151.

1949 (Oct. 10th) U.P.U. As Aden.

S3	10c **dull purple**	.10	.15
S4	15c **indigo**	.70	1.80
	a 'A' of watermark missing £550	-	
S5	25c **orange**	.15	1.50
S6	50c **slate-black**	.30	1.95
S3/6	**set** (4)	1.10	£5

Number issued 10c, 452,690; 15c, 103,653; 25c, 94,452; 50c, 74,218.

BOOKLET PANES

P1	5c CW X4 pane of 10	£1000	-
P2	8c CW X5 pane of 10	£1200	-

BOOKLETS

1935

B1	$1 P1 x 2	£2500	-
B2	$1.30 P1, P2	£3000	-

These booklets are very rare.

PAHANG

All stamps were printed (typo) by De La Rue on chalk-surfaced paper unless otherwise mentioned.

1935-37, Design, Sultan Abu Bakar. Perf 14. Sheets 10 x 10.

X1	1c **black**	.10	.25
X2	2c **green**	£1	.30
X3	4c **orange**	.35	.30
X4	5c **pale brown**	.35	.10
	a brown (/38)	.35	.10
2	6c **red** (1/1/37)	£10	£1
X5	8c **grey**	.30	.10
X6	10c **dull purple**	.75	.10
	a thin striated paper (/41)	-	-
X7	12c **bright ultramarine**	1.50	.75
X8	25c **dull purple and scarlet**	£1	.90
X9	30c **dull purple and orange**	.60	.65
	a thin striated paper (?/41)	-	-
X10	40c **scarlet and dull purple**	.50	1.25
X11	50c **black/emerald**	£2	£2
	a grey/green (/39)	-	.90
X12	$1 **black and red/blue**	1.75	£5
X13	$2 **green and scarlet**	£12	£22
X14	$5 **green and red/emerald**	4.50	£45

1937-41, Perf 13¾ x 14 (C). 1941 values printed (typo) by Harrison & Sons.

1	3c **green** (21/8/41) (sub)	£25	2.50
	a thin striated paper (/41)	8.50	-
3	8c **rose** (11/12/41)	-	-
	a thin striated paper	£2	£40
4	15c **ultramarine** (1/10/41) (sub)	£10	£38
X1/4	**set** (18)	£50	£145
SPX1/4	specimen perf (18)	£360	†

Gum; became brown in Malayan conditions. This is normal. Stamps with white gum, as released to the UK philatelic trade, are worth a premium.

Postmarks; the 1941 new colours/values are priced with 1941 cancellations. Later uses are about one-third of those shown. Faked cancels exist, as is the case with X14.

X9a may not have been used until the post-war period.

2 despite the date of issue, the 6ct was printed by De La Rue in 1935 and hence is listed with the rest of the De La Rue set.

3a many examples were used in Negri Sembilan.

A 2ct in orange and 6ct in grey were to have been issued in 1941, but the Japanese occupation prevented this. Later, mint copies appeared on the market (price £2 each stamp). Those with Singapore postmarks are of doubtful status.

1950 (June 1st)-54 Design, Sultan Sir Abu Bakar. Perf 17½ x 18 (C). Sheets as before.

5	1c **black**	.10	.10
6	2c **orange**	.10	.10
	a pale orange (24/3/54)	£1	.50
7	3c **green**	.15	.50
8	4c **brown**	.85	.10
	a deep brown (24/3/54)	£6	1.50
9	6c **greenish grey**	.25	.20
	a light grey (10/9/53)	.50	.50
10	8c **scarlet**	.25	.90
11	10c **red-purple**	.20	.10
	a deep red-purple (12/6/57)	.10	.10
12	15c **bright ultramarine**	.35	.10
13	20c **black and green**	.25	1.65
14	25c **red-purple and orange**	£1	.10
	a deep red-purple and orange (10/9/53)	.25	.10
	b deep red-purple and yellow-orange (24/3/54)	£3	£1
15	40c **scarlet and red-purple**	.75	4.50
16	50c **black and violet-blue**	.75	.10
	a black and deep blue (17/12/52)	1.50	.10
	b black and pale blue (3/56)	£5	£2
17	$1 **ultramarine and deep red-purple**	1.35	£2
	a ultramarine and red-purple (17/12/52)	2.75	£2
18	$2 **green and carmine-red**	6.50	£13
19	$5 **green and deep brown**	27.50	£55
	a green and sepia (23/3/54)	£60	£70

1952 (Sept. 1st)-56. As before, but new values or colours.

20	5c **magenta**	.25	.40
	a bright magenta (10/9/53)	.25	.15
21	8c **green**	.50	.45
	a deep green (10/9/53)	£1	£1
22	12c **scarlet**	.50	.75
23	20c **blue**	.75	.10
	a deep blue (8/3/56)	£4	1.75
24	30c **scarlet and brown-purple** (5/9/55)	.65	.20
	a scarlet and purple (8/3/56)	£15	3.75
25	35c **scarlet and red-purple**	.30	.15
5/25	**set** (21)	£38	£75

SPECIAL ISSUES

1948 (Dec. 1st) Silver Wedding. As Aden.

| S1 | 10c purple | .10 | .35 |
| S2 | $5 grey-green | 12.50 | £24 |

1949 (Oct. 10th) U.P.U. As Aden.

S3	10c dull purple	.15	.15
S4	15c indigo	.55	.90
S5	25c orange	.20	1.20
S6	50c slate-black	.35	1.50
S3/6	set (4)	1.15	3.40

Numbers issued 10c, 349,564; 15c, 98,795; 25c, 81,776; 50c, 64,661.

BOOKLET PANES

| P1 | 5c X4 pane of 10 | - | - |
| P2 | 8c X5 pane of 10 | - | - |

BOOKLETS

| B1 | $1 1935 two panes of X4 | £2500 | - |
| B2 | $1.30 1935 X4 and X5 | - | - |

There were five printings of B1, the last in 1939, but only two of B2, in 1935 and 1939.

Total produced - B1 19,500; B2 3,500.

PENANG

All stamps were printed (typo) by De La Rue, on chalk-surfaced paper unless otherwise mentioned.

1949 (Feb. 21st)-54 Perf 17½ x 18 (C). Sheets 10 x 10.

1	1c black	.50	.15
2	2c orange	.60	.15
3	3c green	.20	.60
4	4c brown	.20	.10
	a deep brown (12/5/54)	£3	£1
5	6c greenish grey	.50	.15
	a light greenish grey (27/11/52)	1.50	.15
6	8c scarlet	.50	2.75
7	10c red-purple	.20	.10
8	15c bright ultramarine	.75	.20
9	20c black and green	.85	.75
10	25c red-purple and orange	1.10	.45
	a dull red-purple and orange (10/9/53)	£2	£1
11	40c scarlet and red-purple	1.60	£8
12	50c black and violet-blue	2.25	.15
13	$1 blue and deep red-purple	£10	1.50
	a blue and red-purple (13/12/50)	£15	1.50
14	$2 green and carmine-red	£11	1.25
15	$5 green and deep brown	£24	1.80

1952 (Sept. 1st)-54 As before, but new values or colours.

16	5c magenta	1.60	1.80
	a bright magenta (12/5/54)	£2	2.50
17	8c green	1.25	1.25
18	12c scarlet	1.60	4.50
19	20c blue	.85	.75
20	35c scarlet and purple	£1	.75
1/20	set (20)	£55	£24

SPECIAL ISSUES

1948 (Dec. 1st) Silver Wedding. As Aden.

| S1 | 10c purple | .15 | .15 |
| S2 | $5 chocolate | 17.50 | £21 |

1949 (Oct. 10th) U.P.U. As Aden.

S3	10c **dull purple**	.10	.10
S4	15c **indigo**	1.10	2.10
S5	25c **orange**	.25	2.10
S6	50c **slate-black**	.75	2.10
S3/6	**set** (4)	£2	5.75

Number issued 10c, 761,745; 15c, 185,687; 25c, 193,662; 50c, 130,193.

PERAK

All stamps were printed (typo) by De La Rue, on chalk-surfaced paper unless otherwise stated.

1935-37 Design, Portrait (side face) of Sultan Iskandar. Perf 13¾ x 14 (C). Sheets 10 x 10.

X1	1c **black**	.85	.10
X2	2c **green**	.85	.10
X3	4c **orange**	£1	.10
X4	5c **brown**	.35	.10
X5	6c **scarlet** (1/1/37)	£6	2.50
X6	8c **grey**	.50	.10
X7	10c **dull purple**	.40	.10
X8	12c **bright ultramarine**	1.75	.60
X9	25c **dull purple and scarlet**	1.35	.60
X10	30c **dull purple and orange**	1.85	.90
X11	40c **scarlet and dull purple**	2.75	2.75
X12	50c **black/emerald**	£3	.75
X13	$1 **black and red/blue**	1.25	.75
X14	$2 **green and scarlet**	£13	4.25
X15	$5 **green and red/emerald**	£60	£21
X1/15	**set** (15)	£85	£30
SPX1/15	**specimen perf** (15)	£325	†

X4 was issued in coil form.

1938-41 Design, portrait (full face) of Sultan Iskandar. Perf 13¾ x 14 (C). Sheets as before.

2	1c **black** (17/4/39)	£6	.10
3	2c **green** (13/1/39)	3.50	.10
4	2c **orange** (30/10/41)	2.50	£4
	a malformed 'C'	£65	-
	b thin striated paper	1.75	£11
	ba malformed 'C'	£50	-
5	3c **green** (21/8/41)	-	£4
	a thin striated paper	1.35	£4
6	4c **orange** (8/5/39)	£15	.10
7	5c **chocolate** (1/2/39)	£3	.10
8	6c **rose** (1/12/39)	£13	.10
9	8c **slate-grey** (1/12/38)	£13	.10

10	8c **rose-carmine**		
	(18/12/41)	£1	-
	a thin striated paper	.50	£45
11	10c **grey-purple** (17/10/38)	£15	.10
	a thin striated paper	-	-
12	12c **blue** (17/10/38)	£11	.60
13	15c **ultramarine** (sub) (8/41)	£2	£8
	a blue (sub)	£4	£10
14	25c **purple and red**		
	(1/12/39)	£25	£2
15	30c **purple and orange**		
	(17/10/38)	4.50	1.35
	a thin striated paper	£6	£15
16	40c **scarlet and purple**		
	(2/5/38)	£25	1.25
17	50c **black/emerald**		
	(17/10/38)	£15	.50
	a black/green (/41)	£18	.50
18	$1 **black and**		
	carmine/blue (7/40)	£65	£12
19	$2 **green and red**		
	(1/10/40)	£80	£40
20	$5 **green and**		
	carmine/green (1/41)	£150	£240
2/20	**set** (19)	£400	£325
SP2/20	**specimen perf** (19)	£375	†

4a, 4ba R10/10 the left 'C' is distorted

4b, etc thin striated paper. See introduction.

7 was issued in coil form.

8 a change of colour was to take place in 1941. Stamps in grey were printed, but none are known.

1950 (Aug. 17th)-53 Design, Sultan Yussaf Izzuddin. Perf 17½ x 18 (C). Sheets as before.

21	1c **black**	.10	.10
22	2c **orange**	.10	.10
23	3c **green**	.60	.10
	a yellow-green (15/11/51)	£7	4.50
24	4c **dark brown**	.35	.10
	a brown (22/10/53)	.25	.20
	b yellow-brown (20/6/56)	£6	.20
25	6c **greenish grey**	.15	.10
	a grey (22/10/53)	.75	.25
	b silver-grey (20/6/56)	£3	.50
26	8c **scarlet**	.30	1.35
27	10c **purple**	.10	.10
	a claret (20/6/56)	4.50	.35
28	15c **bright ultramarine**	.50	.10

29	20c **black and green**	.75	.40
30	25c **red-purple and orange**	.30	.10
	a red-purple and		
	yellow-orange (20/6/56)	1.50	.10
31	40c **scarlet and red-purple**	2.25	3.75
32	50c **black and violet-blue**	2.25	.10
	a black and blue (20/11/52)	£3	.10
33	$1 **ultramarine and**		
	red-purple	3.50	.60
	a blue and deep red-purple		
	(20/6/56)	4.50	.60
34	$2 **green and carmine-red**	£6	£4
35	$5 **green and deep brown**	£18	£10

1952 (Sept. 1st)-56 As before, but new values or colours.

36	5c **magenta**	.25	1.35
	a bright magenta (10/11/54)	.60	1.35
37	8c **green**	.50	.60
38	12c **scarlet**	.50	£3
39	20c **blue**	.35	.10
40	30c **scarlet and red-purple**		
	(4/9/55)	.90	.15
41	35c **scarlet and red-purple**	.50	.15
21/41	**set** (21)	£35	£24

SPECIAL ISSUES

1948 (Dec. 1st) Silver Wedding. As Aden.

| S1 | 10c **purple** | .10 | .10 |
| S2 | $5 **grey-green** | 11.50 | £19 |

Number issued 10c, 1,199,684; $5, 21,522.

1949 (Oct. 10th) U.P.U. As Aden.

S3	10c **dull purple**	.10	.10
S4	15c **indigo**	.75	1.20
S5	25c **orange**	.15	2.40
S6	50c **slate-black**	.65	2.10
S3/6	**set** (4)	1.50	5.25

Number issued 10c, 1,188,203; 15c, 238,608; 25c, 188,882; 50c, 118,896.

BOOKLET PANES

P1	5c **CW X4** pane of 10	-	-
P2	8c **CW X6** pane of 10	-	-
P3	5c **CW 7** pane of 10	-	-
P4	8c **CW 9** pane of 10	-	-

BOOKLET

B1	$1 **1935 P1** x 2	-	-
B2	$1.30 **1935 P1, P2**	-	-
B3	$1 **1938 P3** x 2	£2800	-
B4	$1.30 **1938 P3, P4**	£3000	-

PERLIS

All stamps were printed (typo) by De La Rue, on chalk-surfaced paper unless otherwise stated.

1949 (Oct. 10th) U.P.U. As Aden.

S3	10c **dull purple**	.15	£1
S4	15c **indigo**	.60	2.40
S5	25c **orange**	.25	1.50
S6	50c **slate-black**	.50	2.25
S3/6	**set** (4)	1.35	6.50

Number issued 10c, 95,230; 15c, 60,844; 25c, 58,119; 50c, 56,981.

1951 (Mar. 26th) Design, Raja Syed Putra. Perf. 17½ x 18 (C). Sheets 10 x 10.

1	1c **black**	.10	.60
2	2c **orange**	.35	.30
3	3c **yellow-green**	.75	£2
4	4c **brown**	.75	.60
5	6c **light grey**	.75	£1
6	8c **scarlet**	1.25	3.75
7	10c **red-purple**	.35	.25
	a deep red-purple (11/5/55)	.75	.25
8	15c **bright ultramarine**	£2	3.75
9	20c **black and yellow-green**	1.50	5.50
10	25c **red-purple and orange**	.85	1.80
11	40c **scarlet and red-purple**	£2	£15
12	50c **black and violet-blue**	£2	3.50
13	$1 **ultramarine and deep red-purple**	3.75	£15
14	$2 **green and carmine-red**	£8	£29
15	$5 **green and deep brown**	£28	£75

1952 (Sept. 1st)-55 As before, but new values or colours.

16	5c **magenta**	.25	1.80
17	8c **green**	.50	2.20
18	12c **scarlet**	.50	2.50
19	20c **blue**	.60	.60
20	30c **scarlet and deep red-purple** (4/9/56)	.85	7.50
21	35c **scarlet and red-purple**	.60	3.30
1/21	**set** (21)	£50	£155

Beware of indistinct cancels, faked postmarks exist.

WATERMARK VARIETY (TYPE A)
(See Introduction for details)

7b	10c **St Edward's Crown**	£12,500	-

SPECIAL ISSUES

1948 (Dec. 1st) Silver Wedding. As Aden.

S1	10c **purple**	.15	1.65
S2	$5 **chocolate**	14.50	£30

SELANGOR

All stamps were printed (typo) by De La Rue, on chalk-surfaced paper unless otherwise stated. Printings subsequent to December 1940 were carried out by Harrison & Sons.

1935-41 Designs, 1c-50c, Mosque at Klang; $1, $2, Sultan Suleiman. Designer, E. J. McNaughton. Perf 14. Sheets 10 x 10.

X1	1c **black** (1/1/36)	.15	.10
	a thin striated paper	-	-
X2	2c **green** (1/1/36)	.45	.10
	a joined script	£30	£15
X3	4c **orange** (2/12/35)	.25	.10
X4	5c **brown** (5/12/35)	.35	.10
4	6c **red** (1/1/37)	2.75	.10
X5	8c **grey** (2/12/35)	.30	.10
X6	10c **purple** (1/1/36)	.30	.10
X7	12c **blue** (1/1/36)	.75	.10
X8	25c **purple and scarlet** (1/4/36)	.50	.35
	a thin striated paper	£2	-
X9	30c **purple and orange** (1/1/36)	.65	.50
	a thin striated paper	£2	-
X10	40c **scarlet and purple** (2/12/35)	.75	.65
X11	50c **black/emerald** (1/2/36)	.50	.15
	a grey-black/green (7/39)	-	.75
X12	$1 **black and deep red/blue** (1/4/36)	£4	.55
	a black and red/blue (12/40)	£4	.55
X13	$2 **green and scarlet** (16/5/36)	£14	5.50
X14	$5 **green and red/green** (16/5/36)	£42	£15

X2 was issued in coil form.

X2a R2/1 'joined script'. Jawi characters at base joined by a scratch.

4 This stamp was printed in 1935 along with the other values, but was not released until 1937.

(a) Perf. 14 x 14½ (C).

1	2c **orange** (21/8/41) (sub)	1.75	.45
	a joined script	£85	£20

1a see X2a.

(b) Perf. 13¾ x 14 (C). Designs, 2c-15c Mosque at Klang; $1, $2 Sultan Hisamud-din Alam Shah.

2	2c **orange** (sub)(21/8/41)	£10	£1
	a joined script	£200	£38
3	3c **green** (sub) (21/8/41)	£6	£5
	a blue-green (sub)	.75	£5
	b thin striated paper (10/41)	£10	£2
5	15c **ultramarine** (1/10/41) (sub)	£6	£22
	a dark ultramarine (sub)	£8	£22
6	$1 **black and scarlet/blue** (15/4/41)	£9	£4
7	$2 **green and crimson** (7/7/41)	£24	£19
X1-7	**set** (20)	£100	£65
SPX1-7	**specimen perf** (19)	£400	†

The 1ct and 10ct also exist on thin striated paper, but all appear to have been overprinted by the Japanese.

2a see X2a.

6 The 1941 $1 was not prepared for UPU distribution in Specimen form, although at least one archival example is known.

Prepared for use but not issued.

8c **red**	£550	-
$5 **green and carmine/ green**	£80	-

These were sent out in 1941. The Japanese occupation prevented issue. The bulk of the $5 were overprinted, but a few examples without overprint leaked out later. The 8ct did not reach Malaya, but one sheet emerged in Australia after the war.

1949 (Sept. 12th) - 55 Design, Sultan Hisamud-din Alam Shah. Perf 17½ x 18 (C). Sheets 6 x 10.

8	1c **black**	.10	.35
9	2c **orange**	.15	.60

10	3c **green**	1.50	£1
11	4c **brown**	.20	.10
	a deep brown (13/11/52)	.30	.25
12	6c **grey**	.50	.30
	a light grey (26/9/51)	.15	.25
	b greenish grey (13/1/52)	.50	.25
13	8c **scarlet**	.50	.60
14	10c **red-purple**	.25	.10
	a deep red-purple (17/8/56)	.10	.10
	b claret (9/5/55)	£2	£1
15	15c **bright ultramarine**	3.25	.10
16	20c **black and green**	1.85	.20
17	25c **red-purple and orange**	£1	.15
18	40c **scarlet and red-purple**	4.50	£4
19	50c **black and violet-blue**	1.50	.10
	a black and blue (13/11/52)	£3	.20
20	$1 **ultramarine and red-purple**	1.50	.35
	a ultramarine and deep red-purple (17/8/55)	1.75	.35
21	$2 **green and carmine-red**	6.50	.35
22	$5 **green and deep brown**	£23	1.35

1952 (Sept. 1st)-55. As before, but new values or colours.

23	5c **magenta**	.25	1.50
	a bright magenta (17/9/53)	.25	.50
24	8c **green**	.40	£1
	a deep green (17/9/53)	£3	£3
25	12c **scarlet**	.40	£2
	a watermark inverted	£375	†
26	20c **blue**	.40	.10
27	30c **scarlet and deep red-purple** (4/9/55)	£1	1.35
28	35c **scarlet and red-purple**	.40	.90
8/28	**set** (21)	£45	£14

SPECIAL ISSUES

1948 (Dec. 1st) Silver Wedding. As Aden.

S1	10c **purple**	.10	.20
S2	$5 **grey-green**	13.50	£12

1949 (Oct. 10th) U.P.U. As Aden.

S3	10c **dull purple**	.15	.10
S4	15c **indigo**	1.10	1.50
S5	25c **orange**	.20	2.50
S6	50c **slate-black**	.50	2.50
S3/6	**set** (4)	1.75	£6

Number issued 10c, 1,346,978; 15c, 268,920; 25c, 233,672, 50c, 155,891.

BOOKLET PANES

P1	5c **X4** pane of 10	-	-
P2	8c **X5** pane of 10	-	-

BOOKLETS

B1	1935 $1	**P1** x 2	£2750	-
B2	1935 $1.30	**P1, P2**	£2750	-

TRENGGANU

All stamps were printed (typo) by De La Rue on chalk-surfaced paper, unless otherwise stated.

1924-1938 Design, Sultan Suleiman. Perf 13¾ x 14 (C). Sheets 120 - 2 panes, each 6 x 10; remainder 6 x 5.

1	1c **black** (/26)	.85	.90
	a ordinary paper (/41)	-	£55
2	2c **green**	.75	1.20
	a ordinary paper (/41)	-	£55
3	3c **green**	£1	.60
4	3c **brown** (/38)	£13	£10
	a chestnut (ordinary paper)(/41)	-	£15
5	4c **rose-red**	1.10	.75
	a scarlet-vermilion (ordinary paper)(/41)	£225	£25
6	5c **grey and deep brown**	£1	£3
7	5c **purple/yellow** (/26)	£1	.75
	a deep reddish purple/ bright yellow paper (/39)	-	-
8	6c **orange** (/26)	£2	.30
	a ordinary paper (/41)	-	£150
9	8c **grey** (/38)	£17	3.50
	a ordinary paper (/41)	-	£25
10	10c **bright blue**	£1	.60
11	12c **bright ultramarine** (/26)	£2	1.95
12	20c **dull purple and orange**	1.10	.90
13	25c **green and deep purple**	1.10	1.80
14	30c **dull purple and black**	1.60	2.25
15	35c **carmine/yellow** (/26)	2.25	3.50
16	50c **green and bright carmine**	4.50	£2
17	$1 **purple and blue/ blue** (/29)	4.50	2.25
18	$3 **green and lake/ green** (/26)	£28	£120
	a green and brown-red/ green (/38)	£100	-
19	$5 **green and red/yellow** (/38)	£225	£2500
20	$25 **purple and blue**	£500	£1300
21	$50 **green and yellow**	£1350	£2600
22	$100 **green and scarlet**	£4900	£5250
1/19	**set** (19)	£275	£1300
SP1/19	**specimen perf or overprinted** (19)	£625	†

11 was also printed on ordinary paper, but is not known without Japanese Occupation overprinted.

19 was placed on sale shortly before the Japanese invasion. Most used examples on the market bear faked cancels; an expert committee certificate is advisable. A few fiscaly-used examples are known from before the Occupation.

1941 (May 1st) As CW 1, etc., but surcharged in black.

23	2c/5c **reddish purple/yellow**	£3	£2
24	8c/10c**blue**	3.50	2.50

A 2c in orange, 3ct blue-green, 6c slate-grey, 8c rose and 15c ultramarine were intended for issue in 1941, but the Japanese invasion prevented this. A few examples leaked out onto the market. The 4ct purple on yellow paper, and $1 black and red on blue paper were also produced, but none are known. Apart from the shade of the 3ct unissued, it is also on ordinary paper.

1949 (Dec. 27th) - 54 Design, Sultan Ismail. Perf 17½ x 18 (C). Sheets 10 x 10.

25	1c **black**	.35	.20
26	2c **orange**	.35	.20
27	3c **green**	1.25	1.50
28	4c **brown**	.15	.20
	a chocolate (21/11/55)	£1	.20
	b pale brown (27/3/57)	£5	.25
29	6c **greenish grey**	.85	.35
	a pale grey (27/3/57)	4.50	£1
30	8c **scarlet**	.30	1.50
31	10c **deep red-purple**	.15	.10
	a red-purple (24/4/51)	.75	.10
	b pale purple (22/5/53)	£1	.10
32	15c **bright ultramarine**	1.75	.20
33	20c **black and green**	£2	2.25
34	25c **red-purple and orange**	1.10	1.20
35	40c **scarlet and red-purple**	3.50	£10
36	50c **black and violet-blue**	£1	1.35
	a black and blue (25/5/53)	£2	£2
37	$1 **ultramarine and deep red-purple**	3.50	5.50
	a blue and red-purple (25/2/53)	£6	£6
38	$2 **green and carmine-red**	£14	£17
39	$5 **green and deep brown**	£25	£36

1952 (Sept. 1st) - 57 As before, but new values or colours.

40	5c **magenta**	.15	£1
	a bright magenta (27/3/57)	.60	£1

41	8c **yellow-green**	.40	£1
	a green (11/8/53)	£7	£10
42	12c **scarlet**	.40	1.65
43	20c **blue**	.40	.25
44	30c **scarlet and deep red-purple** (4/9/55)	.60	1.35
	a scarlet and red-purple (27/6/56)	£2	1.35
45	35c **scarlet and red-purple**	.40	1.35
25/45	**set** (21)	£50	£85

SPECIAL ISSUES

1948 (Dec. 1st) Silver Wedding. As Aden.

S1	10c **purple**	.10	£1
S2	$5 **rose-carmine**	12.50	£25

Number issued 10c, 197,807; $5, 18,446.

1949 (Oct. 10th) U.P.U. As Aden.

S3	10c **dull purple**	.15	.45
S4	15c **indigo**	.95	2.25
S5	25c **orange**	.20	1.50
S6	50c **slate-black**	.50	£2
	a 'C' of watermark missing £550	-	
S3/6	**set** (4)	1.60	5.50

Number issued 10c, 44,913; 15c, 71,742; 25c, 59,987; 50c, 58,755.

POSTAGE DUE STAMPS

1937 (Aug. 10th) Perf 14 x 13¾ (C). Watermark sideways. Uncoated paper. Sheets 120 - 2 panes, each 10 x 6.

PD1	1c **carmine**	3.75	£40
PD2	4c **green**	3.50	£45
PD3	8c **yellow**	27.50	£240
PD4	10c **chocolate**	£55	£75
PD1/4	**set** (4)	£80	£360
SPPD1/4	**specimen perf** (4)	£120	†

PD1-4 beware of faked cancellations on this set, especially the 8ct.

MALDIVE ISLANDS

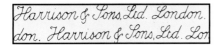

1933 Design, minaret of Juma Mosque, Male.
Printers (photo) Harrisons and Sons Ltd.
Watermark Script 'Harrison and Sons
London', upright. Perf 15 x 14. Sheets 10 x
5.

G1	2c grey	1.50	1.25
G2	3c red-brown	.35	1.65
G3	5c claret	£14	£6
G4	6c scarlet	.75	3.50
G5	10c green	.45	.35
G6	15c black	3.50	£10
G7	25c brown	3.50	£10
G8	50c purple	3.50	£13
G9	1r blue	£5	£12
G1/9	set (9)	£29	£52

As above, but watermark sideways.

G10	2ct grey	£3	£3
G11	3ct red-brown	2.50	£1
G12	5ct claret	£20	£20
G13	6ct scarlet	£5	3.50
G14	10ct green	1.85	£4
G15	15ct black	7.50	£12
G16	25ct brown	5.50	£12
G17	50ct purple	£8	£12
G18	1r blue	£8	£2
G10/18	set (9)	£55	£60

New Currency: 100 Larees = 1 Rupee.

1950 (Dec 24)-52 Design, fishing boat and
palm (except Nos 3, fish and 5, products).
Printers (recess) Bradbury, Wilkinson. Perf 13
¼ x 13 (C). No watermark. Sheets 5 x 10.

1	2l olive-green	1.10	1.80
	a yellowish olive (/52)	£3	4.25

2	3l blue	£5	.40
3	5l green	£5	.40
4	6l red-brown	.65	.75
5	10l scarlet	.65	.60
6	15l orange	.65	.60
7	25l purple	.65	1.35
	a reddish purple (/52)	1.50	1.35
8	50l violet	.65	1.80
	a greyish violet (/52)	1.50	£2
9	1r deep sepia-brown	£6	£19
1/9	set (9)	£18	£24

1952 new designs, fish and local products.

10	3l blue	£1	.35
11	5l emerald	.50	1.20

MALTA

1938 (Feb. 17th) - 44. Designs, historical and contemporary scenes of Malta, and historical personalities. Printers (recess) Waterlow and Sons. Perf. 12½ (L). Sheets ¼d 8 x 15; others, 10 x 6 or 6 x 10.

1	¼d **chocolate**	.10	.10
	a brown (13/3/44)	.10	.10
2	½d **green**	1.35	.20
3	½d **red-brown** (8/3/43)	.25	.20
4	1d **chestnut-brown**	£2	.25
	a deep chestnut-brown (/41)	£2	.25
5	1d **green** (8/3/43)	.30	.10
6	1½d **scarlet**	.60	.20
	a carmine-red (/41)	.75	.20
	b broken cross	£90	£40
7	1½d **slate-black** (8/3/43)	.15	.10
	a broken cross	£42	£35
8	2d **grey-black**	.75	1.20
	a slate-black (/41)	.50	1.20
	b windows at right	£40	£40
	c 'cowlick'	£25	£25
9	2d **scarlet** (8/3/43)	.20	.20
	a windows at right	£35	£30
	b flag at left	£35	£30
	c 'cowlick'	£20	£20
10	2½d **blue**	1.10	.35
11	2½d **violet** (8/3/43)	.30	.10
12	3d **violet**	.75	.50
13	3d **bright blue** (8/3/43)	.20	.15
	a milky blue (4/44)	.25	.15
	b extra window	£18	£15
14	4½d **olive and yellow-brown**	.30	.20
	a olive and orange-brown (13/3/44)	.25	.20
15	6d **olive and scarlet**	.85	.20
16	1/- **black**	.85	.20
17	1/6 **black and olive**	3.50	2.40
18	2/- **pale green and indigo**	2.25	£3
19	2/6 **black and scarlet**	£4	3.25
	a damaged value tablet	£180	£95
20	5/- **brownish black and green**	3.50	4.25
	a semaphore variety	£45	£65
	b black and bright green (13/3/44)	£3	3.25
21	10/- **black and deep carmine**	8.50	£9
1/21	**set** (21)	£28	£22
SP1/21	**specimen perf** (21)	£360	†

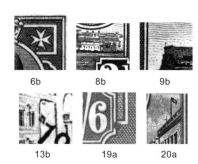

6b   8b   9b

13b   19a   20a

6b, 7a R5/7 (right pane) the cross at top right has a large mark on the bottom segment.

8b, 9a R2/7 five 'windows' on the building at extreme right.

8c, 9c R2/6 'cowlick' and 'extra curl'. R2/6 and 2/7 (above) appear on separate panes. Some sheets exist without the variety.

'cowlick'

9b R5/8 extra flagstaff at the left of the citadel. Progressive, and some exist with the variety touched out.

13b R4/7 (Plate 2) extra window at left of door. Several states.

19a R4/9 area of damage to right of '6'.

20a R2/7 a printer's guide mark known as the 'semaphore variety' by the flagstaff.

SPECIAL ISSUES

1937 (May 12th) Coronation. As Ascension.

S1	½d **green**	.10	.15
S2	1½d **scarlet**	.60	.40
S3	2½d **blue**	.50	.50
S1-3	**set** (3)	1.10	£1
SP S1/3	**specimen perf** (3)	£68	†

The 1½d brown-lake ('carmine-red') shade still recognised by some authorities is, in our opinion, a changeling. Similar items can be found in other colonies' Coronation issues.

1946 (Dec. 3rd). Victory. As Aden (George and Maltese Crosses incorporated in design).

S4	1d **green**	.10	.10
	a watermark inverted	£575	-
S5	3d **deep blue**	.20	.90
SP S4/5	**specimen perf** (2)	£58	†

1948 (Nov. 25th) - 55 Nos. 1, etc., overprinted 'SELF-GOVERNMENT 1947' (diagonally) in black or red to commemorate the inauguration of the new Constitution.

S6	¼d **brown**	.15	.15
S7	½d **red-brown**	.15	.10
	a light red-brown (16/5/50)	.25	.10
	b 'NT' joined	£12	£15
S8	1d **green**	.15	.10
S9	1½d **slate-black** (red)	.75	.15
	a indigo-black (red)		
	(16/5/50)	.60	.10
	b broken cross	£55	£28
	c 'NT' joined	-	-
S10	2d **scarlet**	.60	.10
	a windows at right	£60	£45
	b flag at left	£45	£40
S11	2½d **violet** (red)	.40	.10
S12	3d **blue** (red)	1.25	.10
	a extra window	£25	£15
S13	4½d **olive-green and**		
	yellow-brown	1.25	.90
S14	6d **olive and scarlet**	1.60	.10
	a deep olive-green and		
	scarlet (26/7/55)	£2	.10
	b F damaged	£40	£40
	c F repaired	£40	£40
S15	1/- **black**	1.60	.25
S16	1/6 **black and olive**	1.50	.30
S17	2/- **pale green and**		
	indigo (red)	2.50	1.50
S18	2/6 **black and scarlet**	£6	1.50
	a damaged value tablet	£700	-
S19	5/- **black and green** (red)	£12	2.25
	a semaphore flaw	-	£2400
	b 'NT' joined	£135	£75
S20	10/- **black and carmine**	£12	£13

S7b, 9c, 19b   S14b, c

S7b the 'NT' of 'Government' is joined on R4/10 Plates 4, 5, 6. Plate 6 may be found without the variety.

S9b, S10a, b, S12a, S18a, S19a see previous set.

S9c the 'NT' of Government is joined on R4/6.

S14b/c R3/1 the top bar of 'F' in the overprint was damaged and subsequently repaired. S14c illustrated.

S19b 'NT' joined, R4/10. On one plate only.

1953 (Jan. 8th) As Nos. S8 etc., but colour changed.

S21	1d **light grey** (red)	.25	.10
	a grey (5/11/53)	.50	.10
S22	1½d **green**	.15	.10
	a albino overprint	-	£12000
S23	2d **yellowish ochre**	.15	.10
	a ochre (5/11/53)	.50	.10
	b scratched plate	£85	£80
	c halation flaw	£90	£80
S24	2½d **scarlet**	.25	.90
S25	3d **violet** (red)	.25	.10
S26	4½d **olive and**		
	ultramarine (red)	.25	.55
S6-26	**set** (21)	£38	£20

S22a About ten examples of the albino overprint were found on commercial mail.

S23b   S23c

S23b R5/1 (Plate 2) the scratch runs across the second 'A' of 'MALTA' to the portrait.

S23c R2/5 (Plate 2) a white area behind the king's head (progressive).

1949 (Jan 4th) Silver Wedding. As Aden. (King and Maltese Crosses incorporated in design). £1 value printed (wholly recess).

S27	1d **green**	.25	.10
S28	£1 **bluish slate**	£19	£23

Number Issued 1d, 1,437,500; £1, 44,990.

1949 (Oct. 10th) U.P.U. As Aden. (George and Maltese Crosses incorporated in design).

S29	2½d **dull violet**	.15	.10
S30	3d **indigo**	1.50	.60
S31	6d **carmine-red**	.60	.60
S32	1/- **deep grey**	.60	1.50
S29/32	**set** (4)	£2	2.50

Number Issued 2½d, 615,802; 3d, 377,072; 6d; 421,802; 1/-; 232,633.

1950 (Dec. 1st) Visit of Princess Elizabeth. Printers (recess) Bradbury, Wilkinson. Perf 12 x 11¾ (C). Sheets 6 x 10.

S33	1d **green**	.10	.10
S34	3d **deep ultramarine**	.10	.15
S35	1/- **black**	.35	.90
S33/35	**set** (3)	.45	£1

Number Issued 1d, 1,260,850; 3d, 519,578; 1/-, 286,804.

1951 (July 12th) 7th Centenary of the Scapular. Design, the Virgin Mary handing Carmelite Scapular to St. Simon Stock in 1251. Printers Bradbury, Wilkinson. Perf 12 x 11¾ (C). Sheets 6 x 10.

S36	1d **green**	.10	.20
S37	3d **violet**	.25	.10
S38	1/- **slate-black**	.55	.95
S36/38	**set** (3)	.80	1.10

Number issued 1d, 1,209,560; 3d, 1,185,000; 1/-, 663,570.

POSTAGE DUE STAMPS

1925 (July 20th) - 46 Printers (typo) Bradbury, Wilkinson. Watermark Multiple Script CA (sideways). Perf 12 (2). Sheets 240; four panes, each 6 x 10.

XPD1	½d **emerald-green**	.60	.35
XPD2	1d **violet**	.60	.25
XPD3	1½d **brown**	.75	.50
XPD4	2d **grey**	5.50	.60
XPD5	2½d **orange**	£1	.75
XPD6	3d **blue**	1.85	.75
XPD7	4d **olive-green**	£6	9.50
XPD8	6d **purple**	1.75	2.70
XPD9	1/- **black**	3.25	£7
XPD10	1/6 **carmine**	4.25	£19
XPD1-10	**set** (10)	£23	£38
SPXPD1-10	**specimen overprint set** (10)	£150	†

These stamps are printed on smooth ordinary paper, mostly with streaky brown gum.

1937-46 As above, but on rough paper giving a woolly impression.

PD1	½d **emerald-green** (16/1/41)	£1	.45
PD2	1d **purple** (9/4/43)	£1	.30
PD3	1½d **pale brown** (26/6/46)	1.50	.75
PD4	2d **sepia** (11/4/37)	£6	£1
PD5	2½d **deep orange** (26/6/46)	£2	£1
	a watermark reversed	£65	-
PD6	3d **grey-blue** (26/6/46)	£2	£1
PD7	4d **sage-green** (26/6/46)	£6	£12
PD8	6d **purple-lake** (26/6/46)	£2	£3
PD9	1/- **grey** (9/4/43)	3.50	£10
PD10	1/6 **scarlet** (26/6/46)	£5	£25
PD 1/10	**set** (10)	£27	£50

These printings differ from the original 1925 issue in shade. Subsequently, printings appeared on chalk-surfaced paper.

MAURITIUS

1924 Perf 14 on chalk-surfaced paper. Watermark Multiple Script CA. Printers De La Rue.

G1 50r **dull purple and green** (/24)   £500 £1500

This stamp was still in use in 1938.

1938 (Mar. 2nd) - 48 Printers (typo) De La Rue. Perf. 13¾ x 14 (C). Sheets 120; two panes, each 6 x 10.

1	2c **grey** (9/3/38)	.20	.10
	a deep grey (8/4/43)	.15	.10
	b pearl grey (5/44)	£1	.20
2	3c **reddish purple and scarlet** (27/9/38)	.90	1.20
	a 'Nairac' flaw	£75	-
	b purple-violet and scarlet (8/4/43)	1.50	2.25
	c deep purple and carmine (4/48)	£2	1.75
	d sliced 'S'	£50	£50
3	4c **dull green** (26/1/38)	1.60	1.20
	a dull blue-green (8/4/43)	£1	1.20
	b deep blue-green (4/48)	£2	£5
	c open 'C'	£60	£50
4	5c **violet** (23/2/38)	5.50	.50
	a dull lavender and lavender (/42)	£18	£8
	b deep bright violet (5/44)	1.50	.15
5	10c **carmine-rose** (9/3/38)	1.20	.20
	a deep carmine-red (8/4/43)	£1	.15
	b deep scarlet (5/44)	£1	.15
	c pale scarlet (4/48)	£5	.25
	d topped 'S'	£80	£25
6	12c **deep salmon** (26/2/38)	.75	.15
	a salmon-pink (8/4/43)	.50	.15
	b salmon (8/45)	£1	.20
7	20c **dull blue** (26/2/38)	.40	.10
	a dull greenish blue (8/4/43)	£1	.20
	b blue (4/12/44)	.40	.10
	c broken frame	£275	£150
8	25c **brown-maroon** (ch)	£6	.15
	a maroon (sub)(8/4/43)	£4	.10
	b lake-maroon (ch)(22/5/47)	£7	.15
	c dull maroon (ch) (19/4/48)	£9	.25
	d 'IJ' flaw	£125	£30
9	1r **blackish brown** (ch)	£12	1.50
	a grey-brown (sub) (8/4/43)	£8	.75
	b ditto (ch) (22/5/47)	£14	1.50
	c deep grey-brown (ch)(4/48)	£20	£5
	d battered 'A'	£250	£80

10	2r50 **dull pale violet** (ch)	£15	£15
	a pale lavender (sub)(8/4/43)	£15	£11
	ab broken frame	£550	-
	b dull lavender (ch) (22/5/47)	£18	£18
	c pale violet (F.A.) (ch) (19/4/48)	£26	£24
11	5r **dull olive** (ch)	£16	£18
	a deep olive-green (sub) (8/4/43)	£14	£18
	b deep olive (ch)(19/4/48)	£24	£24
12	10r **purple** (ch)	£22	£27
	a purple (sub)(8/4/43)	£7	£18
	b deep purple (ch)(4/48)	£25	£25
1/12	**set** (12)	£48	£45
SP 1/12	**specimen perf** (12)	£225	†

In many cases, the plate varieties listed occur on many printings. Our listing and pricing is for the cheapest variant; the aim is to keep the listing relatively simple. We do recommend that collectors include different printings of the varieties; our numbers may be expanded; for example the topped 'S' on the 1948 10ct pale scarlet would be '5cd'. There are many other highly significant and collectable plate varieties.

2a damage to the frame on R7/6 RP, named after its discoverer.

2d R2-3/2 RP a pronounced cut to the right side of the 'S' of 'Mauritius'. Less pronounced examples can be found in the same column and are often offered as the variety.

2d

open 'c'   normal

3c the 'c' is more open on R9/6 RP.

4 exists in a faded pale lilac; a changeling.

5d   7c

5d, 15a R4/1 LP and 8/4 RP the top of the 'S' of 'Mauritius' is flattened.

7c, 10ab R9/3 LP the frame above the 'AU' of 'Mauritius' is bent, and badly broken below the 'A'. The 2r 50 shows an earlier state of the variety, which is not so pronounced.

8, 9, 10, 11, 12 the early chalky-paper printings have dark gum - really fresh examples are difficult to locate. Later printings on chalky paper have white gum.

8d   9d

8d R3/6 RP the first 'U' of 'Mauritius' is broken at the base, so as to resemble the letters 'IJ'.

9d R6/1 RP the first 'A' of 'Mauritius' is misshapen. Examples from Plate 1 (CW 9) show a less pronounced state.

1943 As No. 1 etc., but printed on rough paper by Bradbury, Wilkinson (from De La Rue plates). Perf. 14¾ x 14 (C).

13	2c **grey**	.40	.10
14	5c **violet**	£24	.10
15	10c **carmine-red**	£10	£1
	a topped 'S'	£275	£60
16	12c **salmon**	£20	.60
13/16	**set** (4)	£50	1.60

15a see 5d.

1950 (July 1st) Designs, 1c (sugar factory); 3c (aloe plant); 12c (map and dodo); 20c (legend of Paul and Virginie); 25c (Labourdonnais statue); 35c (Government House); 1r (Mauritius Deer); 2r50c (Port Louis); 10r (arms of Mauritius); other values (views and scenes in Colony). Printers (photo) Harrison and Sons. Perf 14¾ x 13¾ (vertical designs) or 13¾ x 14¾ (horizontal designs) (C). Chalk-surfaced paper. Sheets 10 x 6 or 6 x 10.

17	1c **purple-magenta**	.10	.30
18	2c **carmine-lake**	.10	.10
19	3c **pea-green**	.30	2.25
20	4c **deep grey-green**	.10	1.50
21	5c **blue**	.10	.10
	a Q for O	£10	£10
22	10c **scarlet-red**	.15	.45
23	12c **olive**	.75	1.65
24	20c **bright ultramarine**	.50	.10

25	25c **brown-lake**	£1	.25
26	35c **purple-violet**	.20	.10
	a inverted watermark	†	-
27	50c **emerald**	1.35	.30
28	1r **grey-sepia**	3.50	.10
29	2r50 **orange**	7.50	8.50
30	5r **red-brown**	£8	£9
31	10r **mineral blue**	7.50	£18
17/31	**set** (15)	£28	£38

21a R10/5 a flaw on the 'O' of 'Mountain' changes the letter to 'Q'.

26a a single used example is known.

SPECIAL ISSUES

1937 (May 12th) Coronation. As Ascension.

S1	5c **violet**	.20	.15
S2	12c **scarlet**	.25	1.35
S3	20c **blue**	.70	.20
	a line through sword	£40	£30
	b line by sceptre	£40	£30
S1-3	**set** (3)	£1	1.50
SPS1/3	**specimen perf** (3)	£65	†

S3a R2/2 a line runs up the left side of the sword.

S3b R5/3 a line runs vertically left of the sceptre.

Similar varieties, but less pronounced, occurs on R5/2 and 5/6.

S3a   S3b

1946 (Nov. 20th) Victory. As Aden.

S4	5c **lilac**	.10	.45
S5	20c **deep blue**	.10	.15
	a blue	.35	.35
	b flag variety	£14	£18
SP S4/5	**specimen perf** (2)	£55	†

S5b R3/1 a projection from the main tower of Parliament resembles a flag.

1948 (Mar. 22nd) Centenary of first Mauritius Postage Stamp. Design incorporating facsimiles of 'Post Office' stamps, issued 21/9/1847. Printer (recess) Bradbury, Wilkinson. Perf 11½ x 11¼ (C). Sheets 5 x 12.

S6	5c **orange and magenta**	.10	.30
S7	12c **orange and green**	.10	.15
S8	20c **deep blue and grey-blue**	.10	.10
S9	1r **deep blue and**		
	beech-brown	.15	.20
S6/9	**set** (4)	.40	.65
SPS6/9	**specimen perf** (4)	£100	-

1948 (Oct. 25th) Silver Wedding. As Aden.

S10	5c **bright violet**	.10	.10
S11	10r **lake-magenta**	£8	£19

1949 (Oct. 10th) U.P.U. As Aden.

S12	12c **carmine-rose**	.25	£1
S13	20c **indigo**	1.10	1.50
S14	35c **purple**	.30	.90
	a 'A' of watermark missing	-	-
S15	1r **sepia**	.25	.15
S12/15	**set** (4)	1.75	3.25

POSTAGE DUE STAMPS

1933 Printers (typo) Waterlow and Sons. Perf 14¾ x 14 (c). Sheets 6 x10. Off-white paper.

GD1	2c **black**	.60	.30
GD2	4c **violet**	.25	.40
GD3	6c **scarlet**	.30	.50
GD4	10c **green**	.35	.75
GD5	20c **bright blue**	.25	.90
GD1-5	**set** (5)	1.60	2.40

1938-54 as above, later printings and additional values on white paper.

PD1	2ct **black**	£1	.75
PD2	4ct **dull violet**	.40	.50
PD3	6ct **vermilion**	.75	£1
PD4	10ct **pale green**	.60	1.25
PD5	20ct **pale blue**	.40	£2
PD6	50ct **magenta** (1/3/54)	.25	£10
PD7	1r **orange** (1/3/54)	.35	£10
PD1-7	**set** (7)	3.40	£23

BOOKLET PANES

P1	5ct	1950 **pane of 4**	£30	-
P2	50ct	1950 **pane of 4**	£25	-

BOOKLET

B1	5r	**1953 black on white cover**
		P1 x 1, P2 x 2,
		QEII 10c Coronation x 2
		panes of four £125 -

MIDDLE EASTERN FORCES
SEE
BOIC

MONTSERRAT

1938 (Aug. 2nd) Designs, ½d, 3d, 1/-, 5/-, £1 (Carr's Bay); 1d, 1½d, 2½d, (Sea Island Cotton plantation); 2d, 6d, 2/6d, 10/- (Botanic Station, Grove). Printers (recess) De La Rue. Perf 13 x 13¼ (C). Sheets 6 x 10.

1	½d deep green	.85	.75
2	1d rose-carmine	.75	.25
3	1½d purple	3.75	.30
4	2d orange	3.50	.35
5	2½d blue	.25	.35
6	3d chocolate-brown	.60	.25
7	6d purple-violet	2.50	.50
8	1/- deep lake	3.50	.45
	a engraver's slip	£20	-
9	2/6 bluish slate	£7	.75
10	5/- deep rose	£10	£5
1/10	set (10)	£30	£8

1,2 were issued in coils as well as sheets.

8a a engraver's slip appears under R10/5, apparently on the first perforation only.

As No. 1, etc., but Perf. 14 (L).

11	½d deep green (8/42)	.15	.15
	a blue-green (8/45)	.20	.20
12	1d rose-red (8/42)	.20	.20
	a carmine-rose (8/45)	.20	.20
13	1½d purple (8/42)	.15	.30
	a deep brownish purple (/48)	.20	.35
	b 'A' of watermark missing	-	-
14	2d orange (8/42)	.40	.40
	a deep orange (8/45)	.50	.40
15	2½d bright ultramarine (10/43)	.25	.20
	a deep ultramarine (8/45)	.35	.20
16	3d chocolate (/42)	£1	.40
	a deep chocolate (10/43)	£2	2.75
	b red-brown (14/8/45)	.75	.25
	c 'pylon' flaw	-	-
17	6d purple-violet (8/42)	1.25	.35
	a slate-violet (8/45)	1.20	.50
18	1/- deep lake (8/42)	1.50	.75
	a deep red-lake (8/45)	£1	.20
19	2/6 greyish blue black (10/43)	£8	1.50
	a slate-black (8/45)	£7	1.50
20	5/- deep rose (8/42)	£10	2.50
	a bright rose-carmine (10/43)	£12	£2

16b is printed on somewhat thinner paper.

16c R2/2 shows a large flaw, resembling a pylon, on the hill at right. Later printings, or possibly the September 1951 printing only.

1948 (April 1st) Perf 12 (C).

21	10/- blue	£7	£12
22	£1 black	£7	£16
1/22	set (12)	£32	£30
SP1/10, 21/2 specimen perf (12)		£180	†

1951 (Sept. 17th) Designs, 1c, $2.40 (Govt. House); 2c, $1.20 (Sea Island Cotton cultivation); 3c (map of Presidency); 4c, 24c (picking tomatoes); 5c, 12c, (St. Anthony's Church); 6c, $4.80 (Badge of Presidency); 8c, 60c, (cotton ginning). Printers (recess) Bradbury, Wilkinson. Perf 11½ x 11¼ (C). Sheets 5 x 10.

23	1c grey-black	.10	.75
24	2c green	.10	.40
25	3c light chestnut-brown	.15	.40
26	4c red	.15	.25
27	5c bright purple	.15	.40
28	6c sepia	.15	.20
29	8c deep blue	.15	.15
30	12c blue and brown	.15	.20
31	24c carmine and green	.35	.20
32	60c black and red	2.50	1.50
33	$1.20 green and blue	2.50	2.50
34	$2.40 black and green	£2	7.50
35	$4.80 black and deep purple	£8	£11
23/35	set (13)	£15	£23

SPECIAL ISSUES

1937 (May 12th) Coronation. As Ascension.

S1	1d scarlet	.15	.30
S2	1½d light brown	.20	.20
S3	2½d blue	.20	.45
SP S1/3 specimen perf (3)		£38	†

1946 (Nov. 1st) Victory. As Aden.

S4	1½d reddish purple	.10	.10
S5	3d chocolate	.10	.10
SP S4/5 specimen perf (2)		£40	†

1949 (Jan. 3rd) Silver Wedding. As Aden.

S6	2½d **ultramarine**	.10	.10
S7	5/- **rose-carmine**	2.25	3.75

1949 (Oct. 10th) U.P.U. As Aden.

S8	2½d **violet-blue**	.10	.20
S9	3d **brown**	.60	.20
S10	6d **purple**	.20	.20
S11	1/- **purple**	.20	.20
S8/11	**set** (4)	£1	.70

1951 (Feb. 16th) West Indies University College. (See Antigua).

S12	3c **black and claret**	.15	.35
S13	12c **black and violet**	.15	.35

MOROCCO AGENCIES

1. BRITISH CURRENCY
1907-1937 AND 1949-1956

In 1937 unoverprinted stamps of Great Britain gradually replaced the Morocco Agencies issue. In 1949, however, overprinted issues re-appeared for use at Tetuan (in the Spanish zone), the only remaining British Post Office, apart from Tangier, in Morocco. They were finally withdrawn on December 31st 1956.

1949 (Aug 16th) stamps of Great Britain overprinted 'MOROCCO AGENCIES', for use at Tetuan (Spanish Zone).

1	½d **green**	.85	4.50
2	1d **scarlet** (2nd state)	1.50	5.50
3	1½d **red-brown**	1.50	£5
4	2d **dull orange**	1.50	5.50
5	2½d **ultramarine**	1.50	6.50
6	3d **purple-violet**	.75	£1
7	4d **greenish grey**	.25	.75
8	5d **pale brown**	1.50	£9
9	6d **pale purple**	.75	.90
10	7d **emerald-green**	.25	£10
11	8d **deep rose**	1.50	3.75
12	9d **deep olive**	.25	£7
13	10d **deep grey-blue**	.25	4.50
14	11d **deep plum**	.35	£5
15	1/- **bistre-brown**	1.25	3.75
16	2/6 **green**	7.50	£22
	a re-entry	£110	£125
	b T guide	£125	£125
17	5/- **red**	£16	£38
	a T guide	£75	-
1/17	**set** (17)	£33	£120

16a See Great Britain 17a.

16b, 17a - See note after Great Britain 16-21.

Number issued - ½d, 43,483; 1d, 36,829; 1½d, 27,637; 2d, 28,644; 2½d, 30,422; 3d, 51,954; 4d, 42,203; 5d, 25,267; 6d, 42,910; 7d, 29,474; 8d, 24,548; 9d, 33,038; 10d, 28,864; 11d, 29,345; 1/-, 30,910; 2/6, 15,560; 5/-, 13,751.

1951 (May 3rd) As No 1, etc., but colours changed (Nos. 23-4 as Nos. 34-5 of Great Britain), similarly overprinted.

18	½d **orange**	£1	.60
19	1d **ultramarine**	£1	.85

20	1½d **green**	£1	2.25
21	2d **red-brown**	£1	2.40
22	2½d **scarlet**	£1	2.50
23	2/6 **green**	6.50	12.50
24	5/- **red**	6.50	£14
18/24	**set** (7)	£16	£32

Number issued - ½d, 52,227; 1d, 43,557; 1½d, 34,563; 2d, 33,363; 2½d, 50,136; 2/6d, 21,033; 5/-,18,066.

Note: The use in the United Kingdom of stamps overprinted 'Morocco Agencies' (without currency surcharge) was permitted from 1950. Our prices for used stamps are for copies with Morocco Agencies postmarks; stamps with U.K. postmarks are worth much less.

2. SPANISH CURRENCY

1937-40 Stamps of Great Britain, overprinted (in black or blue) 'MOROCCO AGENCIES' and surcharged.

1	5c/½d **deep green** (blue) (10/6/37)	.65	.20
2	10c/1d **deep scarlet** (10/6/37)	.50	.10
3	15c/1½d **deep red-brown** (blue) (4/8/37)	.75	.15
4	25c/2½d **deep ultramarine** (10/6/37)	£1	.75
5	40c/4d **greenish grey** (3/9/40)	£15	£8
6	70c/7d **emerald-green** (3/9/40)	.85	£9
1/6	**set** (6)	£17	£16

Number issued - 5c, 507,142; 10c, 332,503; 15c, 316,234; 25c, 319,884; 40c, 95,866; 70c, 120,769.

1951 (May 3rd)-52. As No. 1, etc., but colours changed, and new values similarly overprinted and surcharged.

7	5c/½d **dull orange**	£1	1.40
8	10c/1d **ultramarine**	1.60	2.50
9	15c/1½d **green**	.90	7.50
10	25c/2½d **scarlet**	.90	2.50
11	40c/4d **light blue** (26/5/52)	.30	5.50
12	1p/10d **deep blue-grey** (16/6/52)	1.10	2.25
7/12	**set** (6)	£5	£20

The 1p/10d (CW 12) has been recorded with the two lines of the overprint spaced 15 mm instead of the normal 13 mm. MOROCCO AGENCIES is further to the left in relation to 1 PESETA than on the normal.

Number issued - 5c, 207,309; 10c, 124,321; 15c, 93,356; 25c, 81,786; 40c, 63,799; 1p, 99,384.

SPECIAL ISSUES

1937 (May 13th) Coronation Issue of Great Britain, overprinted 'MOROCCO AGENCIES' and surcharged.

S1	15c/1½d **dark maroon** (blue)	.40	.40

Number issued - 1,766,723.

1940 (May 6th) Centenary of First Postage Stamp issue of Great Britain, overprinted 'MOROCCO AGENCIES' and surcharged.

S2	5c/½d **deep green** (blue)	.15	1.75
S3	10c/1d **deep scarlet**	1.85	1.50
S4	15c/1½d **deep red-brown** (blue)	.35	£2
S5	25c/2½d **deep ultramarine**	.40	1.50
	a neck flaw retouched	£28	£38
S2/5	**set (4)**	2.50	£6

S5a - See Great Britain S6b.

Number issued - 5c, 543,155; 10c, 289,467; 15c, 242,027; 25c, 195,947.

1948 (April 28th) Silver Wedding Issue of Great Britain, overprinted 'MOROCCO AGENCIES' and surcharged.

S6	25c/2½d **ultramarine**	.60	.20
S7	45p/£1 **deep blue**	8.50	£14

1948 (July 29th) Olympic Games Issue of Great Britain, overprinted 'MOROCCO AGENCIES' and surcharged.

S8	25c/2½d **ultramarine**	.25	£1
S9	30c/3d **violet**	.25	£1
	a crown flaw	£40	£40
S10	60c/6d **reddish purple**	.25	£1
S11	1.20/1/- **bistre-brown**	.30	£1
	a surcharged double	£675	-
S8/11	**set (4)**	.95	3.50

S9a - See Great Britain No. S13a.

S11a - A sheet (120 examples) with the double surcharge was released in London. One example is known used from Tetuan 24.9.48.

Number issued - 25c, 107,309; 30c, 100,020; 60c, 94,278; 120c, 93,304.

3. FRENCH CURRENCY

1937 (June 11th) Stamps of Great Britain overprinted 'MOROCCO AGENCIES' and surcharged.

| 1 | 5c/½d **deep green** (blue) | 1.50 | 1.50 |

Number issued - 806,782.

SPECIAL ISSUES

1937 (May 13th) Coronation Issue of Great Britain overprinted 'MOROCCO AGENCIES' and surcharged.

| S1 | 15c/1½d **dark maroon** (blue) | .20 | .15 |
| | a crack in orb | £15 | £20 |

S1a see Great Britain S1b.

Number issued - 2,203,087.

4. TANGIER

1937 Stamps of Great Britain, overprinted 'TANGIER' in blue or black.

1	½d **deep green** (blue)		
	(11/6/37)	1.25	£1
2	1d **deep scarlet** (11/6/37)	5.50	£1

3	1½d **deep red-brown** (blue)		
	(4/8/37)	1.25	.25
1/3	**set** (3)	£7	£2

Number issued - ½d, 807,805; 1d, 838,219; 1½d, 398,723.

1944-49 (Jan 1st) stamps of Great Britain, similarly overprinted in blue or black. Issued 1/1/49 unless stated.

4	½d **green** (3/5/44)	£7	£3
5	1d **scarlet** (1/10/45)	£7	£2
6	2d **dull orange**	£3	£4
7	2½d **ultramarine**	1.25	£4
8	3d **purple-violet**	.35	.75
9	4d **greyish green**	5.50	6.75
10	5d **pale brown**	1.85	£14
11	6d **pale purple**	.35	.20
12	7d **emerald-green**	.60	£9
13	8d **deep rose**	1.85	£8
14	9d **deep olive**	.75	£8
15	10d **deep grey-blue**	.60	£8
16	11d **deep plum**	1.25	£9
17	1/- **bistre-brown**	.60	1.75
18	2/6 **green**	2.25	£10
19	5/- **red**	£6	£24
20	10/- **ultramarine**	£24	£80
4/20	**set** (17)	£58	£175

Number issued - ½d, 734,338; 1d, 262,605; 2d, 51,517; 2½d, 103,521; 3d, 294,853; 4d, 33,149; 5d, 35,622; 6d, 464,149; 7d, 46,050; 8d, 31,327; 9d, 56,439; 10d, 36,291; 11d, 26,609; 1/-, 214,672; 2/6, 24,629; 5/-, 16,122; 10/-, 11,359.

1950-1 (May 3rd) As No. 4, etc., but colours changed (Nos. 27-29 as Nos. 34-36 of Great Britain), similarly overprinted. Issued 3/5/51 unless stated.

21	½d **dull orange**	.40	.90
22	1d **ultramarine**	.50	1.80
23	1½d **green**	.50	8.50
24	2d **red-brown**	.50	1.50
25	2½d **scarlet**	.50	£3
26	4d **light blue** (21/10/50)	1.75	1.80
27	2/6d **green**	4.75	£3
28	5/- **red**	7.50	£10
29	10/- **ultramarine**	£10	£10
21-29	**set** (9)	£16	£36

Number issued - ½d, 506,283; 1d, 101,853; 1½d, 73,350; 2d, 63,309; 2½d, 132,419; 4d, 73,178; 2/6d, 62,259; 5/-, 38,699; 10/-, 30,305.

SPECIAL ISSUES

1937 (May 13th) Coronation Issue of Great Britain, overprinted 'TANGIER'.

| S1 | 1½d **dark maroon** (blue) | .30 | .30 |

Number issued - 1,397,799.

1940 (May 6th) Centenary of First Postage Stamp Issue of Great Britain, overprinted 'TANGIER'.

S2	½d deep green (blue)	.15	3.75
S3	1d deep scarlet	.25	.35
S4	1½d deep red-brown (blue)	£1	4.50
S2/4	set (3)	1.25	£8

Number issued - ½d, 192,427; 1d, 174,507; 1½d, 139,627.

1946 (June 11th) Victory Issue of Great Britain, overprinted 'TANGIER'.

S5	2½d ultramarine	.30	.40
S6	3d violet	.30	.80

1948 (April 26th) Silver Wedding Issue of Britain, overprinted 'TANGIER'.

S7	2½d ultramarine	.25	.10
	a overprint omitted in pair with normal	£5000	-
	b overprint at top	£175	£175
S8	£1 deep blue	£10	£17

S7a/b - A sheet of stamps was discovered with overprint (normally at the bottom) misplaced, which resulted in the first row missing the overprint entirely, and the rest of the sheet with the overprint near the top of the stamps, and overprints appearing on the lower sheet margin. Forgeries exist of both varieties.

Number issued - 2½d, 192,513; £1, 24,102.

1948 (July 29th) Olympic Games of Great Britain, overprinted 'TANGIER'.

S9	2½d ultramarine	.50	1.20
S10	3d violet	.50	1.35
	a crown flaw	£55	£70
S11	6d reddish purple	.50	1.35
	a 'HLP'	-	-
	b retouch	£175	-
S12	1/- bistre-brown	.50	1.35
S9/12	set (4)	1.80	4.75

S10a - See Great Britain No. S13a.

S11a/b was overprinted on sheets from Cylinder 9 stop; and the 'H.L.P.' variety (See Great Britain S14a/b), in the original and erased states, exists in the Jubilee Line below the last three stamps in the sheet.

Numbers issued - 2½d, 101,965; 3d, 101,638; 6d, 101,175; 1/-, 96,190.

1949 (Oct 10th) U.P.U. Issue of Great Britain, overprinted 'TANGIER'.

S13	2½d ultramarine	.35	1.75
	a lake in India	£40	£60
S14	3d pale violet	.35	1.75
S15	6d reddish mauve	.35	.75
S16	1/- bistre-brown	.35	£2
S13/16	set (4)	1.25	5.50

S13a - See Great Britain No. S16b.

Number issued - 2½d, 81,873; 3d, 74,103; 6d, 77,198; 1/-, 72,404.

Note: The use in the United Kingdom of stamps overprinted 'TANGIER' was permitted from 1950. Our prices for used stamps are for copies with Tangier postmarks. Stamps with U.K. postmarks are worth much less.

MUKALLA
SEE
ADEN STATE

MUSCAT
SEE
BPA IN EA

NAURU

1937-49 Design, 'SS Century' (R.A. Harrison). Engraver, T.S. Harrison. Printers (recess) Commonwealth Bank of Australia. Perf 11¼ (L). Sheets 12 x 10.

1	½d **light brown**	£2	£8
2	1d **yellow-green**	1.25	£2
3	1½d **scarlet-red**	.50	£1
4	2d **orange**	1.10	£5
5	2½d **slate-blue** (/49)	1.50	2.40
	a imperf between vertical pair	£9000	£12500
	b imperf between horizontal pair	£9000	£12500
6	3d **greenish grey**	1.75	8.50
7	4d **sage-green**	£2	£8
8	5d **grey-brown**	2.75	2.50
9	6d **pale violet**	2.75	£3
10	9d **dull olive**	3.75	£12
11	1/- **dull red-lake**	3.75	1.75
12	2/6 **myrtle-green**	£15	£22
13	5/- **claret**	£19	£30
14	10/- **orange-yellow**	£42	£70
1/14	**set** (14)	£90	£160

5a 12 possible pairs; 5b, 10 possible.

Surface gloss tends to disappear in the climate of Nauru. Nevertheless, stamps printed from 1937 onwards can be distinguished from the earlier set (1924-34) by their shades, general smooth and shiny appearance, and white paper. The earlier printings are on matt-surfaced greyish paper and the shades are generally duller.

As No. 1, Perf 14 (L).

15	½d **light brown** (/47)	.75	£6

SPECIAL ISSUE

1937 (May 10th) Coronation. Printers (recess) Australian Note and Stamp Printing Works (John Ash) Perf. 11¼ (L). No watermark. Sheets 8 x 5.

S1	1½d **red**	.20	£1

S2	2d **orange**	.20	1.65
S3	2½d **blue**	.20	£1
	a re-entry	£25	£30
S4	1/- **lake-purple**	.30	£1
S1/4	**set** (4)	.80	£4

S3a R4/4 the upper frameline is clearly doubled.

Number issued S1, 532,500; S2, 40,000; S3, 500,000; S4, 480,000.

NEGRI SEMBILAN
SEE
MALAYA

NEWFOUNDLAND

Imperforate pairs; prices throughout are for examples with gum, except S4c-14b, which are found without gum (S14b is found both with and without gum). Other imperforate pairs exist without gum; these are proofs ex the Perkins Bacon archives. Many other proofs exist, both punched and unpunched.

Prices for pairs, one stamp in pair without watermark, are for instances where no part of the watermark is visible on one of the stamps. Stamps with sideways watermark show the top of the shield pointing left, as seen from the back of the stamp.

1938 (May 12th) Designs, 2c King George VI; 3c Queen Elizabeth (Queen Mother); 4c Princess Elizabeth; 7c Queen Mary. Printer (recess) Perkins Bacon. Perf. 13½ (C). Watermark sideways. Sheets 10 x10.

1	2c **green**	1.50	.75
	a pair, one no watermark	£120	-
	b imperf pair	£85	-
	c watermark sideways inverted	£55	-
2	3c **carmine-red**	.50	.60
	a pair, one no watermark	£200	-
	b imperf pair	£95	-
	c imperf between stamp and margin	£65	-
	d vertical pair, imperf horizontally	-	-
3	4c **light blue**	1.25	.35
	a pair, one no watermark	£85	-
	b imperf pair	£65	-
	c inverted watermark	£48	-
4	7c **deep slate-blue**	.50	£5
	a pair, one no watermark	£120	-
	b imperf pair	£120	-
	c vertical pair, imperf horizontally	£200	-
1-4	**set** (4)	3.25	£6

As CW 2, but perf. 14 (L).

5	3c **carmine-red**	£350	£275

As CW G107, but perf 13½.

5A	5c **violet, Die 1**	£80	-

Die 1   Die 2

This stamp was redrawn, the design being 21mm wide as opposed to G107, which was 20.4mm wide. There is also a difference between the antlers. On Die 1 the tops are offset, whilst on Die 2 they are parallel. It may well have been printed by Waterlow.

1938 (1st Jan.) Design, Fishing Fleet. Perf 13½ (C). Printers (recess) Perkins Bacon.

6	48c **red-brown**	5.50	£6
	a imperf pair	£70	-

1941-9 Designs; 1c, (codfish); 2c, 3c, 4c, 7c, (as CW 2-5, but 2c and 3c redrawn); 5c (Caribou); 8c (Corner Brook Paper Mills); 10c (salmon leaping); 14c (Newfoundland dog); 15c (seal); 20c (Transatlantic Beacon); 24c (ore loading, Bell Is.); 25c (sealing fleet); 48c (fishing fleet). Printers (recess) Waterlow. Perf 12½ (L). Nos. 7-13 watermark sideways. Sheets 10 x 10.

7	1c **dark grey**	.10	1.35
	b imperf pair	£175	-
8	2c **green**	.15	.45
	a watermark sideways inverted	£30	-
	b pair, one no watermark	£120	-
	c imperf pair	£175	-
9	3c **carmine-red**	.15	.20
	a pair, one no watermark	£65	-
	b 'A' flaw	£38	£25
	c watermark sideways inverted	£30	-
	d imperf pair	£175	-
10	4c **dull blue** (shades)	1.25	.25
	a pair, one no watermark	£120	-
	b imperf pair	£200	-
12	5c **purple** (Die 1)	1.35	.50
	a pair, one no watermark	£110	-
	b printed double	£400	-

	c horizontal pair,			
	imperf vertically	£375	-	
	d imperf pair	£125	-	
13	7c **deep slate-blue**	£3	£12	
	a pair, one no watermark	£130	-	
	b imperf pair	£200	-	
14	8c **dull scarlet**	1.10	2.50	
	a pair, one no watermark	£120	-	
	b imperf pair	£200	-	
15	10c **deep sepia**	.85	1.35	
	a imperf pair	£150	-	
16	14c **black**	£3	£5	
	a imperf pair	£200	-	
	b vertical pair, imperf			
	horizontally	£160	-	
17	15c **claret**	£3	£5	
	a aniline ink	£125		
	b imperf pair	£200	-	
18	20c **green**	£3	£5	
	a aniline ink	£125		
	b imperf pair	£200	-	
19	24c **deep blue**	1.50	£14	
	a imperf pair	£180	-	
	b watermark sideways			
	inverted	£45	-	
	c blue (thin paper) (/48)	£6	£9	
20	25c **slate**	4.25	£10	
	a imperf pair	£180	-	
21	48c **brown-lake**	£2	£5	
	a imperf pair	£250	-	
7/21	**set** (14)	£22	£65	

9b R5/9 the 'A' in 'NEWFOUNDLAND' is damaged.

12 see 5A

Stamps of a similar design but perf 13½ were issued in 1932.

1943 (Jan. 2nd) Design, Memorial University College, St. John's. Printers (recess) Canadian Bank Note Co., Ottawa. Perf 12 (L). No watermark. Sheets 200, 2 panes each 10 x 10.

22	30c **rose-carmine**	.75	2.25

1946 (March 21st) As CW 22, but surcharged 'TWO CENTS'.

23	2c/30c **rose-carmine** (23/3/46)	.15	.75

1947 (April 21st) Design, Elizabeth II as Princess. Printers (recess) Waterlow. Perf 12½ (L). Watermark sideways. Sheets 200, two panes each 10 x 10.

24	4c **light blue**	.20	.60
	a horizontally pair,		
	imperf vertically	£275	-
	b imperf pair	£200	-

AIR STAMPS

1943 (June 1st) Design, aeroplane over St. John's. Printers (recess) Canadian Bank Note Co., Ottawa. Perf 12 (L). No watermark. Sheets 10 x 10.

A1	7c **ultramarine**	.25	.60

SPECIAL ISSUES

1937 (May 12th) Coronation. As Antigua. Printers, Bradbury Wilkinson. Perf 11 x 11¾.

S1	2c **green**	.50	1.80
S2	4c **carmine**	.80	2.40
S3	5c **deep purple**	1.50	2.40
S1/3	**set** (3)	2.50	£6
SPS1/3	**specimen perf**	£80	†

1937 (May 12th) Supplementary Coronation Issue. Designs, 1c, (codfish); 3c (map); 7c (caribou); 8c (Corner Brook Paper Mills); 10c (salmon leaping); 14c (Newfoundland Dog); 15c (seal); 20c (Transatlantic beacon); 24c (ore loading, Bell Is.); 25c (sealing fleet); 48c (fishing fleet). Printers (recess) Perkins Bacon. Sheets 10 x 10.

(a) Perf 14¼ (L).

S4	1c **grey**	1.50	.20
	a fish-hook variety	£16	£12
	b pair, one no watermark	£15	£15
	c imperf pair	£85	-
S5	3c **brown-orange** (Die 1)	9.50	2.75
	a pair, one no watermark	£60	-
	b imperf pair	£85	-
	c imperf between		
	(horiz. pair)	£225	-
	d Die 2	4.50	3.30
	e pair, one no watermark	£110	-
	f imperf pair	£90	-
S6	7c **ultramarine**	1.35	.75
	a pair, one no watermark	£50	-
	b medallion re-entry	£45	£45
S7	8c **dull scarlet**	1.50	2.50
	a pair, one no watermark	£50	-
	b imperf pair	£100	-
	c imperf between		
	(horiz. pair)	£650	-
S8	10c **deep sepia**	£3	5.50
	a pair, one no watermark	£78	-
	b imperf pair	£100	-
	c double print	£275	-
S9	14c **black**	.80	2.25
	a pair, one no watermark	£60	-
	b imperf pair	£75	-
S10	15c **claret**	£8	4.25
	a watermark inverted	£60	-
	b pair, one no watermark	£60	-
S11	20c **green**	2.50	£8
	a watermark inverted	£65	-
	b imperf pair	£100	-
	c pair, one no watermark	£50	-
	d extra smokestack	£50	£60
S12	24c **blue**	1.25	1.80
	a pair, one no watermark	£120	-
	b imperf pair	£110	-
S13	25c **slate**	1.10	£2
	a pair, one no watermark	£120	-
	b imperf pair	£150	-
	c bluish slate	£2	2.50
S14	48c **deep purple**	£5	£4
	a pair, one no watermark	£150	-
	b imperf pair	£150	-

(b) Perf. 13¼ (C).

S15	1c **grey**	£14	£35
	a fish-hook variety	£125	-
S16	3c **brown-orange** (Die 1)	4.25	2.50
	a pair, one no watermark	£75	-
	b brown-orange (Die 2)	4.50	2.50
	c pair, one no watermark	£90	-
S17	7c **ultramarine**	£220	£380
	a medallion re-entry	£1500	-
S18	8c **dull scarlet**	4.50	£10
S19	10c **deep sepia**	1.60	£9
	a watermark inverted	£45	-
S20	14c **black**	£14,000	£7500
S21	15c **claret**	£13	£22
	a pair, one no watermark	£110	-
S22	20c **green**	1.60	5.75
	a extra smokestack	£42	£75
S23	24c **blue**	£16	£22
S24	25c **slate**	17.50	£50
S25	48c **deep purple**	£22	£60

(c) Perf. 13¾ (L).

S26	1c **grey**	£2	.45
	a fish-hook variety	£22	-
	b pair, one no watermark	£18	-
S27	3c **brown-orange** (Die 1)	8.50	£4
	a pair, one no watermark	£50	-
	b brown-orange (Die 2)	4.50	3.70
	c pair, one no watermark	£110	-
	d imperf between (vert. pair)	£400	-
S28	7c **ultramarine**	1.50	£1
	a medallion re-entry	£45	£56
	b pair, one no watermark	£50	-
S29	8c **dull scarlet**	1.80	3.30
	a pair, one no watermark	£60	-
S30	10c **deep sepia**	£3	6.75
	a pair, one no watermark	£60	-
S31	14c **black**	.90	2.75
	a pair, one no watermark	£60	-
S32	15c **claret**	8.50	4.50
	a pair, one no watermark	£60	-
	b imperf between (vert. pair)	£550	-
S33	20c **green**	£2	£9
	a pair, one no watermark	£110	-
	b imperf between (vert. pair)	£900	-
	c extra smokestack	£45	£65
S34	24c **blue**	1.25	1.80
	a pair, one no watermark	£120	-
	b imperf between (vert. pair)	£1300	-
S35	25c **slate**	£2	2.25
	a pair, one no watermark	£110	-
	b bluish slate	£3	£4
S36	48c **deep purple**	£5	5.75
	a pair, one no watermark	£170	-
	b imperf between (vert. pair)	£1400	-
S4/36	**set** 11 cheapest perfs (14)	£25	£28

S4a,15a,26a R1/7 and 3/3. Lines of a guide mark protrude from the fish's mouth, resembling a hook.

Die 1   Die 2

S5,16, 27 the main differences between Dies 1 and 2 are to be noted on the King's face. Die 1 shows much less shading on the nose and upper lip.

S6b, 28a R4/8 shows a major re-entry, mainly noticeable in the portrait medallion being doubled at right. There is a similar re-entry on R3/3, although this is not so pronounced.

S11d, S33c R6/5 shows an extra smokestack.

There are a number of re-entries, plate flaws and recut lines affecting many values of this set which are not listed above.

We have seen one example of the 7ct, compound perf 13 ¾ x 14¼.

1939 (June 17th) Royal Visit. Printers (recess) Bradbury, Wilkinson. Perf 13½ x 13¼ (C). No watermark. Sheets 10 x 10.

S37   5c **deep ultramarine**   1.60   .60
         a aniline ink   £175   -

As before, but surcharged. (Nov. 20th) at St. Johns.

S382c/5c **deep ultramarine** (brown) 1.25   .30
            a aniline ink   £175   -

S394c/5c **deep ultramarine** (red)   £1   .60
             a overprint reading 'CENTL' £10 £12
             b aniline ink   £175   -

S39a the overprint reads 'CENTL' on R5/3.

1941 (Dec. 1st) Honour to Sir Wilfred Grenfell (for work in Labrador). Design, Grenfell and his vessel 'Strathcona II'. Printers (recess) Canadian Bank Note Co. Perf. 12 (L). No watermark. Sheets 200 - two panes, each 10 x 10.

S40   5c **light blue**   .15   .60
         a imperforate between stamp
            and left sheet margin   -   -

1947 (June 24rd) 450th Anniversary of John Cabot's dicovery of Newfoundland. Design, Cabot aboard the 'Matthew' off Cape Bonavista. Printers (recess) Waterlow. Perf 12½ (L). Watermark sideways. Sheets 10 x 10.

S41   5c **rose-violet**   .25   .60
         a aniline ink   £125   -
         b imperf between,
            horizontal pair   £200   £300
         c imperf pair   £275   -

Care must be taken when purchasing S41b. Forgeries exist.

POSTAGE DUE STAMPS

1939 (May 1st) Printers (litho) John Dickinson. Perf 10 x 10¼ (L). No watermark. Sheets 10 x 10.

PD1	1c green	1.10	8.50
PD2	2c vermilion	6.50	4.50
PD3	3c ultramarine	2.50	£18
PD4	4c orange	4.50	£16
PD5	5c brown	2.75	£20
PD6	10c purple-violet	£4	£15
PD1/6	set (6)	£19	£75

As before, but Perf 11 x 9 (L).

PD7	2c red (/46)	£7	£15
PD8	3c ultramarine (/49)	6.50	£32
PD9	4c pale orange (/48)	£6	£40

As before, but Perf 11 (L).

PD10	1c green (/49)	1.50	£10

As before, but Perf 11 (L) and watermark 'Arms'.

PD11	10c purple-violet (/49)	£9	£55
	a 'LUE' variety	£85	£250
	b stop after 'DUE'	£60	£175
	c imperf between, vert pair	£700	-
	d ditto, including 'LUE' variety on normal stamp	£1600	-

PD11a R3/3 and 3/8 the inscription reads 'POSTAGE LUE'.

PD11a	PD11b

PD11b R10/1 a full stop appears after 'DUE'.

PD11c Three sheets are reported to exist, each with one horizontal row imperforate between, i.e 30 pairs in total.

PD11d six examples are known.

As before, but perf 9 (L). No watermark.

PD12	3c ultramarine	£750	-

It is reported that twelve different perforation combinations exist.

NEW GUINEA

1932 (June 30th)-34 Printed (recess) John Ash. No watermark, perf 11. sheets 10 x 3.

G56	1d green	£2	.15
G57	1½d claret	£2	£8
G58	2d vermilion	£2	.15
G59	2½d green (14/9/34)	£4	£13
G60	3d blue	2.40	.60
G61	3½d aniline carmine (14/9/34)	£8	£8
G62	4d olive-green	£2	£4
G63	5d deep blue-green	2.50	.50
G64	6d bistre-brown	£3	£2
G65	9d violet	£6	£14
G66	1/- blue-green	£3	6.50
G67	2/- dull lake	2.50	£12
G68	5/- olive-brown	£17	£32
G69	10/- pink	£35	£50
G70	£1 olive-grey	£68	£68
G56/70	set (15)	£145	£200

This set remained in use until 1942.

1932 (June 30th) - 34. As before but overprinted 'AIR MAIL' horizontally in two lines, with silhouette of biplane in black.

G71	½d orange	.35	£1
	a overprint omitted	£100	-
G72	1d green	.75	£1
G73	1½d claret	£1	£5
G74	2d vermilion	£1	.20
G75	2½d green (14/9/34)	£4	1.50
G76	3d blue	£2	1.80
G77	3½d aniline carmine (14/9/34)	£3	£2
G78	4d olive-green	£3	6.50
G79	5d deep blue-green	4.25	£5
G80	6d bistre-brown	£3	£10
G81	9d violet	£4	£6
G82	1/- pale blue-green	£4	£6
G83	2/- dull lake	£6	£32
G84	5/- olive-brown	£32	£40
G85	10/- pink	£60	£55

| G86 | £1 olive-grey | £55 | £38 |
| G71-86 | set (16) | £165 | £190 |

G71a Two sheets are believed to exist. This value was not normally issued without the 'AIR MAIL' overprint.

AIR STAMPS

1935 (May 1st) Design, aeroplane over Bulolo Goldfields. Printers (recess) John Ash. No watermark. Perf 11. Sheets 10 x 3. Inscribed 'POSTAGE'.

| G87 | £2 bright violet | £175 | £100 |
| G88 | £5 emerald-green | £400 | £325 |

Engraved forgeries of both values exist.

1939 (March 1st) As G87/88 but inscribed 'AIR MAIL POSTAGE'. Perf 11¼ (L). No watermark. Sheets 6 x 5.

A1	½d orange	1.50	£4
A2	1d green	1.30	2.75
A3	1½d dull claret	£2	6.50
A4	2d vermilion	£4	£2
A5	3d deep blue	£7	£11
A6	4d sage-green	£7	£5
A7	5d slate-green	6.50	2.50
A8	6d bistre-brown	£14	£14
A9	9d purple-violet	£14	17.50
A10	1/- grey-green	£15	£14
A11	2/- carmine-lake	£32	£32
A12	5/- brown-olive	£70	£70
A13	10/- rose-pink	£225	£190
A14	£1 grey-olive	£50	£70
A1/14	set (14)	£400	£400

SPECIAL ISSUES

1937 (May 18th) Coronation. As Nos. S1-4 of Nauru. Sheets 5 x 6.

S1	2d red	.25	.90
S2	3d blue	.25	£1
	a imperf between stamp and margin	£2250	-
S3	5d green	.25	£1
	a re-entry	£40	£55
S4	1/- lake-purple	.25	1.20
S1/4	set (4)	.90	£4

S2a One sheet lacked the vertical perforations at the left of the first vertical row.

S3a This re-entry is easily visible to the naked eye, as most of the design was duplicated, giving the stamp a deeper shade. R5/2 (Plate 2A).

Number issued 2d, 532,500; 3d, 490,500; 5d, 504,000; 1/-, 480,000.

NEW HEBRIDES

1938 (June 1st)-52 Designs, Island Scene. Designer, J. Kerhor. Printers Bradbury, Wilkinson. Perf 12 (L). Sheets 3 x 10.

1	5c bluish green	1.25	£3
2	10c deep orange	.50	1.35
3	15c purple-violet	1.75	£3
4	20c carmine-rose	.75	1.80
5	25c chocolate-brown	.75	1.80
6	30c deep blue	1.25	1.65
7	40c olive-green	2.25	£4
8	50c lake-maroon	.80	1.65
9	1f carmine/green	£2	5.50
	a deep carmine/blue-green (3/1/51)	£5	£7
10	2f blue/green	£15	£12
11	5f red/yellow	£35	£30
12	10f purple/blue	£100	£50
1/12	set (12)	£150	£105
SP1/12	specimen perf (12)	£200	†

Whilst there are many shades of No. 4, officially the colour was carmine-rose, and we were officially informed that there was only one printing.

1953 (April 30th) Designs, 5c-20c (Canoes under sail); 25c-50c (native carving)); 1f-5f (natives) 5ct-50ct designed by Raoul Serres, 1f-5f designed by L. Hertenberger. Printers (recess) Waterlow and Sons. Perf 12½ (L). Sheets 5 x 10.

13	5c green	.35	.30
14	10c scarlet	.35	.15
15	15c yellow-ochre	.35	.15
16	20c ultramarine	.35	.15
17	25c olive	.30	.15
18	30c brown	.30	.15
19	40c dark sepia	.30	.15
20	50c violet	.50	.15
21	1f orange	2.50	£1
22	2f red-purple	2.50	£5
23	5f scarlet	3.50	£14
13/23	set (11)	£10	£19

SPECIAL ISSUES

1949 (Oct. 10th) U.P.U. As Aden CW S11, but all (recess) by Waterlow and Sons.

S1	10c orange	.15	.60
S2	15c dull violet	.15	.60
S3	30c dull indigo-blue	.15	.60
S4	50c purple	.20	.60
S1/4	set (4)	.60	2.20

POSTAGE DUE STAMPS

1938 (June 1st) As No. 1, etc., but overprinted 'POSTAGE DUE'.

PD1	5c bluish green	£12	£30
PD2	10c deep orange	£12	£30
PD3	20c carmine-rose	£15	£45
PD4	40c olive-green	£20	£50
PD5	1f carmine/green	£22	£60
PD1/5	set (5)	£70	£200
SPPD1/5	specimen perf (5)	£100	†

1953 (April 30th) As No 13, etc., but overprinted 'POSTAGE DUE'.

PD6	5c green	£2	£10
PD7	10c scarlet	£1	£8
PD8	20c ultramarine	2.50	£15
PD9	40c dark sepia	£5	£22
PD10	1f orange	2.25	£22
PD6/10	set (5)	£12	£70

FRENCH NEW HEBRIDES

As an Anglo-French Condominium, many of the stamps were issued in common design but with differing inscriptions, either English ('New Hebrides') or French ('Nouvelles Hebrides'). Each type was equally valid and circulated concurrently. From 1938 both English- and French-inscribed stamps were denominated in a single currency, the gold franc.

The French issues either had no watermark or were on paper watermarked 'RF' in the sheet.

1938 (June 1st) As Nos. 1/12 of New Hebrides but inscribed in French and with cyphers transposed ('RF' at upper right).

F1	5c **bluish-green**	1.50	4.50
F2	10c **deep orange**	1.35	1.50
F3	15c **purple-violet**	1.35	£3
F4	20c **carmine-rose**	1.50	2.50
F5	25c **chocolate-brown**	£3	3.50
F6	30c **deep blue**	£3	3.50
F7	40c **olive-green**	1.75	£6
F8	50c **lake-maroon**	1.35	2.25
F9	1f **carmine/green**	1.50	£4
F10	2f **blue/green**	17.50	£22
F11	5f **red/yellow**	27.50	£38
F12	10f **purple/blue**	£70	£85
F1/F12	**set** (12)	£115	£160
SP1F/12	**specimen perf** (12)	£275	†

1941 (April 15th) Nos. F1/12 overprinted 'France Libre' in allegiance to General de Gaulle.

F13	5c **bluish-green**	1.25	£16
F14	10c **deep orange**	£2	£15
F15	15c **purple-violet**	3.75	£25
F16	20c **carmine-rose**	£10	£20
F17	25c **chocolate-brown**	£11	£25
F18	30c **deep blue**	£11	£23
F19	40c **olive-green**	£11	£25
F20	50c **lake-maroon**	£10	£23

F21	1f **carmine/green**	£11	£23
F22	2f **blue/green**	£10	£23
F23	5f **red/yellow**	8.50	£23
F24	10f **purple/blue**	8.50	£23
F13/F24	**set** (12)	£90	£250

1953 (April 30th) As nos. 13/23 of New Hebrides but inscribed in French and with cyphers transposed ('RF' at lower right).

F25	5c **green**	£1	£2
F26	10c **scarlet**	1.75	£2
F27	15c **yellow-ochre**	1.75	2.25
F28	20c **ultramarine**	1.75	£2
F29	25c **olive**	.60	£2
F30	30c **brown**	.60	2.25
F31	40c **dark sepia**	.85	2.25
F32	50c **violet**	.60	£2
F33	1f **orange**	4.75	£5
F34	2f **red-purple**	£8	£30
F35	5f **scarlet**	£10	£55
F25/35	**set** (11)	£29	£95

SPECIAL ISSUES

1949 (Oct 10th) U.P.U. As Nos. S1/4 of New Hebrides but with 'RF Postes' to left of the globe and right-hand inscription reading 'Union Poste Universelle 1874-1949'.

SF1	10c **orange**	1.50	£5
SF2	15c **dull violet**	£2	£10
SF3	30c **dull indigo-blue**	3.25	£12
SF4	50c **purple**	3.75	£12
SF1/4	**set** (4)	9.50	£35

POSTAGE DUE STAMPS

1938 (June 1st) As No. F1, etc., but overprinted 'CHIFFRE TAXE'.

PDF1	5c bluish-green	£8	£45
PDF2	10c deep orange	£9	£45
PDF3	20c carmine-rose	12.50	£50
PDF4	40c olive-green	£28	£100
PDF5	1f carmine/green	£28	£100
PDF1/5	set (5)	£75	£300
SPPDF1/5	specimen perf (5)	£150	†

1941 (April 15th) As No. PDF1/5, further overprinted 'FRANCE LIBRE'.

PDF6	5c bluish-green	£8	£28
PDF7	10c deep orange	£8	£28
PDF8	20c carmine-rose	£8	£28
PDF9	40c olive-green	£10	£28
PDF10	1f carmine/green	£10	£28
PDF6/10	set (5)	£40	£125

1953 (April 30th) As No. 25F, etc., but overprinted 'TIMBRE-TAXE'.

PDF11	5c green	4.50	£15
PDF12	10c scarlet	3.75	£14
PDF13	20c ultramarine	£11	£24
PDF14	40c dark sepia	7.50	£22
PDF15	1f orange	8.50	£38
PDF11/15	set (5)	£32	£100

NEW ZEALAND

All stamps were printed (recess) on multiple 'NZ Star' watermarked paper unless otherwise mentioned. Two main types of paper were used, previously designated 'Esparto' and 'Woodpulp'; for simplicity, they have been re-designated 'fine' (F) and 'coarse' (C) respectively. These are listed, as they are easily separated; 'fine' being clear white wove paper, 'coarse' being yellowish with a criss-cross weave similar to linen.

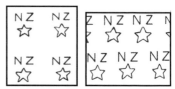

Single watermark   Multiple watermark

1935 Designs, ½d (Pied Fantail); 1d (Kiwi); 1½d (Maori woman); 2d (Maori house); 2½d (Mount Cook); 3d (Maori girl); 4d (Mitre Peak); 5d (swordfish); 6d (harvesting); 8d (Tuatara lizard); 1/- (Tui bird); 2/- (Capt. Cook at Poverty Bay); 3/- (Mount Egmont). Designers, J. Fitzgerald (½d, 4d), C.H. and R.J.G. Collins (1d); M. Matthews (1½d); H.W. Young (2d); L.C. Mitchell (2½d, 3d, 8d, 1/-, 3/-); W.J. Cooch and R.E. Tripe (5d); T.I. Archer (6d); I.F. Calder (9d); I.H. Jenkin (2/-). Printers (recess) De La Rue, except 9d (litho) Waterlow. ½d, 1d. 1½d, 2d, 3d. 6d, 8d, 1/- perf 14 x 13½. 2½d, 5d, 2/-, 3/- perf. 13-14 x 13½ (C); 2½d, perf 14 (L); 4d perf 14 (comb); 9d perf 14 x 14½. All watermark single NZ and star. Sheets: small format, 24 x 10; 6d and 8d 16 x 10; 4d 10 x 8; 5d and 2/- 12 x 10; 2½d and 3/- 6 x 10.

X1	½d green	.75	.90
	a watermark inverted	1.50	£3
X2	1d scarlet (Die 1)	.75	.75
	a watermark inverted	2.75	2.75
X3	1d perf 13½ x 14	£35	£35
X4	1d Die 2	3.75	2.25
	a watermark inverted	£8	2.75
X5	1½d red-brown	£4	9.50
X6	1½d perf 13½ x 14	4.50	5.50
	a wmk inverted & reversed	£15	£20
X7	2d orange	1.50	£1
	a watermark inverted	£180	£55

X8	2½d **chocolate and slate**		
	perf 13-14 x 13½	3.75	£23
	a watermark inverted	£15	£35
X9	2½d **perf 13½ x 14**	3.75	£15
	a watermark reversed	†	£675
X10	3d **brown**	£5	£2
	a watermark inverted	£500	£180
X11	4d **black and brown**	1.50	1.50
	a inverted watermark	£350	£120
X12	5d **ultramarine**		
	perf 13-14 x 13½	£11	£22
	a inverted watermark	-	£180
X13	5d **perf 13½ x 14**	£12	£29
X14	6d **scarlet**	£4	£5
	a inverted watermark	£240	£80
X15	8d **chocolate-brown**	3.75	£9
X16	9d **scarlet and black**	4.75	2.75
X17	1/- **green**	£8	£9
	a inverted watermark	-	£125
X18	2/- **olive-green**		
	perf 13-14 x 13½	£18	£28
	a COQK flaw	£85	£80
	b inverted watermark	£75	£35
X19	2/- **perf 13½ x 14**	£25	£30
	a COQK flaw	£90	£80
X20	3/- **chocolate and yellow-**		
	brown perf 13-14 x 13½	8.50	£30
X21	3/- **perf 13½ x 14**	9.50	£30
	a inverted watermark	†	£160
	b wmk inverted & reversed	£200	£225
X1/X21	**set cheapest perfs** (14)	£68	£120

X3   X4

X4 The die used for this printing has heavy shading in the sky.

X18a/19a R1/4 a short line on the second 'O' of 'COOK' transformed the letter to a 'Q'.

There are many plate varieties affecting this set and, indeed, almost all New Zealand KG VI issues. We list only a small range. Interested parties are referred to Campbell Paterson's Catalogue of New Zealand stamps.

The horizontal perforation of stamps perforated 13-14 x 13½ (C) goes half the length in a gauge of 13, and the other half in a gauge of 14. They are easily distinguishable by eye, having (respectively) broad and narrow points to the teeth.

Cowan paper is white and thick and the watermark is often difficult to see. The mesh, a pattern visible in the paper when viewed from the reverse, is horizontal and the watermark is widely spaced.

Wiggins Teape paper is thin and hard. It has vertical mesh and the watermark is more closely spaced.

1931/40 Design, Arms of Dominion. Designer, H.L. Richardson. Printed (typo) on 'Cowan' paper at the Govt. Printing Office, Wellington, from plates prepared at the Royal Mint, London. Watermark 'NZ Star' (single). Perf 14 (C). Sheets 10 x 8. Paper thick and opaque, mesh horizontal.

F1	1/3d **lemon**	3.50	£24
F2	1/3d **orange-yellow**	£4	£6
F3	2/6d **brown**	7.50	£3
F4	4/- **red**	7.50	£4
F5	5/- **green**	£10	8.50
F6	6/- **carmine**	£15	£9
F7	7/- **blue**	£14	£16
F8	7/6d **olive-grey**	£35	£60
F9	8/- **slate-violet**	£14	£19
P10	9/- **orange**	£15	£18
F11	10/- **carmine-lake**	£12	5.50
F12	12/6d **purple**	£70	£90
F13	15/- **olive**	£35	£25
F14	£1 **pink**	£35	£12
F15	25/- **green-blue**	£250	£385
F16	30/- **brown**	£150	£100
F17	35/- **orange-yellow**	£2500	£3250
F18	£2 **violet**	£175	£40
F19	£2/10 **red**	£200	£325
F20	£3 **green**	£220	£160
F21	£3/10 **rose**	£950	£1100
F22	£4 **light blue**	£220	£110
F23	£4/10 **greenish grey**	£850	£1100
F24	£5 **blue**	£200	£70

1938-40 Design as No. F1, but surcharged so as to render stamps more readily distinguishable from other values of similar colours. Watermark 'NZ Star' (single).

F25	3/6d/3/6d **green** (6/40)	£27	£13
F26	5/6d/5/6d **mauve-lilac** (6/40)	£50	£35
F27	11/-/11/- **yellow** (6/40)	£90	£95
F28	22/-/22/- **vermilion-red**(6/40)	£275	£225
F29	35/-/35/- **orange-yellow**(/39)	£225	£190

1936-39 As F1, on 'Wiggins Teape' paper.

F30	1/3d orange-yellow	£15	2.25
F31	2/6d brown	£45	2.25
F32	4/- red-brown	£55	£6
F33	5/- green	£55	4.50
	a watermark inverted	-	£160
F34	6/- carmine	£55	£22
F35	7/- pale blue	£80	£24
F35a	7/6d olive-grey		
	(unsurfaced paper) (/40)	£90	£190
F36	8/- slate-violet	£85	£32
F37	9/- orange	£90	£48
F38	10/- pale carmine-lake	£85	4.50
F39	15/- olive	£130	£35
F40	£1 pink	£95	£16
F41	30/- brown	£300	£120
F42	35/- orange-yellow	£3400	£3800
F43	£2 purple (/37)	£400	£70
	a watermark inverted	-	-
F44	£3 green	£600	£225
F45	£5 indigo-blue (/37)	£800	£150

1943-52 As F1, but with watermark 'NZ Star' (multiple), and on Wiggins Teape paper. Perf 14 (C).

F47	1/3 yellow-orange (9/43)	£7	1.65
	aa watermark inverted	-	£125
	a error sideways watermark	-	-
	b yellow and black		
	(inverted watermark) (/55)	2.50	£1
	c yellow and black		
	(upright watermark) (/56)	£15	£22
	d yellow and blue		
	(inverted watermark) (/56)	£2	£3
	e yellow and black		
	(/56) perf 14 x 13½	1.25	£2
	f perf 14 x 13½		
	(inverted watermark)	£12	£16
F48	2/6d brown (9/43)	£4	.65
	a watermark inverted	£4	.60
F49	4/- brownish red (11/44)	£10	1.20
	a watermark inverted	£12	1.20
F50	5/- green (9/43)	£10	.60
	a watermark inverted	£12	.60
F51	6/- rose-pink (10/46)	£16	£2
	a watermark inverted	£20	£2
F52	7/- light grey-blue (7/44)	£18	3.50
F53	7/6d olive-green (21/2/50)		
	(watermark inverted)	£30	£40
F54	8/- dark violet-blue (9/43)	£30	£10
	a watermark inverted	£32	£12
F55	9/- brownish orange (1/46)	£16	£25
	a watermark inverted	£32	£25
F56	10/- carmine-red (11/44)	£18	1.50
	a watermark inverted	£22	1.50
F58	15/- sage-green (10/45)	£22	£12
	a watermark inverted	£38	£15
F59	£1 dull pink (10/45)	12.50	2.25
	a watermark inverted	£22	£3
F60	25/- blue (11/44)	£240	£325
	a watermark inverted	£350	£400
F61	30/- brown (1/44)	£150	£90
	a watermark inverted	£140	£85

F63	£2 purple-violet (1/44)	£55	£15
	a watermark inverted	£55	£12
F64	£2/10 red (9/8/51)		
	watermark inverted	£175	£240
F65	£3 green (10/46)	£90	£30
	a watermark inverted	£85	£32
F66	£3/10 rose-red (8/48)	£1600	£1000
	a watermark inverted	£1700	£1000
F67	£4 light blue (watermark		
	inverted) (12/2/52)	£90	£90
	a watermark inverted	†	-
F69	£5 blue-black (10/45)	£225	£48
	a watermark inverted	£125	£38

1944-5 As nos. F25, etc. but watermark 'NZ Star' (multiple).

F70	3/6d/3/6d green Type 1 (11/44)	£10	£4
	a watermark inverted	£19	7.50
	b Type 2 (6/53)	£7	£24
	c Type 2 wmk inverted	£25	£28
F71	5/6d/5/6d mauve-lilac (8/44)	£24	£13
	a watermark inverted	£30	£12
F72	11/-/11/- yellow (/45)	£40	£30
F73	22/-/22/- vermilion-red (/45)	£150	£100
	a watermark inverted	£175	£120

Type 1 Broad capitals - THREE SHILLINGS with serifs.

          Type 1

Type 2 Taller capitals - THREE SHILLINGS without serifs.

          Type 2

F35a, 47e, f, are on 'unsurfaced' paper: the remainder are on chalk-surfaced paper.

Though described as postal fiscals, Nos. F1-73 are postage stamps in the full sense. Values over £5 exist and sometimes these are found postally used.

When purchasing the more expensive stamps, care should be exercised. Fiscally-used stamps have been cleaned and regummed and re-perforated examples can be found, but the main problem is with fiscally-used examples masquerading as postally-used. Often such cancels can be identified by 'Dept.', 'Office' etc. appearing in the postmark. An expert committee certificate is advised for the more expensive items. The fiscally-used examples are far from worthless, in the case of the 'better' stamps, but the collector is advised to pay fractions of the above prices for such stamps.

PICTORIAL ISSUE

1936-43 Pictorial issue. Designs and formats as previously, except 9d sheet format now 120 (10 x 12). Watermark 'NZ Star' (Multiple). Printers, De La Rue. Perf 13-14 x 13½.

1	2½d chocolate and slate	3.50	£13
	a watermark inverted	£20	£45
2	5d ultramarine	8.75	£2
	a watermark inverted	£28	£14

3	2/- **deep olive**	£15	£5
	a watermark inverted	£250	£120
	b COQK flaw	£45	£40
4	3/- **sepia and light chestnut**	£20	5.50
	a watermark inverted	£75	£25

Perf. 14 x 13½.

5	½d **green**	1.50	.10
	a inverted watermark	£3	2.50
6	1d **scarlet** (Die 2)	1.25	.10
	a watermark inverted	£4	2.75
7	1½d **brown**	4.75	3.25
8	2d **orange** (F)	.20	.10
	a inverted watermark	£150	£65
	b orange (C)	.20	.10
	ba watermark inverted	-	-
9	3d **brown**	£14	.75
	a watermark inverted	£45	£35
10	4d **black and sepia**	£3	.40
	a watermark inverted	£10	£12
11	6d **scarlet**	7.50	£1
	a watermark inverted	£32	£14
12	8d **chocolate**	1.75	2.75
	a watermark inverted	-	-
	b watermark sideways	£4	2.75
	c wmk sdys & inverted	£22	£27
13	1/- **green** (F)	1.10	.40
	a inverted watermark	£45	£32
	b green (C)	£3	.65

Perf. 13½ x 14 (C). Printers, De La Rue.

14	2/- **deep olive** (3/39)	£175	1.80
	a COQK flaw	£190	£32

Perf 12½ (L). Printers, Waterlow and Sons or De La Rue.

15	2d **deep orange** (6/41)	2.50	.15
	a inverted watermark	-	-
16	4d **black and sepia-black** (8/41)	£14	£9
	a inverted watermark	†	-
17	5d **dull ultramarine**(F) (7/41)	£8	£3
	a dull ultramarine (C)	£6	2.50
18	6d **red** (10/41)	1.20	2.25
19	8d **chocolate-brown** (watermark sideways)	1.75	£1
20	1/- **deep green** (11/41)	£28	£14
21	2/- **deep olive** (F) (7/41)	£9	5.50
	a COQK flaw	£40	£35
	b deep olive (C)	£15	6.50
	c COQK flaw	£50	£40
22	3/- **sepia and light chestnut** (7/41)	£38	£32

Perf 14 (L). Printers, 2d De La Rue; 4d Waterlow, perforated by De La Rue.

23	2d **deep orange** (6/41)	£12	.75
24	2½d **chocolate and slate** (/42) (line perf)	3.50	£1
	a inverted watermark	£12	-

25	2½d **(comb perf)** (/42)	3.50	£1
26	4d **black and sepia-black**	£28	£70

Perf 14 x 14¾ (L). Printers, De La Rue; perforated by Harrison and Sons.

27	2d **deep orange** (6/41)	£18	£14

Perf 14 x 14¼ (C). Printers, De La Rue.

28	4d **black and sepia** (7/42)	.40	.15
	a watermark inverted	£110	£60
29	6d **red** (C) (6/42)	.60	.15
	a watermark inverted	£225	£180
	b red (F)	£6	1.25
30	8d **chocolate** (watermark sideways) (7/42)	1.50	.90
	a wmk sideways inverted	-	£60

Perf 13¾ x 13½ (C). Printers, De La Rue.

31	2½d **chocolate and indigo-slate** (11/42)	.40	2.50
	a perf 14¼ x 13½	£2	£14
32	5d **dull ultramarine** (11/42)	.80	1.20
	a watermark inverted	£125	£95
	b double print, one albino	£475	-
33	2/- **deep olive** (Plate 1) (10/42)	£5	£1
	a Plate 2 (7/42)	2.75	£1
	ab watermark inverted	-	£125
	b Plate 3 (11/43)	£8	2.50
	c COQK flaw	£80	£35
34	3/- **sepia and brown** (9/42)	£14	£8
	a perf 14¼ x 13½	1.75	1.65
1/34a	**set cheapest** perf (14)	£45	11.50

F - fine paper; C - coarse paper (see note above 1935 set).

Nos. 3b, 14a, 21a, c, 33c for note on 'COQK' flaw see X18.

15 printed by De La Rue and perforated by Waterlow.

17, 21 the 5d and 2/- were printed by Waterlow and De La Rue, and perforated by Waterlow. Other values perf 12½ (L) were printed and perforated by Waterlow.

32b the impression is blurred and the colour is brighter.

33 the ratlines (horizontal lines) in the shrouds differ. Plate 1 shows considerable detail in the lines to the left sailor's hat. Plate 2 is similar but shows less detail. Plate 3 shows very little detail.

Plate 1

Plate 2

Plate 3

33a stamps from the second plate were first to be placed on sale.

1938-41 Design as X16 (Maori Panel) but from plate made by Coulls, Somerville and Wilkie, Wellington. Offset-litho.

Perf 14 x 15 (C). Fine paper, size 18 x 21mm. Watermark 'NZ Star' (multiple) sideways.

35	9d **red and grey** (/36)	£22	£2
	a wmk sideways, inverted and reversed	-	£120

Perf 13¾ x 14¼ (C). Fine paper, size 18 x 21mm. Watermark 'NZ Star' (multiple) upright.

36	9d **red and grey-black** (1/3/38)	£25	£2
	a watermark inverted	£85	£48

Perf 14 x 15 (C). (Chalk-surfaced paper.) Watermark 'NZ Star' (single). Typo (size 17½ x 20½ mm).

37	9d **scarlet and black** (5/41)	£40	£20
	a watermark inverted	†	-

As 37, but watermark 'NZ Star' (multiple). Typo.

38	9d **scarlet and black** (29/9/41)	1.75	2.40
	a watermark inverted	£225	£130

1938-52 Designer, W.J. Cooch. Printers (recess) Bradbury, Wilkinson. Perf 13¾ x 13½ (C). Sheets 24 x 10.

39	½d **emerald-green** (1/3/38) F	£3	.10
	a watermark inverted	£12	2.25
40	½d **orange-brown** (10/7/41) F	.10	.25
	a buff-brown (/42) C	.10	.25
	ab watermark inverted	-	-
41	1d **rose-scarlet** (1/7/38)	£2	.10
	a watermark inverted	£12	2.25
	b scarlet (/39)	£2	.10
	c broken ribbon	£42	£24
42	1d **emerald-green** (2/7/41) E	.10	.10
	a watermark inverted	£35	-
	b pale emerald (2/49) C	.10	.10
	ba watermark inverted	-	£20
43	1½d **red-chocolate** (26/4/38) F	£11	1.95
	ba watermark inverted	£25	3.50
44	1½d **scarlet** (1/2/44) F	.25	.60
	a rose-scarlet (1/2/44) C	.10	.50
	ab watermark inverted	-	£48
45	2d **orange** (1/5/47) C	.15	.10
	a orange-yellow (5/48) C	.35	.10
	ab watermark inverted	£120	£120
	b deep orange (4/49) C	.30	.15
	c thin paper (/50) C	2.50	£1
46	3d **dark grey-blue** (26/9/41) F	.30	.20
	a deep blue (4/49) C	.10	.10
	ab watermark inverted	-	£60
47	4d **purple-mauve** (1/5/47) F	.75	.60
	a purple-lake (/52) C	.40	.60
	b deep purple-lake (/52) C	.50	.60
48	5d **slate-grey** (1/5/47) F	.50	.60
	a grey (/51) C	£1	£1
49	6d **lake-carmine** (1/5/47) F	.50	.10
	a watermark inverted	£80	£24
	b rose-carmine (/50) C	.75	.40
50	8d **violet** (1/5/47) F	.50	.75
	a deep violet (11/48) C	.75	£1
	b thin paper (/50) C	1.50	£1
51	9d **lake-brown** (1/5/47) F	£1	.35
	a deep grey-brown (2/49) C	1.50	.40
	ab watermark inverted	£32	£11
39/51	**set** (13)	£18	£5

F - fine paper; C - coarse paper (see note above 1935 set).

Imperforate stamps come from the Bradbury Wilkinson archives, sold in London in 1990. All printings exist.

41c R6/6, Plate 8. The ribbon above '&' has a large break.

49 the 6d exists printed in pale powder-blue, on normal gummed paper. Status unknown - possibly a trial print.

1941 Nos. 39 and 43 surcharged.

52	1d/½d **emerald-green**		
	(1/5/41)	.75	.10
53	2d/1½d **red-chocolate**		
	(1/5/41)	.85	.10
	a inserted 2	£360	£225

53a R10/10 (certain sheets only) the '2' of the surcharge was inserted by a second overprinting operation. Traces of the first overprinting are generally visible.

COIL-JOIN PAIRS

These are numbered 1-19 on the margins between pairs. All pairs are horizontal, except the 1/- and 1/3d pairs which are vertical. Numbers were either printed in type, or applied by rubber stamp. Prices are for mint pairs.

Rubber-stamped numbers (in red or grey-black);

R1	1d **green**	£8	-
R2	2d **orange**	£8	-
R3	3d **blue**	£8	-
R4	4d **purple-mauve**	£10	-
R5	5d **grey**	£14	-
R6	6d **lake-carmine**	£14	-

Machine-printed numbers (in black);

M1	2d **orange**	£6	-
M2	3d **blue**	£6	-
M3	4d **purple-mauve**	£6	-
M3a	4d **purple-lake**	£9	-
M4	5d **grey**	£6	-
M5	6d **lake-carmine**	£6	-
M6	8d **violet**	£10	-
M7	9d **lake-brown**	£12	-
M8	1/- **watermark upright**	£200	-
M8a	1/- **watermark upright/**		
	sideways combined	£18	-
M8b	1/- **watermark sideways**	£9	
M8c	1/- **watermark upright** (CP2)	£9	-
M9	1/3d **Plate 1** (FP1)	£9	-
M10	1/3d **Plate 2** (FP2)	£9	-

1947 (May 1st) - 52 Design, portrait of King. Printers (recess) De La Rue. Perf 14 x 14½ (C). Watermark sideways unless otherwise mentioned. Coarse paper. Sheets 10 x 16.

54	1/- **chestnut and claret**	.80	.90
	a wmk sideways inverted	£11	£6
	b watermark upright	.25	.50
	c watermark upright		
	CP2 (3/50)	.90	.75
	ca watermark inverted	£55	£18
55	1/3d **chestnut and**		
	ultramarine FP 1	.75	.75
	a wmk sideways inverted	£10	£4
	b FP 2 (3/50)	1.75	£1
	ba wmk sideways inverted	£32	-
	c FP 2 watermark upright		
	(14/1/52)	£1	2.75
	ca watermark inverted	†	-
56	2/- **orange-brown and**		
	deep green	1.75	1.50
	a wmk sideways inverted	£12	£9
	b watermark upright	2.25	£7
57	3/- **deep chestnut and grey**	1.75	£2
	a wmk sideways inverted	£26	£12
	b thin paper (/51)	£3	£3
54/57	**set (4)**	£4	4.25

The watermark is normally with the point of the star pointing to the right, as seen from the reverse of the stamp. Thus the sideways-inverted watermarks have the point of the star pointing to the left.

Centre Plate 1   Centre Plate 2

54, 54b, 56 and 56b were printed from Centre Plate 1, remainder from Centre Plate 2. Plate 1 is generally lightly shaded in the corners; in Plate 2, the shading lines in the corners have been strengthened and are more even and prominent.

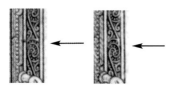

Frame Plate 1   Frame Plate 2

55, b and 55c FP1 and FP2. Frame Plate 2; there is a break in the ornamentation at right. The break was removed by retouching on R13/5.

1950 (July 29th) Design as No F1 (Arms of Dominion).

58	1½d **red**	£2	2.50
	a watermark inverted	.20	.20

The majority had the watermark inverted. The issue was withdrawn 28/11/50.

Number issued 14,543,360.

1952 (Dec 12th) No 43 surcharged 3d.

| 59 | 3d/1d **emerald-green** | .10 | .10 |

Number issued 18,626,640.

1953 (Sept. 11th) No 40 surcharged 1d.

| 60 | 1d/½d **orange-brown** | .10 | .60 |
| | a 'D' omitted | † | - |

Number issued 7,291,440.

SPECIAL ISSUES

1937 (May 13th) Coronation. Printers (recess) Bradbury, Wilkinson. Perf 14 x 13½ (C). Sheets 10 x 12.

S1	1d **carmine**	.15	.10
S2	2½d **deep blue**	.40	1.50
S3	6d **reddish orange**	.55	1.35
S1/3	**set** (3)	£1	2.65

Number issued 1d, 38,455,554; 2½d, 1,564,496; 6d, 2,079,611.

1940 (Jan. 2nd) Centenary of British Sovereignty. Designs, views of New Zealand, etc. Designers, ½d, 3d and 4d (L.C. Mitchell); other values (J. Berry). Printers (recess) Bradbury, Wilkinson. Perf 13½ (C), 2½d perf 14 x 13½ (C), and 5d perf 13½ x 14 (C). Sheets 12 x 10 or 10 x 12, except 2½d and 5d which are 10 x 16.

S4	½d **deep blue-green**	.15	.10
S5	1d **purple-brown and red**	1.20	.10
S6	1½d **blue and mauve-purple**	.15	.35
S7	2d **myrtle-green and sepia**	.60	.10
S8	2½d **myrtle-green and deep blue**	.80	.60
S9	3d **deep purple and crimson-lake**	1.50	.75
S10	4d **chocolate and deep claret**	£6	.90
S11	5d **light blue and brown**	3.50	2.25
S12	6d **emerald and purple-violet**	£5	.75
S13	7d **black and vermilion**	.85	2.50
S14	8d **black and vermilion** (8/3/40)	£5	1.95
S15	9d **sage-green and deep olive**	£3	1.20
S16	1/- **sage-green and deep myrtle**	£6	2.25
S4/16	**set** (13)	£30	£12

Number issued ½d, 36,957,240; 1d, 75,827,040; 1½d, 3,506,240; 2d, 110,219,640; 2½d, 2,038,400; 3d, 7,855,800; 4d, 3,358,800; 5d, 3,280,000; 6d, 5,818,800; 7d, 1,140,000; 8d, 3,359,160; 9d, 2,398,800; 1/, 3,605,520. A small quantity of the ½d value was withdrawn.

1944 (May 1st) As No. S6 but surcharged 'TENPENCE' at the Govt. Printing Office, Wellington.

| S17 | 10d/1½d **blue and mauve-purple** | .10 | .20 |

Number issued 3.842,280.

1946 (April 1st) Peace. Designs, views of New Zealand, Badges of Fighting Services, portraits of Royal Family (2d), HMNZS 'Achilles' and M.V. 'Dominion Monarch' (5d). Designer, J. Berry. Printers, 1½d and 1/- Harrison and Sons (photo) and perf 14 x 14¾ (C); 1d and 2d Bradbury, Wilkinson (recess) and perf 13½ x 13 (C); other values, Waterlow and Sons. Sheets, 1d and 2d 12 x 20; 1½d 16 x 10; 1/-, 6 x 20, others 15 x 8.

S18	½d **dull myrtle and deep brown**	.10	.40
	a 'T' guide	£12	£12
	b watermark inverted	£55	£32
	c dull myrtle and chestnut	.30	.40
	d 'T' guide	£18	£18
S19	1d **emerald-green**	.10	.10
	a watermark inverted	£35	£22
S20	1½d **scarlet** (watermark sideways)	.10	.30
	a wmk. sideways-inverted	.10	.30
S21	2d **purple**	.10	.10
S22	3d **ultramarine and slate-green**	.15	.10
	a plane tail retouch	£7	£8
	b 'T' guide	£10	£10
	c aircraft omitted	£3250	†
S23	4d **olive and deep orange**	.10	.15
	a watermark inverted	£100	£38
S24	5d **green and ultramarine**	.35	.90
	a trailing aerial	£12	£18
S25	6d **chocolate and vermilion**	.10	.20
S26	8d **black and lake**	.10	.20
S27	9d **light blue and black**	.10	.20
	a guide mark	£12	-
S28	1/- **slate-black**	.40	.25
S18/28	**set** (11)	1.50	2.50

S18a   S22a

S22b   S24a

S18a, d R12/3 a printer's 'T' guidemark (sideways) can be found at the centre right of the central vignette. Other positions show faint 'T's at this point, but R12/3 is much stronger.

S22a R2/4 (Plate 42883) and R3/2 (Plate 42796). The tail on the flying boat in the upper right corner has been drawn in. Blocks without a retouch on either position may be found, and are very rare.

S22b R1/1, 1/2 Frame Plate 42856. A 'T' guidemark can be found on the left side of the central vignette, above the bottom left corner.

S22c One sheet was found with the corner folded over, causing the centre to be omitted.

S24a R8/1 (Plate 42794) a plate flaw consists of a straight scratch from the top of the liner to the sea, crossing just below the top of the funnel.

S27a horizontal guideline above the left arm of the cross. R3/3, Pl. 42723.

There are a great many other plate varieties, principally re-entries, to be collected.

Number printed ½d, 9,499,960; 1d, 107,840,000; 1½d, 4,500,000; 2d, 141,840,000; 3d, 12,499,000; 4d, 4,750,000; 5d, 7,999,920; 6d, 7,261,920; 8d, 5,559,960; 9d, 3,249,960; 1/-, 4,500,00.

1948 (Feb. 23rd) Otago Centennial. Designs, views of Otago. Designer, J. Berry. Printers (recess) Bradbury, Wilkinson. Perf 13¼ x 13½ (C), 3d watermark sideways. Sheets 10 x 12 or 12 x 10.

S29	1d **jay-blue and green**	.10	.20
	a missing hand variety	£400	-
	b watermark inverted	£40	£45
S30	2d **green and light brown**	.15	.20
S31	3d **purple-violet**	.15	.35
S32	6d **grey-black and carmine-lake**	.15	.35
	a watermark inverted	-	£150
S29/32	**set** (4)	.30	£1

S29a R12/7 (Plate A2). A lightening of pressure (through a fault in the make-ready) resulted in a gradual disappearance, as printing proceeded, of the Maori's left hand; examples exist where the hand is completely missing.

Number printed 1d, 5,000,000; 2d, 5,000,000 3d, 2,500,000; 6d, 2,500,000. Not all were sold; a small balance of the issue was destroyed.

1950 (Nov. 20th) Canterbury Centenary. Designs and designers, 1d (Anglican Cathedral, Christchurch, J. Berry); 2d (symbolic design depicting arrival of pioneer women, L.C. Mitchell); 3d (John R. Godley, founder of Canterbury, by J.A. Johnstone); 6d (Canterbury University College, J. Berry); 1/- (Timaru, J. Berry). Printers (recess) Bradbury, Wilkinson. Perf 13¼ x 13½ (C). Sheets 12 x 10 or 10 x 12.

S33	1d light blue and grey-green (watermark sideways)	.25	.40
S34	2d brick-red and carmine	.25	.40
S35	3d light and deep blue (watermark sideways)	.25	.50
S36	6d light blue and chocolate	.30	.50
S37	1/- light blue and deep maroon	.30	.65
S33/37	set (5)	1.20	2.20

Number issued 1d, 5,000,000; 2d, 5,000,000; 3d, 2,500,000; 6d, 2,500,000; 1/-, 2,500,00.

HEALTH (CHARITY) ISSUES

The charity surcharge goes to funds providing for childrens' homes and camps throughout New Zealand.

1936 (2nd Nov.) 'Safeguard Health' (Recess) J. Ash. Watermark single NZ and star (sideways). Perf 11. Sheets 6 x 8.

GH9 1d + 1d scarlet   1.10   2.25

Number issued 1,449,980.

1937 (Oct. 1st) 'Boy on Rocks', designers, G. Bull and J. Berry. Printers (recess) Australian Note and Stamp Printers, Melbourne. Watermark single NZ and star. Perf. 11¼ (C). Sheets 8 x 6.

H2 1d+1d scarlet   1.60   2.25

Number issued 1,234,720.

1938 (Oct. 1st) 'Children playing', designer, J. Berry. Printers (recess) Bradbury, Wilkinson. Watermark multiple NZ and star, perf 14 x 13½ (C). Sheets 10 x 8.

H2 1d+1d scarlet   3.25   1.95

Number issued 1,234,720.

1939 (Oct. 16th) 'Boys playing with ball', designer, S. Hall. Printers (recess) Australian Note and Stamp Printers. Watermark single NZ and star. Perf 11¼ (C). Surcharged in black at Govt. Printing Office, Wellington. Sheets 8 x 6.

H3	1d/½d+½d green	2.40	2.75
H4	2d/1d+1d scarlet	2.75	2.75

Changes in postal rates, after printing, were the reason for the surcharges.

Number issued 1d, 482,746; 2d, 516,046.

1940 (Oct. 1st) As before, but without surcharge and values changed.

H5	1d+½d **green**	£5	8.50
H6	2d+1d **light chestnut**	£5	8.50

Number issued 1d, 284,756; 2d, 359,972.

1941 (Oct. 4th) As before, but overprinted 1941 (in black) at Govt. Printing Office, Wellington.

H7	1d+½d **green**	.25	1.35
H8	2d+1d **light chestnut**	.25	1.35

Number issued 1d 349,543; 2d 434,855.

1942 (Oct. 1st) 'Children on swing', designer, etc., as H3-8. Watermark single NZ and star. Sheets 8 x 6.

H9	1d+½d **green**	.15	.75
H10	2d+1d **light chestnut**	.15	.75

Number issued 1d, 720,042; 2d, 942,425.

H 11-28 are all watermarked multiple NZ and star

1943 (Oct. 1st) 'Princesses Margaret and Elizabeth' (triangular design). Designer, J. Berry. Printers (recess) Bradbury, Wilkinson. Perf 12 (L). Sheets 20 x 6.

H11	1d+½d **green**	.10	.90
	a pair imperf horiz	£7000	†
H12	2d+1d **reddish-brown**	.10	.15
	a pair imperf horiz	£10,000	£10,000

Number issued 1d, 3,133,111; 2d, 3,339,686.

1944 (Oct. 9th) 'Princesses Elizabeth and Margret (oblong design). Designed and printed (recess) Bradbury, Wilkinson. Perf 13½ x 13¼ (C). Sheets 12 x 10.

H13	1d+½d **deep green**	.15	.25
H14	2d+1d **deep blue**	.15	.20

Number issued 1d, 3,045,288; 2d, 3,405,260.

1945 (Oct. 1st) 'Peter Pan', designer, J. Berry. Printer, etc. as H13-14. Sheets 10 x 12.

H15	1d+½d **light brown and olive-green**	.10	.15
	a watermark inverted	£45	£42
H16	2d+1d **bistre and carmine**	.10	.15
	a watermark inverted	£120	£55

Number issued 1d, 3,994,633; 2d, 3,994,855.

1946 (Oct. 24th) 'Soldier with child', designer, J. Berry. Printers (recess) Waterlow and Sons. Perf 13½ x 13¼ (C). Sheets 8 x 15.

H17	1d+½d **chestnut and green**	.10	.10
	a watermark inverted	£32	£24
	b chestnut and yellow-green	2.50	3.50
H18	2d+1d **chestnut and sepia-brown**	.10	.10
	a reddish chestnut and sepia-brown	1.75	1.75
	b hat flaw	£12	£12

H18b R8.8 (Pl. 43010) marks on the peak of the soldier's hat.

Many re-entries can be found. From £5 each.

Number issued 1d, 4,500,000; 2d, 5,000,000.

1947 (Oct. 1st) 'Statue of Eros', designer and printer, etc., as H17-18. Sheets 12 x 8.

H19	1d+½d **green**	.10	.10
	a watermark inverted	£42	£38
H20	2d+1d **crimson**	.10	.10
	a watermark inverted	£55	£55

Number issued 1d, 5,500,000; 2d, 6,000,000.

1948 (Oct. 1st) 'Boy watching children play', designer, E. Linzell. Printers (recess) Bradbury, Wilkinson. Perf 13½ x 13¼ (C). Sheets 12 x 10.

H21	1d+½d **ultramarine and deep green**	.10	.15
	a watermark inverted	£48	£28
H22	2d+1d **brown-purple and red**	.10	.15

Number issued 1d, 5,442,851; 2d, 5,903,958.

1949 (Oct. 3rd) 'Nurse with child', designer, J. Berry. Printers (photo) Harrison and Sons. Perf 14 x 14¾ (C). Sheets 20 x 6.

H23	1d+½d **green**	.10	.15
H24	2d+1d **ultramarine**	.10	.15
	a stop omitted	£5	£12

H24a R1/2 the stop normally under 'D' of '1D' is missing.

Number issued 1d, 5,517,034; 2d, 5,999,109.

1950 (Oct. 2nd) 'Princess Elizabeth with Prince Charles', designers, R.S. Phillips and J. Berry, from photo by Marcus Adams, Ltd. Printers (photo) Harrison and Sons. Perf 14 x 14¾ (C). Sheets 20 x 6.

H25	1d+½d **bottle-green**	.10	.15
	a watermark inverted	£4	£4
H26	2d+1d **dull maroon**	.10	.15
	a watermark inverted	£40	£40

Number issued 1d, 5,521,324; 2d, 6,816,448.

1951 (Nov. 1st) 'Yachts of the 'Takapuna' class', designers, J. Berry and R.S. Phillips. Printers (recess) Bradbury, Wilkinson. Perf 13½ x 13¼ (C). Sheets 10 x 12.

H27	1½d+½d **red and yellow**	.15	.60
H28	2d+1d **grey-green & yellow**	.15	.15
	a watermark inverted	£40	£50

Number issued 1½d, 5,100,013; 2d, 6,122,628.

OFFICIAL STAMPS

1936 As X1, etc. (Pictorial Issue), overprinted 'Official' as O1. Watermark 'NZ Star' (single).

XO1	1d **scarlet** (11/36)		
	p 14 x 13½	2.50	.75
	a p 13½ x 14	£50	£45
XO2	1½d **red-brown** (7/36)		
	p 13½ x 14	£14	£20
	a p 14 x 13½	£9500	-
XO4	1/- **green** p 14 x 13½	£19	£35
	a watermark inverted	†	£120

XO2a a block of 4 was officially 'patched in' to a normal sheet.

1938 (July 4th) Design, Arms of Dominion. F5, Watermark single NZ and star overprinted 'Official' ('ff' joined) Perf. 14 (C).

O1	5/- **green**	£80	£70

1937-45 As 10, etc., overprinted 'Official', as O1. Watermark multiple NZ and star. Perf. 13-14 x 13½ (comb).

O2	2½d **chocolate and indigo-slate** (26/7/38) F	£30	£55
O3	2/- **deep olive** (5/37) F	£40	£25
	a COQK flaw	£95	£100

Perf 14 x 13½, 6d 13½ x 14 (comb).

O4	½d **green** (7/37) F	3.50	2.75
O4a	1d **scarlet** (Die 2) F	£4	.30
	ab watermark inverted	£16	£22
O4b	1½d **red-brown** (1/38) F	£12	2.75
O5	2d **orange** (1/38) F	£3	.10
	a orange C	£4	.60
	ab watermark inverted	-	£100
O6	3d **brown** (1/3/38)	£22	£2
	aa watermark inverted	-	£85
O6a	4d **black and sepia** (8/36)	£5	.70
O7	6d **red** (12/37) F	£12	.50
	a watermark inverted	†	-
O8	8d **chocolate-brown** (1/45) F	†	£2200
O9	1/- **deep green** (2/37) F	£22	£1
	aa watermark inverted	-	£160
	a deep green C	£25	£3
O10	2/- **deep olive** (Plate 1) (/44) C	£24	£8
	a Plate 2	£18	£6
	b Plate 3	£18	£6
	c COQK	£225	£150

Some 20 used examples of O8 are known to exist. No mint examples have been found. Used in Whangarei.

Perf. 13½ x 14 (comb).

O11	9d **red and grey-black** (No. 29) (1/3/38)	£40	£25
O12	2/- **deep olive** (/39)	£95	£4
	a COQK flaw	£125	£60

O11 is overprinted in green.

Perf. 14 (L). (2½d line perf (1938), comb perf (1945)).

O13	2d **deep orange** (3/42) F	£25	£10
O14	2½d **chocolate and indigo-slate** (26/7/38) F	£6	£13
	a deep chocolate and indigo-slate (/45) C	£6	£13
O15	4d **black and sepia-black** (8/41) F	£6	2.75

Perf. 14 x 14¼ (Comb).

O16	4d **black and sepia** (10/42)	2.25	.60
	a watermark inverted	-	£120
O17	6d **red perf 14½ x 14** (7/42)	£6	.25
	a Esparto F	£6	.25
O18	8d **chocolate** (watermark sideways) (1/45)	4.25	£10

Perf. 12½ (line).

O19	2d **deep orange** (3/42) F	£80	£35
O20	4d **black and**		
	sepia-black (12/41) F	5.50	4.50
O21	6d **red overprint**		
	at bottom (12/41) F	£7	3.50
	a overprint at top (2/42) F	£6	3.50
O22	8d **chocolate-brown**		
	(watermark sideways)(8/42) F	£6	£10
O23	1/- **deep green** (4/42) F	£14	1.65
O24	2/- **deep olive** (4/42) F	£40	£13
	a COQK flaw	£85	£75
	b deep olive C	£45	£20
	ba COQK flaw	£90	£80

O3a, O10c, O12a, O24a, ba; for 'COQK' flaw
see note after X21.

Perf. 14 x 15 (comb). Chalk-surfaced paper.

O25	9d **black and scarlet**		
	(No 38) (10/43)	£9	£14

**1943 Design, Arms of Dominion type. F50
overprinted 'Official'.**

O26	5/- **green** perf 14 (/43)	£20	3.50
	aa watermark inverted	£20	3.50
	a yellow-green perf		
	14 x 13½ (/61)	£8	£20
O2/O26	set (cheapest perfs)(14) £145		£70

O26 is on chalk-surfaced paper, O26a on
ordinary paper.

**1940 (Issued Jan. 2nd except 8d, Mar. 8th).
S4 etc. (Centenary Issues) overprinted
'Official' (tops of 'ff's not joined); in red on
½d and 3d.**

O27	½d **deep blue-green**	1.25	.20
O28	1d **purple-brown and red**	£3	.10
O29	1½d **blue and mauve-purple**	£2	1.25
O30	2d **myrtle-green and sepia**	£3	.10
O31	2½d **myrtle-green and**		
	deep blue	2.50	1.75
O32	3d **deep purple and**		
	crimson-lake	3.75	.60
O33	4d **chocolate and**		
	deep claret	£18	£1
O34	6d **emerald and**		
	purple-violet	£12	£1
O35	8d **black and vermilion**	£13	£10
O36	9d **sage-green and**		
	deep orange	£6	2.40

O37	1/- **sage-green and**		
	deep myrtle	£22	1.80
O27/O37	set (11)	£80	£18

Numbers printed ½d, 1,082,760; 1d, 3,452,880;
1½d, 361,200; 2d, 6,960,360; 2½d, 241,600; 3d,
904,200; 4d, 481,200; 6d, 661,200; 8d, 240,840;
9d, 241,200; 1/- 372,840. Small quantities of
½d, 1½d and 2½d values were withdrawn, but
the rest were sold.

As before, but 'ff's of overprint joined as
O1, etc.

O38	½d **deep blue-green**	£30	£45
O39	1d **purple-brown and red**	£30	£45
O40	2d **myrtle-green and sepia**	£35	£45
O41	2½d **myrtle-green and**		
	deep blue	£30	£48
O42	3d **deep purple and**		
	crimson-lake	£25	£35
O43	4d **chocolate and**		
	deep claret	£75	£60
O44	6d **emerald and**		
	purple-violet	£40	£45
O45	8d **black and vermilion**	£40	£65
O38/O45	set (8)	£275	£350

R4/3 of the 2½d and R1/10 of the other
values. The variety 'joined ff' occurred
in one consignment only.

**1938-51 King's Head type (32, etc.)
overprinted 'Official', as O1, etc. 1/- and 2/-
all on coarse paper.**

O46	½d **emerald-green** (1/3/38) F£11		1.50
O47	½d **orange-brown** (1/6/46) F	£1	2.40
	a light orange-brown C	1.50	£4
O48	1d **rose-scarlet** (1/7/38)	£11	.10
O49	1d **emerald-green**		
	(10/7/41) F	1.75	.10
	a emerald-green C	1.75	.10
O50	1½d **red-chocolate**		
	(26/7/38) F	£35	£12
O51	1½d **rose-scarlet** (2/4/51) C	£6	4.50
O52	2d **orange** (1/5/47) C	1.50	.10
	a deep orange (/49) C	£4	£1
O53	3d **blue** (16/10/41) F	£5	£1
	a blue C	1.75	.10
O54	4d **purple-mauve** (1/5/47) F	2.25	1.80
	a purple-lake (/50) C	£3	£3
O55	6d **lake-carmine** (1/5/47)F	£6	.30
	a lake-carmine C	£6	.30
O56	8d **violet** (1/5/47)	3.75	£4

O57 9d **reddish brown** (1/5/47) F £4   £4
   a grey-brown C   4.50   £4
O58 1/- **chestnut and claret**
   (watermark upright)(1/5/47) £7   .60
   a watermark sideways
     (1/5/47)   4.25   5.50
   aa wmk sideways inverted   £28   £12
   b plate 2 (watermark upright) £12   4.50
   ba watermark inverted   £65   £24
O59 2/- **orange-brown and**
   green (watermark
   sideways) (1/5/47)   £15   £10
   b watermark upright (1/5/47) £15   £30
O46/O59 **set** (14)   £95   £37

LIFE INSURANCE DEPARTMENT
POSTAGE STAMPS

1937 Designers, W.B. Hudson and J.F. Rodgers. Printers (typo) Govt. Printing Office, Wellington. Perf 14 (C). Watermark 'NZ Star' (single). Cowan paper. Sheets 120; two panes, each 6 x 10.

L1 2d **yellow**   3.50   £5
   a watermark inverted   £22   £30

1937 As before, but perf 14 x 15 on Wiggins Teape paper.

L2 ½d **yellow-green** (3/37)   £4   7.50
L3 1d **scarlet** (3/37)   7.50   £2
L4 6d **pink** (7/37)   £18   £28

1944-47 As before, but watermark 'NZ Star' (mult) and Perf 14 x 15 (C).

L5 ½d **yellow-green** (7/47)   3.25   £6
L6 1d **scarlet-red** (6/44)   1.50   1.50
L7 2d **yellow** (/46)   £8   £14
L8 3d **chocolate** (10/46)   £11   £22
L9 6d **rose-pink** (7/47)   £9   £21
L5/9 **set** (5)   £30   £60

Number printed ½d, 28,920; 1d, 280,920; 2d, 166,440; 3d, 35,040; 6d, 29,400 (13,800 issued).

1947 (Aug. 1st) Designs, lighthouses. ½d, (Castlepoint); 1d, (Taiaroa); 2d, (Cape Palliser); 3d, (Eddystone); 4d, (Stephens Island); 6d, (The Brothers); 1/-, (Cape Brett). Printer (recess) Bradbury, Wilkinson. Watermark 'NZ Star' (multiple), sideways on 1d, 2d, and 2½d). Perf 13¼ x 13½ (C). Sheets 10 x 12 or 12 x 10.

L10 ½d **orange-brown and**
   myrtle   .90   .40
L11 1d **pale blue and olive**   .85   .75
L12 2d **grey-black and**
   dark blue   .85   .60
L13a 2½d **black and blue**
   (4/11/63)   4.50   £8
L14 3d **blue-green and**
   purple-mauve   1.85   .60
L15 4d **orange and brown**   £2   £1
L16 6d **blue and deep brown**   £2   1.65
L17 1/- **blue and chestnut-**
   brown   £2   £2
L10/17 **set** (8)   £14   13.50

9a, 11 The 2½d was printed on very white paper, which was also used for a 1965 printing of the 4d (which has sideways watermark).

EXPRESS DELIVERY STAMPS

1926 Printers (typo) Govt. Printing Office, Wellington. Watermark 'NZ Star' (single). Cowan paper. Perf 14 x 14½. Sheets 6 x 10.

XED2 6d **vermilion and**
   mauve-purple   £25   £18
   a watermark inverted   £110   -

As before, but perf 15 x 14.

XED3 6d **carmine and**
   purple (/36)   £30   £35

As above, but Wiggins Teape paper, perf 14 x 14½.

ED4 6d **carmine and mauve** (/37) £60   £32

As above, but perf 14 x 15.

ED5 6d vermilion and
     bright mauve (4/39)   £100   £225

1939 (Aug. 16th) Designer, J. Berry. Printers
(recess) Govt. Printing Office, Wellington.
Perf. 14 (L). Watermark 'NZ Star' (single).
Sheets as before.

ED5 6d violet   .75   1.50
     a bright violet   .75   £1
     b watermark inverted   £60   -

Number issued 240,000.

POSTAGE DUE STAMPS

1937-8 Designer, W. R. Bock. Printers (typo)
Govt. Printing Office, Wellington. Perf 14 x
15 (C). Watermark 'NZ Star' (single)
sideways. Wiggins Teape, thin hard chalk-
surfaced paper. Sheets 10 x 12.

PD1 ½d red and yellow-green
         (2/38)   £15   £28
PD2 1d red and yellow-green
         (1/37)   £6   2.25
PD3 2d red and yellow-green
         (4/37)   £24   £10
PD4 3d red and yellow-green
         (11/37)   £50   £45
PD1/4 set (4)   £85   £75

1939 (Aug. 16th) Designer, J. Berry. Printers
(typo) Govt. Printing Office, Wellington. Perf
15 x 14 (C). Watermark 'NZ Star' (single)
sideways-inverted. Chalk-surfaced paper.
Sheets 10 x 12.

PD5 ½d turquoise-green   2.50   £3
PD6 1d rose-carmine   1.35   £1
     a watermark sideways   £125   3.75
PD7 2d blue   £3   1.75
PD8 3d orange-brown   £11   £16
     a watermark sideways   £125   -
PD5/8 set (4)   £16   £20

PD6a, 8a the sideways watermark varieties
have the star pointing to the right, as seen from
the back of the stamp.

Number printed ½d, 384,000; 1d, 1,440,000; 2d,
1,440,000; 3d, 456,000.

As before, but watermark 'NZ Star' (multiple).

PD9 1d rose-carmine (watermark
         sideways)(4/49)   £8   £22
PD10 2d blue (watermark
         sideways inverted) (12/46) £4 1.80
     a watermark sideways
         (4/49)   1.40   £6
PD11 3d orange-brown
         (watermark upright) (/43) £24 £22
     aa wmk sideways inverted
         (6/45)   £12   £5
     a watermark sideways
         (28/11/49)   £4   7.50
PD9-11a set (3)   £12   £26

PD9 the used price is for examples dated prior
to 30th September 1951, when the use of
Postage Due stamps officially ceased.

PD11a In the first and second printings, the
star of the watermark was to the left of 'NZ'.
It appears to the right on the printing released
28/11/49.

Number issued 3d, 180,000.

BOOKLET PANES

1935-6 single watermark Pictorials

P1   1935 CW X4 pane of 6
            (advertisement on selvedge) £30   -
        a inverted watermark   -   -

1936-43 multiple watermark Pictorials

P2   1936 CW6 pane of 6
        a inverted watermark   £25   -

1938-44 King's portrait

P3   1938 CW 39 pane of 6   £25   -
        a inverted watermark   £50   -
P4   1938 CW 41 pane of 6   £20   -
        a inverted watermark   £45   -
P5   1938 CW 43 pane of 6   £80   -
        a inverted watermark   £125   -

BOOKLETS (ALL STAPLED)

B1 2/- **1935 black and cream.**
    P1 x 4   £280   -
B2 2/- **1936 black and cream.**
    P2 x 4   £175   -

An interesting study of Die 1 and retouched Die 2, ie Die 3, exists in the booklet panes of this issue from sheets of 180 - specially laid down for booklets.

B3 2/- **1938 black and cream.**
    P4 x 4   £240   -
B4 2/3d **1938 dark blue on**
    light blue. P5 x 3   £225   -
B5 2/- **1939 black on cream.**
    P3 x 2, P4 x 3   £240   -

NIGERIA

1938 (May 1st)-47. Designs, ½d - 1/3d (King's Head with palms). Printers (recess) Bradbury, Wilkinson. Perf 12 (L). Sheets 10 x 12.

1	½d **green**	.10	.10
	a yellow-green (15/11/46)	£4	.10
2	1d **carmine-red**	£8	1.50
	a rose-red (/41)	.35	.20
	ab 'A' of watermark missing	£2000	-
3	1d **mauve-purple**		
	(11/12/44)	.10	.10
	a watermark inverted	-	-
4	1½d **chestnut-brown**	.10	.10
5	2d **black**	.10	1.20
6	2d **rose-red** (11/12/44)	.10	1.20
7	2½d **orange** (28/4/41)	.10	1.20
8	3d **dark blue**	.10	.10
	a deep grey-blue (4/44)	.40	.10
	b watermark sideways	†	£3250
9	3d **black** (11/12/44)	.10	£1
10	4d **orange**	£22	1.80
11	4d **deep blue** (11/12/44)	.10	£2
12	6d **deep plum**	.20	.10
	a purple	.40	.10
13	1/- **sage-green**	.30	.10
	a olive-green (29/9/47)	£1	.10
14	1/3 **turquoise-blue**		
	(13/2/40)	.45	.20
	a light blue (10/2/44)	1.50	.40

1938 (May 5th) Designs, 2/6d (Victoria-Buea Road); 5/- (River Niger at Jebba). Printers (recess) De La Rue. Perf 13 x 11¾ (C). Sheets 6 x 10.

15	2/6 **black and deep blue**	£20	£12
16	5/- **black and orange**	£35	£10

As Nos. 15-16, but Perf 13½ (C).

17	2/6 **black and blue**		
	(6/42)	1.75	2.75
	a black and blackish ultramarine (15/11/46)	£30	£35
18	5/- **black and orange** (8/42)	2.75	£3

As No. 15-16, but Perf 14 (L).

19	2/6d **black and deep blue** (/42)£1		£2	
	a watermark inverted		†	£3250
20	5/- **black and orange** (26/4/48)		3.75	£2

As Nos. 15-16, but Perf 12 (C).

21	2/6 **black and deep blue** (15/8/51)		£1	2.75
22	5/- **black and orange-red** (19/5/49)		2.75	2.50

As No. 1, etc., but Perf 11¾ x 11½ (C).

23	½d **green** (15/2/50)		.85	.35
24	1d **mauve-purple** (15/2/50)		.15	.30
25	1½d **chestnut-brown** (15/11/50)		.10	.10
26	2d **rose-red** (15/2/50)		.10	.30
27	6d **purple** (17/4/51)		.75	.35
28	1/- **olive-green** (15/2/50)		.25	.10
29	1/3 **light blue** (14/6/50)		.85	.45
	a watermark sideways		-	£3500
1/29	**set (cheapest)** (16)		£26	£13
SP1/16	**specimen perf** (15)		£225	†

24 exists as coils, made up from sheets.

Beware of plausible forgeries of the watermark varieties, made from rebacked normal stamps. An expert committee certificate is advisable.

SPECIAL ISSUES

1937 (May 12th) Coronation. As Antigua.

S1	1d **carmine-red**	.50	1.50
S2	1½d **deep brown**	1.10	1.80
S3	3d **blue**	1.10	2.40
S1/3	**set** (3)	2.40	£5
SP S1/3	**specimen perf** (3)	£38	†

1946 (Oct. 21st) Victory. As Aden.

S4	1½d **brown**	.15	.10
	a reddish brown	.35	.35
S5	4d **deep blue**	.15	1.35
SP S4/5	**specimen perf** (2)	£40	†

S4 Plate 1B; S4a Plate 1A

1948 (Dec. 20th) Silver Wedding. As Aden.

S6	1d **magenta-purple**	.15	.20
S7	5/- **orange-brown**	4.75	£9

1949 (Oct. 10th) UPU. As Aden.

S8	1d **magenta**	.10	.20
S9	3d **indigo**	.60	2.25
S10	6d **purple**	.15	2.25
S11	1/- **sage-green**	.25	1.20
S8/11	**set** (4)	£1	5.50

NIUE

1932-38 As Cook Islands CW X1-X6 and 1-3 but with frames altered to include 'NIUE'. Sheets 8 x 10 or 10 x 8. Watermark NZ Star (single).

X1	½d **black and green**	.25	2.25
X2	1d **black and scarlet**	.25	£1
	a watermark inverted	£35	-
X3	2d **black and brown**	.25	£1
	a watermark inverted	£18	£32
X4	2½d **black and blue**	.25	2.50
	a watermark inverted	£35	-
X5	4d **black and bright blue**	.85	2.50
	a watermark inverted	-	-
X6	6d **black and orange**	.35	.45
1	1/- **black and purple-violet** (2/5/38)	£6	£5
2	2/- **black and deep chestnut** (2/5/38)	£6	£11
3	3/- **grey-blue and emerald-green** (2/5/38)	£17	£11
X1/3	**set** (9)	£28	£32

Number issued 1/-, 73,040; 2/-, 36,160; 3/-, 34,880.

1940 (Sept. 2nd) As Cook Islands CW4, but with frame altered to include 'NIUE'. Sheets 8 x 10.

4	3d/1½d **black and purple**	.45	.10

See note after Cook Islands CW 4.

Number issued - 249,520.

1941-2 Design, as PF3 of New Zealand ('Arms of Dominion' type), overprinted 'NIUE' in thin type in blue or red ink. Wiggins Teape paper. Watermark 'NZ Star' (single). Perf 14 (C).

5	2/6 **brown** (4/41)	£45	£60
6	5/- **green** (red) (4/41)	£175	£200
7	10/- **rose-carmine** (6/42)	£50	£150
8	£1 **dull pink** (6/42)	£85	£275
5/8	**set** (4)	£320	£600

Stamps with the overprint in thicker type belong to the 1931-2 issue.

Numbers issued - 5, 8,000; 6, 3,840; 7, 4,000; 8, 3,760.

1944-6 As Cook Islands CW 9-17, with frames altered to include 'NIUE'. Sheets 8 x 10 or 10 x 8. Watermark NZ Star (multiple, sideways on ½d, 1d, 1/- and 2/-).

9	½d **black and green** (9/44)	.25	1.65
10	1d **black and deep scarlet** (12/44)	.25	1.20
11	2d **black and chestnut-brown** (2/46)	£3	4.50
12	2½d **black and slate-blue** (10/45)	.30	.75
13	4d **black and greenish blue** (3/44)	£2	.60
	a watermark inverted and reversed	£12	£15
	b watermark inverted	-	-
14	6d **black and red-orange** (9/44)	£1	.85
15	1/- **black and purple-violet** (9/44)	.75	.50
16	2/- **black and deep chestnut** (6/45)	£4	£2
17	3/- **dull blue and green** (8/45)	7.50	4.50
9/17	**set** (9)	£17	£15

Number issued ½d, 310,800; 1d, 136,480; 2d, 65,760; 2½d, 66,080; 4d, 83,280; 6d, 62,720; 1/-, 54,240; 2/-, 42,560; 3/-, 42,720.

1944-5 As CW 5-8, but watermark NZ Star (multiple).

18	2/6 **brown** (3/45)	1.50	£6
	a watermark inverted (11/51)	7.50	12.50
19	5/- **green** (red) (11/44)	£4	7.50
	a watermark inverted (5/54)	3.50	£9
20	10/- **rose-carmine** (11/45)	£25	£75
	a watermark inverted	£35	£75
21	£1 **pink** (11/45)	£23	£40
18/21	**set** (4)	£55	£115

Number issued 18, 11,920; 18a, 8,000; 19, 19,920; 19a 24,000; 20, 7,600; 20a, 11,920; 21, 12,000.

1950 (July 3rd) Designs, ½d (map of Niue); 1d (Capt. Cook's vessel 'Resolution'); 2d (Alofi Landing); 3d (Native hut); 4d (arch at Hikutavake); 6d (Alofi Bay); 9d (fish spearing); 1/- (cave at Makefu); 2/- (bananas); 3/- (Matapa Chasm). Designer, J. Berry. Printers (recess) Bradbury, Wilkinson. Watermark NZ Star (multiple) (sideways inverted on 1d, 2d, 3d, 4d, 6d and 1/-). Perf 14 x 13½ (C) vertical format, or 13½ x 14 horizontal format. Sheets 12 x 10 or 10 x 12.

22	½d **blue and red-orange**	.10	.60
23	1d **sepia and green**	£1	1.35
24	2d **black and rose-carmine**	.60	£1
25	3d **blue and dull violet**	.10	.15
26	4d **olive-green and chocolate**	.10	.15
27	6d **emerald and orange-chestnut**	.50	.75
28	9d **orange-red and brown**	.10	.85
29	1/- **deep purple and black**	.10	.15
30	2/- **orange-brown and myrtle-green**	1.50	2.85
31	3/- **deep blue and black**	£2	2.85
22/31	**set** (10)	5.50	9.50

SPECIAL ISSUES

1937 (May 13th) Coronation. New Zealand CW S1-3, overprinted 'NIUE'.

S1	1d **carmine**	.15	.10
	a short NIUE	£6	-
S2	2½d **deep blue**	.20	.30
	a short NIUE	£8	-
S3	6d **reddish orange**	.20	.15
	a short NIUE	£8	-
S1/3	**set** (3)	.50	£1

Number issued 1d, 730,429; 2½d, 575,288; 6d, 547,000.

1946 (June 4th) Peace. New Zealand CW S19, S21, S25, S26, overprinted 'NIUE' in black or blue.

S4	1d **emerald-green**	.20	.10
S5	2d **purple** (blue)	.20	.10
S6	6d **chocolate and vermilion**	.20	.50
	a overprint double,		
	one albino	£160	-
S7	8d **black and lake** (blue)	.25	.50
S4/7	**set** (4)	.75	£1

Number printed 1d, 720,00; 2d, 720,000; 6d, 480,000; 8d, 480,000.

NORFOLK ISLAND

All stamps were printed (recess) at the Australian Note and Stamp Printing Works on unwatermarked paper, unless otherwise mentioned.

1947 (June 10th) - 1952 Design, (Ball Bay). Perf. 14 (L). Toned paper. Sheets 5 x 8.

1	½d **orange**		.40	.35
	a brown-orange (/49)		.75	£5
2	1d **purple-violet**		.25	.35
	a imperf. between stamp			
	and margin		-	-
3	1½d **green**		.25	.40
4	2d **mauve-purple**		.25	.25
	a mauve-violet (/52)		.60	.25
5	2½d **bright scarlet**		.40	.20
	a deep carmine-red (/52)		£2	1.50
6	3d **beech-brown**		.35	.40
7	4d **claret**		.85	.25
8	5½d **deep slate**		.35	.20
9	6d **purple-sepia**		.35	.20
	a purple-brown (/52)		1.75	£1
10	9d **magenta**		.60	.25
11	1/- **grey-olive**		.35	.25
12	2/- **deep bistre**		.50	.65

Colour trials in the issued perforation exist. The 1d in emerald, 2d in scarlet, 3d in ultramarine, 6d in chocolate and 1/- in grey-green exist perf 11. These were prepared for issue in 1940, but due to the war their issue did not proceed. Extant examples were stolen from stock prior to destruction.

2a it appears that most examples lack gum.

3 One example is known imperforate between stamp and bottom margin, due to a pre-perforating paper fold.

1956 (Nov) - 1959. As above but new printings and colours, on white paper. Perf. 14 (L).

13	½d **brown-orange**		2.50	£4
	a deep orange (thin paper)			
	(/58)		.80	£6
14	1d **deep violet** (8/57)		2.50	£12
	a dark violet (thin paper)			
	(/58)		£4	£16
15	1½d **deep green**		£4	£15
	a ditto (thin paper) (/58)		£8	£25

16	2d **reddish purple**	£40	£90
17	3d **green** (6/7/59)	5.50	4.50
18	2/- **deep blue** (6/7/59)	£7	£5
1/18	**set** (14)	£15	£12

13-18 were printed by Rotary Recess, similar to contemporary Australian stamps.

Stamps printed by John Ash were to be destroyed, but some exist showing Ash imprints. These were stolen.

Numbers sold ½d 1,736,000; 1d 780,000; 1½d 676,000; 2d 488,000; 2½d 368,000; 3d (CW 6) 488,000; 3d (CW 17) 160,000; 4d 370,000; 5½d 411,000; 6d 360,000; 9d 360,000; 1/- 400,000; 2/- (CW 12) 290,000; 2/- (CW 18) 120,000.

NORTH BORNEO

The stamps current in 1937, from the set first issued in 1925, were as follows: 1c, 2c, 3c, 4c, 5c, 6c, 8c, 10c, 12c, 16c, 18c, 20c/18c, 24c, 25c, 50c, $1, $2, $5, $10.

1939 (Jan. 1st) Designs, 1c (buffalo transport); 2c, 4c, 10c (indigenous fauna); 3c, 6c, 12c, 15c (native inhabitants); 8c (map of Eastern Archipelago); 20c (river scene); 25c (native craft); 50c (Mount Kinabalu); $1-$5 (Arms of North Borneo Co.). Printers (recess) Waterlow and Sons. No watermark. Perf 12½ (L). Sheets 10 x 10.

1	1c **green and red-brown**	1.50	£1
2	2c **purple and greenish blue**	2.20	£1
3	3c **blue-slate and green**	£2	1.25
4	4c **olive and purple-violet**	£5	.30
5	6c **deep blue and claret**	£4	£7
6	8c **red**	£7	£1
7	10c **violet and deep olive**	£20	3.75
8	12c **green and ultramarine**	£18	£4
	a green and light blue	£20	£6
9	15c **green and light brown**	£15	£6
10	20c **deep purple and slate**	£9	£3
11	25c **green and sepia**	£15	£8
	a centre printed double, one sideways and albino	£110	-
12	50c **chocolate and violet**	£15	£7
13	$1 **brown and carmine-rose**	£50	£12
14	$2 **violet and olive-green**	£80	£75
15	$5 **blue-slate and blue**	£225	£190
1/15	**set** (15)	£450	£285
SP1/15	**specimen perf** (15)	£375	†

Waterlow printers' samples overprinted Specimen, and imperf stamps from the printers' archive, exist.

11 A single example is known with centre showing double print, one sideways. 11a is similar but the sideways impression is uninked.

1941 (Feb. 24th) CW 1 and 2 overprinted sideways (in Sandakan) 'WAR TAX'.

16	1c **green and red-brown**	.85	2.25
	a overprinted on front and back	£380	-
17	2c **purple and greenish blue**	3.50	2.50

1945 (Dec. 17th) CW 1-15 overprinted 'BMA' ('British Military Administration').

18	1c green and red-brown	5.50	1.20
19	2c purple and greenish blue	£6	1.20
	a overprint double	£5750	-
20	3c blue-slate and green	.60	.75
21	4c olive and purple-violet	7.50	£10
22	6c deep blue and claret	.60	.75
23	8c red	1.50	.45
24	10c violet and deep olive	1.50	.25
25	12c green and blue	£3	1.80
	a green and ultramarine	4.50	£1
26	15c green and light brown	.75	.60
27	20c deep purple and slate	2.50	£1
28	25c green and sepia	£3	.90
29	50c chocolate and violet	1.75	1.20
30	$1 brown and carmine-rose	£24	£25
31	$2 violet and olive-green	£25	£22
	a overprint double	£3250	-
32	$5 blue-slate and blue	£12	£9
18/32	set (15)	£85	£70

A rectangular boxed cancellation (22 x 19 mm) inscribed 'VICTORIA/DEC 24th/1846-1946/LABUAN' was used at Victoria from December 24th-31st 1946, to commemorate the centenary of the cession of Labuan to Great Britain by the Sultan of Brunei. It may be found on all values of the above set and should not be mistaken for an overprint.

19a the double overprint exists in a vertical pair with the top stamp normal.

28 exists doubly perforated at left.

Number issued 1c, 155,000; 2c, 149,991; 3c, 330,000; 4c, 80,000; 6c, 549,952; 8c, 265,000; 10c, 134,996; 12c, 230,000; 15c, 110,000; 20c, 104,996; 25c, 80,000; 50c, 45,000; $1, 20,000; $2, 20,000; $5, 22,500.

1947 (Dec. 22nd) CW 1-15 overprinted with Royal Cypher (in black or red) to denote change in status to a Crown Colony (15th July 1946).

33	1c green and red-brown (15/12/47)	.10	.60
	a lower bar broken at right	£14	£25
	b lower bar broken at left	£12	£23
34	2c purple and greenish blue	.85	.55

35	3c blue-slate and green (red)	.10	.55
36	4c olive and purple-violet (1/9/47)	.35	.60
	a short overprint bar	£25	£25
37	6c deep blue and claret (red)	.15	.15
38	8c red (1/9/47)	.15	.15
	a lower bar broken at right	£16	£15
39	10c violet and deep olive (15/12/47)	.75	.25
40	12c green and ultramarine	1.25	1.65
	a green and blue	4.50	£5
41	15c green and light brown	1.10	.20
42	20c deep purple and slate	1.50	.55
	a lower bar broken at right	£30	£22
43	25c green and sepia	1.50	.30
	a lower bar broken at right	£45	£22
44	50c chocolate and violet	1.50	.55
	a lower bar broken at right	£45	£22
	b lower bar broken at left	£40	£20
45	$1 brown and carmine-rose	£4	£1
46	$2 violet and olive-green	£10	£11
	a imperf between stamp and left margin	-	-
47	$5 blue-slate and blue (red)	£15	£12
	a lower bar broken at left	£120	-
33-47	set (15)	£35	£27
SP33/47	specimen perf (15)	£225	†

33a, etc. lower bar broken at right R8/3.

33b, 47b lower bar broken at left R8/4, 8/8.

36a R2/2 the top bar, which is intended to block out 'THE STATE OF', is about 1 mm shorter than on the other stamps of the sheet. Illustration shows in pair with normal.

Numbers sold 1c, 906,522; 2c, 655,965; 3c, 395,883; 4c, 1,811,244; 6c, 351,954; 8c, 501,358; 10c, 483,227; 12c, 308,763; 15c, 278,553; 20c, 158,091; 25c, 263,610; 50c, 116,287; $1, 75,248; $2, 38,691; $5, 32,784.

1950 (July 1st)-52 Designs, 1c (Mount Kinabalu); 2c (native musical instrument); 3c, 4c, 5c, 10c, $1, $5 (native industries and occupations); 8c (map); 15c, 30c (native boat); 20c (Bajau Chief); 50c (Clock Tower, Jesselton); $2 (Murut with blowpipe); $10 (Arms of North Borneo Co.). Printers (photo) Harrison and Sons. Watermark Script CA. Perf 14¾ x 13¾ (C). Chalk-surfaced paper. Sheets 10 x 10.

48	1c lake-brown	.10	.75
49	2c grey-blue	.10	.30
50	3c green	.10	.10
51	4c purple-magenta	.10	.10
52	5c purple-violet	.10	.10
53	8c red-scarlet	.75	.55
54	10c purple-brown	.75	.10
55	15c bright ultramarine	£1	.40
	a blue (1/5/52)	1.50	.60
56	20c grey-brown	1.10	.10
57	30c bistre-brown	2.50	.15
58	50c carmine-lake (Jessleton)	.75	2.25
59	50c ditto (Jesselton)		
	(1/5/52)	£6	1.80
60	$1 red-orange	2.25	.60
61	$2 grey-green	4.75	9.75
62	$5 emerald-green	£9	£15
63	$10 mineral blue	£26	£48
48-63	set (16)	£50	£70

59 An error in the spelling of Jesselton necessitated a correction to the design of the 50c value.

SPECIAL ISSUE

1948 (Nov. 1st) Silver Wedding. As Aden.

S1	8c scarlet	.15	.50
S2	$10 dull purple	£13	£22

1949 (Oct. 10th) U.P.U. As Aden.

S3	8c carmine-rose	.30	.20
S4	10c brown	1.60	£1
S5	30c yellow-brown	.65	£1
S6	55c azure	.65	1.65
S3/6	set (4)	2.70	3.50

POSTAGE DUE STAMPS

The 1926-31 set (2c, 3c, 4c, 5c, 6c, 8c, 10c, 12c, 16c) remained current until 1 January 1939.

1939 (Jan 1st) Design, Crest of North Borneo Co. Printers (recess) Waterlow and Sons. Perf. 12½ (L). No watermark. Sheets 10 x 5.

PD1	2c chocolate-brown	£3	£50
PD2	4c carmine-red	£3	£75
PD3	6c purple-violet	£12	£110
PD4	8c green	£13	£200
PD5	10c ultramarine	£35	£325
PD1/5	set (5)	£60	£700
SPPD1/5	specimen perf (5)	£125	†

Beware of faked cancels. No-one should purchase high values in used condition without expert committee opinion.

GERMAN PROPAGANDA LABELS

The 1944 German imitations of the G.B. 1937 Definitives, ½d to 3d (see after Great Britain for details),were also overprinted in black 'LIQUIDATION/OF EMPIRE/BORNEO' within a vertical rectangular frame.

NORTHERN RHODESIA

1938 (Mar. 1st) - 52 Designs, King's head and river scene on the Ambezi, with dug-out canoe, as used by Ba-Lia tribe, with giraffe and elephants in the foreground. Printer (recess) Waterlow and Sons. Perf 12½ (L). Sheets 1-14, 10 x 12; 15-20, 10 x 8.

1	½d **green**	.10	.10
	a C in watermark missing	-	-
	b re-entry to giraffe	£30	-
	c major re-entry	£25	-
2	½d **deep brown** (15/11/51)	.60	.90
3	1d **brown**	.10	.10
	a deep brown (15/3/48)	.75	.45
4	1d **deep green** (15/11/51)	.35	1.20
5	1½d **carmine-red**	£20	.45
	a horizontal pair imperf between	£14000	-
	b 'tick bird'	£4000	£240
6	1½d **brownish yellow** (10/1/41)	.15	.10
	a buff-yellow (3/5/44)	.25	.20
	b 'tick bird'	£55	£30
7	2d **brownish yellow**	£20	£1
8	2d **carmine-red** (10/1/41)	.35	.30
9	2d **purple-claret** (1/12/51)	.25	.90
10	3d **ultramarine**	.20	.20
	a bright ultramarine (15/3/48)	.35	.30
11	3d **scarlet** (1/12/51)	.25	1.65
12	4d **dull purple-violet**	.20	.25
13	4½d **ultramarine** (5/5/52)	£1	£5
14	6d **grey-black**	.20	.10
15	9d **violet** (5/5/52)	£1	4.50
16	1/- **deep orange and black**	1.50	.35
17	2/6 **black and green**	£4	2.75
	a black and blue-green (/42)	5.50	3.25
18	3/- **purple-violet and blue**	£8	£8
19	5/- **grey and dull grey-purple**	£8	£8
	a grey and dull reddish purple (3/5/44)	£10	£8
20	10/- **green and black**	£9	£12
21	20/- **rose-carmine and mauve-purple**	£25	£34
1/21	**set** (21)	£90	£75
SP1/21	**specimen perf** (15)	£325	†

1b re-enty resulting in giraffe with doubled neck. R12/2, Plate 2.

1c the vertical lines at right (trees, elephant, frame) are clearly doubled. R3/3, unnumbered plate.

4 exists in coil form.

5a Very few examples exist. Forgeries are known and an Expert Society Certificate is essential.

1b   5b, 6b

5b, 6b R7/1 a bird-like object near the head of the smaller elephant.

Many values show numerous 'T' guidemarks in the crown. Numerous re-entries exist; we list only the two most outstanding.

1952 (Dec. 10th) As No 2, but perf 12½ x 13¾ (C).

22	½d **deep brown**	.70	3.75

22 exists in coil form.

SPECIAL ISSUES

1937 (May 12th) Coronation. As Antigua.

S1	1½d **carmine-red**	.15	.20
S2	2d **yellow-brown**	.20	.20
S3	3d **blue**	.30	.75
	a hyphen variety	-	-
S1-3	**set** (3)	.60	£1
SP S1/3	**specimen perf** (3)	£48	†

NORTHERN RHODESIA

S3a R9/6 hyphen between 'Northern' and 'Rhodesia'. Constant on a small number of sheets only.

1946 (Nov. 26th) Victory. As Aden.

(a) Perf 13¾ x 14 (C).

S4	1½d **reddish orange**	.35	.45
S5	2d **carmine-red**	.10	.30
SP S4/5	**specimen perf** (2)	£68	†

(b) Perf. 13¾ x 13¼ (C).

S6	1½d **reddish orange**	4.50	7.50

1948 (Dec. 1st) Silver Wedding. As Aden. 20/- printed wholly (recess).

S7	1½d **orange**	.15	.10
S8	20/- **maroon-lake**	£25	£36

Number issued 1½d, 1,268,590; 20/-, 23,135.

1949 (Oct. 10th) U.P.U. As Aden.

S9	2d **carmine-rose**	.10	.20
S10	3d **indigo**	£1	1.50
S11	6d **grey**	.50	£1
S12	1/- **orange**	.35	.60
S9-12	**set** (4)	1.75	£3

Number issued 2d, 306,280; 3d, 208,120; 6d, 239,042; 1/-, 167,602.

POSTAGE DUE STAMPS

1929 Printer (typo) De La Rue. Perf 13¾ x 14 (C). Smooth paper. Sheets of 60.

GD1	1d **grey-black**	1.25	1.50
GD2	2d **grey-black**	£2	£2
GD3	3d **grey-black**	1.50	£18
GD4	4d **grey-black**	4.75	£20

These stamps are printed on thin smooth paper and generally have brown gum.

1945 As before but printed on rough paper.

PD1	1d **black**	£3	£3
PD2	2d **black**	£3	£4
PD3	3d **black**	£3	£20
PD4	4d **black**	£5	£25
PD1/4	**set** (4)	12.50	£47

White gum, thick paper with a coarse impression.

1952 As before, but printed on chalk-surfaced paper.

PD5	1d **black** (23/1/52)	£12	£60
PD6	3d **black** (23/1/52)	3.50	£50

WATERMARK VARIETIES (TYPE A)
(See Introduction for details)

PD5b	1d **St. Edward's Crown**	-	-
PD6a	3d **Missing Crown**	£300	-
PD6b	3d **St Edward's Crown**	£140	-

MKUSHI POSTAGE DUE PROVISIONAL

1953 (Aug.) 1d., (No. 4) is known overprinted in red by typewriter 'Postage Due 1d'.

NYASALAND

1938 (Jan. 1st) - 45 (recess) Waterlow and Sons. Perf 12½ (L). Sheets 6 x 10.

1		½d **green**	.15	£1
2		½d **brown** (15/12/42)	.10	1.35
3		1d **brown**	1.25	.20
4		1d **green** (15/12/42)	.15	£1
5		1½d **carmine**	2.50	£3
6		1½d **grey** (15/12/42)	.15	£4
	a	imperf between stamp and margin	£2500	-
7		2d **grey**	3.75	.75
8		2d **carmine** (15/12/42)	.15	£1
	a	imperf between stamp and margin	£3000	-
	b	'A' of watermark missing	-	-
9		3d **deep blue**	.50	.50
10		4d **magenta**	1.30	£1
11		6d **purple-violet**	1.30	£1
12		9d **sage-green**	1.30	2.25
13		1/- **black and deep orange**	1.75	1.50

6a Sheets numbered 606-8 were imperforate between the right vertical row of 10 and the margin.

8a A sheet was issued with the lower row imperforate between stamp and margin, providing 6 examples of the error.

Typo, De La Rue. Perf. 14 x 13¾ (C). Watermark Multiple Script CA (except No. 18 - Multiple Crown CA). Sheets 12 x 5.

14	2/- **purple and bright blue on grey-blue** (ch)	4.50	8.50
15	2/6 **black and carmine on grey-blue** (ch)	5.50	£10
16	5/- **green and red on yellow** (ch)	£25	£15

a deep green & carmine/pale
yellow (sub) (6/3/44) £40 £75

17 10/- **green and red
on green** (ch) £25 £35

a blue-green and red
on green (sub) (1/38) £150 £225

18 £1 **purple and black/
salmon-red (ch)** £20 £22

a flaw on 'G' £500 -

1/18 **set** (18) £85 £100

SP1/18 **specimen perf** (18) £550 †

14 examples may be found showing a grid-like
background to the central vignette.

17a there is distinct 'flecking' on
the central vignette. This is a
much-misidentified stamp, since
although there was only one printing
of 17, shades exist on chalky
paper).

18a R4/5 a flaw on the 'G' of
'POSTAGE' resembling a serif.

Number printed; 2/-, 164,340; 2/6, 61,740; 5/-,
30,600; 5/- CW 16a 8,460; 10/- 25,440; 10/- CW
17a 4,560; £1 32,220.

**1945 (Sept. 1st) - 52 Designs, ½d, 9d (Lake
Nyasa); 1d (K.A.R. soldier); 1d, (leopard);
1½d, 6d (tea estate); 2d, 1/-, 10/- (map of
Nyasaland, etc.); 3d, 2/- (fishing village); 4d,
2/6 (tobacco plantation); 5/-, 20/- (King
George VI and Badge of Protectorate).
Printers (recess) Bradbury, Wilkinson. Perf
12 (L). Sheets 10 x 6 or 6 x 10.**

19 **½d black and chocolate** .25 .10

20 **1d black and deep green
(soldier)** .10 .40

21 **1d cinnamon and
emerald (leopard)**
(20/10/47) .25 .15

22 **1½d black and greenish slate** .15 .30

23 **2d black and red** .75 .50

24 **3d black and blue** .15 .20

25 **4d black and claret** £1 .50

26 **6d black and violet** 1.50 .55

27 **9d black and olive-green** 1.25 1.80

28 **1/- indigo and myrtle-green** 1.25 .15

29 **2/- green and lake-brown** £4 2.75

30 **2/6 deep green and
grey-blue** 4.25 3.25

31 **5/- mauve and slate** £3 £4

a purple and deep slate
(7/2/52) £5 £5

32 10/- **deep red-claret and
green** £9 £9

33 £1 **scarlet and grey-black** £12 £17

19/33 **set** (15) £35 £37

SP19/33 **specimen perf** (15) £250 †

SPECIAL ISSUES

1937 (May 12th) Coronation. As Antigua.

S1 **½d green** .15 1.20

S2 **1d deep brown** .25 .75

S3 **2d grey-black** .25 1.80

S1/3 **set** (3) .60 3.50

SP S1/3 **specimen perf** (3) £75 †

1946 (Dec. 16th) Victory. As Aden.

S4 **1d pale green** .10 .20

S5 **2d reddish orange** .15 .20

SP S4/5 **specimen perf** (2) £60 †

1948 (Dec. 15th) Silver Wedding. As Aden.

S6 **1d green** .10 .10

S7 **10/- dull purple** £8 £16

1949 (Oct. 10th) U.P.U. As Aden.

S8 **1d green** .15 .15

a 'A' of watermark missing £425 -

S9 **3d deep greenish blue** 1.10 2.40

S10 **6d purple** .25 .45

S11 **1/- dull indigo** .15 .30

S8/11 **set** (4) 1.50 £3

**1951 (May 15th) Diamond Jubilee. Design,
Arms of Territory and original Arms of British
Central Africa. Printers (recess) Bradbury,
Wilkinson. Perf 11 x 11¾ (C). Sheets 12 x 5.**

S12 **2d black and scarlet** .60 .90

S13 **3d black and grey-blue** .60 .90

S14 **6d black and violet** .60 1.20

S15 **5/- black and slate-blue** £2 4.50

S12/15 **set** (4) 3.50 6.75

Number issued 2d,546,591; 3d, 108,211; 6d,
128,140; 5/-, 58,737. Withdrawn August 14th,
1951.

POSTAGE DUE STAMPS

1950 (July 1st) Printers (typo) De La Rue. Perf 13¾ x 14. (C).

PD1	1d **scarlet**	£2	£18
PD2	2d **ultramarine**	7.50	£18
PD3	3d **green**	7.50	£4
PD4	4d **lake**	12.50	£35
PD5	6d **orange**	£18	£110
PD1/5	**set** (5)	£42	£165

Many used examples were cancelled 'by favour'.

PAKISTAN

All stamps are without watermark, except overprinted issues of India. Perforations are comb throughout.

1947 (Oct. 1st) Stamps of India (Nos 20-32 and 13-19) overprinted PAKISTAN at Nasik.

1	3p **slate**	.15	.10
2	½a **purple**	.15	.10
3	9p **green**	.15	.10
4	1a **rose-carmine**	.15	.10
5	1½a **slate-purple** (typo)	.30	.10
	a watermark inverted	-	-
6	2a **vermilion**	.15	.15
7	3a **bright violet**	.15	.15
8	3½a **blue** (typo)	.45	1.40
9	4a **brown**	.15	.15
10	6a **greenish blue**	.50	.75
11	8a **violet-slate**	.20	.35
12	12a **deep crimson**	.50	.15
13	14a **purple**	1.50	£2
14	1r **violet-grey and brown**	1.50	.75
	a pair, with/without ovpt.	£450	-
	b overprint inverted	£120	-
	c overprint double	£300	-
	d watermark inverted	£50	£30
15	2r **reddish purple and brown**	1.50	1.50
16	5r **deep green and deep blue**	2.25	2.50
17	10r **violet-purple and red-claret**	2.25	2.75
18	15r **chocolate and deep green**	£32	£65
19	25r **slate-violet and purple-violet**	£35	£65
1/19	**set** (19)	£70	£100

14a, b these errors were all typographed Karachi prints. As such, they are theoetically beyond the scope of this catalogue but are included for convenience. 14c is reported both from Nasik and Karachi. Similar varieties exist on other values.

1948 As before, but overprinted at Karachi.

20	1a3p **bistre**	.60	1.25

There were a great many local overprints, as well as the Nasik prints listed above. Overprinting (similar to 1-19) was also officially done at the Government Printing Presses at Peshawar and at Karachi from plates made in Lahore and, later, at Karachi. Local handstamps, both rubber and metal, may be found and provide a fertile field for collectors. Early Karachi printings (from unworn plates) are virtually indistinguishable from Nasik prints.

Overprints and handstamps may be found on KGV issues. Forgeries are extensive. Enthusiasts are referred to the book by Ron Doubleday and Usman Ali Isani, 'Pakistan Overprints on Indian Stamps and Postal Stationery 1947-1949'. Potential enthusiasts are advised that the book is heavy!

1948 (Aug. 14th) Designs, 3p, 6p, 9p (scales of Justice); 1a, 1½a, 2a (star and moon facing right); 2½a, 3a, 4a (Lloyds Barrage); 3a, 10a (Karachi Airport); 6a, 8a, 12a (Karachi Port Trust); 1r, 2r, 5r (Salimullah Hostel, Dacca University); 10r, 15r, 25r (Khyber Pass). Printers (recess) De La Rue, Rangoon; 10-25r perforated 13¼ x 13, Security Printing Corp., Karachi, from De La Rue plates. Sheets 21-25, 160; two panes, each 10 x 8; other anna values (except 3a, 10a,) 10 x 8; 28, 32, 35-37, 5 x 16; 38-40, 10 x 6.

21	3p **vermilion-red** 12¼ x 12½	.10	.10
	a perf 13½ (5/54)	.75	.60
	b imperf (pair)	-	-
22	6p **purple-violet** 12¼ x 12½	.60	.10
	a perf 13½ (/54)	1.50	1.65
	b imperf (pair)	-	-
23	9p **myrtle-green** 12¼ x 12½	.20	.10
	a perf 13½ (/54)	1.25	£1
	b imperf (pair)	-	-
24	1a **dark blue** 12¼ x 12½	.10	.30
25	1½a **dull myrtle** 12½	.10	.10
26	2a **vermilion-red** 12¼ x 12½	1.25	.40
27	2½a **green** 14 x 13½	£2	£5
28	3a **green** 13¾ x 14	3.50	.60
	a imperf (pair)	-	-
29	3½a **ultramarine** 14 x 13½	£2	3.50
30	4a **red-brown** 12¼ x 12½	.50	.10
	a imperf (pair)	-	-
31	6a **deep blue** 14 x 13½	£1	.30
32	8a **dark grey** 12¼ x 12½	.50	.75
33	10a **carmine-red** 13¾ x 14	£3	5.50

34	12a **red** 14 x 13½	3.50	.60
35	1r **bright ultramarine**		
	13¾ x 14	£4	.10
	a perf 13½ (/54)	7.50	3.75
36	2r **chocolate-brown**		
	13¾ x 14	£9	.40
	a perf 13½ (5/54)	£12	1.20
37	5r **rose-crimson** 13¾ x 14	£8	£1
	a perf 13½ (5/54)	£6	.15
38	10r **magenta** 14 x 13¾	5.50	£15
	a perf 11¾	£50	£5
	b perf 13¼ x 13 (/51)	£9	1.25
39	15r **blue-green** 14 x13¾	£9	£12
	a perf 11¾	£9	£45
	b perf 13¼ x 13 (27/7/57)	£10	£20
40	25r **purple-violet** 14 x 13¾	£25	£70
	a perf 11¾	£16	£22
	b perf 13¼ x 13		
	(1/11/54)	£24	£21
21/40	**set** (20)	£60	£45

The high values of this set are often offered as genuinely used, when in fact they have fiscal cancels. Usually these are larger than the normal CDSs.

De La Rue's plates for the 3p-5r values were handed over in the early 1950s.

We are advised that minor variations of the perforations listed above exist.

1949 As before, but design altered; moon turned from right to left, from a waning moon to a waxing moon (3a and 10a centres re-drawn). Perf 12½ values printers (recess) De La Rue, perf 13½ values Pakistan Security Printing Corporation. Sheets as before.

44	1a **dark blue**	£2	.50
	a perf 13½ (/52)	2.75	.10
45	1½a **dull myrtle**	1.75	.50
	a perf 13½ (/53)	1.75	.10
	ab printed on gummed side	£40	-
46	2a **vermilion-red**	2.25	.10
	a perf 13½ (/52)	2.25	.10
47	3a **green**	£7	.60
48	6a **deep blue**	£7	1.20
49	8a **dark grey**	£7	1.50
50	10a **carmine-red**	£11	1.95
51	12a **red**	£12	.35
44/51	**set** (8)	£45	5.50

SPECIAL ISSUES

1948 (July 9th) Independence. Designs, 1½a (Constituent Assembly Buildings, Karachi); 2½a (Karachi Airport entrance); 3a (Lahore Fort Gateway); 1r (crescent and stars). All designs incorporating date 15th Aug., 1947. Designer, 1r A.R. Chughtai. Printers (recess) De La Rue. Perf 11¾ (1r) and 13¾ x 14 (other values). Sheets S1-3, 5 x 16; S4 10 x 6.

S1	1½a	deep ultramarine	.60	£1
S2	2½a	green	.60	.15
S3	3a	chocolate-brown	.60	.20
S4	1r	deep scarlet perf 11¾	.60	.40
	a	deep scarlet perf 14 x 13¾	2.25	£13
S1/4		set (4)	£2	1.50

1949 (Sept. 11th) 1st Anniversary, death of M. A. Jinnah. Design, inscription in Arabic (1½a and 3a) and in English (10a). Printers (recess) De La Rue. Perf 13¾ x 14. Sheets 5 x 16.

S5	1½a	brown	1.10	.90
S6	3a	green	1.10	.90
S7	10a	black	£3	£5
S5/7		set (3)	4.75	£6

Number issued S5/6 2,000,000 each; S7, 1,500,000.

1951 (Aug. 14th) 4th Anniversary of Independence. Designs, 2½a and 3½a (vase and plate); 3a and 12a (aeroplane and hourglass); 4a and 6a (leaf pattern in Saracenic style); 8a and 10a (Muslim arch and lamp). Designer, A. R. Chughtai. Printers (recess) De La Rue, later Pakistan Security Printing Corporation. Perf 13 x 13¼. Sheets 8 x 10.

S8	2½a	red	.85	.75
S9	3a	red-purple	.50	.10
S10	3½a	blue (Die 1)	.60	3.25
		a Die 2 (12/56)	1.75	£3
S11	4a	olive-green	.35	.10
S12	6a	brown-orange	.50	.10
S13	8a	deep brown	2.25	.15
S14	10a	purple	.90	1.35
S15	12a	deep green-blue	.90	.10
S8/15		set (8)	£6	£5

Die 1   Die 2

S10a Characters in bottom right tablet redrawn; lower two transposed.

OFFICIAL STAMPS

1947 (Oct. 1st) Official Stamps of India (O9, etc.) overprinted 'PAKISTAN' at Nasik.

O1	3p	slate	1.20	1.35
O2	½a	deep purple	.20	.10
O3	9p	green	2.50	2.25
O4	1a	rose-carmine	.20	.10
		a watermark inverted	-	£15
O5	1½a	slate-purple	.20	.10
		a watermark inverted	£15	£7
O6	2a	vermilion	.20	.15
O7	2½a	purple-violet	3.50	5.75
O8	4a	deep brown	.60	.90
O9	8a	violet-slate	.85	£15
O10	1r	violet-grey and brown	.40	1.50
O11	2r	reddish purple and brown	£3	3.50
O12	5r	deep green and deep blue	£11	£28
O13	10r	violet-purple and red-claret	£32	£85
O1/O13		set (13)	£50	£120

1948 No. O14 of India overprinted 'PAKISTAN' at Karachi.

O13a 1a3p **bistre**   £4   £14

The comments following 1-20 also apply to the Official overprints. Manuscript and typewritten overprints also exist. There are double and inverted overprints, but none are Nasik prints. On the low values, Karachi prints can be difficult to distinguish from Nasik due to the size of the overprints.

1948 (Aug. 14th) No. 21, etc., overprinted 'SERVICE' in black or red.

O14	3p **vermilion-red**	.10	.10
O15	6p **purple-violet (red)**	.10	.10
O16	9p **myrtle-green (red)**	.10	.10
O17	1a **dark blue (red)**	1.75	.10
O18	1½a **dull myrtle (red)**	1.60	.10
O19	2a **vermilion-red**	.75	.10
O20	3a **green**	£12	7.50
O21	4a **red-brown**	.85	.10
O22	8a **dark grey (red)**	1.20	£6
O23	1r **bright ultramarine**	.60	.10
O24	2r **chocolate-brown**	£6	£6
O25	5r **rose-carmine**	£24	£10
O26	10r **magenta** 14 x 13¾	£9	£38
	a perf 11¾	£12	£40
	b perf 13¼ x 13	£9	£48
O14/O26 **set** (13)		£50	£60

1948   1953

Similar issues but with a larger overprint and different perforations were issued in 1953.

1949 No. 44, etc., overprinted 'SERVICE' in black or red.

O28	1a **dark blue (red)**	1.75	.10
O29	1½a **dull myrtle (red)**	1.10	.10
	a overprint inverted	-	£35
O30	2a **vermilion-red**	1.25	.10
	a pair, one overprint omitted	-	£140
	b overprint inverted	-	-
O31	3a **yellow-green**	£15	3.50
O32	8a **dark grey (red)**	£25	12.50
O28/O32 **set** (5)		£40	£14

O30b one example is known.

Considerable care has to be exercised in buying copies of O29a O30a and O30b. An Expert Committee certificate is advisable.

1951 (Aug. 14th) Stamps similar in design, etc., to Nos. S9, S11 and S13, but with the word 'SERVICE' substituted for 'PAKISTAN POSTAGE'.

O33	3a **red-purple**	3.75	£6
O34	4a **olive-green**	£1	.10
O35	8a **deep brown**	£4	2.50
O33/O35 **set** (3)		£8	£8

BAHAWALPUR

One of the Princely States within the Empire of India. Its Muslim ruler acceded to Pakistan on October 3rd 1947, after a brief period of independence following the partition of India on 15th August 1947. Since 1950 the stamps of Pakistan have been used exclusively within the former State, although State stamps are seen with postmarks up to 1953.

All stamps are recess-printed by De La Rue on paper watermarked Multiple Star and Crescent.

The State non-Service stamps are generally found unused as they were never approved for postal use by the Imperial authorities. However, used examples exist, the vast majortiy of which are cancelled to order or forged or illicitly-applied cancellations. Quantities have appeared in various U.K auctions in recent years and must be treated with grave suspicion.

1933 (Feb. 3rd) Centenary of Alliance with Britain. No watermark. Perf 14.

X1   1a black on green   £8   -

Also in 1933, a set of 6 pictorial stamps were printed in quantity. As the State failed to secure approval for postal use they saw some fiscal service on court documents. Mint examples survive, with the three highest denominations being the most common. These three were also overprinted for service use and produced O9-O11. At the beginning of this century the Royal archives were reopened, after protracted legal proceedings following the Amir's death in 1966. This is the source of a few hundred fiscal documents bearing these stamps.

1947 (Aug.) Independence from India. Stamps of India (CW 20-23, 25-32, 13-17 watermark Multiple Star) with the name 'India' blocked out, and overprinted with a Star and Crescent and Persian one-line inscription ('The God-given Kingdom of Bahawalpur'). In red on Nos 2, 4, 6, 8, 9, 11, 12, 16 and 17; remainder in black.

2	3p **slate**	£14	-
3	½a **purple**	£14	-
4	9p **green**	£14	-
5	1a **carmine**	£14	-
6	1½a **dull violet**	£14	-
7	2a **vermilion**	£14	-
	a overprint double	£2400	
8	3a **bright violet**	£14	-
9	3½a **blue**	£14	-
10	4a **brown**	£14	-
11	6a **greenish blue**	£14	-
	a overprint double	£2400	
12	8a **slate-violet**	£14	-
13	12a **lake**	£14	-
14	14a **purple**	£45	-
15	R1 **grey and red-brown**	£18	-
	a overprint double, once albino	£275	
16	Rs2 **purple and brown**	£1600	-
17	Rs5 **green and blue**	£1600	-
18	Rs10 **purple and claret**	£1600	-
2/18	**set** (17 - 3p/10R)	£4800	-
2/15	**set** (14 - 3p/1R)	£220	-

Number issued - 2-15, 480 each; 16-18, 60 each.

There has been considerable philatelic debate over the legitimacy of this issue. Briefly, Imperial India ceased to exist on the stroke of midnight on the 14th August 1947 with the creation of Pakistan and independent India. Theoretically at least, the former Indian States had a choice as to which country they wished to accede. Most decided immediately but a few, including Bahawalpur, deliberated. This State eventually chose Pakistan on the 3rd of October and therefore enjoyed some form of independence in the six-week interim. It is in this interval that 2-18 are said to have been issued. Correspondence from the archive reveals that De La Rue sent dies from England for the Star and Crescent overprint on the 27th June 1947 for approval. It is therefore conceivable that these dies were used to make a trial printing at the Bombay facilities of the printer. This would account for the limited numbers and by the time they were received by the State, Bahawalpur had acceded to Pakistan rendering them obsolete. What is undisputed is that the mint stock was then acquired by a London dealer. It also appears that a few examples were retained by the Amir and used on internal official correspondence in 1947.

2 exists in trial vertical strips of 10; the top 6 stamps with no overprint, 3 with black overprint and the bottom stamp with the overprint double (once in red and once in gold).

6, 10 exists in vertical strips, only the central stamp showing the overprint double.

30	R1	violet and brown	£9	£32
31	R1	green and orange	.85	£13
32	Rs2	green and claret	£28	£55
33	Rs2	black and carmine	.85	£16
34	Rs5	black and violet	£28	£70
35	Rs5	chocolate and ultramarine	.95	£30
36	Rs10	scarlet and black	£15	£75
37	Rs10	brown and green	£1	£35
20/37		set (18)	£90	£430

1948 (Oct. 3rd) First Anniversary of Union with Pakistan. Perf. 13. Sheets 5 x 10.

38	1½a carmine and green	.75	2.75

Number issued - 500,000.

1947 (Dec. 1st) Bicentenary of Abassi dynasty. Watermark sideways. Perf 12½ x 11½. Sheets 5 x 10.

19	½a black and carmine	1.50	£3

Number issued - 500,000.

1948 (April 1st) various palaces and portraits. Watermark sideways on vertical designs. Perf. 12½ (Nos. 20-24): 12½ x 11½ or 11½ x 12½ (Nos. 25-35): 13½ x 14 (36/37). Sheets 5 x 10 or 10 x 5 (except 36-37 - 4 x 10).

20	3p black and blue	£1	£15
21	½a black and claret	£1	£15
22	9p black and green	£1	£15
23	1a black and carmine	£1	£15
24	1½a black and violet	1.50	£12
25	2a green and carmine	1.50	£15
26	4a orange and brown	1.50	£15
27	6a violet and blue	1.75	£15
28	8a carmine and violet	1.75	£15
29	12a green and carmine	1.85	£24
	a green and carmine-lake	£30	-

1948 (Oct. 15th) Centenary of Multan Campaign (Sikh War). Perf. 11½. Sheets 10 x 5.

39	1½a black and lake	.65	6.75

Number issued - 500,000.

1949 (Mar. 3rd) Silver Jubilee of Accession of H.H. The Amir. Various designs. Perf 14. Sheets 5 x 10.

40	3p black and ultramarine	.10	£6
	a imperf pair	£15	-
41	½a black and brown-orange	.10	£6
	a imperf pair	£15	-
42	9p black and green	.10	£6
	a imperf pair	£15	-
43	1a black and carmine	.10	£6
	a imperf pair	£15	-

40/43	set (4)	.30	£22

Number issued - 500,000 each.

1949 (Oct. 10th) 75th Anniversary of U.P.U. Sheets 5 x 10.

(a) Perf 13.

44	9p black and green	.10	.90
	a imperf pair	£10	£14
45	1a black and magenta	.10	.90
	a imperf pair	£10	£14
46	1½a black and orange	.10	.90
	a imperf pair	£10	£14
47	2½a black and blue	.10	.90
	a imperf pair	£10	£14
44/47	set (4)	.40	3.25

(b) Perf 17½ x 17.

48	9p black and green	.75	£14
49	1a black and magenta	.75	£14
50	1½a black and orange	.75	£14
51	2½a black and blue	.75	£14
48/51	set (4)	2.75	£50

OFFICIAL STAMPS

Permission to use State Service stamps on internal official mail was sanctioned by the Imperial authorities for issues from 1945. Later issues are mainly cancelled to order or bear forged or illicitly-applied cancellations.

1933 (Feb. 3rd) CW X1 overprinted with one-line Persian inscription 'SARKARI' ('GOVERNMENT' or 'OFFICIAL') in black probably at Lahore.

XO1	1a black on green	£450	-

XO1 forged overprints exist.

The 1a black and brown (see note under X1) was also prepared for issue with this overprint in black (Price £450).

1945 (Jan 1st) Pictorial stamps as the 1933 unissued values (see note after X1) converted for official postal use by means of a similar overprint in red. Perf 14. Sheets 10 x 10.

O2	½a black and green	£3	8.50
	a black and bluish green	£5	-
O3	1a black and carmine	2.75	6.50
	a 'Sarkark'	£125	£90
	b overprint omitted	-	£675
	c black and bright carmine	£3	-
O4	2a black and violet	1.50	7.50
	a 'Sarkark'	£60	-
O5	4a black and olive	£5	£15
O6	8a black and brown	£12	£11
	a 'Sarkark'	£125	-
	b imperf at right between stamp and margin	£1500	-
O7	R1 black and orange	£12	£11
O2/7	set (6)	£32	£55

O2a, 3c are from later printings, with white gum.

Normal   'Sarkark'

O3a/O6a R6/3 the left up-stroke of the left hand Persian letter is missing, giving the letter the shape of the Persian 'K'. The 4a is also known with an earlier stage of the variety.

O3b the 1a without overprint is known from one sheet issued at, and mostly used from, Rahimya Khan. Most examples have faults.

Numbers issued - 90,000 each.

1945 (Mar. 10th) 1933 unissued 1a, similarly overprinted in red. No watermark.

O8	1a **black and brown**	£30	£45
	a overprint in deep red	£55	£45

1945 (March) 1933 unissued values (see note after X1), similarly overprinted and surcharged in Persian with Hijra date '1363' in black. No watermark.

O9	½a/8a **black and purple**	2.75	£4
	a frame printed double, one albino	-	-
O10	1½a/R1 **black and orange**	£20	6.75
O11	1½a/Rs2 **black and blue**	£65	5.50
O9/11	**set** (3)	£80	£14

O9, O11 are known with overprint and surcharge double.

O10 a single used example with vignette double is recorded.

1945 Nos. O2 and O4 (in changed colours) and O3 overprinted 'SERVICE' in English and Persian (both reading upwards) in black. No watermark.

O12	½a **black and carmine**	.75	6.75
O13	1a **black and carmine**	£1	£8
O14	2a **black and orange**	1.50	£27
	a "SERVICE" omitted	-	-
O12/14	**set** (3)	£3	£37

O14a was caused by a paper fold, part of the overprint appearing on the reverse.

1945 As Nos. 20 and 24 but no watermark. Perf. 14. Sheets 10 x 10.

O15	3p **black and blue**	£2	£7
O16	1½a **black and violet**	£10	£5

1946 (May) Victory. Designer, E. Meronti. Background printed litho. No watermark. Perf. 14. Sheets 5 x 10.

O17	1½a **green and grey**	1.75	2.50
	a green and black	-	-

O17a may be a colour trial. It is certainly rare. Information is solicited.

Number issued - 100,000.

1948 Nos. 20, 23, 25, 26, 31, 33, 35 and 37 overprinted as Nos. O2/7 in red (O18, O22-25) or black (O19-21).

O18	3p	black and blue	.40	£8
O19	1a	black and carmine	.40	7.50
O20	2a	green and carmine	.40	£8
O21	4a	orange and brown	.40	£12
O22	R1	green and orange	.40	£13
O23	Rs2	black and carmine	.40	£18
O24	Rs5	chocolate and ultramarine	.40	£30
O25	Rs10	brown and green	.40	£30
O18/25		set (8)	£3	£115

1949 (Oct. 10th) 75th Anniversary of U.P.U. Nos. 44/51 similarly overprinted in red.

(a) Perf. 13.

O26	9p	black and green	.10	£3
	a	imperf pair	£10	£12
	b	watermark inverted	-	£75
O27	1a	black and magenta	.10	£3
	a	imperf pair	£10	£12
O28	1½a	black and orange	.10	£3
	a	imperf pair	£10	£12
O29	2½a	black and blue	.10	£3
	a	imperf pair	£10	£12
O26/29		set (4)	.40	£11

(b) Perf. 17½ x 17.

O30	9p	black and green	1.25	£20
O31	1a	black and magenta	1.25	£20
O32	1½a	black and orange	1.25	£20
O33	2½a	black and blue	1.25	£20
O30/33		set (4)	4.50	£75

PALESTINE

1932-47 Designs, 2m, 3m, 10m (Rachel's Tomb); 4m, 6m, 8m, 13m, 15m (Dome of the Rock); 5m, 7m, 20m (Tower of David); 50m-£1 (Tiberias overlooking the Sea of Galilee). Designer F. Taylor. Printers (typo) Harrison & Sons. 2m - 20m Perf 13½ x 14½ (C), 50m - £1 Perf 14 (C). Sheets 2m-20m 10 x 25, 50m - £1 10 x 20.

In 1927 this set was first issued with stamps printed on very thin paper, which was replaced by vertically-ribbed paper in 1928. The set contained 4m pink, 7m scarlet, 8m yellow-brown, 13m ultramarine and 90m brown-bistre stamps, which were all obsolete by 1932. The following stamps made up the basic set from 1932 to 1947.

A - 1932-39. Vertically-ribbed paper.

1	2m **grey-blue**	1.25	.10
	a deep blue (/39)	£1	.10
	b Arabic blackout	£15	£15
	c inverted watermark	†	£400
2	3m **yellow-green**	.75	.10
3	4m **violet**	.75	.10
	a F for E flaw	£15	£15
4	5m **orange**	1.50	.10
5	6m **deep green**	.50	.10
	a 'open door' flaw	£6	£6
6	7m **deep violet**	.35	.10
7	8m **scarlet**	.60	.10
	a inverted watermark	-	£400
8	10m **slate**	.75	.10
9	13m **brown-bistre**	£1	.10
	a Arabic 13 with foot	£10	£10
10	15m **ultramarine**	2.25	.10
11	20m **olive**	1.40	.15
12	50m **bright purple**	2.50	.30
	a reversed watermark	-	£325
13	100m **turquoise**	£3	.40
14	200m **violet**	£4	£3
	SP 3, 6-7, 9-10 **Specimen perf** (5)	£200	†

1b the Arabic inscription is partly missing on R4/7.

3a the lower bar of the 'E' in the English inscription is missing at R10/7.

5a, 18a there is a white circular flaw in the centre of the door of the mosque at R10/3.

9a There is a short tail to the Arabic number 3 at R2/16.

B - 1937. Horizontally-ribbed paper.

15	2m **grey-blue**	£250	£5
16	3m **yellow-green**	£2500	£20
17	5m **orange**	£50	.40
	a yellow-orange	£50	£1
18	6m **deep green**	£20	£1
	a 'open door'	£100	£20
19	7m **deep violet**	£35	£2
20	8m **scarlet**	£22	.50
21	10m **slate**	£200	£3
22	15m **ultramarine**	£35	£2

It is thought that these stamps were experimental printings. Used copies date from 1937.

Numerous shades exist, but as contemporary records are incomplete barely any can be allocated to specific printings.

C - 1940-47 White wove paper.

23	2m **grey blue**	£1	.10
24	3m **yellow-green**	.75	.10
	a inverted watermark	-	£180
	b English blackout	£10	£12
25	4m **purple**	.75	.10
	a inverted watermark	-	£325
26	5m **orange**	1.50	.10
	a yellow (18/12/44)	1.75	.15
	ab inverted watermark	£20	£25
27	6m **deep green**	.50	.20
	a blue-green (10/6/46)	.50	.20
28	7m **deep violet**	.35	.10
29	8m **carmine-red**	.60	.20
30	10m **slate**	.75	.10
	a brownish grey (/44)	.75	.10
	b Hebrew blackout	£15	£15
	c 'C' omitted from watermark	-	-
31	13m **brown-bistre**	£1	.10
	a Arabic 13 with foot	£15	£15
32	15m **ultramarine**	£2	.10
	a grey-blue (18/12/44)	£2	.25
	b pale blue (10/6/46)	£2	.25
	c inverted watermark	†	£400
33	20m **yellow-olive**	.75	.15
	a greenish yellow-olive (/47)	1.40	.15
	b inverted watermark	-	£280
34	50m **red-purple**	£1	.20
	a bright red-purple (/41?)	£2	.20
	b horizontal pair imperf between	†	-
35	100m **turquoise**	£1	.40
	a greenish turquoise (18/12/44)	1.50	.40
36	200m **violet**	£5	£3
	a blackish violet (/42?)	£5	£2
37	250m **brown** (15/1/42)	2.50	£2
38	500m **scarlet** (15/1/42)	2.50	£2
39	£1 **black** (15/1/42)	3.50	2.50
	a bluish black	3.50	2.50
	SP 37-39 specimen perf (3)	£125	†

The 3m, 5m, 6m, 7m, 10m, 13m and 20m are known with rough perforations.

24b part of the English inscription is missing at R4/1 on Plate 3.

30b part of the Hebrew inscription is missing (position unknown).

31a see 9a.

33a there is a greenish tinge to the colour of this stamp, best seen in the shading on the wall of the Tower. This stamp is from the sole printing of the 20m Plate 2.

Numerous shades exist, but as records are incomplete and most printings were not released in London it is impossible to allocate them to specific printings.

The Department of Posts and Telegraphs of the Mandate Government suspended services in April 1948. During April and May 1948 a wide variety of provisional issues were released. Numbers 23 to 39 were overprinted at Tiberias, Afula and Nahalal in black or violet ink with the words 'Emergency Post' (in Hebrew) and the name of the appropriate town beneath. Numbers 33/33a also exist with typeset overprint in English 'Government Tohuwabohu'.

Crude forgeries exist of all values on rough paper with glazed yellow gum and pin perforations.

D - Coil stamps. White wove paper. Perf 14½ x 14.

40	5m **deep orange** (/36)	£7	£10
	a thicker teeth on top	£8	£10
	b watermark inverted	£15	£10
	c thicker teeth on top, watermark inverted	†	£10
	d hook on wall	£10	£10
41	10m **slate** (11/38)	£10	£15
	a inverted watermark	-	-

40a at least 172 rolls of the 5m in a deep orange shade were issued with inverted watermark. All used examples known were cancelled in 1938.

40d a mark like a tick appears on early printings in deep orange. At times this flaw can consist of two superimposed tick-like lines.

41 on early printings of the 10m every fourth stamp in the roll had thin top corner teeth.

POSTAGE DUE STAMPS

1938-47 Design, value on unshaded background. Printers (typo) De La Rue. Perf 14 (C).

PD1	1m **deep brown**	.75	.50
PD2	2m **light yellow**	£1	.30
PD3	4m **deep green**	1.25	£1
PD4	6m **greyish brown**	£9	£3
PD5	8m **red-scarlet**	£1	.60
PD6	10m **slate-grey**	.75	.35
PD7	13m **ultramarine**	1.60	£1
PD8	20m **olive-bistre**	1.60	.75
PD9	50m **dark violet**	1.75	.75
SP PD1-9	**specimen opt. or perf (6m) set of 9**	£275	†

As PD1 and PD3, but perf 15 x 14 (C).

PD10	1m **deep brown** (/41)	£28	£50
PD11	4m **deep green** (/41)	£40	£60

BOOKLETS

B1	150m 1937 (?) **red cover** stapled at left; 4 panes of 6: 1 x 2m, 1 x 3m, 1 x 5m, 1 x 15m.	£1250	-

with advertisements on the front and interleaving.

B2	150m 1938 (?) **blue cover** stapled at left; 4 panes of 6: 1 x 2m, 1 x 3m, 1 x 5m, 1 x 15m	£1250	-

with advertisements on the front and interleaving.

B3	120m 1939 (?) **pink cover** 3 panes of 6: 2 x 5m, 1 x 10m	£1200	-

with advertisements on the front and interleaving.

Until 1932 booklets were printed by the Crown Agents and despatched to Palestine. After 1932 booklets were madeup locally. Little is known about locally-produced booklets. The dates given here are provisional and the list may be incomplete.

B2 stamps are known on vertically-ribbed or horizontally ribbed paper.

PAPUA

1932 (Nov. 14th) Various frames. Designers, E. Whitehouse (2d, 4d, 6d, 1/-, 10/-); F. E. Williams (2/-, £1 and frames of other values); Williams and Gibson (photos for remaining vignettes). Sheets 8 x 5. Printers J. Ash (all values): W. C. G. McCracken ½d (CW 1), 1d, 2d, 4d. Perf 11.

G68	½d black and orange	.85	£2
1	½d black and buff (/40)	£10	£16
G69	1d black and green	.85	.40
G70	1½d black and lake	.85	£5
G71	2d scarlet	£6	.20
G72	3d black and blue	1.75	£4
G73	4d olive-green	£4	£6
G74	5d black and slate-green	1.50	£2
G75	6d bistre-brown	3.75	3.75
G76	9d black and lilac	£5	£14
G77	1/- blue-green	2.25	5.50
G78	1/3d black and deep purple	£8	£16
G79	2/- black and slate-green	8.50	£16
G80	2/6d black and maroon	£15	£28
G81	5/- black and olive-brown	£35	£35
G82	10/- lilac	£55	£65
G83	£1 black and olive-grey	£135	£120
G67-83	set (16)	£250	£290

This set remained in use until 1942.

SPECIAL ISSUES

1937 (May 14th) Coronation. Printer J. Ash (Recess). Sheets 5 x 8. Perf 11.

S1	1d green	.25	.15
	a 'Halo' flaw	£25	£30
S2	2d scarlet	.25	.75
S3	3d blue	.25	.75
S4	5d lake-purple	.25	£1
S1-4	set (4)	.90	2.40

S1a R5/2, Plate 1a. A crescent of lighter tone with thinner horizontal lines in the background, following the shape of the back of the head, gives the appearance of a halo.

Numbers issued; S1, 500,000; S2, 490,500; S3, 504,000; S4, 480,000. Remainders were withdrawn on December 31st, 1937.

1938 (Sept. 6th) 50th Anniversary of Declaration of British Possession. Design, Port Moresby. Printers (Recess) J. Ash. Sheets 5 x 8. Perf 11.

S5	2d rose-red	1.50	1.80
S6	3d bright blue	1.50	1.35
S7	5d green	1.50	£2
S8	8d brown-lake	£3	£9
S9	1/- mauve	£9	£10
S5-9	set (5)	£15	£22

Remainders were withdrawn on September 6th, 1939.

1939 (Sept. 6th) - 41 Air Mail. Sheets 5 x 8.

(a) Printers (recess) J. Ash (6 September 1939). Perf 11.

S10	2d rose-red	1.50	£3
S11	3d bright blue	1.50	£6
S12	5d green	1.50	1.50
S13	8d brown-lake	£4	£2
S14	1/- mauve	£5	5.50

(b) Printers (recess) W.C.G. McCracken (2 January 1941). Perf 11½.

S15	1/6 dull olive	£15	£22
S10-15	set (6)	£26	£36

PATIALA
SEE
INDIA

PENANG, PERAK, PERLIS
SEE
MALAYA

PITCAIRN ISLANDS

From 7th June 1927 until the Pitcairn Islands stamps were issued, a New Zealand Postal Agency operated and comtemporary stamps of New Zealand were used and cancelled with a named datestamp.

1940 (Oct. 15th) - 52 Designs, ½d (oranges); 1d (Christian on Bounty, and Pitcairn Is.); 1½d (John Adams and his house); 2d (Bligh and Bounty); 3d (map); 4d (Bounty Bible); 6d (Bounty); 8d (school); 1/- (Christian and Pitcairn Is.); 2/6d (Christian on Bounty and Pitcairn coast). 1d, 3d, 4d, 8d, 2/6d printed (recess) Bradbury, Wilkinson, perf. 11½ x 11¼ (C), sheets 6 x 10; ½d, 1½d, 2d, 6d, 1/- printed (recess) Waterlow and Sons, perf 12½ (L), sheets 5 x 12.

1	½d **red-orange and green**	.20	.35
2	1d **purple and magenta**	.25	.50
	a purple and lake-magenta (4/12/52)	.75	£1
3	1½d **grey and carmine**	.25	.30
	a grey and rose-carmine (13/11/44)	.75	£1
4	2d **green and red-brown**	.90	.90
5	3d **yellow-green and deep blue**	.60	.90
	a watermark inverted	£2600	-
6	4d **black and green** (1/9/51)	£9	6.75
7	6d **chocolate and greenish slate**	2.50	£1
	a brown and greenish slate (13/11/44)	2.50	2.25
8	8d **green and purple** (1/9/51)	£11	4.50
9	1/- **purple-violet and slate-grey**	£2	1.50
10	2/6d **green and red-brown**	5.50	2.50
1/10	**set** (10)	£29	£17
SP 1/10	**specimen perf** (8)	£950	†

SPECIAL ISSUES

1946 (Dec. 2nd) Victory. As Aden.

S1	2d **chocolate-brown**	.30	.20
	a flaw by launch	£25	-
	b flaw retouched	£25	-
S2	3d **deep blue**	.30	.20
	a flagstaff flaw	£25	£24
SPS1/2	**specimen perf** (2)	£275	†

S1a   S1b   S2a

S1a, b R6/3 a very large flaw in the river, retouched with limited success.

S2a R8/2 vertical streak to right of main tower.

1949 (Aus. 1st) Silver Wedding. As Ascension.

S3	1½d **scarlet**	£1	.90
S4	10/- **slate-violet**	£20	£30

1949 (Oct. 10th) U.P.U. As Aden.

S5	2½d **beech-brown**	.50	2.50
S6	3d **indigo**	£4	2.50
S7	6d **green**	£2	2.50
S8	1/- **purple**	£2	2.50
S5/8	**set** (4)	£8	£9

BOOKLETS

B1	4/8d **1940** black on green card, interleaved	
	CW 1-5, 7, 9-10	£2250 -

Booklets have been made up from extra covers supplied to Pitcairn Island. Care is necessary when purchasing. The locals would row out to the visiting ships and sell them booklets for postage. These were sold at 10/- (the extra 5/4d being a charge for rowing out to the ship). The surcharges were in manuscript on the front cover.

ST CHRISTOPHER, NEVIS AND ANGUILLA
SEE
ST. KITTS-NEVIS

ST HELENA

1938 (May 12th) - 1951 Design (Badge of Colony; three-masted sailing vessel, flying St George's Cross, off Headlands, King and Queen Rocks). (Recess) Waterlow and Sons. Perf 12½ (L). Sheets 6 x 10.

1	½d **violet**	.10	.40
2	1d **green**	5.50	1.35
3	1d **orange-yellow** (8/7/40)	.15	.20
	a deep yellow (/45)	£10	£10
4	1d **black and green** (1/11/49)	.60	.90
5	1½d **scarlet**	.15	.75
	a carmine-red (24/5/44)	.15	.25
6	1½d **black and carmine-rose** (1/11/49)	.60	.90
7	2d **orange**	.20	.35
	a pale red-orange (24/5/44)	.10	.10
8	2d **black and carmine** (1/11/49)	.60	.90
9	3d **ultramarine**	£35	£12
10	3d **grey** (8/7/40)	.20	.50
	a slate (25/5/44)	.15	.20
11	4d **ultramarine** (8/7/40)	£1	1.10
	a bright ultramarine (24/5/44)	£1	£1
12	6d **dull light blue**	£1	1.20
	a sky blue (24/5/44)	1.50	1.40
13	8d **sage-green** (8/7/40)	1.60	.60
	a olive-green (24/5/44)	2.25	2.50
	b deep olive-green (8/11/51)	£5	£10
14	1/- **sepia**	£1	£1
	a deep sepia (4/6/50)	.60	.30
15	2/6 **claret**	£9	£4
	a bright claret	£10	£5
16	5/- **light chocolate-brown**	£9	7.50
17	10/- **deep purple**	£9	£11
1/17	**set** (17)	£65	£38
SP1/17	**specimen perf** (14)	£300	†

Nos 1, 3, 5, 7, and 10 are known overprinted 'ROYAL VISIT/29TH. APRIL./1947', but the status of the overprint is doubtful. 3 and 7 have been seen with this overprint preceded by 'FIRST'.

SPECIAL ISSUES

1937 (May 19th) Coronation. As Ascension.

S1	1d **green**	.20	.45
S2	2d **orange**	.25	.25
S3	3d **blue**	.40	.30
S1-3	**set** (3)	.80	.90
SP1/3	**specimen perf** (3)	£65	†

1946 (Oct. 21st) Victory. As Aden

S4	2d **reddish orange**	.20	.30
S5	4d **grey-blue**	.20	.20
SP4/5	**specimen perf** (2)	£65	†

1948 (Oct. 20th) Silver Wedding. As Aden

S6	3d **black**	.15	.20
S7	10/- **slate-violet**	12.50	£23

1949 (Oct. 10th.) U.P.U. As Aden

S8	3d **carmine-rose**	.15	.60
S9	4d **indigo**	1.50	£1
S10	6d **dull olive**	.20	1.35
S11	1/- **slate-black**	.20	.65
S8/11	**set** (4)	1.85	3.30

ST. KITTS-NEVIS

1938 (Aug. 15th)-50 Designs, ½d, 1d, 1½d, 2½d (King's Head) (small format), Perf 13¾ x 14 (C), sheets 120 - two panes, each 6 x 10. 2d, 3d, 1/-, 2/6 (King's Head and Seal of Nevis, Hygiea administering Stream of Life); 6d, 5/- (King's Head and Seal of St. Kitts, Columbus sighting island of St. Christopher) (large format), Perf 13 x 11¾ (C). Printers (typo) De La Rue. Sheets 5 x 12.

1	½d **green**		1.50	.15
	a deep dull green (/43)		.20	.10
	b dull blue-green (/44)		.10	.10
2	1d **red**		£2	.45
	a deep rose-red (4/5/43)		.50	.30
	b rose-red (/41)		.50	.30
	c rose-pink (23/4/47)		£40	£12
	d dull rose-red (/49)		.50	.50
3	1½d **orange**		.30	.20
	a dull orange (/43)		.20	.20
	b pale yellow-orange (/44)		.10	.20
4	2d **scarlet and grey**		£8	£2
	a scarlet and slate (ch) (/40)		£16	£6
5	2½d **pale ultramarine**		1.20	.20
	a ultramarine (4/5/43)		.30	.30
	b bright blue (/44)		.75	.20
6	3d **dull lilac and dull red**		£6	3.75
	a pale dull claret and dull red (ch) (/40)		£6	£5
7	6d **dull green and deep purple**		£2	1.50
8	1/- **greyish black and green**		£3	£1
9	2/6 **greyish black and red**		£9	£6
10	5/- **dull green and red**		£19	£14
SP1/10	**specimen perf** (10)		£175	†

With the exception of Nos. 4a and 6a all the above are on uncoated paper.

No 2c is considerably paler than other printings and care in purchasing should be exercised.

5 The colours can cause some confusion. The ultramarine of the 1938 issue can vary from dull to bright: the paper is thicker than for later issues and the gum generally brown. The 1943 and 1944 printings have white paper and clear gum and have been picked to represent the two main groups of the later printings.

As Nos. 5-10, but perf 14 (L).

11	2d **scarlet and grey** (/41)	.50	1.65	
	a scarlet and deep grey (/42)	£8	£5	
	b scarlet and grey (ch) (28/7/49)	£2	1.95	
12	3d **dull mauve and scarlet** (ch) (/42)	£14	£3	
	a reddish lilac and scarlet (sub) (4/5/43)	1.75	£40	
	b dull reddish lilac and scarlet (sub) (/45)	£15	£12	
	c deep violet and scarlet (ch) (/46)	£55	£40	
	d dull reddish lilac and red (sub) (/47)	£6	5.50	
	e pale dull rose-lilac and red (ch) (/48)	£5	£7	
	f dull mauve and vermilion-red (ch) (7/6/50)	£3	4.75	
13	6d **dull green and dull claret** (ch) (/42)	£25	£8	
	a dull green and deep reddish purple (sub) (/41?)	£4	£1	
	b pale dull green and red-purple (sub) (/43)	£5	£4	
	c pale blue-green and pale reddish purple (sub) (/47)	3.50	£5	
	d pale dull green and reddish purple (ch) (/48)	2.75	2.50	
14	1/- **black and green** (sub) (4/5/43)	1.50	.50	
	a black and green (ch) (28/7/49)	£4	3.50	
15	2/6 **black and scarlet** (ch) (/42)	£60	£5	
	a black and scarlet (sub) (4/5/43)	£6	£3	
	b black and scarlet-vermilion (ch) (/49)	9.50	£5	
16	5/- **greyish green and deep rose-red** (ch) (/42)	£55	£20	
	a dull blue-green and scarlet (sub) (4/5/43)	£10	£9	
	b dull green and vermilion (ch) (7/6/50)	£20	£45	

1948 (Sept. 1st) Design, map of Islands. Frame typo, map litho. Perf. 13¾ x 14 (C). Chalk-surfaced paper. Sheets 6 x 10.

17	10/- **black and deep blue**	£6	£12
18	£1 **black and chocolate-brown**	£6	£14
1/18	**set** (12)	£30	£40

It should be noted that many of the inks used in printing this set were soluble in contact with water. Hence, many used stamps are unclassifiable - 'used on piece' is the ideal way to collect them.

12, 13, 15 and 16 have horizontally-rippled gum. Supplies were sent to the Colony in December 1941, but not put on sale until several months later.

12b has a very poorly-defined head plate. 12c head plate shades of this printing vary considerably, but the deep shade is outstanding.

6d perf 14. CW 13 has horizontally-rippled gum (the dull claret frame helps with used examples). 13d is on very white chalk-surfaced paper. 13, b, and c are relatively close.13a has much the reddest frame and is on very glossy paper with the frame colour showing through to the back. 13b and c appear much pinker. 13c has more blue in the vignette than either 13 or 13a.

The shades listed above are the main sub-divisions. Shades can vary considerably, even within the same printing. For a detailed analysis, see P.L. Baldwin's monograph 'A Study of the King George VI Stamps of St Kitts-Nevis 1938-50', 2nd edition, 1997 published by Murray Payne Ltd.

VARIETIES

Type A   Type B   Type C

Type A: Break in value tablet. A weak area at top right of right value tablet, R12/5. 1947 printing only.

Type B: Break above 'K'. A break in the frame below head oval at 5 o'clock, R12/1 1938 printing only.

Type C: Break in value tablet. A break at base of stroke after '1', in right value tablet. R3/2, 1938-50 printings.

IDENTIFICATION - ST. KITTS 3d, PERF 14

The 3d perf 14 is one of the more difficult KGVI stamps to identify. We hope that this chart will make life a little easier.

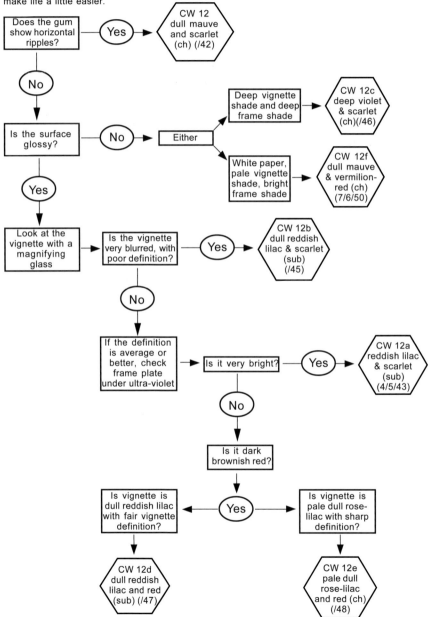

Type D	Type E	Type F

Type D: Break above 'T'. A notch in ornamental frame above 'T'. R2/4, 1942-50 printings.

Type E: Break in frame at left. R7/1, 1942-45 printings.

Type F: Break in value tablet. Notched frame at base of stroke after '5' in right value tablet. R12/3, 1942-45 printings.

Type G	Type H	Type I

Type G: Break above 'I' of 'KITTS'. A large break in frame below head oval at 5 o'clock. R12/5, 1941-45 printings. Often found retouched by hand at the printers.

Type H: Frame flaw. A major frame break occurs at the top right of the frame. R1/3, 1950 printing only.

Type I: Dented frame. A dent occurs above the right value tablet. R2/5 1940-50 printings.

6a	3d	Type I	£55	-
12		Type I	£50	-
12a		Type I	£30	-
12b		Type I	-	-
12c		Type I	-	-
12d		Type A	£120	-
12d		Type I	£35	-
12e		Type I	£35	-
12f		Type I	£30	-
7	6d	Type B	£100	-
8	1/-	Type C	£120	-
14		Type C	£65	-
14a		Type C	£90	-
16	5/-	Type D	£375	-
16a		Type D	£175	-
16b		Type D	£225	-
16		Type E	£375	-
16a		Type E	£175	-
16		Type F	£375	-
16a		Type F	£175	-
16		Type G	£375	-
16a		Type G	£175	-
16b		Type H	£195	-

1952 (June 14th) Designs, 1c (Bath House, Nevis); 2c (Warner Park, St. Kitts); 3c (map of islands); 4c (Brimstone Hill, St. Kitts); 5c (Nevis from sea); 6c (Pinney's Beach, Nevis); 12c (Sir T. Warner's tomb, St. Kitts); 24c (Old Road Bay, St. Kitts); 48c (cotton plantation, Nevis); 60c (Treasury, St. Kitts); $1.20 (salt pond, Anguilla); $4.80 (sugar factory, St. Kitts). Printers (recess) Waterlow and Sons. Perf 12½ (L). Sheets 5 x 10 or 10 x 5.

19	1c olive-green and orange-buff	.10	.90
20	2c emerald-green	.45	.60
21	3c red and violet	.15	.75
22	4c red	.10	.15
23	5c blue and grey	.15	.10
24	6c ultramarine	.15	.10
25	12c blue and brown	.60	.10
26	24c black and deep red	.15	.10
27	48c olive-green and chocolate	£1	1.65
28	60c orange and deep green	.90	1.80
29	$1.20 green and ultramarine	3.50	1.65
30	$4.80 emerald and carmine	£7	£12
19/30	set (12)	£13	£18

SPECIAL ISSUES

1937 (May 12th) Coronation. As Ascension.

S1	1d scarlet	.15	.15
S2	1½d light brown	.20	.10
S3	2½d blue	.30	£1
S1-3	set (3)	.60	1.10
SP S1/3	specimen perf (3)	£65	†

1946 (Nov. 1st) Victory. As Aden.

S4	1½d orange	.10	.10
S5	3d carmine-red	.10	.10
SP S4/5	specimen perf (2)	£60	†

1949 (Jan 3rd) Silver Wedding. As Aden.

S6	2½d ultramarine	.10	.30
S7	5/- rose-carmine	3.50	2.50

1949 (Oct. 10th) UPU. As Aden.

S8	2½d dull violet-blue	.10	.20
S9	3d carmine	£1	1.50
S10	6d reddish mauve	.10	£1
S11	1/- quartz-green	.10	.25
	a 'A' of watermark missing	-	£375
S8/11	set (4)	1.20	2.65

1950 (Nov. 10th) Tercentenary of British Settlement in Anguilla. As nos. 2-8, but nos. S15-17 new printings on chalk-surfaced paper, perf 13x12½ (c) overprinted by the De La Rue in black or red.

S12	1d **rose-red**	.10	.10
S13	1½d **orange**	.10	.30
S14	2½d **blue**	.10	.10
S15	3d **dull purple and red**	.20	.45
	a Type I	£10	£10
S16	6d **dull green and red-purple**	.15	.10
S17	1/- **black and green (red)**	.50	.15
	a Type C	£12	£12
S12/17	**set** (6)	£1	1.10

S15a and S17a see flaw listing after 1938 definitive set.

WATERMARK VARIETIES (TYPE B)
(See Introduction for details)

S13a	1½d **Crown missing**	£1750	-
S13b	**St Edward's Crown**	£850	-

1951 (Feb. 16th) West Indies University College. (See Antigua)

S18	3c **black and orange**	.15	.10
S19	12c **green and lake-magenta**	.15	1.20

ST LUCIA

1938 (Sept. 22nd)-48 Designs, ½d-3d, 8d, 3/-, £1 (King's Head), Printer Waterlow and Sons, Perf 14¾ x 14 (C); 6d (Columbus Sq., Castries); 1/- (Govt. House, Morne Belle Vue), Printer De La Rue, Perf 13½ (C); 2/- (The Pitons); 10/- (Device of Colony), Printer Bradbury, Wilkinson, Perf 12 (L); 5/- (loading bananas on "C.N.S." Liner), Printer Waterlow and Sons. Perf. 12½ (L). Sheets - small format 15 x 8; large format 6 x 10.

1	½d **green**	.80	.10
2	1d **violet**	1.40	.45
3	1d **scarlet** (20/9/48)	.40	.10
4	1½d **scarlet**	.80	.25
5	2d **grey**	1.50	.90
6	2½d **ultramarine**	1.60	.10
7	3d **orange**	.50	.10
8	6d **claret**	2.75	.45
	a bright claret (22/5/43)	£3	.75
	b lake-claret (30/7/45)	1.50	.20
9	1/- **brown**	.60	.20
	a light brown (22/5/43)	.75	.40
10	2/- **blue-black and deep claret**	£2	.75
11	5/- **black and deep purple**	£6	6.75
12	10/- **black/yellow**	4.50	5.50

Designs as No. 1, but perf 12½ and additional values (L).

13	½d **green** (22/5/43)	.10	.10
	a blue-green (8/2/46)	.25	.20
14	1d **violet** (22/9/38)	.10	.10
15	1d **scarlet** (8/4/47)	.10	.10
16	1½d **scarlet** (22/5/43)	.60	.75
17	2d **grey** (22/5/43)	.10	.10
18	2½d **ultramarine** (22/5/43)	.15	.15
	a dull blue (8/2/46)	.10	.10
19	2½d **violet** (8/4/47)	.40	.10
20	3d **orange** (22/5/43)	.10	.10
21	3½d **ultramarine** (1/4/47)	.45	.10

22	8d chestnut-brown		
	(8/2/46)	£2	.20
	a chocolate-brown (8/2/46)	1.75	.20
23	3/- magenta (8/2/46)	£5	£1
24	£1 sepia (8/2/46)	5.50	£5
1/24	set (17) cheapest perfs	£25	£18
SP1/24	specimen perf (17)	£300	†

As Nos. 8-9, but Perf. 12 (C).

25	6d lake-claret (23/2/48)	£1	1.20
26	1/- light brown (23/2/48)	.35	.20

1949 (Oct. 1st) Currency changes. Designs, 1c-16c, as ½d etc. above, Printers (recess) Waterlow, Perf 12½ (L); other values, as 10/- above but name of country below Device of Colony. (Recess) Bradbury, Wilkinson. Perf 11¼ x 11½ (C). Sheets as before.

27	1c green	.10	.10
28	2c deep magenta	.40	.10
29	3c scarlet	.60	1.35
30	4c slate-grey	.50	.10
31	5c violet	.70	.10
32	6c orange	.50	£2
	a imperf between		
	stamp and margin	-	£8000
33	7c ultramarine	1.60	1.75
34	12c brown-lake	2.75	2.25
35	16c deep chocolate	£2	.30
36	24c deep and pale blue	.25	.10
37	48c deep and pale olive	.75	.75
38	$1.20 deep and pale		
	purple-violet	1.10	£5
39	$2.40 deep and pale green	1.50	£10
40	$4.80 deep and pale		
	carmine-red	£5	£12
27/40	set (14)	£16	£32

1949 (Nov. 19th)-52 As Nos. 27, 28, 30 and 34, but 1c perf 14 (L), others. Perf 14¾ x 14 (C).

41	1c green	£1	.25
	a block of four	£60	-
42	2c deep magenta	1.25	.75
	a block of four	£40	-
43	4c grey (/50)	†	£12000
44	12c brown-lake (/52)	£375	£325

32a - A sheet was discovered imperforate between left margin and the first vertical row of stamps. Separated into two singles and three pairs (eight examples in total), they were placed on five covers and postmarked SOUFRIERE 1 Oct., 49. One pair is damaged.

41a, 42a A few 1c and 2c were also issued in sheet form - most being from coils. Almost all examples from the coils have clipped perforations.

43 - Forgeries of this variety exist in mint condition and an expert committee certificate is advised when purchasing this stamp. Most used examples are cancelled at 'PATIENCE'.

SPECIAL ISSUES

1937 (May 12th) Coronation. As Antigua.

S1	1d violet	.15	.20
S2	1½d carmine-red	.25	.15
S3	2½d deep blue	.25	.75
S1/3	set (3)	.60	£1
SPS1/3	specimen perf (3)	£65	†

1946 (Oct. 8th) Victory. As Aden

S4	1d lilac	.10	.10
S5	3½d dull blue	.10	.10
SPS4/5	specimen perf (2)	£55	†

Number Issued; 1d 720,360, 3½d 613,800

1948 (Nov. 26th) Silver Wedding. As Aden

S6	1d scarlet	.10	.10
S7	£1 brownish purple	8.50	£22

1949 (Oct. 10th) U.P.U. As Aden

S8	5c dull violet	.10	.40
S9	6c deep orange	.80	1.35
	a 'A' of watermark missing	£400	-
S10	12c reddish mauve	.10	.15
S11	24c quartz-green	.15	.15
S8/11	set (4)	£1	1.90

Numbers issued (Colony only) - 5c, 38,519; 6c, 31,194; 12c, 7,610; 24c, 7,104

1951 (Feb. 16th) West Indies University College. (See Antigua).

S12	3c black and red	.20	.30
S13	12c black and claret-red	.30	.30

Numbers issued (Colony only) - 3c, 49,972; 12c, 45,500

1951 (June 19th) Castries Reconstruction. Design, Phoenix rising from the flames of burning Castries. Printer (flames typo, frame recess) Bradbury, Wilkinson. Perf 13½ x 13 (C). Sheets 6 x 10.

S14 12c **scarlet and deep blue** .10 .60

1951 (Sept. 25th) New Constitution 1951. Nos. 28, 30, 31, 34 overprinted in black.

S15	2c **deep magenta**	.10	.50
S16	4c **slate-grey**	.10	.35
S17	5c **violet**	.10	.50
S18	12c **brown-lake**	.35	.35
S15/18	**set** (4)	.60	1.50

Numbers issued 2c, 146,000; 4c, 107,420; 5c, 114,011; 12c, 90,918.

POSTAGE DUE STAMPS

Beware of anonymous or dubious cancels, especially where the price differential between mint and used is substantial.

1933-47 Printers (typo) De La Rue. Perf. 13¾ x 14 (C.). Sheets 6 x 10.

PD1	1d **black**	£2	£4
PD2	2d **black**	£8	£5
	a rough paper	£20	-
PD3	4d **black** (25/6/47)	3.50	£35
PD4	8d **black** (25/6/47)	3.50	£40

SPPD1/4 **specimen perf** (4) £120 †

PD 2a the paper in 1933 was smooth. In the early 1940s a printing of the 2d on rough paper was made.

1949 (Oct. 1st) As before, but currency changed. Uncoated paper.

PD5	2c **black**	.90	£18
PD6	4c **black**	1.75	£15
PD7	8c **black**	1.60	£18
PD8	16c **black**	7.50	£50
PD5-8	**set** (4)	£10	£90

1952 (Nov. 27th) Chalk-surfaced paper.

PD9	2c **black**	.10	£6
PD10	4c **black**	.25	£7
PD11	8c **black**	1.50	£28
PD12	16c **black**	2.25	£35
PD9-12	**set (4)**	3.75	£70

WATERMARK VARIETIES (TYPE A)
(See Introduction for details)

PD9a	2c **Crown missing**	£100	-
PD9b	**St Edward's Crown**	£22	-
PD10a	4c **Crown missing**	£160	-
PD10b	**St Edward's Crown**	£32	-
PD11b	8c **St Edward's Crown**	£225	-
PD12b	16c **St Edward's Crown**	£300	-

GERMAN PROPAGANDA LABELS

The 1944 German imitations of the GB 1937 definitives, ½d to 3d (See after Great Britain for details) were also overprinted in black 'LIQUIDATION/OF EMPIRE/Sta. LUCIA' within a vertical rectangular frame.

ST VINCENT

1938 (Mar. 11th) - 47 Designs, ½d, 2d, 3d, 6d, 2/-, £1 (Badge of Colony); 1d (Young's Island and Fort Duvernette); 1½d (Kingstown and Fort Charlotte); 2½d, 3½d, (bathing beach, Villa); 1/- (Victoria Park, Kingstown). Printers (recess) Bradbury, Wilkinson. Perf 12 (L). Sheets 6 x 10 or 10 x 6.

1	½d	**blue and green**	.10	.10
		a blue and blue-green (7/47)	.20	.10
2	1d	**deep blue and lake-brown**	.15	.10
		a deep blue and deep purple-brown (25/9/44)	.10	.10
3	1½d	**emerald & rose-carmine**	.30	.10
		a blue-green and scarlet (/43)	.15	.10
4	2d	**dull green and black**	.50	.30
		a green and grey-black (/43)	.20	.20
5	2½d	**blue-black & blue-green**	.20	.25
		a indigo-black and greenish blue (/43)	£1	.75
		b slate-black and blue-green (6/5/46)	.50	.30
6	2½d	**green and purple-brown** (14/1/47)	.15	.10
7	3d	**orange and deep purple**	.15	.10
		a brownish orange and purple (4/44)	.50	.20
		b orange & dull purple (/47)	£1	.20
8	3½d	**blue-black and blue-green** (1/4/47)	.25	£1
9	6d	**black and deep lake**	.55	.40
		a black & pale purple (4/44)	£2	.25
		b black & bright purple (9/44)	£1	.60
10	1/-	**purple and green**	.50	.40
		a purple-violet and yellow-green (/43)	£1	.50
		b reddish purple and green (7/47)	1.50	.60
11	2/-	**bright blue and deep purple**	£3	.50
		a light blue and purple (7/45)	£4	£1
12	2/6	**red-brown and steel-blue** (14/1/47)	.60	2.25
13	5/-	**crimson and myrtle-green**	£7	£3
		a deep crimson and grey-green (7/45)	£5	1.50
14	10/-	**violet and sepia-brown** (14/1/47)	£2	£5
		a wmk inverted (1947?)	£6500	£2250
15	£1	**purple-violet and black**	£12	£12
		a cold purple and grey-black (4/43)	£12	£9
1/15		**set** (15)	£22	£18
SP1/15		**specimen perf** (15)	£250	†

Printings from 1943 onwards were on thinner, whiter paper than earlier releases.

3 examples with vermilion frames are changelings.

1949 (Mar. 25th) As 1, etc., but currency changed. Sheets 6 x 10.

16	1c	**blue and green**	.10	£1
17	2c	**deep blue and lake-brown**	.10	.30
18	3c	**green and scarlet**	.25	.60
19	4c	**green and black**	.20	.15
20	5c	**green and grey-brown**	.10	.10
21	6c	**orange and deep purple**	.20	.75
22	7c	**blue-black and greenish blue**	2.25	.90
23	12c	**black and deep lake**	.20	.10
24	24c	**purple and green**	.20	.35
25	48c	**blue and deep purple**	1.25	2.40
26	60c	**red-brown & steel-blue**	£1	2.50
27	$1.20	**deep crimson and myrtle-green**	£2	2.50
28	$2.40	**violet and sepia-brown**	£3	£6
29	$4.80	**purple-violet and black**	£6	£12

1952 (June 10th) As 16, etc., but colours changed, and new values. (31 and 33 have designs interchanged in relation to 18 and 21).

30	1c	**green and black**	.15	1.50
31	3c	**orange and deep purple**	.15	1.50
32	4c	**blue and green**	.15	.15
33	6c	**green and scarlet-rose**	.15	1.35
34	10c	**blue-black and greenish blue**	.25	.10
16/34		**set** (19)	£16	£30

SPECIAL ISSUES

1937 (May 12th) Coronation. As Antigua.

S1	1d	**violet**	.15	.75
S2	1½d	**carmine-red**	.20	.75
S3	2½d	**deep blue**	.20	1.35
S1-3		**set** (3)	.50	2.50
SP S1/3		**specimen perf** (3)	£58	†

1946 (Oct. 15th) Victory. As Aden.

S4	1½d **carmine-red**	.10	.10
S5	3½d **deep blue**	.10	.10
SP S4/5	**specimen** perf (2)	£52	†

Number issued; ½d 864,180, 3½d 790,680.

1948 (Nov. 30th) Silver Wedding. As Aden.

S6	1½d **scarlet**	.10	.10
S7	£1 **red-purple**	£11	£15

The £1 'Wedding' stamp was originally printed in black, but as the colony's supply was stolen in transit, another printing in red-purple was made. There is a block of four in black in the Royal Collection.

1949 (Oct. 10th) U.P.U. As Aden.

S8	5c **dull ultramarine**	.10	.10
S9	6c **purple-violet**	.75	1.35
S10	12c **reddish mauve**	.10	1.35
S11	24c **quartz-green**	.10	.60
S9/11	**set** (4)	£1	£3

1951 (Feb. 16th) West Indies University. (See Antigua).

S12	3c **green and red**	.15	.40
S13	12c **black and claret**	.15	£1

1951 (Sept. 21st) New Constitution. 18, etc., overprinted in black.

S14	3c **green and scarlet-rose**	.10	£1
S15	4c **green and black**	.10	.35
S16	5c **green and grey-brown**	.10	.35
S17	12c **black and deep lake**	.60	.75
S14/17	**set** (4)	.80	2.20

Number issued - 3c, 91,098; 4c, 138,992; 5c, 117,329; 12c, 97,204.

SAMOA

1935 (Aug. 7th) Designs, ½d (girl and Kava bowl); 1d (Apia); 2d (river scene); 2½d (chief and wife); 4d (canoe and house); 6d (R. L. Stevenson's home, Vailima); 1/- (R. L. Stevenson's tomb); 2/- (Lake Lanuto'o); 3/- (Falefa Falls). Designers, ½d L.C. Mitchell; 2½d; centre L. C. Mitchell, frame J. Berry; 6d W. J. Cooch; others, J. Berry. Printers (recess) De La Rue. 2d perf 14; others, perf 13½ x 14 (horizontal designs) or perf 14 x 13½ (vertical designs). Watermark 'NZ Star' (single). Sheets 10 x 8 (horizontal designs) or 8 x 10 (vert. designs).

G84	½d **yellow-green**		.10	.20
	a watermark inverted		-	-
G85	1d **black and carmine**		.10	.10
G86	2d **grey-black and orange**	1.75	£2
	a watermark inverted		-	-
	b perf 13½ x 14		£2	2.50
	ba watermark inverted		-	-
G87	2½d **black and deep blue**		.10	.10
G88	4d **black and sepia**		.35	.10
	a grey and sepia		.30	.10
G89	6d **bright magenta**		.20	.10
	a magenta		.25	.10
G90	1/- **violet and grey-brown**	.15	.10
G91	2/- **deep green and**			
	deep brown		.40	.30
G92	3/- **grey-blue and**			
	orange-brown		.75	2.20
G84/92	**set** (9)		3.50	4.75

Number printed - G84, 480,000; G85, 720,000; G86, 240,000; G87, 120,000; G88, 200,000; G89, 156,000; G90, 120,00; G91, 60,000; G92, 60,000.

1935 (Aug. 7th)-42 Arms stamps of New Zealand overprinted 'WESTERN SAMOA' in black or red. Watermark 'NZ Star' (single). Perf 14. Sheets 10 x 8.

(a) Cowan paper.

G93	2/6 **deep brown**		£3	£12
G94	5/- **green**		£7	£15

G95 10/- **carmine-lake** £28 £45
G96 £1 **pink** £28 £70
G97 £2 **bright violet** (R) £75 £250
G98 £5 **indigo-blue** (R) £125 £350

Number overprinted - G93, 7,840; G94, 7,920; G95, 7,760; G96, 7,840.

Values above £5 exist. They were primarily for fiscal purposes although some were undoubtedly cancelled by favour.

(b) Wiggins Teape paper.

G99 5/- **green** (1942) £60 £90
G100 10/- **pale carmine-lake** (41) £60 £100
G101 £2 **bright purple** (R) (42) £300 £500
G102 £5 **indigo-blue** (R) (42) £1200 £1500

Number overprinted - G99, 3,840; G100, 4,000.

1940 (Sept. 2nd) Design, Samoan chief. Printers (recess) Bradbury, Wilkinson. Perf 14 x 13½ (C) . Sheets 10 x 8.

1 3d/1½d **brown** .35 .10

See note after Cook Islands CW4.

Number printed - 400,000.

1942-9 Designs, ½d (Samoan girl with Kava bowl); 2d (river); 2½d (Samoan chief and wife); 5d (Post Office, Apia). Printers (recess); 5d, Bradbury, Wilkinson; other values, De La Rue. Sheets as before. Watermark 'NZ Star' (multiple), 2½d sideways.

(a) Perf 14 x 14½ (C) (2d C and L).

2 ½d **yellow-green** (5/47) .15 £12
3 2d **black and red-orange**
(5/42) 1.50 £4
4 2½d **black and deep blue**
(2/49) £3 £23

(b) Perf 13½ x 14 (C).

5 5d **black and blue**
(8/6/49) 1.10 .30
2/5 **set** (4) £5 £35

3 the 2d value changed from line to comb perforation in August 1945.

Number issued - 2/3, 400,000 each; 4/5, 1,000,000 each.

1945-50 Design as G98, etc overprinted 'WESTERN SAMOA' in red or blue. Perf 14 (C). Watermark 'NZ Star' multiple.

6 2/6 **brown** (6/45) £3 £11
a watermark inverted £7 £10
7 5/- **green** 7.50 £10
a watermark inverted £15 £12
8 10/- **rose-carmine** (4/46) £8 £10
a watermark inverted £20 £22
9 £1 **dull pink** (6/46) £50 £125
10 30/- **brown** (8/48) £85 £240
a watermark inverted - -
11 £2 **violet (red)** (11/47) £90 £200
a watermark inverted £165 £350
12 £3 **green** (8/48) £120 £320
13 £5 **blue-black (red)**
(31/1/50) £140 £350
a watermark inverted £150 £375
6/13 **set** (8) £450 £1150

See note below G98.

Number issued - 6, 44,400; 7, 35,840; 8, 19,520; 9, 8,000; 10, 7,440.

SPECIAL ISSUES

1939 (Aug. 29th) 25th Anniversary of control by New Zealand. Designs, 1d (coastal scene); 1½d (map); 2½d (dancing party); 7d (Robert Louis Stevenson). Designer, 1d and 1½d J. Berry, 2½d and 7d L. C. Mitchell. Printers (recess) Bradbury, Wilkinson. Perf 14 x 13½ (C) Sheets 8 x 10 or 10 x 8. Watermark 'NZ Star (multiple).

S1 1d **sage and scarlet** .50 .15
S2 1½d **light blue and chestnut** .85 .45
S3 2½d **red-brown and deep blue** .75 .60
S4 7d **violet and greenish slate** £4 2.40
S1/4 **set** (4) 5.50 3.25

Number printed - S1, 240,000; S2, 160,00; S3, 120,000; S4, 120,000.

1946 (June 1st) Peace. New Zealand CW S19, etc., overprinted 'WESTERN SAMOA' in black or blue.

S5	1d **emerald-green**	.20	.10
	a watermark inverted	£125	-
S6	2d **purple (blue)**	.20	.10
S7	6d **chocolate and**		
	vermilion	.20	.10
S8	8d **black and**		
	lake (blue)	.20	.10
S5/8	**set** (4)	.70	.40

Number printed - S5, 720,000; S6, 720,000; S7, 528,000; S8, 480,000.

SARAWAK

1934 (May 1st). Design, Sir Charles Vyner Brooke. Printers (recess) Bradbury, Wilkinson. No watermark. Perf 12. Sheets 10 x10.

G74	1c **purple**	.60	.10
G75	2c **green**	.75	.10
G76	3c **black**	.60	.10
G77	4c **bright purple**	£1	.10
G78	5c **violet**	£1	.10
	a imperf. between		
	stamp and margin	-	†
G79	6c **carmine**	1.35	.35
G80	8c **red-brown**	1.10	.10
G81	10c **scarlet**	1.50	.25
G82	12c **blue**	1.50	.15
G83	15c **orange**	£3	£6
G84	20c **olive-green and**		
	carmine	2.75	.75
G85	25c **violet and orange**	2.75	.90
G86	30c **red-brown and violet**	2.75	1.50
G87	50c **violet and scarlet**	3.50	.45
G88	$1 **scarlet and sepia**	1.10	.45
G89	$2 **bright purple and**		
	violet	£9	£11
G90	$3 **carmine and green**	£19	£24
G91	$4 **blue and scarlet**	£19	£40
G92	$5 **scarlet and red-brown**	£24	£40
G93	$10 **black and yellow**	12.50	£45

G78a one sheet was imperforate between the left hand margin and the first vertical row.

1941 (Mar. 1st). As before, but new colours.

1	2c **black**	1.90	£1
2	3c **deep green**	3.50	2.75
3	6c **maroon-brown**	3.75	£5
4	8c **carmine**	£4	.10
5	12c **deep orange**	£3	£3
6	15c **deep blue**	£4	£9
G74/6	**set** (26)	£115	£175
SPG74/6	**specimen perf** (26)	£475	†

2 on paper watermarked Multiple Script CA, see CW 29a.

Sarawak was occupied by the Japanese from December 17th, 1941 to September 9th, 1945. Nos. G74/93 and 1/6 remained in use until they were replaced by overprinted Japanese stamps on October 1st, 1942.

During the occupation, Sarawak, North Borneo and Brunei were administered as a single territory (North Borneo), and the stamps of all three States were later overprinted and used throughout the whole area.

Immediately following the re-occupation by Australian Forces, internal mail was carried free and bore neither stamps nor postmarks; but from October 29th, 1945 Australian stamps (1d, 3d, 6d, 1/-) were used on external mail.

At Baram (alternative name Marudi), Australian stamps were not available and the Civil Affairs Officer (C. B. Murray) produced a provisional stamp, typed on paper cut from a ruled accounts book. The typed inscription was in four lines, 'Postage Paid/15 cents/ C.A.O./ MARUDI'. Each example was initialled by Mr. Murray and cancelled with the District Office mark and the Baram cds (in black or violet). '8 cents' labels also exist.

1945 (Dec. 17th) British Military Administration. Nos. G74/93 and 1/6 overprinted 'BMA' in black sans-serif letters (in red on CW 8, 11, 18 and 26). Setting 10 x 10.

7	1c **deep purple**	.60	.35
8	2c **black**	1.10	.75
	a overprint double	£8000	£6000
9	3c **deep green**	.60	.90
10	4c **purple-magenta**	1.10	.20
	a overprint double, once albino	£1500	–
11	5c **violet**	1.60	.60
12	6c **maroon-brown**	1.50	.45
13	8c **carmine**	6.50	8.50
14	10c **red**	.75	.40
15	12c **deep orange**	1.25	2.25
16	15c **deep blue**	2.75	.25
17	20c **olive-green and deep carmine**	1.50	1.65
18	25c **purple-violet and orange**	1.75	1.65
19	30c **red-brown and violet**	3.25	1.65
20	50c **violet and deep red**	.60	.20
21	$1 **scarlet and sepia**	1.25	1.80
22	$2 **deep magenta and violet**	4.50	£9
23	$3 **carmine and green**	£11	£45
24	$4 **blue and red**	12.50	£30
25	$5 **scarlet and chocolate**	£80	£145
26	$10 **black and deep yellow**	£75	£145
7/26	**set** (20)	£190	£350

8a the two overprints are close together.

During the period of Military Administration the area continued to be administrated as a single territory, and the North Borneo BMA stamps were also sold in Sarawak. These BMA issues were withdrawn from sale in Sarawak on April 25th, 1946, although they remained valid for use until July 31st 1946; and they continued in use in North Borneo and Brunei until 1947.

Numbers issued - 7, 65,000; 8, 80,000; 29, 1,300,000; 30, 420,000; 31, 440,000; 32, 780,000, 33, 210,000; 34/35/38 330,000 each; 36, 170,000; 37, 220,000; 39, 160,000; 40, 130,000; 41, 75,000.

1947 (April 16th). Crown Colony status. Nos. G74/92 and 1/6 reprinted on Watermark Multiple Script CA paper, and overprinted in black or red (Nos. 28, 29 and 35-38) with Royal Cypher.

27	1c **deep purple**	.10	.20
28	2c **black**	.10	.10
29	3c **deep green**	.10	.10
	a albino overprint	£5250	–
30	4c **purple-magenta**	.10	.10
31	6c **maroon-brown**	.15	.55
32	8c **carmine**	.50	.10
33	10c **red**	.15	.15
34	12c **deep orange**	.25	.60
35	15c **deep blue**	.25	.25
36	20c **olive green and deep carmine**	£1	.30
37	25c **purple-violet and orange**	.30	.20
38	50c **violet and deep red**	.60	.25
39	$1 **scarlet and sepia**	.75	.55
40	$2 **deep magenta and violet**	1.35	£2
41	$5 **scarlet and chocolate**	1.75	£2
27/41	**set** (15)	6.75	6.50
SP27/41	**specimen perf** (15)	£240	†

1950 (Jan. 3rd) - 52 Designs, 1c (Trogonoptera brookiana butterfly); 2c (Tarsier); 3c (Kayan tomb); 4c, 8c, 12c, 50c (indigenous peoples); 6c, 15c, $1 (local occupations); 10c (pangolin); 10c, $2 (map of Sarawak); 20c (rice barn); 25c (pepper vines); $5 (Arms of Sarawak). Recess ($5 Arms typo) Bradbury, Wilkinson. Perf 11¾ x 11½ or 11½ x 11¾ (C). Watermark Multiple Script CA. Sheets 10 x 10.

42	1c greenish grey-black	.20	.20
	a black (20/11/52)	.60	.60
43	2c orange-vermilion	.15	.25
44	3c green	.15	.35
45	4c sepia-brown	.20	.15
46	6c deep turquoise-blue	.20	.10
47	8c carmine-red	.35	.20
48	10c orange (pangolin)	.85	2.75
49	10c orange (map) (1/2/52)	.85	.30
50	12c purple-violet	1.75	.90
51	15c blue	1.25	.10
52	20c chocolate and vermilion	1.25	.20
53	25c green and carmine	1.75	.20
54	50c chocolate and purple-violet	2.50	.20
55	$1 myrtle and sepia	£10	2.70
56	$2 blue and deep carmine	£14	£9
57	$5 yellow, black, red and deep purple	11.50	£9
42/57	set (16)	£40	£24

48 an error in the drawing of the anteater necessitated replacement.

SPECIAL ISSUES

1946 (May 18th) Centenary of Brooke Dynasty. Design, portraits of Sir James Brooke, Sir Charles Vyner Brooke and Sir Charles Brooke in three panels. Recess, Bradbury, Wilkinson. Perf 12 (L). No watermark. Sheets 10 x 10.

S1	8c lake-carmine	£1	.60
S2	15c deep blue	1.10	1.20

S3	50c black and red	1.10	1.50
S4	$1 black and sepia	1.25	£16
S1/4	set (4)	£4	£17
SP S1/4	specimen perf (4)	£130	†

Japanese occupation of the territory prevented the intended issue in 1941.

Numbers issued - S1, 295,200; S2, 111,750; S3, 80,350; S4, 46,500.

1948 (Oct. 25th) Silver Wedding. As Aden.

S5	8c scarlet	.15	.20
S6	$5 chocolate	£20	£27

1949 (Oct. 10th) U.P.U. As Aden.

S7	8c carmine-rose	.60	.35
S8	15c indigo	1.75	1.50
S9	25c green	£1	.75
S10	50c dull violet	£1	£4
S7/10	set (4)	£4	£6

Five covers are known from Simunjan postmarked 21st September, having been used early in error.

SEYCHELLES

1938-49 Designs, 2c, 9c, 18c, 25c, 50c, 1r50 (Coco-de-mer palm); 3c, 12c, 15c, 30c, 75c, 2r25 (tortoise); 6c, 20c, 45c, 1r, 5r (fishing pirogue). Printers (photo) Harrison and Sons. Perf 14¾ x 13¾ (C), vertical designs; 13¾ x 14¾, horizontal designs. Chalk-surfaced paper, unless otherwise indicated. Sheets 8 x 15 or 15 x 8.

1	2c **purple-brown** (10/2/38)	.45	.25
	a purple-chocolate (sub) (18/11/42)	.15	£1
2	3c **green** (1/1/38)	3.50	1.20
3	6c **deep orange** (1/1/38)	£4	£2
4	9c **scarlet-red** (10/2/38)	£6	1.65
5	12c **mauve-purple** (1/1/38)	£14	.75
6	20c **blue** (1/1/38)	£15	3.75
7	25c **yellow-bistre** (1/1/38)	£18	8.50
8	30c **lake-claret** (10/2/38)	£18	£6
9	45c **chocolate** (10/2/38)	£8	1.50
	a brown-purple (sub) (18/11/42)	1.25	1.25
	b brown-purple (5/4/49)	£9	£8
10	50c **grey-violet** (10/2/38)	£5	.35
	a grey-violet (sub) (18/11/42)	.80	£2
11	75c **grey-blue** (10/2/38)	£30	£24
12	1r **yellow-green** (10/2/38)	£45	£35
13	1r50 **ultramarine** (1/2/38)	£12	2.75
	a ultramarine (sub) (18/11/42)	2.25	5.75
	ab watermark inverted	£2250	†
14	2r25 **olive** (10/2/38)	£18	6.75
	a olive (sub) (18/11/42)	£10	£10
15	5r **brownish red** (10/2/38)	£8	5.50
	a brownish red (sub) (18/11/42)	£10	£20

As before, but colours changed and new values. Sheets 6 x 10 or 10 x 6 (a 1949 printing of CW 25 was released in sheets 8 x 6, the last two vertical rows having been removed).

16	3c **orange** (8/8/41)	.50	.60
	a orange (sub) (18/11/42)	.25	.90
17	6c **dull grey-green** (8/8/41)	1.40	.75
	a watermark inverted	£900	-
	b green (sub) (18/11/42)	.25	1.35
	c green (5/4/49)	3.75	.75
	d moon flaw	£50	-
	e moon retouch	£25	-

18	9c **dull grey-blue** (8/8/41)	£5	.25
	a dull grey-blue (sub) (18/11/42)	£6	.90
	b dull blue (sub) (19/1145)	£3	1.80
	c dull blue (5/4/49)	£8	3.75
	d watermark inverted	-	-
19	15c **brownish carmine** (8/8/41)	£5	.25
	a brownish red (sub) (18/11/42)	2.75	2.25
20	18c **mauve-magenta** (8/8/41)	£4	.35
	a mauve-magenta (sub) (18/11/42)	£3	1.65
	b rose-magenta (5/4/49)	£11	£10
21	20c **yellow-bistre** (8/8/41)	£5	.40
	a 'fishing net' flaw	£150	-
	b yellow-bistre (sub) (18/11/42)	1.25	1.80
	ba 'fishing net' flaw	£95	£70
22	30c **blue** (8/8/41)	£5	.30
	a blue (sub) (18/11/42)	£1	2.75
23	50c **bright violet** (13/6/49)	1.75	1.50
24	75c **grey-lilac** (8/8/41)	£4	2.40
	a grey-lilac (sub) (18/11/42)	1.10	2.40
25	1r **grey-black** (8/8/41)	£8	1.95
	a grey-black (sub) (18/11/42)	£1	2.40
1/25	**set** (25)	£175	£95
SP1/25	**specimen perf** (24)	£450	†

SP 1/25 the 50ct bright violet (CW 23) was not issued in specimen form.

In general, many of the 'substitute paper' variations listed above do react to the silver test. However, the reaction is not very strong on most of these. Other indications may help; the early chalky papers often have rippled gum, and the late ones are on very white paper. The substitute paper issues often have a grainy appearance.

13ab three mint examples are known.

17d   17e

17d, e an area of damage occurs on R3/1, to the right of the value, later retouched in more than one operation.

18d one mint and one used example are known.

20b this release fluoresces strongly under UV.

'Madam Joseph' faked cancellations are frequently encountered.

21b

21ba R6/2 a substantial flaw by the hand of the standing figure resembles a thrown fishing-net.

1952 (Mar. 3rd) Designs, 2c, 40c, 10r (sailfish); 3c, 25c, 2r25 (tortoise); 9c, 50c, 1r50 (Coco-de-mer palm); 15c, 20c, 45c (pirogue); 18c, 1r, 5r (map). Printers (photo) Harrison and Sons. Perf 13¾ X 14¾ horizontal designs, 14¾ x 13¾ vertical designs. Sheets 10 x 5 or 5 x 10.

26	2c lilac	.30	.45
27	3c red-orange	.30	.20
28	9c grey-blue	.30	£1
29	15c deep yellow-green	.25	.45
30	18c terracotta-pink	.75	.15
31	20c orange-yellow	.60	.90
32	25c vermilion-pink	.35	£1
33	40c dull ultramarine	.50	.90
34	45c lake-brown	.50	.20
35	50c violet-magenta	.60	£1
36	1r grey-black	1.75	£2
37	1r50 blue	£4	8.50
38	2r25 olive	6.50	£9
39	5r dull red	£7	9.75
40	10r green	£12	£25
26/40	set (15)	£32	£55

WATERMARK VARIETIES (TYPES A AND B)
(See introduction for details)

26a	2c Crown missing	£525	-
26b	St Edward's Crown	£95	-
27a	3c Crown missing	£400	-
27b	St Edward's Crown	£120	-
28a	9c Crown Missing	£750	-
28b	St Edward's Crown	£230	-
29a	15c Crown missing	£525	-
29b	St Edward's Crown	£200	-
30a	18c Crown missing	£700	-
30b	St Edward's Crown	£230	-
31a	20c Crown missing	£850	-
31b	St Edward's Crown	£300	-
32a	25c Crown missing	£1100	-
32b	St Edward's Crown	£300	-

33a	40c Crown missing	£1200	-
33b	St Edward's Crown	£500	-
34a	45c Crown missing	£1200	-
34b	St Edward's Crown	£325	-
35a	50c Crown missing	£1250	-
35b	St Edward's Crown	£400	-
36b	1r St Edward's Crown	£1050	-
37b	1r50 St Edward's Crown	£1900	-
38b	2r25 St Edward's Crown	£1100	-
39b	5r St Edward's Crown	£750	-

SPECIAL ISSUES

1937 (May 12th) Coronation. As Antigua.

S1	6c sage-green	.20	.10
	a pale bistre-sage	2.75	£2
	b bronze-bistre	£8	7.50
S2	12c orange	.35	.30
S3	20c deep blue	.40	.60
S1-3	set (3)	.85	.90
SP S1/3	specimen perf (3)	£68	†

1946 (Sept 23rd) Victory. As Aden.

S4	9c light blue	.10	.10
S5	30c deep blue	.15	.10
	a lamp on mast	£18	£20
SP S4/5	specimen perf (2)	£58	†

S5a R1/5 a sizeable mark at the top of the mast. Not to be found on all sheets.

1948 (Nov. 11th) Silver Wedding. As Aden.

S6	9c light blue	.10	.35
	a line left of crown	£18	£24
S7	5r rose-carmine	6.50	£21

S6a an oblique line to the left of the crown occurs on R1/3.

1949 (Oct. 10th) U.P.U. As Aden but all recess.

S8	18c magenta	.10	.15
S9	50c purple-violet	.85	.90
S10	1r grey	.25	.15
S11	2r25 sage-green	.15	.75
S8/11	set (4)	1.20	1.80

POSTAGE DUE STAMPS

1951 (Mar. 1st) Design adapted from that of Australia. Recess (border) and typo (value) Bradbury, Wilkinson. Perf 11¾ x 11½ (C). Thick, rough paper. Value scarlet. Sheets 6 x 10.

PD1	2c **carmine**	.40	£1
PD2	3c **green**	£1	£1
PD3	6c **ochre**	£1	.90
PD4	9c **red-orange**	£1	.90
PD5	15c **purple**	.85	£8
PD6	18c **deep blue**	.85	£8
PD7	20c **deep brown**	.85	£8
PD8	30c **lake-brown**	.85	£5
PD1/8	**set (8)**	£6	£30

SIERRA LEONE

1938-51 Designs, ½d, 1d, 3d, 4d, 1/-, 2/- and £1 (view of Freetown); 1½d, 2d, 5d, 6d, 1/3d, 5/- and 10/- (rice harvesting). Printers (recess) Waterlow and Sons. Perf 12½ (L). Watermark sideways. Sheets 5 x 12.

1	½d **black and green** (1/5/38)	.10	.25
	a black and emerald-green (13/1/44)	.30	.40
2	1d **black and brown-lake** (1/5/38)	.20	.35
	a vertical pair, imperf. between	†	-
	b light reddish lake (11/44)	.40	.50
3	1½d **scarlet** (1/5/38)	£10	.60
4	1½d **purple-mauve** (1/2/41)	.15	.60
	a mauve (13/11/44)	.30	.35
5	2d **purple-mauve** (1/5/38)	£20	1.80
6	2d **scarlet** (1/2/41)	.15	1.20
	a bright scarlet (4/46)	.30	1.20
7	3d **black and ultramarine** (1/5/38)	.20	.30
	a black and bright ultramarine (3/53)	.30	.30
8	4d **black and chocolate** (20/6/38)	.85	2.75
	a black and red-brown (23/5/50)	£1	2.75
9	5d **sage-green** (20/6/38)	1.75	2.40
	a olive-green (6/3/44)	£2	2.75
10	6d **grey** (20/6/38)	.60	.30
11	1/- **black and sage-green** (20/6/38)	1.50	.40
	a black and olive-green (5/5/49)	1.10	.40
12	1/3 **orange-yellow** (1/7/44)	.35	.35
13	2/- **black and sepia** (20/6/38)	2.50	1.65
	a black and deep sepia (23/5/50)	2.25	1.65
14	5/- **chocolate-brown** (20/6/38)	£6	£7
	a reddish brown (19/3/45)	£4	£8
15	10/- **emerald** (20/6/38)	£12	8.50
	a bright emerald (13/1/45)	£14	8.50
16	£1 **indigo** (20/6/38)	£9	£15
	a dark blue (11/12/47)	£10	£18
	b dark steel-blue (19/12/51)	£14	£25
1/16	**set** (16)	£55	£40
SP 1/16	**specimen perf** (16)	£250	†

2a forged pairs exist mint. Two used pairs are reported to exist, one of which is postmarked Freetown, April 18th 1939. The other is fiscally used.

There are a number of interesting re-entries on Centre Plate 3 of the 'view of Freetown' design; notably R11/2, where the boat at left has the mast doubled, and 11/5 (Plate 3) where the sky at lower right is doubled. Frame Plate re-entries are also met with; there are a number of strong examples on the 1/- value.

SPECIAL ISSUES

1937 (May 12th) Coronation. As Antigua.

S1	1d **orange**	.35	.60
S2	2d **deep purple**	.45	.60
S3	3d **deep blue**	.85	2.40
S1-3	**set** (3)	1.50	3.25
SP S1/3	**specimen perf** (3)	£65	†

1946 (Oct. 1st) Victory. As Aden.

S4	1½d **lilac**	.10	.10
S5	3d **ultramarine**	.10	.20
SP S4/5	**specimen perf** (2)	£60	†

1948 (Dec. 1st) Silver Wedding. As Aden.

S6	1½d **magenta-purple**	.10	.10
S7	£1 **bluish slate**	9.50	£12

1949 (Oct. 10th) U.P.U. As Aden.

S8	1½d **dull purple**	.10	.30
S9	3d **indigo**	£1	3.30
S10	6d **grey**	.25	£4
S11	1/- **sage-green**	.20	.60
S8/11	**set** (4)	1.40	7.50

SINGAPORE

All definitive stamps were printed (typo) by De La Rue, on chalk-surfaced paper.

1948 (Sept. 1st) Design as Straits Settlements with 'SINGAPORE' in lower panel. Perf 13¾ x 14 (C). Sheets 10 x 10.

1	1c **black**	.10	.60
2	2c **orange**	.10	.40
3	3c **green**	.20	.90
4	4c **brown**	.10	.90
5	6c **grey**	.20	.60
6	8c **scarlet** (1/10/48)	.25	.60
7	10c **red-purple**	.15	.10
8	15c **bright ultramarine** (1/10/48)	£5	.10
9	20c **black and green** (1/10/48)	2.50	.45
10	25c **red-purple and orange** (1/10/48)	3.25	.25
11	40c **scarlet and deep purple** (1/10/48)	4.50	3.50
12	50c **black and blue** (1/1/0/48)	1.50	.10
13	$1 **blue and deep purple** (1/10/48)	£5	2.50
14	$2 **green and carmine-red** (25/10/48)	£24	£3
15	$5 **green and deep brown** (1/10/48)	£55	3.50
1/15	**set** (15)	£90	£15

Postal forgeries of the 50ct, $1 and $2 exist on unwatermarked paper, perf 14x14½. Prices from £250.

1949-55 As 1-15, but perf 17½ x 18 (C).

16	1c **black** (21/5/52)	.75	2.50
17	2c **orange** (31/10/49)	.75	1.20
	a orange-yellow (10/12/52)	£2	1.30
18	4c **brown** (1/7/49)	.75	.10
	a deep brown (24/5/51)	2.25	.10
19	6c **greenish grey** (10/12/52)	£1	1.20
	a grey (10/11/53)	1.25	£2
20	10c **red-purple** (9/2/50)	.30	.10
	a pale red-purple (10/12/52)	.60	.10
	b deep red-purple (21/4/55)	£1	.20
21	15c **violet-blue** (9/2/50)	£8	.10

22	20c **black and green**		
	(31/10/49)	£4	2.25
23	25c **red-purple and orange**		
	(9/2/50)	£1	.10
	a deep red-purple and		
	orange (21/4/55)	£2	.20
24	40c **scarlet and red-purple**		
	(/51)	£22	£10
25	50c **black and violet-blue**		
	(9/2/50)	£4	.10
	a black and blue		
	(21/5/52)	£6	.10
26	$1 **blue and red-purple**		
	(31/10/49)	£8	.15
	a blue and deep red-purple		
	(19/11/53)	£10	.15
27	$2 **green and carmine-red**		
	(24/5/51)	£45	.75
	a watermark inverted	-	-
28	$5 **green and deep brown**		
	(19/12/51)	£85	£1
	a watermark inverted	-	-

24 released in London 24/5/51, but on sale in Singapore some months earlier.

WATERMARK VARIETY (TYPE B)
See introduction for details

26b	$1 **St Edward's Crown**	£9000	-
27b	$2 **St Edward's Crown**	£12,000	-

1952 (Sept. 1st) - 53 As 16, etc., but new values or colours.

29	5c **magenta**	1.50	1.25
	a bright magenta		
	(19/11/53)	£2	1.25
30	8c **yellow-green**	3.75	2.50
	a green (25/8/53)	5.75	£3
31	12c **scarlet**	£5	£8
32	20c **blue**	3.50	.10
	a violet-blue (25/8/53)	7.50	.25
34	35c **scarlet and purple**	3.25	.60
16/34	**set** (18)	£160	£29

SPECIAL ISSUES

1946 Victory stamps in the Crown Colony design with face values of 8ct and 15ct were prepared, but never issued. None are known outside archival collections.

1948 (Dec. 1st) Silver Wedding. As Aden.

S1	10c **purple**	.35	.60
S2	$5 **chocolate**	£55	£30

1949 (Oct. 10th) UPU. As Aden.

S3	10c **dull purple**	.35	.40
S4	15c **indigo**	£3	2.50
S5	25c **orange**	£3	1.80
S6	50c **slate-black**	£3	1.95
S3/6	**set** (4)	8.50	£6

Number issued 10c, 2,580,544; 15c, 577,261; 25c, 681,908; 50c, 409,401.

GERMAN PROPAGANDA LABELS

The 1944 German imitations of the Great Britain 1937 definitives ½d to 3d (see after Great Britain for details) were also overprinted in black 'LIQUIDATION/OF EMPIRE/SINGAPORE' within a vertical rectangular frame.

SOLOMON ISLANDS

1939 (Feb. 1st)-51 Designs, ½d (spears and shield); 1d (native policeman and chief); 1½d (Auki Is.); 2d (native house, Reef Islands); 2½d (Roviana canoe); 3d (Roviana canoes); 4½d, 10/- (native house and palms); 6d (coconut plantation); 1/- (breadfruit); 2/- (Tinakula volcano); 2/6 (Bismarck Scrub Fowl); 5/- (Malaita canoe). Printers (recess) De La Rue, 2d., 3d., 2/-, 2/6, Perf 13½(C); Waterlow and Sons, other values, Perf 12½ (L). Sheets 6 x 10 or 10 x 6, 5 x 12 or 12 x 5.

1	½d	**deep blue and green**	.10	.60
	a	bright blue and deep green (5/42)	.25	£1
2	1d	**deep brown and violet**	.15	.90
3	1½d	**myrtle and lake-carmine**	£1	£1
	a	dark myrtle and bright lake-carmine (10/45)	.35	£1
4	2d	**chestnut and grey-black**	£1	1.40
	a	red-brown and grey-black (5/43)	.45	£1
5	2½d	**magenta and olive-green**	1.25	1.35
	a	deep magenta and deep olive-green (5/46)	1.75	1.75
	b	imperf. bet. vertical pair £15,000		-
6	3d	**black and ultramarine**	.60	£1
	a	slate-black and bright ultramarine (5/43)	£3	£5
7	4½d	**yellow-green and chocolate**	£2	£8
8	6d	**slate-violet and deep claret**	.35	.60
	a	deep slate and deep reddish purple (12/46)	£2	£2
	b	slate-violet and purple-claret (29/11/51)	£4	£4
9	1/-	**green and black**	.60	.60
10	2/-	**black and orange**	5.50	3.50
	a	slate-black and red-orange (5/43)	£10	£10
11	2/6	**black and dull purple-violet**	£12	£3
	a	slate-black and purple-violet (5/43)	£14	£7
12	5/-	**emerald-green and red**	£14	£7
13	10/-	**sage-green and magenta** (27/4/42)	£2	5.50
1/13		**set** (13)	£35	£30
SP1/13		**specimen perf** (13)	£300	†

5b A part sheet was found by a U.S. serviceman and taken back to the U.S.A.

Number issued - No. 7, 70,000.

1951- 54 As Nos. 4a and 6 but Perf 12 (C).

14	2d	**red-brown and grey** (7/11/51)	.15	£1
	a	Indian red and black (16/6/54)	£1	1.75
15	3d	**black and ultramarine** (29/11/51)	.70	1.50

SPECIAL ISSUES

1937 (May 13th) Coronation. As Antigua.

S1	1d	**violet**	.15	.75
S2	1½d	**carmine-red**	.15	.35
S3	3d	**deep blue**	.25	.30
S1-3		**set** (3)	.50	1.25
SP S1/3		**specimen perf** (3)	£45	†

Numbers issued - S1, 631,480; S2, 301,420; S3, 507,600.

1946 (Oct. 15th) Victory. As Aden.

S4	1½d	**carmine-red**	.10	.75
S5	3d	**deep blue**	.10	.15
SP S4/5		**specimen perf** (2)	£60	†

Number issued - S4, 778,500; S5, 768,240.

1949 (March 14th) Silver Wedding. As Aden.

S6	2d	**black**	.25	.30
	a	handkerchief flaw	£22	£22
S7	10/-	**lake-magenta**	£5	5.25

S6a a flaw on the King resembles a handkerchief on R1/6.

Numbers printed - S6, 373,000; S7, 125,000.

1949 (Oct. 10th) U.P.U. As Aden.

S8	2d	**beech-brown**	.25	.60
S9	3d	**indigo**	1.10	.90
S10	5d	**green**	.25	£1
S11	1/-	**slate-black**	.25	£1
S8/11		**set** (4)	1.65	3.20

Number printed - S8, 455,000; S9, S10, S11, 340,000 each.

POSTAGE DUE STAMPS

1940 (Sept. 1st) Printers (typo) Bradbury, Wilkinson. Perf 12 (L). Sheets 12 x 10.

PD1	1d emerald	3.25	4.25
PD2	2d deep red	3.50	4.25
PD3	3d brown	3.50	6.75
PD4	4d deep blue	5.50	£7
PD5	5d deep green	£6	£12
PD6	6d magenta	£6	£10
PD7	1/- violet	£7	£18
PD8	1/6 turquoise-green	14.50	£30
PD1/8	set (8)	£45	£85
SPPD1/8	specimen perf (8)	£140	†

SOMALILAND PROTECTORATE

1938 (May 10th) Designs, ½a-3a (Blackhead sheep); 4a-12a (Greater Kudu antelope); 1r-5r (map). All with head of King, facing left. Printers (recess), Waterlow and Sons. Perf 12½ (L). Sheet formats: anna values 8 x 15; rupee values 6 x 10.

1	½a green	.30	£3
2	1a scarlet-red	.20	1.25
3	2a lake	1.20	£2
4	3a blue	£7	£10
5	4a deep brown	2.50	£6
6	6a violet	£5	7.50
7	8a grey	1.75	7.50
8	12a reddish orange	£5	£15
9	1r green	4.50	£45
10	2r purple	£8	£45
11	3r blue	£9	£28
12	5r black	£10	£28
	a horizontal pair, imperf between	£16,000	†
1/12	set (12)	£50	£180
SP1/12	specimen perf (12)	£175	†

Used prices are for examples with postmarks dated prior to August 19th 1940, when the territory was occupied by Italian Forces, and quantities of the issue were looted. Forged Berbera CDSs dated 15 AU 38 are frequent, and other forged CDSs exist.

The Italian occupation ended on March 16th, 1941; and from July 1st, 1941, contemporary stamps of Aden were used in British Somaliland until the new definitive set was issued on April 27th, 1942.

1942 (April 27th) As CW 1, etc., but portrait changed to full face. Sheet formats: anna values 8 x 15; rupee values 10 x 6.

13	½a green	.10	.25
14	1a scarlet-red	.10	.10
15	2a lake	.30	.15
16	3a blue	£1	.15
17	4a deep brown	1.40	.20
18	6a violet	1.40	.15
19	8a grey	1.50	.15
20	12a reddish orange	1.50	.30
21	1r green	1.25	£1
22	2r purple	1.25	£4
23	3r blue	2.75	7.25
24	5r black	5.50	£5
13/24	set (12)	£16	£17
SP13/24	specimen perf (12)	£175	†

1951 (April 1st) CW 13, etc., surcharged in black or red, to bring in line with changed currency (100 Cents = 1 Shilling).

25	5c/½a green	.15	1.20
26	10c/2a lake	.15	.60
27	15c/3a blue	.85	1.75
28	20c/4a deep brown	£1	.15
	a sepia-brown	1.50	£12
29	30c/6a violet	.85	.60
30	50c/8a grey	1.25	.15
31	70c/12a red-orange	£2	3.50
	a vermilion	£3	£5
32	1s/1r green	£1	.75
33	2s/2r purple	2.75	£11
34	2s/3r blue	4.50	£4
35	5s/5r black (red)	6.50	6.75
25/35	set (11)	£19	£27

Examples of a 5ct/1a scarlet value were prepared but never issued. The only apparent survivors are in the Crown Agent's Record Album, the Crown Agent's Inspector's Album, the Foreign & Commonwealth collection and a plate block of four in the Royal Collection. 359 examples which had been intended for the UPU were destroyed; it is not known what happened to the remainder.

First Day covers of the 1951 Currency change set seem to be without the 2s/2r purple. Has anyone any information as to the actual date of issue of this stamp?

SPECIAL ISSUES

1937 (May 13th) Coronation. As Ascension.

S1	1a scarlet	.10	.30
S2	2a grey-black	.25	1.20

S3	3a blue	.55	.75
S1/3	set (3)	.80	£2
SP S1/3	specimen perf (3)	£65	†

Number printed - S1, 490,000; S2, 394,000; S3, 390,000.

1946 (Oct. 15th) Victory. As Aden.

(a) Perf 13¾ x 14 (C).

S4	1a carmine-red	.10	.10
S5	3a deep blue	.10	.10
SP S4/5	specimen perf (2)	£35	†

(b) Perf. 13¾ x 13¼ (C).

S6	1a carmine-red	£6	£38

S6 there was no colonial release. All used examples were sent out from London by collectors and dealers.

1949 (Jan 28th) Silver Wedding. As Aden.

S7	1a scarlet	.10	.10
S8	5r grey-black	1.85	2.50

1949 (Oct. 10th) U.P.U. As Aden, but surcharged in black or red.

S9	1a/10c carmine-rose	.10	.25
S10	3a/30c indigo (red)	.60	1.65
S11	6a/50c purple	.15	1.65
S12	12a/1/- orange	.45	£1
SP9/12	set (4)	1.20	£4

This issue was not put on sale in the Protectorate until October 24th.

SOUTH AFRICA

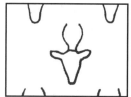

All stamps were printed (roto) at the Govt. Printing Works, Pretoria, on paper with "Springbok's Head" watermark and printed alternately in English and Afrikaans, unless otherwise mentioned. The rotogravure printing procedure produced some characteristics which are not generally encountered in King George VI philately. For instance, there are a large number of positional varieties throughout the reign, and many definitives exist with inverted watermarks. There are also a large number of shades.

Collectors who wish to study South African stamps of the period are urged to acquire 'The Stamps of the Union of South Africa 1910-61', Reijger Publishers (Pty.) Ltd, 1986, usually referred to as 'The South African Handbook'. This work, for instance, does not give a detailed listing of shades but does indicate that they exist. You, the collector, should make your own decisions as to whether you wish to collect a range of the shades.

More collectors 'put off' South Africa until last in their King George VI collections than any other area, with the possible exception of the Indian States. The reason for this is that it is perceived as too complicated. It isn't; it is quite easily understood. The key lies in recognising and understanding the process of 'screening'. A good magnifying glass is essential.
1. Unscreened; lines in solid colour. Dots cannot be seen in the make-up of any lines.
2. Frame screened; outer section of design composed of dots, giving uneven edges to apparently solid lines. Inner portion of design in solid colour.

unscreened   screened

3. Centre screened; outer section solid, inner portion dotted.
4. Fully screened; design composed of dots throughout.

South African stamps are best collected in horizontal pairs to illustrate the se-tenant language format. We do not stock (nor do we recommend that collectors bother with) singles or vertical pairs, except in the cases of Postage Dues, two values from each of the War Effort sets and the 1949 Voortrekker Monument set, each of which was inscribed bilingually.

Certain coils were produced in vertical format and these are indicated in the text. All prices listed are for horizontal pairs, unless otherwise stated.

1930-45 'SUIDAFRIKA' in one word. Designs; ½d (Springbok's head), 1d (Van Riebeeck's ship "Dromedaris"), 1½d (gold mine), 2d (Union Buildings), 3d (Groote Schuur), 4d (native kraal), 6d (orange tree), 1/- (gnus), 2/ 6d and 5/- (ox-wagons), 10/- (Table Mountain and Bay). ½d, 1d and 6d perf 14¾ x 14, other values perf 14. Sheets, ½d, 1d and 6d 12 x 20; large format 6 x 20.

X1	½d **black and green** (5/30)	1.75	1.80
	a watermark inverted	1.75	1.80
	b vertical strip of four (two English, two Afrikaans)	£28	-
	c tete-beche pair	£775	-
	d 'cobweb' variety	£25	-
	e '$' variety	£25	-
X2	1d **black and carmine** (Die I) (4/30)	2.25	1.80
	a watermark inverted	2.25	1.80
	b tete-beche pair	£950	-
	c frame omitted (single)	£350	-
X3	1d **black and deep carmine** (Die 2)(/32)	£25	2.25
	a watermark inverted	£20	2.50
X4	2d **grey and lilac** (4/31)	£12	£13
	a watermark inverted	8.50	5.50
	b tete-beche pair	£4000	-
	c frame omitted (single)	£2250	-
X5	2d **dark blue and violet** (/38)	£140	£50
X6	3d **black and red** (/31)	£32	£50
	a watermark inverted	£15	£38
	b window flaw	£90	

X7	3d **blue** (/33)	£9	4.25
	a watermark inverted	£3	3.75
	b window flaw	£28	-
	c centre omitted	£20000	-
	d frame omitted (single)	£10000	-
X8	4d **brown (Type 1)** (11/32)	£140	£100
	a watermark inverted	£15	£20
	b spear flaw	£90	-
	c brown (shades) (Type 2) (/36)	1.50	£2
	ca 'monkey'	£25	-
	cb watermark inverted	6.50	5.50
X9	6d **green and orange** (/31)	6.50	2.75
	a watermark upright (/32)	£20	£10
X10	1/- **brown and deep blue** (14/9/32)	£40	£30
	a watermark inverted	£17.50	£16
	b twisted horn	£140	-
X11	2/6 **green and brown** (/32)	£40	£65
	a watermark inverted	£100	£120
	b blue and brown (/45)	£12	£8

X1d

X1e

X1d cyl.1, R9/5.

X1e cyl.2, R10/9.

The 1d, on unwatermarked paper or on paper with trefoil watermark, exists from Darmstadt Trial printings.

X2, X3 Dies 1 and 2 are differentiated by the spacing of the shading lines in the side panels. Die 1 has them closer together than Die 2.

Die 1   Die 2

X6b, 7b a large extra window appears on the building above 'U' of 'SOUTH' on R20/4, printings up to 1937.

X7c, d The 3d blue was printed from two cylinders, for the frame and vignette. The background clouds are part of the frame plate. We have been shown a block with two total and two partial omissions from the 1937 printing.

Type 1

Type 2

X8ca

X8, X8c Types 1 and 2 are differentiated by the shading of the scroll to left of the right value tablet '4d'. In Type 1, the curl underneath the scroll is solid; Type 2 has an additional white line.

X8ca R2/2.

X8b the spear flaw is in the form of an almost vertical line by the standing figure at left of hut. R9/2.

X10b R1/5 (cyl. 7020). The topmost horn appears twisted.

X8b

X10b

1933-54 SUID-AFRIKA (with hyphen). Designs, etc., as before.

Unscreened.

3	½d **grey and green** (Type 1) (watermark inverted) (/35)	2.25	1.20
	a watermark upright	4.50	4.50
	b perf. 13½ x 14 (watermark inverted)	£18	£40
	ba watermark upright	£18	£40
4	½d **grey and green** (Type 2) (4/37)	£4	1.35
	a grey and blue-green (Type 2) (/37)	2.50	.75
	b deep grey and dull blue-green (cross-hatched) (11/47)	£25	£25
	ba bush tick and fly	£75	-
5	1d **grey and red** (4/34)	.85	1.20
	a watermark inverted	.85	1.20
	b perf. 13½ x 14 (watermark upright)	£19	£38
	ba watermark inverted	£19	£38
	c frame omitted (single)	£225	-
	d imperf (pair)	£120	-
	e St Elmo's fire	£15	£10
7	2d **blue and violet** (11/38)	£35	£23
8	2d **grey and purple-lilac** (5/41)	£20	£55
10	6d **green and vermilion** (Type 1) (10/37)	£25	£20
	a falling ladder	£120	£150
	b molehill	£80	£80
	c Type 2 (6/38)	£15	.60
	d Type 3 (/46)	£7	.50
11	1/- **brown and chalky blue** (2/39)	£20	£9
	a frame omitted (single stamp)	£4000	-
13	5/- **black and green** (10/33)	£25	£45
	a watermark inverted	£60	£90
	b black and blue-green (9/44)	£16	£11
	c broken yoke pin	£65	£55

Frame only screened.

14	½d **grey and green** (/47)	£1	2.50
	a bush tick and fly	£24	-

Centre only screened.

| 20 | 2d **slate and purple-violet** (1st State) (3/45) | £6 | 1.50 |

	a slate and violet		
	(2nd State)(10/46)	£6	3.50
	b slate and bright violet		
	(2nd State) (/47)	£2	£6
21	3d **ultramarine** (2/40)	5.50	£2
23	10/- **deep blue and sepia**		
	(8/39)	£25	£10
	a blue and blackish		
	brown (8/39)	£18	3.50
	b ultramarine and grey-black	£18	3.50

Fully screened.

25	½d **sepia-grey and green**		
	(2/49)	.80	2.50
	a bushtick and fly	£25	-
	b 'charcoal' and		
	grey-green (12/49)	£5	£3
26	1d **grey and**		
	magenta-rose (9/50)	1.10	2.50
27	1d **grey-black and carmine**		
	(re-drawn) (22/2/51)	.70	.90
28	1½d **bright gold and**		
	slate-green (11/36)	1.50	1.40
	a watermark inverted	.75	£1
	aa shading on mine		
	dump omitted	£125	£125
	b yellow-buff and		
	grey-green (/40)	£3	£2
	c broken chimney	£15	£15
	d flag on chimney	£15	£15
29	2d **slate-blue and**		
	purple (3/50)	£2	£7
30	3d **dull blue** (4/49)	1.50	3.75
31	3d **blue** (3/51)	1.75	£3
	a flying saucer	£35	£35
	b deep intense blue (/54)	£125	-
32	6d **green and red-orange**		
	(1/50)	1.75	.90
	a green and brown-orange		
	(/51)	1.50	.60
33	1/- **sepia and slate-blue**		
	(1/50)	4.50	£6
	a sepia-black and		
	deep violet-blue (4/52)	£8	£9
34	2/6 **green and brown**		
	(8/49)	£4	£18
35	5/- **black and green** (9/49)	£20	£45
	a rain	£65	£60

3 - Type 1   4 - Type 2

3, 4   Type 1/2. In Type 2, the number of shading lines around the buck's head is reduced from over 40 to 28. The vertical lines at top and bottom of the frame have also been replaced by horizontal ones.

3b, ba, 5b, ba from sheets prepared for the production of coils.

4b   The panels running along top and bottom of stamps have diagonal lines running left-right and right-left, forming a cross-hatched effect.

4ba, 14a, 25a a large black mark on the buck's left ear and a spot towards the end of the nose. On the first of the two cross-hatched issues, there was a white patch on the ear, which was subsequently retouched so that it appeared as a dark patch. R3/4, then 3/1 from May 1948. In April 1949 the flaw moved to an English-inscribed stamp; in August 1949 it moved to R2/4 and reverted to a white flaw.

5e R15/4 (Issue 21) a large red blob in the rigging below the top pennant.

Type 1   Type 2

Type 3

10/c/d   Types 1/2/3. In Type 1,

'SUID-AFRIKA' measures 16½mm; in Types 2 and 3, it is 17mm. Type 1 has faint lines behind the orange tree. Types 1 and 2 have the 'question mark' scrolls below the country name at top opened up; Type 3 has these closed. Types 1 and 2 measure 18½ x 22½mm, Type 3 18mm x 22mm (the inked portion of the design).

10a   10b

10a   R5/10 probably the largest KG VI plate flaw.

10b   R20/11 a large green flaw to the right of the trunk.

13c   R18/5 the second horizontal pin from the top of the rod at left has the right portion broken off.

| 20 - State 1 | 20a - State 2 |

20, 20a, 20b - Not only do the shades differ from Nos. 7 and 8, but the Union Buildings are depicted from another angle. In the 1st State the top of the '2' of the value merges with the surrounding circle: in the 2nd State the '2' is cut clear. Previous 2ds were unscreened.

21, 30 - The centre of each is screened. In 21, the shading in the scrolls above '3D' is clear ; in 30, indistinct.

21   30

23a the centre of this stamp has an all-over 'wash' of colour.

25b when held obliquely to the light, the centre resembles a charcoal drawing inside a shiny frame.

27 the design has been reduced from 18 x 22mm to 17½mm x 21½mm. Small design changes were also made.

28, a the dots making up the design of the central vignette are, in fact, part of the design and not due to screening. To avoid confusion, these stamps are listed as 'fully screened'.

28 some sheets from the first printing showed the shading on the mine dump partially or completely omitted.

28c the left chimney is broken at the point where it crosses the mine dump. R11/6, cyl. 62

28d a 'flag' on the small chimney at right. R20/2, cyl. 62.

31 now printed in one operation (previously two), the centre and frame screens are of a regular pattern. The clouds are well defined.

31a On Cyl. 17 R17/2 a blue line can be found in the sky to the left of the trees.

31b an extremely deep dark shade, with large perforation holes. We recommend an expert committee certificate be obtained when purchasing this stamp.

35a R20/6 four strong diagonal lines at right resemble rain.

1941-51 As Nos. 28 and 29, but reduced in size. Perf. 14 x 14¾. Watermark sideways.

36	1½d **yellow-buff and**		
	blue-green (8/41)	1.20	£1
	a "waffle" print (8/41)	£25	£12
	b yellow-buff background omitted	£3250	-
37	2d **slate-blue and plum** (4/50)	.15	.60

36a the very coarse exterior screen used resulted in the variety, which shows as a distinct 'grid' pattern in the frame.

1943-52 Coils. Designs as Nos. 4 and 5, but redrawn and printed in monocolour. Perf. 14¾ x 14 (C).

38	½d **blue-green** (18/2/43)	1.50	£3
	a green (clear impression) (/49)	1.50	£3
39	1d **carmine-magenta** (9/43)	1.75	2.50
	a uncoloured blotch	£22	£35
	b carmine-red (clear impression) (/49)	1.75	2.50
	c blazing sun	£8	£12

38a, 39b have a much finer screen than other printings and the details of the design can be clearly seen.

39a   39c

39a   R19/3 a large blotch appears at the right side one-third of the way up. Later printings only.

39c   the sun at the right side has lost all definition.

1948 (April 1st) Design as No. 36, but format altered. Perf 14 around each vertical pair and rouletted 6½ internally. Watermark sideways.

40   1½d **yellow-buff and blue-green**   1.50   3.50

Priced for units of four, because they were printed se-tenant vertically as well as horizontally.

1948 Design as No. X1, but printed from plates of 1926 issue. 'SUIDAFRIKA' without hyphen. Sheets 9 x 20. Perf 14¾ x 14 (C).

41   ½d **grey and dull grey-green** (5/48)   .85   £9

A special printing made to use up a stock of paper already cut.

1952-4   Perf. 14 (C). Screened.

46   4d **brown** (22/8/52)   2.25   £7
47   5/- **black and yellow-green** (1/54)   £25   £58

47 redrawn 'South Africa'. The serifs at the tops of the 'A's, and the projections at each side of the base of the 'U' have been removed. However, colour difference should be sufficient for identification.

SPECIAL ISSUES

1937 (May 12th) Coronation. Perf. 14 (C) Watermark sideways. Sheets 20 x 6.

S1	½d **dark grey and green**	.40	.75
	a watermark inverted	.40	.75
	b line through country names	£18	£22
S2	1d **grey-black and carmine** (Cyl. 55)	£3	1.50
	a ditto (Cyl. 30a)	.40	.60
	ab watermark inverted	.40	.60
S3	1½d **orange and greenish-blue**	.40	.50
	a watermark inverted	.40	.50
	b "Mouse" variety	£10	£12
S4	3d **ultramarine**	.75	1.80
	a watermark inverted	.75	1.80
S5	1/- **red-brown and blue**	1.50	2.75
	a watermark inverted	1.50	2.75
	b missing hyphen	£32	£35
	c dot in place of hyphen	£16	£18
S1/5	**set (5)**	£3	£6

Watermarks. The 'normal' sideways watermark has the horns pointing to the right, while the 'inverted' shows them pointing to the left: each as seen from the back of the stamp.

S1b   R6/2-3 a strong scratch runs through 'AFRICA' and 'AFRIKA'. Later printings only.

S2   S2a

S2, a   Cyl. 55. Relatively clear impression. Greyish shading around head. Front lobe and back of ear clearly outlined. Face and neck entirely shaded (watermark facing right only, as seen from reverse). Cyl. 30a (as used for centres of all other values in set). Inferior impression. Deeper shading around head, except behind. Ear not outlined. Shading of face and neck patchy (watermark facing right or left).

S3b R4/1 a blotch on the ornaments left of 'SUID' resembles a mouse.

S5b   S5c

S5b R2/13 the hyphen between 'SUID-AFRIKA' is completely obliterated.

S5c R4/17 the hyphen is almost entirely omitted, leaving just a dot.

Number printed (pairs) - ½d, 13,018,500; 1d, 21,156,000; 1½d, 2,392,500; 3d, 1,980,100; 1/-, 1,477,500.

(Reduced Size)

1938 (Dec. 14th) Voortrekker Centenary Memorial Fund. Designs, ½d (ploughing); 1d (wagon); 1½d (signing treaty); 3d (Memorial). ½d, 1d perf 14; 1½d, 3d perf 14¾ x 14. Surcharge for Memorial Fund. **Sheets 6 x 20.**

S6	½d+½d **slate-blue and green**	£6	£3
S7	1d+1d **deep blue and carmine**	£7	3.50
S8	1½d + 1½d **chocolate and deep green**	£9	£6
S9	3d+3d **blue**	£10	£6
S6/9	**set** (4)	£30	£16

Number printed (pairs) - ½d, 6,144,000; 1d, 11,550,000; 1½d, 3,564,000; 3d, 2,100,000.

1938 (Dec. 14th) Great Trek (Voortrekker) Commemoration. Designs, 1d (wagon wheel); 1½d (Voortrekker family). Designer, W.H. Coetzer. Perf 14¾ x 14. Sheets 6 x 20.

S10	1d **slate-blue and carmine**	£3	2.50
	a third nut	£25	£20
S11	1½d **dull green and chestnut**	£4	2.50
	a lower frame pale	£10	£10

S10a R15/5 extra nut in wheel rim.

S11a R20/1-6 all stamps in the bottom row show the lower portion of the frame much paler.

Number printed (pairs) - 1d, 4,380,000; 1½d, 5,344,000.

1939 (July 17th) 250th Anniversary of Landing of the Huguenots. Designs, ½d (Old Vicarage, Paarl); 1d (dawning light); 1½d (Huguenot dwelling). ½d and 1d perf 14, 1½d perf 14¾ x 14. Surcharge for Commemoration Fund. **Sheets 6 x 20.**

S12	½d+½d **brown and green**	2.50	£4
S13	1d+1d **green and carmine**	£6	£4
S14	1½d+1½d **blue-green and purple**	12.50	8.50
S12/14	**set** (3)	£19	£15

Number printed (pairs) - ½d, 2,490,000; 1d, 1,344,000; 1½d, 1,290,000 (includes quantities overprinted for South West Africa).

1941-42 War Effort (large size). Designs, members of forces, ordnance, etc. 2d, 4d and 6d perf 14, watermark sideways; other values, perf 14¾ x 14 and watermark upright. 2d and 1/- bilingual. Sheets; S15/17 12 x 20; others 20 x 6 or 6 x 20.

S15	½d **green** (19/11/41)	.75	£2
	a blue-green (7/42)	1.50	2.25
S16	1d **carmine** (3/10/41)	.90	£2
	a stain on uniform	£19	£25
S17	1½d **myrtle-green** (12/1/42)	.70	1.80
S18	2d **violet** (15/9/41)	.40	.45
S19	3d **blue** (1/8/41)	£10	£25
	a woman smoking	£55	-

S20	4d **orange-brown** (20/8/41)	£11	£15
	a red-brown (6/42)	£15	£24
S21	6d **red-orange** (3/9/41)	£6	8.50
S22	1/- **chocolate** (27/10/41)	1.60	.60
S15/22	**set** (8)	£28	£50

S16a   S19a

S16a R14/11 a large red 'stain' appears centrally above the crossed arms.

S19a R18/2 an apparent wreath of smoke from the W.A.C.'s mouth.

1942-5 War Effort ("Bantams"). Designs as S15, etc., but reduced in size. ½d, 1d, 3d and 4d in units of three, other values in pairs. Prices for units or pairs as issued. 3d, 4d, 1/- watermark sideways. Sheets S24/25/28/29, 20 x 18 or 18 x 20; others, 20 x 12 or 12 x 20.

Perf 14 (externally) and Roul 13 (internally).

S23	1½d **red-brown** (8/42)	.75	2.50
	a right side background missing	£3	£5
	b ear flap	£12	-
	c roul. 13 and 6½ (se-tenant)	£8	£12

Perf 14¾ x 14 or 14 (externally) and Roul 6½ (internally). 4d and 1/- Bilingual.

S24	½d **blue-green** (10/42)	£1	.90
	a upper background missing	£4	£8
	c roulette omitted	£650	-
	d deep green (3/43)	1.25	1.35
	e upper background missing	£6	£9
	f deep greenish blue (7/44)	.85	£1
	g upper background missing	£5	£9
	h background added	£10	£14
S25	1d **carmine** (1/43)	.65	.90
	a roulettes omitted	£475	-
	b left roulette omitted	£675	-
	c bright carmine (3/44)	.45	.75
S26	1½d **red-brown** (3/43)	.30	1.35
	a right side background missing	2.50	£5
	b roulettes omitted	£225	-
	c ear flap	£10	-

S27	2d **violet** (shades) (2/43)	.40	.60
	a roulette omitted	£575	-
	b '2/6d' flaw	£30	£30
	c line on cap	£30	£30
S28	3d **blue** (10/42)	£3	£11
S29	4d **green** (10/42)	7.50	£7
	a unshaded corner	£9	£11
S30	6d **red-orange** (10/42)	£1	1.25
	a whiter flame	£5	£6
S31	1/- **chocolate** (11/42)	6.50	2.50
	a bursting shell	£45	-
	b mark by 'L'	£45	-
	c upper background missing	£10	£12
	d background added	£20	£25
S24/31	**set of 8 units**	£15	£18

Early printings bore "War Savings" slogans in the same colour as the stamp on the margins, but in 1944 these were printed in violet on the ½d, 1d and 4d values. In 1945 these slogans were replaced by lines and figures ('240' and '360' according to the number of stamps in the sheet) for the ½d (green), 1d (both violet and carmine), 2d and 6d (violet). All values except the 6d are known with misplaced slogans (printed on the stamps themselves).

S23a   S23b   S27b

S23a, S26a shading omitted at right at every 2nd stamp in last column.

S23b, S26c, Cyl. 43 R13/3 line by head.

normal   S24a

S24a,e,g, S31b the shading of the background on the upper part of all stamps on the first horizontal row is absent. S24h shows extensive retouching to the top of the design, correcting the omission.

S26a Upper right corner background missing.

S27b Cyl. 6931 R19/1 line above 'D' of '2D', making it resemble '2/6d'. From issues 1 and 2.

S27c Cyl. 39 R12/11 line on cap below value.

S29a all stamps in the bottom row show the lower left corner unshaded.

S30a all stamps in the last vertical column show the flame with less orange.

S31a   S31b

S31a R11/20 above the right armoured car, a number of dots give the appearance of a bursting shell.

S31b R8/2 large mark by 'L' of 'POSSEEL'.

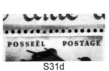

S31c   S31d

S31c upper background missing on all stamps in top row. Later some retouching occurred.

1943-6 War Effort. Design, signaller. Perf 14¾ x 14 (C). Sheets 20 x 12.

S32	1/3d **olive-brown** (2/1/43)	£5	£4
	a **deep sepia** (5/46)	1.75	£4

1945 (Dec. 3rd) Victory. Designs, 1d (soldier with flag); 2d (ploughing); 3d (star-gazing). Perf 14 (C). Sheets 6 x 20.

S33	1d **deep brown and carmine**	.10	.75
	b barbed wire	£8	£12
S34	2d **slate-blue and purple-violet**	.10	.75
S35	3d **deep blue and blue**	.10	.90
S33/35	**set** (3)	.30	2.20

S33b a flaw resembling a ring of barbed wire R9/6.

Number printed (pairs) - 1d, 14,117,880; 2d, 19,441,920; 3d, 4,367,640 (includes quantities overprinted for South West Africa).

1947 (Feb. 17th) Royal Visit. Designs, portraits of Royal Family. Perf 14¾ x 14 (C). Sheets - S36, 12 x 20; others 6 x 20.

S36	1d **deep slate and carmine**	.10	.20
	a whiskers	£6	£6
S37	2d **purple-violet** (Cyl. 6912)	£1	1.50
	a bird on '2'	£5	£6
	b purple-violet (Cyl. 39)	.10	.35
S38	3d **deep blue**	.10	.35
	a blinded princess	£5	6.50
S36/38	**set** (3)	.25	.80

S36a R16/12 a flaw on the cheek gives the appearance of side-whiskers.

Cylinder 6912   Cylinder 39

S37 the scroll is shaded above and below the words SOUTH AFRICA, giving a bevelled appearance. There is no break in the small scroll at the bottom left corner on stamps with Afrikaans inscription. Also there are 9 dots in the centre of the flower at the left hand side on all stamps (Cyl. 6912).

S37a   S38a

S37a R10/6 (Cyl. 6912) a large mark on the '2' resembles a bird.

S37b the scroll is plain and unshaded. There is a break in the small scroll near the join to the large scroll at the left bottom corner on Afrikaans stamps. There are only 8 dots in the centre of the left-hand flower (Cyl. 39).

S38a R19/2 (Cyl. 6912) a smudge across the eyes of Princess Elizabeth.

Number printed (pairs) - 1d, 18,562,400; 2d, 22,392,120; 3d, 4,317,900 (includes quantities overprinted for South West Africa).

1948 (April 26th) Silver Wedding. Design, portrait of King and Queen (from photographs by Dorothy Wilding) framed by silver leaves (Leucadendron Argenteum). Perf. 14 (C). Sheets 6 x 20.

| S39 | 3d **silver and deep blue** | .20 | .75 |
| | a large spot on King's forehead | £6 | £11 |

S39a A large spot appears on R20/2.

Number printed (pairs) - 5,070,000 (includes quantity overprinted for South West Africa).

1949 (May 2nd) Centenary of Arrival in Natal of British Settlers. Design, 'Wanderer' lying off Durban. Perf. 14¾ x 14 (C). Sheets 6 x 20.

S40	1½d **pale claret**	.40	.50
	a deep claret	.40	.50
	b 'V' by mainmast	6.50	£7
	c 'pennant' flaw	6.50	£7

Sheets of S40 bear Cyl. No. 29; those of S40a have no cyl. number.

S40b R14/2 (both cylinders) a 'V' on its side appears at the top of the mainmast.

S40c R17/5 (both cylinders) a line streaming aft from from the foremast.

Number issued (pairs) - 24,976,740.

1949 (Oct. 1st) U.P.U. Perf. 14 x 14¾ (C). Watermark sideways. Sheets 20 x 6.

S41	½d **blue-green**	.25	.60
S42	1½d **brownish lake**	.25	.60
	a watch on wrist	£6	£6
S43	3d **bright ultramarine**	.30	.60
	a 'G' variety	£24	-
	b 'lake' in East Africa	£24	-
S41/43	**set** (3)	.70	1.60

S42a   S43a   S43b

S42a R4/8 a mark on the left wrist resembles a wristwatch.

S43a R1/1 the 'C' of 'AFRICA' resembles a 'G'.

S43b R2/19 a large white spot above 'POS' resembles a lake.

Number printed (pairs) - ½d, 12,101,580; 1½d, 17,244,300; 3d, 2,413,620.

1949 (Dec. 1st) - 50 Inauguration of Voortrekker Monument. Designs (bilingual inscriptions); 1d (Voortrekkers on way to Natal); 1½d (Monument); 3d (Triptych). Perf 13¾ x 14 (C). Sheets 6 x 20.

S44	1d **magenta**	.10	.10
S45	1½d **bluish green**	.10	.10
S46	3d **deep slate-blue**	.10	.10
S44/46	**set** (3)	.25	.25

Numbers printed - 1d, 21,585,480; 1½d, 32,205,720; 3d, 3,187,680.

OFFICIAL STAMPS

1938-49 Designs, 2d (as X5); 1/- (as X10); 2/6 (as X11, X11a), overprinted OFFICIAL (at right) and OFFISIEEL (reading downwards).

O1	2d **dark blue and**		
	violet (/39)	£75	£60
O2	1/- **brown and deep blue**		
	(wmk inverted)(/37)	£22	£50
	a twisted horn	£230	-
	b watermark upright	£30	£70
O3	2/6 **green and brown** (/39)	£30	£80
	a watermark inverted (/37)	£250	£300
O4	2/6 **blue and brown** (/47)	£20	£65
	a diaresis (R6/2)	£600	£675
	b diaresis (R6/3)	£600	£675

O2 - The overprint measures 21mm between lines. Stamps with overprint measuring 19mm were issued in 1932.

O3 - The overprint measures about 21mm. Stamps with overprint measuring 17½-18mm belong to the 1933 issue.

O4a diaresis (two dots) above final 'E' of 'Offisieel' on stamp inscribed 'Suid Afrika' R6/2.

O4b diaresis (two dots) above final 'E' of 'Offisieel' on stamp inscribed 'South Africa' R6/3.

1937-51 As No. 4, etc., overprinted as before with OFFISIEEL to left.

O5	½d **grey and green** (No. 3)(/37)	3.50	£17
	a watermark inverted (/36)	£15	£22
	b grey and green		
	(No. 4) (7/38)	£2	£12
	c grey and green		
	(No. 14) (/49)	2.50	£6
	ca bushtick and fly	£40	-

	d sepia and grey-green		
	(No. 25) (/49)	2.75	£6
O6	1d **grey and red**		
	(No. 5) (/38)	£2	1.80
	a watermark inverted (/35)	2.25	3.75
	b St Elmos' fire	-	-
O7	1½d **bright gold and slate-**		
	green (wmk inverted)		
	(No. 28) (9/37)	£22	£20
	a watermark upright	£13	£15
	b yellow-buff and		
	blue-green (No. 28a) (/42)	£18	£7
	c broken chimney	-	-
O8	1½d **yellow-buff and**		
	blue-green (No. 36)		
	(/47) (14½ mm opt.)	1.20	£6
	a diaresis over second		
	'E' of 'OFFISIEEL'	£450	£225
	b yellow-buff and blue-green		
	(16mm opt.) (No. 36) (/50)	£1	£7.50
O9	2d **blue and violet**		
	(No. 7) (/38)	£68	£24
O10	2d **slate and violet**		
	(No. 20a) (/47)	2.75	£15
	a diaresis over second		
	'E' of 'OFFISIEEL'	£375	£500
	b slate and bright violet		
	(No. 20b) (/49)	£4	£10
O11	6d **green and vermilion**		
	(Type 1) (No. 10) (/38)	£35	£30
	aa falling ladder	£600	-
	a Type 2 (No. 10a) (/40)	£6	£6
	b Type 3 (No. 10c) (/48)	£2	£5
O12	1/- **brown and chalky**		
	blue (No. 11) (3/40)	£35	£30
	a diaresis over second		
	'E' of 'OFFISIEEL'		
	(both stamps)	£1500	£1100
	b ditto (English stamp only)	£1100	£750
	c misplaced overprint		
	strip of 6 across sheet	-	-
	d sepia and slate-blue		
	(No. 33) (6/50)	£6	£17
O13	5/- **black and green**		
	(No. 13) (/48)	£30	£100
	a broken yoke-pin	£125	-
	b rain	£125	-
O14	10/- **ultramarine and grey-**		
	black (No. 23a) (7/48)	£50	£175

For details of plate varieties see main listing.

O8b the width between lines of overprint is approximately 16¼mm instead of not quite 15mm, as in O8. The lettering is bolder and more widely spaced.

O8a, O10a, O12a two dots over second 'E' of 'OFFISIEEL'. The position in the sheet varies. The variety can be found overprinted on stamps inscribed in both languages on the 1/- value.

O10 stamps exist with overprint in two different founts, one larger, with the letters more widely spaced than the other; these can be found se-tenant.

O12b   first stamp with 'Official' at both left and right, last stamp 'Offisieel' at both left and right. R6/1-2 (11.47).

013a and O13b, see 13c and 35a.

1940 Designs as before but with 'OFFICIAL' at left.

O15	5/- **black and green**		
	(No. 13) (/40)	£60	£85
O16	10/- **blue and sepia**		
	(No. 23) (3/40)	£225	£325

1944-48 As O5a, etc., second 'E' of 'OFFISIEEL' with diaresis.

O17	½d **grey and green**		
	(No. 4) (10/44)	£20	£18

O17 'OFFICIAL' of overprint is at left and reads upwards.

1944 No. 36, etc., overprinted as before, but with overprint reading upwards. O19 'OFFICIAL' at right, O18-19a at left.

O18	1½d **yellow-buff and blue-**		
	green (No. 36a) (/49)	£35	£50
O19	2d **grey and purple-lilac**		
	(No. 8) (3/44)	5.50	£19
O19a	2d **blue-slate and purple**		
	(No. 37) (/50)	£2250	-

1950 No. 36 overprinted sideways: 'OFFICIAL' at top, 'OFFISIEEL' at bottom.

O19b	1½d **yellow-buff and**		
	blue-green	£850	-

It is reported that one sheet was sold over a post office counter, but positive information is lacking as to the issue of this variety.

1950-3 No. 25c, etc., overprinted with new font ('OFFICIAL' at right, reading downwards).

O20	½d **grey and green (No. 4)**	.50	£4
	a sepia-grey and		
	green (No. 25)	.35	£1
	ab bushtick and fly	-	-
O21	1d **grey and red (No. 5)** (9/50)	.50	3.50
O22	1d **grey and magenta-rose**		
	(No. 26) (6/51)	.50	£2
O23	1d **grey-black and carmine**		
	(No. 27) (1/52)	.60	1.25
O24	1½d **yellow-buff and blue-**		
	green (No. 36) (2/51)	£1	2.50
O25	2d **slate-blue and plum**		
	(No. 37) (8/50)	.50	1.25
	a overprint inverted	£800	-
O26	6d **green and red-orange**		
	(No. 32) (11/50)	.75	2.50
	a green and brown-orange		
	(No. 32a) (1/51)	.85	£2
O27	1/- **sepia and slate-blue**		
	(No. 33) (9/50)	2.50	£12
	a sepia-black and		
	deep violet-blue (No. 33a)	£110	£120
O28	2/6 **green and brown**		
	(No. 34) (11/50)	£4	£22
O29	5/- **black and blue-green**		
	(No. 13a) (7/51)	£80	£75
	a 'rain'	-	-
	b black and yellow-green		
	(No. 47) (2/2/53)	£30	£60
O30	10/- **ultramarine and**		
	grey-black (No. 23a)(11/50)	£35	£150
O20/O30	**set of 9 pairs**	£68	£225

O20ab see 4ba.

O25a appeared on the market long after the Official overprints were withdrawn; little is known of the status of this error.

O29a see 35a.

POSTAGE DUE STAMPS

1932-42 Design, value on white background (small "d" after figure), bilingual frame. Perf 14¾ x 14 (C). Sheets 120 - two panes, each 6 x 10.

XPD1	½d **black and blue-green** (/34)	1.25	1.25
	a watermark inverted	£1	£1
XPD2	1d **black and carmine**		
	(watermark inverted) (/34)	£1	.10
PD1	2d **black and deep**		
	purple (/37)	£14	.10
	a watermark inverted	£13	.30
	b 2d doubled	£250	£20

XPD4 3d **deep blue and blue**
(watermark inverted) (/35) £4 .20
a indigo and milky blue
(watermark inverted) (/42)£35 £2
ab watermark upright £25 £2
PD2 6d **deep green and**
bright orange
(watermark inverted) (/38) 6.50 £2

XPD1 is unscreened.

PD1 this stamp replaced one which had value (typo) and frame (roto), and can be distinguished by the screened appearance of the value, which thus differs from the solid appearance of the previous issue. The digit is also thicker.

PD1b see note after PD11.

1943-47 Design, value in colour on white background. Bilingual frame. Units of three, Perf. 14¾ x 14 (C) (externally) and Roul. 6½ (internally). Sheets 360 - six panes, each 6 x 10.

PD3 ½d **deep green** (9/47) 7.50 £30
PD4 1d **carmine** (20/4/43) £5 3.50
a bright carmine (/46) £4 3.50
PD5 2d **deep violet** (/43) £3 £7
a bright violet (/46) £7 £30
PD6 3d **deep blue** (/45) £25 £50
PD3/6 **set of 4 units** £35 £80

1948-9 As Nos. PD1-2 but with capital 'D' after value. Bilingual frame. Perf. 14¾ x 14 (C).

PD7 ½d **black and**
deep green (/48) £3 £8
PD8 1d **black and red** (/48) £8 3.50
PD9 2d **black and violet** (/49) £8 3.50
a 2d doubled £45 £24
PD10 3d **blue-black and**
grey-blue (/48) £7 £11
a split 'D' £140 £175
PD11 6d **deep green and**
bright orange (/48) £11 £5
PD7/11 **set (5)** £33 £28

PD1b/9a/14a, c R15-16/5-6 have the value thicker than normal, and the centre of the 'D' narrower. This is caused by a double image being reproduced during the preparation of the diapositive.

PD10a the 'D' of the value tablet is split on R7/5 of every fourth sheet.

1950-8 Design as 1948 issue, but hyphenated 'SUID-AFRIKA'. Perf. 14¾ x 14 (C).

PD13 1d **black and red** (3/50) .35 .20
PD14 2d **black and violet** (4/51) .25 .15
a 2d doubled £6 £6
b black and reddish
violet (12/52) .50 .45
c 2d doubled £7 £7
d centre omitted £2400 -
PD15 3d **deep blue and blue**
(3/50) 2.25 1.50
a split 'D' £65 -
PD16 4d **deep green and**
light emerald (2/58) £6 £9
a major retouch £45 £60
PD17 6d **deep green and**
bright orange (5/50) £3 £6
PD18 1/- **dark brown and**
red-brown (2/58) £6 £9
PD13/18 **set (6)** £16 £23

PD14a, c see note after PD11.

PD15a see PD10a.

PD16a R1/1 a flaw on the '4' was partially covered by a crude retouch.

BOOKLET PANES

1930-41. All prices for mint panes.

P1 ½d **1935 pane of 6 (adverts)**
CW 3a £20 -
P2 1d **1935 pane of 6 (adverts)**
CW 5 £12 -
P3 ½d **1937 pane of 6 (blank)**
CW 4 £36 -
P4 1d **1937 pane of 6 (blank)**
CW 5 £12 -
P5 ½d **1937 pane of 2 CW 4** 2.50 -
P6 1d **1937 pane of 2 CW 5** 2.50 -
P7 ½d **1938 pane of 6 CW 4** £15 -

P8	1d **1938 pane of 6 CW 5**	£15	-	
P9	1½d **1941 pane of 4 CW 28**	£30	-	

Panes may be found with margins at top and bottom as well as at sides. These may be blank or bear slogans, or advertisements.

P5-9 have no additional selvedge.

1948 Postal Slogan Booklet issue. Panes surrounded at top, bottom and side by borders printed with Postal Slogans.

P10	½d **pane of 6 CW 14**	£3	-
P11	1d **pane of 6 CW 5**	£3	-
P12	1½d **pane of 6 CW 36**	£4	-

1951 issue with additional blank selvedge opposite binding selvedge.

P13	½d **pane of 6 CW 25**	£3	-
P14	1d **pane of 6 CW 26**	£3	-
P15	2d **pane of 6 CW 37**	£3	-

BOOKLETS

All Booklets are stitched at left.

B1	2/6d **1930 black on pink**		
	'FIRESTONE TYRES' advertisement		
	2 panes of 6 X1,		
	4 panes of 6 X2	£1400	-
B2	3/- **1931 black on pink**		
	'SMITHS COOPERAGE' advertisement		
	2 panes of 6 X2		
	3 panes of 6 X4	£1500	-
B3	2/6d **1935 black on lemon**		
	first 'DRY FOOT' advertisement		
	2 x P1, 4 x P2	£200	-
B4	2/6d **1937 black on lemon**		
	2 x P3, 4 x P4	£475	-
B5	6d **1937 red on white 'Razor'**		
	2 x P5, 2 x P6	£6	-
B6	3d **1938 blue 'Razor'**		
	1 x P5, 1 x P6	£30	-
B7	2/6d **1938 black on buff**		
	(Arms at top left)		
	2 x P7, 4 x P8	£450	-
B8	2/6d **1939 black on buff**		
	(Arms at top centre)		
	2 x P7, 4 x P8	£450	-
B9	2/6d **1939 green on buff**		
	2 x P7, 4 x P8	£2000	-
B10	2/6d **1940 blue on buff**		
	2 x P7, 4 x P8	£90	-
B11	2/6d **1941 blue on buff**		
	2 x P7, 4 x P8,		
	2 x P9	£120	-
B12	3/- **1948 black on buff**		
	2 x P10, 2 x P11,		
	2 x P12	£20	-
B13	3/6d **1951 black-brown on buff**		
	2 x P13, 2 x P14,		
	2 x P15	£12	

B5 may be found with coarse stitching (5 stitches) or fine stitching (7 stitches).

SOUTH WEST AFRICA

All stamps were printed in Afrikaans and English (alternately), and are priced as horizontal pairs unless otherwise stated. Overprints on South Africa, formats as South Africa.

1931-54 Perf 14 x 13½. Designs, flora, fauna and scenery. Printer (recess) Bradbury, Wilkinson. Watermark Springbok's Head. Panes 6 x 10.

X1	½d **black and emerald**	1.25	1.50
X2	1d **indigo and red**	1.10	1.50
X3	2d **blue and brown**	.35	£3
	a watermark inverted	£350	-
X4	3d **pale blue and blue**	.35	2.50
X5	4d **green and purple**	.75	4.25
X6	6d **blue and brown**	.75	£6
X7	1/- **chocolate and blue**	1.10	£8
X8	1/3 **violet and yellow**	£3	£7
X9	2/6 **carmine and grey**	£10	£15
X10	5/- **green and brown**	£8	£25
X11	10/- **brown and emerald**	£25	£32
X12	20/- **lake and deep green**	£38	£45
X1/12	**set** (12)	£80	£135

1937 (Mar 1st) - 52 Design, train, aeroplane and R.M.S. 'Capetown Castle' exemplifying methods of mail transport. Printer (recess) Bradbury, Wilkinson. Perf 13¾ x 13½ (C). Sheets as before.

1	1½d **purple-brown**	£11	2.50
	a deep purple-brown (/52)	£11	2.50

AIR STAMPS

1931 As nos. X1-12 but inscribed 'AIR MAIL'. 3d with monoplane, 10d with biplane, each over Windhock.

A1	3d **brown and blue**	£14	£20
A2	10d **black and purple-brown**	£22	£48

SPECIAL ISSUES

See South Africa for details of special issues and varieties common to both countries. The overprints are (typo).

1937 (May 12th) Coronation. Printers (recess) Bradbury, Wilkinson. Perf 13½ x 13¾ (C). Watermark sideways. Centres black. Sheets 120 - two panes, each 10 x 6.

S1	½d **emerald-green**	.20	.10
S2	1d **red**	.20	.10
S3	1½d **orange**	.20	.10
S4	2d **brown**	.20	.10
S5	3d **blue**	.25	.10
S6	4d **deep purple**	.25	.15
	a re-entry	£20	£20
S7	6d **yellow**	.25	1.80
S8	1/- **grey**	.30	1.95
S1/8	**set** (8)	1.70	£4

S6a R6/3, lower pane. The leaves and frame at lower left are doubled. The stamp is inscribed in Afrikaans.

1938 (Dec. 14th) Voortrekker Centenary Memorial. CW S6-9 of South Africa, overprinted 'SWA'.

S9	½d+½d **slate-blue & green**	4.50	£15
S10	1d+1d **deep blue & carmine**	£12	£12
S11	1½d+1½d **chocolate and deep green**	£12	£18
S12	3d + 3d **dull blue**	£24	£48
S9/12	**set** (4)	£45	£85

Numbers overprinted (pairs) - 10,000 each value.

1938 (Dec 14th) Great Trek (Voortrekker). CW S10-11 of South Africa, overprinted 'SWA'.

S13	1d **slate-blue and carmine**	£5	£12
	a third nut	£35	£40

S14 1½d **dull green and chestnut** 7.50 £15
    a lower frame pale £15 £25

Number overprinted (pairs) - 1d, 240,000; 1½d, 120,000.

1939 (July 17th) 250th Anniversary of the Huguenots' landing in South Africa. CW S12-14 of South Africa, overprinted 'SWA'.

S15 ½d+½d **sepia & deep green** £7 £9
S16 1d+1d **deep green & carmine** £9 £9
S17 1½d+1½d **dull green and**
        deep purple £15 £9
S15/17 **set** (3) £28 £24

1941-2 War Effort (large size). CW S15-22 of South Africa, overprinted 'SWA'.

S18 ½d **green** (19/11/41) .35 2.70
S19   a blue-green (/42) .30 1.50
S19 1d **carmine** (3/10/41) .25 £2
    a stain on uniform £10 £18
S20 1½d **myrtle-green** (21/1/42) .25 2.25
S21 2d **violet (single)** (15/9/41) .25 £1
S22 3d **blue** (8/41) £10 £14
    a woman smoking £48 £50
S23 4d **orange-brown** £3 £10
    a red-brown (/42) £8 £17
S24 6d **deep orange** (9/41) 3.50 £5
S25 1/- **chocolate (single)**
    (27/10/41) .80 1.20
S18/25 **set** (8) 16.50 £33

The overprint on the 3d and 1/- values is larger than that used for the others.

1942-5 War Effort 'Bantams'. CW S24-31 of South Africa, overprinted 'SWA'. Prices for units of 3 or pairs, perforated around the outside and rouletted between.

S26 ½d **blue-green** (10/42) .25 3.30
    a upper background missing £5 £10
    c deep green 2.25 4.50
    d upper background missing £6 £10
    e deep greenish blue (/44) £2 £4
    f upper background missing £6 £10
    g background added £10 £14
S27 1d **carmine** (1/43) 1.50 3.25
    a bright carmine (/45) 1.50 3.25
S28 1½d **reddish brown** (8/42) .25 .90
    a right side background
    missing £5 £6
S29 2d **purple-violet** (1/43) £4 3.25
    a '2/6d' flaw £25 £25
    b overprint middle of stamp £14 £14
S30 3d **blue** (10/42) 1.50 £11
S31 4d **green** (11/42) £1 12.50
    a overprint inverted £575 £400
    b unshaded corner £2 £16
S32 6d **red-orange** (10/42) 2.75 1.80
    a overprint inverted £475 -
    b much whiter flame £4 £4

S33 1/- **chocolate**
    (large overprint) (12/42) £5 £14
    a bursting shell £40 £50
    b upper background missing £12 £15
    ba upper background added £20 £28
    c overprint inverted £450 £225
    d chocolate
    (small overprint) (/44) £2 3.50
    da bursting shell £20 £25
    db smoking 'L' £20 £25
    dc upper background missing £12 £14
    dd upper background added £16 £20
    de overprint inverted £360 £250
S26/33 **set** (8) £12 £35

Large Overprint   Small Overprint

The overprint on the 1½d and the 1/- is in large type (as used for S34).

There are variations in the overprint types on the 6d value.

1943-6 War Effort. CW S32 of South Africa, overprinted 'SWA'.

S34 1/3 **olive-brown** (2/1/43) £6 £14
    a deep sepia (/46) £6 £14

1945 (Dec 3rd) Victory. CW S33-5 of South Africa, overprinted 'SWA'.

S35 1d **deep brown and**
    carmine .10 .45
    a overprint inverted £290 £300
    b barbed wire £10 £12
S36 2d **slate-blue and**
    purple-violet .15 .45
S37 3d **deep blue and blue** .75 £1
S35/37 **set** (3) .90 1.75

1947 (Feb 17th) Royal Visit. CW S36-38 of South Africa, overprinted 'SWA'.

S38 1d **deep slate and carmine** .10 .10
    a whiskers £5 £5
S39 2d **purple-violet (Cyl 6912)** .10 .15
    a bird on '2' £5 £7
S40 3d **deep blue** .10 .15
    a blinded princess £6 £9
S38-40 **set** (3) .30 .35

1948 (Apr 26th) Silver Wedding. CW S39 of South Africa, overprinted 'SWA'.

S41 3d **silver and dark blue** .50 .25
    a large spot on King's
    forehead £5 £6

1949 (Oct 1st) U.P.U. CW S41-3 of South Africa, overprinted 'SWA'.

S42	½d **deep blue-green**	.40	1.35
S43	1½d **brownish lake**	.40	£1
	a gauntlet on wrist	£10	£12
S44	3d **bright ultramarine**	.60	.60
	a 'G' variety	£24	-
	b 'lake' in East Africa	£24	-
S42/44	**set** (3)	1.25	2.65

Numbers overprinted (pairs) - ½d, 847,440; 1½d, 847,380; 3d, 607,980.

1949 (Dec 1st) Inauguration of Voortrekker Monument. CW S44-46 of South Africa, overprinted (roto) 'SWA'. Printed bilingually and priced for singles.

S45	1d **lake-magenta**	.10	.10
S46	1½d **dull green**	.10	.10
S47	3d **deep slate-blue**	.10	.35
S45/47	**set** (3)	.25	.50

Number overprinted (pairs) - ½d, 847,440; 1½d, 847,380; 3d, 607,980.

OFFICIAL STAMPS

The easiest way to identify the Official stamps is by the shape of the 'O' in the overprint.

O1 the 'O' is thin and oval.

O2-O6 the 'O' is thicker but still oval.

O7-O11 the 'O' is round.

O12-O16a the 'O' is round and thicker; the ink is also deeper vermilion colour rather than scarlet.

1938 (July 1st) CW 1 overprinted 'OFFICIAL' and 'OFFISIEEL' in red.

O1	1½d **purple-brown**	£13	£30

Stamps with forged double overprint exist.

1945-50 Pictorial Issue of 1931, overprinted in red as CW O1 but in a smaller and thicker type. Printers (recess) Breadbury, Wilkinson. Perf 13¾ x 13½ (C).

O2	½d **black and emerald** (/45)	£6	£18
	a overprint in dark red	£10	£20
O3	1d **dark blue and scarlet** (/50)	£5	£11
	a overprint double	£400	-
O4	1½d **purple-brown** (/45)	17.50	£30
	a overprint double	-	-
	b overprint in dark red (/50)	17.50	£30
O5	2d **blue-black and sepia-brown** (/47)	£375	£550
O6	6d **blue and olive-brown** (/45)	£10	£35
	a overprint in dark red (/50)	£12	£35
O1-4, 6	**set of 4**	£44	£85

1951 (Nov. 15th) As CW O3, etc., but overprint in changed font.

O7	½d **black and emerald**	-	-
	a overprints transposed	†	£2000
O8	1d **dark blue and scarlet**	2.50	£12
	a overprints transposed	£45	£150
	b block of four, one pair normal, one pair transposed	£55	£180
O9	1½d **purple-brown**	£12	£17
	a overprints transposed	£45	£55
	b block of four, one pair normal, one pair transposed	£55	£75
O10	2d **blue-black and sepia-brown**	1.50	12.50
	a overprints transposed	£40	£140
	b block of four, one pair normal, one pair transposed	£45	£160
O11	6d **dark blue and olive-brown**	1.50	£29
	a overprints transposed	£15	£100
	b block of four, one pair normal, one pair transposed	£25	£135
O8/O11	**set** (4 pairs)	£16	£65

O7a-O11a the overprint in English appears on stamps inscribed in Afrikaans, and vice versa.

O7a one used pair is known. We have yet to see any further example of O7a. It is possible that the pair came from a trial sheet.

O8b-O11b the transposed overprint occurs in two forms:

(1) Each vertical row of 10 overprinted 'Official' or 'Offisieel' right down the column. This caused the stamps in every alternate row to be transposed (values existing thus, 1½d and 6d).

(2) Top half of sheet set correctly, but row 6 across the sheet set as the row above it. This caused the lower 5 rows of sheet to be set all transposed (values existing thus 1d, 1½d, 2d, and 6d).

1952 As CW O8/O11, but overprint in thicker type in deep vermilion ink.

O12	½d **black and green**	£8	£14
O13	1d **blue and scarlet**	3.50	£12
O14	1½d **brown**	£12	£17
	a overprints transposed	-	-
O15	2d **blue and brown**	1.50	£14
O16	6d **blue and olive-brown**	2.50	£30
	a overprints transposed	-	-
O12/16	**set** (5)	£25	£80

POSTAGE DUE STAMPS

1931 (Feb 23rd) inscribed bilingually, and priced as singles.

D1	½d **black and green**	.50	£5
D2	1d **black and red**	.50	£1
D3	2d **black and violet**	.50	1.75
D4	3d **black and blue**	£2	£10
D5	6d **black and grey**	£6	£15
D1/5	**set** (5)	£9	£30

SOUTHERN RHODESIA

All stamps were printed (recess) by Waterlow and Sons on unwatermarked paper, unless otherwise mentioned. Many variants of archival proofs exist.

1937 (Nov. 25th) - 50. Perf 14 (L). Sheets 10 x 6 (except Nos. 1-3 which were printed in sheets of 240; four panes, each 10 x 6.

1	½d **yellow-green**	.25	.10
	a green (/50)	.25	.10
2	1d **red**	.25	.10
3	1½d **reddish brown**	.45	.20
	a deep red-brown (/45)	.45	.20
4	4d **deep orange**	.65	.10
5	6d **dark grey**	.65	.30
6	8d **turquoise-green**	£1	1.95
7	9d **light blue**	.75	.60
8	10d **purple**	1.10	1.65
9	1/- **black and green**	1.35	.10
	a double print of frame, once albino	£1600	-
10	1/6 **black and deep orange**	5.50	1.50
11	2/- **black and deep brown**	£8	.35
12	2/6 **deep ultramarine and purple**	£5	£4
13	5/- **deep blue and green**	£10	1.50
1/13	**set** (13)	£30	£11

1, 2 exist from coils.

9a The uninked plate has broken the surface fibres of the paper, blurring the lines of the design and resulting in a much brighter shade.

Later printings of all values exist on a much thinner paper than the original 1937 printings.

Withdrawn June 30th 1954.

1935-41 Design, view of Victoria Falls (with inscription 'Postage and Revenue'). Perf 14 (L).

14	2d **deep green and chocolate**, perf 12½ (/35)	£2	£9
	a perf 14 (/41)	1.10	.10
15	3d **dark blue**, perf 14 (1/38)	£2	.75

1950 As CW 14, but perf 14 x 13¾ (C).

16	2d **deep green and light chocolate**	£2	£2

SPECIAL ISSUES

1937 (May 12th) Coronation. Design, Victoria Falls with train in foreground. Perf 12 ½ (L). Sheets 6 x 10.

S1	1d **olive-green and rose-carmine**	.30	.60
S2	2d **emerald and sepia**	.30	£1
S3	3d **purple-violet and blue**	1.60	5.50
	a imperf between stamp and top margin	-	-
S4	6d **black and purple**	.85	2.25
S1/4	**set** (4)	2.75	8.50

Number issued 1d, 3,587,294; 2d, 932,710; 3d, 370,440; 6d, 480,588.

Withdrawn August 31st, 1937.

1940 (June 3rd) British South Africa Company's Golden Jubilee. Designs, ½d (Arms of Company); 1½d (Cecil Rhodes); other values (views and scenes in territory). Designers, ½d, 1d, 1½d, 3d Mrs L.E. Curtis; 2d, 4d, 6d, 1/- Mrs. I. Mount. Rhodes's portrait, S. P. Kendrick. Perf 14 (L). Sheets 10 x 6, or 6 x 10.

S5	½d **grey-violet and green**	.10	.40
S6	1d **violet-slate and red**	.10	.10
S7	1½d **black and chocolate-brown**	.10	.50
	a shaded collar	£15	£26
S8	2d **green and violet**	.15	.40
S9	3d **black and deep blue**	.15	.90
	a cave flaw	£32	£65
S10	4d **green and light brown**	£1	1.75
S11	6d **grey-green and sepia**	.60	1.75
S12	1/- **green and deep steel-blue**	.60	1.25
S5/12	**set** (8)	2.50	6.50

S7a   S9a

S7a R6/1 Rhodes's left collar has extra lines of shading.

S9a a flaw resembles a cave in the mountain on R6/6.

Numbers printed - S5, 7,012,000; S6, 9,734,000; S7, 3,239,000; S8, 168,000; S9, 363,000; S10, 200,00; S11, 350,000; S12, 282,000.

Withdrawn October 31st, 1944.

1943 (Nov 1st) Anniversary of Occupation of Matabeleland. Design, Mounted pioneer. Printers (roto) Government Stamp Printers, Pretoria. Wmk. 'Springbok's Head' sideways. Perf 14 (C). Sheets 10 x 6.

S13	2d **brown and deep green**	.10	.60
	a sepia-brown and deep green	.10	.60
	b narrow stamp	1.25	£2
	c cauliflower ear	£14	£15
	d line under saddlebag	£14	£15

13b the 8th stamp in each of the six rows is narrower (1mm) than other stamps on most sheets, as occurs also with stamps of South Africa which were similarly perforated.

13c   13d

S13c R1/8 (Plate 1B) there is a large retouch affecting the brim of the hat.

S13d R6/10 (Plate 1A) a white line appears under the saddlebag.

Withdrawn October 31st, 1944.

1947 (April 1st) Royal Visit. Designs, portraits of Royal Family. Perf 14 (L). Sheets 6 x 10.

S14	½d **black and green**	.15	.35
S15	1d **black and carmine-red**	.15	.35

1947 (May 8th) Victory. Designs, portraits of Royal Family. Perf 14 (L). Sheets S16, 240 in four panes, each 10 x 6; S17/19, 10 x 6.

S16	1d **carmine-red**	.10	.10
S17	2d **slate**	.10	.10
	a double print	£1600	-
	b part double print	£750	-
	c damaged frame	£65	-
S18	3d **deep blue**	.40	.95
S19	6d **orange**	.15	.85
S16/19	set (4)	.65	1.80

S17b the top and right hand side of the head, the frame at right and part of the lettering are doubled. One part sheet is reported to exist.

S17c The frame is damaged on the right hand side, R1/10 sheet A. This variety seems to be far scarcer than should logically be the case. We have yet to see a used example.

Withdrawn November 8th, 1947.

1949 (Oct. 10th) U.P.U. As Aden CW S9/10, but inscribed 'SOUTHERN RHODESIA'. Sheets 5 x 12.

S20	2d **green-slate**	.35	.15
S21	3d **slate-blue**	.40	2.50

Withdrawn January 10th, 1950.

1950 (Sept. 12th) Diamond Jubilee of Colony. Perf 14 (L). Sheets 5 x 12.

S22	2d **emerald and grey-sepia**	.25	.75

Number issued - 2,819,032. (Number printed - 4,650,000).

Withdrawn December 31st, 1950.

POSTAGE DUE STAMPS

1951 (Oct. 1st) Postage Due stamps of Great Britain, overprinted 'SOUTHERN RHODESIA'.

PD1	½d **emerald-green**	1.50	£10
PD2	1d **cobalt**	1.40	1.50

PD3	2d **agate**	1.25	1.25
PD4	3d **violet**	1.35	1.75
PD5	4d **grey-green**	£90	£400
PD6	4d **light blue**	.85	2.25
PD7	1/- **blue**	1.25	2.75
PD1/7	**set** (7)	£90	£400
PD1-4,6, 7 set (6)		£7	17.50

Numbers overprinted - ½d, 222,720; 1d, 671,040; 2d, 229,120; 3d, 922,880; 4d PD5, 109,680; PD6, 1,839,360; 1/- 672,240.

PD5 many 'used' examples bear anonymous cancels. This error of colour was issued to Fort Victoria and Gwelo post offices only. An expert opinion is desirable.

BOOKLET PANES

| P1 | ½d **1937 pane of 6** | £20 | - |
| P2 | 1d **1937 pane of 6** | £25 | - |

BOOKLET

B1   2/6d **1937 black on yellow cover**
P1 x 4
P2 x 3 from £200

There were 6 printings of these interesting booklets. Students are referred to *The Rhodesian Philatelist*, No. 8, page 119 for further details.

SUDAN

All stamps of Sudan, except where otherwise stated, were printed by De La Rue and Co. Watermarked 'SG' unless stated.

 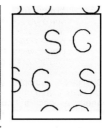

1927-40 (Typo) Watermark Multiple "SG". Perf. 14. 1m - 15m small format, sheets 240 (4 panes of 60); 2p - 20p large format, sheets 120 (2 panes of 60). Chalky paper unless otherwise stated. Perf 14.

G8	1m **black and orange**	.35	.10
	a (sub) (/41)	.35	.10
G9	2m **orange and chocolate**	.35	.10
	a (sub) (/41)	.75	.10
G10	3m **mauve and green**	.35	.10
	a (sub) (/41)	1.35	.20
G11	4m **green and chocolate**	.30	.10
	a (sub) (/41)	1.75	.25
	b watermark inverted	£50	£50
G12	5m **brown and black**	.30	.10
	a (sub) (/41)	1.25	.10
G13	10m **red and black**	.75	.10
	a (sub) (/41)	1.75	.10
G14	15m **blue and chestnut**	1.60	.10
	a watermark inverted	†	£165
	b (sub) (/41)	1.25	.10
G15	2p **purple and yellow**	£2	.10
	a (sub) (/41)	£3	.10
G16	3p **red-brown and blue** (1/1/40)	2.35	.10
	a (sub) (/41)	£6	.10
G17	4p **ultramarine and grey** (2/11/36)	1.75	.10
G18	5p **chestnut and green**	.60	.10
	a (sub) (/41)	3.25	1.65
G19	6p **green-blue and black** (2/11/36)	£4	£1
	a (sub) (/41)	£20	1.80
G20	8p **emerald and black** (2/11/36)	£4	£2
	a (sub) (/41)	£22	£3
G21	10p **black and violet**	2.50	.10
	a black and bright violet (sub) (/41)	4.50	.50
G22	20p **pale blue and blue** (17/10/35)	£3	.10
	a (sub) (/41)	£3	.10
G8/22	**set** (15)	£22	3.75

The chalky paper printings are almost invariably on thick paper with brown, streaky gum, while the ordinary (substitute) paper printings are on very white paper.

1936-7 Air Stamps. As 1931-5 issue, but perf 11¾ x 12½ instead of 14. Watermark sideways.

G54 15m **chocolate and brown**
(4/3/37)   1.80   .10
G55 2p **black and deep**
orange   £2   £10
G56 2½p **magenta and blue** (/36) 1.25 .10
    a aniline centre   £4   £2
    ba watermark reversed   £100   -
    bb watermark sideways
    inverted, and reversed   -   £140
G57 3p **black and grey**
(4/3/37)   .40   .25
G58 3½p **black and dull violet** 1.20   £9
    a watermark sideways
    inverted, and reversed   †   -
G59 5p **black and ultramarine**
(4/3/37)   1.75   .20
G60 7½p **myrtle-green and**
turquoise-green   1.75   £6
G61 10p **deep sepia and**
greenish blue   1.75   £14
    a watermark sideways
    inverted and reversed   £120   -
G54/61 **set** (8)   £11   £35

The sideway/inverted/reversed varieties show the top of the G to the right as seen from the reverse.

Number sold - 15m, 90,000; 2p, 3½p, 7½p, 10p, 15,000 each; 2½p, 175,000; 3p, 120,000; 5p, 48,000.

1938 (July 1st) Air Stamps. Surcharged in English and Arabic by De La Rue.

(a) Perf 14 (L)

G62 3p/3½p **black and dull violet** £16   £32

G63 3p/7½p **myrtle-green and**
turquoise-green   £3   £4
    a watermark sideways
    inverted, and reversed £50   £50
    b watermark reversed   -   -
G64 5p/10p **deep sepia and**
greenish blue   .85   2.75
    a watermark reversed   -   -

(b) Perf 11¾ x 12½ (C).

G65 5m/2½p **magenta and blue** 1.75   .10
    a watermark sideways
    inverted   -   £85
    b watermark reversed   -   -
G66 3p/3½p **black and dull violet** £350 £425
G67 3p/7½p **myrtle-green and**
turquoise-green   £350   £425
G69 5p/10p **deep sepia and**
greenish blue   £350   £425

G68, the formerly-listed 5p on 2½p perf 11¾ x12½, is from a trial sheet.

Number sold - perf 14; 3p on 3½p, 17,650; 3p on 7½p, 37,750; 5p on 10p, 32,400.

Perf 11¾ x 12½; 5m, 171,350; 3p on 3½p, 3p on 7½p, 5p on 10p, usually stated to be 100 each.

1940-41 Provisionals. G13, G12 and G20 surcharged in English and Arabic (4½p and 5m in English only) at Khartoum.

2   5m/10m **red and black**
(c) (25/2/40)   .60   .45
    a extra Arabic "M"   £35   £50
    b missing dots   £35   £50
    c short 'mim'   £35   £50
    d broken 'lam'   £35   £50
    e inserted "5"   £125   -
3   4½p/5m **brown and black**
(c) (9/2/41)   £24   5.50
4   4½p/8p **emerald and black**
(c) (12/12/40)   £20   5.50

2 was issued when it became apparent that De La Rue could not supply a new printing of the 5m in time to avoid exhaustion of stocks in Sudan.

2a R5/1, left panes. An extra "M" makes the Arabic read "MALMIME"

2b R8/6, right panes. The two diamond-shaped dots below the Arabic are missing.

2c R3/1, right panes. The downstroke at left is shortened.

2d R6/2, right panes. The upstroke 'lam' is broken.

2e R4/5, lower right pane. The "5" of the surcharge was inserted by a second operation in a small number of sheets.

3, 4 were provisional issues for Forces' Mail.

1941 (Mar - Aug.) Design, Tuti Island, on the Nile near Khartoum. Designer, Miss H.M. Hebbert. Printers (litho) Security Press, Nasik, India. Small format, perf 14 x 13¾ (C), sheets; 120 in six panes, each 4 x 5. Large format, perf 13¾ x 14 (C), sheets; 10 x 8. No watermark.

5	1m slate and orange	1.50	2.40
6	2m orange and chocolate-brown	1.50	2.40
7	3m mauve and green	1.60	.10
8	4m slate-green and chocolate-brown	.40	.35

9	5m olive-brown and black	.15	.10
10	10m crimson-rose and black	6.50	2.20
11	15m ultramarine and chestnut (25/3/41)	.75	.10
12	2p purple-maroon and orange	3.25	.35
13	3p red-brown and dark blue (25/3/41)	.60	.10
14	4p ultramarine and black (23/3/41)	1.75	.10
15	5p red-chestnut and deep green	3.25	5.75
16	6p green-blue and black	£11	.40
17	8p dull emerald-green and black	9.50	.40
18	10p deep slate and purple	£36	.45
19	20p dull blue and dark blue	£35	£22
5/19	set (15)	£100	£33

An emergency issue made necessary by the difficulty of obtaining supplies of normal issues from Great Britain owing to the war. Where no date is mentioned, the stamps were issued on 10/8/41.

The 3p and 4p values have been seen with frame double, and Stagg records the 5m with centre double. Others may exist and reports are welcome. Such double prints frequently appear on stamps printed by Nasik.

Number sold - (Issue date 25/3/41) 15m, 422,400; 3p 306,800; 4p, 115,580.

(Issue date 10/8/41) 1m, 2m 52,680 each; 3m 51,480; 4m 51,120; 5m 2,051,520; 10m 31,680; 15m 422,400; 2p 52,080; 3p 306,800; 4p 115,580; 5p 10p, 21,840; 8p 22,000; 20p 10,960.

1948 (Jan 1st) Design as CW G8, etc., but with inscription on bottom panel altered. Sheets, small format, 10 x 10; large format, 10 x 5. Chalk-surfaced paper unless otherwise stated. Perf 14.

20	1m black and orange	.15	2.50
21	2m orange and chocolate	.40	2.75
22	3m mauve and deep green	.15	£4
23	4m green and chocolate-brown	.25	.90

24	5m	olive-brown and black	3.50	1.35
		a watermark inverted	£50	-
25	10m	dull rose and black	2.75	.10
		a centre inverted	†	-
26	15m	ultramarine and red-chestnut	2.50	.10
27	2p	purple-maroon and orange	4.25	1.50
28	3p	red-brown and dark blue	3.75	.20
29	4p	ultramarine and black	£2	£1
30	5p	dull orange and grey-green	£2	2.40
31	6p	turquoise-green and black	2.25	£2
32	8p	green and black (sub)	2.25	£2
33	10p	grey-black and purple-mauve (sub)	£5	£3
		a black and red-mauve (6/48)	£20	3.75
34	20p	blue and deep blue (sub)	2.25	.30
		a perf 13¼ x 13	£20	£130
35	50p	carmine-red and ultramarine	3.25	1.50
20/35		set (16)	£33	£23

25a   one used example, which is very slightly damaged, is known, postmark dated 1951.

1951 (Sept. 1st) Designs, scenes, customs and fauna of Sudan. Designers, Col. W. L. Atkinson (1m, 2m, 4m, 5m, 10m, 3p, 3½p, 20p); Col. E.A. Stanton (50p); other values from photographs. Printers (typo) De La Rue. 1m to 15m, perf 13¾ x 14 (C), sheets 10 x 10; other values, perf 13¼ x 13 (C), sheets 5 x 10 or 10 x 5. Chalk-surfaced paper.

36	1m	black and orange	1.25	.90
37	2m	black and blue	1.25	.75
38	3m	black and green	£4	2.40
39	4m	black and light green	1.25	2.40
40	5m	black and purple	1.10	.10
		a black and red-purple	£3	.50
41	10m	black and azure	.15	.10
42	15m	black and light red	2.50	.10
		a black and brown-orange	2.50	.10
43	2p	blue and light blue	.15	.10
		a dark blue and very pale blue	2.25	.20
44	3p	brown and dark ultramarine	5.50	.10
		a brown and deep blue	£5	£1

45	3½p	emerald and brown	1.25	.10
		a light emerald and brown	£2	.10
46	4p	ultramarine and black	1.10	.10
		a deep blue and black	3.75	.10
47	5p	brown and emerald	.35	.10
48	6p	light blue and black	4.25	1.50
		a deep blue and black	£8	£4
49	8p	blue and brown	£7	2.50
		a deep blue and brown	£8	2.50
50	10p	black and deep green	.75	.40
51	20p	green and black	3.50	£2
52	50p	carmine and black	7.50	£2
36/52		set (17)	£38	£14

This set had a long life. The shades listed above did not appear until the early 1960s, but are so strong that they demand inclusion. There are shades of other values.

AIR STAMPS

See also G54/69 above.

1950 (July 1st) - 51 Design, views and scenes. Printers (recess) De La Rue. Perf 12 (C). Sheets 5 x 10.

A16	2p	black and grey-green	2.35	.90
A17	2½p	blue and red-orange	.50	.75
A18	3p	lake and deep blue	1.85	.75
A19	3½p	deep chocolate and light brown	1.60	2.25
A20	4p	light brown and light blue	.75	1.65
A21	4½p	black and ultramarine	1.25	2.25
		a black and dull blue (6/51)	6.50	4.50
A22	6p	black and carmine-red	1.50	1.95
A23	20p	black and purple-lake	1.10	3.30
A16/23		set (8)	£6	12.50

SPECIAL ISSUES

1948 (Oct. 1st) Golden Jubilee of 'Camel Postman' stamps. Printers De La Rue. Perf 12¾ x 13 (C). Chalk-surfaced paper. Sheets 10 x 5.

S1 2p **black and grey-blue**
(Type I) .10 .10
a ditto (Type II) .20 .20

Type I    Type II

Type I. Behind the camel's neck, a circular unshaded portion has the appearance of a setting sun and the white patch on the ground is entirely irregular in shape.

Type II. The sky is entirely shaded in, and on the ground the top of the white patch behind the front legs of the camel finishes in a straight line.

Both types are to be found on sheets of either Plates 1 or 2, but the number of examples of each type in a sheet is not constant.

1948 (Dec. 23rd) Opening of Legislative Assembly. Printers De La Rue. Perf 12¾ x 13 (C). Chalk-surfaced paper. Sheets 10 x 5.

S2 10m **carmine-rose and black** .25 .10
S3 5p **dull orange and
deep green** .50 .90

POSTAGE DUE STAMPS

1948 (Jan. 1st) Design, Gunboat "Zafir". Perf 14 x 13¾ (C). Chalk-surfaced paper, with new Arabic inscription as above. Sheets 10 x 10.

PD1 2m **black and dark orange** .85 £30
PD2 4m **chocolate and green** 1.75 £32
PD3 10m **green and mauve** £9 £12
PD4 20m **ultramarine and carmine** £9 £20
PD1/4 **set (4)** £19 £85

OFFICIAL STAMPS

1936-46 G8-G22 (Watermark Multiple SG) overprinted "SG" in black by De La Rue. The letters are 2mm and 2½mm in height on Millieme and Piastre values respectively. Chalk-surfaced paper unless otherwise stated.

O1 1m **black and orange**
(sub) (22/11/46) 1.25 £6
a overprint double † £130
O2 2m **orange and chocolate**
(sub) (1/3/45) 1.50 £4
a orange and chocolate - £50
O3 3m **mauve and deep
green** (28/1/37) 1.75 .10
O3a 4m **green and chocolate**
(9/36) £2 1.80
a ditto (sub) - -
O4 5m **olive-brown and black**
(5/3/40) 1.85 .10
a ditto (sub) £12 .25

O5 10m **carmine-red and black**
(1/6/46) .85 .10
O6 15m **blue and chestnut-brown**
(12/6/37) 4.25 .20
a ditto (sub) £30 1.80
O7 2p **purple-maroon and**
orange (30/3/37) 7.50 .10
a ditto (sub) £19 .60
O8 3p **red-brown and**
dark blue (sub) (1/4/46) 3.75 1.65
O9 4p **ultramarine and black**
(1/4/46) £17 3.50
a ditto (sub) £30 2.50
O9b 5p **dull orange and**
grey-green (9/36) £8 .10
c ditto (sub) £38 2.85
O10 6p **turquoise-blue and**
black (sub) (1/4/46) 4.75 4.25
O11 8p **emerald-green and**
black (sub) (1/4/46) 3.25 £23
O12 10p **grey-black and**
purple (1/9/37) 17.50 £10
a black and mauve (sub) £26 £4
O13 20p **blue and deep**
blue (sub) (29/6/46) £15 £16
O1/13 **set** (15) £80 £55

1948 (Jan 1st) CW 20, etc., overprinted "SG"
in black.

O14 1m **black and orange** .15 2.50
O15 2m **orange and chocolate** .60 .10
O16 3m **mauve and deep green** £2 £5
O17 4m **green and**
chocolate-brown 1.85 2.75
O18 5m **olive-brown and black** 1.75 .10
O19 10m **dull rose and black** 1.75 1.65
O20 15m **ultramarine and**
red-chestnut £2 .10
O21 2p **purple-maroon**
and orange £2 .10
O22 3p **red-brown and**
dark blue £2 .10
O23 4p **ultramarine and black** 1.60 .10
a ditto perf. 13¼ x 13 £6 £10
O24 5p **dull orange and**
grey-green 2.50 .10
O25 6p **turquoise-blue and**
black 1.75 .10
O26 8p **turquoise-green and**
black (sub) 1.75 £3
O27 10p **grey-black and**
purple-mauve (sub) 3.25 .15
O28 20p **blue and deep**
blue (sub) 2.35 .15
O29 50p **carmine-red and**
ultramarine £32 £36
O14/29 **set** (16) £55 £45

1950 (July 1st) - 51 CW A16-A23 overprinted
"SG" in black or red.

OA30 2p **black and**
grey-green (red) 7.50 £2

OA31 2½p **blue and red-orange** .75 £1
OA32 3p **lake and deep blue** .40 .60
OA33 3½p **deep chocolate and**
light brown .40 4.75
OA34 4p **light brown and**
light blue .40 4.50
OA35 4½p **black and**
ultramarine (red) £2 £10
a black and dull blue
(red) (4/51) £6 12.50
OA36 6p **black and**
carmine-red (red) .50 2.50
OA37 20p **black and**
purple-lake (red) 2.50 7.50
OA30/37 **set** (8) £13 £30

1951 (Sept. 1st) - 58 CW 35-52, overprinted
"SG" in black or red.

O38 1m **black and orange (red)** .25 2.25
O39 2m **black and blue (red)** .25 .60
O40 3m **black and green (red)** 4.25 £9
O41 4m **black and**
light green (red) .10 3.50
O42 5m **black and purple (red)** .10 .10
O43 10m **black and azure (red)** .10 .10
O44 15m **black and light**
red (red) .50 .10
O45 2p **dark blue and**
light blue .10 .10
a overprint inverted £575 -
b dark blue and
very pale blue .85 .10
O46 3p **brown and dark**
ultramarine £8 .10
a brown and deep blue £8 1.20
O47 3½p **emerald and brown** .15 .10
a light emerald and brown 2.25 1.80
O48 4p **ultramarine and black** 1.50 .10
a deep blue and black 1.75 .10
O49 5p **brown and emerald** .15 .10
O50 6p **light blue and black** .35 1.65
a deep blue and black £5 4.80
O51 8p **blue and light brown** .50 .10
a deep blue and light brown £3 £2
O52 10p **black and**
deep green (red) .35 .10
O53 10p **black and**
deep green (black) ('58) £8 1.80
O54 20p **green and black** .75 .20
a overprint inverted - £2200
O55 50p **carmine and black** 1.75 .75
O38/55 **set** (18) £24 £18

S.G. S.G.

1951   1957-60

The 1951 set was overprinted with the thick type,
above. Later printings (1957-60) of the 5m, 10m
and 15m received a thinner overprint with
smaller stops.

SWAZILAND

1938 (April 1st) - 42. Printer (recess) De La Rue. Perf 13¼ x 13 (C). Watermark multiple Script CA. Off-white paper for 1938-39 printings; thin, very white paper from 1940. Sheets 10 x 6.

1	½d **green**	£1	.75
	a bright green (11/40)	1.50	1.25
2	1d **scarlet**	1.25	.75
	a carmine	1.50	.75
	b scarlet, white paper (11/40)	£4	1.75
3	1½d **light blue**	1.75	.45
4	2d **light brown**	£1	.75
	a reddish brown (10/38)	2.50	1.50
5	3d **ultramarine**	£4	£1
	a deep blue (10/38)	£5	£1
6	4d **orange**	£3	1.35
7	6d **reddish magenta**	£6	1.65
	a reddish purple	£10	3.50
8	1/- **olive**	£6	1.25
	a grey-olive (12/40)	£8	1.75
9	2/6 **violet**	£8	2.50
10	5/- **brownish grey**	£18	£9
11	10/- **sepia**	£22	3.75
1/11	**set** (11)	£65	£21
SP1/11	**specimen perf** (11)	£175	†

As CW 3 but perf 14 (L) and on thin white paper.

12	1½d **light blue** (1/42)	1.15	.60

1942-54. As CW 1, etc., but perf 13¼ x 13¾ (C). Thin white paper.

13	½d **yellowish green** (/43)	.20	£2
	a green (/48)	.15	1.65
	b bronze-green (/50)	£1	£5
14	1d **scarlet** (/43)	.40	£1
	a rose-carmine (/47)	.40	£1
15	1½d **light blue** (/42)	.20	.90
	a bright light blue (/48)	.25	.60
	b jay blue (/49)	1.50	£2
	c printed on gummed side	£2400	-
16	2d **light brown** (/43)	.25	.40
	a yellow-brown (/45)	.15	.30
	b fawn (/45)	2.50	2.50
17	3d **violet-blue** (/43)	2.25	£5
	a light ultramarine (/46)	£10	£11
	b deep blue (/47)	£6	£7
	c steel blue (/52)	£12	£14

18	4d **orange** (/43)	.25	.85
	a bright orange (/48)	.25	£1
19	6d **bright purple** (/43)	2.50	2.75
	a reddish purple (/44)	£2	.90
	b mauve (/47)	£2	£1
	c claret (/54)	£3	£4
20	1/- **greenish olive** (/43)	.65	1.25
	a olive (/44)	£4	£2
	b brown-olive (/49)	£2	1.25
	c deep greyish olive (/54)	£2	1.25
21	2/6 **violet** (/43)	9.50	1.80
	a reddish violet (/49)	£9	6.75
	b purple-violet (/51)	£9	£8
22	5/- **slate** (/43)	£20	£40
	a grey (/44)	£18	£9
	b grey-black (/52)	£18	£9
23	10/- **sepia** (/43)	3.50	3.75
	a greyish sepia (/47)	£8	£4
13/23	**set** (11)	£33	£24

There was some variation from the perforation measurements given above.

SPECIAL ISSUES

1937 (May 12th) Coronation. As Antigua.

S1	1d **carmine-red**	.25	1.50
S2	2d **brown**	.25	.15
S3	3d **blue**	.25	.45
S1/3	**set** (3)	.70	1.90
SPS1/3	**specimen perf** (3)	£68	†

1945 (Dec. 3rd) Victory. CW S33-5 of South Africa, overprinted 'SWAZILAND'.

S4	1d **deep brown and carmine**	.30	.50
	a barbed wire	£10	£12
S5	2d **slate-blue and violet**	.30	.50
S6	3d **deep blue and blue**	.30	1.50
S4-6	**set** (3)	.85	2.25

S4a R9/6 see details under South Africa.

1947 (Feb. 17th) Royal Visit. As Basutoland, CW S7-10.

S7	1d **scarlet**	.10	.10
S8	2d **green**	.10	.10
S9	3d **ultramarine**	.10	.10
S10	1/- **dull mauve**	.10	.10
S7/10	**set** (4)	.35	.35
SP S7/10	**specimen perf** (4)	£80	†

1948 (Dec. 1st) Silver Wedding. As Aden.

S11	1½d **ultramarine**	.25	.40
S12	10/- **brownish purple**	£16	£23

1949 (Oct. 10th) U.P.U. As Aden.

S13	1½d **dull ultramarine**	.10	.15
	a 'A' of watermark missing	-	-
S14	3d **indigo**	£1	£2
S15	6d **reddish mauve**	.15	.40

S16 1/- **sage-green**   .15 1.10
     a 'A' of watermark missing   -   -
S13/16 **set** (4)   1.25 3.30

POSTAGE DUE STAMPS

1933-48 Printers (typo) De La Rue. Perf 13¾ x 14 (C). Watermark multiple Script CA. Sheets 6 x 10.

PD1 1d **carmine** (2/1/33)   .30   £8
     a deep carmine (/47)   .20 £10
PD2 2d **purple and pale purple**
     (2/1/33)   1.25 £18
     a purple and purple-violet
     (/46)   1.25 £18
     b dull violet (2/48)   1.75 £20
SP PD1/2 **specimen perf** (2)   £35   †

While the designs of the 1946 printings were similar to the stamps originally issued in 1933, they were not only printed on rough paper but the 1d was a deeper shade of carmine (the '1d' is also thicker and the stop under 'd' larger), and the 2d is also of a darker shade, particularly the '2d' in the centre.

1951 As before, but printed on chalk-surfaced paper.

PD3 1d **deep carmine** (24/10/51) .15 £12
PD4 2d **purple-violet** (22/5/57) 2.25 £28
     a thick 'd'   £35   -

Watermark variety (Type A)
See introduction for details.

PD3b 1d **St Edward's Crown**   £220   -

PD4a See Basutoland PD2b

TOKELAU ISLANDS

The islands were administered by, and used the stamps of, Western Samoa, from 1925 until they became a Dependency of New Zealand.

1948 (June 22nd) Designs, ½d (Atafu village and maps); 1d (Nukunono hut and map); 2d (Fakaofo village and map). Designer, J. Berry. Printers (recess) Bradbury, Wilkinson. Watermark 'N.Z. Star' (multiple). Perf 13½ x 13¼ (C). Sheets 12 x 10.

1   ½d **lilac and deep cinnamon**.10 .45
2   1d **chestnut and**
     myrtle-green   .10   .30
     a watermark inverted   £220   -
3   2d **deep emerald and deep**
     blue   .10   .30
1/3 **set** (3)   .25   .95

Numbers printed: 1 1,100,000 (of which 887,520 were surcharged in 1956 and 1967), 2 and 3 2,000,000 each.

TONGA

All stamps were printed (recess) by De La Rue unless otherwise stated.

1943 (Jan.) Watermark Tortoises. Perf. 14 (L). Sheets 10 x 6.

1	1½d **grey-black**	.50	2.75

The design of this stamp is slightly larger than that of the 1935 printing. Also the perforation was previously 14 x 13¾ (C).

Stamps current up to the 1942-3 issue were as follows; 1897 issue 1d, 3d, 6d, 2/6d and 5/-, 1920-35 issue ½d, 1½d, 2d, 2½d, 5d, 7½d, 10d and 1/-.

1942 (Sept. 18th) - 49 Design, ½d (arms of Tonga); 1d (Ovava tree); 2d, 2½d and 1/- (Queen Salote); 3d (prehistoric Trilith, Haamonga); 6d (coral); 2/6 (parrot); 5/- (Vavau harbour). Printed by De la Rue. Watermark multiple Script CA (sideways on 5/-). Sheets 10 x 6 or 6 x 10.

(a) Perf 13¾ x 14.

2	½d **green**	.15	1.80
	a 'A' of watermark missing	£450	-
3	1d **grey-black and carmine-red** (1/10/46)	1.50	1.80
	a black and deep scarlet (30/3/49)	1.25	1.80
	b lopped branch	£40	£40

(b) Perf 14 (L).

4	1d **black and carmine-red**	1.25	1.80
	a lopped branch	£40	£45
5	2d **black and purple-violet (Die II)**	3.50	1.65

6	2½d **ultramarine**	.80	1.20
	a wide D variety	£25	£35
	b value recut	£25	£35
7	3d **black and yellow-green**	.30	2.75
8	6d **red-scarlet**	1.75	1.35
9	1/- **slate-black and chestnut**	£2	2.20
	a retouched hyphen (smaller)	£25	£22
	b grey-black and chestnut (30/3/49)	£8	£15
10	2/6 **deep purple** (30/1/43)	£14	£18
11	5/- **black and brown-orange** (30/1/43)	£7	£34
1/11	**set** (9)	£27	£58
SP2, 4/11	**specimen perf** (9)	£150	†

(c) Perf 13¾ (C).

12	2d **grey-black and purple-violet (Die III)** (30/3/49)	3.50	£6
13	1/- **slate-grey and chestnut** (23/4/47)	£3	£4

Hand-retouching to various plate varieties occurred. Because of the possibility of forgery, they are not detailed here, but they are of great interest.

3 was line-perforated 13.8 x 14.2. 3a was comb-perforated 14, and alone has printer's imprint and Plate number on the bottom selvedge.

Normal   'Lopped Branch'

3b, 4a R8/5 the branch at extreme right is shortened. All printings after 1944.

Die II   Die III

5, 12 In Die III, the ball of the '2' is larger than in Die II and there is a spur on the left side of the 'U'. The lettering is taller, and the foot of the '2' extends to the right of the body of the numeral.

6a R4/10 the 'D' in the value panel is broader.

normal   6a

6b R1/1 the '2½' in the value tablet has been re-cut.

9, 13 the '1' in the value panel is made up of a number of lines; in the case of 9b these lines have been retouched with numerous small circles, giving a 'corncob' effect, separately carried out on each stamp in the sheet.

9a The second hyphen is smaller on R3/5.

SPECIAL ISSUES

1938 (Oct. 12th) 20th Anniversary of Queen Salote's Accession. Design, full-length portrait of Queen Salote (lower panel dated '1918-38'). Printers De la Rue. Perf. 13¾ (L). Watermark Tortoises. Sheets 10 x 6.

S1	1d black and carmine-red	.50	£3
S2	2d black and purple-violet	5.50	2.50
S3	2½d black and ultramarine	5.50	3.50
S1-3	set (3)	£10	£8
SP S1/3	specimen perf (3)	£50	†

1944 (Jan. 25th) Silver Jubilee of Queen Salote's Accession. Design, as CW S1, etc., but date on lower panel altered to '1918-1943'. Printers De la Rue. Perf. 13¾ (L). Sheets 10 x 6.

S4	1d black and carmine	.10	.75
S5	2d black and purple-violet	.10	.75
S6	3d black and deep green	.10	.75
S7	6d black and orange	.50	1.20
S8	1/- black and chocolate	.35	1.20
S4/8	set (5)	£1	4.25
SP S4/8	specimen perf (5)	£68	†

There are numerous cases of scratched initials appearing on the top selvedge of this issue. In addition, it is possible to find part of a portrait (an unadopted head of the King) on the top selvedge. This is most often found on the 2d value. The issue provides an interesting study in wartime printing practices.

S4 some were printed in aniline ink, not easily discernable except in ultra-violet light.

S5 examples with frames in blue are changelings which can be easily created, and are not colour trials, as has been claimed.

Number issued - 1d, 245,180; 2d, 177,560; 3d, 101,160; 6d, 76,684; 1/-, 82,147.

1949 (Oct. 10th) U.P.U. (See Aden for details).

S9	2½d dull violet-blue	.10	.60
S10	3d deep olive	£1	2.25
S11	6d carmine-red	.10	.35
S12	1/- beech-brown	.15	.35
S9/12	set (4)	1.20	3.25

Number issued - 2½d, 141,790; 3d, 116,240; 6d, 114,500; 1/-, 100,340.

1950 (Nov. 1st) Queen Salote's 50th Birthday. Designs, portraits. Designer, James Berry. Printers (photo) Waterlow and Sons. Perf 12½ (L). Watermark multiple Script C.A. Chalk-surfaced paper. Sheets 12 x 5 or 5 x 12.

S13	1d rose-red	.40	1.50
S14	5d green	.40	1.50
S15	1/- purple-violet	.40	1.65
S13/15	set (3)	.75	4.25

Number issued - 1d, 107,510; 5d, 74,850; 1/-, 72,230.

1951 (July 2nd) 50th Anniversary of the Treaty of Friendship between Tonga and Great Britain. Designs, ½d (map); 1d (Palace, Nuku'alofa); 2½d (beach view); 3d (H.M.N.Z.S. "Bellona"); 5d (Tongan flag); 1/- (Arms of G.B. and Tonga). Designer, James Berry. Printers (recess) Waterlow and Sons. 3d perf. 12½ (L), other values perf 13¼ x 13½ (C). Sheets 12 x 5 or 5 x 12.

S16	½d green	.10	1.80
S17	1d black and carmine	.10	2.10
S18	2½d olive-green and brown	.15	1.80
S19	3d yellow and blue	1.25	1.80
S20	5d carmine and green	1.40	.60
S21	1/- orange and violet	1.40	.75
S16/21	set (6)	£4	£8

TRANSJORDAN

Recess-printed, except where stated.

1939 Design, Emir Abdullah. Printer, Perkins Bacon. Watermark Multiple Script CA. Perf 13¼ x 13 (C). Sheets 10 x 10.

1	1m chestnut	£4	2.40
2	2m slate-green	£5	1.50
3	3m yellow-green	£8	2.50
4	4m rose-carmine	£40	£17
5	5m orange	£30	£2
6	10m red	£60	2.50
7	15m ultramarine	£18	£3
8	20m olive-green	£30	£8
1/8	set (8)	£175	£35

An unheralded printing, shown by postmarked copies, to have been placed on sale in 1939, with mint copies turning up from time to time in post office stocks proving that there had been no general release. Similar stamps, perforated 14, were issued from 1927.

1942 Design as CW 1, etc., but with Arabic inscriptions altered. Printer (litho) Survey Dept., Cairo. Perf 13¼ x 13½. (C). No watermark. Sheets 10 x10.

9	1m chocolate-brown	.60	2.75
10	2m grey-green	1.10	1.50
11	3m green	1.35	2.75
12	4m rose-carmine	1.35	2.75
13	5m orange	£2	.75
14	10m scarlet	2.50	1.75
15	15m deep ultramarine	£6	1.75
16	20m olive-green	£15	£15
9/16	set (8)	£27	£26

Forgeries exist on whiter paper with uneven perforations.

Number issued - 9, 122,500; 10, 155,000; 11/12, 100,000 each; 13, 218,00; 14, 107,500; 15, 68,000; 16, 43,000.

1943-7 Design as CW 1, etc., but printed by Bradbury Wilkinson. Watermark Multiple Script CA, Perf 12 (L).

17	1m red-brown (2/1/43)	.10	.45
18	2m blue-green (2/1/43)	1.25	.60
	a grey-green (/43)	1.75	.80
19	3m green (2/1/43)	£1	.75
	a yellow-green (/43)	1.25	£1
20	3m rose-carmine (12/5/47)	.25	.25
21	4m rose-carmine (2/1/43)	.85	.75
	a deep rose-carmine (30/4/45)	£1	£1
22	4m green (12/5/47)	.25	.25
23	5m orange (2/1/43)	.85	.15
	a yellow-orange (3/4/44)	.85	.15
24	10m vermilion-red (2/1/43)	1.50	.75
25	10m pale violet (12/5/47)	.25	.25
26	12m scarlet (12/5/47)	.75	£8
27	15m blue (2/1/43)	1.50	.30
28	15m olive-green (12/5/47)	£1	1.50
29	20m sage-green (3/4/44)	1.50	.60
	a deep olive-green (30/4/45)	1.75	.60
30	20m blue (12/5/47)	£1	1.50
31	50m lake (3/4/44)	1.50	.60
32	90m bistre (3//4/44)	2.20	£3
33	100m blue (3/4/44)	2.25	1.20
34	200m violet (3/4/44)	£4	£6
35	500m brown (3/4/44)	5.50	7.50
36	£1 grey-black (3/4/44)	£12	£14
17/36	set (20)	£35	£45
SP20/30	specimen perf (6)	£175	†

The Specimen set consists of the six 1947 new colours and values.

26 this is a difficult stamp to find genuinely used. Beware of faked cancellations.

POSTAGE DUE STAMPS

1939 Printer, Perkins Bacon. Perf 13¼ x 13 (C). Watermark Multiple Script CA. Sheets 10 x 10.

PD1	1m chestnut	£65	£60

Similar stamps, but perforated 14, were issued in 1929.

1942 (Dec. 22nd) Design as CW PD1, but Arabic inscription altered (taller). Printer (litho) Survey Dept., Cairo. Perf 13¼ x 13½ (C). No watermark. Sheets as before.

PD3	1m chestnut	2.25	£15
PD4	2m orange	£6	6.50
PD5	10m red	8.50	£5
PD 3/5	set (3)	£15	£24

Forgeries: see note after 9-16.

1944 Design as CW PD1. Printer, Bradbury, Wilkinson. Perf 12 (L). Watermark multiple Script CA. Sheets as before.

PD6	1m light brown	.50	£5
PD7	2m orange	.50	£3
PD8	4m yellow-orange	.50	£4
PD9	10m carmine-red	1.75	£6
PD10	20m olive-green	£38	£60
PD6/10	set (5)	£38	£70

TRINIDAD AND TOBAGO

1935-37 (recess) Bradbury, Wilkinson. Watermark Multiple Script CA (sideways). Sheets 6 x 10. Perf 12¾.

G105	1c blue and green	.15	.10
G106	2c ultramarine and yellow-brown	.50	.10
G107	3c black and scarlet	1.40	.20
G108	6c sepia and blue	4.50	3.50
G109	12c black and violet	£5	4.50
G110	24c black and olive-green	£7	7.50
G105/10	set (6)	£16	£14

1938 (May 2nd) - 50 Designs, 1c (First Boca); 2c (Imperial College of Tropical Agriculture); 3c (Mount Irvine Bay, Tobago); 4c (War Memorial, Memorial Park); 5c (G.P.O. and Treasury); 6c (Raleigh discovering Lake Asphalt); 8c (Queen's Park, Savannah); 12c (Town Hall, San Fernando); 24c (Government House); 60c (Blue Basin Waterfall). Printers (recess) Bradbury, Wilkinson. Perf 11½ x 11 ¼ (C). Sheets 5 x 12.

1	1c deep blue and pale green	.40	.20
	a violet-blue and pale green (21/6/50)	.40	.20
2	2c dark blue and light brown	.50	.15
	a indigo and chestnut-brown (12/11/45)	.50	.15
3	3c black and red	£5	.60
4	3c green and chocolate-brown (1/4/41)	.20	.15
	a green and purple-brown (18/9/44)	.15	.15
	b green and deep purple-brown (16/3/49)	.30	.15
	c 'A' of watermark missing	-	-
5	4c brown	£12	£1

6	4c **scarlet** (1/4/41)		.25	.60
	a scarlet-rose (6/42)		.20	.60
	b deep scarlet-rose			
	(16/3/49)		£5	£1
7	5c **deep claret** (1/5/41)		.20	.10
	a magenta (22/9/47)		.35	.10
8	6c **sepia-brown and**			
	blue		1.25	.50
	a sepia-brown and			
	grey blue (22/9/47)		1.25	.50
	b sepia-brown and			
	bright blue (16/3/49)		1.25	.75
9	8c **sage-green and**			
	deep orange		1.25	.60
	a sage-green and			
	red-orange (10/43)		1.25	.60
	b 'A' of watermark missing £575			-
10	12c **black and reddish violet** £11			1.20
	a black and deep violet (/42) £5			£1
	b black and deep			
	purple-violet (18/9/44)		1.25	.10
11	24c **black and olive-green**		1.25	.10
	a black and deep olive			
	(18/9/44)		1.50	.10
12	60c **myrtle-green and**			
	carmine		4.50	.90
	a dark myrtle and			
	carmine (10/43)		5.50	.90

1940-2 Design, portrait of King, with palms. Perf 12 (L). Printers, Bradbury, Wilkinson. Sheets 12 x 10.

13	$1.20 **bluish green** (2/1/40)		£6	.90
	a green (6/42)		£7	.60
14	$4.80 **carmine-rose** (21/2/40)		£15	£27
	a bright carmine-rose (10/47)		£15	£27
1/14	**set** (14)		£40	£30
SP1/14	**specimen perf** (13)		£225	†

SPECIAL ISSUES

1937 (May 12th) Coronation. As Ascension.

S1	1c **green**		.10	.35
S2	2c **yellow-brown**		.15	.10
S3	8c **orange**		.45	1.35
S1/3	**set** (3)		.65	1.60
SP S1/3	**specimen perf** (3)		£75	†

1946 (Oct. 1st) Victory. As Aden

S4	3c **dark brown**		.10	.10
	a reddish brown		.25	.25
S5	6c **deep blue**		.10	.90
SP4/5	**specimen perf** (2)		£60	†

S4 from Plate A1, S4a from Plate B1.

Numbers issued S4, 2,233,860, S5, 1,003,800

1948 (Nov. 22nd) Silver Wedding. As Aden.

S6	3c **chestnut-brown**		.10	.10
S7	$4.80 **rose-carmine** (all recess)	12.50	£19

1949 (Oct. 10th) U.P.U. As Aden

S8	5c **magenta**		.15	.60
S9	6c **indigo**		£1	1.35
S10	12c **purple**		.25	.90
S11	24c **sage-green**		.25	.75
S8/11	**set** (4)		1.50	3.25

1951 (Feb. 16th) West Indies University College. (See Antigua). Inscribed 'TRINIDAD' only.

S12	3c **green and brown**		.15	.75
S13	12c **black and purple-violet**	.15	.75

POSTAGE DUE STAMPS
(Inscribed 'TRINIDAD')

1923-45 (typo) De La Rue. Watermark multiple Script CA. Perf 13¾ x 14. Sheets 6 x 10.

GD1	1d **black**		.80	1.65
GD2	2d **black**		£2	.90
GD3	3d **black** ('25)		£2	2.40
GD4	4d **black** ('29)		£2	14.50
GD5	5d **black** ('44)		17.50	£75
GD6	6d **black** ('45)		£30	£32
GD7	8d **black** ('45)		£22	£120
GD8	1/- **black** ('45)		£40	£95
	a upright diagonal		£85	£175
GD1/8	**set** (8)		£110	£300
SPGD1/8	**specimen perf** (8)	£135	†

GD2/4 Early printings were on smooth paper, whereas the 1940 printings were on rough paper.

GD8a See Gold Coast PD 7a.

1947 (Sept. 1st) Designs, etc., as before, but currency changed. Ordinary paper.

PD7	2c **black**		1.85	2.85
PD8	4c **black**		.75	1.80
PD9	6c **black**		1.75	4.50
PD10	8c **black**		.60	£19
PD11	10c **black**		.85	3.25
PD12	12c **black**		£1	£14

PD13	16c **black**	£1	£30
PD14	24c **black**	4.25	£6
PD7/14	**set** (8)	£11	£75
SP PD7/14	**specimen perf** (8)	£125	†

1953-61 Chalk-surfaced paper.

PD15	2c **black** (20/1/53)	.10	2.25
PD16	4c **black** (10/8/55)	2.25	£3
PD17	6c **black** (20/1/53)	.15	4.50
PD18	8c **black** (10/9/58)	.15	£16
PD19	10c **black** (10/8/55)	2.50	£10
PD20	12c **black** (20/1/53)	.20	£13
PD21	16c **black** (22/8/61)	£6	£35
PD22	24c **black** (10/9/55)	3.75	£30
PD15/22	**set** (8)	13.50	£100

WATERMARK VARIETIES (TYPE A)
(See introduction for details)

PD15a	2c **Crown missing**	£60	-
PD15b	**St Edward's Crown**	£20	-
PD17a	6c **Crown Missing**	£240	-
PD17b	**St Edward's Crown**	£55	-
PD20a	12c **Crown Missing**	£300	-
PD20b	**St Edward's Crown**	£100	-

GERMAN PROPAGANDA LABELS

The 1944 German imitation of the G.B. 1937 Definitives, ½d to 3d (see after Great Britain for details), were also overprinted "LIQIDATION/OF EMPIRE/TRINIDAD" within a vertical rectangular frame.

TRISTAN DA CUNHA

Originally occupied by Great Britain in 1816 to prevent its possible use as a base to rescue Napoleon from St. Helena, the island was declared a dependency of St.Helena on January 3rd, 1938.

There was no Post Office until stamps were issued in 1952; mail was despatched by visiting ships either without stamps or with G.B. (or other Commonwealth issues) often cancelled with an undated circular postmark in black, blue or red. (See illustration below).

There are a number of types of circular, oval and rectangular cancellations and collectors should refer to the handbook "The Postal History of Tristan da Cunha" by G. Crabb, published 1980.

During the 1939-45 War the island was known as H. M. S. Atlantic Isle and there was a certain volume of mail from Service personnel.

1952 (Jan. 1st) No. 1, etc., of St. Helena, overprinted 'TRISTAN DA CUNHA'. Sheets 6 x 10 (overprint settings 3 x 5).

1	½d **violet**	.10	1.80
2	1d **black and green**	.40	.90
3	1½d **black and carmine-rose**	.40	.90
4	2d **black and carmine**	.40	.90
5	3d **slate**	.40	.90
6	4d **ultramarine**	£2	1.50
7	6d **sky-blue**	£2	1.50
8	8d **deep olive-green**	£2	£4
9	1/- **deep sepia**	£2	1.20
10	2/6 **claret**	£8	£8
11	5/- **light chocolate-brown**	£10	£12
12	10/- **deep purple**	£25	£20
1/12	**set** (12)	£45	£48

Inverted overprints are bogus.

TURKS AND CAICOS ISLANDS

1938 (June 18th) - 45 Designs, based on photographs by E. Neil Coverley: ¼d to 1/- (salt raking); 2/- to 10/- (salt industry). (Recess) Waterlow and Sons. Perf 12½ (L). Designs, 2/-, 5/-, 10/- V. Sheets 10 x 6.

1	¼d **black**	.10	.10
2	½d **yellow-green**	1.75	.10
	a medallion flaw	£25	-
	b green (6/42)	.85	.50
3	1d **chocolate-brown**	.30	.10
	a red-brown (12/11/45)	.30	.10
4	1½d **scarlet**	.30	.10
	a carmine-red (12/11/45)	.30	.10
5	2d **grey**	.40	.20
	a slate-grey (6/11/44)	.40	.20
6	2½d **orange**	£2	.50
	a deep orange (6/11/44)	1.50	1.35
7	3d **blue**	.30	.25
	a bright ultramarine (6/11/44)	.30	.20
8	6d **mauve**	£8	1.35
9	6d **sepia** (9/2/45)	.20	.15
10	1/- **bistre**	2.25	5.50
11	1/- **grey-olive** (9/2/45)	.20	.15
12	2/- **deep rose-carmine**	£20	8.50
	a bright rose-carmine (6/11/44)	£8	£11
13	5/- **yellow-green**	£25	£13
	a blue-green (6/11/44)	£16	£14
14	10/- **bright violet**	£12	5.50
	a violet (/44)	£12	4.50
1/14	**set** (12)	£50	£22
SP 1/14	**specimen perf** (14)	£200	†

Papers are particularly useful in identifying the shades of this set. Thick creamy paper indicates an early printing; thin, whiter paper a later one.

2a a flaw at bottom of the medallion on R3/7.

1950 (Aug. 1st) Designs, by Anne Deed: ½d, 5/- (salt industry); 1d (Salt Cay); 1½d (Caicos Mail); 2½d (sponge diving); 3d (South Creek); 4d (map of Islands); 6d (Grand Turk Lighthouse); 1/- (Gov. House); 1/6 (Cockburn Harbour); 2/- (Gov. Offices); 10/- (Badge of Dependency). (Recess) Waterlow and Sons. Perf 12½ (L). Sheets 6 x 10.

15	½d **green**	.35	.25
16	1d **red-brown**	.35	.45
17	1½d **carmine**	.50	.35
18	2d **red-orange**	.40	.25
19	2½d **olive-grey**	.50	.30
20	3d **bright blue**	.25	.25
21	4d **black and rose-red**	1.20	.40
22	6d **black and blue**	.80	.30
23	1/- **black and slate-green**	.50	.25
24	1/6 **black and scarlet-red**	£4	£2
25	2/- **emerald and ultramarine**	1.25	2.75
26	5/- **blue and black**	£8	£5
27	10/- **black and deep lilac**	£10	£11
15/27	**set** (13)	£25	£21

SPECIAL ISSUES

1937 (May 12th) Coronation. As Ascension.

S1	½d **green**	.10	.10
S2	2d **slate**	.30	.40
S3	3d **blue**	.30	.40
S1/3	**set** (3)	.60	.80
SP S1/3	**specimen perf** (3)	£65	†

Shades exist.

1946 (Nov. 4th) Victory. As Aden.

S4	2d **black**	.10	.10
S5	3d **deep blue**	.10	.10
SP S4/5	**specimen perf** (2)	£60	†

1948 (Sept. 13th) Silver Wedding. As Aden.

S6	1d **chestnut-brown**	.10	.10
S7	10/- **dull purple**	4.75	8.50

ZANZIBAR

1948 (Dec. 14th) Anniversary of Separation from Bahamas. Designs, by Anne Deed: ½d, 2d (Badge of Colony); 3d (Blue Ensign); 6d (map of Islands); other values (portraits of Victoria and George VI). (Recess) Waterlow and Sons. Perf 12½ (L). Designs, ½d, 2d, V. Sheets 10 x 6 or 6 x 10.

S8	½d grey-green	.60	.10
S9	2d carmine-red	.60	.10
S10	3d dull blue	.85	.10
S11	6d purple-violet	.60	.20
S12	2/- black and blue	.60	1.20
S13	5/- black and deep emerald	.75	£3
S14	10/- black and chocolate-brown	1.10	£3
S8/14	set (7)	4.50	£7

1949 (Oct. 10th) U. P. U. As Aden.

S15	2½d red-orange	.10	£1
S16	3d indigo	1.10	.35
S17	6d dull brown	.15	.45
S18	1/- sage-green	.10	.20
S15/18	set (4)	1.30	1.80

1936-52 Design, 5ct - 50ct Sultan Kalif bin Harub; 1/- - 7/6 sailing canoe; 10/- Dhow. Printers (recess) De La Rue. Watermark Multiple Script CA. Perf 14 x 14. Sheets 10 x 10 (1ct - 50ct); 12 x 5 or 5 x 12 (shilling values).

X1	5c green	.10	.10
X2	10c black	.10	.10
X3	15c red	.10	.75
X4	20c brown-orange	.10	.10
X5	25c purple/yellow	.10	.10
X6	30c deep ultramarine	.10	.10
X7	40c sepia-brown	.10	.10
X8	50c lake	.15	.10
X9	1/- green	.25	.10
X10	2/- slate	.60	£1
X11	5/- scarlet	£9	3.50
X12	7/6 blue	12.50	£16
X13	10/- green and brown	£13	£13
X1/13	set (13)	£32	£32
SP X1/13	specimen perf (13)	£120	†

1946-51 As above, but Perf. 14 x 13½ (C).

1	5c green (19/6/47)	£1	£1
2	10c black (19/6/47)	£1	£1
3	15c carmine-red (24/5/51)	£3	£4
4	20c brown-orange (15/11/46)	£1	£1
5	25c purple/yellow (22/3/48)	£4	£6
6	30c deep ultramarine (19/6/47)	£1	£1
7	40c sepia-brown (24/5/51)	£3	£6
8	50c lake (15/11/46)	£3	£1
1/8	set (8)	£15	£19

Similar stamps, but with 'CENTS' in seriffed capitals were issued in 1926.

SPECIAL ISSUES

1936 (Dec. 9th) Silver Jubilee of Sultan. Printers (recess) De La Rue. Perf 14. Sheets 10 x10.

S1	10c black and olive-green	1.50	.20
S2	20c black and bright purple	2.25	1.20
S3	30c black and deep ultramarine	£7	.20
S4	50c black and orange-vermilion	£7	2.50
S1/4	set (4)	£16	3.75
SPS 1/4	specimen perf (4)	£70	†

1944 (Nov. 20th) Bicentenary of Al-Busaid Dynasty. Printers (recess) De La Rue. Perf 14 (L). Sheets 10 x 10.

S5	10c ultramarine	.45	£2
	a C of watermark missing	£450	-
S6	20c brick-red	.60	£2
	a C of watermark missing	£450	-
S7	50c grey-green	.60	.20
S8	1/- deep purple-slate	.60	.40
	a A of watermark missing	-	-
S5/8	set (4)	£2	£4
SP S5/8	specimen perf (4)	£75	†

1946 (Nov. 11th) Victory. Nos. 2 and 6 overprinted in red. Perf 14 x 13½ (C).

S9	10c black	.10	.30
S10	30c ultramarine	.15	.30
SP S9/10	specimen perf (2)	£50	†

1949 (Jan. 10th) Silver Wedding. As Aden.

S11	20c orange	.15	.90

S12	10/- chocolate	11.50	£18

1949 (Oct. 10th) U.P.U. As Aden.

S13	20c red-orange	.15	1.80
S14	30c indigo	.85	.90
	a C of watermark missing	£550	-
S15	50c reddish mauve	.50	1.80
S16	1/- quartz-green	.50	2.70
S13/16	set (4)	1.80	6.50

POSTAGE DUE STAMPS

1936-46 Printers (typo) de La Rue. Perf 13¾ x 14 (c). Sheets 10 x 10.

XPD1	5ct violet	3.25	6.50
XPD2	10ct scarlet	2.75	1.65
XPD3	20ct green	1.10	3.50
XPD4	30ct brown	£6	£14
XPD5	40ct ultramarine	4.50	£18
XPD6	1/- grey	£6	£19
XPD1-6	set (6)	£22	£60
SPXPD1-6	specimen perf (6)	£75	†

As above but rough paper (woolly impression).

PD1	5c purple-violet (/46)	£3	£6
PD2	10c crimson-red	£3	£3
PD3	20c myrtle-green	£3	£5
PD4	30c chocolate-brown	£8	£12
PD5	40c dull ultramarine	£8	£20
PD6	1/- slate-grey	£8	£25
PD1/6	set (6)	£30	£75

Stamps on white, chalk-surfaced paper were issued from 1956 onwards.

1937 Coronation
Total number of issuing territories 59   Mint   £90
(202 stamps)   Used   £150

1946 Victory
Total number of issuing territories 62   Mint   £30
(cheapest perforations)   Used   £50
(164 stamps)

1947 Royal Visit
Total number of issuing territories 6   Mint   £2.25
(20 stamps)   Used   £3.00

1948 Royal Silver Wedding
Total number of issuing territories 69   Mint   £900
(138 stamps)   Used   £1250

1948 Olympic Games
Total number of issuing territories 6   Mint   £11
(24 stamps)   Used   £30

1949 Universal Postal Union
Total number of issuing territories 78   Mint   £150
(310 stamps)   Used   £300

1951 BWI University
Total number of issuing territories 14   Mint   £6.50
(28 stamps)   Used   £17

1951 BWI New Constitution
Total number of issuing territories 4   Mint   £2.50
(16 stamps)   Used   £6.00

Coronation 1937	Victory 1946	Royal Visit 1947	Silver Wedding 1948	Olympic Games 1948	UPU 1949	BWI University 1951	New Constitution 1951
Great Britain	Great Britain		Great Britain	Great Britain	Great Britain		
Aden	Aden		Aden		Aden		
	A/Seyiun		A/Seyiun		A/Seyiun		
	A/Shihr		A/Shihr		A/Shihr		
Antigua	Antigua		Antigua		Antigua	Antigua	
Ascension	Ascension		Ascension		Ascension		
	Australia				Australia		
Bahamas	Bahamas		Bahamas		Bahamas		
			Bahrain	Bahrain	Bahrain		
Barbados	Barbados		Barbados		Barbados	Barbados	
Basutoland	Basutoland	Basutoland	Basutoland		Basutoland		
Bechuanaland	Bechuanaland	Bechuanaland	Bechuanaland		Bechuanaland		
Bermuda	Bermuda		Bermuda		Bermuda		
B. Guiana	B. Guiana		B. Guiana		B. Guiana	B. Guiana	
B. Honduras	B. Honduras		B. Honduras		B. Honduras	B. Honduras	
			BPA in EA	BPA in EA	BPA in EA		
B. Virgin Is	B. Virgin Is		B. Virgin Is		B. Virgin Is	B. Virgin Is	
					Brunei		
	Burma						
Canada							
Cayman Is	Cayman Is		Cayman Is		Cayman Is		
Ceylon	Ceylon				Ceylon		
Cook Is	Cook Is						
Cyprus	Cyprus		Cyprus		Cyprus		
Dominica	Dominica		Dominica		Dominica	Dominica	Dominica
Falkland Is	Falkland Is		Falkland Is		Falkland Is		
	Falk Is Depds		Falk Is Depds		Falk Is Depds		
Fiji	Fiji		Fiji		Fiji		
Gambia	Gambia		Gambia		Gambia		
Gibraltar	Gibraltar		Gibraltar		Gibraltar		
Gilbert & Ellice Is	Gilbert & Ellice Is		Gilbert & Ellice Is		Gilbert & Ellice Is		
Gold Coast	Gold Coast		Gold Coast		Gold Coast		
Grenada	Grenada		Grenada		Grenada	Grenada	Grenada
Hong Kong	Hong Kong		Hong Kong		Hong Kong		
	India				India		
	Hyderabad						
Jamaica	Jamaica		Jamaica		Jamaica	Jamaica	
K.U.T.	K.U.T.		K.U.T.		K.U.T.		
			Kuwait	Kuwait	Kuwait		
Leeward Is	Leeward Is		Leeward Is		Leeward Is	Leeward Is	
M/Straits							
			M/Johore		M/Johore		
			M/Kedah		M/Kedah		
			M/Kelantan		M/Kelantan		
			M/Malacca		M/Malacca		
			M/N Sembilan		M/N Sembilan		
			M/Pahang		M/Pahang		
			M/Penang		M/Penang		

Coronation 1937	Victory 1946	Royal Visit 1947	Silver Wedding 1948	Olympic Games 1948	UPU 1949	BWI University 1951	New Constitution 1951
			M/Perak		M/Perak		
			M/Perlis		M/Perlis		
			M/Selangor		M/Selangor		
			M/Trengganu		M/Trengganu		
Malta	Malta		Malta		Malta		
Mauritius	Mauritius		Mauritius		Mauritius		
Montserrat	Montserrat		Montserrat		Montserrat	Montserrat	
M/Agencies(F)							
M/Agencies(S)			M/Agencies(S)	M/Agencies(S)			
M/Tangier	M/Tangier		M/Tangier	M/Tangier	M/Tangier		
Nauru							
Newfoundland[1]							
New Guinea							
					New Hebrides		
					N. Hebrides(F)		
New Zealand	New Zealand						
Nigeria	Nigeria		Nigeria		Nigeria		
Niue	Niue						
			N Borneo		N Borneo		
N Rhodesia	N Rhodesia		N Rhodesia		N Rhodesia		
Nyasaland	Nyasaland		Nyasaland		Nyasaland		
	P/Bahawalpur				P/Bahawalpur[2]		
Papua							
	Pitcairn Is		Pitcairn Is		Pitcairn Is		
St Helena	St Helena		St Helena		St Helena		
St Kitts	St Kitts		St Kitts		St Kitts	St Kitts	
St Lucia	St Lucia		St Lucia		St Lucia	St Lucia	St Lucia
St Vincent	St Vincent		St Vincent		St Vincent	St Vincent	St Vincent
	Samoa						
			Sarawak		Sarawak		
Seychelles	Seychelles		Seychelles		Seychelles		
Sierra Leone	Sierra Leone		Sierra Leone		Sierra Leone		
			Singapore		Singapore		
Solomon Is	Solomon Is		Solomon Is		Solomon Is		
Somaliland	Somaliland		Somaliland		Somaliland		
South Africa	South Africa	South Africa	South Africa		South Africa		
S W Africa	S W Africa	S W Africa	S W Africa		S W Africa		
S Rhodesia	S Rhodesia	S Rhodesia			S Rhodesia		
Swaziland	Swaziland	Swaziland	Swaziland		Swaziland		
					Tonga		
T & Tobago	T & Tobago		T & Tobago		T & Tobago	T & Tobago	
Turks & Caicos	Turks & Caicos		Turks & Caicos		Turks & Caicos		
	Zanzibar		Zanzibar		Zanzibar		

(1) Newfoundland. Original set of 3 in Crown Colonies design plus additional set of 11.

(2) Pakistan (Bahawalpur). Postage set of 4 (U.P.U.) plus Official set of 4.

Commonwealth and British Empire Stamps 1840-1970, Stanley Gibbons (2009)

Printings of King George VI Colonial Stamps - W. J. W. Potter (in collaboration with Lt.-Col. R. C. M. Shelton) (1952)

British Empire Postage Stamp Booklet (Evaluation & Study) - H. R. Work (1958)

Fundamentals of Philately - L. N. and M. Williams (1971)

Specimen Stamps of the Crown Colonies 1857-1948 - Marcus Samuel (1976)

Madame Joseph Forged Postmarks - Derek Worboys edited by Roger B. West (1994); Madame Joseph Revisited, Brian Cartwright, RPSL 2005

King George VI Collectors' Society Study Papers (various)

King George VI Large Key Type Stamps of Bermuda, Leeward Islands, Nyasaland - Robert W. Dickgiesser and Eric P. Yendall (1985); The KGVI Large Key Type Revenue and Postage High Value Stamps 1937-1953, Eric P. Yendall, RPSL (2008).

The Postal Agencies in Eastern Arabia and The Gulf - Neil Donaldson (1975)

Specialised Stamp Catalogue of the Falkland Island & Dependencies 1800-1996 - Stefan Heijtz (2006)

A Study of the Hong Kong Definitive Adhesives of King George VI - Nick Halewood and David Antscherl (1992)

Stamps of Ireland - Specialised Catalogue - Dave MacDonnell & Ian Whyte

A Handbook of King George VI Issues of Kenya, Uganda and Tanganyika - R. D. Berrington (1955?)

Standard Catalogue of Malaysia, Singapore, Brunei Stamps and Postal History - Steven Tan.

Loose Leaf Catalogue of New Zealand Stamps 1985 to the Present Day - Campbell Paterson Ltd.

The God Given Kingdom of Bahawalpur - Ron Wood (1990)

A Study of the King George VI Stamps of St. Kitts-Nevis 1938-1950 - P.L. Baldwin (1997).

The Stamps of the Union South Africa 1910-1961 Handbook Catalogue, Definitive Edition - S. J. Hagger (1986).

Australian Commonwealth Specialists' Catalogue, King George VI, Brusden-White, 2006.

Newfoundland Specialised Stamp Catalogue, John M. Walsh and John G. Butt, 6th edition (2006).

Gibraltar; Collecting King George VI, Edmund Chambers, Gibralter Study Circle (2003).

The KGVI Postage and Revenue Stamps of Northern Rhodesia, Drysdall, Lane and Cheston, Rhodesia Study Circle (2006).

Pakistan Overprints on Stamps and Postal Stationery. 1947-9, Doubleday and Isani (1993).

Many periodicals and other publications, especially Geosix; Gibbons Stamp Monthly, articles written by Richard Lockyer; the Malayan Philatelist, and many other Specialist Society Publications.

If you would like to know what exists in the way of literature on your favourite subject please feel free to ask us for details.

Over many years, we have built relationships with customers who are friends as well as clients. Many have taken the option of disposing of their collections through us, because the full range of options Murray Payne can offer (outright purchase, Private Treaty or auction) provides the best opportunity for maximising returns from disposal; the same applies to philatelic estates.

You need to make arrangements for your philatelic holdings in the event of your death. Your collection needs to be professionally valued; Murray Payne Ltd can carry this out for your executors with sympathy and discretion.

You should lodge with your will a copy of a letter instructing your executor/ trustee to appoint us (or, of course, another company of your choice) to value your collection. This can be in the form of a codicil to your will or in a separate letter of instruction. Keep another copy with your collection. An example of such a letter follows:

It is my wish, without imposing any legal obligation on my executors/ trustees, that Murray Payne Ltd of P.O. Box 1135, Axbridge, Somerset BS26 2EW should be consulted and instructed to prepare a valuation of my philatelic collection, and arrange disposal (if appropriate).

Sign and date the letter; lodge a copy with your solicitor. Keep another with your collection and send a third to us. If you have any queries, don't hesitate to contact us.